The Works of Philo Judaeus
Volume II
By Philo Judaeus
Translated By Charles Duke Yonge
This edition edited by Anthony Uyl

Woodstock, Ontario, 2017

The Works of Philo Judaeus: Volume II

The Works of Philo Judaeus: Volume II
By Philo Judaeus
The contemporary of Josephus, translated from the Greek
Translated By Charles Duke Yonge
This edition edited by Anthony Uyl

Originally Published by:
London, H. G. Bohn, 1854-1890.

The text of The Works of Philo Judaeus: Volume II is all in the Public Domain. The layout and Devoted Publishing logo are Copyright ©2017 Devoted Publishing. This edition is published by Devoted Publishing a division of 2165467 Ontario Inc.

**What kind of philosophies do you have?
Let us know!**

Visit our online store: www.devotedpublishing.com
Contact us at: devotedpub@hotmail.com
Visit us on Facebook: @DevotedPublishing

Published in Woodstock, Ontario, Canada 2017

For bulk educational rates, please contact us at the above email address.

ISBN: 978-1-77356-124-0

Table of Contents

ON MATING WITH THE PRELIMINARY STUDIES ... 4
- Footnotes: ... 20

ON FLIGHT AND FINDING ... 21
- Footnotes: ... 40

ON THE CHANGE OF NAMES ... 42
- Footnotes: ... 65

ON DREAMS, THAT THEY ARE GOD-SENT ... 67
- BOOK 1 ... 67
  - Footnotes: ... 90
- BOOK 2 ... 92
  - Footnotes: ... 114

ON ABRAHAM ... 116
- Footnotes: ... 140

ON JOSEPH ... 141
- Footnotes: ... 165

ON THE LIFE OF MOSES, I ... 166
- Footnotes: ... 198

ON THE LIFE OF MOSES, II ... 199
- Footnotes: ... 225

THE DECALOGUE ... 227
- Footnotes: ... 243

THE SPECIAL LAWS, I ... 244
- Footnotes: ... 277

THE SPECIAL LAWS, II ... 279
- THE FIRST FESTIVAL ... 283
- THE SECOND FESTIVAL ... 285
- THE THIRD FESTIVAL ... 292
- THE FOURTH FESTIVAL ... 293
- THE FIFTH FESTIVAL ... 293
- THE SIXTH FESTIVAL ... 294
- THE SEVENTH FESTIVAL ... 295
- THE EIGHTH FESTIVAL ... 296
- THE NINTH FESTIVAL ... 297
- THE TENTH FESTIVAL ... 298
  - Footnotes: ... 304

ON MATING WITH THE PRELIMINARY STUDIES [805]

I

I. (1) "But Sarah the wife of Abraham had not borne him any child. And she had an Egyptian handmaiden, who name was Hagar. And Sarah said unto Abraham, Behold, the Lord has closed me up, so that I should not bear children; go in unto my handmaiden that thou mayest have children by Her." [806] (2) The name Sarah, being interpreted, means "my princedom." And the wisdom which is in me, and the temperance which is in me, and the particular justice, and each of the other virtues which belong to me alone, are the princedom of me alone. For such virtue, being a queen from its birth, rules over and governs me who have determined on obeying it. (3) Now this virtue, Moses (making a most paradoxical assertion) reports, as being both barren and also most prolific, since he affirms that the most populous of all nations is sprung from it. For, in real truth, virtue is barren with respect to all things which are evil, but is so exceedingly prolific of good things, that it stands in no need of the art of the midwife, for it anticipates it by bringing forth before its arrival. (4) Therefore animals and plants, after considerable intervals and interruptions, bring forth their appropriate fruits, once, or at most twice a year; according to the number of times which nature has appointed each of them, and which is properly adapted to the seasons of the year. But virtue without any interruption, without any interval or any cessation, is continually bringing forth at all times and on all occasions, not indeed children, but virtuous reasonings, and irreproachable counsels, and praiseworthy actions.

II

II. (5) But neither is wealth, which it is not possible to employ, of any advantage to its possessors, nor is the fertility of wisdom of any service to us, unless it also brings forth such things as are serviceable to us. For some persons it judges to be in every respect worthy of living in its company; but others appear to have not yet arrived at such an age, as to be able to support so highly praised and well regulated a charge; whom, however, it permits to enter upon the preliminaries of marriage, holding out to them a hope that they may hereafter consummate the wedlock. (6) Sarah therefore, the virtue which rules over my soul, has brought forth, but, she has not brought forth for me (for I should never as yet have been able, since I am quite young, to receive her offspring); she has brought forth, I say, wisdom, and the doing of just actions, and piety, by reason of the multitude of illegitimate children whom the vain opinions have brought forth to me. For the education of the offspring, and the constant superintendence and incessant care which they require, have compelled me to neglect the legitimate children, who are really citizens. (7) It is well, therefore, to pray that virtue may not only bring forth, since she is prolific even without a prayer, but that she may bring for us; in order that we, receiving a share of her seed and of her offspring, may be happy. For she is accustomed to bring forth children to God alone, restoring with burning gratitude the first fruits of all the blessings which she has received, to him, who, as Moses says, "opened her Womb," [807] which was at all times virgin. (8) For he also says that the lamp, that archetypal model after which the copy is made, shines in one part, that is to say, in the part which is turned towards God. [808] For since that completes the number of seven, and stands in the middle of the six branches, which are divided into two lots of three each, acting as body-guards to it on either side, it sends its rays upwards toward that one being, namely God, thinking its light too brilliant for mortal sight to be able to stand its proximity.

III

III. (9) On this account he does not say that Sarah did not bring forth at all, but only that she did not bring forth for him, for Abraham. For we are not as yet capable of becoming the fathers of offspring of virtue, unless we first of all have a connection with her handmaiden; and the handmaiden of wisdom is the encyclical knowledge of music and logic, arrived at by previous instruction. (10) For as in houses there are vestibules placed in front of staircases, and as in cities there are suburbs, through which one must pass in order to enter into the cities; so also the encyclical branches of instruction are placed in front of virtue, for they are the road which conducts to her. (11) And as you must know that it is common for there to be great preludes to great propositions, and the greatest of all propositions is virtue, for it is conversant about the most important of all materials, namely, about the universal life of man; very naturally, therefore, that will not employ any short preface, but rather it will use as such, grammar, geometry, astronomy, rhetoric, music, and all the other sorts of contemplation which proceed in accordance with reason; of which Hagar, the handmaid of Sarah, is an emblem, as we will proceed to show. (12) "For Sarah," says Moses, "said unto Abraham, Behold, the Lord has closed me up, so that I may not bear children. Go in unto my handmaiden, that thou mayest have children by her." Now, we must take out of the present discussion those conjunctions and connections of body with body which have pleasure for their end. For this is the connection of the mind with virtue, which is desirous to have children by her, and which, if it cannot do so at once, is at all events taught to espouse her handmaid, namely, intermediate instruction.

IV

IV. (13) And here it is worth while to admire wisdom, by reason of its modesty, which has not thought fit to reproach us with the slowness of our generation, or our absolute barrenness. And this, too, though the oracle says truly that she brought forth no child, not out of envy, but because of the unsuitableness of our own selves. For, says she, "The Lord has closed me up so, that I may not bear children." And she no longer adds the words, "to you," that she may not appear to mention the misfortunes of others, or to reproach them with theirs. (14) "Therefore," says she, "go thou in to my handmaiden," that is to say, to the intermediate instruction of the intermediate and encyclical branches of knowledge, "that you may first have children by her;" for hereafter you shall be able to enjoy a connection with her mistress, tending to the procreation of legitimate children. (15) For grammar, by teaching you the histories which are to be found in the works of poets and historians, will give you intelligence and abundant learning; and, moreover, will teach you to look with contempt on all the vain fables which erroneous opinions invent, on account of the ill success which history tells us that the heroes and demigods who are celebrated among those writers, meet with. (16) And music will teach what is harmonious in the way of rhythm, and what is ill arranged in harmony, and, rejecting all that is out of tune and all that is inconsistent with melody, will guide what was previously discordant to concord. And geometry, sowing the seeds of equality and just proportion in the soul, which is fond of learning, will, by means of the beauty of continued contemplation, implant in you an admiration of justice. (17) And rhetoric, having sharpened the mind for contemplation in general, and having exercised and trained the faculties of speech in interpretations and explanations, will make man really rational, taking care of that peculiar and especial duty which nature has bestowed upon it, but upon no other animal whatever. (18) And dialectic science, which is the sister, the twin sister of rhetoric, as some persons have called it, separating true from false arguments, and refuting the plausibilities of sophistical arguments, will cure the great disease of the soul, deceit. It is profitable, therefore, to aide among these and other sciences resembling them, and to devote one's especial attention to them. For perhaps, I say, as has happened to many, we shall become known to the queenly virtues by means of their subjects and handmaidens. (19) Do you not see that our bodies do not use solid and costly food before they have first, in their age of infancy, used such as had no variety, and consisted merely of milk? And, in the same way, think also that infantine food is prepared for the soul, namely the encyclical sciences, and the contemplations which are directed to each of them; but that the more perfect and becoming food, namely the virtues, is prepared for those who are really full-grown men.

V

V. (20) Now the first characteristics of the intermediate instruction are represented by two symbols, the race and the name. As to race, the handmaiden is an Egyptian, and her name is Hagar; and this name, being interpreted, means "emigration." For it follows of necessity that the man who delights in the encyclical contemplations, and who joins himself as a companion to varied learning, is as such enrolled under the banners of the earthly and Egyptian body; and that he stands in need of eyes in order to see and to read, and of ears in order to attend and to hear, and of his other external senses, in such a manner as to be able to unfold each of the objects of the external sense. (21) For it is not natural to suppose that the subject of judgment can possibly be comprehended without some power which is to judge; and the power which judges of the objects of the external sense is the external sense, so that without the external sense it would not be possible for any thing in that world which is perceptible by the external sense to be accurately known, though those are the matters which are the principal field for philosophical speculation. But the external sense, being that portion of the soul which most resembles the body, is deeply rooted in the entire vessel of the soul; and the vessel of the soul is, by a figurative way of speaking, called Egypt. (22) And there is one characteristic derived from her race, which the handmaiden of virtue possesses. But what or what kind of characteristic that is which is derived from the name, we must now proceed to consider. The intermediate instruction has the same rank and classification as a sojourner. For all knowledge, and wisdom, and virtue, are the only real native and original inhabitants and citizens of the universe. And all the others kinds of instruction, which obtain the second, and third, and lowest honours, are on the confines, between foreigners and citizens. For they are not connect with either race without some alloy, and yet again they are not connected with both according to a certain community and participation. (23) For they are sojourners from the fact of their passing their time among citizens; but from the fact of their not being settled inhabitants, they also resemble foreigners. In the same manner, according to my idea, as adopted children, inasmuch as they inherit the property of those who have adopted them, resemble real legitimate children; but inasmuch as they were not begotten by them, they resemble strangers. The same relation, then, that a mistress has to her handmaidens, or a wife, who is a citizen, to a concubine, that same relation has virtue, that is Sarah, to education, that is Hagar. So that very naturally, since the husband, by name Abraham, is one who has an admiration for contemplation and knowledge; virtue, that is Sarah, would be his wife, and Hagar, that is all kinds of encyclical accomplishments, would be his concubine. (24) Whoever, therefore, has acquired wisdom from his teachers, would never reject Hagar. For the acquisition of all the preliminary branches of education is wholly necessary.

VI

VI. But if any one, having determined on perseveringly enduring labours in the cause of virtue, devotes himself to continued study, practising and meditating without intermission, that man will marry two citizens, and also an equal number of concubines, the handmaidens of the citizens. (25) And each of these has a different appearance and a different nature. For instance, of the two citizen wives, one is a most healthy and well established and peaceful motion, whom from the circumstances the historians called Leah: and the other resembles a whetstone and is called Rachel, in the pursuit of whom the mind, which is fond of labour and fond of exercises, is much sharpened and excited; and the name, being interpreted, means the "sight of profanation;" not because she sees profanely, but, on the contrary, because she thinks the things which are seen and which are the objects of the external senses, not brilliant but common and profane in comparison of the pure and untainted nature of those things which are invisible and which are only discernible by the intellect. (26) For since our soul is composed of two parts, and since the one contains the rational faculties, and the other the irrational ones, it follows that each part must have its own peculiar virtue, Leah being the virtue of the rational part, and Rachel of the irrational. (27) For the one trains us, by means of the external senses and the parts of speech, to look contemptuously upon all things which it is proper to disregard, such as glory, and wealth, and pleasure, which the principal and general multitude of common men look upon as things to be admired and striven for, their sense of hearing being corrupted, and the tribunal of all the other external senses being corrupted likewise. (28) But the other teaches us to turn away from that uneven and rough road which is never approached by souls that love virtue, and to go smoothly along the smooth road without any stumbling and without meeting any hindrances in the path. (29) Therefore the handmaiden of the former of the two citizen wives will necessarily be the power of interpretation as exercised by means of the organs of speech, and also the rational invention of sophisms, deceiving man by a well-imagined plausibility; and its necessary nourishment is meat and drink. (30) The historian has recorded for us the names of the two handmaidens, calling them Zilpah and Billah. [809] The name Zilpah, being interpreted, means "a mouth going forth," a symbol of that nature which interprets and speaks. But Billah means "a swallowing," which is the first and most necessary support of all mortal animals. For it is by swallowing that our bodies are established firmly, and the cables of life are attached to this action as to a sure foundation. (31) Accordingly the practiser of virtue lives with all the aforesaid powers, with some as with free women and citizens, and with others as slaves and concubines. For he is enamoured of the motion of Leah; and a smooth (leia) motion existing in a body would be calculated to produce health, and, when existing in a soul, it would produce virtue and justice. But he loves Rachel, wrestling with his passions, and preparing himself for a struggle of temperance, arraying himself in opposition to all the objects of the external senses. (32) For there are two kinds of advantage, either that according to which we enjoy blessings, as in peace, or else that which comes from arraying one's self in opposition to and from removing evils as in war. Now Leah is the wife according to whom it happens to the husband to enjoy the elder, and more important, and dominant blessings; and Rachel the wife, according to whom he obtains what resemble the sports of war. Such then is his way, if left with his citizen wives. (33) But the practiser of virtue also wants Billah, that is, swallowing, but as a slave and a concubine; for without food and vitality, living well could not possibly be the lot of man, since things indifferent are always the foundation of what is better; and he also wants Zilpah, that is to say, interpretation by means of utterance, in order that the rational part itself may, in a twofold manner, contribute to perfection, both from the fountain existing in the intellect, and also from the stream flowing therefrom in the organ of the voice.

VII

VII. (34) But these men were husbands of many wives and concubines, not only of such as were citizens, as the sacred scriptures tell us. But Isaac had neither many wives nor any concubine at all, but only his first and wedded wife, who lived with him all his life. (35) Why was this? Because the virtue acquired by teaching, which Abraham pursues, requires many things, both such as are legitimate according to prudence, and such also as are illegitimate according to the exegetical contemplations of preliminary instruction. And there is also a virtue which is made perfect by practice, to which Jacob appears to have been devoted; for exercises consist of many and various dogmas and doctrines, some leading and others following, some leading the way, and others arriving later, and bringing at one time more serious, and at other times lighter labours. (36) But the self-instructed race, of which Isaac was a partaker, the excellent country of the mastery over the passions, has received as its share a nature simple, and unmixed, and unalloyed, standing in no need of either practice or instruction in which there is need of the concubine sciences, and not only of the citizen wives; for when God has showered down from above that most requisite benefit of knowledge, self-taught, and having no need of a preceptor, it would be impossible any longer for a man to live with the slavish and concubine arts, having a desire for bastard doctrines as his children. For the man who has arrived at this honour, is inscribed as the husband of the mistress and princess virtue; and she is called in the Greek language, perseverance, but among the Hebrews her name is Rebekkah. (37) For he who, by reason of the happy constitution of his own nature and by the prolific fertility of his soul, has attained to wisdom without encountering labour or enduring hardship, stands in need of no further improvement; (38) for he has at hand the perfect gifts of God, inspired by means of those most ancient graces, and he wishes and prays that they may remain lasting. In reference to which, it appears to me to be that the Author of all goodness gave him perseverance as his wife, in order that his mercies might endure for ever to the man who had her for his wife.

VIII

VIII. (39) Now recollection only comes in the second rank after memory, as inferior to it; and he who recollects is inferior to him who remembers; for the latter resembles a man in an uninterrupted state of good health, but the other is like a man recovering from a disease, for forgetfulness is a disease of the memory; (40) and it follows inevitably that the man who exerts his recollection has previously forgotten what he now recollects. Therefore the sacred scriptures call memory Ephraim, which name, being interpreted, means "fruit-bearing." But the Hebrews call recollection, after forgetfulness, Manasseh; (41) for, in good truth, the soul of the man who remembers does bear as fruit the things which he has learned, losing nothing of them; but the soul of the man who exerts recollection, is only escaping from forgetfulness, by which it was detained before it recollected; therefore a citizen wife, memory, lives with the man who is endowed with remembrance. But the concubine recollection, a Syrian by birth, insolent and overbearing, lives with the man who forgets; for the meaning of the name Syria, is "sublimity;" (42) and the son of the concubine recollection is Machir, as the Hebrews call him; but the Greeks interpret the name to mean "of the father." For those who recollect a thing think that the mind is the father and cause of their recollecting, and do not consider that this same endowment of the mind did also before contain "forgetfulness," though it never would have received it if it had had memory in its power. (43) For it is said in the scripture, "And the sons of Manasseh were Ashriel whom she bare, but his concubine, the Aramitess, bare Machir; and Machir was the father Gilead." [810] And Nachor, also, the brother of Abraham, had two wives, one a citizen and the other a concubine. And the name of the citizen was Milcah; and the name of the concubine was Rumah. (44) But let no one who is in his senses suspect that the wise legislator recorded this as a historical genealogy, but it is rather an explanation of things which are able to benefit the soul by means of symbols. And when we have translated the names into our own language, we shall understand the real meanings intended to be conveyed by them. Come, then, let us now investigate each of them.

IX

IX. (45) The name Nachor, being interpreted, means "a rest from light;" and Milcah means "princess;" and Rumah means "she who sees something." Therefore, to have light in the mind is good; but cessation from light, and tranquillity, and immobility is not perfect good, for it is advantageous to have evils tranquil, but it is desirable to have blessings in motion; for what advantage is there in a man's having a tuneful voice, if he keeps silent? (46) or in his having the skill of a flute player, if he does not play the flute? or of his knowing the harp, if he does not strike it? or, in short, what good is there in any artist whatever, if he does not exercise his art? for theoretical knowledge, without putting it in practice, is of no advantage whatever to those who possess it. For a man, though skilful in the contest of the pancratium, or in boxing, or in wrestling, would derive no advantage from his athletic prowess if his hands were tied behind him; and he who was thoroughly practised in running would derive no advantage from his fleetness of foot if he were afflicted with the gout, or if he were to meet with any other injury to his feet. (47) And the light of the soul, which is the most brilliant and the most like the sun, is knowledge; for as the eyes are lightened up by beams, so is the mind made brilliant by wisdom, and becomes gradually accustomed to see more acutely from being continually anointed with new speculations. Therefore, Nachor is interpreted "a cessation from light," very naturally; (48) for, inasmuch as he is a relation of the wise Abraham, he partakes of that light which is according to wisdom; but inasmuch as he did not join him in his emigration from the crated to the uncreated being, from the world to the Creator of the world, he has acquired only a lame and imperfect knowledge, intermittent and delaying, or rather put together like a lifeless statue; (49) for he does not depart and quit his abode in the Chaldaean country, that is to say, he does not separate himself from the speculations concerning astronomy; honouring that which is created rather than him who created it, and the world in preference to God; or rather, I should say, looking on the world itself as an absolute independent God, and not as the work of an absolute God.

X

X. (50) And he takes Milcah for his wife, not being some queen who by the dispensations of fortune governs some nation of men, or some city, but only one who bears a common name, the same as here. For, just as a person would not be widely wrong who called the world, as being the most excellent of all created things, the king of the objects of the external sense; so, also, one may call the knowledge which is conversant about the heaven, which knowledge those who study astronomy and the Chaldaeans possess in an eminent degree, the queen of all the sciences. (51) This, therefore, is the wife who is a citizen; but the concubine is she who sees one only of all existing things at a time, even though it may be the most worthless of all. It is given, therefore, to the most excellent race to see the most excellent of things, namely, the really living God; for the name Israel, being interpreted, means "seeing God." But to him who aims at the second prize, it is allowed to see that which is second best, namely, the heaven which is perceptible by the external senses, and the harmonious arrangement of the stars therein, and their truly musical and wellregulated motion. (52) The third class are the sceptics, who do not apply themselves to the most excellent objects, either of the intellect or of the external senses, which exist in nature, because they are always occupying themselves with petty sophistries, and small cavils, and criticisms. These have for their companions the concubine Rumah, who sees something which is very minute, because they are unable to approach the investigation of better things, by means of which they might benefit their own life. (53) For, as among physicians that which is called theoretical medical skill, is a long way from doing any good to those that are sick--for diseases are cured by medicines, and by operations, and by regimen, and not by discussions or theories; so also in philosophy, there is a set of word-traffickers and word-eaters, who have neither the will nor the skill to heal a life which is full of infirmities, but who, from their very earliest infancy to the extremity of old age, are not ashamed to cavil, and quibble, and wrangle about figurative expressions, as if happiness consisted in an interminable and profitless minuteness of accuracy in the matter of nouns and verbs, and not in the improving and ameliorating the moral character, the true fountain of the persons' disposition; and in expelling the vices, and driving them out of its boundaries, and establishing the virtues as settlers within them.

XI

XI. (54) Now the wicked also have a desire for concubines, that is, for vain opinions and doctrines; accordingly Moses tells us that Thimna, the concubine of Eliphah the son of Esau, bore Amalek to Eliphah. [811] Alas, for the eminent ignobleness of the descendant! And you will see this ignobleness the more clearly, if you abandon the idea that this expression is used about a man, and rather consider the soul, with a kind of anatomical dissection. (55) The historian then calls the irrational and immoderate desires and impetuosity of the passions, Amalek; now the name Amalek, being interpreted, means "the people looking up." For as the power of fire consumes the materials which are offered to it, so in the same manner does passion, when boiling over lick up and destroy everything with which it meets. (56) And the father of this passion is very properly described as Eliphah; for this name, being interpreted, means "God has scattered me." But does it not follow that when God scatters, and disperses, and discards the soul, banishing it from himself, irrational passion is at once engendered? For He plants the mind which can really behold him, and which is really attached to God, the vine of a good kind, stretching out its roots so as to make them everlasting, and giving it abundance of fruit for the acquisition and enjoyment of the virtues. (57) On which account Moses prays, saying, "Bring them in and plant them In,"[812] in order that those divine shoots may not be ephemeral, but long-lived and lasting for ever and ever. And banishing the unjust and ungodly soul, he disperses it and drives it to a distance from himself to the region of the pleasures and appetites and acts of injustice; and this region is, with exceeding appropriateness, called the region of the impious, more fitly than that one which is fabled as existing in the shades below. For indeed, the real hell is the life of the wicked, which is audacious, and flagitious, and liable to all kinds of curses.

XII

XII. (58) There is also in another place the following sentence deeply engraven: "When the Most High came down to scatter the nations, as he dispersed the sons of Adam,"[813] he drove out all earthly dispositions, which had no desire to see any good thing from heaven; depriving them of house and city, and rendering them truly wanderers on the face of the earth. For no house, nor city, nor anything else which relates to society and participation, is preserved for any one of the wicked; but they are deprived of all settled habitation, and dispersed abroad, being moved in every direction, and living a life of continued emigration, and not being able to become settled any where. (59) Therefore the wicked man has for his children, wickedness, by his wife who is a citizen, and passion by his concubine; for the whole soul, like a free citizen, is a companion of reason, but that which is open to reproach brings forth wickedness. But the nature of the body is a concubine, by means of whom the birth of the passion is beheld; and the body is the region of the pleasures and passions, and it is called Thamnah, (60) which name, being interpreted, signifies a "fluctuating abandonment." For the soul becomes faint and powerless by reason of the passions having received much tossing about and agitation from the body, on account of the violent storm which bursts forth from immoderate impetuosity. (61) But as the head is the chief of all the aforementioned parts of an animal, so is Esau the chief of this race, whose name is at one time interpreted "an oak," and at another, "a thing made." It is interpreted an oak, in reference to his being unbending, and implacable, and obstinate, and stiffnecked by nature, and having folly for his chief fellow counsellor, and being as such of a truly oaken character. And it is interpreted "a thing made," inasmuch as a life according to folly is an invention and a fable, full of tragic pomp and vain boasting; and, on the other hand, of mockery and comic ridicule, having in it nothing sound, being full of falsehood, having utterly cast off truth, and disregarding as a thing of no value, that nature which is void of distinctive qualities, or of particular species, but plain and sincere, which the practiser of virtue loves. (62) And Moses bears witness to this, when he says that "Jacob was a man without artifice, dwelling in a House;"[814] so that he who is contrary to him, must necessarily be destitute of a house, the companion of invention, and of things made, and of fabulous nonsense, or rather be himself a theatre and a fable.

XIII

XIII. (63) The connection therefore between the reason which is devoted to contemplation and those powers which are citizen wives, or concubines, has here been explained to the best of my power. We must now proceed to investigate what follows, and endeavour to frame a proper connection for an argument. "Abraham," says the sacred historian, "listened to the voice of Sarah."[815] For it is necessary for him who is a learner to be obedient to the injunctions of virtue: (64) but yet all men are not so obedient, but only those who are inspired with an exceedingly vehement love for knowledge. Since almost every day the places where there is anything to hear and the theatres are crowded, and those who study philosophy go on without ever stopping to take breath in one long continued discussion about virtue. (65) But still what advantage is derived from all that is said? For men, instead of attending, turn their mind in other directions, some to marine and mercantile affairs, others to rents and agriculture; some to public honours and affairs of state, some to the gains to be derived from each different profession and art, others to revenging themselves upon their enemies, others again to the enjoyments to be derived from the indulgence of the amorous appetites, and in short every body is under the influence of some distracting idea or other; so that, as far as the subjects of the discussion are concerned, they are completely deaf, and are present with their bodies only, but are at a distance as to their minds, being in no particular different from images or statues. (66) And if any persons do attend, they sit all that time only listening, and when they have departed they do not recollect a word of what has been said, but they have come in fact rather to be pleased through the medium of their hearing than with the view of deriving any solid advantage; so that their soul has not been able to comprehend anything or to become pregnant with any new idea, and even the cause which at first excited their pleasure soon ceases and their attention is extinguished. (67) There is a third kind of persons to whom what is said is for a time attended to and remembered, as if still sounding in their ears; but still they are found to be sophists rather than philosophers: of these men the language indeed is praiseworthy but the life is blameable; for they are powerful at speaking, but have no ability to do what is best. (68) It is therefore hardly possible to find a man who is inclined to attend and endowed with a good memory, honouring deeds rather than words; as is testified to in the praise of the man fond of hearing in the words, "He listened to the voice of Sarah." For he is not represented merely as hearing but also as listening to: and this last is a particularly felicitous expression to indicate one who approves of and is influenced by what he hears. (69) And the expression, "to the voice," is not inconsiderately or incorrectly used in preference to saying--he listened to Sarah speaking. For it is the especial character of a learner to listen to the voice and words of his teacher; for by these alone is he taught. But he who acquires what is good by practice, and solitary meditation, and not by instruction, does not attend to what is said but rather to those who say it, imitating the lives of those men in their actions which are in each particular irreproachable. (70) For it is said, in the case of Jacob when he was sent away to form a marriage among his kinsmen, "Jacob listened to his mother and his father, and went into Mesopotamia." [816] He listened not to their voice, nor to their words, for it was fitting that he who was an imitator of their actions should be a practiser of virtue not a listener to speeches. For this is the peculiar character of one who is being taught, but the other is the mark of one who is enduring labours, in order that from this instance we may comprehend the difference between a practiser and a learner, the one being regulated with regard to him who is speaking, and the other with regard to his speech.

XIV

XIV. (71) Therefore, continues the sacred historian, Sarah, the wife of Abraham, having taken Hagar, the Egyptian woman, her own handmaiden, ten years after Abraham had begun to dwell in the land of Canaan, gave her to Abraham her "husband, to be his Wife." [817] Wickedness is by nature an envious, and bitter, and evil-disposed thing, but virtue is gentle, and inclined to communion, and friendly; wishing in every possible manner to benefit those who are well disposed, either by its own power or by the means of others. (72) So now accordingly, as we are not able to become the fathers of children by prudence, she espouses us to her own handmaiden, encyclical instruction, as I have said before, and all but endures to be the bridesmaid and manager of the marriage; for it is said that Sarah herself took this woman and gave her to her own husband. (73) And here it is worth while to raise the question why it is that now again Moses calls the wife of Abraham Sarah, when he had already repeatedly told us what her name was before; for he was not a writer who ever indulged in that worst description of prolixity, tautology. What, then, are we to say? Since she is about to betroth to him the handmaiden of wisdom, encyclical instruction, he says that she did not forget the duty which she owed to her mistress, but knew that she was, both in law and in her master's feelings, his wife, and that she herself was only such because of necessity and the force of opportunity. And this happens to every man who is fond of learning. And he who has experienced it may be looked upon as the most trustworthy witness to this fact. (74) At all events I, when I was first excited by the stimulus of philosophy to feel a desire for it, when I was very young connected myself with one of her handmaidens, namely, grammar; and all the offspring of which I became the father by her, such as writing, reading, and the acquaintance with the works of the poets and historians, I attributed to the mistress. (75) And at a subsequent time, forming connection with another of her handmaidens, geometry, and admiring her beauty (for she had beautiful symmetry and proportions in all her parts), I still appropriated none of the offspring, but carried them to the citizen wife, and bestowed them on her. (76) I was desirous also to form a similar connection with a third, and she was full of good rhythm, well arranged, and well limbed, and was called music. And by her I became the parent of diatonic, and chromatic, and harmonic, and combined and separate melodies, and all the different concords belonging to fourths and to fifths, and to the diapason. And, again, I concealed none of all these things, in order that my legitimate citizen wife might become wealthy, being ministered unto by a multitude of ten thousand servants; (77) for some men, being attracted by the charms of handmaidens, have neglected their true mistress, philosophy, and have grown old, some in poetry, and others in the study of painting, and others in the mixture of colours, and others in ten thousand other pursuits, without ever being able to return to the proper mistress; (78) for each act has its own peculiar brillliancies, certain attractive powers, by which some persons are allured and overcome, forgetting all the covenants which they have made with philosophy; but he who abides by the agreements which he has made, provides every thing from all quarters with a view to pleasing her. Very appropriately, therefore, does the sacred scripture, admiring his good faith in respect of his legitimate wife, say that even now Sarah was his true wife, inasmuch as he only took his handmaid into his bed out of complaisance towards her; (79) and, indeed, in the same manner as the encyclical branches of education contribute to the proper comprehension of philosophy, so also does philosophy aid in the acquisition of wisdom; for philosophy is an attentive study of wisdom, and wisdom is the knowledge of all divine and human things, and of the respective causes of them. Therefore, just as encyclical accomplishments are the handmaidens of philosophy, so also is philosophy the handmaiden of wisdom; (80) but philosophy teaches temperance with regard to the belly, and temperance with regard to the parts below the belly, and also temperance and restraint of the tongue. Now these qualities are said to be worthy of praise for their own sakes, but they would appear more respectable still if they were cultivated for the sake of doing honour to and giving pleasure to God. We must, therefore, always remember the legitimate mistress when we are about to espouse her handmaidens; and let us be said indeed to be the husbands of the latter, but still let our legitimate mistress be our real wife, and not merely called such.

XV

XV. (81) Again, she gives Hagar to him, not the first moment that he arrives in the country of the Canaanites, but after he has abode there ten years. And what the meaning of this statement is we must investigate in no careless manner. Now, at the beginning of our existence, our soul dwelt among the passions alone as its fosterbrethren, griefs, pains, fears, desires, and pleasures, which reach it through the medium of the external senses, before reason was as yet able to see good and evil, and to distinguish accurately the points wherein these things differ from one another, but while it was still wavering and hesitating, and as it were closing its eyes in profound sleep; (82) but as time advances, when advancing out of the age of infancy we are on the point of becoming young men, then, without any delay, the double trunk of virtue and wickedness springs forth out of one root, and we attain to a comprehension of them both, but still we by all means choose one of the two; those who are well disposed choosing virtue, and those of the contrary character choosing wickedness. (83) These things, now, being previously sketched out in this manner, we must become aware that Egypt is the symbol of the passions and the land of the Canaanites, the emblem of the wickednesses; so that it is in strict accordance with natural probability that God, after having roused his people and made them depart from Egypt, leads them into the country of the Canaanites; (84) for the man, as I have said before, at his very earliest birth had the Egyptian passions assigned to him to dwell among, being deeply rooted in pleasures and in pains; and at a subsequent time he departs as if to found a colony, and migrates towards wickedness. His reason now being inclined to a more acute sight, and comprehending accurately both the opposite extremes of good and evil, but nevertheless choosing the worse part, because it has a great share in mortal nature, to which what is evil is in some degree akin, as also the contrary, namely, good, is akin to the divine nature.

XVI

XVI. (85) But these are the different countries of each respective nature; passions, that is to say, Egypt, being the country of the age of childhood; and wickedness, that is the land of Canaan, being the country of the age of youth. But the sacred scripture, although it is well acquainted with the different countries of the mortal race, suggests to us what ought to be done and what will be advantageous to us, enjoining us to hate the heathen, and their laws, and their customs, in that passage where he says, (86) "And the Lord spake unto Moses, saying, Speak unto the children of Israel, and say unto them, I am the Lord your God; ye shall not behave according to the customs of Egypt in which ye dwelt among them, and ye shall not walk in their laws. Ye shall do my judgments, and ye shall not do according to the customs of the land of Canaan, into which I am leading you to dwell there. And he shall keep my commandments, and ye shall walk in them. I am the Lord your God. And ye shall keep all my commandments and my judgments, and ye shall do them. He that doeth them the same shall live in them. I am the Lord your God: and ye shall keep all my commandments and my Judgments." [818] (87) Therefore, real true life, above everything else, consists in the judgments and commandments of God, so that the customs and practices of the impious must be death: but there are some races which take no note of passions and wickednesses, from whom the multitudes of impious persons and wickedness are sprung. (88) Therefore, ten years after our departure to settle in the land of the Canaanites let us marry Hagar, since from the first moment that we become rational beings, we seek for ignorance and a deficiency of knowledge which is pernicious in its own nature; but at a subsequent period, and at a perfect number, namely, the legal number of the decade, we come to feel a desire for that instruction which is able to benefit us.

XVII

XVII. (89) But the sons of the musicians have accurately and carefully investigated the question respecting the decade; and the most sacred Moses has composed a hymn, with no slight degree of skill, attributing the most excellent things to this number of the decade, such as prayers, first-fruits, the continual and unceasing offerings of the priests, the observance of the passover, the atonement, [819] the remission of debts, and the return to the ancient allotments of property at the end of every fifty years; [820] the preparation and furnishing of the indissoluble tabernacle, [821] and ten thousand other things which it would take a long time to enumerate. However, we must not pass over the most important points. (90) In the first place he represents Noah to us (and this man is the first who is specially entitled just, in the holy scriptures), as the tenth in succession from him who was formed out of the earth, not intending by this statement to indicate the number of years that had elapsed, but rather to show clearly that as the decade is the most perfect boundary and end of the numbers which proceed onwards from the unit, so also just in the soul is the perfection and true end of the actions of human life. (91) For the number three when multiplied by itself so as to make nine, the oracles have pronounced to be the most warlike of numbers; but when one is added to it so as to complete the number ten, then they receive it as a friendly one. (92) And as a proof of this, they allege the kingdoms of the nine kings, [822] (when the civil war was fanned into a flame, the four passions rising up against the five outward senses, and when the entire soul, like a city, was in danger of being subjected to an utter overthrow and destruction,) which the wise Abraham, appearing as the tenth king, put an end to, by joining in the warfare. (93) He then caused a calm instead of a storm, and health instead of disease, and life, if one may speak the plain truth, instead of death, showing himself as the trophy-bearer of God who giveth the victory, to whom also he consecrated the tenths as a grateful offering on account of his victory. (94) Moreover, he also separates off the tenth of all the cattle which come "under the Rod," [823] I mean by this under instruction, and of all those which are of a tame and tractable sort, pronouncing them to be holy by an express provision of the law. In order that so, by many concurrent testimonies, we may learn the particular and especial appropriateness of the number ten to God, and of the number nine to our mortal race.

XVIII

XVIII. (95) But also it is expressly ordered, that men should offer as first fruits the tenths, not only of animals, but also of all the things which grow up out of the earth; "For," says the scripture, "every tenth of the earth from the seed and from the fruit of every tree, is holy to the Lord: and every tenth of oxen and sheep, and everything of any cattle which passes under the rod, of all these the tenth shall be holy to the Lord." (96) You see that he thinks that it is proper to make an offering, by way of first fruits from the corporeal mass that is around us, which is really earthly and wooden; for life, and durability, and increase, and good health, fall to his share through the divine grace. You see also, that again an express command is given to offer first-fruits from all the irrational animals that are around ourselves; and by these are meant the outward senses. For to see, and to hear, and to smell, and to taste, and also to touch are divine gifts, for which it is our duty to give thanks. (97) But not only are we taught to thank the giver of all goodness for these earthly, and wooden, and corporeal things, and for the irrational animals, the outward senses, but also for the mind, which, to speak with strict propriety, is man in man, the better in the worse, the immortal in the mortal. (98) On this account I think it is, that God ordered to be consecrated the whole of the firstborn, the tenth, I mean the tribe of Levi, taking them in exchange for the first-born, for the preservation and protection of holiness, and piety, and sacred ministrations, which all have reference to the honour of God. For the first and best thing in ourselves is our reason, and it is very proper to offer up the first-fruits of our cleverness, and acuteness, and comprehension, and prudence, and of all our other faculties which we have in connection with our reason as first-fruits to God, who has bestowed upon us this great abundance of power of exerting our intelligence. (99) From this consideration it was, that Jacob, the practiser of virtue, at the beginning of his prayers, says: "Of all that thou givest me, I will set apart and consecrate a tenth to Thee." [824] And the sacred scripture, which was written after the prayers on occasion of victory, which Melchisedek, who had received a self-instructed and self-taught priesthood, makes, says: "For he gave him a tenth of all Things." [825] assigning to him the outward senses the faculty of feeling properly, and by the same sense of speech the faculty of speaking well, and by the senses connected with the mind the faculty of thinking well. (100) Very beautifully, therefore, and at the same time most unavoidably, does the sacred historian tell us in the fashion of an incidental narrative, when the memorial of that heavenly and divine food was consecrated in the golden urn, that "gomer was the tenth part of three Measures." [826] For in us men there appear to be three measures, the outward senses, and speech, and mind. The outward sense being the measure of the objects of outward sense, speech being the measure of nouns and verbs, and of whatever is said; and the mind being the measure of those things which can only be perceived by the intellect. (101) We must therefore offer first-fruits of each of these three measures as a sacred tenth, in order that our powers of speaking, and of feeling, and of comprehending, may be seen to be irreproachable and sound, in reference to and in connection with God. For this is the true and just measure, and the things that relate to ourselves are false and unjust measures.

XIX

XIX. (102) Very appropriately, therefore, in the case of sacrifices also, the tenth part of the measure of fine wheat flour will be brought upon the altar, together with the victims. But the number of nine, which is what is left of the number ten, will remain among us. (103) And the daily sacrifice of the priests corresponds also to these facts. For it is expressly commanded to them to offer every day the tenth part of an Ephah [827] of fine wheat flour. For, passing over the ninth number, the god who was only discernible by the outward senses and by opinion, they learnt to worship the tenth, who is the only living and true God. (104) For the world had nine portions assigned to it, eight in heaven, namely the portion of the fixed stars and the seven planets which are all borne forward in the same arrangement, and the ninth being the earth in conjunction with the air and water. For of these things there is only one bond and connection, though they admit all kinds of various changes and alterations. (105) Therefore men in general have paid honours to these nine portions, and to the world which is compounded of them. But the perfect man honours only that being who is above the nine, and who is their creator, being the tenth portion, namely God. For having examined into the whole of his works, he has felt a love for the creator of them, and he has become anxious to be his suppliant and servant. On this account the priest offers up a tenth every day to the tenth, the only and everlasting God. (106) This is, to speak properly, the spiritual passover of the soul, the passing over of all the passions and of every object of the outward senses to the tenth, which is the proper object of the intellect, and which is divine. For it is said in the scripture: "On the tenth day of this month let each of them take a sheep according to his house;[828] in order that from the tenth, there may be consecrated to the tenth, that is to God, the sacrifices which have been preserved in the soul, which is illuminated in two portions out of the three, until it is entirely changed in every part, and becomes a heavenly brilliancy like a full moon, at the height of its increase at the end of the second week, and so is able not only to guard, but even to sacrifice uninjured and faultless improvements, that is to say, propitiations. (107) For this propitiation also is established in the tenth day of the month, when the soul addresses its supplications to the tenth portion, namely to God, and has learnt, by its own sagacity and acuteness, the insignificance and nothingness of the creature, and also the excessive perfection and pre-eminent excellence in all good things of the uncreated God. Therefore God becomes at once propitious, and propitious too, even without any supplications being addressed to him, to those who abase and humble themselves, and who are not puffed up with vain arrogance and self-opinion. (108) This is remission and deliverance, this is complete freedom of the soul, shaking off the wanderings in which it wandered, and fleeing for a secure anchorage to the one nature which cannot wander, and which rises up to return to the lot which it formerly received when it had brilliant aspirations, and when it vigorously toiled in labours which had virtuous ends for their object. For then admiring it for its exertions, the holy scripture honoured it, giving it a most especial honour, and immortal inheritance, a place namely in the imperishable race. (109) This is what the wise Abraham supplicates for, when that which in word indeed is the land of Sodom, but in real fact is the soul made barren of all good things and blinded as to its reason, is about to be burnt up, in order that if the memorial of justice, namely the Tenth [829] part be found in it, it may obtain a short of amnesty. Therefore he begins his supplication with a prayer for pardon, connected with the number fifty, and terminates with the number ten, the lowest number for whose deliverance he can dare to entreat.

XX

XX. (110) From which consideration it appears to me to have been, that Moses, after the appointment of chiliarchs, or commanders of thousands, and of centurians, and of captains of fifties,[830] thought proper to appoint captains of ten over all, in order than if the mind was not able to be improved by means of the elder orders, it might at least be purified by these last in order. (111) And the son of the man who was devoted to learning, learnt a very beautiful doctrine when he went on that admirable embassy, asking in marriage for the self-taught wise man that most appropriate sister, namely, perseverance. For he takes ten camels,[831] a reminder of the number ten, that is to say, of right instruction, from among many and, indeed, infinite memorials of the Lord. (112) He also takes of his good things, evidently not silver, nor any gold, nor any other of those things which consist of perishable materials; for Moses never gave the favourable apellation of good to any of these things, but those genuine good things which are the only good things of the soul; and those he appropriates for the use of his journey, and for his purposes of traffic, namely, instruction, improvement, study, desire, admiration, enthusiasm, prophecy, and the love of doing good actions; (113) to which objects, a man who devotes all his care, and who practices the actions calculated to ensure their attainment, when he is about, as it were, to anchor in a safe harbour after having been tossed in a stormy sea, will take two earrings, each of a drachm in weight, and two golden armlets of ten shekels weight of gold for the arms of her who is sought in Marriage. [832] Oh the divine ornament! We may understand that the drachm means the faculty of hearing, and the unbroken unit, and the attractive nature; for it is not becoming for hearing to have leisure to attend to anything except to that speech alone which sets forth in a suitable manner the virtues of the one and only God. And the ten shekels weight of gold mean attempts at works; for the actions, in accordance with wisdom, are established in perfect numbers, and every one of them is more precious than gold.

XXI

XXI. (114) Something of this kind, now, is the contribution made by the princes, selected and appointed with reference to worth and merit, which they made when the soul being properly prepared and adorned by philosophy, was celebrating the festival of the dedication in a sacred and becoming manner, giving thanks to God its teacher and its guide; for it "offers up a censer full of frankincense, ten golden shekels in Weight," [833] in order that the wise man alone may judge of the odours which are exhaled by prudence and by every virtue. (115) But when they appear to be made propitious, then Moses will sing a sacred hymn over them, saying, "The Lord has smelt the smell of a sweet savour," using the word to smell here as equivalent to approving of; for God is not formed like a man, nor has he any need of nostrils, or of any other organ parts. (116) But as he proceeds onwards he speaks also of the divine abode, the tabernacle, and its ten Curtains;" [834] for, in fact, the compound edifice of entire wisdom has been assigned the perfect number, the number ten. And wisdom is the court and palace of the all governing and only absolute and independent king. (117) Accordingly, this is his abode, discernible only by the intellect; but the world is perceptible by the outward senses; since Moses made the curtains of such things as are symbols of the four elements, for they were made of fine flax, and of hyacinthine colour, and of purple, and of scarlet, â"four numbers, as I have said before. Now the fine flax is an example of the earth, for the flax grows out of the earth; and the hyacinthine colour is a symbol of the air, for it is black by nature; purple (porphyra), again, is a symbol of the water; for the cause of this dye is derived from the sea, being the shell-fish of the same name (heÂ porphyra); and scarlet is a symbol of fire, for it most nearly resembles a flame. (118) Again, that omnipotent overseer and ruler of the universe reproved the state of Egypt, when rebellious against the rein, when it was extolling with grandiloquent words the mind as an adversary of God, and bestowing on it all the ensigns of kingly authority, such as the throne, the sceptre, the diadem; and chastised it with ten stripes and severe punishment. (119) And in the same manner, also, he promises the wise Abraham that he will work for him the overthrow and complete destruction of ten Nations [835] exactly, neither more nor less, and that he will give the country of those who are thus destroyed to his descendants; in every instance choosing to employ the number ten, both for praise and for blame, and also for honour and for punishment. And yet why do we mention these things? (120) For what is more important than this is the fact, that Moses gave laws to that sacred and divine assembly in a code of ten commandments in all. And these are the commandments which are the generic heads, and roots, and principles of the infinite multitude of particular laws; being the everlasting source of all commands, and containing every imaginable injunction and prohibition to the great advantage of those who use them.

XXXII

XXXII. (121) Very naturally, therefore, is the connection of Abraham with Hagar, placed at the end of ten years after his arrival in the land of the Chaldeans. For it does not follow that the first moment that we become endowed with reason, while our intellect is still in a somewhat fluid state, we are able at once to derive encyclical instruction. But when we have attained to intelligence and acuteness of comprehension, then we no longer have a light and superficial mind, but rather a firm and solid intellect which we can exercise on every subject. (122) And it is for this reason that the expression which follows is added, in connection with the former statement, "And he went in unto Hagar." For it was becoming for the scholar to go to his teacher, who was a man of learning, in order to learn such branches of instruction as are suited to the nature of man. For now, also, the pupil is represented as going to the place where he may obtain learning; but learning very often anticipates him and runs forward to meet him, having driven out envy from her habitation, and she attracts those towards her who are well inclined to her. (123) Accordingly, one may read that virtue, that is Leah, went forward to meet the practiser of virtue, and said unto him, "To-day you shall come in to Me," [836] when he was returning from the fields. For where was the man who had the care of the seeds and plants of knowledge found to come, except to that virtue which he himself had cultivated?

XXIII

XXIII. (124) But there are times when virtue, as if making experiment of those who come to her as pupils, to see how much eagerness they have, does not come forward to meet them, but veiling her face like Tamar, sits down in the public road, giving room to those who are traveling along the road to look upon her as a harlot, in order that those who are over curious on the subject may take off her veil and disclose her features, and may behold the untouched, and unpolluted, and most exquisite, and truly virgin beauty of modesty and chastity. (125) Who then is he who is fond of investigating, and desirous of learning, and who thinks it not right to leave any of those things which are disguised or concealed unconsidered and examined? Who is he, I say, but the chief captain and king, he who abides and rejoices in the agreements which he has made with God, by name Judah? For says the scripture, "He turned aside out of his road to her, and said unto her, Suffer me to come in unto thee," (but he was not inclined to offer her any violence), and to see what is that power which is thus veiled, and for what purpose it is thus adorned; (126) and after they had come together it is written, "And she conceived;" but the name of the person is not expressly mentioned. For art conceives and carries along with it him who is learning it, persuading him to feel amorously inclined towards her; and also he who is learning carries with him her who is teaching him, whenever he is fond of learning. (127) And it often happens that he who professes some one of the indifferent branches of knowledge, when he meets with a pupil of good natural qualifications, boasts of his success in teaching, thinking that he, by himself and alone, is the cause of his pupil's facility in learning. And then, becoming elated and puffing himself up, he holds his head high, and draws his eyebrows and becomes full of pride, and asks very high terms from those who desire to become his pupils; but those whom he perceives to be poor but still to be eager for instruction, he rejects and repels, as if he were the only person who had found a treasure of wisdom. (128) This is the meaning of the expression, "to conceive," namely, to be full of pride, and to be puffed up with arrogance beyond all moderation, on which account some persons have appeared to dishonour the queen of all the intermediate and indifferent branches of knowledge, virtue, who deserves to be honoured, even for her own sake. (129) All the souls, therefore, which, in connection with prudence, are pregnant of real things, do nevertheless bring forth, separating and distinguishing between things previously in confusion, like Rebekkah; for she having conceived in her womb ideas of two nations, the knowledge of virtue and the knowledge of wickedness, having a fortunate labour separated and distinguished between the nature of each; but those which have conceived without prudence either miscarry or else bring forth an offspring inclined to evil contention and sophistry, always either aiming darts and arrows at others, or having darts and arrows aimed at themselves. (130) And may we not say that this is natural? for some fancy that they are just conceiving, and others they they are actually pregnant, which is a very different thing; for those who think that they are already pregnant attribute their pregnancy and the birth of their offspring to themselves, and pride themselves upon it; but those who look upon themselves as now conceiving, admit that they have of themselves nothing which they can call peculiarly their own, but they receive the seed and the prospects of posterity which are showered upon them from without, and they admire him who bestows it, and repel the greatest of evils, namely self-love, by that perfect good, piety towards the gods.

XXIV

XXIV. (131) In this manner also the seeds of the legitimate wisdom, which exists among men, were sown, "For there was," says the same historian, "a man of the tribe of Levi, named Amram, who took to wife one of the daughters of Levi, and had her, and she conceived and brought forth a male child; and seeing that he was a goodly child they concealed him for three Months."[837] (132) This is Moses, the purest mind, the child that is really goodly; the child that received at the same time all legislative and prophetic skill by the means of inspired and heaven-bestowed wisdom; who, being by birth a member of the tribe of Levi, and being flourishing both in the things relating to his mother and in those affecting his father, clings to the truth; (133) and the greatest profession ever made by the author and chief of this tribe is this, for he makes bold to say, that "the only God is alone to be honoured by me;" and nothing besides of all the things that are inferior to Him, neither earth, nor sea, nor rivers, nor the nature of the air, nor the nature of the winds, nor the changes of the atmosphere, nor the appearances of any animals or plants, nor the sun, nor the moon, nor the multitude of the stars moving in well-arranged revolutions, nor the whole heaven, nor the entire world. (134) This is a boast of a great and magnanimous soul, to rise above all creation, and to overleap its boundaries, and to cling to the great uncreated God alone, according to his sacred commands, in which we are expressly enjoined "to cleave unto Him."[838] Therefore he, in requital, bestows himself as their inheritance upon those who do cleave unto him, and who serve him without intermission; and the sacred scripture bears its testimony in behalf of this assertion, where it says, "The Lord himself is his Inheritance." [839] (135) Thus the souls which are already pregnant are naturally likely to bring forth children, rather than those which are now receiving the seed. But as the eyes of the body do oftentimes see obscurely, and often on the other hand see clearly, so in the same manner does the eye of the soul, at times, receive the particular impressions conveyed to it by things in a most confused and indistinct manner, and at other times it beholds them with the greatest purity and clearness; (136) therefore an indistinct and not clearly manifested conception resembles an embryo which has not yet received any distinct character or similitude within the womb: but that which is clear and distinctly visible, is like one which is completely formed, and which is already fashioned in an artistic manner as to both its inward and its outward parts, and which has already received its suitable character. (137) And with respect to these matters the following law has been enacted with great beauty and propriety: "If while two men are fighting one should strike a woman who is great with child, and her child should come from her before it is completely formed, he shall be muleted in a fine, according to what the husband of the woman shall impose on him, and he shall pay the fine deservedly. But if the child be fully formed, he shall pay life for Life." [840] For it was not the same thing, to destroy a perfect and an imperfect work of the mind, nor is what is only likened by a figure similar to what is really comprehended, nor is what is only hoped for similar to what really exists. (138) On this account, in one case, an uncertain penalty is affixed to an uncertain action; in another, a definite punishment is enacted by law against an act which is perfected, but which is perfected not with respect to virtue, but with reference to what is done in an irreproachable manner, according to some act. For it is not she who has just received the seed, but she who has been for some time pregnant, who brings forth this offspring, professing boasting rather than modesty. For it is impossible that she who has been pregnant some time should miscarry, since it is fitting that the plant should be conducted to perfection by him who sowed it; but it is not strange if some mishap should befall the woman who was pregnant, since she was afflicted with a disease beyond the art of the physician.

XXV

XXV. (139) And do not suppose that Hagar is represented as beholding herself as pregnant, by the words, "seeing that she had conceived," but as beholding her mistress Sarah; for afterwards she speaks of herself, and says, "Seeing that she was pregnant, she was despised before Her." [841] Why so? (140) Because the intermediate and indifferent arts, and the sciences in accord with them, see indeed of what they are pregnant, but they nevertheless see in every respect but dimly; but the sciences comprehend clearly and very distinctly. For science is something beyond art, having derived from reason a certain firmness and exemption from error; (141) for this is the definition of art, a system of comprehensions well practised with reference to some desirable end, the word desirable being very properly added by reason of the abundance of evil arts. But the definition of science is a safe and firm comprehension, which, through reason, is not liable to any error. (142) Therefore we call music and grammar, and other pursuits, arts; for those also who are made perfect in them, as musicians, or grammarians, are called artists. But we call philosophy and the other virtues, sciences, and those who are possessed of the knowledge of them we call scientific; for they are prudent, and temperate, and philosophical, not one of whom is ever deceived in the doctrines of a philosophy which he himself has cultivated, any more than the artists, whom I have mentioned before, err in their speculations with respect to their indifferent arts. (143) For as the eyes see, and still the mind sees more clearly by means of the eyes; and as the ears hear, but nevertheless the mind hears better through the medium of the ears; and as the nostrils smell, and yet the soul smells more precisely through the instrumentality of the nostrils; and in like manner, as the other external senses comprehend their respective appropriate objects, still the mind comprehends them also more purely and distinctly by their ministration. For to speak properly, it is the mind which is the eye of eyes, the hearing of hearing, and the more pure external sense of each of the external senses, using them as ministers in a court of justice, and itself deciding on the nature of the objects submitted to it, so as to approve of some and to reject others. In the same way, those that are called the intermediate arts, resembling the faculties of the body, indulge in contemplations according to certain simple observations of them, but the sciences do so with greater accuracy and with exceedingly careful investigation. (144) For the same relation that the mind bears to the outward sense, that same does science bear towards art; for, as has been said before, the soul is as it were the outward sense of the outward sense; therefore each of them has attracted to itself some slight things of nature, concerning which it labours and occupies itself, geometry having appropriated lines, and music sounds, and philosophy the whole nature of existing things. For this world is its subject matter, and so is the whole essence, both visible and invisible, of existing things. (145) What then is there wonderful if the soul, which sees both the whole and the parts, sees them too better than they do, as if it were furnished with larger and more acute eyes? Very naturally, therefore, proper philosophy will behold intermediate instruction its handmaiden, and she that she is pregnant, more than the other will see that she is.

XXVI

XXVI. (146) And yet even this is not unknown to any one, namely, that philosophy has bestowed upon all the particular sciences their first principles and seeds, from which speculations respecting them appear to arise. For it is geometry which invented equilateral and scalene triangles, and circles, and polygons, and all kinds of other figures. But it was no longer geometry that discovered the nature of a point, and line, and a superficies, and a solid, which are the roots and foundations of the aforementioned figures. (147) For from whence could it define and pronounce that a point is that which has no parts, that a line is length without breadth; that a superficies is that which has only length and breadth; that a solid is that which has the three properties, length, breadth, and depth? For these discoveries belong to philosophy, and the consideration of these definitions belongs wholly to the philosopher. (148) Again, to write and read is the undertaking of this more imperfect kind of grammar, which some people, perverting the name of, call grammatistica. But to the most perfect kind of grammar belongs the explanation of the great works of the poets and historians. When, therefore, men are going through the different parts of speech, and they not in so doing trying to drag over to themselves and appropriate as a kind of accessory the discoveries of philosophy? (149) For it is the peculiar province of philosophy to inquire what a conjection, what a noun, what a verb, what a common noun, what a particular noun, what is deficient in a speech, what is superfluous, what is an affirmative, what an interrogative, what an indirect question, what is a comprehensive expression, what is a supplicatory form of address. For this is a science which has been compounded for the purpose of the investigation of independent propositions, and axioms, and categorems. (150) But, moreover, has not the whole question of semi-vowels, or vowels, or such elements as are completely mute, and the consideration of the sense in which each of these expressions is ordinarily used, and in short every notion connected with the voice, and the elements, and the parts of speech, been thoroughly worked out and brought to an accurate system by philosophy? And those thieves, after having as it were carried off a few drops from her torrent, and having sought to impregnate their own shallow souls with what they have stolen, are not ashamed to bring forth her resources as their own.

XXVII

XXVII. (151) On which account, being elated and proud, they disregard the mistress to whom in reality the authority and the complete confirmation of their contemplations belong. But she, perceiving their neglect, will convict them, and will speak freely to them, and say, "I am treated unjustly, and in utter violation of our agreement, as far as depends on you who transgress the covenants entered into between us; (152) for from the time that you first took to your bosom the elementary branches of education, you have honoured above measure the offspring of my handmaiden, and have respected her as your wife, and you have so completely repudiated me that you never by any chance came to the same place with me. And perhaps this may be only a suspicion of mine respecting you, arising from your open connection with my servant, which leads me to conjecture your alienation from myself, though it is not really manifest. But if your disposition is contrary to that which I suspect, still it is impossible for any one else to know this, but it is easy to God alone." (153) On which account she says very appropriately, "May God judge between thee and me; [842] not making haste to condemn him beforehand as having done her wrong, but intimating a doubt, that perhaps he may speedily do her right, which in point of fact is seen to be the case not long afterwards, when he, excusing himself and remedying her doubts, says to her, "Behold thy handmaiden is in thy hands, do unto her as it seemeth good to thee." (154) For also, when he calls her her handmaiden, he confesses both facts, both that she is a slave and also that she is a child; for the name of the handmaiden (paidiskeÂ) suits both these circumstances. At the same time also, he confesses the contrary things, opposing the child to the fullgrown woman, and the mistress to her slave, all but crying out in plain words: I embrace indeed encyclical instruction as a younger maiden and as a handmaiden, but I honour knowledge and prudence as full-grown and a mistress. (155) And the expression, "She is in thy hands," means, she is in thy power and subject to thee. And this is also a symbol of something else of this nature, namely, that the qualities of the handmaiden come to the hands of the body; for the encyclical branches of knowledge have need of the bodily organs and faculties; but the qualities of the mistress reach the soul; for the things which belong to prudence and knowledge come under the province of reason; (156) so that in proportion as the mind is more powerful and more efficacious than, and in short superior to, the hand, in the same proportion also do I look upon knowledge and wisdom as more admirable than encyclical accomplishment, and I honour them in a higher degree. Do thou, therefore, O thou who both art the mistress, and who art so accounted by me, take all my encyclical instruction and use it as thy handmaid, doing to it as it shall seem good to thee; (157) for I am not unaware that whatever pleases thee is in all respects good even though it may not always be pleasant, and is useful even though it be far removed from being agreeable.

But admonition and reproof are both good and profitable to those who stand in need of correction, which indeed the holy scriptures call by another name, and denominate affliction.

XXVIII

XXVIII. (158) On which account the historian presently adds, "And she afflicted her;" an expression equivalent to, she admonished and corrected her. For a sharp spear is very profitable for those who are corrupted by over security and indolences, just as it is of use with restive horses; since they can scarcely be subdued and made manageable by the whip and by gentle leading. (159) Do you not see how they are utterly unaffected by the prizes proposed to Them? [843] They are fat, they are stout, they are sleek, they breathe hard; then they take up the actions of impiety, miserable and wretched men that they are, seeking a melancholy reward, being proclaimed and crowned as conquerors by ungodliness. For by reason of the prosperity which was constantly flowing gently towards them, they looked upon themselves as silver or golden gods, after the fashion of adulterated money, forgetting the real and true coinage. (160) And Moses testifies to this view of the matter when he says, "He got fat, he became stout, he became swollen, and forsook God who had created Him." [844] So that if excessive relaxation begets the greatest of all evils, impiety, its contrary, affliction, in accordance with the law produces that perfect good, much praised correction; (161) and proceeding outward from this point, he also calls the unleavened bread the symbol of the first festival, "the bread of Affliction." [845] And yet who is there who does not know that feasts and festivals produce cheerful joy and delectation, and not affliction? (162) But it is plain that he is here using in a perverted sense this word for the labour of him who is the corrector. For the most numerous and greatest blessings are usually acquired by laborious practice and exercise, and by vigorously excited labour. But the festival of the soul is emulation, which is labour to attain those things which are most excellent and which are brought to perfection; on which account it is expressly commanded to "eat the unleavened bread with bitter Herbs;" [846] not by way of an additional dish, but because men in general look upon the fact of being prevented from swelling and boiling over with their appetites, but being forced to contract and restrain them as a grievous thing, thinking it a bitter thing to unlearn the indulgence of their passions, which is the real feast and festival of a mind which loves honourable contests.

XXIX

XXIX. (163) It is for this reason that the law, as it appears to men, was given in a place which is called Bitterness; for to do wrong is pleasant, but to act justly is laborious. And this is the most unerring law; for the sacred history says, "And after they had gone out from the passions of Egypt they came to Marah: and they were not able to drink of the water at Marah, for it was bitter. On this account the name of that place was called Bitterness. And the people murmured against Moses, saying, What shall we drink? And Moses cried unto the Lord; and the Lord showed him a stick, and he cast it into the water, and the water was made sweet. And then he gave him justification and judgment, (164) and then he tempted Him." [847] For the invisible trial and proofs of the soul are in labouring and in enduring bitterness; for then it is hard to know which way it will incline; for many men are very speedily fatigued and fall away, thinking labour a terrible adversary, and they let their hands fall out of weakness, like tired wrestlers, determining to return to Egypt to the indulgence of their passions. (165) But others, with much endurance and great vigour, supporting the fearful and terrible events of the wilderness pass through the contest of life, keeping their life safe from overthrow and from destruction, and rising up in vigorous contest against the necessities of nature, such as hunger, thirst, cold, and heat, which are in the habit of reducing other persons to slavery, and subduing them with great exuberance of strength. (166) And the cause of this is not merely labour, but also the sweetness with which it is combined; for the scripture says, "And the water was made sweet." But sweet and pleasant labour is called by another name, fondness for labour; for that which is sweet in labour is the love of, and desire for, and admiration of, and friendship for, what is honourable. (167) Let no one, therefore, reject such affliction as this, and let no one think that the table of festivity and cheerfulness is called the bread of affliction for injury rather than for advantage; for the soul which is rightly admonished is supported by the doctrines of instruction.

XXX

XXX. (168) This unleavened cake is so sacred that it is enjoined in the holy scriptures, "to place in the innermost part of the temple, on the golden table, twelve loaves of unleavened bread, corresponding in number to the twelve tribes; and those loaves shall be called the shew-Bread."[848] (169) And again, it is in the law expressly "forbidden to offer any leaven or any honey upon the Altar;"[849] for it is a difficult thing to consecrate as holy either the sweetnesses of the pleasures according to the body, or the light and unsubstantial elations of the soul, since they are by their own intrinsic nature profane and unholy. (170) Does not, then, the prophetic word, by name Moses, very rightly speak in dignified language when he says, "Thou shalt remember all the road by which the Lord God led thee in the wilderness, and how he afflicted thee, and tried thee, and proved thee, that he might know what was in thy heart, and whether thou wouldest keep his commandments. Did he not afflict thee and oppress thee with hunger, and feed thee with manna which thy fathers know not, that he might make thee know that man shall not live by bread alone, but by every word that proceedeth out of the mouth of God?"[850] (171) Who, then, is so impious as to conceive that God is one who afflicts, and who brings that most pitiable death of hunger upon those who are not able to live without food? For God is good, and the cause of good things, bounteous, the saviour, the supporter, the giver of wealth, the giver of great gifts, driving out wickedness from the sacred boundaries; for thus did he drive out the burdens of the earth, Adam and Cain, from paradise. (172) Let us, then, not be led aside by words, but let us consider and examine what meaning is intended to be conveyed under figurative expressions, and pronounce that the words "he afflicted," are equivalent to "he instructed, and he admonished, and he corrected." And when it is said that he oppressed them with hunger, it does not mean that he caused a deficiency of meat and drink, but of pleasures, and desires, and fear, and grief, and acts of injustice, and, in short, of all things which are the works of wickedness or of the passions. (173) And what is said immediately afterwards is an evidence of this: "He fed thee with manna." Is it, then, proper to call that food which, without any exertion or hardship on his part, and without any trouble of his is given to man, not out of the earth as is usual, but from heaven, a marvellous work, afforded for the benefit of those who are to be permitted to avail themselves of it, the cause of hunger and affliction, and not rather, on the contrary, the cause of prosperity and happiness, of freedom from fear, and of a happy state of orderly living? (174) But men in general and the common herd think that those who are nourished on the word of God live in a miserable and wretched manner; for they are without the taste of the allnourishing food of wisdom; but they are not aware that they are living in the height of happiness.

XXXI

XXXI. (175) Thus, therefore, there is a certain description of affliction which is profitable, so that its very most humiliating form, even slavery, is accounted a great good. And there is a father who is recorded in the sacred writings as having prayed for this, for his son, namely, the most excellent Isaac for the foolish Esau; (176) for he says somewhere, "By thy sword shalt thou live, and thou shalt serve thy Brother."[851] Judging that destiny to be the most advantageous one for a man who had chosen war rather than peace, and who was as it were constantly armed and engaged in battle, by reason of the sedition and disorder constantly existing in his soul, the destiny namely of being a subject and a servant, and of obeying all the commands which the lover of temperance should lay upon him. (177) And it is from this consideration, as it appears to me that one of the disciples of Moses, by name the peaceful, who in his native language is called Solomon, says, "My son, neglect not the instruction of God, and be not grieved when thou art reproved by him; for whom the Lord loveth he chasteneth; and scourgeth every son whom he Received."[852] Thus, then, scourging and reproof are looked upon as good, so that by means of it agreement and relationship with God arise. For what can be more nearly related than a son is to his father, and a father to his son? (178) But that we may not seem to be too prolix connecting one argument with another, we will, besides what we have already said, just add one most evident proof that a certain description of affliction is the work of virtue. For there is such a law this, "Thou shalt not afflict any widow or orphan, but if thou dost afflict them with wickedness." ... What does this mean? Is it then possible to be afflicted by something else? For if afflictions were the work of wickedness alone, then it would be superfluous to add what would be admitted by all, and which would be understood without any such addition. (179) But, you will most certainly say, I know that men are reproved by virtue, and instructed by wisdom; on which account I do not blame every kind of affliction, but I very greatly admire that which is the work of justice and of the law; for that corrects by means of punishment, but that which proceeds from folly and wickedness and is pernicious, I do, as becomes me, detest, and pronounce real evil. (180) When, therefore, you hear that Hagar was afflicted by Sarah, you must not suppose that any of those things befell her, which arise from rivalry and quarrels among women; for the question is not here about woman, but about minds; the one being practised in the branches of elementary instruction, and the other being devoted to the labours of virtue.

Footnotes:

805. Yonge's title, A Treatise on the Meeting for the Sake of Seeking Instruction.
806. Gen 16:1.
807. Gen 29:31.
808. Exod 25:31.
809. Gen 30:1.
810. 1Chr 7:14.
811. Gen 36:12.
812. Exod 15:17.
813. Deut 32:8.
814. Gen 25:27.
815. Gen 16:2.
816. Gen 28:7.
817. Gen 16:3.
818. Lev 18:1.
819. Lev 23:27.
820. Lev 25:9.
821. Exod 26:1.
822. Gen 14:1.
823. Lev 27:32.
824. Gen 28:22.
825. Gen 14:20.
826. Exod 16:36.
827. Exod 10:20.
828. Exod 12:3.
829. Gen 18:32.
830. Exod 18:25.
831. Gen 24:10.
832. Gen 24:22.
833. Num 7:14.
834. Exod 26:1.
835. Deut 7:1.
836. Gen 30:16.
837. Exod 2:1.
838. Deut 30:20.
839. Deut 10:9.
840. Exod 21:22.
841. Gen 16:4.
842. Gen 16:5.
843. this is scarcely sense, but the truth probably is that the passage is corrupt. Mangey proposes one or two emendations, but they are not very satisfactory.
844. Deut 32:15.
845. Deut 16:3.
846. Exod 12:8.
847. Exod 15:23.
848. Exod 25:30.
849. Lev 2:11.
850. Deut 8:2.
851. Gen 27:40.
852. Prov 3:11.

Philo Judaeus

ON FLIGHT AND FINDING [853]

I

I. (1) "And Sarah afflicted her, and she fled from before her face. And the angel of the Lord found her sitting by a fountain of water in the wilderness, by a fountain which is in the way to Shur. And the angel of the Lord said unto her: æThou handmaiden of Sarah, whence art thou come? and whither art thou going?' And she answered and said: æI am fleeing from the face of Sarah, my mistress.' And the angel of the Lord said unto her: æReturn unto thy mistress, and be thou humbled beneath her hands.' And the angel of the Lord said unto her: æBehold, thou art with child, and thou shalt bring forth a son, and shall call his name Ishmael, because the Lord has heard the cry of thy humiliation. He shall be a rude man; his hand shall be against every man, and every man's hand against Him." [854] (2) Having in our former treatise spoken what was becoming respecting the preliminary branches of education, and respecting affliction, we will now proceed in regular order to discuss the topic of fugitives. Now Moses often mentions persons who flee, as here he says concerning Hagar, that being afflicted she fled from the face of her mistress. (3) I think therefore that there are three causes for flight--hatred, fear, and shame. Now women leave their husbands out of hatred, and for the same reason men desert their wives. But children flee from their parents, and servants from their masters, out of fear. And lastly, friends avoid their companions out of shame, when they have done anything which is displeasing to them. And before now I have known instances of fathers who have led a life of effeminate luxury, reverencing the austere and philosophical lives of their sons, and out of shame preferring to live in the country rather than in the city. (4) Now of all these three causes, one may find instances revealed in the sacred scriptures. Accordingly, Jacob, the practiser of virtue, fled from his father-in-law Laban out of hatred, and from his brother Esau out of fear, as I shall show presently. (5) But Hagar flees out of shame. And a proof of this is, that the angel, that is the word of God, met her, with the intent to recommend her what she ought to do, and to guide her in her return to her mistress's house. For he encouraged her, and said unto her: "The Lord has heard the cry of thy humiliation," which you uttered, not out of fear, nor yet out of hatred. For the one is the feeling of an ignoble soul, and the other of one which loves contention, but under the influence of that copy of temperance and modesty, shame. (6) For it was natural, if she had fled out of fear, that he would have encouraged her mistress, who was holding out threats to alarm her, to comfort her, and to restore her to tranquillity. For then it would have been safe for the fugitive to return, and not before. But no one intercedes for her to her mistress, inasmuch as she was already appeased by herself. But this angel, who is reproof, at the same time friendly and full of advice, out of his goodwill teaches her not to feel only shame, but also to entertain confidence, for that modesty is but half a virtue, when separated from proper boldness.

II

II. (7) Therefore the account which follows will show these characteristics more accurately. But we must return to the heads of the question which we have already set forth, and begin with those who flee under the influence of hatred. "For," says the scripture, "Jacob concealed his purpose from Laban the Syrian, so as not to tell him that he was fleeing, and he fled, he and all that he Had." [855] (8) What then was the cause of his hatred? For perhaps you are desirous to hear this. There are some persons who make themselves gods of substance destitute of all distinctive quality, and species, and shape, neither knowing the cause which puts things in motion, nor showing any anxiety to learn of those who do know, but being contented with their ignorance and want of understanding of the most important kind of learning, which was in fact the first and only thing of which it was absolutely necessary to labour for the understanding. (9) Laban now is one of this kind of persons; for the sacred scriptures attribute to him a flock devoid of all distinctive marks. And matter, without any distinctive characteristics, is without any marks in the universe, and so is in men the soul, which is destitute of learning and which has no instructors. (10) But there are others who belong to a better portion, who say that the mind has come and arranged everything, bringing the disorder which arose from an ochlocracy among all existing things, into the order established by the legitimate authority of kingly power. Of this company Jacob is a follower, who presides over the marked and party-coloured flock. On the other hand the species in the universe is distinguished by marks and is of varied colour, and so also in men is the mind which has been well instructed and which is fond of learning. (11) And he who is marked, and who is the companion of true kingly power, having received a great deal of the social affection from nature, goes to him who has no distinguishing marks, and who, as I have said, makes himself gods of the material powers, and who thinks that besides them there is no effectual cause of anything, to teach him that his opinions are not correct. (12) For the world has been created, and has by all means derived its existence from some extraneous cause. But the word itself of the Creator is the seal by which each of existing things is invested with form. In accordance with which fact perfect species also does from the very beginning follow things when created, as being an impression and image of the perfect word. (13) For the animal when first created is imperfect as to quantity; and a proof of this is the gradual growth which takes place at each successive age. But it is perfect as to quality. For the same quality remains in it, as having been stamped upon it by the divine word which abides permanently and never charges.

III

III. (14) But seeing that he is dumb with respect to learning and to all desirable and legitimate authority, he very naturally thinks of flight. For he is afraid that in addition to not being able to derive any advantage, he may even be injured. For all connections with the foolish injures us, and very often the soul against its will becomes stamped with the impression of their insanity of mind. And, in truth, instruction is naturally a thing inimical to ignorance, and so is industry to indifference. (15) In reference to which fact the powers devoted to practice and meditation, when they are set free, cry out, giving a full account of the causes of their hatred: "Have we not any longer a share and an inheritance in the house of our father? Are we now accounted aliens by him? For he has sold us, and he has eaten up and devoured our money. All the wealth and all the glory which God took from our father shall belong to us and to our Children." [856] (16) For those who are free both in name and also in their minds do not consider any foolish person as either rich or glorious, but look upon all such persons, so to say, as inglorious and poor, even if they exceed the fortune of wealthy kings. For they do not say that they will have the riches of their father, but the riches which have been taken away; nor do they say that they shall possess his glory, but the glory which has been taken away from him. (17) But the wicked man is deprived of all genuine riches and of all true and honourable glory; for these blessings are procured by wisdom, and temperance, and the kindred dispositions of the soul, and are inherited by those souls which love virtue. (18) Therefore, it is not the things which belong to the wicked man, but those of which he is destitute, that are the abundance and the glory of the good. And he is destitute of virtues which are their possession, in order that what is said in another place may be consistent with the passage already quoted: "Let us sacrifice the abominations of Egypt to the Lord our God." [857] For the virtues are perfect and blameless offerings, and so are the actions in accordance with virtue, which the Egyptian body, being devoted to the passions, abominates; (19) for, as in this passage, those things which, according to the principles of natural philosophy, are reckoned profane among the Egyptians are called sacred by the Israelites who see acutely, and are all offered as sacrifices; so, in the same manner, the man who is the companion of virtue will be the heir of those things of which every foolish man is deprived and destitute. And these things are true glory, which in fact differs in no respect from knowledge, and wealth, not blind wealth, but that which is the most sharpsighted of all existing things, which never receives any base money, not even anything whatever devoid of life unless it be thoroughly tried and approved. (20) Very naturally, therefore, that person will flee from him who has no participation in divine blessings, who even in the matters in which he accuses another does without perceiving it accuse himself also, when he says, "If thou hadst told me I would have sent thee Away." [858] For this very thing was a worthy cause for your being deserted, if you, being the servant of an infinite number of masters, pretending to have been invested with command and authority, proclaimed liberty to others. (21) But I, says he, did not take a man as my assistant in the road which leads to virtue, but I listened to the divine oracles which enjoined me to depart from hence, and which even now continues to direct my course. (22) And how would you have sent me away? surely, as you boast, using pompous language, with a joy which to me would have been sorrowful, with music which would have been no music, with dances, and noises destitute of articulate sound and of reason, striking blows on the soul through the medium of the ears, and with the harp, and with sounds unsuited to the lyre, and unsuited to harmony, not being so much organs, as the actions of a whole life. But these are the things by reason of which I meditated flight; but you, as it seems, contemplated dragging me back from my flight, in order that I might return on account of the deceitful and seductive nature of the external senses, by which I was scarcely able to permit myself to be carried forward.

IV

IV. (23) Hatred then, was the cause of the flight which I have been here describing; but fear was the cause of the one which I am about to mention. For, says the sacred historian, Rebekkah said unto Jacob, "Behold, Esau thy brother threateneth to kill thee: now therefore, my son, hear my voice, and rise up, and flee to Laban my brother, to Charran, and dwell with him certain days, until the anger of thy brother is turned away, and he forget what thou hast done unto him; and then I will send again, and fetch thee back from Thence." [859] (24) For it was worth while to fear, lest the worse portion of the soul, lying in an ambuscade, or else moving forwards openly to the attack, might overthrow and cast down the better part; and so the counsel of the right-minded perseverance, Rebekkah, was very good. (25) But she says, when you see the bad man coming in with great impetuosity, against virtue, and making great account of those things which it is more proper to disregard, such as wealth, glory, and pleasure, and praising the performance of actions of injustice, as being the cause of all the advantages before mentioned: for we see that those who act unjustly, are, for the most part, men possessed of much silver, and of much gold, and of high reputation. Do not then, turn away to the opposite road, and devote yourself to a life of penury, and abasement, and austerity, and solitude; for, by doing so, you will irritate your adversary, and arm a more bitter enemy against yourself. (26) Consider, therefore, now by what conduct you may avoid his attacks; apply yourself to the same things, I do not mean the same pursuits, but to the same things which are the efficient causes of those things which have been mentioned; to honours, to offices of authority, to silver, to gold, to possessions, to money, to colours, to forms, to exceeding nicety; and when you meet with such things, then, like a skilful workman, impress the most beautiful appearance on the material substances: and perfect a most excellent work. (27) Do you not know, that if a man unacquainted with navigation, takes the management of a ship, which might otherwise have reached the harbour in safety, he overturns it? but that a man, skilful as a pilot, has often saved a ship which otherwise must have been lost? And also, some sick persons, owing to the unskilfulness of their medical attendants, have been severely afflicted with disease; while others, through the skill of their doctors, have escaped from dangerous sicknesses? And why need I have been prolix on this point; for always the things which are done with skill, are a conviction of those which are done unskilfully; and the true praise of the one is an unerring accusation of the other.

V

V. (28) If therefore, you wish to convict a wicked man, who is also possessed of great wealth, do not disdain an abundance of money; for the unhappy man will soon show himself in his true colours, either as an illiberal and slavish-minded skin-flint, and parer of people by usury, or else as a profligate and intemperate spendthrift, very ready to devour and to squander, and a most zealous companion of harlots and brothel-keepers, and pimps, and of every kind of profligate company. (29) But you will rather bestow your contributions on those who are in want of friends, and will do favours to, and bestow your liberality on, your country, and will assist to portion out the daughters of needy parents, giving them, in addition to their inheritance, a most sufficient dowry; and in fact, very nearly throwing all your own property into the common stock, you will invite to a participation in it all who are worthy of favour. (30) And, in the same manner, when you wish to reprove any wicked man who is mad with a high opinion of himself and full of boasting, while you are able yourself to attain to distinguished honours, do not disdainfully reject the praise of the multitude: for by so doing you will trip up and supplant the miserable man who takes long strides, and who gives himself airs. For he will abuse his own renown for the purpose of behaving with insolence and contumely to others who are better than he, promoting those who are worse, so as to set them above them; while you, on the contrary, will give all worthy persons a share in your renown, giving in this manner security to those who are good, and by your admonitions improving those who are not so good. (31) And if you ever to go a drinking party or to a costly entertainment, go with a good confidence; for you will put to shame the intemperate man by your own dexterity. For he, falling on his belly, and opening his insatiable desires even before he opens his mouth, will glut himself in a most shameless and indecorous manner, and will seize the things belonging to his neighbour, and will lick up everything without thinking. And when he is completely sated with eating, then drinking, as the poets say, with his mouth open, he will make himself an object for the laughter and ridicule of all those who behold him. (32) But do you adopt a moderate course without being compelled thereto, and if ever you are constrained to indulge yourself in things beyond moderation, still make reason the governor of the necessity, and never go so far as to change pleasure into unpleasantness, but, if we may speak in such a manner, be drunk in a sober manner.

VI

VI. (33) And here therefore truth may not unreasonably blame those who, without any examination, abandon the business and means of regulating a civil life, and who say that they have learnt to despise glory and pleasure; for those men are behaving insolently, and do not really despise these things, making an open boast of their sordid, and melancholy, and stern appearance, and putting forth their austere and dirty way of living as a bait, as if they were lovers of orderly behaviour, and modestly, and endurance; (34) but they are not able to deceive those who look into them with greater accuracy, and who pierce within their disguise, and who are not led astray by outward show; for having removed these veils and coverings from the others, they see what is treasured up and concealed within, and learn what kind of qualities and nature are theirs: and if they are good they admire them, and if they are evil they ridicule them, and hate them because of their hypocrisy. (35) Let us then say to such persons, "Are ye zealous admirers and imitators of a life which hates mixing with and joining in the society of others, a solitary and uncompanionable life? For what specimen of virtue have you ever exhibited while living in the society of others? Do ye disdain money? Have you, then, who have been professed money-dealers, been desirous to act justly? Professing to disregard the pleasures of the belly and of the parts beneath the belly, have you behaved with moderation when you have had abundant opportunities of indulging these appetites? Do you despise glory? Then, when you have been placed in situations of authority, have you cultivated an affable humility? Perhaps you have ridiculed a participation in the affairs of state, not considering how useful an employment that is." (36) Have you then first exercised yourselves in, and directed your attention to, the public and the private business of life? and having become skilful politicians and experienced economists by means of the kindred virtues of economical and political science, have you, in your exceeding abundance of these things, prepared for your migration to another and a better kind of life? For it is proper to go through a practical life before beginning the theoretical one: as being a sort of rehearsal of the more perfect contest and exhibition. In this way it is possible to escape from the charge of hesitation and indolence. (37) Thus also an express injunction is given to the Levites to fulfil their works till the time that they are fifty years of age; and after they are released from all active ministrations, to consider and contemplate each particular thing, receiving as a reward for their welldoing in active life, another life which delights only in knowledge and contemplation. (38) And at other times it is necessary that those who think themselves worthy to claim the just things of God, should first of all fulfil their human duties; for it is great folly to expect to attain to what is of greater importance, while one is unable properly to discharge what is of less consequence. First of all, therefore, be ye known for your virtue among men, that you may also become established by that which relates to God." This is the advice which perseverance gives to the man inclined to the practice of virtue; but we must now examine her several expressions with accuracy.

VII

VII. (39) "Behold," says she, "Esau thy brother threatens thee." But is it not natural for that disposition, hard as oak and obstinate through ignorance, by name Esau, who offers the baits of mortal life to lead you to your destruction; such baits, I mean, as wealth, glory, pleasure, and other kindred temptations, to seek to kill thee? But do you, O my child! flee from this contest at present, for you have not as yet had complete strength for it given to you, but still the nerves of your soul, like those of a child, are somewhat soft and weak. (40) And it is for this reason that she calls him "my child," while is a name of affection, and also one which indicates his tender age; for we look upon the disposition which is inclined to the practice of virtue, and which is young, as worthy of affection in comparison of the fullgrown man. But such a person is worthy to carry off the prizes which are proposed for children, but he is not yet able to win the prizes offered for the men. But the best contest for men to engage in is the service of the only God. Therefore if, even before we have been completely purified, (41) but while we appear only to have proceeded so far as to wash off the things which defile our life, we have arrived at the vestibule of God's service, we departed again more quickly than we approached, not being able to endure the austere way of living dictated by that service, nor the sleepless desire to please God, nor the continual and unwearied labour; (42) flee, therefore, at this present time from what is best and from what is worst. What is worst are the fabulous inventions, the unmetrical and inharmonious poems, the conceptions and persuasions which from ignorance are hard and stubborn, of which Esau is the namesake. What is beset is the offering; for the race inclined to service is an offering meet to God, being consecrated to him alone in the great chief priesthood; (43) for to dwell with what is evil is most pernicious, and to dwell with perfect good is most dangerous. Accordingly Jacob both flees from Esau, and also dwells apart from his parents; for being fond of practising virtue and still labouring at it, he flees from wickedness, and yet is unable to live in company with perfect virtue so as to have no need of an instructor.

VIII

VIII. (44) On which account we read, "He will depart to Laban," not to him as the Syrian, but as the brother of his mother; that is to say, he will go to the brilliancies of life; for Laban, being interpreted, means "white." And when he has arrived there he will not hold his head too high, from being puffed up with the happy events of fortune; for the word Syrian, being translated, means "sublime." But now he does not recollect the Syrian Laban, but the brother of Rebekkah; (45) for the means of life being given to a bad man, inflate and raise up to great height the mind which is devoid of wisdom, which is called the Syrian; but if they are bestowed on a lover of instruction, then they make the mind inclined to abide by the steady and solid doctrines of virtue and excellence. This is the brother of Rebekkah, that is to say, of perseverance, and he dwells in Charran, which name, being interpreted, means "holes," a symbol of the external senses; for he who is still moving about in mortal life has need of the organs of the external senses. (46) "Dwell, therefore," says she, "O my child, with him," not all thy life, but "certain days;" that is to say, learn to be acquainted with the country of the external senses; know thyself and thy own parts, and what each is, and for what end it was made, and how it is by nature calculated to energise, and who it is who moves through those marvellous things, and pulls the strings, being himself invisible, in an invisible manner, whether it is the mind that is in thee, or the mind of the universe. (47) And, when you have become thoroughly acquainted with yourself, then examine accurately also the peculiar qualities of Laban; the things which are accounted brilliant instances of the success of empty glory; but do not you be deceived by any one of them, but like a good workman adapt them all in a skilful manner to your own necessities; for if, while immersed in this political and much confused life, you display a stable and wellinstructed disposition, I will send for you from thence that you may receive the same prize which also your parents received: and the prize is the unchangeable and unhestitating service of the only wise God.

IX

IX. (48) And his father also gives him similar precepts, adding a few trifling injunctions; for he says, "Rise up and flee into Mesopotamia, to the house of Bethuel, the father of thy mother, and from thence take a wife to thyself of the daughters of Laban thy mother's Brother." [860] (49) Again, he also forbears to speak of Laban as a Syrian, but he calls him Rebekkah's brother, who is about to form a connection with the practiser of virtue by means of intermarriage. Flee, therefore, into Mesopotamia, that is to say, into the middle of the rapid torrent of life, and take care not to be washed away and swollowed up by its whirlpools, but standing firmly, vigorously repel the violent, impetuous course of affairs which overflows and rushes upon thee from above, from both sides, and from every quarter; (50) for you will find the house of wisdom a calm and secure haven, which will gladly receive you when you are anchored within it. But Bethuel in the sacred scriptures is called wisdom; and this name, being translated, means "the daughter of God;" and the legitimate daughter, always a virgin, having received a nature which shall never be touched or defiled, both on account of her own orderly decency, and also because of the high dignity of her Father. (51) And he calls Bethuel the father of Rebekkah. How, then, can the daughter of God, namely, wisdom, be properly called a father? is it because the name indeed of wisdom is feminine but the sex masculine? For indeed all the virtues bear the names of women, but have the powers and actions of full-grown men, since whatever is subsequent to God, even if it be the most ancient of all other things, still has only the second place when compared with that omnipotent Being, and appears not so much masculine as feminine, in accordance with its likeness to the other creatures; for as the male always has the precedence, the female falls short, and is inferior in rank. (52) We say, therefore, without paying any attention to the difference here existing in the names, that wisdom, the daughter of good, is both male and a father, and that it is that which sows the seeds of, and which begets learning in, souls, and also education, and knowledge, and prudence, all honourable and praiseworthy things. And from this source it is that Jacob the practiser of wisdom, seeks to procure a wife for himself; for from what other quarter she he seek a partner rather than from the house of wisdom? and where else should he find an opinion free from all reproach, with which to live all his life? [...] [861]

X

X. (53) But Moses has spoken more accurately about flights when he was establishing the law with respect to homicides, in which he goes through every species of homicide, that of intentional murder, that of unintentional slaying, that of murder by deliberate attack, or by crafty treachery. Repeat the law: "If any man strike another and he die, the striker shall die the death." And if a man do it not intentionally, but if God delivers him into his hand, then I will give thee a place to which he who has slain another shall flee. And if any one set upon his neighbour to slay him by treachery, and flee away, thou shalt drag him even from the altar to put him to Death." [862] (54) Knowing very well that the law is here adding no superfluous word from any indescribable impetuosity in its description of the matter, I doubted within myself why it does not merely say that he who has slain another shall die, and why it has added, that he shall die the death; (55) for how else does any one die, who dies at all, except dying the death? Therefore, betaking myself for instruction to a wise woman, whose name is Consideration, I was released from my difficulty, for she taught me that some persons who are living are dead, and that some who are dead are still live: she pronounced that the wicked, even if they arrive at the latest period of old age, are only dead, inasmuch as they are deprived of life according to virtue; but that the good, even if they are separated from all union with the body, live for ever, inasmuch as they have received an immortal portion.

XI

XI. (56) Moreover, she confirmed this opinion of hers by the sacred scriptures, one of which ran in this form: "You who cleave unto the Lord your God are all alive to this Day:" [863] for she saw that those who sought refuge with God and became his suppliants, were the only living persons, and that all others were dead. And Moses, it seems, testifies to the immortality of those persons, when he adds, "You are all alive to this day;" (57) and this day is interminable eternity, from which there is no departure; for the period of months, and years, and, in short, all the divisions of time, are only the inventions of men doing honour to number. But the unerring proper name of eternity is "today;" for the sun is always the same, without ever changing, going at one time beneath the earth, and at another time above the earth, and by him it is that day and night, the measures of time, are distinguished. (58) She also confirmed her statement by another passage in scripture of the following purport: "Behold, I have set before thy face life and death, and good and Evil." [864] Therefore, O all-wise man, good and virtue mean life, and evil and wickedness mean death. And in another passage we read, "This is thy life, and thy length of days, to love the Lord thy God." [865] This is the most admirable definition of immortal life, to be occupied by a love and affection for God unembarrassed by any connection with the flesh or with the body. (59) Thus, the priests, Nadab and Abihu, die in order that they may live; taking an immortal existence in exchange for this mortal life, and departing from the creature to the uncreated God. And it is with reference to this fact that the symbols of incorruptibility are thus celebrated: "Then they died before the Lord;"[866] that is to say, they lived; for it is not lawful for any dead person to come into the sight of the Lord. And again, this is what the Lord himself has said, "I will be sanctified in those who come nigh unto Me." [867] "But the dead," as it is also said in the Psalms, "shall not praise the Lord," [868] (60) for that is the work of the living; but Cain, that shameless man, that fratricide, is no where spoken of in the law as dying; but there is an oracle delivered respecting him in such words as these: "The Lord God put a mark upon Cain, as a sign that no one who found him should kill Him." [869] Why so? (61) Because, I imagine, wickedness is an evil which can never end, but which is kindled and is never able to be extinguished; so that the lines of the poet may well be applied to wickedness--

And she is of no mortal race,
But an immortal foul disgrace.

Immortal, indeed, as to the life among us on earth, since with reference to the life with God it is lifeless and dead, and as some one has said, more worthless and odious than dung.

XII

XII. (62) But it was by all means necessary that different regions should be assigned to different things, the heaven to good things, the earth to what is evil; for the tendency of good is to soar on high, and if it ever comes down to us, for its Father is very bounteous, it still is very justly anxious to return again to heaven. But if evil remains here, living at the greatest possible distance from the divine choir, always hovering around mortal life, and unable to die from among the human race. (63) This, too, one of the most eminent among the men who have been admired for their wisdom has asserted, speaking in a magnificent strain in the Theaetetus, where he says, "But it is impossible for evils to come to and end. For it is indispensable that there should always be something in opposition to God. And it is equally impossible that it should have a place in the divine regions; but it must of necessity hover around mortal nature and this place where we live; on which account we ought to endeavor to flee from this place as speedily as possible. And our flight will be a likening of ourselves to God, to the best of our power. And such a likening consists of being just and holy in conjunction with Prudence." [870] (64) Very naturally, therefore, Cain, the symbol of wickedness, will not die, for wickedness must of necessity be always alive in the mortal race of mankind; so that the expression, "to die the death," is not incorrectly spoken of the homicide, for the reasons which have here been given.

XIII

XIII. (65) And the expression, "not intentionally, but if God deliver him into his hand," is used with exceeding propriety with reference to those who commit an unintentional homicide; for it seems to Moses here, that our intentional actions are the fruit of our own mind and will, but that our unintentional actions proceed from the will of God. I mean by this, not our sins, but, on the contrary, those things which are the punishment of our sins; (66) for it is not becoming for God himself to inflict punishment, as being the first and most excellent Lawgiver; but he punishes by the ministry of others, and not by his own act. It is very suitable to his character that he himself should bestow his graces, and his free gifts, and his great benefits, inasmuch as he is by nature good and bountiful. But it is not fitting that he should inflict his punishments further than by his mere command, inasmuch as he is a king; but he must act in this by the instrumentality of others, who are suitable for such purposes. (67) And the practicer of virtue, Jacob, bears his testimony in support of this doctrine of mine, where he says, "The God who has nourished me from my youth up, the angel who delivered me from all my Evils." [871] For the most ancient benefits, those by which the soul is nourished, he attributes to God, but the more recent ones, which are caused by the errors of the soul, he attributes to the servant of God. (68) On this account, I imagine it is, that when Moses was speaking philosophically of the creation of the world, while he described everything else as having been created by God alone, he mentions man alone as having been made by him in conjunction with other assistants; for, says Moses, "God said, Let us make man in our Image." [872] The expression, "let us make," indicating a plurality of makers. (69) Here, therefore, the Father is conversing with his own powers, to whom he has assigned the task of making the mortal part of our soul, acting in imitation of his own skill while he was fashioning the rational part within us, thinking it right that the dominant part within the soul should be the work of the Ruler of all things, but that the part which is to be kept in subjection should be made by those who are subject to him. (70) And he made us of the powers which were subordinate to him, not only for the reason which has been mentioned, but also because the soul of man alone was destined to receive notions of good and evil, and to choose one of the two, since it could not adopt both. Therefore, he thought it necessary to assign the origin of evil to other workmen than himself, --but to retain the generation of good for himself alone.

XIV

XIV. (71) On which account, after Moses had already put in God's mouth this expression, "Let us make man," as if speaking to several persons, as if he were speaking only of one, "God made man." For, in fact, the one God alone is the sole Creator of the real man, who is the purest mind; but a plurality of workmen are the makers of that which is called man, the being compounded of external senses; (72) for which reason the especial real man is spoken of with the article; for the words of Moses are, "The God made the man;" that is to say, he made that reason destitute of species and free from all admixture. But he speaks of man in general without the addition of the article; for the expression, "Let us make man," shows that he means the being compounded of irrational and rational nature. (73) In accordance with this he has also not attributed the blessing of the virtuous and the cursing of the wicked to the same ministers, though both these offices receive praise. But since the blessing of the good has the precedence in panegyrics, and the affixing curses on the wicked is in the second rank of those who are appointed for these duties (and they are the chiefs, and leaders of the race, twelve in number, whom it is customary to call the patriarchs), he has assigned the better six, who are the best for the task of blessing, namely, Simeon, Levi, Judah, Issachar, Joseph, and Benjamin; and the others he has appointed for the curses, namely, the first and last sons of Leah, Reuben, and Zabulon, and the four bastard sons by the handmaidens; (74) for the chiefs of the royal tribe, and of the tribe consecrated to the priesthood, Judah and Levi, are reckoned in the former class. Very naturally, therefore, does God give up those who have done deeds worthy of death to the hands of others for punishment, wishing to teach us that the nature of evil is banished to a distance from the divine choir, since even punishment, which, though a good, has in it some imitation of evil, is confirmed by others. (75) And the expression, "I will give thee a place to which he who has slain a man unintentionally shall flee," appears to me to be spoken with exceeding propriety; for what he calls a place is not a region filled by the body, but is rather, in a figure, God himself, because he, surrounding all things, is not surrounded himself, and because he is that to which all things flee for refuge. (76) It is proper, therefore, for him who appears to have been involuntarily changed to say that this change has come upon him by the divine will, just as it is not proper for him to say so who has done evil of his own accord; and he says that he will give this place, not to him who has slain the man, but to him with whom he is conversing, so that the inhabitant of it shall be one person, but he who flees to it for refuge another; for God has given his own word a country to inhabit, namely, his own knowledge, as if it were a native of it. But to the man who is under the pollution of involuntary error he has given a foreign home as to a stranger, not a country as to a citizen.

XV

XV. (77) Having now said thus much in a philosophical spirit with respect to involuntary offences, he proceeds to legislate concerning the man who rises up to attack another, or who treacherously plots his death, saying, "But if any one attacks his neighbour so as to slay him by treachery, and he flees to God," that is to say to the place which has already been spoken of under a figure, from which life is given to all men. For he says also in another passage: "Whosoever shall flee thither shall live." (78) But is not everlasting life a fleeing for refuge to the living God? and is not a fleeing from his presence death? But if anyone sets upon another, he by all means is committing iniquity by deliberate purpose, and that which is done with treachery is liable to be accounted among voluntary actions, just as, on the other hand, that which is done without treachery is not subject to blame. (79) There is nothing therefore of the wicked actions which are done secretly, and treacherously, and of malice aforethought, which we can properly say are done through the will of God, but they are done only through our own will. For, as I have said before, the storehouses of wickedness are in us ourselves, and those of good alone are with God. (80) Whosoever therefore flees for refuge, that is to say, whosoever accuses not himself, but God as the cause of his offence, let him be punished, being deprived of that refuge to the altar which tends to salvation and security, and which is meant for suppliants alone. And is not this proper? For the altar is full of victims, in which there is no spot, I mean of innocent and thoroughly purified souls. But to pronounce the Deity the cause of evil is a spot which it is hard to cure, or rather which is altogether incurable. (81) Those who have cultivated such a disposition as to be lovers of themselves rather than lovers of God, may remain in a distance from the sacred places, in order that as polluted and impure persons, they may not behold, not even from a distance, the sacred flame of the evil which is unextinguishably set on fire, and purified, and dedicated to God with entire and perfect power. (82) Very beautifully, therefore, did one of the wise men of old, hastening on to this same conclusion, find confidence to say that "God is in no respect and in no place unjust, but he is the most righteous being possible. There is nothing that more nearly resembles him than the man who is as just as possible. Around him is the strength, and the real ability, and power of man, and also nothingness and unmanliness. For the knowledge of him is wisdom and true virtue; but the ignorance of him is real ignorance and manifest wickedness. And all other things which appear to be cleverness or wisdom, if they be displayed in political affairs are troublesome, and if in acts, are Sordid. [873]

XVI

XVI. (83) Therefore, having further commanded the unholy man who is a speaker of evil against divine things to be removed from the most holy places and to be given up to punishment, he proceeds to say, "Whosoever hateth his father or his mother, let him Die." [874] And in a similar strain he says, "He who accuseth his father or his mother, let him die." (84) He here all but cries out and shouts that there is no pardon whatever to be given to those who blaspheme the Deity. For if they who bring accusations against their mortal parents are led away to death, what punishment must be think that those men deserve who venture to blaspheme the Father and Creator of the universe? And what accusation can be more disgraceful than to say that the origin of evil is not in us but in God? (85) Drive away, therefore, drive away, O ye who have been initiated in, and who are the hierophants of, the sacred mysteries, drive away, I say, the souls which are mixed and in a confused crowd, and brought together promiscuously from all quarters, those unpurified and still polluted souls, which have their ears not closed, and their tongues unrestrained, and which bear about all the instruments of their misery ready prepared, in order that they may hear all things, even those which it is not lawful to hear. (86) But they who have been instructed in the difference between voluntary and involuntary offences, and who have received a tongue which speaketh good things instead of one which delighteth in accusation, when they do right are to be praised, and when they err contrary to their intention, they are not greatly to be blamed, for which reason cities have been set apart for them to flee unto for refuge.

XVII

XVII. (87) And it is worth while to examine with all the accuracy possible into some necessary points relating to this place. They are four in number. One, why it is that the cities which were set apart for the fugitives were not chosen out of those cities which the other tribes received as their portion, but only out of those which were assigned to the tribe of Levi. The second point is, why they were six in number, and neither more nor fewer. The third is, why three of them were beyond Jordan, and the other three in the land of the Canaanites. The fourth is, why the death of the high priest was appointed to the fugitives as a limit, after which they might return. (88) We must, therefore, say what is suitable on each of these heads, beginning with the first order. It is with exceeding propriety that the command is given to flee only to those cities which have been assigned to the tribe of Levi; for the Levites themselves are in a manner fugitives, inasmuch as they, for the sake of pleasing God, have left parents, and children, and brethren, and all their mortal relations. (89) Therefore the original leader of the company is represented as saying to his father and mother, "I have not seen you, and my brethren I do not know, and my sons I Disown," [875] in order to be able to serve the living God without allowing any opposite attraction to draw him away. But real flight is a deprivation of all that is nearest and dearest to man. And it introduces one fugitive to another, so as to make them forget what they have done by reason of the similarity of their actions. (90) Either, therefore, it is for this reason alone, or perhaps for this other also, that the Levitical tribe of the persons set apart for the service of the temple ran up, and at one onset slew those who had made a god of the golden calf, the pride of Egypt, killing all who had arrived at the age of puberty, being inflamed with righteous danger, combined with enthusiasm, and a certain heaven-sent inspiration: "And every one slew his brother, and his neighbour, and him that was nearest to Him." [876] The body being the brother of the soul, and the irrational part the neighbour of the rational, and the uttered speech that which is nearest to the mind. (91) For by the following means alone can that which is most excellent within us become adapted for and inclined to the service of him who is the most excellent of all existing beings. In the first place, if a man be resolved into soul, the body, which is akin to it as a brother, being separated and cut off from it, and also all its insatiable desires; and in the second place when the soul has, as I have already said, cast off the irrational part, which is the neighbour of the rational part; for this, like a torrent, being divided into five channels, excites the impetuosity of the passions through all the external senses, as so many aqueducts. (92) Then, in regular order, the reason removes to a distance and separates the uttered speech which appeared to be the nearest to it of all things, in order that speech, according to the intention, might alone be left, free from the body, free from the entanglements of the outward senses, and free from all uttered speech; for when it is left in this manner existing in a solitary manner, it will embrace that which alone is to be embraced with purity, and in such a way that it cannot be drawn away. (93) In addition to what has been said above, we must also mention this point, that the tribe of Levi is the tribe of the ministers of the temple and of the priests, to whom the service and ministration of holy things is assigned; and they also perform sacred service who have committed unintentional homicide, since, according to Moses, "God gives into their Hands" [877] those who have done things worthy of death, with a view to their execution. But it is the duty of the one body to know the good, and of the other body to chastise the wicked.

XVIII

XVIII. (94) These then are the reasons on account of which they who have committed unintentional homicide fly only to those cities which belong to the ministers of the temple. We must now proceed to mention what these cities are, and why they are six in numbers. Perhaps we may say that the most ancient, and the strongest, and the most excellent metropolis, for I may not call it merely a city, is the divine word, to flee to which first is the most advantageous course of all. (95) But the other five, being as it were colonies of that one, are the powers of Him who utters the word, the chief of which is his creative power, according to which the Creator made the world with a word; the second is his kingly power, according to which he who has created rules over what is created; the third is his merciful power, in respect of which the Creator pities and shows mercy towards his own work; the fourth is his legislative power, by which he forbids what may not be done. [...](96) And these are the very beautiful and most excellently fenced cities, the best possible refuge for souls which are worthy to be saved for ever; and the establishment of them is merciful and humane, calculated to excite men, to aid and to encourage them in good hopes. Who else could more greatly display the exceeding abundance of his mercy, all of the powers which are able to benefit us, towards such an exceeding variety of persons who err by unintentional misdeeds, and who have neither the same strength nor the same weakness? (97) Therefore he exhorts him who is able to run swiftly to strain onwards, without stopping to take breath, to the highest word of God, which is the fountain of wisdom, in order that by drinking of that stream he may find everlasting life instead of death. But he urges him who is not so swift of foot to flee for refuge to the creative power which Moses calls God, since it is by that power that all things were made and arranged; for to him who comprehends that everything has been created, that comprehension alone, and the knowledge of the Creator, is a great acquisition of good, which immediately persuades the creature to love him who created it. (98) Him, again, who is still less ready he bids flee to his kingly power; for that which is in subjection is corrected by the fear of him who rules it, and by necessity which keeps it in order, even if the child is not kept in the right way by love for his father. Again, in the case of him who is not able to reach the boundaries which have been already mentioned, in respect of their being a long way off, there are other goals appointed for them at a shorter distance, the cities namely of the necessary powers, the city of the power of mercy, the city of the power which enjoins what is right, the city of the power which forbids what is not right: (99) for he who is already persuaded that the deity is not implacable, but is merciful by reason of the gentleness of his nature, then, even if he has previously sinned, subsequently repents from a hope of pardon. And he who has adopted the notion that God is a lawgiver obeys all the injunctions which as such he imposes, and so will be happy; and he who is last of all will find the last refuge, namely, the escape from evil, even though he may not be able to arrive at a participation in the more desirable good things.

XIX

XIX. (100) These, then, are the six cities which Moses calls cities of refuge, five of which have had their figures set forth in the sacred scriptures, and their images are there likewise. The images of the cities of command and prohibition are the laws in the ark; that of the merciful power of God is the covering of the ark, and he calls it the mercy-seat. The images of the creative power and of the kingly power are the winged cherubim which are placed upon it. (101) But the divine word which is above these does not come into any visible appearance, inasmuch as it is not like to any of the things that come under the external senses, but is itself an image of God, the most ancient of all the objects of intellect in the whole world, and that which is placed in the closest proximity to the only truly existing God, without any partition or distance being interposed between them: for it is said, "I will speak unto thee from above the mercyseat, in the midst, between the two Cherubim." [878] So that the word is, as it were, the charioteer of the powers, and he who utters it is the rider, who directs the charioteer how to proceed with a view to the proper guidance of the universe. (102) Therefore, he who is so far removed from committing any intentional misdeeds, that he is even free from all unintentional offence, will have God himself for his inheritance, and will dwell in him alone. But those who fall into errors which proceed not from wilful purpose, but which are done without premeditation, will have the aforesaid places of refuge in all abundance and fulness. (103) Now of the cities of refuge there are three on the other side of Jordan, which are at a great distance from our race. What cities are they? The word of the Governor of the universe, and his creative power, and his kingly power: for to these belong the heaven and the whole world. (104) But those which, as it were, participate in us, and which are near to us, and which almost touch the unfortunate race of mankind which is alone capable of sinning, are the three on this side of the river; the merciful power, the power which enjoins what is to be done, the power which prohibits what ought not to be done: for these powers touch us. (105) For what need can there be of prohibition to persons who are not likely to do wrong? And what need of injunction to people who are not by nature inclined to stumble? And what need of mercy can those persons have who will absolutely never do wrong at all? But our race of mankind has need of all these things because it is by nature inclined and liable to offences both voluntary and involuntary.

XX

XX. (106) The fourth and last of the points which we proposed to discuss, is the appointing as a period for the return of the fugitives the death of the high priest, which, if taken in the literal sense, causes me great perplexity; for a very unequal punishment is imposed by this enactment on those who have done the very same things, since some will be in banishment for a longer time, and others for a shorter time; for some of the high priests live to a very old age, and others die very early, (107) and some are appointed while young men, and others not until they are old. And again of those who are convicted of unintentional homicide, some have been banished at the beginning of the high priest's entrance into office, and some when the high priest has been at the very point of death. So that some are deprived of their country for a very long time, and others suffer the same infliction only for a day, if it chance to be so; after which they lift up their heads, and exult, and so return among those whose nearest relations have been slain by them. (108) This difficult and scarcely explicable perplexity we may escape if we adopt the inner and allegorical explanation in accordance with natural philosophy. For we say that the high priest is not a man, but is the word of God, who has not only no participation in intentional errors, but none even in those which are involuntary. (109) For Moses says that he cannot be defiled neither in respect of his father, that is, the mind, nor his mother, that is, the external sense; [879] because, I imagine, he has received imperishable and wholly pure parents, God being his father, who is also the father of all things, and wisdom being his mother, by means of whom the universe arrived at creation; (110) and also because he is anointed with oil, by which I mean that the principal part of him is illuminated with a light like the beams of the sun, so as to be thought worthy to be clothed with garments. And the most ancient word of the living God is clothed with the word as with a garment, for it has put on earth, and water, and air, and fire, and the things which proceed from those elements. But the particular soul is clothed with the body, and the mind of the wise man is clothed with the virtues. (111) And it is said that he will never take the mitre off from his head, he will never lay aside the kingly diadem, the symbol of an authority which is not indeed absolute, but only that of a viceroy, but which is nevertheless an object of admiration. Nor will he "rend his clothes;" (112) for the word of the living God being the bond of every thing, as has been said before, holds all things together, and binds all the parts, and prevents them from being loosened or separated. And the particular soul, as far as it has received power, does not permit any of the parts of the body to be separated or cut off contrary to their nature; but as far as depends upon itself, it preserves every thing entire, and conducts the different parts to a harmony and indissoluble union with one another. But the mind of the wise man being thoroughly purified, preserves the virtues in an unbroken and unimpaired condition, having adapted their natural kindred and communion with a still more solid good will.

XXI

XXI. (113) This high priest, as Moses says, "shall not enter into any soul that is dead." But the death of the soul is a life according to wickedness; so that he must never touch any pollution such as folly is fond of dealing with. (114) And to him also "a virgin of the sacred race is joined;" that is to say, an opinion for ever pure, and undefiled, and imperishable; for he "may never become the husband of a widow, or of one who has been divorced, or of one who is a profane person, or of one who is a harlot," since he is always proclaiming an endless and irreconcileable war against them. For it is a hateful thing to him to be widowed with respect to virtue, and to be divorced and driven away by her; and in like manner all persuasion of this kind is profane and unholy. But that promiscuous evil abandoned to many husbands, and to the worship of many gods, that is, a harlot, he does not think fit even to look upon, being content with her who has chosen for herself one husband and father only, the all-governing God. (115) There is a certain extravagance of perfection visible in this disposition. He has Known [880] the man who has vowed the great vow in some instances offending unintentionally, even if not of deliberate purpose; for he says, "But if any one die before him suddenly, he shall be at once polluted." For if of things without deliberation anything coming from without strikes down suddenly, such things do at once pollute the soul, but not with a pollution which remains for any length of time, inasmuch as they are unintentional actions. And about these actions the high priest (standing above them, as he also does above those which are voluntary) is indifferent. (116) But I am not saying this at random, but for the sake of proving that the period of the death of the high priest is a most natural termination of exile to be appointed by the law, so as to allow of the return of the fugitives. (117) As long, therefore, as this most sacred word lives and survives in the soul, it is impossible for any involuntary error to enter into it; for it is by nature so framed as to have no participation in, and to be incapable of admitting any kind of error. But if it dies (not meaning by this that it is itself destroyed, but that it is separated from our soul), then a return is at once granted to intentional offences. (118) For if while the word remained and was healthy in us, error was driven to a distance, by all means, when the word departs, error will be introduced. For the undefiled high priest, conscience, has derived from nature this most especial honour, that no error of the mind can find any place within him; on which account it is worth our while to pray that the high priest may live in the soul, being at the same time both a judge and a convictor, who having received jurisdiction over the whole of our minds, is not altered in his appearance or purpose by any of those things which are brought under his judgment.

XXII

XXII. (119) Having now, therefore, said what was proper on the subject of fugitives, we will proceed with what follows in the regular order of the context. In the first place it is said, "The angel of the Lord found her in the Way," [881] pitying the soul which out of modesty had voluntarily committed the danger of wandering about, and very nearly becoming a conductor of her return to opinion void of error. (120) It is desirable also not to pass over in silence the things which are said in a philosophical strain by the lawgiver on the subject of discovery and investigation; for he represents some persons as neither investigating nor discovering anything, others as succeeding in both these paths, others as having chosen only one of them; of which last class some who seek do not find, and others find without having sought. (121) Those, then, who have no desire for either discovery or investigation have shamefully debased their reason by ignorance and indifference, and though they had it in their power to see acutely, they have become blind. Thus he says that "Lot's wife turning backwards became a pillar of Salt;" [882] not here inventing a fable, but pointing out the proper nature of the event. (122) For whoever despises his teacher, and under the influence of an innate and habitual indolence forsakes what is in front of him, by means of which it may be in his power to see, and to hear, and to exert his other powers, so as to form a judgment in things of nature, and turns his head round so as to keep his eyes on what is behind him, that man has an admiration for blindness in the affairs of life, as well as in the parts of the body, and becomes a pillar, like a lifeless and senseless stone. (123) For, as Moses says, "such men have not hearts to understand, nor eyes to see, nor ears to Hear," [883] but make the whole of their life blind, and deaf, and senseless and mutilated in every respect, so as not to be worth living, caring for none of those matters which deserve their attention.

XXIII

XXIII. (124) And the leader of this company is the king of the region of the body. "For," says Moses, "Pharaoh turned himself about and went into his house, and did not set his heart to this thing Either," [884] which statement is equivalent to, he did not take notice of anything whatever, but allowed himself to become dried up like a plant which has no care taken of it by the farmer, and to lose his fertility and become barren. (125) Those then who take counsel, and consider matters, and who investigate everything carefully, sharpen and rouse their minds: and the mind being duly exercised bears its appropriate fruit of cleverness and intelligence, by means of which the power of repelling all deceitful things is acquired. But the man who is an enemy to consideration blunts and breaks the edges of his wisdom; (126) we must therefore discard the truly senseless and lifeless company of such men as these, and choose those who exert their powers of consideration and discovery. And presently the political disposition is introduced, which, without being at all over ambitious of glory, has a desire for that better generation, which the virtues have received as their inheritance, and which consequently seeks and finds it; (127) for, says the scripture, "A man found Joseph in the plain, and asked him saying, What seekest thou; and he said, I am seeking my brothers; tell me where they are feeding their flocks: and the man said unto him, They are departed from hence; for I heard them saying, Let us go into Dothan; and Joseph went after his brethren and found them in Dothan." [885] (128) The name Dothan is interpreted, "a sufficient abandonment," being a symbol of the soul which has in no slight degree but altogether escaped those vain opinions, which resemble the pursuits of women rather than those of men. On which account virtue, that is Sarah, is very beautifully described as having given up "the manner of Women," [886] which is the object of pursuit to those men who live an unmanly and truly feminine life. But the wise man is also "added when Leaving," [887] according to Moses, speaking most strictly in accordance with nature. For the deprivation of empty opinion must necessarily be the addition of true opinion. (129) But if any one, passing his days in a mortal, and promiscuous, and variously formed life, and having abundant resources of wealth and riches, considers and inquires concerning that better generation which looks only to what is good, he is worthy of being received, if the dreams and visions of those things, which are fancied to be and which appear to be good, do not again overwhelm him and immerse him in luxury. (130) For if he abides in contemplation of the soul without any adulteration, proceeding and following in the track of the things which he is seeking, he will never give up his search till he has attained to the objects of his wishes; (131) but he will find none of the things which he desires among the wicked. Why not? Because they departed from hence. Having abandoned the studies of their friends they have changed their abode from the country of the pious, and settled in the desert of the wicked. But the real man, the convictor that dwells in the soul says this, who when he sees the soul in perplexity, and considering and investigating deeply, exerts a prudent care in its behalf, that it may not wander and so miss the right road.

XXIV

XXIV. (132) I very greatly wonder at those persons also, I mean at him who is fond of asking questions about what is in the middle between two extremes, and who says, "Behold the fire and the wood, but where is the lamb for the burnt Offering?" [888] And also at him who answers, "My son, God will provide himself a lamb for a burnt offering," and who afterwards finds what is given as a ransom; "For behold a single ram was caught by his horns in a shrub of Sabec." (133) Let us therefore consider what it is that he who is seeking doubts about, and what he who answers reveals, and in the third place what the thing is which was found. Now what the inquirer asks is something of this kind:--Behold the efficient cause, the fire; behold also the passive part, the material, the wood. Where is the third party, the thing to be effected? (134) As if he said, --Behold the mind, the fervid and kindled spirit; behold also the objects of intelligence, as it were so much material or fuel; where is the third thing, the act of perceiving? Or, again, --Behold the sight, behold the colour, where is the act of seeing? And, in short, generally, behold the external sense, behold the thing to be judge of; but where are the objects of the external sense, the material, the exertion of the feeling? (135) To him who puts these questions, answer is very properly made, "God will provide for himself." For the third thing is the peculiar work of God; for it is owing to his providential arrangement that the mind comprehends, and the sight sees, and that every external sense is exerted. "And a ram is found caught by his horns;" that is to say, reason is found silent and withholding its assent; (136) for silence is the most excellent of offerings, and so is a withholding of assent to those matters of which there are not clear proofs; therefore this is all that ought to be said, "God will provide for himself,"--he to whom all things are known, who illuminates the universe by the most brilliant of all lights, himself. But the other things are not to be said by creatures over whom great darkness is poured; but quiet is a means of safety in darkness.

XXV

XXV. (137) Those also who have inquired what it is that nourishes the soul, for as Moses says, "They knew not what it was," learnt at last and found that it was the word of God and the divine reason, from which flows all kinds of instinctive and everlasting wisdom. This is the heavenly nourishment which the holy scripture indicates, saying, in the character of the cause of all things, "Behold I rain upon you bread from Heaven;" [889] (138) for in real truth it is God who showers down heavenly wisdom from above upon all the intellects which are properly disposed for the reception of it, and which are fond of contemplation. But those who have seen and tasted it, are exceedingly delighted with it, and understand indeed what they feel, but do not know what the cause is which has affected them; and on this account they inquire, "What is this which is sweeter than honey and whiter than snow?" And they will be taught by the interpreter of the divine will, that "This is the bread which the Lord has given them to Eat." [890] (139) What then is this bread? Tell us. "This," says he, "is the word which the Lord has appointed." This divine appointment at the same time both illuminates and sweetens the soul, which is endowed with sight, shining upon it with the beams of truth, and sweetening with the sweet virtue of persuasion those who thirst and hunger after excellence. (140) And the prophet also having himself inquired what was the cause of meeting with success, finds it to be associated with the only God; for when he was doubting and asking, Who am I, and what am I, that I shall deliver the seeing race of Israel from the disposition hostile to God, which seems to be a king? (141) He is taught by the oracle that, "I will be with thee." And, indeed, inquiries into individual matters have a certain elegant and philosophical kind of meditation in them; for how can they avoid it? But the inquiry into the nature of God, the most excellent of all things, who is incomparable, and the cause of all things, at once delights those who betake themselves to its consideration, and it is not imperfect inasmuch as he, out of his own merciful nature, comes forward to meet it, displaying himself by his virgin graces, and willingly to all those who are desirous to see him. Not, indeed, such as he is, for that is impossible, since Moses also turned away his face, [891] for he feared to see God face to face; but as far as it is possible for created nature to approach by its own power those things which are only discernible to the mind. (142) And this also is written among the hortatory precepts, for, says Moses, "Ye shall turn unto the Lord your God, and shall find him, when ye seek him with all your heart, and with all your Soul."[892]

XXVI

XXVI. (143) Having now spoken at sufficient length on this point also, let us proceed in regular order to consider the third head of our subject, in which the seeking existed, but the finding did not follow it. At all events Laban, who examined the entire spiritual house of the practiser of virtue, "did not," as Moses says, "find the Images," [893] for it was full of real things, and not of dreams and vain fantasies. (144) Nor did the inhabitants of Sodom, blind in their minds, who were insanely eager to defile the holy and unpolluted reasonings, "find the road which led to This" [894] object; but, as the sacred scriptures tell us, they were wearied with their exertions to find the door, although they ran in a circle all around the house, and left no stone unturned for the accomplishment of their unnatural and impious desires. (145) And before now some persons, wishing to be kings instead of doorkeepers, and to put an end to the most beautiful thing in life, namely order, having not only failed in obtaining the success which they hoped to meet with through injustice, but have even been compelled to part with that which they had in their hands; for the law tells us that the companions of Korah, who coveted the priesthood, lost both what they wished for and what they had: (146) for as children and men do not learn the same things, but there are institutions adapted to each age, so also there are by nature some souls which are always childish, even though they are in bodies which have grown old; and on the other hand, there are some which have arrived at complete perfection in bodies which are still in the prime and vigour of early youth. But those men will deservedly incur the imputation of folly who desire objects too great for their own nature, since everything which is beyond one's power will vanish away through the intensity of its own vehemence. (147) And so Pharaoh also, when "seeking to kill Moses," [895] the prophetic race, will never find him, although he has heard that a heavy accusation is brought against him, as if he has attempted to destroy all the supreme authority of the body by two attacks, (148) the first of which he made upon the Egyptian disposition, which was fortifying pleasure as a citadel against the soul; for "having smote him," with an accidental instrument that came to hand, "he buried him in the Sand," [896] thinking that the two doctrines, of pleasure being the first and greatest good, and of atoms being the origin of the universe, both proceed from the same source. The second attack he made upon him who was cutting into small pieces the nature of the good, and assigning one portion to the soul, another to the body, and another to external circumstances; for he wishes the good to be entire, being assigned to the best thing in us, the intellect alone, as its inheritance, and not being adapted to anything inanimate.

XXVII

XXVII. (149) Nor does he, who is sent forth to search for that virtue which is invincible and embittered against the ridiculous pursuits of men, by name Tamar, find her. And this failure of his is strictly in accordance with nature; for we read in the scripture, "And Judah sent a kid in the hands of his shepherd, the Adullamite, to receive back his pledge from the woman, and he found her not: and he asked the men of the place, Where is the harlot who was in Aenan by the wayside? and they said, There is no harlot in this place. And he returned back to Judah, and said unto him, I have not found her, and the men of the place say that there is no harlot there. And Judah said, Let her keep the things, only let me not be made a laughing-stock, I because I have sent the kid, and you because you have not found Her." [897] Oh, the admirable trial! oh, the temptation becoming sacred things! (150) Who gave the pledge? Why the mind, forsooth, which was eager to purchase the most excellent possession, piety towards God, by three pledges or symbols, namely a ring, and an armlet, and a staff, signifying confidence and sure faith; the connection and union of reason with life, and of life with reason; and upright and unchanging instruction on which it is profitable to rely. (151) Therefore he examines the question as to whether he had properly given this pledge. What, then, is the examination? To throw down some bait having an attractive power, such as glory, or riches, or bodily health, or something similar, and to see to which it will incline, like the balance in a scale; for if there is any inclination to any one of these things the pledge is not sure. Therefore he sent a kid in order to recover back his pledge from the woman, not because he had determined by all means to recover it, but only in the case of her being unworthy to retain it. (152) And when will this be? when she willingly exchanges what is of importance for what is indifferent, preferring spurious to genuine good. Now the genuine good things are faith, the connection and union of words with deeds, and the rule of right instruction, as on the other hand the evils are, faithlessness, a want of such connection between words and deeds, and ignorance. And spurious goods are those which depend upon appetite devoid of reason; (153) for "when he sought her he did not find her;" for what is good is hard to be found, or, one may even say, is utterly impossible to be found in a confused life. And if one inquires whether the soul, which is a harlot, is in every place of virtue, one will be distinctly told that it is not, and that it has not been previously; for a common, unchaste, and wanton, and utterly shameless woman, selling the flower of her beauty at a low price, and making her external parts both bright with purifications and washings, but leaving her inward parts unclean and vile, and being like pictures painted with colours about the face because of the absence of all natural beauty; she who pursues that promiscuous evil called the vice of having many husbands, as if it were a good, coveting polygamy, and laying herself open for infinite variety, and being mocked and insulted at the same time by ten thousand bodies and things, "is not there." (154) He, then, who sent the messenger to inquire, hearing this, having removed envy to a distance from himself, and being gentle in his nature, rejoices in no moderate degree, and says, "Perhaps, then, according to my prayer, she is truly a virtuous mind, a citizen wife, excelling in modesty, and chastity, and all other virtues, cleaving to one husband alone, being content with the administration of one household, and rejoicing in the authority of one husband; and if she is such an one, let her keep what I have given her--the instruction and the connection of reason with life and of life with reason, and, what is the most necessary of all things, surety and faith. (155) But let us not be laughed at as appearing to have given gifts which were not merited, while we think that we gave what is most suitable to the soul; for I, indeed, did what was proper for a man to do who wished to make experiment of and to test her disposition, throwing out a bait and sending a messenger; but he has showed me that her nature is not easily caught. (156) And it is not clear to me why it is not easily caught; for I have seen ten thousand persons of the extremely wicked class doing the same things as those who are extremely good, but not with the same purpose, since the one class has truth and the other only hypocrisy, and it is very hard to distinguish the one from the other, for very often reality is overpowered by appearance.

XXVIII

XXVIII. (157) Also the person who loves virtue seeks a goat by reason of his sins, but does not find one; for, already, as the sacred scripture tells us, "it has been Burnt." [898] Now we must consider what is intimated under this figurative expression--how never to do any thing wrong is the peculiar attribute of God; and to repent is the part of a wise man. But this is very difficult and very hard to attain to. (158) Accordingly the scripture says that "Moses sought and sought again" a reason for repentance for his sins in mortal life; for he was very anxious to find a soul which was stripped if sin, and coming forward naked of all offence without shame. But nevertheless he did not find one, the flame, I mean by this the very quickly moving irrational desire, rushing inwards and devouring the whole soul. (159) For what is smaller in numbers is usually overpowered by what is more numerous, and what is slower by what is more speedy, and what is to come hereafter by what is present. Now what is contracted in quantity, and slow, and future, is repentance; what is numerous, and swift, and continuous in human life is, iniquity. Very naturally, therefore, when any one falls into error, he says that he is unable to eat of what is offered by reason of his sins, so that his conscience will not permit him to be nourished by repentance; on which account it is said in the scripture, "Moses heard, and it pleased Him." [899] (160) For the things which relate to the creature are very far removed from the things which relate to God; for to the creature only those things which are visible are known, but to God, even those things which are also invisible. And that man is crazy who, speaking falsely instead of truly, while still committing iniquity, asserts that he has repented. It is like as if one who had a disease were to pretend that he was in good health; for he, as it seems, will only get more sick, since he does not choose to apply any of the remedies which are conducive to health.

XXIX

XXIX. (161) On one occasion Moses was urged on, by a desire of learning, to investigate the causes through which the most necessary of things in the world are brought to perfection; for seeing how many things come to an end, and are produced afresh in creation, being again destroyed, and again abiding, he marvelled, and was amazed, and cried out, saying, "The bush (batos) burns, and is not Consumed." [900] (162) For he does not trouble his head about the inaccessible (abatos) country as being the abode of divine natures. But now that he is about to undertake a labour which will have no success and no end, he is relieved by the mercy and providence of God, the Saviour of all men, who has given warning out of his holy shrine, "Do not approach near this place," which is equivalent to, Do not approach this consideration; for it is a business requiring more labour, and more energy, and care, and fondness for investigation than can be suited to human power. But be content with admiring what is created; and do not be overcurious about the causes why each thing is created or destroyed. (163) "For the place," says God, "on which thou standest is holy Ground."[901] What kind of place is that? Is it not plain that it is that which relates to the principles of causes, which is the only one that he has adapted to the divine natures, not thinking any more competent to aim at a clear understanding of the principle of causes? (164) But he who, out of his desire for learning, has raised his head above the whole world begins to inquire concerning the Creator of the world who this being is who is so difficult to see and whose nature it is so difficult to conjecture, whether he is a body, or an incorporeal being, or something above these things, or whether he is a simple nature like a unit, or a compound being or any ordinary existing thing. And when he sees how difficult to ascertain, and how difficult to understand this is, he then prays to be allowed to learn from God himself who God is; for he has never hoped to be able to learn this from any other of the beings that are around him. (165) But nevertheless, though inquiring into the essence of the living God he has heard nothing. For, says, God, "thou shalt see my back parts, but my face thou shalt not Behold." [902] For it is sufficient for the wise man to know the consequences, and the things which are after God; but he who wishes to see the principal essence will be blinded by the exceeding brilliancy of his rays before he can see it.

XXX

XXX. (166) Having now said thus much concerning the third head of our subject, we will proceed to the fourth and last of the propositions we proposed to examine, according to which discovery sometimes comes to meet us without there having been any search. To this order belongs every self-taught and self-instructed wise man; for such an one has not been improved by consideration, and care, and labour, but from the first moment of his birth he has found wisdom ready prepared and showered upon him from above from heaven, of which he drinks an unmixed draught and on which he feasts, and continues being intoxicated with a sober intoxication with correctness of reason. (167) This is the man whom the law calls Isaac, whom the soul did not conceive at one time and bring forth at another, for says the scripture, "having conceived him she brought him Forth," [903] as if without any consideration of time. For it was not a man who was now being thus brought forth, but a conception of the purest character, beautiful rather in its nature than in consequence of any study; for which reason also she who brings him forth is said to have given up the usual manner of women, that is to say her usual, and reasonable, and human customs. (168) For the self-taught race is something new, and beyond any description, and truly divine, existing not by any human conceptions, but by some inspired frenzy. Are you ignorant that the Hebrews stand in no need of midwives for their delivery? But they, as Moses says, "bring forth before the midwives can arrive," by which is meant that they have nature alone for a coadjutor, without having any need of methods, or arts, or sciences. And Moses gives very beautiful and very natural definitions of what is taught a man by himself; one being such a thing as is speedily discovered, the other what God himself has given us; (169) accordingly, that which is taught by others requires a long time, but what is taught a man by himself is quick, and in a manner independent of time. And the one again has God for its expounder, but the other has man. Now the first definition he has placed in the question, "What is this that thou has found so quickly, O my Son?" [904] But the other is contained in the answer to this question, "What the Lord God gave unto me."

XXXI

XXXI. (170) There is also a third definition of what is taught a man by himself, namely that which of its own accord rises upwards. For it is said in the hortatory injunctions, "Ye shall not sow, neither shall ye reap those things which arise from the earth of their own Accord." [905] For nature has not need of any art since God himself sows those things, and by his agricultural skill brings to perfection, as if they grew of themselves, things which do not grow of themselves, except inasmuch as they stand in need of no human assistance whatever. (171) But this is not so much a positive exhortation as an announcement of his opinion, for if he had been giving a positive recommendation he would have said, "Do not sow, and do not reap:" but as he is only giving his opinion, he says, "Ye shall not sow, neither shall ye reap." For as to those things with which we meet by the voluntary bounty of nature, of these we cannot find either the beginnings or the ends in ourselves as if we were the cause of them: therefore the beginning is the seed-time and the end the harvest time. (172) And it is better to understand these things thus: every beginning and every end is spontaneous, that is to say, it is the work of nature and not of ourselves. For instance; what is the beginning of learning. It is plain that it is a nature in the person who is taught which is well calculated to reeive the particular subjects of meditation submitted to him. Again what is the beginning of being made perfect? If we are to speak plainly without keeping anything back, it is nature. Therefore he who teaches is also indeed to effect improvement, but it is God alone, the most excellent nature of all, who is able to conduct one to supreme perfection. (173) He who is bred up among such doctrines as these has everlasting peace, and is released from wearisome and endless labours. And according to the lawgiver there is no difference between peace and a week; for in each creation lays aside the appearance of energising and rests. (174) Very properly, therefore, is it said, "And the sabbath of the law shall be food for you," speaking figuratively. For the only thing which is really nourishing and really enjoyable is rest in God; which confers the greatest good, undisturbed peace. Peace, therefore, among cities is mixed up with civil war; but the peace of the soul has no mixture in it of any kind of difference. (175) And the lawgiver appears to me to be recommending most manifestly that kind of discovery which is not preceded by any search, in the following words, "When the Lord thy God shall lead thee into the land which he swore to thy fathers that he would give thee, large and beautiful cities which thou buildest not, houses full of all good things which thou filledst not, cisterns hewn out of the quarries which thou hewedst not, vineyards and olive gardens which thou plantedst Not." [906] (176) You see here the ungrudging abundance of all the great blessings which are ready, and poured forth for man's possession and enjoyment. And the generic virtues are here likened to cities, because they are of the most comprehensive kind; and the specific virtues are likened to houses, because they are contracted into a narrower circle; and the souls of a good disposition are likened to cisterns, which are well inclined to receive wisdom, as the cisterns are calculated to receive water; and the improvement, and growth, and production of fruit, are compared to vineyards and olive gardens; and the fruit of knowledge is a life of contemplation, which produces unmixed joy, equal to that which proceeds from wine; and a light appreciable only by the intellect, as if from a flame of which oil is the nourishment.

XXXII

XXXII. (177) Having now said thus much on the subject of discovery, we will proceed in due order to what comes next in the context. Moses proceeds, "Therefore the angel of the Lord found her sitting by a fountain of water." Now a fountain is spoken of in many senses; in one manner our mind is meant by a fountain, in another the rational habit and instruction; in a third sense a bad disposition is intimated; in a fourth sense a good disposition, the contrary of the preceding; in a fifth sense, the Creator and Father of the universe is himself thus spoken of in a figure; (178) and there are passages written in the sacred scriptures which give proof of these things. What they are we must now consider. Now in the very beginning of the history of the law there is a passage to the following effect: "And a fountain went up from the earth, and watered all the face of the Earth."[907] (179) Those men, then, who are not initiated in allegory and in the nature which loves to hide itself, liken the fountain here mentioned to the river of Egypt, which every year overflows and makes all the adjacent plains a lake, almost appearing to exhibit a power imitating and equal to that of heaven; (180) for what the heaven during winter bestows on the other countries, the Nile affords to Egypt at the height of summer; for the heaven sends rain from above upon the earth, but the river, raining upward from below, which seems a most paradoxical statement, irrigates the corn-fields. And it is starting from this point that Moses has described the Egyptian disposition as an atheistical one, because it values the earth above the heaven, and the things of the earth above the things of heaven, and the body above the soul; (181) but, however, we shall have an opportunity of speaking on these subjects hereafter when occasion permits. But at present, for we must study not to be too prolix, we had better have recourse to an explanation which may be drawn from looking on the words as used figuratively; and we may say that the meaning of the statement that "a fountain went up and watered all the face of the earth," is something of this kind. (182) The dominant part of us, like a fountain, pours forth many powers through the veins of the earth as it were, till they reach the organs of the external senses, that is to say, the eyes, and ears, and nostrils, and other organs; and these organs in every animal are situated about the head and face. Therefore, the face, which is the dominant portion of the soul; making the spirit, which is calculated for seeing, reach to the eyes, that which has the power of hearing reach the ears, the spirit of smelling reach the nostrils, that of taste the mouth, and causing that of touch to pervade the whole surface of the body.

XXXIII

XXXIII. (183) There are also many various fountains of instruction, by means of which most nutritious reasonings have sprung up like the trunks of palm-trees; "for," says Moses, "they came to Aileim, and in Aileim there were twelve fountains of water and seventy trunks of palm-trees. And they pitched their tents there by the side of the Water."[908] The name Aileim is interpreted to mean "vestibules," a symbol of the approach to virtue. For as vestibules are the beginning of a house, so also are the encyclical preliminary branches of instruction the beginning of virtue, (184) and twelve is the perfect number, of which the circle of the zodiac in the heaven is a witness, studded as it is with such numbers of brilliant constellations. The periodical revolution of the sun is another witness, for he accomplishes his circle in twelve months, and men also reckon the hours of the day and of the night as equal in number to the months of the year, (185) and the passages are not few in which Moses celebrates this number, describing the twelve tribes of his nation, appointing by law the offering of the twelve cakes of shewbread, and ordering twelve stones, on which inscriptions are engraved, to be woven into the sacred robe of the garment, reaching down to the feet of the high-priest, on his oracular dress. (186) He also celebrates the number seven, multiplied by the number ten; at one time speaking of the seventy palm-trees by the fountains, and in other passages he speaks of the elders, who were only seventy in number, to whom the divine and prophetical Spirit was vouchsafed. And again, it is the same number of heifers which are sacrificed at the solemn festival of the feast of tabernacles,[909] in a regular and proper division and order, for they are not all sacrificed together, but in seven days, the beginning being made with thirteen bulls; for thus, by every day subtracting one till they come to the number seven, the arranged number of seventy is properly completed. (187) And when they have come to the gates of virtue, the preliminary liberal sciences, and have seen the fountains, and the stems of the palmtrees growing by them, they are said to pitch their tents, not by the palm-trees, but by the waters. Why is this? Because those who carry off the prizes of perfect virtue are adorned with palm-leaves and with fillets; but those who are still exercising themselves in the preliminary branches of instruction, as people thirsting for learning, settle themselves by the side of those sciences which are able to bedew and irrigate their souls.

XXXIV

XXXIV. (188) Such then are the fountains of intermediate instruction. Let us now consider the fountain of folly, concerning which the lawgiver speaks thus, "Whosoever shall lie with a woman who is sitting apart has uncovered her fountain, and she has uncovered the issue of blood; they shall both be Destroyed."[910] Here he calls the external sense a woman, representing the mind as her husband. (189) When therefore the woman, having forsaken her legitimate husband, settles near those objects of the external sense which allures and destroys, and embraces them all in this amorous manner; then therefore, if the mind be turned to sleep when it is necessary that it should be awakened, it has uncovered the fountain of the external sense, that is itself, that is to say, it has rendered itself, without a covering and without a wall, and easy to be plotted against. (190) But nevertheless the woman also has uncovered the fountain of her blood, for every external sense, when flowing towards the external object appreciable by it, is cheered and restrained by being under the dominion of the reason; and it is left in a solitary condition, being deprived of any proper governor. And as the most terrible misfortune for a city is to be without walls, so the most unfortunate state for a soul is to be without a guardian. (191) When, then, is it without a guardian? Is it not when the sight is without any covering, being poured forth upon the objects of sight; and when the hearing is without a covering, being occupied in drinking in all kinds of sounds; and when the sense of smell is uncovered, and the kindred powers are left to themselves, and so are most ready to suffer whatever the invading enemy may be disposed to inflict? And that speech is uncovered and uttered which speaks ten thousand things in an unseasonable manner, without any thing to restrain its impetuosity; therefore flowing on unrestrainedly, it overturns many noble purposes and plans of life which were previously sailing on erect as though in calm weather. (192) This is that great deluge in which "the cataracts of heaven were opened"58—by heaven I here mean the mind—and the fountains of the bottomless pit were revealed; that is to say, of the outward sense; for in this way alone is the soul overwhelmed, iniquities being broken up and poured over it from above, as from the heaven of the mind, and the passions irrigating it from below, as from the earth of the outward senses. (193) For which reason Moses forbids a man to uncover the nakedness of his father or of his mother,[911] well knowing how great an evil it is not to check and to conceal the offences of the mind and of the external senses, but to bring them forward and display them as though they were good actions.

XXXV

XXXV. (194) These are the fountains of errors. We must now examine that of prudence. To this one it is that perseverance, that is to say, Rebecca, descends;[912] and after she has filled up the whole vessel of her soul she goes up again, the lawgiver, most strictly in accordance with natural truth, calling her return an ascent; for whoever brings his mind to descend from over-arrogant haughtiness is raised to a great height of virtue. (195) For Moses says, "And having gone down to the fountain, she filled her ewer, and went up again." This is that divine wisdom from which all the particular sciences are irrigated, and all the souls which love contemplation are are filled with a love of what is most excellent; (196) and to this fountain the sacred scripture most appropriately assigns name, calling it "judgment" and "holy." For says the historian, "Having turned back, they came to the fountain of judgment; this is the fountain of Caddes,"[913] and the interpretation of the name Caddes is holy. It all but cries out and shouts that the wisdom of God is holy, bringing with it nothing of the earth, and that it is the judgment of the universe by which all contrarieties are separated from one another.

XXXVI

XXXVI. (197) We must now speak also concerning that highest and most excellent of fountains which the Father of the universe spake of by the mouths of the prophets; for he has said somewhere, "They have left me, the fountain of life, and they have digged for themselves cisterns already worn out, which will not be able to hold Water;"[914] (198) therefore, God is the most ancient of all fountains. And is not this very natural? For he it is who has irrigated the whole of this world; and I am amazed when I hear that this is the fountain of life, for God alone is the cause of animation and of that life which is in union with prudence; for the matter is dead. But God is something more than life; he is, as he himself has said, the everlasting fountain of living. (199) But the wicked having fled away, and having passed their time without ever tasting the draught of immortality, have digged, insane persons that they are, for themselves, and not first for God, having preferred their own actions to the heavenly and celestial things, and the things which proceed from care to those which are spontaneous and ready. (200) Then they dig, not as the wise men Abraham and Isaac did, making wells, but cisterns, which have no good nutritious stream belonging to and proceeding from themselves, but requiring an influx from without, which must proceed from instruction. While the teachers are always pouring into the ears of their disciples all kinds of doctrines and speculations of science altogether, admonishing them to retain them in their minds, and to preserve them when faithfully committed to memory. (201) But now they are but worn-out cisterns, that is to say, all the channels of the ill-educated soul are broken and leaky, not being able to hold and to preserve the influx of those streams which are able to profit.

XXXVII

XXXVII. (202) We have now then said as much as the time will permit us to say on the subject of the fountains, and it is with great accuracy and propriety that the sacred scriptures represent Hagar as found at the fountain, and not as drawing water from it: for the soul has not as yet made such an advance as to be fit to use the unmixed draught of wisdom; but it is not forbidden from making its abode in its neighbourhood. (203) And all the road which is made by instruction is easy to travel, and most safe, and most solid, and strong, on which account the scripture tells us that she was found in the road leading to Shur; and the name Shur being interpreted means a wall or a direction. Therefore its convicter, speaking to the soul, says, "Whence comest thou, and whither goest thou?" And it says, not because it doubts, and not so much by the way of asking a question, as in a downcast and reproachful spirit, for an angel cannot be ignorant of anything that concerns us, and a proof of this is, (204) that he is well acquainted even with the things that are in the womb, and which are invisible to the creature, inasmuch as he says, "Behold thou art with child, and thou shalt bring forth a son, and shalt call his name Ishmael;" for to know that that which is conceived is a male child does not belong to human power, any more than it does to foretell the destruction of life which the child who is not yet born will adopt, namely, that it will be rude life, and not that of a citizen or of a polished man. (205) The expression, "Whence comest thou?" is said by way of reproving the soul, which is fleeing from the better and dominant opinion, of which she is the handmaiden, not in name more than in fact, and by remaining in subjection to which she would gain great glory. And the expression, "And whither goest thou?" means, you are running after uncertain things, having discarded and thrown away confessed good. (206) It is well, therefore, to praise her for rejoicing at this admonition. And she shows a proof of her delighting in it, by not bringing any accusation against her mistress, and by attributing the cause of her running away to her own self, and by her making no reply to the second question, "Whither goest thou?" for it is a matter of uncertainty; and it is both safe and necessary to restrain one's self from speaking of what is uncertain.

XXXVIII

XXXVIII. (207) Therefore the convicter of the soul approving of her in respect of her obedience says, Return unto thy mistress; for the government of the teacher is profitable to the disciple, and servitude in subjection to wisdom is advantageous to her who is imperfect; and when thou returnest, "be thou humbled under her hands:"--a very beautiful humiliation, comprehending the destruction of irrational pride. (208) For thus, after a gentle travail, thou wilt bring forth a male child, by name Ishmael, corrected by divine admonitions; for Ishmael, being interpreted, means "the hearing of God;" and hearing is considered as entitled to only the second prize after seeing; but seeing is the inheritance of the legitimate and first-born son, Israel; for the name Israel, being interpreted, means "seeing God." For it is possible for a man to hear false statements as though they were true, because hearing is a deceitful thing; but seeing is a sense which cannot be deceived, by which a man perceives existing things as they really are. (209) But the angel describes the characteristics of the disposition which is born of Hagar, by saying that he will be a rude man; as if he had said that he would be a man wise about rude matters, and not as yet thought worthy of that which is the truly divine and political portion of life: and this is virtue, by means of which it is the nature of the moral character to be humanised. And by his saying, "His hand shall be against every man, and every man's hand against him," he means to describe the design and plan of life of a sophist, who professes an overcurious scepticism, and who rejoices in disputatious arguments. (210) Such a man shoots at all the followers of learning, and in his own person opposes all men, both publicly and privately, and is shot at by all who very naturally repel him as if they were acting in defence of their own offspring, that is to say, of the doctrines which their soul has brought forth. (211) He also adds a third characteristic of him, saying, "He shall dwell before the face of all his brethren." In these words all but expressly declaring that he will wage an everlasting battle and war against them, face to face, for ever. Therefore the soul, which is pregnant with sophistical reasoning, says to the convicter who is addressing her, "Thou art God, who hast beheld me:" an expression equivalent to, Thou art the creator of my plans and of my offspring. (212) And may we not look upon this as a very natural reply on her part? For of these souls which are free, and, as it were truly citizens, the Creator is free, and a deliverer; but of slavish minds, slaves are the creators. And the angels are the servants of God, and are considered actual gods by those who are in toil and slavery; on this account, says Moses, she called the well, "The well where I saw in front of me." (213) But O, thou soul! advancing in wisdom and plunging deep into the knowledge of the elementary parts of encyclical instruction, thou wast not able to see the cause of thy knowledge in instruction as in a mirror. But the most appropriate place for such a well is in the midst, between Caddes and Barad; and the name Barad, being interpreted, means "in common," and Caddes means "holy;" for the person who is in a state of imprisonment is on the confines between what is holy and what is profane, fleeing from what is wicked, and being not yet able to live in the company of what is perfectly good.

Footnotes:

853. Yonge's title, A Treatise on Fugitives.
854. Gen 16:8.
855. Gen 16:8.
856. Gen 31:14.
857. Exod 8:26.
858. Gen 31:27.
859. Gen 27:42.
860. Gen 28:2.
861. the rest of this chapter is lost.
862. Exod 21:12.
863. Deut 4:4.
864. Deut 30:15.
865. Deut 30:20.
866. Lev 10:2.
867. Lev 10:3.
868. Ps 113:25.
869. Gen 4:15.
870. plato, Theaetetus, p. 176.
871. Gen 48:15.
872. Gen 1:26.
873. Plato, Theoetetus, p. 176.
874. Exod 21:15.
875. Deut 33:9.
876. Exod 32:26.
877. Exod 21:31.
878. Exod 25:22.
879. Lev 21:11.
880. there is some obscurity in the sense here. Mangey proposes instead of hoide pou, to read oudepou, but it does not seem any more intelligible than that in the text.
881. Gen 16:7.
882. Gen 19:26.
883. Deut 29:4.
884. Exod 7:23.
885. Gen 37:15.
886. Gen 18:11.
887. Gen 25:17.
888. Gen 22:7.
889. Exod 16:4.
890. Exod 16:15.
891. Exod 3:6.
892. Deut 4:29.
893. Gen 31:33.
894. Gen 19:11.
895. Exod 2:15.
896. Exod 2:12.
897. Gen 38:20.
898. Lev 10:16.
899. Lev 16:20.
900. Exod 3:2.
901. Exod 3:5.
902. Exod 33:23.
903. Gen 21:2.
904. Gen 27:20.

905. Gen 25:11.
906. Deut 6:10.
907. Gen 2:6.
908. Exod 15:27.
909. Num 29:13.
910. Lev 20:18.
911. Lev 18:7.
912. Gen 24:15.
913. Gen 14:7.
914. Jer 2:13.

ON THE CHANGE OF NAMES [915]

I

I. (1) "Abraham was ninety and nine years old; and the Lord appeared unto Abraham, and said unto him, I am thy God." [916] The number of nine, when added to the number ninety, is very near to a hundred; in which number the self-taught race shone forth, namely Isaac, the most excellent joy of all enjoyments; for he was born when his father was a hundred years old. (2) Moreover the first fruits of the tribe of Levi are given up to the priests; [917] for they having taken tithes, offer up other tenths from them as from their own fruits, which thus comprise the number of a hundred; for the number ten is the symbol of improvement, and the number a hundred is the symbol of perfection; and he that is in the middle is always striving to reach the extremity, exerting the inborn goodness of his nature, by which he says, that the Lord of the universe has appeared to him. (3) But do not thou think that this appearance presented itself to the eyes of the body, for they see no things but such as are perceptible to the outward senses; but those objects of the outward senses are compounded ones, full of destruction; but the Deity is not a compound object, and is indestructible: but the eye which receives the impression of the divine appearance is the eye of the soul; (4) for besides this, those things which it is only the eyes of the body that see, are only seen by them because they take light as a coadjutor, and light is different, both from the object seen and from the things which see it. But all these things which the soul sees of itself, and through its own power, it sees without the cooperation of any thing or any one else; for the things which the soul does thus comprehend are a light to themselves, (5) and in the same way also we learn the sciences; for the mind, applying its never-closing and never-slumbering eye to their doctrines and speculations, sees them by no spurious light, but by that genuine light which shines forth from itself. (6) When therefore you hear that God has been seen by man, you must consider that this is said without any reference to that light which is perceptible by the external senses, for it is natural that that which is appreciable only by the intellect should be presented to the intellect alone; and the fountain of the purest light is God; so that when God appears to the soul he pours forth his beams without any shade, and beaming with the most radiant brilliancy.

II

II. (7) Do not, however, think that the living God, he who is truly living, is ever seen so as to be comprehended by any human being; for we have no power in ourselves to see any thing, by which we may be able to conceive any adequate notion of him; we have no external sense suited to that purpose (for he is not an object which can be discerned by the outward sense), nor any strength adequate to it: therefore, Moses, the spectator of the invisible nature, the man who really saw God (for the sacred scriptures say that he entered "into the Darkness," [918] by which expression they mean figuratively to intimate the invisible essence), having investigated every part of every thing, sought to see clearly the much-desired and only God; (8) but when he found nothing, not even any appearance at all resembling what he had hoped to behold; he, then, giving up all idea of receiving instruction on that point from any other source, flies to the very being himself whom he was seeking, and entreats him, saying, "Show my thyself that I may see thee so as to know Thee." [919] But, nevertheless, he fails to obtain the end which he had proposed to himself, and which he had accounted the most all-sufficient gift for the most excellent race of creation, mankind, namely a knowledge of those bodies and things which are below the living God. (9) For it is said unto him, "Thou shalt see my back parts, but my face shall not be beheld by Thee." [920] As if it were meant to answer him: Those bodies and things which are beneath the living God may come within thy comprehension, even though every thing would not be at once comprehended by thee, since that one being is not by his nature capable of being beheld by man. (10) And what wonder is there if the living God is beyond the reach of the comprehension of man, when even the mind that is in each of us is unintelligible and unknown to us? Who has ever beheld the essence of the soul? the obscure nature of which has given rise to an infinite number of contests among the sophists who have brought forward opposite opinions, some of which are inconsistent with any kind of nature. (11) It was, therefore, quite consistent with reason that no proper name could with propriety be assigned to him who is in truth the living God. Do you not see that to the prophet who is really desirous of making an honest inquiry after the truth, and who asks what answer he is to give to those who question him as to the name of him who has sent him, he says, "I am that I Am," [921] which is equivalent to saying, "It is my nature to be, not to be described by name:" (12) but in order that the human race may not be wholly destitute of any appellation which they may give to the most excellent of beings, I allow you to use the word Lord as a name; the Lord God of three natures--of instruction, and of holiness, and of the practice of virtue; of which Abraham, and Isaac, and Jacob are recorded as the symbols. For this, says he, is the everlasting name, as if it has been investigated and discerned in time as it exists in reference to us, and not in that time which was before all time; and it is also a memorial not placed beyond recollection or intelligence, and again it is addressed to persons who have been born, not to uncreated natures. (13) For these men have need of the complete use of the divine name who come to a created or mortal generation, in order that, if they cannot attain to the best thing, they may at least arrive at the best possible name, and arrange themselves in accordance with that; and the sacred oracle which is delivered as from the mouth of the Ruler of the universe, speaks of the proper name of God never having been revealed to any one, when God is represented as saying, "For I have not shown them my Name;" [922] for by a slight change in the figure of speech here used, the meaning of what is said would be something of this kind: "My proper name I have not revealed to them," but only that which is commonly used, though with some misapplication, because of the reasons abovementioned. (14) And, indeed, the living God is so completely indescribable, that even those powers which minister unto him do not announce his proper name to us. At all events, after the wrestling match in which the practicer of virtue wrestled for the sake of the acquisition of virtue, he says to the invisible Master, "Tell me thy Name;" [923] but he said, "Why askest thou me my name?" And he does not tell him his peculiar and proper name, for says he, it is sufficient for thee to be taught my ordinary explanations. But as for names which are the symbols of created things, do not seek to find them among immortal natures.

III

III. (15) Therefore do not doubt either whether that which is more ancient than any existing thing is indescribable, when his very word is not to be mentioned by us according to its proper name. So that we must understand that the expression, "The Lord was seen by Abraham," [924] means not as if the Cause of all things had shone forth and become visible, (for what human mind is able to contain the greatness of his appearance?) but as if some one of the powers which surround him, that is to say, his kingly power, had presented itself to the sight, for the appellation Lord belongs to authority and sovereignty. (16) But when our mind was occupied with the wisdom of the Chaldaeans, studying the sublime things which exist in the world, it made as it were the circuit of all the efficient powers as causes of what existed; but when it emigrated from the Chaldaean doctrines, it then knew that it was moving under the guidance and direction of a governor, of whose authority it perceived the appearance. (17) On which account it is said, "The Lord," not the living God, "was seen;" as if it had been meant to say, the king appeared, he who was from the beginning, but who was not as yet recognized by the soul, which, indeed, was late in learning, but which did not continue for ever in ignorance, but received a notion of there being an authority and governing power among existing things. (18) And when the ruler has appeared, then he in a still greater degree benefits his disciple and beholder, saying, "I am thy God;" [925] for I should say to him, "What is there of all the things which form a part of creation of which thou art not the God?" But his word, which is his interpreter, will teach me that he is not at present speaking of the world, of which he is by all means the creator and the God, but about the souls of men, which he has thought worthy of a different kind of care; (19) for he thinks fit to be called the Lord and Master of bad men, but the God of those who are in a state of advancement and improvement; and of those which are the most excellent and the most perfect, both Lord and God at once. On which account, having made Pharaoh the very extreme instance of impiety, he has never once called himself his Lord or his God; but he calls the wise Moses so, for he says to him, "Behold I give thee as a god to Pharaoh." [926] But he has in many passages of the sacred oracles delivered by him, called himself Lord. (20) For instance, we read such as passage as this: "Thus says the Lord;" [927] and at the very beginning we read, "The Lord spake unto Moses, saying, I am the Lord, say unto Pharaoh, the king of Egypt, all the things which I say unto Thee." [928] (21) And Moses, in another place, says, "Behold, when I go forth out of the city I will spread out my hands unto the Lord, and the sounds shall cease, and the hail, and there shall be no more rain, that thou mayest know that the earth is the Lord's;" that is to say, every thing that is made of body or of earth, "and that thou," that is the mind which bears in itself the images of things, "and thy servants," that is the particular reasonings which act as body-guards to the mind, "for I know that ye do not yet fear the Lord;" [929] by which he means not the Lord who is spoken of commonly and in different senses, but him who is truly the Master of all things. (22) For there is in truth no created Lord, not even a king shall have extended his authority and spread it from one end of the world even to the other end, but only the uncreated God, the real governor, whose authority he who reverences and fears receives a most beneficial reward, namely, the admonitions of God, but utterly miserable destruction awaits the man who despises him; (23) therefore he is held forth as the Lord of the foolish, striking them with a terror which is appropriate to him as ruler. But he is the God of those who are improved; as we read now, "I am thy God, I am thy God, be thou increased and Multiplied." [930] And in the case of those who are perfect, he is both together, both Lord and God; as we read in the ten commandments, "I am the Lord thy God."[931] And in another passage it is written, "The Lord God of our Fathers." [932] (24) For he thinks it right for the wicked man to be governed by a master as by a lord; that, being in a state of alarm and groaning, he may have the fear of a master suspended over him; but him who is advancing in improvement he thinks deserving to receive benefits as from God in order that by means of these benefits he may arrive at perfection; and him who is complete and perfect he thinks should be both governed as by the Lord, and benefited as by God; for the last man remains for ever unchangeable, and he is, by all means and in all respects, the man of God: (25) and this is especially shown to be the fact in the case of Moses; for, says the scripture, "This is the blessing which Moses, the man of God, Blessed." [933] O the man that thus thought worthy of this all-beautiful and sacred recompense, to give himself as a requital for the divine Providence! (26) But do not thou think that he is in the same sense a man and the man of God; for he is said to be a man as being a possession of God, but the man of God as boasting in and being benefited by him. And if thou wishest to have God as the inheritance of thy mind, then do thou in the first place labour to become yourself an inheritance worthy of him, and thou wilt be such if thou avoidest all laws made by hands and voluntary.

IV

IV. (27) But it is not right to be ignorant of this thing either, that the statement, "I am thy God," [934] is made by a certain figurative misuse of language rather than with strict propriety; for the living God, inasmuch as he is living, does not consist in relation to anything; for he himself is full of himself, and he is sufficient for himself, and he existed before the creation of the world, and equally after the creation of the universe; (28) for he is immovable and unchangeable, having no need of any other thing or being whatever, so that all things belong to him, but, properly speaking, he does not belong to anything. And of the powers which he has extended towards creation for the advantage of the world which is thus put together, some are spoken of, as it were, in relation to these things; as for instance his kingly and his beneficent power; for he is the king of something, and the benefactor of something there being inevitably something which is ruled over and which receives the benefits. (29) Akin to these powers is the creative power which is called God: for by means of this power the Father, who begot and created all things, did also disperse and arrange them; so that the expression, "I am thy God," is equivalent to, "I am thy maker and creator;" (30) and it is the greatest of all possible gifts to have him for one's maker, who has also been the maker of the whole world. The soul, indeed, of the wicked man he did not make, for wickedness is hateful to God; and the soul, which is between good and bad, he made not by himself alone, according to the most sacred historian Moses, since that, like wax, was about to receive the different impressions of good and evil. (31) On which account it is said in the scriptures, "Let us make man in our own image," that if it receives a bad impression it may appear to be the work of others, but if it receives a good impression it may then appear to be the work of him who is the Creator only of what is beautiful and good. By all means, therefore, that must be a good man to whom he says, "I am thy God," as he has had him alone for his creator without the cooperation of any other being. (32) Moreover he brings up with this that doctrine which is established in many other passages, showing that God is the creator only of those men who are virtuous and wise; and the whole of this company has voluntarily deprived itself of the abundant possession of external things, and has neglected those things which are dear to his flesh. (33) For the athletes of vigorous health and high spirit have erected their servile bodies as a sort of fortification against the soul, but those men who have been devoted to the pursuit of instruction, and who are pale, and weak, and emaciated, having overloaded the vigour of the body with the power of the soul, and if one must tell the plain truth, being entirely dissolved into one species of soul, have through the energy of their minds become quite disentangled from the body. (34) Therefore that which is earthly is very naturally destroyed and overwhelmed when the entire mind resolves in every particular to make itself acceptable to God. But the race of these persons is rare and scarcely to be found, and one may almost say is unable to exist; and the following oracle, which is given with respect to Enoch, proves this: "Enoch pleased God, and he was not Found;" [935] (35) for by what kind of contemplation could a man attain to this good thing? What seas must he cross over? What islands, or what continents, must he visit? Must he dwell among Greeks or among the barbarians? (36) Are there not even to the present day some of those persons who have attained to perfection in philosophy, who say that there is no such thing as wisdom in the world, since there is also no such thing as a wise man? for that from the very beginning of the creation of mankind up to the present moment, there has never been any one who could be considered entirely blameless, for that it is impossible for a man who is bound up in a mortal body to be entirely and altogether happy. (37) Now whether these things are said correctly we will consider at the proper time: but at present let us stick to the subject before us, and follow the scripture, and say that there is such a thing as wisdom existing, and that he who loves wisdom is wise. But though the wise man has thus an actual existence he has escaped the notice of us who are wicked: for what is good will not unite with what is bad. (38) On this account it is that "the disposition which pleased God was not found;" as if in truth it has a real existence, but was concealed and had fled away to avoid any meeting in the same place with us, since it is said to have been translated; the meaning of which expression is that it emigrated and departed from its sojourn in this mortal life, to an abode in immortal life.

V

V. (39) These men then, being mad with this divinely inspired madness, were made more ferocious; but there are others who are companions of a more manageable and humanised wisdom. By those men piety is practised to a most eminent degree, and the observance due to man is not neglected. And the sacred oracles are witnesses of this in which Abraham is addressed (the words being put in the mouth of God), "Thou shalt be pleasing in my Sight," [936] that is to say, thou shalt be pleasing, not only to me but also to my works, in my eyes as judge, and overseer, and superintendant; (40) for if you honour your parents, or show mercy to the poor, or do good to your friends, or fight in defence of your country, or pay proper attention to the common principles of justice towards all men, you most certainly are pleasing to those with whom you associate, and you are also acceptable in the sight of God: for he sees all things with an eye which never slumbers, and he unites to himself with especial favour all that is good, and that he accepts and embraces. (41) Therefore the practicer of virtue, even while praying, proves the very same thing, saying, "The God to whom my fathers were Acceptable," [937] and he adds the words "before him," for the sake of giving you to know the difference, the real practical difference between the expression, "to please God," by itself, and the same words with the addition of the sentence, "before him." For the one expression gives both meanings, and the other only one. (42) Thus also Moses, in his exhortatory admonitions, recommends his disciples such and such things, saying, "Thou shalt do what is pleasing before the Lord thy God," [938] as if he were to say, Do such things as we shall be worthy to appear before God, and what he when he sees them will accept. And these things are wont to appear equally pure both externally and Internally. [939] (43) And proceeding onwards from thence he wove the tent of the tabernacle with two boundaries of space, placing a veil between the two, in order to separate what is within from what is without. And also he gilded the sacred ark, the place wherein the laws were kept, both within and without; and he gave the great high priest two robes, the inner one made of linen, and the other one beautifully embroidered, with one robe reaching to the feet. (44) For these and such things as these are symbols of the soul which in its inner parts shows itself pure towards God, and in its exterior parts shows itself without reproach in reference to the world which is perceptible to the outward senses and to this life: with great felicity therefore was this said to the victorious wrestler, when he was about to have his brows crowned with the garlands of victory: and the declaration made with respect to him was of the following tenor, "You have been mightily powerful both with God and with Men;" [940] (45) for to have a good reputation with both classes, namely, with the uncreated God and with the creature, is the task of no small mind, but, if one must say the truth, it is one fit for that which is in the confines between the world and God. In short, it is necessary that the good man should be an attendant of God, for the creature is an object of care to the Ruler and Father of the universe; (46) for who is there who does not know, that even before the creation of the world God was himself sufficient to himself, and that he remained as much a friend as before after the creation of the world, without having undergone any change? Why then did he make what did not exist before? Because he was good and bounteous. Shall we not then, we who are slaves, follow our master, admiring, in an exceeding degree, the great first Cause of all things, and not altogether despising our own nature?

VI

VI. (47) But after he has said, "Be thou pleasing to me before me," he adds further, "and be thou blameless," using here a natural consequence and connection of the previous sentence. Do thou therefore all the more apply thyself to what is good that thou mayest be pleasing; and if thou canst not be pleasing, at all events abstain from open sins, that thou mayest not incur reproach. For he who does right is praiseworthy, and he who avoids doing wrong is not to be blamed. (48) And the most important prize is assigned to those who do right, namely, the prize of feeling that they are acceptable to God: but the second prize belongs to those who do no sin, that, namely, of avoiding blame; and, perhaps, in the case of the mortal race of mankind, the doing no sin is set down as equivalent to doing right; for who, as Job says is "pure from pollution, even if his life be but one single day Long?" [941] (49) In fact, the things which pollute the soul are infinite in number, and it is impossible completely to wash them away and to efface their stains; for there are, of necessity, left disasters which are akin to every mortal man, which it is natural indeed to weaken, but impossible wholly to eradicate. (50) Does any one therefore seek a just, or prudent, or temperate, or, in short, any perfectly good man, in this confused life? Be content if you find one who is not wholly unjust, or foolish, or intemperate, or cowardly, or who is not utterly worthless; for the avoidance of evil is a thing with which to be content, but the complete acquisition of the virtues is unattainable to any man, such as is endowed with our nature. (51) It was therefore with great reason that it was said, "and be thou blameless," the speaker thinking that it is a great addition towards a happy life to live without sin and without reproach; but the man who has deliberately chosen this way of life, promises to leave his inheritance in accordance with the covenant, such as is becoming to God to give, and to a wise man to accept, (52) for he says, "I will place my covenant between me and between Thee;" [942] and covenants and testaments are written for the advantage of those who are worthy of the gift, so that a testament is a symbol of grace, which God has placed between himself who proffers it and man who receives it; (53) and this is the very extravagance of beneficence, that there is nothing between God and the soul except his own virgin grace. And I have written two commentaries on the whole discussion concerning testaments, and for that reason I now deliberately pass over that subject, for the sake of not appearing to repeat what I have said before; and also at the same time, because I do not wish here to interrupt the connected course of this discussion.

VII

VII. (54) And immediately afterwards it is said, "And Abraham fell on his face:" was he not about, in accordance with the divine promises, to recognize himself and the nothingness of the race of mankind, and so to fall down before him who stood firm, by way of displaying the conception which he entertained of himself and of God? Forsooth that God, standing always in the same place, moves the whole composition of the world, not by means of his legs, for he has not the form of a man, but by showing his unalterable and immovable essence. (55) But man, being never settled firmly in the same place, admits of different changes at different times, and being tripped up, miserable man that he is (for, in fact, his whole life is one continued stumble), he meets with a terrible fall; (56) but he who does this against his will is ignorant, and he who does it voluntarily is docile; on which account he is said to fall on his face, that is to say, in his outward senses, in his speech, in his mind, all but crying out loudly and shouting that the outward sense has fallen, inasmuch as it was unable, by itself, to feel as it should, if it had not been aroused by the providence of the Saviour, to take hold of the bodies which lay in its way. And speech too has fallen, being unable to give a proper explanation of anything in existence, unless he who originally made and adapted the organ of the voice, having opened its mouth and enabled its tongue to articulate, should strike it so as to produce harmonious sounds. Moreover, the king of all the mind has fallen, being deprived of its comprehension, unless the Creator of all living things were again to raise it up and re-establish it, and furnishing it with the most acutely seeing eyes, to lead it to a sight of incorporeal things.

VIII

VIII. (57) Therefore admiring this same disposition when thus taking to flight, and submitting to a voluntary fall by reason of the confession which it had made respecting the living God, namely, that he stands in truth and is one only, while all other things beneath him are subject to all kinds of motions and alterations, he speaks to it, and allows it to enter into conversation with him, saying, "And I, behold my covenant is with Thee." [943] (58) And this expression conceals beneath its figurative words such a meaning as this: There are very many kinds of covenants, which distribute graces and gifts to those who are worthy to receive them; but the highest kind of covenant of all is I myself: for God, having displayed himself as far as it was possible for that being to be displayed who cannot be shown by the words which he has used, adds further, "And I too, behold my covenant;" the beginning and fountain of all graces is I myself. (59) For on some persons God is in the habit of bestowing his graces by the intervention of others; as, for instance, through the medium of earth, water, air, the sun, the moon, heaven, and other incorporeal powers. But he bestows them on others through himself alone, exhibiting himself as the inheritance of those who receive him, whom from that he thinks worthy of another appellation: (60) for it is said in the scripture, "Thy name shall not be called Abram, but Abraham shall thy name be." Some, then, of those persons who are fond of disputes, and who are always eager to affix a stain upon what is irreproachable, on things as well as bodies, and who wage an implacable war against sacred things, while they calumniate everything which does not appear to preserve strict decorum in speech, being the symbols of nature which is always fond of being concealed, perverting it all so as to give it a worse appearance after a very accurate investigation, do especially find fault with the changes of names. (61) And it is only lately that I heard an ungodly and impious man mocking and ridiculing these things, who ventured to say, "Surely they are great and exceeding gifts which Moses says that the Ruler of the universe offers, who, by the addition of one element, the one letter alpha, a superfluous element; [944] and then again adding another element, the letter rho, appears to have bestowed upon men a most marvellous and great benefit; for he has called the wife of Abram Sarrah instead of Sarah, doubling the Rho," and connecting a number of similar arguments without drawing breath, and joking and mocking, he went through many instances. (62) But at no distant period he suffered a suitable punishment for his insane, wickedness; for on a very slight and ordinary provocation he hanged himself, in order that so polluted and impure a person might not die by a pure and unpolluted death.

IX

IX. But we may justly, in order to prevent any one else from falling into the same error, eradicate the erroneous notions which have been formed on the subject, arguing the matter on the principle of natural philosophy, and proving that these things which are here said are worthy of all attention. (63) God does not bestow on men mutes and vowels, or, in short, nouns and verbs; since when he created plants and animals, he summoned them before man as their governor, that he might give each of them their appropriate names by a reference to the knowledge which he had of all things; for, says the scripture, "Whatever Adam called any thing, that was the name Thereof."[945] (64) Therefore since God did not think fit to take upon himself even the active imposition of the names, but entrusted the task to a wise man, the author of the whole race of mankind, it is reasonable to suppose that he himself gave and arranged the different parts, and syllables, and letters of nouns, disposing not only the vowels, but even the mutes, and that he did this too to make a show of liberality and exceeding beneficence? It is impossible to say so. (65) But such things as these are the characteristic marks of different powers; small marks of great powers, marks perceptible by the outward senses of powers which are indistinct; and the powers themselves are discerned in most excellent doctrines, in true and pure conceptions, in the improvement of souls. And it is easy to see a proof of this if we make a beginning with the man who is here spoken of as having his name changed; (66) for the name Abram, being interpreted, means "sublime father," but Abraham means the "elect father of sound;" and how these names differ from one another we shall know more clearly if we first of all read what is exhibited under each of them. (67) Now using allegorical language, we call that man sublime who raises himself from the earth to a height, and who devotes himself to the inspection of high things; and we also call him a haunter of high regions, and a meteorologist, inquiring what is the magnitude of the sun, what are his motions, how he influences the seasons of the year, advancing as he does and retreating back again, with revolutions of equal speed, and investigating as he does the subjects of the radiance of the moon, of its shape, of its waning, of its increase, and of the motion of the other stars, whether fixed or wandering; (68) for the inquiry into these matters belongs not to an ill-conditioned or barren soul, but to one which is eminently endowed by nature, and which is able to produce an entire and perfect offspring; on which account the scripture calls the meteorologist, "father," inasmuch as he is not unproductive of wisdom.

X

X. (69) Now the symbols represented by the name of Abram are thus accurately defined; those conveyed under the name of Abraham are such as we shall proceed to demonstrate. The meanings now are three, "the father," and "elect," and "of sound." Now by the word "sound" here, we mean uttered speech; for the sounding organ of the living animal is the organ of speech. Of this faculty we say that the father is the mind, for it is from the mind, as from a fountain, that the stream of speech proceeds. The word "elect" belongs to the mind of the wise man, for whatever is most excellent is found in him; (70) therefore the man devoted to learning and occupied in the contemplation of sublime subjects, was sketched out according to the former characteristic marks, but the philosopher, or I should rather say the wise man, was exhibited in accordance with those of which we have just given an outline. Think not, then, any longer that the Deity bestows a change of names, but consider that what he gives is a correction of the moral character by means of symbols; (71) for having invited the nature of heaven, and whom some call a mathematician, to a participation in virtue, he made him wise and called him so. For having given an appropriate name to his transformed disposition, he named him, as the Hebrews would call it, "Abraham," but in the language of the Greeks, "the elect father of sound;" (72) for says he, On what account dost thou investigate the motions and periods of the stars? and why hast thou bounded up so high from the earth to the heavens? Is it merely that you may indulge your curiosity with respect to those matters? And what advantage could accrue to you from all this curiosity? What destruction of pleasure would is cause? What defeat of appetite? What dissolution of pain or fear? What eradication of the passions which disturb and agitate the soul? (73) For as there is no advantage in trees unless they are productive of fruit, so in the same way there is no use in the study of natural philosophy unless it is likely to confer upon a man the acquisition of virtue, for that is its proper fruit. (74) On which account some of the ancients have compared the discussion and consideration of philosophy to a field, and have likened the physical portion of it to the plants, the logical part to the hedges and fences, the moral part to the fruit, (75) thinking that the walls which are built around for the sake of protecting the fruit have been erected by the possessors of the land, and that the plants have been created for the sake of the production of fruit; thus, therefore, they said that in philosophy it is requisite for the consideration of the physical and the logical part of philosophy to be referred to the moral part, by which the moral character is improved, which as a desire at the same time for both the acquisition and the use of virtue. (76) This is the lesson which we have been taught concerning the man who in word indeed had his name changed, but who in reality changed his nature from the consideration of natural to that of moral philosophy, and who abandoned the contemplation of the world itself for the knowledge of the Being who created the world; by which knowledge he acquired piety, the most excellent of all possessions.

XI

XI. (77) We will now speak of his wife, Sarah, for she too had her name changed to Sarrah by the addition of the one element, the letter rho. These, then, are the names, and we must now explain what they mean. Sarah, being interpreted, signifies "my authority," but Sarrah signifies "princess;" the former name, (78) therefore, is a symbol of specific virtue, but the latter of generic virtue. But in proportion as genus is superior to species in regard of quantity, in the same proportion does the latter name excel the former; for species is something small and perishable, but genus is numerous and immortal, (79) and the intention of God is to bestow great and immortal things instead of such as are small and perishable, and this is a task suited to his dignity. Now the prudence which exists in the virtuous man is the authority of himself alone, and he who has it would not err if he were to say, my authority is the prudence which is in me; but that which has stretched out this authority is generic prudence, not any longer the authority of this or that person, but absolute intrinsic authority; therefore that which exists only in species will perish at the same time with its possessor, but that which, like a seal, has stamped it with an impression, is free from all mortality, and will remain for ever and ever imperishable. (80) Thus also those arts which exist only in species perish along with those who have acquired them, such as geometricians, grammarians, and musicians, but the generic arts remain exempt from destruction. And, again, he gives an additional sketch of his meaning when he teaches by the same name that every virtue is a princess, and a queen, and a ruler of all the affairs of life.

XII

XII. (81) But it has also happened that Jacob had his name changed to Israel; and this, too, was a felicitous alteration. Why so? Because the name Jacob means "a supplanter," but the name Israel signifies "the man who sees God." Now it is the employment of a supplanter, who practices virtue, to move, and disturb, and upset the foundations of passion on which it is established, and whatever there is of any strength which is founded on them. But these things are not brought about without a struggle or without severe labour; but only when any one, having gone through all the labours of prudence, then proceeds to practise himself in the exercises of the soul and to wrestle against the reasonings which are hostile to it, and which seek to torment it; but it is the part of him who sees God not to depart from the sacred contest without the crown of victory, but rather to carry off the prize of triumph. (82) And what more flourishing and more suitable crown could be woven for the victorious soul than one by which it will be able acutely and clearly to behold the living God? At least a beautiful prize is thus proposed for the soul which delights in the practice of virtue, namely, the being endowed with sight adequate to the clear comprehension of the only thing which is really worth beholding.

XIII

XIII. (83) And it is worth while here to raise the question why Abraham, from the time that his name was changed, is always thought worthy of this same appellation, and is no longer called by his former name; but Jacob, who is also called Israel, is nevertheless called Jacob too, as he was before the change of his name; and, indeed, is called Jacob oftener than Israel. We must say, then, that these facts are characters by which it is seen that the virtue which is taught differs from that which is acquired by practice; (84) for the man who is improved by instruction, having received a happy and virtuous nature, uses that virtue alone which, by means of memory co-operating with it, implants in him an absence of forgetfulness, so that he comprehends and takes firm hold of all the things which he has once learnt; but he who practices virtue, since he is continually exercising himself, stops to take breath, and relaxes his efforts for a while, collecting himself and recovering the vigour which was a little impaired by his exertions, just as those men do who have oiled their bodies for the contests in the arena. For these men, also, labouring at their training exercises, in order to prevent their powers being utterly broken down, anoint themselves with oil on account of the violent and continued nature of their exercise. (85) Then the man who is improved by instruction, having an immortal monitor, receives from him a harmonious and imperishable advantage, without suffering any change; but the practiser of virtue is impelled to action by his own inclination alone, and he exercises himself in it, and labours at it in order to change that passion, which is akin to a created being; and even if he attains to perfection, he still, being fatigued, returns to his ancient kind of labour; (86) for he is more inclined to endure toil, but the other is more fortunate, for he has another person as a teacher. But this man, by his own unassisted efforts, investigates, and inquires, and pushes his examination, investigating the mysteries of nature with great earnestness, and exerting continual and incessant labour. (87) For this reason God, who never changes, altered the name of Abraham, since he was about to remain in a similar condition, in order that that which was to be firmly established might be confirmed by him who was standing firmly, and who was remaining in the same state in the same manner. But it was an angel who altered the name of Jacob, being the Word, the minister of God; in order that it might be confessed and ascertained, that there is none of the things whose existence is subsequent to that of the living God, which is the cause of unchangeable and unvarying firmness. ... but of that harmony which, as in a musical instrument, contains the intensity and relaxation of sounds so as to produce an artistical combination of melody.

XIV

XIV. (88) But, there being three leaders and authors of this race, the two at each extremity of it had their names changed, namely Abraham and Jacob: but the one in the middle, Isaac, always retained the same appellation. Why was this? Because both that virtue which is derived from teaching and that which is attained to by practice, admit of improvement and advancement: for the man who receives instruction desires a knowledge of those matters of which he is ignorant and he who applies himself to practice desires the crowns of victory, and the prizes which are proposed to his industrious and contemplation-loving soul. But the race which is self-taught and which derives all its learning from its own diligence inasmuch as it exists rather by nature than by study, was at the very beginning introduced as equal, and perfect, and even, there being no number whatever deficient of those which tend to completeness. (89) Nor indeed does Joseph have any such need, he who is the president of the necessities of the body; for he also changes his name, being called Psonthomphanech by the king of the country. And what the meaning of these names is we must explain; the name Joseph, being interpreted, signifies "an addition." For things which are put by the side are an addition to those which exist by nature; for instance, gold, silver, possessions, revenues, the ministrations of servants, abundant treasure of heirlooms, and furniture, and other superfluities, and the infinite multitude of the different efficients of pleasure which some persons possess; (90) the provider and superintendant of which was called Joseph, or addition, by a very felicitous nomenclature: since he had undertaken the superintendence of the things which were to be brought in from without, and added to the natural things previously existing in the course of nature. And the sacred scriptures testify that this is the case, showing that he was the purveyor of the food of all the corporeal region, Egypt, having stored it up in his treasure-houses.

XV

XV. (91) Such a person as this, then, Joseph is recognized as being by his distinctive marks and name. Let us now see what sort of person is indicated by the name Psonthomphanech. Now this name being interpreted means, "a mouth judging in an answer;" for every foolish person thinks that the man who is very rich and overflowing with external possessions, must at once be wise and sensible, competent to give an answer to any question which any one puts to him, and competent also of his own head to deliver advantageous and sagacious opinions. And, in short, by such men prudence is supposed to be identical with good fortune, while one ought, on the contrary, to consider good fortune as consisting in being prudent; for it is fitting that what is unstable should be under the direction of that which stands firmly. (92) And indeed his father gave to his own uterine brother the name of Benjamin: [946] but his mother called him the son of her sorrow, speaking most completely in accordance with nature. For the name Benjamin being interpreted means, "the son of days:" and the day is illuminated by the light of the sun which is perceptible by the outward senses: and to this we liken vain glory. (93) For that has a certain brilliancy appreciable by the outward senses in the praises which it receives from the multitude and from the common herd of men, in formally enrolled decrees, in the erection of statues and images, in purple robes and golden crowns, in chariots and teams of four horses, and processions of the multitude. He therefore who is an admirer and desirer of such things is very appropriately called a son of days: that is to say, of that light which is perceptible by the outward senses and of the brilliancy which attends vain glory. (94) This felicitous and appropriate name the elder word and real father imposes on him; but the soul which has suffered gives him a name suited to what she has suffered. For she calls him the son of her sorrow. Why so? Because those men who are borne about by vain glory are supposed indeed to be happy, but in real truth are unhappy. (95) For the things which oppose their happiness are numerous, envy, discontent, emulation, continual strife, irreconcileable enmities lasting till death, hostilities handed down in succession to one's children's children--a destiny not at all to be desired. (96) Very necessarily therefore did the divinely inspired prophet represent that vain glory as dying in the very act of bringing forth; for says he, "Rachel died, having had a bad Delivery." [947] Since, in truth and reality, the sowing and generation of vain glory perceptible by the outward senses is the death of the soul.

XVI

XVI. (97) And what shall we say of the sons of Joseph, Ephraim and Manasseh? Are they not, in strict accordance with nature, compared to the two eldest sons of Jacob, Reuben and Simeon? For the scripture says, "Thy two sons who were born in Egypt, before that I came into Egypt, belong to me; Ephraim and Manasseh shall be to me as Reuben and as Simeon." [948] Let us now then see in what manner the one pair are likened to the other pair. (98) Reuben is the symbol of a good natural disposition, for the name being interpreted means, "A seeing son;" since every one who is endowed with tolerable acuteness of mind and a good disposition is capable of seeing; and Ephraim, as we have already frequently said in other places, is a symbol of memory, for his name being interpreted signifies, "productiveness of fruit," and the most excellent fruit of the soul is memory; and there is no one thing so nearly akin to another as remembering is to a man of good natural endowments. (99) Again, the name of Simeon is a symbol of learning and instruction; for, being interpreted, it signifies "listening," and it is the especial part of a learner to listen and attend to what is said. But Manasseh is a symbol of "recollection," for thus that art is called, from forgetfulness; (100) for it must of necessity happen to the man who has advanced out of forgetfulness to recollect, and recollecting especially belongs to learning, for very often his notions escape from the man who is learning, as out of weakness he is unable to retain them, and then again they return to him as at the beginning. The condition therefore which arises from this escaping of his notions is denominated forgetfulness, and that which arises from their returning to him is called recollection. (101) Now is not memory very naturally spoken of as connected with good natural endowments, and recollection as akin to learning? And, indeed, the same relation which Simeon bears to Reuben, that is to say, learning to natural endowment, the same does Manasseh bear to Ephraim, and the same does recollection bear to memory. (102) For as the man of good natural endowments is better than he who is only a learner, for the one resembles the sense of seeing, the other that of hearing, and hearing is always reckoned as entitled to a lesser honour than seeing; so also, he who is endowed with a good memory is at all times superior to him who only recollects, because the one is combined with forgetfulness, but the other continues unalloyed and unadulterated from beginning to end.

XVII

XVII. (103) And indeed the scriptures at one time call the father-in-law of the first prophets Jother, and at another time Raguel-Jother, when pride is flourishing and at its height; for the name Jother being interpreted means "superfluous," and pride is superfluous in an honest and sincere life, turning into ridicule, as it does, all that is equal and necessary to life, and honouring the unequal things of excess and covetousness. (104) This passion honours human things above divine, and customs above laws, and profane above sacred things, and mortal above immortal things, and, in short, appearances above reality; and it even ventures of its accord to pass on into the rank of counsellors, suggesting to the wise man not to teach those things which alone are worthy to be known, namely, "the commandments of God, and the Law," [949] but to study the covenants and contracts of men with one another, which are almost the causes of the society which exists among them being so little sociable. But the great man is obedient in all things, thinking that little things are adapted to little people, and that great things are justly added to the great; (105) but very often this man who is wise in his own conceit, and who, passing over from the herds which the blind had assigned to him for him to guide, having sought out the divine herd, becomes no small portion of it; admiring the leader of nature, and marvelling at his way of leading which he employs in his care of his own flocks, for the name Raguel being interpreted, signifies the "pastoral care of God." [950]

XVIII

XVIII. (106) The main part has now been explained; we will now proceed to adduce the proofs. In the first place the scripture represents him as the cultivator of judgment and of justice, for the name Midian, being interpreted, means "out of judgment." And this is said in a twofold sense, for some times it signifies both selection and rejection, such as usually happens to those who are competitors in those contests which are called sacred; for numbers as they appear not qualified, are rejected by the masters of the games. (107) These are the men who have been initiated in the unholy rites of Beelphegor,[951] and having widened all the mouths of the body to enable them to receive the streams which are poured into them from without, for the name Beelphegor is interpreted "the mouth above the skin," for they have overwhelmed the mind, the governor of the body, and have sunk it down to the lowest depth, so that it can never emerge, nor even hold up its head in ever so slight a degree. (108) And it suffered this until Phineas, the lover of peace and manifest priest of God, came as a champion of his own accord, being by nature a hater of all that is evil, and filled with an admiration and desire for what is good; and as he took a coadjutor, that is to say, the well sharpened and sharp-edged sword, competent to investigate and examine everything, he could not be deceived, but exerting a vigorous strength, he pierced passion through her womb, that it might not hereafter bring forth any divinely caused evil. (109) Now between these men and the seeing race there is a terrible war, in which no one of the combatants differed in language,[952] but each returned home unwounded and safe, crowned with the garlands of victory.

XIX

XIX. (110) This now is one of the things which are shown by the name of Midian; another is that more excellent and judicial species which by the affinity of marriage is connected with the prophetic race. The scripture then says, "The priest of judgment and justice" (that is to say, of Midian) "has seven Daughters;"[953] (111) by which seven daughters are frequently intimated the powers of the irrational part of the soul, the power of generation and the voice, and the five outward senses, tending the flocks of their father; for by means of these seven powers it is that all the progresses and increases of their father, the mind, exist in the perceptions which are produced from him. These, then, coming each to its appropriate object, the power of sight to colours and shapes, the sense of hearing to sounds, the faculty of smelling to scents, taste to flavours, and all the other faculties to those objects which are adapted for their exercise do in a manner imbibe some of the external objects of the outward senses, until they have filled all the channels of the soul, and from these channels they give drink to the sheep of their father; I mean by these sheep that most pure flock of the reason which bears safety and ornament at the same time. (112) But the companions of envy and jealousy, the leaders of the wicked herd coming up, drive them away from that use of their powers which is in accordance with nature, for some conduct these things which are without, inwards to the mind as to a judge and a king, in order that they may do well from having the most excellent of governors; (113) but others take the opposite side, pursuing and proclaiming the exact contrary, while it is possible for the mind to be drawn towards them, and to give up the flock which was entrusted to it to Feed.[954] Until the good disposition, devoted to virtue and inspired by God, which for awhile has appeared to be resting in inactivity, by name Moses, holds his shield over them and defends them from those who would attack them, nourishing the flock of his father on wholesome words, (114) and they having escaped the attack of the enemies of intellect who admire only the external appendages, like people in tragedies, go no longer to Jother but to Raguel, for they have abandoned all connections with pride, and having connected themselves with lawful persuasion, choosing to become a portion of the sacred flock, of which the divine word is the leader, as his name shows, for it signifies the pastoral care of God.

XX

XX. (115) But while he is taking care of his own flock, all kinds of good things are given all at once to those of the sheep who are obedient, and who do not resist his will; and in the Psalms we find a song in these words, "The Lord is my shepherd, therefore shall I lack Nothing;"[955] (116) therefore the mind which has had the royal shepherd, the divine word, for its instructor, will very naturally ask of his seven daughters, "Why is it that you have contended with such great haste to come hither this Day?"[956] for formerly, when you met with the objects of the outward sense, remaining a long time outside, you were a long time in returning again by reason of the manner in which you were allured by them, but now I do not know what it is that has happened to you, but you are speedy in your return, contrary to your usual custom. (117) Therefore they will say that there were not the same causes why they should run back with such exceeding speed, making the double course from the objects of the outward sense and to the objects of the outward sense, without stopping to take breath, and with excessive impetuosity;

but that the cause was rather the man who delivered them from the shepherds of the wild flock. And they call Moses an Egyptian, a man who was not only a Hebrew, but even a Hebrew of the very purest race, of the only tribe which is consecrated, because they are unable to rise above their own nature; (118) for the outward senses, being on the confines between the objects of the intellect and those of the outward senses, we must be content if they aim at both of them, and are not allured by the objects of the outward sense alone. And to think that they are inclined only to attend to the things which are purely objects of the intellect is great folly; on which account they give him both these names, since when they call him a man, they indicate the things which are within the province of reason alone to contemplate, and when they call him an Egyptian, they indicate the objects of the external senses. (119) When they had heard this, he will again inquire, "Where is the man?" In what part of you is the reasonable species dwelling? Why have you left it so easily, and have not rather after having once met with it, preserved that which was the most beautiful of possessions, and the most advantageous for yourselves? (120) But even if you have not done so before, at least call it to you now, that it may eat of and be supported by your improvement and your close connection with him; for perhaps he will even dwell with you, and will bring with him the winged, and divinely inspired, and prophetical race by name Zipporah.

XXI

XXI. (121) Thus much we have thought fit to say on this subject. But, moreover, Moses also changes the name of Hosea into that of Joshua; displaying by his new name the distinctive qualities of his character; (122) for the name Hosea is interpreted, "what sort of a person is this?" but Joshua means "the salvation of the Lord," being the name of the most excellent possible character; for the habits are better with respect to those persons who are of such and such qualities from being influenced by them: as, for instance, music is better in a musician, physic in a physician, and each art of a distinctive quality in each artist, regarded both in its perpetuity, and in its power, and in its unerring perfection with regard to the objects of its speculation. For a habit is something everlasting, energising, and perfect; but a man of such and such a quality is mortal, the object of action, and imperfect. And what is imperishable is superior to what is mortal, the efficient cause is better than that which is the object of action; and what is perfect is preferable to what is imperfect. (123) In this way the coinage of the above mentioned description was changed and received the stamp of a better kind of appearance. And Caleb himself was changed wholly and entirely; "For," as the scripture says, "a new spirit was in Him;" [957] as if the dominant part in him had been changed into complete perfection; for the name Caleb, being interpreted, means "the whole heart." (124) And a proof of this is to be gathered from the fact that the mind is changed, not by being biassed and inclining in one particular direction or the other, but wholly and entirely in the direction which is good; and that, even if there is any thing which is not very praiseworthy indeed, it makes that to depart by arguments conducive to repentance; for, having in this manner washed off all the defilements which polluted it, and having availed itself of the baths and purifications of wisdom, it must inevitably look brilliant.

XXII

XXII. (125) But it happens to the arch-prophet to have many names: for when he interprets and explains the oracles which are delivered by God, he is called Moses; and when he prays for and blesses the people, he is called the man of God; [958] and when Egypt is paying the penalty of its impious actions, he is then denominated the god of him who is the king of the country, namely, of Pharaoh. [959] And why is all this? (126) Because to alter a code of laws for the advantage of those who are to use them is the part of a man who is always handling divine things, and having them in his hands; and who is called a lawgiver by the allknowing God, and who has received from him a great gift--the interpretation of the sacred laws, and the spirit of prophecy in accordance with them. For the name Moses, being translated, signifies "gain," and it also means handling, for the reasons which I have already enumerated. (127) But to pray and to bless are not the duties of any ordinary man, but they belong to one who has not admitted any connection with created things, but who has devoted himself to God, the governor and the father of all men. (128) And any one must be content to whom it has been allowed to use the privilege of blessing. And to be able also to procure good for others belongs to a greater and more perfect soul, and is the profession of one who is really inspired by God, which he who has attained to may reasonably be called God. But also, this same person is God, inasmuch as he is wise, and as on this account he rules over every foolish person, even if such foolish person be established and strengthened by a haughty sceptre, and be ever so proud on this account; (129) for the Ruler of the universe, even though some persons are about to be punished for intolerable acts of wickedness, nevertheless is willing to admit some intercessors to mediate on their behalf, who, in imitation of the merciful power of the father, exercise their power of punishment with more moderation and humanity; but to do good is the peculiar attribute of God.

XXIII

XXIII. (130) Having now discussed at sufficient length the subject of change and alteration of names, we will turn to the matters which come next in order in our proposed examination. Immediately after the events which we have just mentioned, came the birth of Isaac; for after God had given to his mother the name of Sarrah instead of Sarah, he said to Abraham, "I will give unto thee a Son." [960] We must consider each of the things here indicated particularly. (131) Now he who is properly said to give any thing whatever must by all means be giving what is his own private property. And if this is true beyond controversy, then it would follow that Isaac must not have been a man, but a being synonymous with that most exquisite joy of all pleasures, namely, laughter, the adopted son of God, who gave him as a soother and cheerer to the most peace-loving souls; (132) for it is absurd to suppose that there was one who was a man, and another of whom bastard and illegitimate offspring were descended: and, indeed, Moses calls the man of an intellect devoted to virtue a god, when he says, "The Lord, seeing that Leah was hated, opened her Womb."[961] (133) For having felt compassion and pity for virtue as being hated by the race of mankind, and for the soul which loves virtue, he makes the nature which loves beauty barren, but opens the fountain of fecundity and gives it a prosperous labour. (134) But Tamar, when she became pregnant of divine seeds, and did not know who it was who had sown them (for it is said that at that time "she had covered her face," as Moses did when he turned away, having a reverential fear of beholding God), still when she saw the tokens and the evidences and decided within herself that it was not a mortal man who gave these things, cried out, "To whomsoever these things belong, it is by him that I am with Child." [962] (135) Whose was the ring, or the pledge, or the seal of the whole, or the archetypal appearance, according to which all the things, though devoid of species and of distinctive quality, were all stamped and marked? And whose again was the armlet, or the ornament; that is to say, destiny, the link and analogy of all things which have an indissoluble connection? Whose, again, was the staff, the thing of strong support, which wavers not, which is not moved; that is to say, admonition, correction, instruction? Whose is the sceptre, the kingly power? (136) does it not belong to God alone? Therefore, the disposition inclined to confession, that is to say, Judah, being pleased at her possessed and inspired condition, speaks freely, saying, "She has spoken justly, because I gave her in marriage to no mortal Man;" [963] thinking it an impious thing to pollute divine with profane things.

XXIV

XXIV. (137) And wisdom, which, after the fashion of a mother, has conceived and brought fourth the self-taught race, points out that it is God who is the sower of it; for, after the offspring is brought forth, she speak magnificently, saying, "The Lord has caused me Laughter;" [964] an expression equivalent to, he has fashioned, he has made, he has begotten Isaac, since Isaac is the same with laughter. (138) But it does not belong to every one to hear this sound, since the evil of superstition is very widely spread among us, and has overwhelmed many unmanly and ignoble souls; on which account she adds, "For whoever hears this will not rejoice with me." As if those persons were very few whose ears are opened and pricked up so as to be inclined to the reception of these sacred words, which teach that it is the peculiar employment of the only God to sow and to beget what is good; to which words all other persons are deaf. (139) And I know that this illustrious oracle was formerly delivered from the mouth of the prophet. "Thy fruit has been found from me: who is wise and will understand these things? who is prudent and will know Them?" [965] But I have observed, and comprehended, and admired him who causes to resound, and who himself, invisible as he is, does in an invisible manner strike the organ of the voice; being amazed also at the same time at what was uttered. (140) For if there be any good thing among existing things, that, or I should rather say the whole heaven and the whole world, if one must tell the truth, is the fruit of God; being preserved upon his eternal and everflourishing nature as upon a tree. But it belongs to wise and understanding men to understand and to confess such things as these, and not to the ignorant.

XXV

XXV. (141) We have now then explained what is meant by the words, "I will give unto thee." We must now explain the words, "out of her." Some now have understood them as meaning that which exists out of her, thinking that it has been most correctly decided by right reason that the soul never displays any peculiar beauty of its own, but only such as comes to it from without, in accordance with the greatness of the good will of God who showers his graces upon it. (142) But others understand these words to mean instant rapidity; for that the words (ex auteÂs, which we have translated) "out of her," are here equivalent to, "at once, immediately, without any delay, without hesitation." And it is in this way that the gifts of God usually come to men, outstripping the differences of time. There is a third class of persons who say, that virtue is the mother of all created good, without having received the seed of it from any mortal man; (143) and to those who ask, whether she who is barren has an offspring (for the holy scriptures, which some time ago represented Sarrah as barren, now confess that she will become a mother); this answer must be given, that a woman who is barren cannot, in the course of nature, bring forth an offspring, just as a blind man cannot see, nor a deaf man hear; but that the soul, which is barren of bad things, and which is unproductive of immoderate license of the passions and vices, is alone very nearly attaining to a happy delivery, bringing forth objects worthy of love, namely, the number seven, according to the hymn which is sung by Grace, that is, by Hannah, who says, "she who was barren hath born seven, and she who had many children has become weak:" [966] (144) and what she means by, "She who has many children," is the mind, which being pregnant of mixed and promiscuous reasonings, from all quarters confused together, by reason of the multitudes which crowd around her, and of the disorder which they cause, brings forth incurable evils; and by "she who was barren," she means that the mind which had never received any mortal seed, as if it were productive of offspring, but has avoided and shunned all association and all connection with the wicked, and clings to the seventh, and to the most peaceful numbers in accordance with it, for it deserves to be pregnant of it, and to be called its mother.

XXVI

XXVI. (145) This then is the meaning of the words, "out of her." We must now consider the third point, namely, what that is which is called her son. In the first place, then, there is this worthy of our admiration, that God does not say that he will give her many children, but that he will give her one only. And why is this? Because it is the nature of what is good to be investigated, not so much with respect to its number or magnitude, as with respect to its power; (146) for musical precepts, to take them for an instance, or rules of grammar, or of geometry, or of justice, or of wisdom, or of manly courage, or of temperance, are very numerous indeed; but the science itself of music, or grammar, or geometry, and still more the virtue of justice, or temperance, or wisdom, or manly courage, is only one thing, the loftiest perfection, in no respect differing from the archetypal model, after which all those numerous and countless precepts were formed. (147) And this is why he only says that he will give her one son. And now he called it a son, not speaking carelessly or inconsiderately, but for the sake of showing that it is not a foreign, or a supposititious, nor an adopted, nor an illegitimate child, but a legitimate child, a proper citizen, inasmuch as a foreign child cannot be the offspring of a truly citizen soul, for the Greek word teknon (son), is derived from tokos (bringing forth), by way of showing the kindred by which children are, by nature, united to their parents.

XXVII

XXVII. (148) And, says God, "I will bless her, and she shall be a mother of Nations;" [967] because, not only is generic virtue divided into its proximate species, and into individuals subordinate to the species, as if into nations; but also because, as there are nations of living animals, so in a manner are there nations of things, to which virtue is a very great advantage; (149) for all things which are devoid and destitute of wisdom are mischievous, just as all places upon which the sun does not shine are of necessity dark; for it is by virtue that a farmer is able to pay better attention to his crops, and by virtue that a charioteer drives his chariot in the horse-races so as to avoid falling; and by virtue too, that a pilot and a steersman guides his vessel in its voyage. (150) Virtue again has caused houses, and cities, and countries to be inhabited in a better manner, making men competent to manage houses and cities, and fit to associate with one another. Virtue has also introduced most excellent laws, and has sown the seeds of peace everywhere; since, from the contrary habit, things of a contrary character do naturally arise--war, lawlessness, bad constitutions, confusion, unnecessary voyages, overthrows, that which, in science, is the most grievous of all diseases, namely, cunning, from which, instead of art, all kinds of evil artifice has flowed. Very necessarily, therefore, will virtue be divided among all nations, which are large and collected systems of living beings and things taken together, for the advantage of those who receive her.

XXVIII

XXVIII. (151) Immediately afterwards it is said, "And kings of the nations shall be born of her." For those with whom she is pregnant and whom she brings forth are all rulers; not because they have been elected as such for a short period by lot, which is an uncertain thing, or by the show of hands of men who are for the most part bribed, but because they have been destined and appointed so for everlasting by nature herself. (152) And these are not my words only, but those of the most holy scriptures, in which certain persons are introduced as saying to Abraham, "Thou art a king from God among Us;" [968] not out of consideration for his resources (for what resources could a man have who was an emigrant and who had no city to inhabit, but who was wandering over a great extent of impassable country?), but because they saw that he had a royal disposition in his mind, so that they confessed, in the words of Moses, that he was the only wise king. (153) For in real truth the wise man is the king of those who are foolish, since he knows what he ought and what he ought not to do; and the temperate man is the king of the intemperate, as he has attained to no careless or inaccurate knowledge of what relates to choice and avoidance. Also the brave man is king over the cowardly, inasmuch as he has thoroughly learnt what he ought to endure and what he ought not. So too the just man is king of the unjust, as he is possessed of the knowledge of undeviating equality as to what is to be distributed. And the holy man is king over the unholy, as he is possessed with the most just and excellent notions of God.

XXIX

XXIX. (154) It was natural then for the mind, being puffed up by these promises, to be elated and raised to an undue height in its own estimation; and accordingly, by way of producing conviction in us, who were accustomed to hold up our heads at the slightest trifles, "it falls down and immediately laughs the laughter of the soul," looking mournful as to its face, but smiling in its mind a great and unmixed joy having entered into it: (155) and both these feelings, namely, to laugh and also to fall, do at the same time occur to a wise man who inherits good things beyond his expectation; the one being his fate, as a proof that he is not over-proud because of his thorough knowledge of his mortal nothingness; and the other, by way of a confirmation of his piety on account of his looking upon God as the sole cause of all graces and of all good things. (156) Let, then, the creature fall down and wear a melancholy countenance very naturally; for it has no stability in its own nature, and as far as that goes is easily dissolved; but let it be raised up again by God, and laugh, for he alone is the support and joy of it. (157) And here any one may reasonably express a doubt how it is possible for any one to laugh when laughter had not as yet come among one branch of the creation; for Isaac is laughter, who, according to the account under our consideration at present, was not yet born. For just as it is impossible to see without eyes, or to hear without ears, or to smell without nostrils, or to exert any other of the external senses without the organs adapted to each respectively, or to comprehend without the reason, so also it is not likely that a person can have laughed, if laughter had not as yet been made. (158) What, then, are we to say? Nature foreshows many of the things which are hereafter to happen by certain symbols. Do you not see how the young bird, before it commits itself to the air, is fond of fluttering its wings and shaking its pinions, giving a previous happy indication of its hope that it will be able to fly? (159) And have you never seen a lamb, or a kid, or an ox, while still young, and before his horns are as yet grown and noticed, if by chance any one irritates him, how he opposes him, and moves forward to defend himself with those parts in which nature has planted his arms for defence? (160) And in the battles which take place with wild beasts, the bulls do not at once gore the adversaries who are opposed to them, but standing well apart, and relaxing their neck in a moderate degree and bending their heads on one side, and looking fierce, as it were, they then, after a truce, rush on with the determination of persevering in the contest. And this sort of conduct those who are in the habit of inventing new words call "sparring," being a sort of sham attack before the real one.

XXX

XXX. (161) And the soul is subject to many things of much the same kind. For when something good is hoped for it rejoices beforehand, so that in a manner it rejoices before its joy, and is delighted before its delight. And one may also compare this to what happens with respect to plants; for they, too, when they are about to bear fruit, bud beforehand and flower previously, and are green previously. (162) Look at the cultivated vine, how marvellously it is furnished by nature with young shoots, and tendrils, and suckers, and leaves redolent of wine, which, though they utter no voice, do nevertheless indicate the joy of the tree at the coming fruit. And the day also laughs in anticipation of the early dawn, when the sun is about to rise; for one ray is a messenger of another, and one beam of light, as the forerunner of another though more obscure, is still a herald of that which shall be brighter. (163) Therefore, joy accompanies a good when it is already arrived, and hope while it is expected. For we rejoice when it is come, and we hope while it is coming; just as in the case also with the contrary feelings; for the presence of evil brings us grief, and the expectation of evil generates fear, and fear is nothing more than grief before grief, as hope is joy before joy. For the same relation that, I imagine, fear bears to grief, that same does hope bear to joy. (164) And the external senses afford very manifest proofs of what has now been said; for smell, sitting as it were in front of taste, pronounces judgment beforehand on almost every thing which is eaten and drunk; from which fact some persons have very felicitously named it the foretaster, having a regard to its employment. And so hope is by nature adapted to have as it were a foretaste of the coming good; and to represent it to the soul, which is to have a firm possession of it. (165) Moreover, when any one who is engaged in a journey is hungry or thirsty, if he on a sudden sees a fountain or all kinds of trees weighed down with eatable fruits, he is at once filled with a hope of enjoyment, not only before he has either eaten or drunk, but before he has either come near them or gathered of them. And do we then think that we are able to feast on the nourishment of the body before we receive it, but that the food of the mind is not able to render us cheerful beforehand, even when we are on the very point of feasting on it?

XXXI

XXXI. (166) He laughed then very naturally, even though laughter did not as yet appear to have been scattered among the human race: and not only did he laugh but the woman also laughed; for it is said presently, "And Sarrah laughed in herself, saying, There has never up to the present time come any good unto me of its own accord without care on my part; but he who has promised is my Lord, and is older than all creation, and him I must of necessity believe." (167) And at the same time it also teaches us that virtue is naturally a thing to be rejoiced at, and that he who possesses it is at all times rejoiced; and, on the contrary, that vice is a painful thing, and that he who possesses that is most miserable. And do we even now marvel at those philosophers who affirm that virtue consists in apathy? (168) For, behold, Moses is found to be the leader of this wise doctrine, as he represents the good man as rejoicing and laughing. And in other passages he not only speaks of him in that way, but also of all those who come to the same place with him; for he says, "And when he seeth thee he will rejoice in Himself;" [969] as if the bare sight of a good man were by itself sufficient to fill the mind with cheerfulness while the soul would cast off its most fearful burden, sorrow. (169) But it is not allowed to every wicked man to rejoice, as it is said in the predictions of the prophet, "There is no rejoicing for the wicked, says God." [970] For this is truly a divine saying and oracle, that the life of every wicked man is melancholy, and sad, and full of unhappiness, even if with his face he pretends to feel happiness; (170) for I should not say that the Egyptians rejoiced in reality when they heard that the brethren of Joseph were come, but that they only feigned joy, putting on a false appearance like hypocrites; for no convictor, when standing by and pressing upon a foolish man is a pleasure to him, just as no physician is to an intemperate man who is sick; for labour attends on what is useful, and laziness on what is hurtful. And those who prefer laziness to labour are very naturally hated by those who advise them to a course which will be useful and laborious. (171) When, therefore, you hear that "Pharaoh and all his servants rejoiced on account of the arrival of Joseph's Brethren," [971] do not think that they rejoiced in reality, unless perhaps in this sense, that they expected that he would become changed from the good things of the soul in which he had been brought up, and would come over to the profitless appetites of the body, having adulterated the ancient and hereditary coinage of that virtue which was akin to him.

XXXII

XXXII. (172) The mind, then, which is devoted to pleasure, having entertained these hopes, does not think that it is sufficient to attract the younger men, and those who are as yet only attending the school of temperance, by its allurements; but it looks upon it as a terrible thing, if it cannot also bring over the elder reasoning, the more impetuous passions of which have now passed their prime; (173) for in a subsequent passage Joseph says to them, proposing injuries to them as though they were benefits, "Now, therefore, bringing with you your father and all your possessions, come hither to Me;" [972] speaking in this way of Egypt and of that terrible king who drags back all our paternal inheritance and the good things which really belong to us and which have advanced beyond the body (for by nature they are free), endeavoring by force to surrender them to a very bitter prison, having, as the holy scripture tells us, "appointed as guardian of the prison Pentaphres, the eunuch and chief Cook," [973] who was a man in great want of all that is good, and who had been deprived of the generative parts of the soul; and who was also unable to sow and to plant any of those things which bear upon instruction; but who like a cook slew the living animals, and cut them up and divided them in different portions limb by limb, and who wallowed about in dead and lifeless bodies and things equally, and who, by his superfluous preparations and refinements, excited and stirred up the appetites of the profitless passions, while it was natural to expect that those who were able to tame them should mollify. (174) And he also says, "I will give unto you all the good things of Egypt, and you shall eat of the marrow of the Earth." [974] But we will say unto him, We who keep our eyes fixed on the good things of the soul do not desire those of the body. For that most delicious desire of the former things, when once implanted in the mind, is well calculated to engender a forgetfulness of all those things which are dear to the flesh.

XXXIII

XXXIII. (175) Something like this, then, is the falsely named joy of the foolish. But the true joy has already been described, which is adapted only to the virtuous, "Therefore, falling down he Laughed." [975] Not falling from God, but from himself; for he stood near the unchangeable God, but he fell from his own vain opinion. (176) On which account that pride which was wise in its own conceit, having been thrown down, and the feeling which is devoted to God having been raised in its place, and been established around the only unalterable being, he, immediately laughing, said in his mind, "Shall a child be born to one who is a hundred years old, and shall Sarrah, who is ninety years old, have a child?" (177) Do not fancy, my good friend, that the word, "he said" not with his mouth but "in his Mind," [976] has been added for no especial use; on the contrary, it is inserted with great accuracy and propriety. Why so? Because it seems by his saying, "Shall a child be born to him who is a hundred years old?" that he had a doubt about the birth of Isaac, in which he was previously stated to believe; as what was predicted a little before showed, speaking thus, "This child shall not be thy heir, but he who shall come out of thee;" and immediately afterward he says, "Abraham believed in the Lord, and it was counted to him for righteousness." (178) Since then it was not consistent for one who had already believed to doubt, he has represented the doubt as of no long continuance, extending only as far as the mouth of the tongue, and stopping there at the mind which is endowed with such celerity of motion; for, says the scripture, "he said in his mind," which nothing, and no person ever so celebrated for swiftness of foot, could ever be able to outstrip, since it outruns even all the winged natures; (179) on which account the most illustrious of all of the Greek poets appears to me to have said:--

"Swift as a winged bird or fleeter Thought." [977]

Showing by these words the exceeding speed of its promptitude, placing the thought after the winged bird as a sort of climax; for the mind advances at the same moment to very many things and bodies, hurrying on with indescribable impetuosity, and without a moment's lapse of time it speeds at once to the borders of both earth and sea, bringing together and dividing infinite magnitudes by a single word; and at the same time it soars to such a height above the earth, that it penetrates through the air and reaches even the aether, and scarcely stops at the very furthest circle of the fixed stars. (180) For the fervid and glowing heat of that region does not suffer to to rest tranquil; on which account, overleaping many things, it is borne far beyond every boundary perceptible by the outward senses, to that which is compounded of ideas and appearances by the law of kindred. On which account in the good man there is a slight change, indivisible, unapportionable, not perceptible by the outward senses, but only by the intellect, and being in a manner independent of them.

XXXIV

XXXIV. (181) But, perhaps, some one may say, What then? is he who has once believed bound never to admit the slightest trace, or shadow, or moment of incredulity at all? But this man appears to me to have nothing else in his mind except an idea of proving the creature uncreated, and the mortal immortal, and the corruptible incorruptible, and man, if it be lawful to say so, God. (182) For he says that the belief which man has once conceived ought to be so firm as in no respect to differ from that which is entertained of the truly living God and which is complete in every part; for Moses, in his greater hymn, says, "God is faithful, and there is no unrighteousness in Him." [978] (183) And it is great folly to fancy that the soul of man is able to contain the virtues of God, which never vary and which are established on the most solid footing; for it is sufficient, and one must be content to have been able to acquire the images of them, though they are inferior to the archetypal patterns by many and large numbers. (184) And is not this reasonable? for it follows of necessity that the virtues of God must be pure and unmixed, since God is not a compound being, inasmuch as he is a single nature; on the other hand, the virtues of men must be mixed with some alloy, since we ourselves are compounds, the divine and human nature being combined in us, and adapted together according to the principles of perfect music; and that which is composed of many separate things has a natural attraction to each of its parts. (185) But he is happy to whom it has happened that for the greater portion of his life he has inclined towards the more excellent and more divine part; for that he should have done so all his life is impossible, since at times the mortal weight which is opposed to him has preponderated in the opposite scale, and impending over his mind, has kept watch for the opportunities of coming upon his reason at an unfavourable time, so as to drag it back again.

XXXV

XXXV. (186) Abraham therefore believed in God; but he believed as a man; that you may be aware of the peculiar attribute of mortals, and may learn that his fall did not happen to him in any other way than in consequence of the ordinances of nature. And if it was of short duration and only momentary, it is a thing to be thankful for: for many other men have been so overturned by the violence and impetuosity of error, and by its irresistible force, that they have been utterly destroyed for ever. (187) For know, my good man, that, according to the most holy Moses, virtue is not perfect in the human body, but it suffers something like torpor, and is often ever so little lame. For says the scripture, "The broader part of his thigh became torpid, on which he was Lame." [979] (188) And perhaps some man of an over-confident disposition may come forward and say that this is not the language of one who disbelieves, but of one praying, so that if that most excellent of all the happy feelings were about to be produced, it would not be brought forth according to any other number than that of ninety years, that so the perfect good might arrive at its production according to perfect numbers. (189) But the aforesaid numbers are perfect, and especially according to the sacred scriptures. And let us consider each of them: now first of all there is the son of the just Noah and the ancestor of the seeing race, and he is said to have been a hundred years old when he begat Arphaxad, [980] and the meaning of the name of Arphaxad is, "he disturbed sorrow." At all events it is a good thing that the offspring of the soul should confuse, and disorder, and destroy that miserable thing iniquity, so full of evils. (190) But Abraham also planted a field, [981] using the ratio of an hundred for the measurement of the ground: and Isaac found some barley yielding a hundred Fold. [982] And Moses also made the vestibule of the sacred tabernacle in a hundred arches, [983] measuring out the distance towards the east and towards the west. (191) Moreover the ratio of a hundred is the first fruit of the first fruit which the Levites assign to those who are consecrated to the priesthood; [984] for after they have taken the tenth from the nation they are enjoined to give unto the priests a sacred tenth of the whole share, as if from their own possessions. (192) And if a person were to consider, he might find many other instances to the praise of the aforesaid number brought forward in the law of Moses, but for the present what have been enumerated are sufficient. But if from the hundred you set aside the tenth part as a sacred first fruit to God who produces, and increases, and brings to perfection the fruit of the soul--for how can it be anything but perfect, inasmuch as it is on the confines between the first and the tenth, in the same manner in which the Holy of Holies is separated by the veil in the middle. [...] [985] by which those things which are of the same genus are divided according to the differences in species?

XXXVI

XXXVI. (193) Therefore the good man was speaking and saying things which were really good in his mind. But the bad man at times interprets good things in a very excellent manner, but nevertheless does shameful things in a most shameful one, as Shechem does who is the offspring of folly. For he is the son of Hamon his father, and the name Hamon, being translated, means "an ass," but the Shechem means "a shoulder" when interpreted, the symbol of labour. But that labour of which folly is the parent is miserable and full of suffering, as, on the other hand, that labour is useful to which prudence is related. (194) Accordingly the holy scriptures tell us that, "Shechem spake according to the mind of the virgin, having first humbled Her." [986] It is not said then, with great purpose and accuracy, that he spake according to the mind of the damsel, for the purpose of showing distinctly that he acted in a contrary manner to that in which he spoke? For Dinah means "incorruptible judgment:" justice the attribute seated by God, the everlasting virgin; for the name Dinah, being interpreted, means either thing, "judgment" or "justice." (195) Fools, then, laying violent hands upon and attempting to defile her, by means of their daily designs and practices, by their plausibility of speech escape conviction. Therefore they must either act in a manner consistent with the language that they hold, or else they must hold their tongues while committing iniquity. For it is said, "Silence is one half of evil:" as Moses says when rebuking the man who accounted the creature worthy of the principal honour, and the immortal God worthy only of the second place, "Thou hast sinned, be silent." (196) For to use bombastic language, and to boast of one's evil deeds, is a double sin: and men in general are very prone to this; for they are constantly saying what is pleasing to the ever-virgin virtue, and such things as are just: but they never omit any opportunity of insulting and violating her when they are able. For what city is there which is not full of those who are continually celebrating the praises of virtue?--(197) men who weary the ears of those who hear them by everlastingly dwelling on such subjects as these; wisdom is a necessary good; folly is pernicious; temperance is desirable; intemperance is hateful; courage is a thing proper to be cultivated; cowardice must be avoided; justice is advantageous; injustice is disadvantageous; holiness is honourable; unholiness is shameful; piety towards the gods is praiseworthy; impiety is blameable; that which is most akin to the nature of man is to design, and to act, and to speak virtuously; that which is most alien from his nature is to do the contrary of all these things. (198) By continually stringing together these and similar aphorisms they deceive the courts of justice, and the council chambers, and the theatres, and every assembly and company which they meet; as men who put beautiful masks on ugly faces, with the intention of not being discovered by those who see them. (199) But it is of no use; for some persons will come endowed with great vigour, and occupied with a real zeal and admiration for virtue, and who will strip them of all their coverings, and disguises, and appendages which they had woven round themselves by the evil artifice of plausible speeches, and will display their soul naked by itself as it really is, and will make themselves acquainted with the secret things of their nature which are hidden as it were in recesses. And then having brought to light all its shame and all the reproaches to which it is liable, they will display them in broad daylight to every one, and show what sort of thing it is, how disgraceful and ridiculous, and what a spurious kind of beauty it has disguised itself with by means of its appendages and coverings. (200) And those who are prepared to avenge themselves on such profane and impure dispositions are Simeon and Levi, [987] two indeed in number, but only one in mind; on which account, in his blessings of his sons, their father numbers them together under one classification, on account of the harmonious character of their unanimity and of their violence in one and the same direction. But Moses does not make any mention of them afterwards as a pair, but classes the whole tribe of Simeon under that of Levi, combining together two essences, of which he made one impressed as it were with one idea and appearance, hearing to doing.

XXXVII

XXXVII. (201) When, therefore, the virtuous man knew that the promise was uttering things full of reverence and prudent caution, according to his own mind, he admitted both these feelings into his breast, namely, faith in God, and incredulity as to the creature. Very naturally therefore he says, using the language of entreaty, "Would that this Ishmael might live before Thee," [988] using each word of those which he utters here with deliberate propriety, namely, the "this," the "might live," the "before thee." (202) For it is no small number of persons who have been deceived by the similarity of the names of different things, and we had better examine here what I am saying. The name of Ishmael, being interpreted, means "the hearing of God," but some men listen to the divine doctrines to their benefit, and others listen to both his admonitions and to those of others only to their destruction. Do you recollect the case of the soothsayer Balaam? [989] He is represented as hearing the oracles of God, and as having received knowledge from the Most High, (203) but what advantage did he reap from such hearing, and what good accrued to him from such knowledge? In his intention he endeavored to injure the most excellent eye of the soul, which alone has received such instruction as to be able to behold God, but he was unable to do so by reason of the invincible power of the Saviour; therefore, being overthrown by his own insane wickedness, and having received many wounds, he perished amid the heaps of wounded, [990] because he had stamped beforehand the divinely inspired prophecies with the sophistry of the soothsayers. (204) Very righteously, therefore, does the good man pray that this his only son, Ishmael, may be sound in mind and health, because of those persons who do not listen in a sincere spirit to the sacred admonitions, whom Moses has expressly forbidden to come into the assembly of the Ruler of the universe, (205) for those men are broken as to the generative parts of their minds, or are even rendered completely impotent in that respect, who magnify their own minds, and their external sense, as the only causes of all the events which take place among men; and there are others who are lovers of a system of polytheism, and who honour the company which is devoted to the service of many gods, being the sons of a harlot, having no knowledge of the one husband and father of the virtue-loving soul, namely, God; and are not all these men very properly driven away and banished from the assembly of God? (206) They appear to me very much to resemble those parents who accuse their sons of intemperance in wine, for they say, "This our son is Disobedient," [991] indicating, by the addition of the word "this," that they have other sons likewise who are temperate and self-denying, and who obey the injunctions of right reason and instruction; for these are the most genuine parents, by whom it is a most disgraceful thing to be accused, and a most glorious thing to be praised. (207) Then as to the words, "This is Aaron and Moses, whom God directed to lead the children of Israel out of Egypt," [992] and the expression, "These are those who conversed with Pharaoh the king." Let us not think that they are used superfluously, or that they do not convey some intimations beyond the mere open meaning of the words; (208) for since Moses is the purest mind, and Aaron is his speech, and moreover, since the mind has been taught to think of divine things in a divine manner, and since the speech has learnt to interpret holy things in holy language, the sophists imitating them, and adulterating the genuine coinage, say, that they also conceive rightly, and speak in a praiseworthy manner about what is most excellent. In order, therefore, that we may not be deceived by a placing of the base money in juxtaposition with the good, by reason of the similitude of the impression, he has given us a test by which they may be distinguished. (209) What then is the test? To bring out of the region of the body the mind, endowed with the power of seeing, fond of contemplation and philosophical; for he who can do this is the same Moses; and he who is unable really to do so, but who is only said to be able, and who makes professions with infinite pomp and magnitude of language, is laughed at. But he prays that Ishmael may live, not meaning to refer to the life in conjunction with the body, but he prays that the divine voice, dwelling for evermore in his soul, may awaken and vivify it.

XXXVIII

XXXVIII. (210) And he indeed prays that the hearing of sacred words and the learning of sacred doctrine may live, as has been already said; but Jacob, the practiser of virtue, prays that the good natural disposition may live; for he says, "May Reuben live and not Die,"[993] does he then here pray for immortality for him, a thing impossible for man to attain to? (211) Surely not, we must then explain what it is which he intends to signify. All the lessons and all the admonitions of instruction are built up and established on the nature which is calculated to receive instruction, as on a foundation previously laid; but if there is no natural foundation previously in existence, everything is useless; for men, by nature destitute of sense, would not appear at all to differ from a stock or a lifeless stone; for nothing could possibly be adapted to them so as to cleave to them, but everything would rebound and spring back as from some hard body. (212) But on the other hand, we may see the souls of those who are well endowed by nature, like a well-smooth waxen tablet, neither too solid nor too tender, moderately tempered, and easily receiving all admonitions and all lessons, and themselves giving an accurate representation of any impression which has been stamped upon them, being a sort of distinct image of memory. (213) It was therefore indispensable to pray that a good natural disposition, free from all disease and from all mortality, should be joined to the rational race; for they are but few who partake of the life according to virtue, which is the most real and genuine life. I do not mean of the common herd of men only, for of them there is not one who partakes of real life: but even of those to whom it has been granted to shun the objects of human desire, and to live to God alone. (214) On which account the practiser of virtue, that courageous man, marvelled greatly, if any one being borne along the middle of the stream of life, was not dragged down by any violence, but was able to withstand the flow of abundant wealth coming over him, and to stem the impetuosity of immoderate pleasure, and to avoid being carried away by the whirlwind of vain opinion. (215) At all events Jacob does not speak to Joseph more than the sacred scripture speaks to every one who is vigorous in his body, and who is seen to be immersed amid abundant treasures, and riches, and superfluities, and to be overcome by none of them, when he says, "For still thou livest," uttering a most marvellous sentiment, and one which is quite beyond the daily life of us who, if we have fallen in with ever so slight a breeze which bears us towards the good fortune, immediately set all sail and became greatly elated, and being full of great and high spirits, hurry forward with all our speed to the indulgence of our passions, and never will check our unbridled and immoderately excited desires until we run ashore and are wrecked as to the whole vessel of our souls.

XXXIX

XXXIX. (216) Very beautifully therefore, do we pray that this Ishmael may live. Therefore, Abraham adds, "May he live before God," looking upon it as the perfection of all happiness for the mind to be accounted worthy of him who is the most excellent of all beings, as its inspector and overseer; (217) for if, while the teacher is present the pupil cannot go wrong, and if a monitor being at hand is of service to the learner, and if while an elder person is present the younger man is adorned by modesty and temperance, and if the presence of his father or of his mother have often prevented a son when about to commit sin, even though they are only beheld by him in silence, then what excess of good must we imagine that man to enjoy, who believes that he is always watched and beheld by God? for while he fears and reverences and looks up to the dignity of him as being present, he will flee from committing iniquity with all his might. (218) But when he prays that Ishmael may live, he does not despair of the birth of Isaac, as I have already said, but he believes in God; for it does not follow that what it is possible for God to give, it is also possible for man to receive, since to God it is easy to give the most numerous and important benefits, but to us it is not easy to accept of the gifts which are proffered to us; (219) for we must be content, if, by means of labour and diligence, we obtain a share of those good things which are familiar and customary to us. But there is no hope that we can attain to those which come of their own accord, and from some ever ready and previously prepared source,

Philo Judaeus

without any art, or in short, any human contrivance whatever; for inasmuch as these things are divine, they must of necessity be found out by more divine and unadulterated natures, such as have no connection with any mortal body. (220) And Moses has shown that every one, to the best of his power, ought to make grateful acknowledgments for benefits received; for instance, that the clever man ought to offer up as a sacrifice his acuteness and wisdom; the eloquent man should consecrate all his excellences of speech, by means of psalms and a regular enumeration of the greatness and panegyric on the living God; and to proceed with each species, he who is a natural philosopher should offer up his natural philosophy; he who is a moral philosopher should make an offering of his ethical philosophy; he who is skilful in any art or science should dedicate to God his knowledge of the arts and sciences. (221) Thus again a sailor and a pilot should dedicate their successful voyage; the agricultural farmer, his productive crops; the stock-farmer, the prolific increase of his flocks and herds; the physician, the good health of his patients; the commander of an army, his success in war; the magistrate or the king will offer up his administration of the laws or his sovereign power. And, in short, the man who is not blinded by self-love, looks upon the only true maker of all things, God, as the cause of all the good things affecting his soul, or body, or his external circumstances. (222) Let no one therefore, of those who seem to be somewhat obscure and humble, from a despair of any better hope, hesitate to become a suppliant to God. But even if he no longer looks forward to any great advantages, still let him, to the best of his power, give God thanks for the blessings which he has already received, (223) and in effect, those which he has received are countless; his birth, his life, his soul, his food, his outward senses, his imagination, his inclinations, his reason; and reason is a very short word, but a most perfect and admirable thing, a fragment of the soul of the universe, or, as it is more pious to say for those who study philosophy according to Moses, a very faithful copy of the divine image.

XL

XL. (224) It is right also to praise those inquirers after truth, who have endeavored to tear up and carry off the whole trunk of virtue, root and branch: but since they have not been able to do it, have at least taken either a single shoot, or a single bunch of fruit, as a specimen and portion of the whole tree, being all that they were able to Bear. [994] (225) It is a desirable thing, indeed, to associate at once with the entire company of the virtues; but if this be too great an indulgence to be granted to human nature, let us be content if it has fallen to our lot to be connected with any one of the particular virtues, as a portion of the whole band, such as temperance, or courage, or justice, or humanity; for the soul may produce and bring forth some good from even one of them, and so avoid being barren and unproductive of any. (226) But will you impose any such injunctions as these on your own son? Unless you treat your servants with gentleness, do not treat those of the same rank as yourself socially. Unless you behave decorously to your wife, never bear yourself respectfully to your parents. If you neglect your father and your mother, be impious also towards God. If you delight in pleasure, you must not keep aloof from covetousness. Do you desire great riches? Then be also eager for vain-glory. (227) For what more need we add? Need you not desire to be moderate in some things unless you are able to be so in all? Would not your son say to you in such a case, My father, what do you mean? Do you wish your son to become either perfectly good or perfectly bad, and will you not be content if he keeps the middle path between the two extremes? (228) Was it not for this reason that Abraham also, at the time of the destruction of Sodom, began at fifty and ended at Ten? [995] Therefore, propitiating and supplicating God, entreat him that if there could be found among his creatures a complete remission so as to give them liberty, of which the sacred number of fifty is a symbol, at least the intermediate instruction which is equal in number to the decade, might be accepted for the sake of the deliverance of the soul which was about to be condemned. (229) But those who are instructed have many more opportunities of prayer than those who are destitute of teachers, and those who are well initiated in encyclical accomplishments have more opportunities than those who are unmusical and illiterate, inasmuch as they from their childhood almost have been imbued with all the lessons of virtue, and temperance, and all kinds of excellence. Wherefore, even if they have not entirely got rid of and effaced old marks of iniquity so as to wear a completely clean appearance, at least they have purified themselves in a reasonable and moderate degree. (230) And it is something like this that Esau seems to have said to his father, "Have you not one blessing for me, O my father? Bless me, bless me, also, O my Father!" [996] For different blessings have been set apart for different persons, perfect blessings for the perfect, and moderate blessings for the imperfect. As is the case also with bodies; for there are different exercises appropriate to those which are in health, and to those which are sick. And also different regimens of food, and different systems of living, and not the same. But some things are suitable to the one kind that they may not become at all diseased; and other things are good for the other sort, they they may be changed and rendered more healthy. (231) Since, therefore, there are many good things existing in nature, give me that which appears to be best adapted to my circumstances, even if it be the most trifling thing possible; looking at this one point alone, whether I shall be able to bear what is given me with equanimity, and not, like a wretched person, sink under and be overwhelmed by it. (232) Again, what do we imagine to be meant by the words, "Will not the hand of the Lord be Sufficient?" [997] Do they not signify that the powers of the living God penetrate everywhere for the purpose of conferring benefits, not only on those who are noble, but on those also who appear to be in a more obscure condition, to whom also God gives such things as are suitable to the measure and weight of the soul of each individual, conjecturing and measuring in his own mind with perfect equality what is proportionate to the circumstances and requirements of each.

XLI

XLI. (233) But what makes an impression on me in no ordinary degree is the law which is enacted with respect to those who put off their sins and seem to be repentant. For this law commands that the first victim which such persons offer shall be a female sheep without spot. But, if it proceeds, "his hand is not strong enough to bring a sheep, then for the trespass which he has committed he shall bring two turtle doves or two young pigeons, one for his trespass and one for a burnt offering; (234) and if his hand cannot find a pair of turtle doves or two young pigeons, then he shall bring as his gift the tenth part of an ephah of fine flour for a sin offering; he shall not pour oil upon it, nor shall he place any frankincense thereon, because it is a sin offering; and he shall bring it to the priest, and the priest having taken it from him shall take a full handful of it, and place it as a memorial on the Altar." [998] (235) God therefore here is propitiated by three different kinds of repentance, by the aforesaid beasts, or by the birds, or by the while flour, according, in short, to the ability of him who is being purified and who repents. For small offences do not require great purifications, nor are small purifications fit for great crimes; but they should be equal, and similar, and in due proportion. (236) It is worth while, therefore, to examine what is meant by this purification which may be accomplished in three ways. Now it may almost be said that both offences and good actions are perceived to exist in three things; in intention, or in words, or in actions. On which account Moses, teaching in his hortatory admonitions that the attainment of good is not impossible nor even very difficult, says, (237) "It is not necessary to soar up to heaven, nor to go to the borders of the earth and sea, for the attainment of it, but it is near, yea, and very Near."[999] And then in a subsequent passage he shows it all but to the naked eye as one may say, where he says, "Every action is in thy mouth, or in thy heart, or in thy Hands:" [1000] meaning under this symbolical expression, in thy words, or in they designs, or in thy actions. For he means that human happiness consists in wise design, and good language, and righteous actions, just as the unhappiness arises from the contrary course. (238) For both well-doing and wrong-doing exist in the same regions, in the heart, or in the mouth, or in the hand; for some persons decide in the most righteous, and sagacious manner, some speak most excellently, some do only what ought to be done: again, of the three sources of error the most unimportant is to design to do what ought not to be done, the most grievous is to do what is iniquitous, the middle evil is to speak improperly. (239) But it often happens that even what is least important is the most difficult to be removed; for it is very hard to bring an agitated state of the soul to tranquillity; and one may more easily check the impetuosity of a torrent than the perversion of the soul which is hurrying in a wrong direction, without restraint. For innumerable notions coming one upon the other like the waves of a stormy sea, bearing everything along with them, and throwing everything into confusion, overturn the whole soul with irresistible violence. (240) Therefore the most excellent, and most perfect kind of purification is this, not to admit into one's mind any improper notions, but to regulate it in peace and obedience to law, the ruler of which principles is justice. The next kind is, not to offend in one's language either by speaking falsely, or by swearing falsely, or by deceiving, or by practicing sophistry, or by laying false informations; or, in short, by letting loose one's mouth and tongue to the injury of any one, as it is better to put a bridle and an insuperable chain on those members.

XLII

XLII. (241) But why it is a more grievous offence to say what is wrong than only to think it, is very easy to see. For some times a person thinks without any deliberate previous intention of so thinking, but inconsiderately: for he is compelled to admit ideas in his mind which he does not wish to admit; and nothing which is involuntary is blameable: (242) but a man speaks intentionally, so that if he utters words which are not proper he is unhappy and is committing offence, since he does not even by chance choose to say anything that is proper, and it would be more for his advantage to adopt that safest expedient of silence: and, in the second place, anyone who is not silent can be silent if he pleases. (243) But what is even a still more grievous offence than speaking wrongly, is unjust action. For the word, as it is said, is the shadow of the deed; and how can an injurious deed help being more mischievous than a shadow of the same character? On this account Moses released the mind, even when it yielded to many involuntary perversions and errors, from accusations and from penalties, thinking that it was rather acted upon by notions which forced their way into it, than was itself acting. But whatever goes out through the mouth that he makes the utterer responsible for and brings him before the tribunal, since the act of speaking is one which is in our own power. (244) But the investigation to which words are subject is a much more moderate one, and that with which words are united is a more vigorous one. For he imposes severe punishments on those who commit gross offences, and who carry out in action, and utter with hasty tongues what they have been designed in their unjust minds.

XLIII

XLIII. (245) Therefore he has called the purifying victims which are to be offered up for the three offenders, the mind, speech, and the action, a sheep, and a pair of turtle doves or pigeons, and the tenth part of a sacred measure of fine flour; thinking it fit that the mind should be purified by a sheep, the speech by winged creatures, and the action by fine flour: Why is this? (246) Because, as the mind is the most excellent thing in us, so also is the sheep the most excellent among irrational animals, inasmuch as it is most gentle, and also as it gives forth a yearly produce in its fleece, for the use and also for the ornament of mankind. For clothes keep off all injury from both cold and heat, and also they conceal the unmentionable parts of nature, and in this way they are an ornament to those who use them: (247) therefore the sheep, as being the most excellent of animals, is a symbol of the purification of the most excellent part of man, the mind. And birds are an emblem of the purification of speech: for speech is a light thing, and winged by nature, flying and penetrating in every direction more swiftly than an arrow. For what is once said can never be re-called; [1001] but being borne abroad, and running on with great swiftness, it strikes the ears and penetrates every sense of hearing, resounding loudly: but speech is of two kinds, one true and the other false; (248) on which account it appears to me to be here compared to a pair of turtle doves or young pigeons: and of these birds one he says is to be looked upon as a sin offering, since the speech which is true is wholly and in all respects sacred and perfect, but that which is false is very wrong and requires correction. (249) Again, as I have already said, fine flour is a symbol of the purification of activity, but it is sorted from the commoner sort by the hands of the bakers, who make the business their study. On which account the law says, "And the priest having taken an entire handful, shall place it on the altar as a memorial of them," by the word handful, indicating both the endeavor and the action. (250) And he speaks with exceeding accuracy with respect to the sheep, when he says, "And if his hand be not strong enough to supply a sheep;" but with respect to the birds he says, "And if he cannot find a bird." Why is this? Because it is a sign of very great strength and of excessive power, to get rid of the errors of the mind: but it does not require any great strength, to check the errors of words; (251) for, as I have said already, silence is a remedy for all the offences that can be committed by the voice, and every one may easily practise silence; but yet, by reason of their chattering habits and want of moderation in their language, many people cannot find out how to impose a limitation on their speech.

XLIV

XLIV. (252) Since the, the virtuous man has been bred up among and practised in these and similar divisions and discriminations of things, does he not rightly appear to pray that Ishmael may live, if he is not as yet able to become the father of Isaac? (253) What then does the merciful God say? To him who asks for one thing he gives two, and on him who prays for what is less he bestows what is greater; for, says the historian, he said unto Abraham, "Yea, behold, Sarrah thy wife shall bring forth a Son." [1002] Very felicitous and significant is this answer, "Yea;" for what can be more suitable to and more like the character of God, than to promise good things and to ratify that promise with all speed! (254) But what God promises every foolish man repudiates; therefore the sacred scriptures represent Leah as hated, and on this account it is that she received that name; for Leah, being interpreted, means "repudiating and labouring," because we all turn away from virtue and think it a laborious thing, by reason of its very often imposing commands on us which are not pleasant. (255) But nevertheless, she is thought worthy of such an honourable reception from the prince, that her womb is opened by him, so as to receive the seed of divine generation, in order to cause the production of honourable pursuits and actions. Learn therefore, O soul, that Sarrah, that is, virtue, will bring forth to thee a son; and that Hagar, or intermediate instruction, is not the only one who will do so; for her offspring is one which has its knowledge from teaching, but the offspring of the other is entirely self-taught. (256) And do not wonder, if God, who brings forth all good things, has also brought forth this race, which, though rare upon the earth, is very numerous in heaven. And you may learn this also from other things of which man consists: do the eyes see from having been taught to do so? And what do the nostrils do? Do they smell by reason of their having learnt? And do the hands touch, or the feet advance, in accordance with the commands or recommendations of instructors? (257) Again, do the appetites and imaginations (and these are the first moving powers and persuasions of the soul) exist in consequence of teaching? And has our mind gone as a pupil to any sophist, in order to learn to think and to comprehend? All these things repudiate all kinds of instruction, and avail themselves only of the spontaneous gifts of nature to exert their appropriate energies. (258) Why then do you any longer wonder if God showers upon men virtue, unaccompanied by any labour or suffering, such as stand in need of no superintending care or instruction, but is from the very beginning entire and perfect? And if you wish to receive any testimony in corroboration of this view, can you find any more trustworthy than that of Moses? And he says that the rest of mankind derive their food from earth, but that he alone who is endowed with the power of sight, derives his from heaven. (259) And men occupied in agriculture co-operate to produce the food from the earth; but God, the only cause and giver, rains down the food from heaven without the cooperation of any other being. And, indeed, we read in the scriptures, "Behold, I rain upon you bread from Heaven." [1003] Now what nourishment can the scriptures properly say is rained down, except heavenly wisdom? (260) which God sends from above upon those souls which have a longing for virtue, God who possesses a great abundance and exceeding treasure of wisdom, and who irrigates the universe, and especially so on the sacred seventh day which he calls the sabbath; for then, he says, that there is an influx of spontaneous good things, not rising from any kind of art, but shooting up by their own spontaneous and self-perfecting nature, and bearing appropriate fruit.

XLV

XLV. (261) Virtue, therefore, will bring thee forth a legitimate male child, far removed from all effeminate passions; and thou shalt call the name of thy son by the name of the passion which thou feelest in regard to him; and thou wilt by all means feel joy; so that thou shalt give him a name which is an emblem of joy, namely, Laughter. (262) As grief and fear have their appropriate expressions which the passion, when more than usually violent and predominant, gives utterance to; so also, good counsels and happiness compel a man to employ a natural expression of them, for which no one could find out more appropriate and felicitous names, even if he were very skilful in the imposition of names. (263) On which account God says, "I have blessed him, I will increase him, I will multiply him, he shall beget twelve Nations;" [1004] that is to say, he shall beget the whole circle and ring of the sophistical preliminary branches of education; but I will make my covenant with Israel, that the race of mankind may receive each kind of virtue, the weaker part of them receiving both that which is taught by others, and that which is learnt by one's self, and the stronger part that which is ready and prepared.

XLVI

XLVI. (264) "And at that time," says he, "she shall bring forth a son to Thee;" [1005] that is to say, wisdom shall bring forth joy. What time, O most marvellous being, are you pointing out? Is it that which cannot be indicated by the thing brought forth? For that must be the real time, the rising of the universe, the prosperity and happiness of the whole earth, and of heaven, and of all intermediate natures, and of all animals, and of all plants. (265) On which account Moses also took courage to say to those who had run away, and who did not dare to enter upon a war in the cause of virtue against those who were arrayed against it, "The Lord has departed from them, but the Lord is in Us;" [1006] for he here almost confesses in express words that God is time, who stands aloof and at a distance from every impious person, but walks among those souls which cultivate virtue. (266) "For," says he, "I will walk among you, and I will be your God." [1007] But those who say that what is meant by time is only the seasons of the year are misapplying the names with great inaccuracy, like men who have not studied the nature of things with any care, but have gone on to a great degree at random.

XLVII

XLVII. (267) But by way of amplifying the beauty of the creature to be born, he says that it shall be born the next year, indicating by the term, "the next Year," [1008] not a difference of time, such as is measured by lunar or solar periods, but that which is truly marvellous, and strange, and new, being an age which is very different from those which are visible to the eyes and perceptible to the outward senses, being investigated in incorporeal things appreciable only by the intellect, which, in fact, is the model and archetype of time. But an age is a name given to the life of the world, intelligible only by the intellect, as time is that given to the life of the world, perceptible by the outward senses. (268) And in this year the man who had sown the graces of God so as to produce many more good things, in order that the greatest possible number of persons worthy to share them might participate in them, finds also the barley producing a Hundredfold. [1009] But he who has sown does usually also reap. (269) And he sowed, displaying the virtue, the enemy of envy and wickedness; he is, however, here said to find, not to reap. For he who has made the ear of his good deeds more productive and full, was a different person, having laid up an abundance of greater hopes well prepared, and he also proposed more abundant advantages to all those who sought them, encouraging them to hope to find them.

XLVIII

XLVIII. (270) And the words, "He finished speaking to Him," [1010] are equivalent to saying, he made his hearer perfect, though he was devoid of wisdom before, and he filled him with immortal lessons. But when his disciple became perfect, the Lord went up and departed from Abraham, showing, not that he separated himself from him; for the wise man is naturally an attendant of God, not wishing to represent the spontaneous inclination of the disciple in order that as he had learnt while his teacher was no longer standing by him, and without any necessity urging him, giving of his own accord a specimen of himself, and displaying a voluntary and spontaneous eagerness to learn, he might for the future exert his energies by himself; for the teacher assigns a model to him who has learnt by voluntary study without any suggestions from other quarters, stamping on him a most durable species of indelible recollection.

Footnotes:

915. Yonge's title, A Treatise on the Question Why Certain Names in the Holy Scripture Are Changed.
916. Gen 17:1.
917. Num 18:26.
918. Exod 20:21.
919. Exod 33:13.
920. Exod 33:23.
921. Exod 3:14.
922. Exod 6:3.
923. Gen 32:29.
924. Gen 17:1.
925. Gen 17:2.
926. Gen 7:1.
927. Exod 7:17.
928. Exod 6:29.
929. Exod 9:29.
930. Gen 17:1, also 35:2.
931. Exod 20:2.
932. Deut 4:1.
933. Deut 33:1.
934. Gen 17:1.
935. Gen 5:24.
936. Gen 17:3.
937. Gen 48:15.
938. Deut 12:28.
939. this passage is given up by Mangey as corrupt and quite unintelligible. Mangey corrects it and gives a Latin translation which I have followed.
940. Gen 32:28.
941. Job 14:4.
942. Gen 17:2.
943. Gen 17:4.
944. the text here is very corrupt. Mangey adopts the emendations of Markland, and I have followed his translation.
945. Gen 2:19.
946. Gen 35:18.
947. Gen 35:16.
948. Gen 48:5.
949. Exod 18:11.
950. Exod 2:18.
951. Num 25:3.
952. Exod 31:29.
953. Exod 2:16.
954. this passage is very corrupt in the original. I have followed Mangey in adopting the

corrections of Marsland.
955. Ps 23:1.
956. Exod 2:18.
957. Num 14:24.
958. Deut 33:1.
959. Exod 7:1.
960. Gen 17:16.
961. Gen 29:31.
962. Gen 38:25.
963. Gen 17:26.
964. Gen 21:6.
965. Hos 14:9.
966. 1Sam 2:5.
967. Gen 17:16.
968. Gen 23:6.
969. Exod 4:14.
970. Isa 47:22.
971. Gen 45:16.
972. Gen 45:18.
973. Gen 39:1.
974. Gen 45:18.
975. Gen 17:17.
976. Gen 17:20.
977. Homer, Odyssey 8.171.
978. Deut 32:4.
979. Gen 32:25.
980. Gen 11:10.
981. Gen 21:33.
982. Gen 26:12.
983. Exod 27:9.
984. Num 18:28.
985. there is an hiatus in the text here.
986. Gen 34:3.
987. Deut 33:6.
988. Gen 17:18.
989. Num 24:17.
990. Num 31:8.
991. Deut 21:20.
992. Exod 6:26.
993. Deut 33:6.
994. Num 13:25.
995. Gen 18:32.
996. Gen 27:28.
997. Num 11:23.
998. Lev 5:5.
999. Deut 30:10.
1000. Deut 30:14.
1001. this resembles what is said by Horace in A. P. 390 and in Epist. l. 18.71.
1002. Gen 17:19.
1003. Exod 16:4.
1004. Gen 17:20.
1005. Gen 15:10.
1006. Num 14:9.
1007. Lev 26:12.
1008. Gen 18:10.
1009. Gen 26:12.
1010. Gen 17:22.

ON DREAMS, THAT THEY ARE GOD-SENT [1011]

BOOK 1

I

I. (1.1) The treatise before this one has contained our opinions on those visions sent from heaven which are classed under the first species; in reference to which subject we delivered our opinion that the Deity sent the appearances which are beheld by man in dreams in accordance with the suggestions of his own nature. But in this treatise we will, to the best of our power, describe those dreams which come under the second species. (1.2) Now the second species is that in which our mind, being moved simultaneously with the mind of the universe, has appeared to be hurried away by itself and to be under the influence of divine impulses, so as to be rendered capable of comprehending beforehand, and knowing by anticipation some of the events of the future. Now the first dream which is akin to the species which I have been describing, is that which appeared on the ladder which reached up to heaven, and which was of this kind. (1.3) "And Jacob dreamed, and behold a ladder was firmly planted on the earth, the head of which reached up to heaven; and the angels of God were ascending and descending on it. And behold there was a ladder firmly planted on the earth, and the Lord was standing steadily upon it; and he said, I am the God of Abraham thy father, and the God of Isaac: be not afraid. The earth on which thou art sleeping I will give unto thee and unto thy seed, and thy seed shall be as the dust of the earth, and it shall be multiplied as the sand on the seashore, and shall spread to the south, and to the north, and to the east; and in thee shall all the kindreds of the earth be blessed, and in thy seed also. And, behold, I am with thee, keeping thee in all thy ways, by whichever thou goest, and I will bring thee again into this land; because I will not leave thee until I have done everything which I have said unto Thee." [1012] (1.4) But the previous considerations of the circumstances of this vision require that we should examine them with accuracy, and then perhaps we shall be able to comprehend what is indicated by the vision. What, then, are the previous circumstances? The scripture tells us, "And Jacob went up from the well of the oath, and came to Charran, and went into a place and lay down there until the sun arose. And he took one of the stones of the place and placed it at his head, and went to sleep in that place." And immediately afterwards came the dream. (1.5) Therefore it is well at the outset to raise a question on these three points:--One, What was the well of the oath, [1013] and why was it called by this name? Secondly, What is Charran, and why, after Jacob had departed from the well beforementioned, did he immediately go to Charran? Thirdly, What was the place, and why, when he was in it, did the sun at once set, and did he go to sleep?

II

II. (1.6) Let us then at once begin and consider the first of these points. To me, then, the well appears to be an emblem of knowledge; for its nature is not superficial, but very deep. Nor does it lie in an open place, but a well is fond of being hidden somewhere in secret. Nor is it found with ease, but only after great labour and with difficulty; and this too is seen to be the case with sciences, not only with such as have great and indescribable subjects of speculation, but even with respect to such as are the most insignificant. (1.7) Choose, therefore, whichever art you please; not the most excellent, but even the must obscure of all, which perhaps no one who has been bred a free man in the whole city would ever study of his own accord, and which scarcely any servant in the field would attend to, who, against his will, was a slave to some morose and ill-tempered master who compelled him to do many unpleasant things. (1.8) For the matter will be found to be not a simple one, but rather one of great complications and variety, not easy to be seized upon, but difficult to discover, difficult to master, hostile to delay, and indolence and indifference, full of earnestness and contention, and sweat, and care. For which reason "those who dig in this well say that they cannot find even water in it;" because the ends of science are not only hard to discover, but are even altogether undiscoverable; (1.9) and it is owing to this that one man is more thoroughly skilled in grammar or in geometry than another, because of its being impossible to circumscribe, increase, and extend one within certain limits; for there is always more that is left behind than what comes to be learnt; and what is left watches for and catches the learner, so that even he who fancies that he has comprehended and mastered the very extremities of knowledge would be considered but half perfect by another person who was his judge, and if he were before the tribunal of truth would appear to be only beginning knowledge; (1.10) for life is short, as some one has said, but art is long; of which that man most thoroughly comprehends the magnitude, who sincerely and honestly plunges deeply into it, and who digs it out like a well. And such a man, when he is at the point of death, being now grey-headed and exceedingly old, it is said, wept, not that he feared death as being a coward, but out of a desire for instruction, as feeling that he was now, for the first time, entering upon it when he was finally departing from life. (1.11) For the soul flourishes for the pursuit of knowledge when the prime vigour of the body is withering away from the lapse of time; therefore, before one has arrived at one's prime and vigour by reason of a more accurate comprehension of things, it is not difficult to be tripped up. But this accident is common to all people who are fond of learning, to whom new subjects of contemplation are continually rising up and striving after old ones, the soul itself producing many such subjects when it is not barren and unproductive. And nature, also, unexpectedly and spontaneously displaying a great number to those who are gifted with acute and penetrating intellects. Therefore the well of knowledge is shown to be of this kind, having no boundary and no end. (1.12) We must now explain why it was called the well of the oath. Those matters which are doubted about are decided by an oath, and those which are uncertain are confirmed in the same manner, and so, too, those which want certification receive it; from which facts this inference is drawn, that there is no subject respecting which any one can make an affirmation with greater certainty than he can respecting the fact that the race of wisdom is without limitation and without end. (1.13) It is well, therefore, to enrol one's self under the banners of one who discusses these matters without an oath; but he who is not very much inclined to assent to the assertions of another will at least assent to them when he has made oath to their correctness. But let no one refuse to take an oath of this kind, well knowing that he will have his name inscribed on pillars among those who are faithful to their oaths.

III

III. (1.14) However, enough of this. The next thing must be to consider why it is that as four wells had been dug by the servants of Abraham and Isaac, the fourth and last was called the well of the oath. (1.15) May it not be that sacred historian here desires to represent, in a figurative manner, that as in the universe there are four elements of which this world is composed, and as there are an equal number in ourselves, of which we have been fashioned before we were moulded into our human shape, three of them are capable of being comprehended somehow or other, but the fourth is unintelligible to all who come forward as judges of it. (1.16) Accordingly, we find that the four elements in the world are the earth, and the water, and the air, and the heaven, of which, even if some are difficult to find, they are still not classed in the utterly undiscoverable portion. (1.17) For that the earth, because it is a heavy, and indissoluble, and solid substance, is divided into mountains and champaign districts, and intersected by rivers and seas, so that some portion of it consists of islands, and some portions are continent. And again, some of it has a shallow and some a deep soil; and some is rough, and rugged, and strong, and altogether barren; and some is smooth and delicate, and exceedingly fertile; and besides all these facts we know a great number of others relative to the earth. (1.18) And again, there is the water, which we know has many of the aforesaid qualities in common with the earth, and many also peculiar to itself; for some of it is sweet, and some brackish, and some is mixed up of various characteristics; and some is good to drink, and some is not drinkable; and, moreover, neither of these last qualities is invariable with respect to every creature, but there are some to which it is the one and not the other, and vice versa. Again, some water is by nature cold, and other water naturally hot; (1.19) for there is in all sorts of places an infinite number of springs pouring forth hot water, not on the land only but even in the sea: at all events, there have appeared before now veins pouring up warm water in the middle of the sea, which all the enormous efflux of salt water in all the sea that encircles the world, pouring over them from all eternity, has never been able to extinguish, nor even in the least degree to diminish. (1.20) Again, we know that the air has an attractive nature, yielding to such bodies as surround it in an altitude of resistance, being the organ of life, and breath, and sight, and hearing, and all the rest of the external senses, admitting of rarification, and condensation, and motion, and tranquillity, and changes, and variations of every kind, by which it is altered and modified, and generating summers and winters, and the seasons of autumn and spring, by means of which the circle of the year is the last brought to a conclusion.

IV

IV. (1.21) All these things, then, we feel: but the heaven has a nature which is incomprehensible, and it has never conveyed to us any distinct indication by which we can understand its nature; for what can we say? that it is solid ice, as some persons have chosen to assert? or that it is the purest fire? or that it is a fifth body, moving in a circle having no participation in any of the four elements? For what can we say? Has that most remote sphere of the fixed stars any density in an upward direction? or is it merely a superficies devoid of all depth, something like a plane figure? (1.22) And what are the stars? Are they masses of earth full of fire? For some persons have said that they are hills, and valleys, and thickets, men who are worthy of a prison and a treadmill, or of any place where there are instruments proper for the punishment of impious persons; or are they, as some one has defined them, a continuous and dense harmony, the closely packed, indissoluble mass of aether? Again, are they animated and intelligent? or are they destitute alike of mind and vitality? Have they their motions in consequence of any choice of their own? or merely because they are compulsory? (1.23) What, again, are we to say of the moon? Does she show us a light of her own, or a borrowed and illegitimate one, only reflected from the rays of the sun? or is neither of these things true, but has she something mixed, as it were, so as to be a sort of combination of her own light and of that which belongs to some other body? For all these things, and others like them, belonging to the fourth and most excellent of the bodies in the world, namely, the heaven, are uncertain and incomprehensible, and are spoken of in accordance with conjectures and guesses, and not with the solid, certain reasoning of truth, (1.24) so that a person might venture to swear that no mortal man will ever be able to comprehend any one of these matters clearly. At all events, the fourth and dry well was called the well of the oath on this account, because the search after the fourth element in the world, that is to say the heaven, is without any result, and is in every respect fruitless.

V

V. But let us now see in what manner that fourth element in us is by nature in such an especial and singular manner incomprehensible. (1.25) There are, then, four principal elements in us, the body, the external sense, the speech, and the mind. Now of these, three are not uncertain or unintelligible in every respect, but they contain some indication in themselves by which they are comprehended. (1.26) Now what is my meaning in this statement? We know already that the body is divisible into three parts, and that it is capable of motion in six directions, inasmuch as it has three dimensions, in length, in depth, in breadth; and twice as many motions, namely six, the upward motion, the downward motion, that to the right, that to the left, the forward, and the backward motion. But, moreover, we are not ignorant that it is the vessel of the soul; and we are also aware that it is subject to the changes of being young, of decaying, of growing old, of dying, of undergoing dissolution. (1.27) And with respect to the outward senses, we are not, so far as that is concerned, utterly dull and mutilated, but we are able to say that that also is divided into five divisions, and that there are appropriate organs for the development of each sense formed by nature; for instance, the eyes for seeing, the ears for hearing, the nostrils for smelling, and the other organs for the exercise of the respective senses to which they are adapted, and also that we may call these outward senses messengers of the mind which inform it of colours, and shapes and sounds, and the peculiar differences of vapours, and flavours, and, in short, which describe to it all bodies, and all the distinctive qualities which exist in them. They also may be looked upon as body-guards of the soul, informing it of all that they see or hear; and if anything injurious attacks it from without, they foresee it, and guard against it, so that it may not enter by chance and unawares, and so become the cause of irremediable disaster to their mistress. (1.28) Again, the voice does not entirely escape our comprehension; but we know that one voice is shrill and another deep; that one is tuneful and harmonious, and another dissonant and very unmusical; and again, one voice is more powerful, and another less so. And they differ also in ten thousand other particulars, in kind, in complexion, in distance, in combined and separate tension of the tones, in the symphonies of fourths, of fifths, and of the diapason. (1.29) Moreover, there are some things which we know also with respect to that articulate voice which has been allotted to man alone of all animals, as, for instance, we know that it is emitted by the mind, that it receives its articulate distinctness in the mouth, that it is by the striking of the tongue that articulate utterance is impressed upon the tones of the voice, and which renders the uttered sound not only a bare, naked, useless noise, void of all characteristic, and that it discharges the office of a herald or interpreter towards the mind which suggests it.

VI

VI. (1.30) Now then is the fourth element which exists within us, the dominant mind, comprehensible to us in the same manner as these other divisions? Certainly not; for what do we think it to be in its essence? Do we look upon it as spirit, or as blood, or, in short, as any bodily substance! But it is not a substance, but must be pronounced incorporeal. Is it then a limit, or a species, or a number, or a continued act, or a harmony, or any existing thing whatever? (1.31) Is it, the very first moment that we are born, infused into us from without, or is it some warm nature in us which is cooled by the air which is diffused around us, like a piece of iron which has been heated at a forge, and then being plunged into cold water, is by that process tempered and hardened? (And perhaps it is from the cooling process [psyxis] to which it is thus submitted that the soul [heÂ psycheì] derives its name.) What more shall we say? When we die, is it extinguished and destroyed together with our bodies? or does it continue to live a long time? or, thirdly, is it wholly incorruptible and immortal? (1.32) Again, where, in what part does this mind lie hid? Has it received any settled habitation? For some men have dedicated it to our head, as the principal citadel, around which all the outward senses have their lairs; thinking it natural that its body-guards should be stationed near it, as near the palace of a mighty king. Some again contend earnestly in favour of the position which they assign it, believing that it is enshrined like a statue in the heart. (1.33) Therefore now the fourth element is incomprehensible, in the world of heaven, in comparison of the nature of the earth, of the water, and of the air; and the mind in man, in comparison of the body and the outward sense, and the speech, which is the interpreter of the mind; may it not be the case also, that for this reason the fourth year is described as holy and praiseworthy in the sacred scriptures? (1.34) For among created things, the heaven is holy in the world, in accordance with which body, the imperishable and indestructible natures revolve; and in man the mind is holy, being a sort of fragment of the Deity, and especially according to the statement of Moses, who says, "God breathed into his face the breath of life, and man became a living Soul."[1014] (1.35) And it appears to me, that it is not without reason that both these things are called praiseworthy; for these two things, the heaven and the mind, are the things which are able to utter, with all becoming dignity, the praises, and hymns, and glory, and beatitude of the Father who created them: for man has received an especial honour beyond all other animals, namely, that of ministering to the living God. And the heaven is always singing melodies, perfecting an all-musical harmony, in accordance with the motions of all the bodies which exist therein; (1.36) of which, if the sound ever reached our ears, love, which could not be restrained, and frantic desires, and furious impetuosity, which could not be put an end to or pacified, would be engendered, and would compel us to give up even what is necessary, nourishing ourselves no longer like ordinary mortals on the meat and drink, which is received by means of our throat, but on the inspired songs of music in its highest perfection, as persons about to be made immortal through the medium of their ears: and it is said that Moses [1015] was an incorporeal hearer of these melodies, when he went for forty days, and an equal number of nights, without at all touching any bread or any water.

VII

VII. (1.37) Therefore the heaven, which is the archetypal organ of music, appears to have been arranged in a most perfect manner, for no other object except that the hymns sung to the honour of the Father of the universe, might be attuned in a musical manner; and we hear that virtue, that is to say, Leah,[1016] after the birth of her fourth son, was no longer able to bring forth any more, but restrained, or perhaps I should say, was restrained, as to her generative powers; for she found, I conceive, all her generative power dry and barren, after she had brought forth Judah, that is to say, "confession," the perfect fruit: (1.38) and the phrase, "Leah desisted from bearing children," differs in no respect from the statement, that the children of Isaac found no water in the fourth Well."[1017] Since it appears from both these figurative expressions, that every creature thirsts for God, by whom all their births take place, and from whom nourishment is bestowed to them when they are born. (1.39) Perhaps therefore some petty cavilling critics will imagine that all this statement about the digging of the wells is a superfluous piece of prolixity on the part of the lawgiver: but those who deserve a larger classification, being citizens not of some petty state but of the wide world, being men of more perfect wisdom, will know well that the real question is not about the four wells, but about the parts of the universe that the men who are gifted with sight, and are fond of contemplation exercise their powers of investigation; namely, about the earth, the water, the air, and the heaven. (1.40) And examining each of these matters with the most accurately refined conception, in three of them they have found some things within the reach of their comprehension; on which account they have given these names, injustice, enmity, and latitude to what they have discovered. But in the fourth, that is to say in heaven, they have found absolutely nothing whatever, which they could comprehend; as we explained a little time ago: for the fourth is found to be a well destitute of water, and dry; and for the reason above mentioned it is called a well.

VIII

VIII. (1.41) We will now investigate what comes next, and inquire what Charran is, and why the man who went up from the well came to it. Charran then, as it appears to me, is a sort of metropolis of the outward senses: and it is interpreted at one time a pit dug, at another time holes; one fact being intimated by both these names; (1.42) for our bodies are in a manner dug out to furnish the organs of the outward senses, and each of the organs is a sort of hole for the corresponding outward sense in which it shelters itself as in a cave: when therefore any one goes up from the well which is called the well of the oath, as if he were leaving a harbour, he immediately does of necessity come to Charran: for it is a matter of necessity that the outward senses should receive one who comes on an emigration from that most excellent country of knowledge, unbounded as it is in extent, without any guide. (1.43) For our soul is very often set in motion by is own self after it has put off the whole burden of the body, and has escaped from the multitude of the outward senses; and very often too, even while it is still clothed in them. Therefore by its own simple motion it has arrived at the comprehension of those things which are appreciable only by the intellect; and by the motion of the body, it has attained to an understanding of those things which are perceptible by the outward senses; (1.44) therefore, if any one is unable altogether to associate with the mind alone, he then finds for himself a second refuge, namely, the external senses; and whoever fails in attaining to a comprehension of the things which are intelligible only by the intellect is immediately drawn over to the objects of the outward senses; for the second organ is always to the outward senses, in the case of those things which are not able to make a successful one as far as the dominant mind. (1.45) But it is well for man not to grow old or to spend all his time in this course either, but rather, as if they were straying in a foreign country like sojourners, to be always seeking for a second migration, and for a return to their native land. Therefore Laban, knowing absolutely nothing of either species or genus, or form, or conception, or of anything else whatever which is comprehended by the intellect alone, and depending solely on what lies externally visible, and such things as come under the notice of the eyes, and the ears, and the other hundred faculties, is thought worthy of Charran for his country, which Jacob, the lover of virtue, inhabits as a foreign land for a short time, always bearing in his recollection his return homewards; (1.46) therefore his mother, perseverance, that is Rebecca, says to him, "Rise up and flee to Laban, my brother, to Charran, and dwell with him certain Days." [1018] Do you not perceive then that the practiser of virtue will not endure to live permanently in the country of the outward senses, but only to remain there a few days and a short time, on account of the necessities of the body to which he is bound? But a longer time and an entire life is allotted to him in the city which is appreciable only by the intellect.

IX

IX. (1.47) In reference to which fact, also, it appears to me to be that his grandfather also, by name Abraham, so called from his knowledge, would not endure to remain any great length of time in Charran, for it is said in the scriptures that "Abraham was seventy-five years old when he departed from Charran;" [1019] although his father Terah, which name being interpreted means, "the investigation of a smell," lived there till the day of is Death. [1020] (1.48) Therefore it is expressly stated in the sacred scriptures that "Terah died in Charran," for he was only a reconnoitrer of virtue, not a citizen. And he availed himself of smells, and not of the enjoyments of food, as he was not able as yet to fill himself with wisdom, nor indeed even to get a taste of it, but only to smell it; (1.49) for as it is said that those dogs which are calculated for hunting can by exerting their faculty of smell, find out the lurking places of their game at a great distance, being by nature rendered wonderfully acute as to the outward sense of smell; so in the same manner the lover of instruction tracks out the sweet breeze which is given forth by justice, and by any other virtue, and is eager to watch those qualities from which this most admirable source of delight proceeds, and while he is unable to do so he moves his head all round in a circle, smelling out nothing else, but seeking only for that most sacred scent of excellence and food, for he does not deny that he is eager for knowledge and wisdom. (1.50) Blessed therefore are they to whom it has happened to enjoy the delights of wisdom, and to feast upon its speculations and doctrines, and even of the being cheered by them still to thirst for more, feeling an insatiable and increasing desire for knowledge. (1.51) And those will obtain the second place who are not allured indeed to enjoy the sacred table, but who nevertheless refresh their souls with its odours; for they will be excited by the fragrances of virtue like those languid invalids who, because they are not as yet able to take solid food, nevertheless feed on the smell of such viands as the sons of the physicians prepare as a sort of remedy for their impotency.

X

X. (1.52) Therefore, having left the land of the Chaldaeans, Terah is said to have migrated to Charran; bringing with him his son Abraham and the rest of his household who agreed with him in opinion, not in order that we might read in the account of the historical chronicles that some men had become emigrants, leaving their native country and becoming inhabitants of a foreign land as if it were their own country, but in order that a lesson of the greatest importance to life and full of wisdom, and adapted to man alone, might not be neglected. (1.53) And what is the lesson? The Chaldaeans are great astronomers, and the inhabitants of Charran occupy themselves with the topics relating to the external senses. Therefore the sacred account says to the investigator of the things of nature, why are you inquiring about the sun, and asking whether he is a foot broad, whether he is greater than the whole earth put together, or whether he is even many times as large? And why are you investigating the causes of the light of the moon, and whether it has a borrowed light, or one which proceeds solely from itself? Why, again, do you seek to understand the nature of the rest of the stars, of their motion, of their sympathy with one another, and even with earthly things? (1.54) And why, while walking upon the earth do you soar above the clouds? And why, while rooted in the solid land, do you affirm that you can reach the things in the sky? And why do you endeavour to form conjectures about matters which cannot be ascertained by conjecture? And why do you busy yourself about sublime subjects which you ought not to meddle with? And why do you extend your desire to make discoveries in mathematical science as far as the heaven? And why do you devote yourself to astronomy, and talk about nothing but high subjects? My good man, do not trouble your head about things beyond the ocean, but attend only to what is near you; and be content rather to examine yourself without flattery. (1.55) How, then, will you find out what you want, even if you are successful? Go with full exercise of your intellect to Charran, that is, to the trench which is dug, into the holes and caverns of the body, and investigate the eyes, the ears, the nostrils, and the other organs of the external senses; and if you wish to be a philosopher, study philosophically that branch which is the most indispensable and at the same time the most becoming to a man, and inquire what the faculty of sight is, what hearing is, what taste, what smell, what touch is, in a word, what is external sense; then seek to understand what it is to see, and how you see; what it is to hear, and how you hear; what it is to smell, or to taste, or to touch, and how each of these operations is ordinarily effected. (1.56) But it is not the very extravagance of insane folly to seek to comprehend the dwelling of the universe, before your own private dwelling is accurately known to you? But I do not as yet lay the more important and extensive injunction upon you to make yourself acquainted with your own soul and mind, of the knowledge of which you are so proud; for in reality you will never be able to comprehend it. (1.57) Mount up then to heaven, and talk arrogantly about the things which exist there, before you are as yet able to comprehend, according to the words of the poet,

> "All the good and all the evil
> Which thy own abode contains;"

and, bringing down that messenger of yours from heaven, and dragging him down from his search into matters existing there, become acquainted with yourself, and carefully and diligently labour to arrive at such happiness as is permitted to man. (1.58) Now this disposition the Hebrews called Terah, and the Greeks Socrates; for they say also that the latter grew old in the most accurate study by which he could hope to know himself, never once directing his philosophical speculations to the subjects beyond himself. But he was really a man; but Terah is the principle itself which is proposed to every one, according to which each man should know himself, like a tree full of good branches, in order that these persons who are fond of virtue might without difficulty gather the fruit of pure morality, and thus become filled with the most delightful and saving food. (1.59) Such, then, are those men who reconnoitre the quarters of wisdom for us; but those who are actually her athletes, and who practise her exercises, are more perfect. For these men think fit to learn with complete accuracy the whole question connected with the external senses, and after having done so, then to proceed to another and more important speculation, leaving all consideration of the holes of the body which they call Charran. (1.60) Of the number of these men is Abraham, who attained to great progress and improvement in the comprehension of complete knowledge; for when he knew most, then he most completely renounced himself in order to attain to the accurate knowledge of him who was the truly living God. And, indeed, this is a very natural course of events; for he who completely understands himself does also very much, because of his thorough appreciation of it, renounce the universal nothingness of the creature; and he who renounces himself learns to comprehend the living God.

XI

XI. (1.61) We have now, then, explained what Charran is, and why he who left the well of the oath came thither. We must now consider the third point which comes next in order, namely, what the place is to which this man came; for it is said, "He met him in the Place." [1021] (1.62) Now place is considered in three ways: firstly, as a situation filled by a body; secondly, as a divine word which God himself has filled wholly and entirely with incorporeal powers; for says the scripture, "I have seen the place in which the God of Israel Stood," [1022] in which alone he permitted his prophet to perform sacrifice to him, forbidding him to do so in other places. For he is ordered to go up into the place which the Lord God shall choose, and there to sacrifice burnt offerings and sacrifices for salvation, and to bring other victims also without spot. (1.63) According to the third signification, God himself is called a place, from the fact of his surrounding the universe, and being surrounded himself by nothing whatever, and from the fact of his being the refuge of all persons, and since he himself is his own district, containing himself and resembling himself alone. (1.64) I, indeed, am not a place, but I am in a place, and every existing being is so in a similar manner. So that which is surrounded differs from that which surrounds it; but the Deity, being surrounded by nothing, is necessarily itself its own place. And there is an evidence in support of my view of the matter in the following sacred oracle delivered with respect to Abraham: "He came unto the place of which the Lord God had told him: and having looked up with his eyes, he saw the place afar Off." [1023] (1.65) Tell me, now, did he who had come to the place see it afar off? Or perhaps it is but an identical expression for two different things, one of which is the divine world, and the other, God, who existed before the world. (1.66) But he who was conducted by wisdom comes to the former place, having found that the main part and end of propitiation is the divine word, in which he who is fixed does not as yet attain to such a height as to penetrate to the essence of God, but sees him afar off; or, rather, I should say, he is not able even to behold him afar off, but he only discerns this fact, that God is at a distance from every creature, and that any comprehension of him is removed to a great distance from all human intellect. (1.67) Perhaps, however, the historian, by this allegorical form of expression, does not here mean by his expression, "place," the Cause of all things; but the idea which he intends to convey may be something of this sort; --he came to the place, and looking up with his eyes he saw the very place to which he had come, which was a very long way from the God who may not be named nor spoken of, and who is in every way incomprehensible.

XII

XII. (1.68) These things, then, being defined as a necessary preliminary, when the practiser of virtue comes to Charran, the outward sense, he does not "meet" the place, nor that place either which is filled by a mortal body; for all those who are born of the dust, and who occupy any place whatever, and who do of necessity fill some position, partake of that; nor the third and most excellent kind of place, of which it was scarcely possible for that man to form an idea who made his abode at the well which was entitled the "well of the oath," where the self-taught race, Isaac, abides, who never abandons his faith in God and his invisible comprehension of him, but who keeps to the intermediate divine word, which affords him the best suggestions, and teaches him everything which is suitable to the times. (1.69) For God, not condescending to come down to the external senses, sends his own words or angels for the sake of giving assistance to those who love virtue. But they attend like physicians to the disease of the soul, and apply themselves to heal them, offering sacred recommendations like sacred laws, and inviting men to practice the duties inculcated by them, and, like the trainers of wrestlers, implanting in their pupils strength, and power, and irresistible vigour. (1.70) Very properly, therefore, when he has arrived at the external sense, he is represented no longer as meeting God, but only the divine word, just as his grandfather Abraham, the model of wisdom, did; for the scripture tells us, "The Lord departed when he had finished conversing with Abraham, and Abraham returned to his Place." [1024] From which expression it is inferred, that he also met with the sacred words from which God, the father of the universe, had previously departed, no longer displaying visions from himself but only those which proceed from his subordinate powers. (1.71) And it is with exceeding beauty and propriety that it is said, not that he came to the place, but that he met the place: for to come is voluntary, but to meet is very often involuntary; so that the divine Word appearing on a sudden, supplies an unexpected joy, greater than could have been hoped, inasmuch as it is about to travel in company with the solitary soul; for Moses also "brings forward the people to a meeting with God," [1025] well knowing that he comes invisibly towards those souls who have a longing to meet with him.

XIII

XIII. (1.72) And he subsequently alleges a reason why he "met the place;" for, says he, "the sun was Set." [1026] Not meaning the sun which appears to us, but the most brilliant and radiant light of the invisible and Almighty God. When this light shines upon the mind, the inferior beams of words (that is of angels) set. And much more are all the places perceptible by the external senses overshadowed; but when he departs in a different direction, then they all rise and shine. (1.73) And do not wonder if, according to the rules of allegorical description, the sun is likened to the Father and Governor of the universe; for in reality nothing is like unto God; but those things which by the vain opinion of men are thought to be so, are only two things, one invisible and the other visible; the soul being the invisible thing, and the sun the visible one. (1.74) Now he has shown the similitude of the soul in another passage, where he says, "God made man, in the image of God created him." And again, in the law enacted against homicides, he says, "Whoso sheddeth man's blood, by man shall his blood be shed in requital for that blood, because in the image of God did I make Him." [1027] But the likeness of the sun he only indicates by symbols. (1.75) And it is easy otherwise by means of argument to perceive this, since God is the first light, "For the Lord is my light and my Saviour," [1028] is the language of the Psalms; and not only the light, but he is also the archetypal pattern of every other light, or rather he is more ancient and more sublime than even the archetypal model, though he is spoken of as the model; for the real model was his own most perfect word, the light, and he himself is like to no created thing. (1.76) Since, as the sun divides day and night, so also does Moses say that God divided the light from the darkness; for "God made a division between the light and between the Darkness." [1029] And besides all this, as the sun, when he arises, discovers hidden things, so also does God, who created all things, not only bring them all to light, but he has even created what before had no existence, not being their only maker, but also their founder.

XIV

XIV. (1.77) And the sun is also spoken of in many passages of holy writ in a figurative manner. Once as the human mind, which men build up as a City [1030] and furnish, who are compelled to serve the creature in preference to the uncreated God, of whom it is said that, "They built strong cities for Pharaoh and Peitho," [1031] that is, for discourse; to which persuasion (to peithein) is attributed, and Rameses, or the outward sense, by which the soul is devoured as if by moths; for the name Rameses, being interpreted, means, "the shaking of a moth;" and On, the mind, which they called Heliopolis, since the mind, like the sun, has the predominance over the whole mass of our body, and extends its powers like the beams of the sun, over everything. (1.78) But he who appropriates to himself the regulation of corporeal things, by name Joseph, takes the priest and minister of the mind to be his father-in-law; for says the scripture, "he gave him Aseneth, the daughter of Peutephres, the priest of Heliopolis, for his Wife." [1032] (1.79) And, using symbolical language, he calls the outward sense a second sun, inasmuch as it shows all the objects of which it is able to form a judgment to the intellect, concerning which he speaks thus, "The sun rose upon him when he passed by the appearance of God." [1033] For in real truth, when we are no longer able to endure to pass all our time with the most sacred appearances, and as it were with incorporeal images, but when we turn aside in another direction, and forsake them, we use another light, that, namely, in accordance with the external sense, which is real truth, is in no respect different from darkness, (1.80) which, after it has arisen, arouses as if from sleep the senses of seeing, and of hearing, and also of taste, and of touch, and of smell, and sends to sleep the intellectual qualities of prudence, and justice, and knowledge, and wisdom, which were all awake. (1.81) And it is for this reason that the sacred scripture says, that no one can be pure before the evening, [1034] as the disorderly motions of the outward senses agitate and confuse the intellect. Moreover, he establishes a law for the priests also which may not be avoided, combining with it an expression of a grave opinion when it says, "He shall not eat of the holy things unless he has washed his body in water, and unless the sun has set, and he has become Pure." [1035] (1.82) For by these words it is very clearly shown that there is no one whatever completely pure, so as to be fit to be initiated into the holy and sacred mysteries, to whose lot it has fallen to be honoured with these glories of life which are appreciable by the external senses. But if any one rejects these glories, he is deservedly made conspicuous by the light of wisdom, by means of which he will be able to wash off the stains of vain opinion and to become pure. (1.83) Do you not see that even the sun itself produces opposite effects when he is setting from those which he causes when rising? For when he rises everything upon the earth shines, and the things in heaven are hidden from our view; but, on the other hand, when he sets then the stars appear and the things on earth are overshadowed. (1.84) In the same manner, also, in us, when the light of the outward senses rises like the sun, the celestial and heavenly sciences are really and truly hidden from view; but when this light is near setting, then the starlike radiance of the virtues appears, when the mind is pure, and concealed by no object of the outward senses.

XV

XV. (1.85) But according to the third signification, when he speaks of the sun, he means the divine word, the model of that sun which moves about through the heaven, as has been said before, and with respect to which it is said, "The sun went forth upon the earth, and Lot entered into Segor, and the Lord rained upon Sodom and Gomorrah brimstone and fire." (1.86) For the word of God, when it reaches to our earthly constitution, assists and protects those who are akin to virtue, or whose inclinations lead them to virtue; so that it provides them with a complete refuge and salvation, but upon their enemies it sends irremediable overthrow and destruction. (1.87) And in the fourth signification, what is meant by the sun is the God and ruler of the universe himself, as I have said already, by means of whom such offences as are irremediable, and which appear to be overshadowed and concealed, are revealed; for as all things are possible, so, likewise, all things are known to God. (1.88) In reference to which faculty of his it is that he drags those persons who are living dissolutely as regards their souls, and who are in a debauched and intemperate manner, cohabiting with the daughters of the mind the outward senses, as prostitutes and harlots, to the light of the sun, in order to display their true characters; (1.89) for the scripture says, "And the people abode in Shittim;" now the meaning of the name Shittim is, "the thorns of passion;" which sting and wound the soul. "And the people was polluted, and began to commit whoredom with the daughters of Moab," [1036] and those who are called daughters are the outward senses, for the name Moab is interpreted, "of a father;" and the scripture adds, "Take all the chiefs of the people, and make an example of them unto the Lord in the face of the sun, and the anger of the Lord shall be turned from Israel." [1037] (1.90) For he not only desires that the wicked deeds which are hidden shall be made manifest, and therefore turns upon them the beams of the sun, but he also by this symbolical language calls the father of the universe the sun, that being by whom all things are seen beforehand, and even all those things which are invisibly concealed in the recesses of the mind; and when they are made manifest, then he promises that he who is the only merciful being, will become merciful to the people. (1.91) Why so? Because, even if the mind, fancying that though it does wrong it can escape the notice of the Deity as not being able to see everything, should sin secretly and in dark places, and should after that, either by reason of its own notions or through the suggestions of some one else, conceive that it is impossible that anything should be otherwise than clear to God, and should disclose itself and all its actions, and should bring them forward, as it were, out of the light of the sun, and display them to the governor of the universe, saying, that it repents of the perverse conduct which it formerly exhibited when under the influence of foolish opinion (for that nothing is indistinct before God, but all things are known and clear to him, not merely such as have been done, but even such are merely hoped or designed, by reason of the boundless character of his wisdom), it then is purified and benefited, and it propitiates the chastiser who was ready to punish it, namely, conscience, who was previously filled with just anger towards it, and who now admits repentance as the younger brother of perfect innocence and freedom from sin.

XVI

XVI. (1.92) Moreover, it appears that Moses has in other passages also taken the sun as a symbol of the great Cause of all things, of which I seen an instance in the law which is enacted with respect to those who borrow on pledges: let us recite the law, "If thou takest as a pledge the garment of thy neighbour, thou shalt give it back before the setting of the sun: for it is his covering, it is his only covering of his nakedness, in which he lies down. If he cries unto me I will hearken unto him, for I am Merciful." [1038] (1.93) Is it not natural that those who fancy that the lawgiver displays such earnestness about a garment should, if they do not reproach him, at least make a suggestion, saying, "What are ye saying, my good men? Do ye affirm that the Creator and ruler of the world calls himself merciful with respect to so trivial a matter, as that of a garment not being restored to the borrower by the lender?" (1.94) These are the opinions and notions of men who have never had the least conception or comprehension of the virtue of the almighty God, and who, contrary to all human and divine law, impart the triviality of human affairs to the uncreate and immortal nature, which is full of happiness, and blessedness, and perfection; (1.95) for in what respect do those lenders act unreasonably, who retain in their own hands the pledges which are deposited with them as security, until they receive back their own which they have lent? The debtors are poor, some one will perhaps say, and it is right to pity them: would it not have been reasonable and better to enact a law in accordance with which a contribution should be made to assist their necessities, rather than allow them to appear as debtors, or else one which should forbid the lending on pledges at all? But the law which has permitted the lending on pledges, cannot fairly be indignant against those who will not give up the pledges which they have received before the proper time, as if they were acting unjustly. (1.96) But if any one having come, so to say, to the very farthest limits of poverty, and, being clothed in rags, loads himself with new debts, neglecting the pity which he receives from the bystanders, which is freely bestowed, upon those who fall into such misfortunes, in their own houses, and in the temples, and in the market-place, and everywhere; (1.97) such a one brings and offers to his creditor, the only covering which he had for his shame, with which he has been wont to cover the secret parts of his nature, as a pledge for something. For what, I pray? Is it for some other and better garment? For no one is unprovided with necessary food as long as the springs of the rivers bubble up, and the torrents flow abundantly, and the earth gives forth its annual fruits. (1.98) Again, is any creditor so covetous of riches, or so very cruel, or so perverse, as not to be willing to contribute a tetradrachm, or even less, to one in distress? Or is any one so stingy as to be willing to lend it, but to refuse to give it? or as to take the only garment that the poor man has as a pledge? which indeed under another name may fairly be called running away with a man's clothes; [1039] for men who do this are accustomed to put on other peoples' clothes, and steal them, and to leave the proper owners naked. (1.99) And why has the law provided so carefully that the debtor may not be without his clothes by night, and that he may not lie down to sleep without them, but has not paid the same attention to the fact of his being indecorously naked by day? Are not all things concealed by night and darkness, so as to cause less shame, or rather none at all at that time, but are they not disclosed by day and by light, so as then to compel persons to blush more freely? (1.100) And why does the law not use the expression "to give," but "to restore?" For restoration takes place with respect to the property of other persons, but pledges belong rather to those who have lent on them than to those who have borrowed on them. Moreover, do you not perceive that the law has not enjoined the debtor, who has received back his garment that it may serve as bed-clothes, to bring it back again to his creditor at the return of daylight? (1.101) And, indeed, if the exact propriety of the language be considered, even the most stupid person may see that there is something additional meant beyond what is formally expressed. For the injunction rather resembles a maxim than a recommendation. For, if a person had been giving a recommendation, he would have said: "Give back to your debtor, at the approach of evening, the garment which has been pledged to you, if it be the only garment that he is possessed of, that he may have something with which to cover himself at night." But one who was laying down a maxim would speak thus; as indeed the law does here, "For it is his garment, the only covering of his nakedness, in which he will lie down to sleep."

XVII

XVII. (1.102) These things then, and other things of the same kind, may be urged in reply to those assertors of the literal sense of a passage; and who superciliously reject all other explanations. We will now, in accordance with the usual laws of allegorical speaking, say what is becoming with respect to these subjects. We say, therefore, that a garment here is spoken of symbolically, to signify speech; for clothes keep off the injuries which are wont to visit the body, from cold and heat, and they also conceal the unmentionable parts of nature, and moreover, a cloak is a fitting garment for the body. (1.103) In much the same manner, speech has been given to man by God, as the most excellent of gifts; for in the first place, it is a defensive weapon against those who would attack him with innovations. For as nature has fortified all other animals with their own appropriate and peculiar means of defence, by which they are able to repel those who attempt to injure them, so also has it bestowed upon man that greatest defence and most impregnable protection of speech, with which, as with a panoply, every one who is completely clothed, will have a domestic and most appropriate bodyguard; and employing it as a champion, will be able to ward off all the injuries which can be brought against him by his enemies. (1.104) In the second place, it is a most necessary defence against shame and reproach; for speech is very well calculated to conceal and obscure the faults of men. In the third place, it conduces to the whole ornament of life: for this is the thing which improves every one, and which conducts every one to what is best; (1.105) for there are many disgraceful and mischievous men, who take conversation as a pledge, and deprive its proper owners of it, and utterly cut off what they ought to seek to increase; like men who ravage the lands of their enemies, and who attempt to destroy their corn and all the rest of their crops, which, if it were left unhurt, would be a great advantage to those who would use it. (1.106) For some men carry on an irreconcilable and never-ending war against rational nature, and utterly extirpate its every shoot and beginning, and destroy all its first appearances of propagation, and render it, as one may say, utterly unproductive and barren of all good practices. (1.107) For sometimes, when it is borne onwards towards sacred instruction with irresistible impetuosity, and when it is smitten with a love of the speculations of true philosophy, they--out of jealousy and envy, fearing lest, when it has derived strength from its noble aspirations and has been elevated to a splendid height, it may overwhelm all their petty cavils and plausible devices against the truth, like an irresistible torrent--turn its energy in another direction by their own evil artifices, guiding it in another channel to vulgar and illiberal acts: and very often they seek to blunt it or to hedge it in, and in this way leave the nobility of its nature uncultivated, just as at times wicked guardians of orphan children have rendered a deep-soiled and fertile land barren. And these most pitiless of all men have not been restrained by shame from stripping the man of his only garment, namely, speech; "For," says the scripture, "it is his only covering."--What is a man's only covering, except speech? (1.108) For, as neighing is the peculiar attribute of a horse, and barking of a dog, and lowing of an ox, and roaring of a lion, so also is speaking, and speech itself, the peculiar property of man: for this is what man has received above all other animals as his peculiar gift, as a protection, a bulwark, and panoply, and wall of defence; he being, of all living creatures, the most beloved of God.

XVIII

XVIII. (1.109) On which account the scripture adds, "This is the only covering of his nakedness;" for what can so becomingly overshadow and conceal the reproaches and disgraces of life, as speech? For ignorance is a disgrace akin to irrational nature, but education is the brother of speech, and an ornament properly belonging to man. (1.110) In what then will a man lie down to rest? That is to say, in what will a man find tranquillity and a respite from his labours, except in speech? For speech is a relief to our most miserable and afflicted race. As therefore, when men have been overwhelmed by grief, or by fear, or by any other evil, tranquillity, and constancy, and the kindness of friends have often restored them; so it happens, not often, but invariably, that speech, the only real averter of evil, wards off that most heavy burden which the necessities of that body in the which we are bound up, and the unforeseen accidents of external circumstances which attack us, impose upon us; (1.111) for speech is a friend, and an acquaintance, and a kinsman, and a companion bound up within us; I should rather say, fitted close and united to us by some indissoluble and invisible cement of nature. On this account it is, that it forewarns us of what will be expedient for us, and when any unexpected event befalls us it comes forward of its own accord to assist us; not only bringing advantage of one kind only, such as that which he who is an adviser without acting, or an agent who can give no advice, may supply, but of both kinds: (1.112) for he does not display a half-complete power, but one which is perfect in every part. Inasmuch, as even if it were to fail in his endeavour, and in any conceptions which may have been formed, or efforts which may have been made, it still can have recourse to the third species of assistance, namely, consolation. For speech is, as it were, a medicine for the wounds of the soul, and a saving remedy for its passions, which, "even before the setting of the sun," the lawgiver says one must restore: that is to say, before the all-brilliant beams of the almighty and all-glorious God are obscured, which he, out of pity for our race, sends down from heaven upon the human mind. (1.113) For while that most Godlike light abides in the soul, we shall be able to give back the speech, which was deposited as a pledge, as if it were a garment, in order that he who has received this peculiar possession of man, may by its means conceal the discreditable circumstances of life, and reap the benefit of the divine gift, and indulge in a respite combined with tranquillity, in consequence of the presence of so useful an adviser and defender, who will never leave the ranks in which he has been stationed. (1.114) Moreover, while God pours upon you the light of his beams, do you hasten in the light of day to restore his pledge to the Lord; for when the sun has set, then you, like the whole land of Egypt,[1040] will have an everlasting darkness which may be felt, and being stricken with blindness and ignorance, you will be deprived of all those things of which you thought that you had certain possession, by that sharp-sighted Israel, whose pledges you hold, having made one who was by nature exempt from slavery a slave to necessity.

XIX

XIX. (1.115) We have discussed this subject at this length with no other object except that of teaching that the mind, which is inclined to practice virtue, having irregular motions towards prolificness and sterility, and as one may say, being in a manner always ascending and descending, when it becomes prolific and is elevated to a height is illuminated with the archetypal and incorporeal beams of the rational spring of the all-perfecting sun; but when it descends and becomes unproductive, then it is again illuminated by those images of those beams, the immortal words which it is customary to call angels. (1.116) On which account we now read in the scripture, "He met the place; for the sun was Set."[1041] For when those beams of God desert the soul by means of which the clearest comprehensions of affairs are engendered in it, then arises that second and weaker light of words, and the light of things is no longer seen, just as is the case in this lower world. For the moon, which occupies the second rank next to the sun, when that body has set, pours forth a somewhat weaker light than his upon the earth; (1.117) and to meet a place or a word is a most sufficient gift for those who cannot discern that God is superior to every place or word; because they have not a soul wholly destitute of light, but because, since that most unmixed and brilliant light has set, they have been favoured with one which is alloyed. "For the children of Israel had light in all their Dwellings,"[1042] says the sacred historian in the book of Exodus, so that night and darkness were continually banished from them, though it is in night and darkness that those men live who have lost the eyes of the soul rather than those of the body, having no experience of the beams of virtue. (1.118) But some persons--supposing that what is meant here by the figurative expression of the sun is the external sense and the mind, which are looked upon as the things which have the power of judging; and that which is meant by place is the divine word--understand the allegory in this manner: the practiser of virtue met with the divine word, after the mortal and human light had set; (1.119) for as long as the mind thinks that it attains to a firm comprehension of the objects of the intellect, and the outward sense conceives that it has a similar understanding of its appropriate objects, and that it dwells amid sublime objects, the divine word stands aloof at a distance; but when each of these comes to confess its own weakness, and sets in a manner while availing itself of concealment, then immediately the right reason of a soul well-practised in virtue comes in a welcome manner to their assistance, when they have begun to despair of their own strength, and await the aid which is invisibly coming to them from without.

XX

XX. (1.120) Therefore, the scripture says in the next verses, "That he took one of the stones of the place and placed it at his head, and slept in that Place." [1043] Any one may wonder not only at the interior and mystical doctrine contained in these words, but also at the distinct assertion, which gives us a lesson in labour and endurance: (1.121) for the historian does not think it becoming, that the man who is devoted to the study of virtue should adopt a luxurious life, and live softly, imitating the pursuits and rivalries of those who are called indeed happy, but who are in reality full of all unhappiness; whose entire life is a sleep and a dream, according to the holy lawgiver. (1.122) These men, after they have during the whole day been doing all sorts of injustice to others, in courts of justice, and council halls, and theatres, and everywhere, then return home, like miserable men as they are, to overturn their own house. I mean not that house which comes under the class of buildings, but that which is akin to the soul, I mean the body. Introducing immoderate and incessant food, and irrigating it with an abundance of pure wine, until the reason is overwhelmed, and disappears; and the passions which have their seat beneath the belly, the offspring of satiety, rise up, being carried away by unrestrained frenzy, and falling upon, and vehemently attacking all that they meet with, are only at last appeased after they have worked off their excessive violence of excitement. (1.123) But by night, when it is time to turn towards rest, having prepared costly couches and the most exquisite of beds, they lie down in the most exceeding softness, imitating the luxury of women, whom nature has permitted to indulge in a more relaxed system of life, inasmuch as their maker, the Creator of the universe, has made their bodies of a more delicate stamp. (1.124) Now no such person as this is a pupil of the sacred word, but those only are the disciples of that who are real genuine men, lovers of temperance, and orderliness, and modesty, men who have laid down continence, and frugality, and fortitude, as a kind of base and foundation for the whole of life; and safe stations for the soul, in which it may anchor without danger and without changeableness: for being superior to money, and pleasure, and glory, they look down upon meats and drinks, and everything of that sort, beyond what is necessary to ward off hunger: being thoroughly ready to undergo hunger, and thirst, and heat, and cold, and all other things, however hard they may be to be borne, for the sake of the acquisition of virtue. And being admirers of whatever is most easily provided, so as to not be ashamed of ever such cheap or shabby clothes, think rather, on the other hand, that sumptuous apparel is a reproach and great scandal to life. (1.125) To these men, the soft earth is their most costly couch; their bed is bushes, and grass, and herbage, and a thick layer of leaves; and the pillows for their head are a few stones, or any little mounds which happen to rise a little above the surface of the plain. Such a life as this, is, by luxurious men, denominated a life of hardship, but by those who live for virtue, it is called most delightful; for it is well adapted, not for those who are called men, for those who really are such. (1.126) Do you not see, that even now, also, the sacred historian represents the practiser of honourable pursuits, who abounds in all royal materials and appointments, as sleeping on the ground, and using a stone for his pillow; and a little further on, he speaks of himself as asking in his prayers for bread and a cloak, the necessary wealth of nature? like one who has at all times held in contempt, the man who dwells among vain opinions, and who is inclined to revile all those who are disposed to admire him; this man is the archetypal pattern of the soul which is devoted to the practice of virtue, and an enemy of every effeminate person.

XXI

XXI. (1.127) Hitherto I have been uttering the praises of the man devoted to labour and to virtue, as it occurred to me naturally; but now we must examine what is symbolically signified under the expressions made use of. Now it is well that we should know, that the divine place and the sacred region are full of incorporeal intelligences; and these intelligences are immortal souls. (1.128) Taking then one of these intelligences, and selecting one of them according as it appears to be the most excellent, this lover of virtue, of whom we are speaking, applies it to our own mind, to it as to the head of a united body; for, indeed, the mind is in a manner the head of the soul; and he does this, using the pretext indeed as if he were going to sleep, but, in reality, as being about to rest upon the word of God, and to place the whole of his life as the lightest possible burden upon it; (1.129) and it listens to him gladly, and receives the labourer in the paths of virtue at first, as if he were going to become a disciple; then when he has shown his approbation of the dexterity of his nature, he gives him his hand, like a gymnastic trainer, and invites him to the gymnasia, and standing firmly, compels him to wrestle with him, until he has rendered his strength so great as to be irresistible, changing his ears by the divine influences into eyes, and calling this newly-modelled disposition Israel, that is, the man who Sees. [1044] (1.130) Then also he crowns him with the garland of victory. But this garland has a singular and foreign, and, perhaps, not altogether a wellomened name, for it is called by the president of the games torpor, for it is said, that the breadth became Torpid [1045] of all the rewards and of the proclamations of the heralds, and of all those most wonderful prizes for pre-eminent excellence which are had in honour; (1.131) for the soul which has received a share of irresistible power, and which has been made perfect in the contests of virtue, and which has arrived at the very furthest limit of what is honourable, will never be unduly elated or puffed up by arrogance, nor stand upon tiptoes, and boast as if it were well to make vast strides with bare feet; but the breadth which was extended wide by opinion, will become torpid and contracted, and then will voluntarily succumb and yield to tameness, so as being classed in an inferior order to that of the incorporeal natures, it may carry off the victory while appearing to be defeated; (1.132) for it is accounted a most honourable thing to yield the palm to those who are superior to one's self, voluntarily rather than through compulsion; for it is incredible how greatly the second prize in this contest is superior in real dignity and importance to the first prize in the others.

XXII

XXII. (1.133) Such then may be said, by way of preface, to the discussion of that description of visions which are sent from God. But it is time now to turn to the subject itself, and to investigate, with accuracy, every portion of it. The scripture therefore says, "And he dreamed a dream. And behold a ladder was planted firmly on the ground, the head of which reached to heaven, and the angels of God were ascending and descending along It." [1046] (1.134) By the ladder in this thing, which is called the world, is figuratively understood the air, the foundation of which is the earth, and the head is the heaven; for the large interior space, which being extended in every direction, reaches from the orb of the moon, which is described as the most remote of the order in heaven, but the nearest to us by those who contemplate sublime objects, down to the earth, which is the lowest of such bodies, is the air. (1.135) This air is the abode of incorporeal souls, since it seemed good to the Creator of the universe to fill all the parts of the world with living creatures. On this account he prepared the terrestrial animals for the earth, the aquatic animals for the sea and for the rivers, and the stars for the heaven; for every one of these bodies is not merely a living animal, but is also properly described as the very purest and most universal mind extending through the universe; so that there are living creatures in that other section of the universe, the air. And if these things are not comprehensible by the outward senses, what of that? For the soul is also invisible. (1.136) And yet it is probable that the air should nourish living animals even more than the land or the water. Why so? Because it is the air which has given vitality to those animals which live on the earth and in the water. For the Creator of the universe formed the air so that it should be the habit of those bodies which are immovable, and the nature of those which are moved in an invisible manner, and the soul of such as are able to exert an impetus and visible sense of their own. (1.137) Is it not then absurd that that element, by means of which the other elements have been filled with vitality, should itself be destitute of living things? Therefore let no one deprive the most excellent nature of living creatures of the most excellent of those elements which surrounds the earth; that is to say, of the air. For not only is it not alone deserted by all things besides, but rather, like a populous city, it is full of imperishable and immortal citizens, souls equal in number to the stars. (1.138) Now of these souls some descend upon the earth with a view to be bound up in mortal bodies, those namely which are most nearly connected with the earth, and which are lovers of the body. But some soar upwards, being again distinguished according to the definitions and times which have been appointed by nature. (1.139) Of these, those which are influenced by a desire for mortal life, and which have been familiarised to it, again return to it. But others, condemning the body of great folly and trifling, have pronounced it a prison and a grave, and, flying from it as from a house of correction or a tomb, have raised themselves aloft on light wings towards the aether, and have devoted their whole lives to sublime speculations. (1.140) There are others, again, the purest and most excellent of all, which have received greater and more divine intellects, never by any chance desiring any earthly thing whatever, but being as it were lieutenants of the Ruler of the universe, as though they were the eyes and ears of the great king, beholding and listening to everything. (1.141) Now philosophers in general are wont to call these demons, but the sacred scripture calls them angels, using a name more in accordance with nature. For indeed they do report (diangellousi) the injunctions of the father to his children, and the necessities of the children to the father. (1.142) And it is in reference to this employment of theirs that the holy scripture has represented them as ascending and descending, not because God, who knows everything before any other being, has any need of interpreters; but because it is the lot of us miserable mortals to use speech as a mediator and intercessor; because of our standing in awe of and fearing the Ruler of the universe, and the all-powerful might of his authority; (1.143) having received a notion of which he once entreated one of those mediators, saying: "Do thou speak for us, and let not God speak to us, lest we Die." [1047] For not only are we unable to endure his chastisements, but we cannot bear even his excessive and unmodified benefits, which he himself proffers us of his own accord, without employing the ministrations of any other beings. (1.144) Very admirably therefore does Moses represent the air under the figurative symbol of a ladder, as planted solidly in the earth and reaching up to heaven. For it comes to pass that the evaporations which are given forth by the earth becoming rarefied, are dissolved into air, so that the earth is the foundation and root of the air, and that the heaven is its head. (1.145) Accordingly it is said that the moon is not an unadulterated consolidation of pure aether, as each of the other stars is, but is rather a combination of the aether-like and air-like essence. For the black spot which appears in it, which some call a face, is nothing else but the air mingled with it, which is by nature black, and which extends as far as heaven.

XXIII

XXIII. (1.146) The ladder therefore in the world which is here spoken of in this symbolical manner, was something of this sort. But if we carefully investigate the soul which exists in men, the foundation of which is something corporeal, and as it were earth-like, we shall find that the foundation to be the outward sense; and the head to be something heavenly, as it were the most pure mind. (1.147) But all the words of God move incessantly upwards and downwards through the whole of it, dragging it upwards along with them whenever they soar aloft, and separating it from whatever is mortal, and exhibiting to it a sight of those things which alone are worthy of being beheld; but yet not casting it down when they descend. For neither is God himself, nor the word of God, worthy of blame. But they join with them in their descent, by reason of their love for mankind and compassion for our race, for the sake of being their allies and rendering them assistance, in order that by breathing in a saving inspiration they may recall to life the soul which was still being tossed about in the body as in the river. (1.148) Now the God and governor of the universe does by himself and alone walk about invisibly and noiselessly in the minds of those who are purified in the highest degree. For there is extant a prophecy which was delivered to the wise man, in which it is said: "I will walk among you, and I will be your God." [1048] But the angels--the words of God--move about in the minds of those persons who are still in a process of being washed, but who have not yet completely washed off the life which defiles them, and which is polluted by the contact of their heavy bodies, making them look pure and brilliant to the eyes of virtue. (1.149) But it is plain enough what vast numbers of evils are driven out, and what a multitude of wicked inhabitants is expelled in order that one good man may be introduced to dwell there. Do thou, therefore, O my soul, hasten to become the abode of God, his holy temple, to become strong from having been most weak, powerful from having been powerless, wise from having been foolish, and very reasonable from having been doting and childless. (1.150) And perhaps too the practiser of virtue represents his own life as like to a ladder; for the practice of anything is naturally an anomalous thing, since at one time it soars up to a height, and at another it turns downwards in a contrary direction; and at one time has a fair voyage like a ship, and at another has but an unfavourable passage; for, as some one says, the life of those who practise virtue is full of vicissitudes: being at one time alive and waking, and at another dead or sleeping. (1.151) And perhaps this is no incorrect statement; for the wise have obtained the heavenly and celestial country as their habitation; having learnt to be continually mounting upwards, but the wicked have received as their share the dark recesses of hell, having from the beginning to the end of their existence practised dying, and having been from their infancy to their old age familiarised with destruction. (1.152) But the practisers of virtue, for they are on the boundary between two extremities, are frequently going upwards and downwards as if on a ladder, being either drawn upwards by a more powerful fate, or else being dragged down by that which is worse; until the umpire of this contention and conflict, namely God, adjudges the victory to the more excellent class and utterly destroys the other.

XXIV

XXIV. (1.153) There is also in this dream another sort of similitude or comparison apparent, which must not be passed over in silence; the affairs of mankind are naturally compared to a ladder, on account of their irregular motion and progress: (1.154) for as some one or other has said; "One day has cast one man down from on high and destroyed him, and another it has raised up, nothing that belongs to our human race being formed by nature so as to remain long in the same condition, but all such things changing with all kinds of alteration. (1.155) Do not men become rulers from having been private individuals, and private individuals from having been rulers, poor from having been rich, and very rich from having been very poor; glorious from being despised, and most illustrious from having been infamous?" [...] A very beautiful way of life: for it is very possible that the being whose habitation is the whole world, may dwell with you also, and take care of your house, so that it may be completely protected and free from injury for ever; (1.156) and there is such a way as this in which human affairs move upwards and downwards, meeting with an unstable and variable fortune, the anomalous character of which, unerring time proves by evidence which is not indistinct but manifest and legible.

XXV

XXV. (1.157) But the dream also represented the archangel, namely the Lord himself, firmly planted on the ladder; for we must imagine that the living God stands above all things, like the charioteer of a chariot, or the pilot of a ship; that is, above bodies, and above souls, and above all creatures, and above the earth, and above the air, and above the heaven, and above all the powers of the outward senses, and above the invisible natures, in short, above all things whether visible or invisible; for having made the whole to depend upon himself, he governs it and all the vastness of nature. (1.158) But let no one who hears that he was firmly planted thus suppose that any thing at all assists God, so as to enable him to stand firmly, but let him rather consider this fact that what is here indicated is equivalent to the assertion that the firmest position, and the bulwark, and the strength, and the steadiness of everything is the immoveable God, who stamps the character of immobility on whatever he pleases; for, in consequence of his supporting and consolidating things, those which he does combine remain firm and indestructible. (1.159) Therefore he who stands upon the ladder of heaven says to him who is beholding the dream, "I am the Lord God of Abraham thy father, and the God of Isaac; be not Afraid." [1049] This oracle and this vision were also the firmest support of the soul devoted to the practice of virtue, inasmuch as it taught it that the Lord and God of the universe is both these things also to his own race, being entitled both the Lord and God of all men, and of his grandfathers and ancestors, and being called by both names in order that the whole world and the man devoted to virtue might have the same inheritance; since it is also said, "The Lord himself is his Inheritance." [1050]

XXVI

XXVI. (1.160) But do not fancy that it is an accidental thing here for him to be called in this place the God and Lord of Abraham, but only the God of Isaac; for this latter is the symbol of the knowledge which exists by nature, which hears itself, and teaches itself, and learns of itself; but Abraham is the symbol of that which is derived from the teaching of others; and the one again is an indigenous and native inhabitant of his country, but the other is only a settler and a foreigner; (1.161) for having forsaken the language of those who indulge in sublime conversations about astronomy, a language imitating that of the Chaldaeans, foreign and barbarous, he was brought over to that which was suited to a rational being, namely, to the service of the great Cause of all things. (1.162) Now this disposition stands in need of two powers to take care of it, the power that is of authority, and that of conferring benefits, in order that in accordance with the authority of the governor, it may obey the admonitions which it receives, and also that it may be greatly benefited by his beneficence. But the other disposition stands in need of the power of beneficence only; for it has not derived any improvement from the authority which admonishes it, inasmuch as it naturally claims virtue as its own, but by reason of the bounty which is showered upon it from above, it was good and perfect from the beginning; (1.163) therefore God is the name of the beneficent power, and Lord is the title of the royal power. What then can any one call a more ancient and important good, than to be thought worthy to meet with unmixed and unalloyed beneficence? And what can be less valuable than to receive a mixture of authority and liberality? And it appears to me that it was because the practiser of virtue saw that he uttered that most admirable prayer that, "the Lord might be to him as God;" [1051] for he desired no longer to stand in awe of him as a governor, but to honour and love him as a benefactor. (1.164) Now is it not fitting that even blind men should become sharpsighted in their minds to these and similar things, being endowed with the power of sight by the most sacred oracles, so as to be able to contemplate the glories of nature, and not to be limited to the mere understanding of the words? But even if we voluntarily close the eye of our soul and take no care to understand such mysteries, or if we are unable to look up to them, the hierophant himself stands by and prompts us. And do not thou ever cease through weariness to anoint thy eyes until you have introduced those who are duly initiated to the secret light of the sacred scriptures, and have displayed to them the hidden things therein contained, and their reality, which is invisible to those who are uninitiated. (1.165) It is becoming then for you to act thus; but as for ye, O souls, who have once tasted of divine love, as if you had even awakened from deep sleep, dissipate the mist that is before you; and hasten forward to that beautiful spectacle, putting aside slow and hesitating fear, in order to comprehend all the beautiful sounds and sights which the president of the games has prepared for your advantage.

XXVII

XXVII. (1.166) There are then a countless number of things well worthy of being displayed and demonstrated; and among them one which was mentioned a little while ago; for the oracles calls the person who was really his grandfather, the father of the practiser of virtue, and to him who as really his father, it has not given any such title; for the scriptures says, "I am the Lord God of Abraham thy father," but in reality Abraham was his grandfather; and then proceeds, "And the God of Isaac," and in this case he does not add, "thy father:" (1.167) is it not then worth while to examine into the cause of this difference? Undoubtedly it is; let us then in a careful manner apply ourselves to the consideration of the cause. Philosophers say that virtue exists among men, either by nature, or by practice, or by learning. On which account the sacred scriptures represent the three founders of the nation of the Israelites as wise men; not indeed originally endowed with the same kind of wisdom, but arriving rapidly at the same end. (1.168) For the eldest of them, Abraham, had instruction for his guide in the road which conducted him to virtue; as we shall show in another treatise to the best of our power. And Isaac, who is the middle one of the three, had a self-taught and self-instructed nature. And Jacob, the third, arrived at this point by industry and practice, in accordance with which were his labours of wrestling and contention. (1.169) Since then there are thus three different manners by which wisdom exists among men, it happens that the two extremes are the most nearly and frequently united. For the virtue which is acquired by practice, is the offspring of that which is derived from learning. But that which is implanted by nature is indeed akin to the others, for it is set below them, as the root for them all. But it has obtained its prize without any rivalry or difficulty. (1.170) So that it is thus very natural for Abraham, as one who had been improved by instruction, to be called the father of Jacob, who arrived at his height of virtue by practice. By which expression is indicated that not so much the relationship of one man to the other, but that the power which is fond of hearing is very ready for learning; the power which is devoted to practice being also well suited for wrestling. (1.171) If, however, this practiser of virtue runs on vigorously towards the end and learns to see clearly what he previously only dreamed of in an indistinct way, being altered and re-stamped with a better character, and being called Israel, that is, "the man who sees God," instead of Jacob, that is, "the supplanter," he then is no longer set down as the son of Abraham, as his father, of him who derived wisdom from instruction, but as the son of Israel, who was born excellent by nature. (1.172) These statements are not fables of my own invention, but are the oracle written on the sacred pillars. For, says the scripture: "Israel having departed, he and all that he had came to the well of the oath, and there he sacrificed a sacrifice to the God of his father Isaac." [1052] Do you not now perceive that this present assertion has reference not to the relationship between mortal men, but, as was said before, to the nature of things? For look at what is before us. At one time, Jacob is spoken of as the son of his father Abraham, and at another time he is called Israel, the son of Isaac, on account of the reason which we have thus accurately investigated.

XVIII

XVIII. (1.173) Having then said: "I am the Lord God of Abraham, the father and the God of Isaac," he adds: "Be not afraid," very consistently. For how can we any longer be afraid when we have thee, O God, as our armour and defender? Thee, the deliverer from fear and from every painful feeling? Thee, who hast also fashioned the archetypal forms of our instruction while they were still indistinct, so as to make them visible, teaching Abraham wisdom, and begetting Isaac, who was wise from his birth. For you condescended to be called the guide of the one and the father of the other, assigning to the one the rank of pupil, and to the other that of a son. (1.174) For this reason, too, God promised that he would not give him the land. I mean by the land here, all-prolific virtue, on which the practiser rests from his contests and sleeps, from the fact of the life according to the outward sense being lulled asleep, and that of the soul being awakened. Receiving gladly peaceful repose there, which he did not obtain without war, and the afflictions which arise from war, not by means of bearing arms and slaying men; away with any such notion! but by overthrowing the array of vices and passions which are the adversaries of virtue. (1.175) But the race of wisdom is likened to the sand of the sea, by reason of its boundless numbers, and because also the sand, like a fringe, checks the incursions of the sea; as the reasonings of instruction beat back the violence of wickedness and iniquity. And these reasonings, in accordance with the divine promises, are extended to the very extremities of the universe. And they show that he who is possessed of them is the inheritor of all the parts of the world, penetrating everywhere, to the east, and to the west, to the south, and to the north. For it is said in the scripture: "He shall be extended towards the sea, and towards the south, and towards the north, and towards the East." [1053] (1.176) But the wise and virtuous man is not only a blessing to himself, but he is also a common good to all men, diffusing advantages over all from his own ready store. For as the sun is the light of all those beings who have eyes, so also is the wise man light to all those who partake of a rational nature.

XXIX

XXIX. (1.177) "For in thee shall all the nations of the earth be blessed." And this oracle applies to the wise man in respect of himself, and also in respect of Others. [1054] For if the mind which is in me is purified by perfect virtue, and if the tribes of that earthly part which is about me are purified at the same time, which tribes have fallen to the lot of the external senses, and of the greatest channel of all, namely the body; and if any one, either in his house, or in his city, or in his country, or in his nation, becomes a lover of wisdom, it is inevitable that that house, and that city, and that country, and that nation, must attain to a better life. (1.178) For, as those spices which are set on fire fill all persons near them with their fragrance, so in the same manner do all those persons who are neighbours of and contiguous to the wise men catch some of the exhalations which reach to a distance from him, and so become improved in their characters.

XXX

XXX. (1.179) And it is the greatest of all advantages to a soul engaged in labours and contests, to have for its fellow traveller, God, who penetrates everywhere. "For behold," says God, "I am with Thee." [1055] Of what then can we be in need while we have for our wealth Thee, who art the only true and real riches, who keepest us in the road which leads to virtue in all its different divisions? For it is not one portion only of the rational life which conducts to justice and to all other virtue, but the parts are infinite in number, from which those who desire to arrive at virtue can set out.

XXXI

XXXI. (1.180) Very admirably therefore is it said in the scripture: "I will lead thee back to this land." For it was fitting that the reason should remain with itself, and should not depart to the outward sense. And if it has departed, then the next best thing is for it to return back again. (1.181) And perhaps also a doctrine bearing on the immortality of the soul is figuratively intimated by this expression. For the soul, having left the region of heaven, as was mentioned a little while before, came to the body as a foreign country. Therefore the father who begot it promises that he will not permit it to be for ever held in bondage, but that he will have compassion on it, and will unloose its chains, and will conduct it in safety and freedom as far as the metropolis, and will not cease to assist it till the promises which he has made in words are confirmed by the truth of actions. For it is by all means the peculiar attribute of God to foretell what is to happen. (1.182) And why do we say this? for his words do not differ from his actions; therefore the soul which is devoted to the practice of virtue, being set in motion, and roused up to the investigations relating to the living God, at first suspected that the living God existed in place; but after a short space it became perplexed by the difficulty of the question, and began to change its opinion. (1.183) "For," says the scripture, "Jacob awoke and said, Surely the Lord is in this place, and I knew it not;" and it would have been better, I should have said; not to know it, than to fancy that God existed in any place, he whom himself contains all things in a circle.

XXXII

XXXII. (1.184) Very naturally, therefore, was Jacob afraid, and said in a spirit of admiration, "how dreadful is this Place." [1056] For, in truth, of all the topics or places in natural philosophy, the most formidable is that in which it is inquired where the living God is, and whether in short he is in any place at all. Since some persons affirm that everything which exists occupies some place or other, and others assign each thing a different place, either in the world or out of the world, in some space between the different bodies of the universe. Others again affirm that the uncreated God resembles no created being whatever, but that he is superior to everything, so that the very swiftest conception is outstripped by him, and confesses that it is very far inferior to the comprehension of him; (1.185) wherefore it speedily cries out, This is not what I expected, because the Lord is in the place; for he surrounds everything, but in truth and reason he is not surrounded by anything. And this thing which is demonstrated and visible, this world perceptible by the outward senses, is nothing else but the house of God, the abode of one of the powers of the true God, in accordance with which he is good; (1.186) and he calls this world an abode, and he has also pronounced it with great truth to be the gate of heaven. Now, what does this mean? We cannot comprehend the world which consists of various species, in that which is fashioned in accordance with the divine regulations, appreciable only by the intellect, in any other manner than by making a migration upwards from this other world perceptible by the outward senses and visible; (1.187) for it is not possible either to perceive any other existing being which is incorporeal, without deriving our principles of judgment from bodies. For while they are quiet, their place is perceived, and when they are in motion we judge of their time; but the points, and the lines, and the superficies, and in short the boundaries. [...] [1057] as of a garment wrapped externally around it. (1.188) According to analogy, therefore, the knowledge of the world appreciable by the intellect is attained to by means of our knowledge of that which is perceptible by the outward senses, which is as it were a gate to the other. For as men who wish to see cities enter in through the gates, so also they who wish to comprehend the invisible world are conducted in their search by the appearance of the visible one. And the world of that essence which is only open to the intellect without any visible appearance or figure whatever, and which exists only in the archetypal idea which exists in the mind, which is fashioned according to its appearance, will be brought on without any shade; all the walls, and all the gates which could impede its progress being removed, so that it is not looked at through any other medium, but by itself, putting forth a beauty which is susceptible of no change, presenting an indescribable and exquisite spectacle.

XXXIII

XXXIII. (1.189) But enough of this. There is another dream also which belongs to the same class, that one I mean about the spotted flock, which the person who beheld it relates after he had awoke, saying, "The angel of God spake unto me in a dream, and said, Jacob; and I said, What is it? And he said unto me, Look up with thine eyes, and see the goats and the rams mounting on the flocks, and the she-goats, some white, and spotted, and ring-straked, and speckled: for I have beheld all that Laban does unto thee. I am that God who was seen by thee in the place of God, where thou anointedst the pillar, and vowedst a vow unto me. Now therefore, rise up and depart out of the land, and go into the land of thy birth, and I will be with Thee." [1058] (1.190) You see here, that the divine word speaks of dreams as sent from God; including in this statement not those only which appear through the agency of the chief cause itself, but those also which are seen through the operation of his interpreters and attendant angels, who are thought by the father who created them to be worthy of a divine and blessed lot: (1.191) consider, however, what comes afterwards. The sacred word enjoins some persons what they ought to do by positive command, like a king; to others it suggests what will be for their advantage, as a preceptor does to his pupils; to others again, it is like a counsellor suggesting the wisest plans; and in this way too, it is of great advantage to those who do not of themselves know what is expedient; to others it is like a friend, in a mild and persuasive manner, bringing forward many secret things which no uninitiated person may lawfully hear. (1.192) For at times it asks some persons, as for instance, Adam, "Where art thou?" And any one may properly answer to such a question, "No where?" Because all human affairs never remain long in the same condition, but are moved about and changed, whether we speak of their soul or their body, or of their external circumstances; for their minds are unstable, not always having the same impressions from the same things, but such as are diametrically contrary to their former ones. The body also is unstable, as all the changes of the different ages from infancy to old age show; their external circumstances also are variable, being tossed up and down by the impetus of everagitated fortune.

XXXIV

XXXIV. (1.193) When, however, he comes into an assembly of friends, he does not begin to speak before he has first accosted each individual among them, and addressed him by name, so that they prick up their ears, and are quiet and attentive, listening to the oracles thus delivered, so as never to forget them or let them escape their memory: since in another passage of scripture we read, "Be silent and Listen." [1059] (1.194) In this manner, too, Moses is called up to the bush. For, the scripture says, "When he saw that he was turning aside to see, God called him out of the bush, and said, Moses, Moses: and he said, What is it, Lord?" [1060] And Abraham also, on the occasion of offering up his beloved and only son as a burnt-offering, when he was beginning to sacrifice him, and when he had given proof of his piety, was forbidden to destroy the self-taught race, Isaac by name, from among men; (1.195) for at the beginning of his account of this transaction, Moses says that "God did tempt Abraham, and said unto him, Abraham, Abraham; and he said, Behold, here am I. And he said unto him, Take now thy beloved son Isaac, whom thou lovest, and offer him up." And when he had brought the victim to the altar, then the angel of the Lord called him out of heaven, saying, "Abraham, Abraham," and he answered, "Behold, here am I. And he said, Lay not thy hand upon the child, and do nothing to Him." [1061] (1.196) Also the practiser of virtue is also called one of this company dear to God, being deservedly accounted worthy of the same honour; for, says the scripture, "The angel of God said to me in my sleep, Jacob: and I answered, and said, What is It?" [1062] (1.197) But after he has been called he exerts his attention, endeavouring to arrive at an accurate knowledge of the symbols which are displayed to him; and these symbols are the connection and generation of reasonings, as flocks and herds. For, says the scripture, "Jacob, looking up with his eyes, saw the goats and rams leaping upon the shegoats and upon the sheep." (1.198) Now the hegoat is the leader of the flock of goats, and the ram is the leader of the flock of sheep, and these two animals are symbols of perfect reasonings, one of which purifies and cleanses the soul of sins, and the other nourishes it and renders it full of good actions. Such then are the leaders of the flocks in us, namely, reasons; and the flocks themselves, resembling the sheep and goats whose names they bear, rush forwards and hasten with zeal and earnestness towards justice. (1.199) Therefore, looking up with the eye of his mind, which up to that time had been closed, he saw the perfect and thoroughly sharpened reasons analogically resembling the goats and rams, prepared for the diminution of offences and the increase of good actions. And he beheld how they leap upon the sheep and the goats, that is on those souls which are still young and tender, and in the vigour of youth, and beautiful in the flower of their age; not pursuing irrational pleasure, but indulging in the invisible sowing of the doctrines of prudence. (1.200) For this is a marriage which is blessed in its children; not uniting bodies, but adapting perfect virtues to well-disposed souls. Therefore do all ye right reasons of wisdom leap up, form connections, sow seed, and pass by no soul which you see rich and fertile, and welldisposed, and virgin; but inviting it to association and connection with you, render it perfect and pregnant; for so you will become the parents of all kinds of good things, of a male offspring, white, variegated, ring-straked, and speckled.

XXXV

XXXV. (1.201) But we must now examine what power each of these offspring has. Now those which are purely white (dialeukoi) are the most beautiful and the most conspicuous: the word dia being often prefixed in composition by way of adding force to the word, so that the words diadeÂlon and diaselmion are commonly used to signify what is very conspicuous (delÌon) and very remarkable (episeÌmon); (1.202) therefore the meaning here is that the first-born offspring of the soul which has received the sacred seed, is purely white; being like light in which there is no obscurity, and like the most brilliant radiance: like the unclouded beam which might proceed from the rays of the sun in fine weather at mid-day. Again, by the statement that some are variegated, what is meant is, not that the flocks are marked by such a multiform and various spottedness as to resemble the unclean leprosy, and which is an emblem of a life unsteady and tossed about in any direction by reason of the fickleness of the mind, but only that they have marks drawn in regular lines and different characters, shaped and impressed with all kinds of well approved forms, the peculiarities of which, being multiplied together and combined properly, will produce a musical harmony. (1.203) For some persons have looked upon the art of variegating as so random and obscure a matter, that they have referred it to weavers. But I admire not only the art itself, but the name likewise, and most especially so when I look upon the divisions of the earth and the spheres in heaven, and the differences between various plants and various animals, and that most variegated texture, I mean the world; (1.204) for I am compelled to suppose, that the maker of this universal textile fabric was also the inventor of all varied and variegating science; and I look with reverence upon the inventor, and I honour the art which he invented, and I am amazed at the work which is the result, and this too, though it is but a very small portion of it which I have been able to see, but still, from the portion of which has been unfolded to me, if indeed I may say that it has been unfolded, I hope to form a tolerably accurate judgment of the whole, guiding my conjectures by the light of analogy. (1.205) Nevertheless I admire the lover of wisdom for having studied the same art, collecting and thinking fit to weave together many things, though different, and proceeding from different sources, into the same web; for taking the first two elements from the grammatical knowledge imparted to children, that is to say, reading and writing, and taking from the more perfect growth of knowledge the skill which is found among poets, and the comprehension of ancient history, and deriving certainty and freedom from deception from arithmetic and geometry, in which sciences there is need of proportions and calculations; and borrowing from music rhyme, and metre, and harmonies, and chromatics, and diatonics, and combined and disjoined melodies; and having derived from rhetoric invention, and language, and arrangement, and memory, and action; and from philosophy, whatever has been omitted in any of these separate branches, and all the other things of which human life consists, he has put together in one most admirably arranged work, combining great learning of one kind with great learning of another kind. (1.206) Now the sacred scripture calls the maker of this compound work Besaleel, which name, being interpreted, signifies "in the shadow of God;" for he makes all the copies, and the man by name Moses makes all the models, as the principal architect; and for this reason it is, that the one only draws outlines as it were, but the other is not content with such sketches, (1.207) but makes the archetypal natures themselves, and has already adorned the holy places with his variegating art; but the wise man is called the only adorner of the place of wisdom in the oracles delivered in the sacred scriptures.

XXXVI

XXXVI. And the most beautiful and varied work of God, this world, has been created in this its present state of perfection by all-wise knowledge; and how can it be anything but right to receive the art of variegating as a noble effort of knowledge? (1.208) the most sacred copy of which is the whole word of wisdom, which will bear about in its bosom the things of heaven and of earth, from which the practiser of virtue elaborates his notions of various things. For after the white sheep he immediately beheld the variegated animals, stamped with the impression of instruction. (1.209) The third kind are the ring-straked and speckled; and what man in his senses would deny that these also are, as to their genus, variegated? but still he is not so very eager about the varieties of the members of the flocks, as about the road which leads to virtue and excellence; (1.210) for the prophet intends that he who proceeds along this road shall be besprinkled with dust and water; because it is related that the earth and water being kneaded together and fashioned into shape by the Creator of man, was formed into one body, not being made by hand, but being the work of invisible nature. (1.211) Therefore it is the first principle of wisdom not to forget one's self, and always to keep before one's eyes the materials of which one has been compounded; for in this way a man will get rid of boasting and arrogance, which of all evils is the one most hated by God; for who that ever admits into his mind the recollection that the first principles of his formation are dust and water, would ever be so puffed by vanity as to be unduly elated? (1.212) On this account the prophet has thought it fit that those who are about to offer sacrifice shall be sprinkled with the aforesaid things; thinking no one worthy to appear at a sacrifice who has not first of all learnt to know himself, and to comprehend the nothingness of mankind, and the elements of which he is composed, conjecturing from them that he himself is utterly insignificant.

XXXVII

XXXVII. (1.213) These three signs, the white, the variegated, and the ring-straked and speckled, are as yet imperfect in the practiser of virtue, who has not himself as yet attained to perfection. But, in the case of him who is perfect, they also appear to be perfect. And in what manner they appear so we will examine. (1.214) The sacred scripture has appointed that the great High Priest, when he was about to perform the ministrations appointed by the law, should be besprinkled with water and ashes in the first place, that he might come to a remembrance of himself. For the wise Abraham also, when he went forth to converse with God, pronounced himself to be dust and ashes. In the second place, it enjoins him to put on a tunic reaching down to his feet, and the variouslyembroidered thing which was called his breastplate, an image and representation of the lightgiving stars which appear in heaven. (1.215) For there are, as it seems, two temples belonging to God; one being this world, in which the high priest is the divine word, his own firstborn son. The other is the rational soul, the priest of which is the real true man, the copy of whom, perceptible to the senses, is he who performs his paternal vows and sacrifices, to whom it is enjoined to put on the aforesaid tunic, the representation of the universal heaven, in order that the world may join with the man in offering sacrifice, and that the man may likewise co-operate with the universe. (1.216) He is now therefore shown to have these two things, the speckled and the variegated character. We will now proceed to explain the third and most perfect kind, which is denominated thoroughly white. When this same high priest enters into the innermost parts of the holy temple, he is clothed in the variegated garment, and he also assumes another linen robe, made of the very finest flax. (1.217) And this is an emblem of vigour, and incorruptibility, and the most brilliant light. For such a veil is a thing very difficult to be broken, and it is made of nothing mortal, and when it is properly and carefully purified it has a most clear and brilliant appearance. (1.218) And these injunctions contain this figurative meaning, that of those who in a pure and a guileless spirit serve the living God, there is no one who does not at first depend upon the firmness and obstinacy of his mind, despising all human affairs, which allure men with their specious bait, and injure them, and produce weakness in them. In the next place, he aims at immortality, laughing at the blind inventions with which mortals delude themselves. And last of all, he shines with the unclouded and most brilliant light of truth, no longer desiring any of the things which belong to false opinion, which prefer darkness rather than light.

XXXVIII

XXXVIII. (1.219) The great high priest of the confession, then, may have now been sufficiently described by us, being stamped with the impressions above-mentioned, the white, the variegated, and the ring-straked and speckled. But he who is desirous of the administration of human affairs, by name Joseph, does not, as it appears, claim for himself any of the extreme characteristics, but only that variegated one which is in the middle between the others. (1.220) For we read that Joseph had a "coat of many Colours," [1063] not being sprinkled with the sacred purifications, by means of which he might have known that he himself was only a compound of dust and water, and not being able to touch that thoroughly white and most shining raiment, virtue. But being clothed in the much-variegated web of political affairs, with which the smallest possible portion of truth is mixed up; and also many and large portions of plausible, probable, and likely falsehoods, from which all the sophists of Egypt, and all the augurs, and ventriloquists, and sorcerers spring; men skilful in juggling, and in incantations, and in tricks of all kinds, from whose treacherous arts it is very difficult to escape. (1.221) And it is on this account that Moses very naturally represents this robe as stained with blood; since the whole life of the man who is mixed up in political affairs is tainted, warring on others and being warred against, and being aimed at, and attacked, and shot at by all the unexpected chances which befall him. (1.222) Examine now the man who has great influence with the people, on whom the affairs of the city depend. Do not be alarmed at those who look with admiration upon him; and you will find many diseases lurking within him, and you will see that he is entangled in many disasters, and that fortune is dragging him violently in different directions, though he bends his neck the other way, and resists, although invisibly, and in fact that fortune is seeking to overthrow and destroy him; or else the people themselves are impatient at his supremacy, or he is exposed to the attacks of some more powerful rival. (1.223) And envy is a formidable enemy, and one hard to be shaken off, clinging also to everything that is called good fortune, and it is not easy to escape from it.

XXXIX

XXXIX. (1.224) What reason is there then for our congratulating ourselves on the administration of political affairs as if we were clothed in a garment of many colours, deceived by its external splendour, and not perceiving its ugliness, which is kept out of sight, and hidden, and full of treachery and guile? (1.225) Let us then put off this flowery robe, and put on that sacred one woven with the embroideries of virtue; for thus we shall escape the snares which want of skill, and ignorance, and want of knowledge, and education lay for us, of which Laban is the companion. (1.226) For when the sacred word has purified us with the sprinklings prepared beforehand for purification, and when it has adorned us with the select reasonings of true philosophy, and, having led us to that man who has stood the test, has made us genuine, and conspicuous, and shining, it blames the treacherous disposition which seeks to raise itself up to invalidate what is said. (1.227) For the scripture says: "I have seen what Laban does unto Thee," [1064] namely, things contrary to the benefits which I conferred on you, things impure, wicked, and altogether suited to darkness. But it is not right for the man who anchors on the hope of the alliance of God to crouch and tremble, to whom God says, "I am the God who was seen by thee in the place of God." (1.228) A very glorious boast for the soul, that God should think fit to appear to and to converse with it. And do not pass by what is here said, but examine it accurately, and see whether there are really two Gods. For it is said: "I am the God who was seen by thee;" not in my place, but in the place of God, as if he meant of some other God. (1.229) What then ought we to say? There is one true God only: but they who are called Gods, by an abuse of language, are numerous; on which account the holy scripture on the present occasion indicates that it is the true God that is meant by the use of the article, the expression being, "I am the God (ho Theos);" but when the word is used incorrectly, it is put without the article, the expression being, "He who was seen by thee in the place," not of the God (tou Theou), but simply "of God" (Theou); (1.230) and what he here calls God is his most ancient word, not having any superstitious regard to the position of the names, but only proposing one end to himself, namely, to give a true account of the matter; for in other passages the sacred historian, when he considered whether there really was any name belonging to the living God, showed that he knew that there was none properly belonging to him; but that whatever appellation any one may give him, will be an abuse of terms; for the living God is not of a nature to be described, but only to be.

XL

XL. (1.231) And a proof of this may be found in the oracular answer given by God to the person who asked what name he had, "I am that I Am,"[1065] that the questioner might know the existence of those things which it was not possible for man to conceive not being connected with God. (1.232) Accordingly, to the incorporeal souls which are occupied in his service, it is natural for him to appear as he is, conversing with them as a friend with his friends; but to those souls which are still in the body he must appear in the resemblance of the angels, though without changing his nature (for he is unchangeable), but merely implanting in those who behold him an idea of his having another form, so that they fancy that it is his image, not an imitation of him, but the very archetypal appearance itself. (1.233) There is then an old story much celebrated, that the Divinity, assuming the resemblance of men of different countries, goes round the different cities of men, searching out the deeds of iniquity and lawlessness; and perhaps, though the fable is not true, it is a suitable and profitable one. (1.234) But the scripture, which at all times advances its conceptions with respect to the Deity, in a more reverential and holy tone, and which likewise desires to instruct the life of the foolish, has spoken of God under the likeness of a man, though not of any particular man; (1.235) attributing to him, with this view, the possession of a face, and hands, and feet, and of a mouth and voice, and also anger and passion, and moreover, defensive weapons, and goings in and goings out, and motions upwards and downwards, and in every direction, not indeed using all these expressions with strict truth, but having regard to the advantage of those who are to learn from it; (1.236) for the writers knew that some men are very dull in their natures, so as to be utterly unable to form any conception whatever of God apart from a body, whom it will be impossible to admonish if they were to speak in any other style than the existing one, of representing God as coming and departing like a man; and as descending and ascending, and as using his voice, and as being angry with sinners, and being implacable in his anger; and speaking too of his darts and swords, and whatever other instruments are suitable to be employed against the wicked, as being all previously ready. (1.237) For we must be content if such men can be brought to a proper state, by the fear which is suspended over them by such descriptions; and one many almost say that these are the only two paths taken, in the whole history of the law; one leading to plain truth, owing to which we have such assertions as, "God is not as a Man;"[1066] the other, that which has regard to the opinions of foolish men, in reference to whom it is said, "The Lord God shall instruct you, like as if a man instructs his Son."[1067]

XLI

XLI. (1.238) Why then do we any longer wonder, if God at times assumes the likeness of the angels, as he sometimes assumes even that of men, for the sake of assisting those who address their entreaties to him? so that when he says, "I am the God who was seen by thee in the place of God;"[1068] we must understand this, that he on that occasion took the place of an angel, as far as appearance went, without changing his own real nature, for the advantage of him who was not, as yet, able to bear the sight of the true God; (1.239) for as those who are not able to look upon the sun itself, look upon the reflected rays of the sun as the sun itself, and upon the halo around the moon as if it were the moon itself; so also do those who are unable to bear the sight of God, look upon his image, his angel word, as himself. (1.240) Do you not see that encyclical instruction, that is, Hagar, says to the angel, "Art thou God who seest Me?"[1069] for she was not capable of beholding the most ancient cause, inasmuch as she was by birth a native of Egypt. But now the mind begins to be improved, so as to be able to contemplate the governor of all the powers; (1.241) on which account he says himself, "I am the Lord God,"[1070] I whose image you formerly beheld instead of me, and whose pillar you set up, engraving on it a most sacred inscription; and the inscription indicated that I stood alone, and that I established the nature of all things, bringing disorder and irregularity into order and regularity, and supporting the universe firmly, so that it might rest on a firm and solid foundation, my own ministering word.

XLII

XLII. (1.242) For the pillar is the symbol of three things; of standing, of dedication, and of an inscription: now the standing and the inscription have been described, but the dedication it is necessary should be explained to all men. (1.243) For heaven and the world are an offering dedicated to God who made them; and all the cosmopolitan and God-loving souls, which dedicate and consecrate themselves to him, not allowing any mortal thing to drag them in an opposite direction, are never weary of hallowing their own life, and adorning it with every kind of beauty as a meet offering for him. (1.244) And he is a foolish man who does not set up a pillar to God, but who erects one to himself instead, attributing stability to the things of creation, which is tossed about in every direction, and thinking those things worthy of inscriptions and panegyrics, which are in reality full of matter for blame and accusation, and which as such had better never have been mentioned in an inscription at all, or if they had, had better have been speedily erased again. (1.245) On which account the holy scripture says distinctly, "Thou shalt not set up a pillar to Thyself;"[1071] for in truth there is nothing belonging to man that is stable, no, not though some persons persist even so obstinately in affirming it. (1.246) But they not only think that they stand firmly, but also that they are worthy of honours and inscriptions, forgetting him who is alone worthy of honour, and who is alone firmly fixed; for while they are turning aside and wandering away from the path which leads to virtue, the outward sense leads them still more astray, that is to say, the woman who is akin to them, she also compels them to run ashore; (1.247) therefore, the whole soul, like a ship,[1072] being shut in all around, is offered up as a pillar; for the sacred scriptures tell us that Lot's wife having turned back to look behind her, became a pillar of salt, (1.248) and this is said very naturally and fitly; for if any one does not look forwards at those things which are worthy of being seen and heard (and these things are the virtues and the actions done in accordance with virtue), but looks backwards at the things which are behind him, at deaf glory, and blind riches, and senseless vigour of body, and an empty elegance of mind, pursuing these objects only, and such as are akin to them, he will lie as a lifeless pillar melting away by itself; for salt is not a thing to preserve his firmness.

XLIII

XLIII. (1.249) Very admirably therefore does the practiser of virtue, having learnt by continued study that creation is a thing in its own nature moveable, but that the uncreated God is unchangeable and immoveable, erect a pillar to God, and anoint it after he has erected it; for God says, "Thou hast anointed my Pillar."[1073] (1.250) But do not fancy that that stone was anointed with oil, but understand rather that that opinion, that God is the only being who stands firmly, was thoroughly hardened by exercise, and established in the soul by the science of wrestling, not that science by which bodies are made fat, but that by which the mind acquires strength and irresistible vigour; (1.251) for the man who is eager in the pursuit of good studies and virtuous objects is fond of labours, and fond of exercises; so that very naturally, having worked out the science of training which is the sister of the art of medicine, he anoints and brings to perfection all the reasonings of virtue and piety, and dedicates them, as a most beautiful and lasting offering to God. (1.252) For this reason, after mentioning the dedication of the pillar, God adds that, "Thou vowedst a vow to me." Now a vow also is, to speak properly, a dedication, since he who makes a vow is said to offer up, as a gift to God, not only his own possessions, but himself likewise, who is the owner of them; (1.253) for says the scripture, "the man is holy who nourishes the locks of the hair of his head; who has vowed a vow." But if he is holy he is undoubtedly an offering to God, no longer meddling with anything unholy or profane; (1.254) and there is an evidence in favour of my argument, in the conduct of the prophetess, and mother of a prophet, Hannah, whose name being translated, signifies grace; for she says that she gives her son, "Samuel, as a gift to the Holy One,"[1074] not dedicating him more as a human being, than as a disposition full of inspiration, and possessed by a divinely sent impulse; and the name Samuel being interpreted means, "appointed to God." (1.255) Why then, O my soul, do you any longer waste yourself in vain speculations and labours? and why do you not go as a pupil to the practiser of virtue, taking up arms against the passions, and against vain opinion, to learn from him the way to wrestle with them? For as soon as you have learnt this art, you will become the leader of a flock, not of one which is destitute of marks, and of reason, and of docility, but of one which is well approved, and rational, and beautiful, (1.256) of which, if you become the leader, you will pity the miserable race of mankind, and will not cease to reverence the Deity; and you will never be weary of blessing God, and moreover you will engrave hymns suited to your sacred subject upon pillars, that you may not only speak fluently, but may also sing musically the virtues of the living God; for by these means you will be able to return to your father's house, being delivered from a long a profitless wandering in and foreign land.

Footnotes:

1011. Yonge's title, A Treatise on the Doctrine that Dreams Are Sent from God.
1012. Gen 28:12.
1013. Gen 26:33.
1014. Gen 2:7.
1015. Exod 24:18.
1016. Gen 29:35.
1017. Gen 26:32.
1018. Gen 27:43.
1019. Gen 12:4.
1020. Gen 17:32.
1021. Gen 28:11.
1022. Exod 24:10.
1023. Gen 22:4.
1024. Gen 18:33.
1025. Exod 19:17.
1026. Gen 28:11.
1027. Gen 9:6.
1028. Ps 26:1.
1029. Gen 1:4.
1030. Gen 1:4.
1031. Gen 11:4.
1032. Gen 41:45.
1033. Gen 32:31.
1034. Lev 4:31.
1035. Lev 22:6.
1036. Num 25:1.
1037. Num 25:4.
1038. Exod 22:26.
1039. the Greek word is loÂpodyteoÌ. A loÌpodyteÌs was one who frequented the baths for the purpose of stealing the clothes of the bathers.
1040. Exod 10:21.
1041. Gen 28:11.
1042. Exod 10:23.
1043. Gen 28:11.
1044. the marginal note in our Bible translates Israel, "a prince of God."
1045. Gen 32:25; where, however, the expression of the Bible is "the hollow of Jacob's thigh was out of joint."
1046. Gen 28:12.
1047. Exod 20:19.
1048. Lev 26:12.
1049. Gen 28:13.
1050. Deut 10:9.
1051. Gen 28:21.
1052. Gen 46:1.
1053. Gen 28:14.
1054. the text is very corrupt here. I have followed Mangey's reading and translation.
1055. Gen 28:15.
1056. Gen 28:16.
1057. there is an hiatus here, which cannot be filled up satisfactorily. The whole of the rest of the chapter is pronounced by Mangey to be obscure and corrupt, and almost unintelligible.
1058. Gen 31:11.
1059. Deut 27:9.
1060. Exod 3:4.
1061. Gen 22:1.
1062. Gen 31:10.
1063. Gen 37:3.
1064. Gen 31:12.
1065. Exod 3:14.
1066. Num 23:19.
1067. Deut 1:31.
1068. Gen 31:13.

1069. Gen 16:13.
1070. Gen 31:13.
1071. Deut 16:22.
1072. Mangey thinks that this passage is corrupt, and proposes to alter naus into apnous, "dead," but it seems unnecessary.
1073. Gen 31:13.
1074. 1Sam 1:28.

BOOK 2

I

I. (2.1) In describing the third species of dreams which are sent from God, we very naturally call on Moses as an ally, in order that as he learnt, having previously been ignorant, so he may instruct us who are also ignorant, concerning these signs, illustrating each separate one of them. Now this third species of dreams exists, whenever in sleep the mind being set in motion by itself, and agitating itself, is filled with frenzy and inspiration, so as to predict future events by a certain prophetic power. (2.2) For the first kind of dreams which we mentioned, was that which proceeded from God as the author of its motion, and, as some invisible manner prompted us what was indistinct to us, but well known to himself. The second kind was when our own intellect was set in motion simultaneously with the soul of the universe, and became filled with divine madness, by means of which it is allowed to prognosticate events which are about to happen; (2.3) and for this reason the interpreter of the sacred will very plainly and clearly speaks of dreams, indicating by this expression the visions which appear according to the first species, as if God, by means of dreams, gave suggestions which were equivalent to distinct and precise oracles. Of the visions according to the second species he speaks neither very clearly nor very obscurely; an instance of which is afforded by the vision which was exhibited of the ladder reaching up to heaven; for this version was an enigmatical one; nevertheless, the meaning was not hidden from those who were able to see with any great acuteness. (2.4) But these visions which are afforded according to the third species of dreams, being less clear than the two former kinds by reason of their having an enigmatical meaning deeply seated and fully coloured, require the science of an interpreter of dreams. At all events all the dreams of this class, which are recorded by the lawgiver, are interpreted by men who are skilled in the aforesaid art. (2.5) Whose dreams then am I here alluding to? Surely every one must see to those of Joseph, and of Pharaoh king of Egypt, and to those which the chief baker and chief butler saw themselves; (2.6) and it may be well at all times to begin our instruction with the first instances. Now the first dreams are those which Joseph beheld, receiving two visions from the two parts of the world, heaven and earth. From the earth the dream about the harvest; and that is as follows, "I thought that we were all binding sheaves in the middle of the field; and my sheaf stood Up." [1075] (2.7) And the other relates to the circle of the zodiac, and is, "They worshipped me as the sun and the moon and the eleven stars." And the interpretation of the former one, which was delivered with great violence of reproof, is as follows, "Shall you be a king and reign over us? or shall you be a lord and lord it over us?" The interpretation of the second is again full of just indignation, "Shall I, and thy mother, and thy brethren come and fall down upon the ground and worship thee?"

II

II. (2.8) Let these things be laid down first by way of foundation; and on this foundation let us raise up the rest of the building, following the rules of that wise architect, allegory, and accurately investigating each particular of the dreams; but first we must mention what it is requisite should be attended to before the dreams. Some persons have extended the nature of good over many things, and others have attributed it to the most excellent Being alone; some again have mixed it with other things, while others have spoken of it as unalloyed. (2.9) Those then who have called only what is honourable good, have preserved this nature free from alloy, and have attributed it only to what is most excellent, namely to the reason that is in us; but those who have mixed it have combined it with three things, the soul, the body, and external circumstances. And they who act thus are persons of a somewhat effeminate and luxurious way of life, being bred up the greater part of their time, from their earliest infancy, in the women's apartments and among the effeminate race which is found in the women's apartments. But those who argue differently are men inclined to a harder regimen, being bred up from their boyhood among men, and being themselves men in their minds, embracing what is right in preference to what is pleasant, and devoting themselves to nourishment fit for athletes for the sake of strength and vigour, not of pleasure. (2.10) Moses moreover represents two persons as leaders of these two companies. The leader of the noble and good company is the self-taught and self-instructed Isaac; for he records that he was weaned, not choosing to avail himself at all of tender, and milk-like, and childish, and infantine food, but only of such as was vigorous and perfect, inasmuch as he was formed by nature, from his very infancy, for acts of virtue, and was always in the prime and vigour of youth and energy. But the leader of the company, which yields and which is inclined to softer measures, is Joseph; (2.11) for he does not indeed neglect the virtues of the soul, but he likewise shows anxiety about the stability and permanence of the body, and also desires an abundance of worldly treasures; and it is in strict accordance with natural truth, that he is represented as drawn in different directions, since he proposes to himself many different objects in life; and being attracted by each of them, he is kept in a state of commotion and agitation, without being able to stand firm. (2.12) And his case is not like that of cities, which having made a truce enjoy peace, and yet after a time are again attacked, so as to gain the victory and to be defeated alternately; for at times a great influx of riches and glory coming upon them, subdues all their cares for the body and the soul, but afterwards, being repelled by both these things, they are conquered by the adversary; (2.13) and in the same manner all the pleasures of the body coming upon the soul in a compact array overwhelm and efface all the objects of the intellect one after the other; and then, after a short time, wisdom, changing its course and blowing in the opposite direction with a fresh and violent breeze, causes the stream of the pleasures to slacken, and altogether moderates all the eagerness, and impetuosity, and rivalry of the external senses. (2.14) Such a circle then of never-ending war revolves around the soul, subject as it is to so many changes; for when one enemy has been destroyed, then immediately there springs up another more powerful, after the fashion of the many-headed hydra; for they say, that in the case of this monster, instead of the head which was cut off another sprung up, by which statement they mean to intimate the multiform, and prolific, and almost invincible character of undying wickedness. (2.15) Do not, therefore, answer [...] Joseph [...] [1076] but know that he is the image of multiform and mixed knowledge. For there appears in him a rational species of continence, which is of the masculine kind, being fashioned in accordance with his father Jacob; (2.16) and also that kind which is devoid of reason is likewise visible, that of the outward sense I mean, being made in the likeness of his maternal race, according to Rachel. There appears in him also the seed of bodily pleasures, which his association with the chief butlers, and chief bakers, and chief cooks has stamped upon him. There is, also visible the seed of vain opinion, on which he mounts as on a chariot by reason of his levity, being puffed up, and elated, and raising himself to a height to the destruction of equality.

III

III. (2.17) Now the character of Joseph is sketched out by the foregoing outlines. But each of his dreams must be investigated with accuracy; and first of all we must examine the one about the sheaves. "I thought," says he, "that we were all binding sheaves." The expression, "I thought," is clearly that of a person who is not certain, but who is hesitating and supposing with some amount of indistinctness, not of one who sees positively and clearly; (2.18) for it is very natural for persons just awakening out of a deep sleep, and still dozing at it were, to say, "I thought;" but not so for people who are thoroughly awake, and who can see distinctly. (2.19) And the practiser of virtue, Jacob, does not say, "I thought," but his language is, "Behold, a ladder firmly set, the head of which reached up to Heaven." [1077] And again he says, when "the sheep conceived I saw them with my eyes in my sleep, and behold the he-goats and the rams leapt upon the ewes and upon the she-goats, white, and variegated, and ring-straked, and Speckled." [1078] (2.20) For it happens of necessity that the sleeping conceptions also of those who think what is honourable and eligible for its own sake and more distinct and more pure, just as their waking actions are also more deserving of approbation.

IV

IV. (2.21) But when I hear Jacob relating his dream I marvel at his having fancied that he was binding up the sheaves, and not reaping the corn; for the one is the task of the lower classes and of servants, but the other is the occupation of the employers, and of men more skilled in agriculture. (2.22) For to be able to distinguish what is necessary from what is mischievous, and what is nutritious from what is not so, and what is genuine from what is spurious, and useful fruit from a worthless root, not only in reference to those things which the land bears, but also in those which the intellect bears, is the work of most perfect virtue. (2.23) Accordingly the holy scripture represents those who see, that is the sons of Israel, as reaping, and what is a most extraordinary thing, as reaping not barley or wheat, but the harvest itself; accordingly the language of Moses is, "When you reap your harvest, you shall not wholly reap the corners of your Harvest." [1079] (2.24) For he means here that the virtuous man is not merely the judge of things which differ from one another, and that he does not only distinguish the things from which some produce is derived from the produce itself; but that he is able also to distinguish while reaping the harvest, to remove this opinion of his ability to distinguish, and to eradicate a man's own opinion of himself; because he is firmly persuaded, and believes Moses when he affirms that "judgment belongs to God Alone,"[1080] with whom are the comparisons and distinctions between all things; to whom it is well for a man to confess that he is inferior, a confession more glorious than the most renowned victory. (2.25) Now the reaping a harvest is like cutting a second time what has been cut already; which when some persons fond of novelty applied themselves to they found a circumcision of circumcision, and a purification of purification;[1081] that is to say, they found that the purification of the soul was itself purified, attributing the power of making bright to God, and never fancying that they themselves were competent, without the assistance of the divine wisdom, to wash and cleanse a life which is full of stains. (2.26) Akin to this is the double cave, which is a symbol of the twofold and excellent recollections (the one existing in reference to the creature, and the other to the Creator), in which the virtuous man is bred up, contemplating the things which are in the world, and being also fond of inquiring about the father who made them; (2.27) and it is owing to these twofold recollections, in my opinion, that the double symphony in music, that of the double diapason, was invented. (2.28) For it was necessary that the work and the creator should be made happy in two most perfect melodies, and not both in the same one. For since the excellencies which were to be celebrated by them differed from one another, it followed of necessity that the melodies and symphonies should likewise differ from one another. The combined symphony being assigned to the world, which is a compound creation, composed of many different parts; and the disjoined melody being appropriated to him who, as to his essence, is separated from every creature, namely, to God. (2.29) Moreover, the interpreter of the sacred will again enunciates an opinion friendly to virtue, saying that it is not proper "to thoroughly reap every corner of the harvest field;" remembering the original proposition, according to which he agreed that "the tribute belonged to the Lord,"[1082] to whom the authority and the conformation of these things also belong; (2.30) but he who is uninitiated in reaping boasts, so far as to say, "I thought that I was with the others binding up the sheaves which I had Reaped."[1083] And he does not consider that this is the occupation of servants and unskilled hands, as I have said a little while ago. (2.31) But this word sheaves is an allegorical expression by which affairs are really meant, such as each man takes in hand for the support of his house, in which he hopes to live and dwell for ever.

V

V. (2.32) There are, therefore, an infinite number of differences between sheaves, that is to say, between such affairs as support a house. There are also a countless host of differences between those who gather and take up the sheaves in their hand, so that it is impossible to mention or even to imagine them all. Still it is not out of place to describe a few of them by way of example, which he too mentioned, when he was recounting his dream. (2.33) For he says to his brethren, "I thought that we were binding up sheaves." Now, of brethren he has ten, who are sons of the same father as himself, and one who is by the same mother; and the name of each individual among them is an emblem of some most necessary thing. Reuben is an emblem of natural acuteness, for he is called "the son who sees," being in so far as he is a son not perfect, but in so far as he is endowed with the faculty of sight and sees acutely, he is naturally well qualified. (2.34) Simeon is an emblem of learning, for his name being interpreted means, "listening." Levi is a symbol of virtuous energies and actions, and of holy ministrations. Judas is an emblem of songs and hymns addressed to God. Issachar, of wages which are given for good work; but perhaps the works themselves are their own perfect reward. Zabulon is a symbol of light, since his name means the departure of night; and when the night departs and leaves us, then of necessity light arises. (2.35) Dan is a symbol of the distinction between, and division of, different things. Gad is an emblem of the invasion of pirates, and of a counter attack made upon them. Asser is a symbol of natural wealth, for his name being interpreted, signifies "a calling blessed," since wealth is accounted a blessed possession. (2.36) Napthali is a symbol of peace, for all things are open and extended by peace, as on the other hand they are closed by war; and his name being interpreted means, "widening," or "that which is opened." Benjamin is an emblem of young and old times; for being interpreted his name means "the son of days," and both young time and old time are measured by days and nights. (2.37) Accordingly, every one of them takes up in his hand what belongs to himself; and having taken it up, binds all the parts together; the man well endowed by nature taking up the parts of dexterity, and perseverance, and memory, of which good natural endowments consist; the man who has learnt well takes up the parts of listening, tranquillity, and attention; the man willing to endeavour takes up courage and a happy confidence which does not shrink from danger; (2.38) the man inclined to gratitude takes up praises, panegyrics, hymns, and blessings, both in speaking and in singing; the man who is eager for wages takes up unhesitating industry, most enduring gratitude, and care, armed with a promptitude which is not to be despised; (2.39) he who pursues light rather than darkness takes up wakefulness and acuteness of sight; the man who is an admirer of the division of and distinction between things takes up wellsharpened reasons so as not to be deceived by things similar to one another as if they were identical, impartiality so as not to be led away by favour, and incorruptibility; (2.40) he who, in something of a piratical fashion, lays ambuscades against those who counterplot against him, takes up deceit, cajolery, trickery, sophistry, pretence, and hypocrisy, which being in their own nature blamable, are nevertheless praised when employed against the enemy; he who studies to be rich in the riches of nature takes up temperance and frugality; he who loves peace takes up obedience to law, a good reputation, freedom from pride, and equality.

VI

VI. (2.41) It is of these things, then, that the sheaves of his brethren by the same father are composed and bound up; but the sheaf of his uterine brother is composed of days and of time, which are the causes of nothing, as if they were the causes of all things. (2.42) But the dreamer and interpreter of dreams himself, for he united both characters, makes a sheaf of empty opinion as of the greatest and most brilliant of possessions and the most useful to life. For which reason it is originally by his dreams, which are things dear to night, that he is made known to the king of the bodily country, and not by any performance of conspicuous actions, which require day for their exhibition. (2.43) After that, he is appointed overseer or governor of all Egypt, and is honoured with the second rank in the kingdom, and made inferior in honour only to the king. All which things are in the eye of wisdom, if that were the judge, more inglorious and more ridiculous than even defeat and dishonour. (2.44) After that he puts on a golden necklace, a most illustrious halter, the circlet and wheel of interminable necessity, not the consequence and regular order of things in life, nor the connection of the affairs of nature as Thamar was; for her ornament was not a necklace, but an armlet. Moreover, he assumes a ring, a royal gift which is no gift, a pledge devoid of good faith, the very contrary gift to that which was given to the same Thamar by Judah the son of the seeing king, Israel; (2.45) for God gives to the soul a seal, a very beautiful gift, to show that he has invested with shape the essence of all things which was previously devoid of shape, and has stamped with a particular character that which previously had no character, and has endowed with form that which had previously no distinctive form, and having perfected the entire world, he has impressed upon it an image and appearance, namely, his own word. (2.46) But Joseph also mounts the second chariot, being puffed up with elation of mind and vain arrogance. And he is regulator of the provisions, laying up and preserving the treasures for the body, and providing it with food from all quarters: and this is a very formidable fortification against the soul. (2.47) Moreover, his deliberate choice of life, and the life which he admires, is testified to in no slight degree by his name; for Joseph, being interpreted, means "addition;" and vain opinion is always adding what is spurious to what is genuine, and what is the property of others to what is one's own, and what is false to what is true, and what is superfluous to what is adequate, and luxury to what is sufficient to support existence, and pride to life.

VII

VII. (2.48) Consider now what it is which I am here desirous to prove. We are nourished by meat and drink, even though the meat be the most ordinary corn, and the drink plain water from the stream. Moreover, besides this, vain opinion has added to it an infinite number of varieties of cakes, and cheese-cakes, and sweetmeats, and costly and various mixtures of an indescribable multitude of wines, for the enjoyment of pleasure rather than for a participation in necessary food properly prepared. (2.49) Again, the necessary seasonings for eating, are leeks, [1084] and vegetables, and many fruits of trees, and cheese, and other things of that sort; and if you wish to include carnivorous men, we must, besides, add fish and meat to these items. (2.50) Would it not, then, have been sufficient to broil these things upon the coals, or to roast them at the fire, and then eat them at once, after the fashion of those true heroes of old times? But the epicure is eager not only for such things as these, but he takes vain opinion for his ally, and excites the gluttonous passions which are within him, and seeks out and hunts all about for confectioners and pastrycooks of high reputation in their art. (2.51) And they, bringing forward the different baits for his miserable stomach, which have been invented after long consideration, and preparing all kinds of peculiar flavours, and arranging them in due order, tickle, and allure, and subdue the tongue. Then, immediately they circumvent that foundation of the outward senses, the taste, by means of which the banquet-hunter in a very short time is rendered a slave instead of a free man. (2.52) For who is there who does not know that clothes were originally made as a defence against the injuries which might arise to the body from cold and heat? as the poets say somewhere:--

"Taming the wind in the winter."

(2.53) Who, therefore, thinks of costly purple garments? Who cares about transparent and thin summer robes? Who wishes for a garment delicate as a spider's web? Who is eager to have embroidered for him apparel flowered over with dyes and brocaded figures, by those who are skilful in sewing and weaving cunning embroidery, and are superior in their handwork to the imitative skill of the painter? Who, I say? Who, but vain opinion.

VIII

VIII. (2.54) And, indeed, it is for the same reasons that we had need of houses, requiring them also for protection against the attacks of wild beasts, or of men more savage in their nature than even wild beasts. Why is it, then, that we adorn the pavements and floors with costly stones? And why do we travel over Asia, and Africa, and all Europe, and the islands, searching for pillars and capitals, and architraves, and selecting them with reference to their superior beauty? (2.55) And why are we anxious for, and why do we vie with one another in specimens of Doric, and Ionic, and Corinthian sculpture, and in all the refinements which luxurious men have devised in addition to the existing customs, adorning the capitals of their pillars? And why do we furnish our chambers for men and for women with golden ornaments? Is it not all from our being influenced by vain opinion? (2.56) And yet, for sound sleep, the mere ground was sufficient (since, even to the present day, the accounts tell us that the gymnosophists, among the Indians, sleep on the ground in accordance with their ancient customs); and if it were not, at all events a couch made of carefully chosen stones or plain pieces of wood, would be a sufficient bed; (2.57) but now the poles of our ladders are ornamented with ivory feet, and workmen inlay our beds with costly mother-of-pearl and variegated tortoise-shell, at great expense of labour, and money, and time: and some beds are even made of solid silver or solid gold, and inlaid with precious stones, with all kinds of flowery work, and embossed golden ornaments strewed about them, as if for mere display and magnificence, and not for daily use. The contriver of all which is again the same vain opinion. (2.58) Again: why need we seek for more in the way of ointment than the juice pressed out of the fruit of the olive? For that softens the limbs, and relieves the labour of the body, and produces a good condition of the flesh; and if anything has got relaxed or flabby, it binds it again, and makes it firm and solid, and it fills us with vigour and strength of muscle, no less than any other unguent. (2.59) But the pleasant unguents of vain opinion, are set up in opposition to those that are merely useful, on which the perfumers work, and to which vast regions contribute, such as Syria, Babylon, the Indians, and the Scythians; in which nations the origins of all perfumes are found.

IX

IX. (2.60) Again, with respect to drinking; what more could man really have need of than the cup of nature wrought with the perfection of art? Now such a cup our own hands supply, which, if any one brings together and forms into a hollow, applying them closely to his mouth, while another pours in the liquid to be drank, he gets not only a remedy for his thirst, but also a most indescribable pleasure. (2.61) Still, if one were absolutely in need of something else, would not the ivy cup of the agricultural labourer be sufficient? and why should it be requisite to have recourse to the arts of other eminent artists? And what can be the use of providing a countless multitude of gold and silver goblets, it if be not for the gratification of boastful and vain-glorious arrogance, and of vain opinion raising itself to an undue height? (2.62) Again, when men wear crowns, they are not content with fragrant garlands of laurel, or ivy, or violets, or lilies, or roses, or of any three whatever, or of any flower, neglecting all the gifts of God, which he bestows upon us as the various seasons of the year, but they put golden crowns on their heads, which are a very grievous weight, wearing them in the middle of the crowded marketplace without any shame. And what can we think of such men, but that they are slaves of vain opinion, in spite of their asserting themselves not only to be free, but even to be rulers over many other persons? (2.63) The day would fail me if I were to go through all the varieties of human life; and yet, why need I dwell on the subject with prolixity? For who is there who has not heard, or who has not seen, such men as these? Who is there who does not associate with, and who is not familiar with them? So that the sacred scripture has very appropriately named "addition" the enemy of simplicity and the companion of pride; (2.64) for as superfluous shoots do grow on trees, which are a great injury to the genuine useful branches, and which the cultivators destroy and cut out from a prudent foreknowledge of what is necessary: so likewise the life of falsehood and arrogance often grows up by the side of the true life devoid of pride, of which, to this day, no cultivator has been found who has been able to cut away the injurious superfluous growth by the roots. (2.65) Therefore the practisers of wisdom, knowing this in the first instance by the outward sense, and secondly, pursuing it by the mind, cry out loudly and say, "A wicked beast has seized and devoured Joseph." [1085] (2.66) But does not that most ferocious beast, the various pride which springs up in the life of men living in irregularity and confusion, whose chief workmen are covetousness and unscrupulous cunning, devour every one who comes within his reach? Therefore grief will be added to them, even while they are alive, as though they were dead, since they have a life worthy of lamentation and mourning, since Jacob mourns for Joseph, even while he is alive.

(2.67) But Moses will not allow the sacred reasonings about Nadab to be bewailed;[1086] for they have not been carried off by a savage beast, but have been taken up by unextinguishable violence and imperishable light; because, having discarded all fear and hesitation, they had duly consecrated the fervent and fiery zeal, consuming the flesh, and very easily and vehemently excited towards piety, which is unconnected with creation, but is akin to God, not going up to the altar by the regular steps, for that was forbidden by law, but proceeding rapidly onwards with a favourable gale, and being conducted up even to the threshold of heaven, becoming dissolved into ethereal beams like a whole burnt-offering.

X

X. (2.68) Therefore, O thou soul, that art obedient to thy teacher! thou must cut off thine hand and thy power when it begins to take hold of the parts of generation; that is to say, of things created, or of human pursuits; (2.69) for very often ... to cut off the hand which has laid hold of the privy Parts,"[1087] in the first place, because it has gladly received the pleasure which it ought rather to hate; and, secondly, because it has thought that the faculty of propagating seed was in our own power, and also, because it has attributed to the creature that power which belongs to the Creator. (2.70) Dost thou not see that the earthly mass, Adam, when it lays its hands upon the two trees, dies, because it has preferred the number two to the unit, and because it has admired the creature in preference to the Creator? But do thou go forth beyond the reach of the smoke and the tempest, and flee from the ridiculous pursuits of mortal life as a fearful whirlpool, and do not, as the proverb has it, touch them even with the tip of thy finger. (2.71) And when thou hast girded thyself up for the sacred ministrations, having made broad thy whole hand and thy whole power, then take a firm hold of the speculations of instruction and wisdom; for the command is of this kind, "If a soul brings a gift or a sacrifice, the gift shall be of fine wheaten Flour."[1088] After that the lawgiver adds: "And when he has taken a full handful of the fine wheaten flour, with the oil, and with all the frankincense, he places the memorial on the altar of sacrifice." (2.72) Is not this a very beautiful and appropriate expression of Moses, to call that soul incorporeal which is about to offer sacrifice, but not to call the double mass which consists of mortality and immortality by any such name? For that which vows the vow--that which is full of gratitude--that which offers such sacrifices as are truly without spot, is one thing only, namely, the soul. (2.73) What then is the offering of the incorporeal soul? What is the fine wheaten flour, a symbol of the mind purified by the suggestions of instruction, which is able to render the friend of education free from all disease, and life free from all reproach? (2.74) From which the priest taking a handful within his whole hand, that is to say, with the whole grasp of his mind, is commanded to offer up the whole soul itself, full of the most unalloyed and pure doctrines, as the most excellent of sacrifices, fat and in good condition, rejoicing in divine light, and redolent of the exhalations which are given forth by justice, and by the other virtues, so as always to enjoy a most fragrant, and delicious, and happy life; for the oil and the frankincense, of which the priest takes a handful with the white meat, contain a figurative assertion of this.

XI

XI. (2.75) It is on this account that Moses set apart an especial festival for the sheaf; however, not for every sheaf, but for that which came from the sacred land. "For when," says he, "you come into the land which I give unto you, and when you reap its harvest, you shall bring sheaves as a first fruit of your harvest to the Priest."[1089] (2.76) And the meaning of this injunction is, when, O mind, you come into the country of virtue, which it is fitting should be offered up to God alone, being a land good for pasture, a land of rich soil, a land which beareth fruit, and when you reap the fruit (either that afforded by the land spontaneously or that which thou hast sown), which has been brought to perfection by the God who gives perfection; carry it not home to thy house; that is to say, do not store it up, and do not attribute to thyself the cause of the crop which has arisen to thee, before thou has offered the first fruits to the Cause of all wealth, and to him who persuaded thee to study the operations which confer riches. (2.77) And it is enjoined that you shall offer the "first fruits of your own harvest;" not of the harvest of the land, in order that we may reap and gather in the harvest for ourselves; dedicating to God all good and nutritious, and beneficial fruits.

XII

XII. (2.78) But the man who is at the same time initiated in dreams and also an interpreter of dreams, is bold to say that his sheaf rose and stood upright; for in real truth, as spirited horses lift their necks high, so all who are companions of vain opinion place themselves above all things, above all cities, and laws, and national customs, and above all the circumstances which affect each individual of them. (2.79) Then proceeding onwards from being demagogues to being leaders of the people, and overthrowing the things which belong to their neighbours, and setting up and establishing on a solid footing what belongs to themselves, that is to say, all such dispositions as are free and by nature impatient of slavery, they attempt to reduce these also under their power; (2.80) on which account the dreamer adds, "And your sheaves turning towards my sheaf made obeisance unto It." [1090] For the lover of modesty marvels at and fears the stiffnecked, and the cautious person fears the self-willed man, and he who reverences holiness fears that which is impious both for himself and for others. (2.81) And is not this reasonable? For inasmuch as the good man is a spectator, not only of human life but also of all the things which exist in the world, he knows how many things are accustomed to be caused by necessity, and chance, and opportunity, and violence, and authority; and what numbers of propositions, and what great instances of prosperity proceeding onwards with rapidity towards heaven, the same causes have shaken and overthrown; (2.82) so that he will of necessity take up caution as a shield, as a protection to prevent his suffering any sudden and unexpected evil; for as I imagine what a wall is to a city, that caution is to an individual. (2.83) Do not these men then talk foolishly, are they not mad, who desire to display their inexperience and freedom of speech to kings and tyrants, at times daring to speak and to do things in opposition to their will? Do they not perceive that they have not only put their necks under the yoke like brute beasts, but that they have also surrendered and betrayed their whole bodies and souls likewise, and their wives and their children, and their parents, and all the rest of the numerous kindred and community of their other relations? And is it not lawful for the charioteer, and also for the passenger, with all freedom to spur, and to urge forward, and to check, and to hold back, according as he desires to arrange things, so as to make them greater or smaller. (2.84) Therefore, being pricked with goads, and flogged, and mutilated, and suffering all the cruelties which can be inflicted in an inhuman and pitiless manner before death, all together, they are led away to execution and put to death.

XIII

XIII. (2.85) These are the rewards of unseemly freedom of speech, not of that which is accounted such by right-thinking judges, but of that license which is full of folly, and insanity of mind, and of incurable distemper. What do you mean? Does anyone, when he sees a storm at its height, and a violent gale opposing him, and a hurricane raging tempestuously, and the sea full of vast waves, when he ought to anchor his ship, does anyone, I say, at such a moment weigh anchor and put to sea? (2.86) What pilot, or what captain of a ship, was ever so drunk and intoxicated, as, while all the dangers which I have just enumerated were threatening him, to be willing to set sail, lest, if his vessel became water-logged by the sea breaking over it from above, it might be swallowed up with all its crew? For, if he had been inclined to meet with a voyage free from danger, it was in his power to wait for calm weather and a smooth and favourable breeze. (2.87) What would one say, suppose anyone were to see a bear or a lion coming on with violence, and, while he might pacify and tame him, were to provoke him and make him savage, in order to give up himself as an unpitied meal and feast to those ravenous monsters? (2.88) Unless indeed anyone will assert that it is of no use to anyone to oppose the asps and serpents of Egypt, and all the other things which ... destructive poison ... inflict inevitable death on those who are once bitten by them; for that men must be content to use incantations, and so to tame those beasts, and by such means to avoid suffering any evil from them. (2.89) Moreover, are there not certain men who are more savage and more treacherous than boars, or serpents, or asps? whose treacherous and malignant disposition it is impossible to escape otherwise than by gentleness and caresses? Therefore the wise Abraham will offer adoration to the sons of Cheth, and their name being interpreted, means "admiring," because the occasion persuades him to do so. (2.90) For he has not come to this action of adoration because he honours person who, by nature, and by hereditary qualities, and by their own habits, are enemies to reason, and who miserably waste the coinage of the soul, namely instruction, corrupting, and adulterating, and clipping it, but because he fears their present power and their scarcely conquerable strength, and is on his guard not to provoke them, he takes refuge in that great and powerful possession and weapon of virtue, that most excellent place of abode for wise souls, the double cave, which he could not occupy while warring and fighting, but only by acting as a champion and servant of reason. (2.91) What? Do not we also, when we are spending our time in the market-place, frequently wonder at the masters, and also at the beasts of burden? But we wonder at these two classes, with different and not the same feelings. For we look upon the masters with honour, and upon the beasts of burden with fear, lest some injury should be done to us by them. (2.92) And when an opportunity offers, it is a good thing to attack our enemies and put down their power; but when we have no such opportunity, it is better to be quiet; but if we wish to find perfect safety as far as they are concerned, it is advantageous to caress them.

XIV

XIV. (2.93) On which account it is even now proper to praise those persons who do not yield to the president of vain opinion but who withstand him and say, "Shall you be a king and rule over Us?" [1091] For they do not see him actually in possession of kingly power, they do not see him as yet kindled like a flame, and shining and blazing in the unlimited fuel, but only smouldering like a spark, dreaming of glory, and not visibly having attained to it; (2.94) for they also suggest favourable hopes to themselves as if they will not be able to be overcome by him; for which reason they say, "Shall you reign over us?" Which is equivalent to saying, Do you expect to be a king over us while we are living, existing, strong, and breathing? Perhaps, indeed, you may make yourself master of such as are weak people, but with respect to us who are strong you will be looked upon us as a subject. (2.95) And, indeed, this is the natural state of the case. For when right reason is powerful in the soul, vain opinion is put down; but when right reason is weak, vain opinion is strong. As long, therefore, as the soul has its own power still safe, and as long as it is not mutilated in any part of it, it may well have confidence to attack and aim its arrows at the pride which resists it, and it may indulge in freedom of speech, saying, "You shall not be a king, you shall not be a lord either over us, or during our lifetime over others; (2.96) but we, with our body-guards and shield-bearers, the offspring of wisdom, will overthrow your attacks and baffle your threats with one single sally of ours. In reference to which circumstances it is said, "They began to hate him because of his dreams and because of his words." (2.97) But are not all the images which pride sets up and worships mere words and dreams, while, on the contrary, those things alone deserve to be called actions and real energies which are referable to correct life and right reason? And the one class are worthy of hatred as being false, and the other class deserve friendship as being full of desirable and lovely truth. (2.98) Let no one, therefore, venture to bring accusations against the virtues of such men, as if they exhibited a specimen of an inhuman and unbrotherly disposition; but let any one who is disposed to do so, learn that it is not a man who is now being judged of, but the disposition which exists in the soul of each individual, which is mad on the subject of glory and arrogant pride; let him embrace these men who have adopted irreconcileable enmity and hatred towards this disposition, and let him never love what is hated by them. (2.99) Knowing thoroughly that such judges are never deceived so as to wander from a sound opinion, but that, having learnt from the beginning to understand who is the true king, namely, the Lord, they indignantly refuse to worship him who deprives God of his honour, and seeks to appropriate it to himself, and who invites his fellow servants to do him service.

XV

XV. (2.100) On which account they say with confidence, "Shall you be a king and reign over us?" Are you ignorant that we are not independent, but that we are under the government of an immortal king, the only God? And why should you be a lord and lord it over us? for are we not under domination, and have we not now, and shall we not have for ever, and ever the same one Lord? in being whose servants we rejoice more than any one else can do in his liberty; for to be the servant of God is the most excellent of all things which are honoured in creation. (2.101) I, therefore, should pray that I myself also might be able to abide firmly in the things which have been decided by these men; overseers of things, not of bodies, and just, and sober all their lives, so as never to be deceived by any of those things which are accustomed to deceive mankind. (2.102) But up to this time I am in a state of intoxication, and I am labouring under much uncertainty, and I have need of a staff and of a guide like a blind man; for if I had a staff to support me, then, perhaps, I might neither stumble nor fall. (2.103) But if any persons who are conscious that they are but inconsiderate and precipitate, pay no attention to and do not care to follow those who have investigated all necessary matters with diligence and circumspection, nor, though they themselves are ignorant of the road, submit to the guidance of those who are acquainted with it, let them know that they have entered a course which is very difficult to travel through, and that they are entangled in it, and will not be able to advance further; (2.104) but I am so bound by treaties to these men, the moment I have a little recovered from my intoxication, that I think the same person both a friend and an enemy. But at present I will drive from me and hate that dreamer no less than they do; for no one in his senses could blame me for this, that the majority of opinions and votes does always prevail; (2.105) but when he changes to a better course of life, and no longer dreams, and no longer worries himself by entangling himself in the vain imaginations of the slaves of vain opinion, and when he no longer dreams about night, and darkness, and the changes of uncertain matters which cannot be guessed at; (2.106) he, then, having awakened from deep sleep, continues awake and receives certainty instead of indistinctness, and truth instead of false conceptions, and day instead of night, and light instead of darkness, and rejects an Egyptian wife, that is to say, the pleasure of the body, when she invites him to come in to her, and to enjoy her conversation, out of an indescribable love of continence and admiration for piety, (2.107) and asserts his right to a share in those kindred and inherited blessings from which he appeared to be alienated, again desiring to recover that portion of virtue which properly belongs to him. For proceeding by small and gradual improvements, as if he were now established on the summit and perfection of his own life, he cries out, what indeed he knows to a certainty from what has happened to him, that he "belongs to God,"[1092] and that he belongs no more to any object of external sense which can affect any creature; (2.108) and then his brethren will come to a permanent reconciliation with him, changing their hatred into friendship, and their malignity into good will. But I who am the follower of these men, for I have learnt to obey them as a servant obeys his master, will never cease to praise him for his change of mind. (2.109) Since Moses, also, that priest of sacred things, preserves his change of mind as what is worthy of love and of being preserved in men's recollection, from being forgotten, by the symbol of the Bones [1093] which he did not think proper to have buried in Egypt for ever, looking upon it as a hard thing, if the soul put forth any beautiful flower to suffer that to wither away, and to be overwhelmed and destroyed by the torrents which the Egyptian river of the passions, namely the body, which is incessantly flowing through all the outward senses, sends forth.

XVI

XVI. (2.110) The vision, therefore, which appeared proceeding from the earth, with reference to the sheaves and the interpretation thereof, has now been sufficiently discussed. It is time now to consider the other vision; and to examine how that is interpreted by the art of the explanation of dreams. (2.111) "He saw then," says the scripture, "a second dream, and he related it to his father, and to his brethren, and he said, I saw that the sun, and the moon, and the eleven stars worshipped me. And his father rebuked him, and said, What is this dream that thou hast dreamed? Shall I, and thy mother, and thy brethren, come forward and advance, and fall down to the earth and worship thee? And his brethren were jealous of him; but his father regarded his Words." [1094] (2.112) The studiers of sublime wisdom now say that the zodiac, the greatest of all circles in heaven, is studded with twelve animals (zoÂdia), from which it has derived its name. And that the sun and the moon are always revolving around it, and go through each of the animals, not indeed with equal rapidity, but in unequal numbers and periods; the one doing so in thirty days, and the other in as near as may be a twelfth part of that time, that is in two days and a half; (2.113) therefore, he who saw this heaven-sent vision, thought that he was being worshipped by eleven stars, ranking himself among them as the twelfth, so as to complete the whole circle of the zodiac. (2.114) And I recollect having before now heard some man who had applied himself to learning in no careless or indolent spirit, say that men were not the only beings which went mad with vain opinions, but that the stars did so too. And they also, said he, contend with one another for precedence, and those which are the greater claim to be attended by the lesser stars as their guards; (2.115) these matters, however, we may leave for the studiers of sublime subjects to investigate, and to settle how much truth and how much random assertion there is in them. But we say, that the lover of indiscriminate study, and unreasonable contention, and vain opinion, being always puffed up by folly, wishes to assert a precedence, not only over men, but also above the nature of all existing things; (2.116) and he thinks that all things were created for his sake, and that it is necessary that everything, whether earth or heaven, or water or air, should bring him tribute; and he has gone to such an extravagant pitch of folly, that he is not able to reason upon such matters as even a young child might understand, and to see that no artist ever makes the whole for the sake of the part, but rather makes the part for the sake of the whole. Now the part of the whole is the man, so that he is properly asserted to have been made for the sake of perfecting the world in which he is rightly classed.

XVII

XVII. (2.117) But some persons are full of such exceeding folly, that they are indignant if the whole world does not follow their intentions: for this reason Xerxes, the king of Persia, being desirous to strike terror into his enemies, made a display of very mighty undertakings, altering the whole face of nature; (2.118) for he changed the nature of the elements of the earth and of the sea, giving land to the sea and sea to the land, by joining the Hellespont with a bridge, and breaking up Mount Athos into deep gulfs, which, being filled with sea, became so many new and artificially-cut seas, being entirely changed from the ancient course of nature. (2.119) And having worked wonders with respect to the earth, according to his wishes, he mounted up upon daring conceptions, like a miserable man as he was, contracting the guilt of impiety, and seeking to soar up to heaven, as if he would move what cannot be moved, and would subjugate the host of heaven, and, as the proverb has it, he began with a sacred thing. (2.120) For he aimed his arrows at the most excellent of the heavenly bodies, the sun, the ruler of the day, as if he had not himself been wounded by the invisible dart of insanity, not only because of his desiring things which were impossible, but such as were also most impious, either of which is a great disgrace to him who attempts them. (2.121) It is related, also, that the very populous nation of the Germans, and theirs is a country where the sea is subject to the ebb and flow of the tide, ran down to the reflux which occurs in their country with great impetuosity, and drawing their naked swords charged and encountered the billowy sea as if it were a phalanx of enemies: (2.122) and these men deserve to be hated because they dare impiously to take up the arms of enemies against the free and invincible parts of nature; but they deserve also to be ridiculed for attempting what is impossible, as if they thought it practicable to wound the water as though it were a living animal, or to stab it and kill it. And again, one should grieve at the sight of such men, and fear, and flee out of fear at their attacks, and submit to all the affections of the soul which are conversant with pleasures and pains.

XVIII

XVIII. (2.123) Moreover, it is only a very short time ago that I knew a man of very high rank, one who was prefect and governor of Egypt, who, after he had taken it into his head to change our national institutions and customs, and in an extraordinary manner to abrogate that most holy law guarded by such fearful penalties, which relates to the seventh day, and was compelling us to obey him, and to do other things contrary to our established custom, thinking that that would be the beginning of our departure from the other laws, and of our violation of all our national customs, if he were once able to destroy our hereditary and customary observance of the seventh day. (2.124) And as he saw that those to whom he offered violence did not yield to his injunctions, and that the rest of our people was not disposed to submit in tranquillity, but was indignant and furious at the business, and was mourning and dispirited as if at the enslaving, and overthrow, and utter destruction of their country; he thought fit to endeavour by a speech to persuade them to transgress, saying: (2.125) "If an invasion of enemies were to come upon you on a sudden, or the violence of a deluge, from the river having broken down all its barriers by an inundation, or any terrible fire, or a thunderbolt, or famine, or pestilence, or an earthquake, or any other evil, whether caused by men or inflicted by God, would you still remain quiet and unmoved at home? (2.126) And would you still go on in your habitual fashion, keeping your right hand back, and holding the other under your garments close to your sides, in order that you might not, even without meaning it, do anything to contribute to your own preservation? (2.127) And would you still sit down in your synagogues, collecting your ordinary assemblies, and reading your sacred volumes in security, and explaining whatever is not quite clear, and devoting all your time and leisure with long discussions to the philosophy of your ancestors? (2.128) Nay: rather shaking off all these ideas, you would gird yourselves up for the preservation of yourselves, and of your parents, and of your children, and, if one must tell the plain truth, of your possessions and treasures, to save them from being utterly destroyed. (2.129) And, indeed, I myself, am," said he, "all the evils which I have just enumerated: I am a whirlwind, I am war, and deluge, and thunderbolt, and the calamity of famine, and the misery of pestilence, and an earthquake which shakes and overthrows what stood firm before, not being merely the name of a necessity of fate, but actual, visible power, standing close to you." (2.130) What then can we say that a man who says, or who merely thinks such things as these, is? Is he not an evil of an extraordinary nature? He surely must be some foreign calamity, brought from over the sea, or from some other world, since he, a man in every respect miserable, has dared to compare himself to the all-blessed God. (2.131) We must likewise add, that he is daring here to utter blasphemies against the sun, and the moon, and the rest of the stars, whenever anything which had been looked for according to the seasons of the year, either does not happen at all, or is brought about with difficulty; if, for instance, the summer causes too much heat, or the winter too excessive a cold, or if the spring or autumn were unseasonable, so that the one were to become barren and unfruitful, and the other to be prolific only in diseases. (2.132) Therefore, giving all imaginable license to an unbridled mouth and abusive tongue, such a man will reproach the stars as not bringing their customary tribute, all but claiming for the things of earth the reverence and adoration of the heavenly bodies, and for himself above them all, in proportion as he, as being a man, looks upon himself as superior to the other animals.

XIX

XIX. (2.133) Such men then are classed by us as the very teachers of vain opinion. Let us now in turn look at their followers by themselves. These men are always laying plots against the practisers of virtue, and when they see them labouring to make their own life pure with guileless truth, and to exhibit it, as one may say, to the light of the moon, or of the sun, as able to stand inspection, they endeavor by deceit, or even by open violence, to hinder them, trying to drive them into the sunless country of impious men, which is occupied by deep night, and endless darkness, and ten thousand tribes of images, and appearances, and dreams, and then, having thrust them down thither, they compel them to fall down and worship them as masters. (2.134) For we look upon the practiser of virtue as the sun, since the one gives light to our bodies, and the other to the things which belong to the soul: and the education which such a man uses we look upon as the moon, for the use of each is most pure and most useful in the night; and the brethren are those virtuous reasonings which are the offspring of instruction, and of a soul devoted to the practice of virtue, all of which make straight the right path of life, and which they, therefore, by all kinds of wary and cunning wrestlings, seek to overcome, and to trip up, and overthrow, and break the neck of, because they have determined neither to think nor to say anything sound themselves. (2.135) For this reason his father rebukes this intractable youth (I do not mean Jacob, but right reason, which is older even than he), saying, (2.136) "What is this dream which thou hast dreamt?" but thou hast not seen any dream at all; hast thou fancied that things which are free by nature are to be of necessity slaves to human things, and that things which are rulers are to become subjects? and, what is more paradoxical still, subject, not to anything else but to the very things which they govern? and to be the slaves of no other things except those very things which are their own slaves? unless indeed a change of all the established things to their direct contraries is to take place, by the power of God, who is able to effect all things, and to move what is immovable, and to fix what is in a constant state of agitation. (2.137) Since on what principle can you be angry with or reproach a man who sees a vision in his sleep? For he will say, I did not see it intentionally, why do you bring accusations against me, for errors which I have not committed from any deliberate purpose? I have related to you what fell upon me and made an impression on my mind suddenly, and without my desiring it. (2.138) But the present question is not about dreams, but about things which resemble dreams; which, to those whose minds are not highly purified appear great, and beautiful, and desirable things; while they are, in reality, trifling, and obscure, and deserving of ridicule, in the eyes of honest judges of the truth.

XX

XX. (2.139) Shall I then, says he, I, that is to say, right reason, come to you? And shall the soul, which is both the mother and nurse of the company devoted to learning virtuous instruction, also come to thee? (2.140) And are the offspring of us too to come likewise? And are we all to stand in a row, laying aside all our former dignity, and holding up our hands and praying to thee? And are we then to prostrate ourselves on the ground, and endeavour to propitiate and adore thee? But may the sun never shine upon such transactions, since deep darkness is suited to evil deeds, and brilliant light to good deeds. And what could be a greater evil than for pride, that deceiver and beguiler, to be praised and admired, instead of sincere and honest simplicity? (2.141) And it is with great propriety that the statement is added, "And his father took notice of his words." For it is the occupation of a soul which is not young, nor barren, nor wholly unfruitful, but rather of one which is really older and able to beget offspring, to cohabit with prudent caution, and to despise and overlook nothing whatever, but to have a reverential fear of the power of God, from which we cannot escape, and which we cannot overcome; and to look all around to see what its very end shall be. (2.142) For this reason they say, that the sister of Moses also (and she is called Hope by us, when speaking in a figurative manner) was contemplated at a distance by the sacred scriptures, inasmuch as she kept her eyes fixed on the end of life, hoping that some good fortune might befall her, sent by the Giver of all good from above, from heaven; (2.143) for it has often happened that many persons, after having taken long voyages, and having sailed over a great expanse of sea with a fair wind, and without any danger, have suddenly been shipwrecked in the harbour itself, when they have been on the very point of casting anchor; (2.144) and many persons too, who have successfully come to the end of formidable wars of long duration, and have come off unwounded so as never to have received even a scratch on the surface of the skin, but to have escaped whole and entire as if they had only been at some popular assembly or national festival, having returned home with joy and cheerfulness, have been plotted against in their houses by those who, of all the world, least ought to have done so; being, as the proverb says, like oxen slain in their stall.

XXI

XXI. (2.145) As these unexpected events, which no one could ever have anticipated, do frequently happen in this manner and overthrow people, so also do they often drive the powers of the soul in a contrary direction to the proper one, and drag it in an opposite way, according to their power, and compel it to change its course: for what man, who has ever descended into the arena of life, has come off without a fall? (2.146) And who is there who has never been tripped up in that contest? He is happy who has not often been so. And for whom has not fortune laid snares, blowing upon him at intervals, and collecting its strength, that it may twine itself around him, and speedily carry him off before its adversary is ready for the contest? (2.147) Do we not know, that some persons have come from infancy to old age who have never been sensible of any irregularity, whether it be from the happy condition of their nature, or from the care of those who brought them up and educated them, or owing to both circumstances? But then, being filled with profound peace in themselves, which is real peace, and the archetypal model of that which exists in cities, and being considered happy on that account, because they have never had a notion, not even in a dream, of the intestine war which arises from the violence of the passions, and which is the most piteous of all wars, have at last, at the very close of their lives, run on shore and made shipwreck, either through some intemperance of language or some insatiable gluttony, or some incontinent licentiousness of the parts below the belly. (2.148) For some, while--

"Still on the threshold of extreme old age,"

have admired the youthful, unhonoured, detestable, and disgraceful life of debauches; and others have given in to the cunning, and wicked, and calumnious, and desperate way of life of others, pursuing the first fruits of quarrelsome curiosity, when they ought rather to have discarded such habits now, even if they had been familiar to them. (2.149) For which reason one ought to propitiate God, and to supplicate him perseveringly, that he will not pass by our miserable race, but that he will allow his saving mercy to be everlastingly shown towards us; for it is difficult for those who have tasted unalloyed peace to be prevented from glutting themselves with it.

XXII

XXII. (2.150) But, come now, this hunger is lighter evil than thirst, inasmuch as it has love and desire for its comforters; but when, through the desire of drinking, it is necessary to satisfy one's self with that other fountain, the water of which is dirty and unwholesome, then it is indispensable for the drinkers, being filled with a bitter-sweet pleasure, to live an unenviable life, betaking themselves to pernicious things as though they were advantageous, from ignorance of what is really desirable. (2.151) But the impetuous course of these evils is most grievous when the irrational powers of the soul attack the powers of the reason and get the better of them; (2.152) for as long as the herds of oxen obey their drivers, and the flocks obey their shepherds, and the goats obey the goatherds, the herds and all belonging to them go on well; but when the herdsmen who are appointed to look after the cattle become weaker than the beasts committed to their care, then everything goes wrong, and instead of regularity there arises irregularity, and disorder in the place of order, and confusion instead of steadiness, and disturbance in the place of good arrangement, since there is no longer any lawful superintending power properly established; for if there had been such a thing, it would have been destroyed before this time. (2.153) What then? Do we not think that even in ourselves there is a herd of irrational cattle, inasmuch as the irrational multitude of the soul is deprived of reason, and that the shepherd is the governing mind? But as long as that is vigorous and competent to act as the manager of the herd, everything goes on in a just, and prosperous, and advantageous manner; (2.154) but when any weakness or want of power supervenes to the king, then it follows of necessity that the subjects also labour with a like infirmity; and when they most completely seem to be in enjoyment of liberty, then they are a prize, lying most entirely ready for any one who pleases to contend for it to seize; for the natural course is for anarchy to be treacherous, and for government to be salutary, especially in a state where law and justice are honoured. And this is such a state as is consistent with reason.

XXIII

XXIII. (2.155) We have now, then, spoken with sufficient accuracy about the dreams of vain opinion. Now, the different species of gluttony are conversant about drinking and eating. But the one has no need of any great variety, while the other requires a countless number of seasonings and sauces. These things, then, are referred to two managers. The matters relating to excessive drinking are referred to the chief butler, and those which belong to luxurious eating to the chief baker. (2.156) Now these men are, with excessive propriety, recorded to have seen visions of dreams one night; for they, each of them, labour to gratify the same need of their master, providing not simple food, but such as is accompanied with pleasure and extraordinary gratification; and each of them, separately, labours about half the food, but the two together are employed about the whole, and the one part draws on the other; (2.157) for men, when they have eaten, immediately desire drink; and men who have drunk immediately wish to eat; so that it is in no slight degree on this account that a vision is ascribed to them both at the same time. (2.158) Therefore the chief butler has the office of ministering to the appetite for wine, and the chief baker to the voracity. And each of them sees in his vision what relates to his own business: the one sees wine and the plant which engenders wine, namely the vine; the other sees white bread lying on dishes, and himself serving up the Dishes.[1095] (2.159) Now perhaps it may be proper first of all to examine the first dream. And it is as follows:--"In my sleep there was a vine before me; and on the vine were three branches, and it flourished and brought forth shoots, and there were on it ripe bunches of grapes. And Pharaoh's cup was in my hand, and I took the bunch of grapes and pressed it into the cup, and I gave the cup into Pharaoh's Hand." [1096] (2.160) He speaks here in an admirable manner, and the expression, "in my sleep," is quite correct. For, in real truth, he who follows not so much the inebriety which arises from wine as that which proceeds from folly, being indignant at an upright and wakeful position, like people asleep, is thrown down and relaxed, and shuts the eyes of his soul, not being able either to see or to hear anything which is worthy of being seen or of being heard. (2.161) And being overthrown, he goes on a blind and guideless (I will not say path, but pathless) way through life, being pricked with thorns and briars; and sometimes too he falls down steep places, and tumbles down upon other people, so as to hurt both them and himself in a pitiable manner. (2.162) But the deep and long-enduring sleep in which every wicked man is held, removes all true conceptions, and fills the mind with all kinds of false images, and unsubstantial visions, persuading it to embrace what is shameful as praiseworthy. For at one time it dreams of grief as joy, and does not perceive that it is looking at the vine, the plant of folly and error. (2.163) "For," says the chief butler, "the vine was before me," the desired object was before him who desired it, wickedness was before the wicked man: which we, foolish men that we are, cultivate, without being aware that we are doing so to our own injury, the fruit of which we eat and drink, classing it under both species of food, which, as it would seem, we appropriate, not for one half the evils that affect us for the whole of our complete and entire misfortunes.

XXIV

XXIV. (2.164) But it is desirable not to be ignorant that the intoxication which proceeds from the vine does not affect all who indulge in it in a similar manner, but very often affects different people in contrary ways, so that it makes some better and others worse than they are naturally. (2.165) For in the case of some men, it relaxes the sternness and moroseness of their character, and relieves them of their cares, and assuages their anger and their sorrow, and brings their dispositions into a milder mood, and makes their souls placable. But of others again, it cherishes the angry passions, and binds their pain firmly, and excites their feelings of love, and stimulates their rudeness; rendering the mouth talkative, their tongue unbridled, emancipating their external senses from all restraint, rendering their passions furious, and their whole mind violent and excited towards every object. (2.166) So that the condition of the men firstmentioned appears to resemble an untroubled calm in fine weather, or a waveless tranquillity at sea, or a most peaceful and steady state of affairs in a city. But the condition of those whom I have last described, is more like a violent and unremitting gale, or a sea tossed by a storm into vast billows, or a sedition, an evil more fearful than even interminable and irreconcileable war. (2.167) Therefore, of these two banquet parties, the one is filled with laughter, with men promising amusement, and hoping for good fortune, and enjoying cheerfulness, and pleasant language, and mirth, and joy, and freedom from anxiety; (2.168) but the other is full of melancholy, and seriousness, and downcast looks, and offences, and reproaches, and wounds; of men gnashing their teeth, looking fiercely at one another, barking, strangling one another, contending with one another in every conceivable way, mutilating one another's ears and noses, and whatever parts of the body they can reach, displaying the intoxication of their whole life and their drunkenness in this unholy contest, with every kind of unseemly behaviour.

XXV

XXV. (2.169) It would therefore be naturally consistent to consider next that the vine is the symbol of two things: of folly, and of mirth. And each of these two, though it is indicated by many circumstances, we will explain in a few words, to avoid prolixity. (2.170) When any one leading us along the road, deserted by the passions and by acts of wickedness, the rod, that is, of philosophy, has led right reason to a height, and placed it like a scout upon a watch-tower, [1097] and has commanded it to look around, and to survey the whole country of virtue, and to see whether it be blessed with a deep soil, and rich, and productive of herbage and of fruit, since deep soil is good to cause the learning which has been sown in it to increase, and to make the doctrines which have been planted in it, and which have grown to trees, to form solid trunks, or whether it be of a contrary character; and also to examine into actions, as one might into cities, and see whether they are strongly fortified, or whether they are defenceless and deprived of all the security which might be afforded by walls around them. Also to inquire into the condition of the inhabitants, whether they are considerable in numbers and in valour, or whether their courage is weak and their numbers scanty, the two causes acting reciprocally on one another. (2.171) Then because we were not able to bear the weight of the whole trunk of wisdom, we cut off one branch and one bunch of grapes, and carried it with us as a most undeniable proof of our joy, and a burden very easy to be borne, wishing to display at the same time the branch and the fruit of excellence to those who are gifted with acuteness of mental sight, to show them, that is, the strongly-shooting and grapebearing vine.

XXVI

XXVI. (2.172) They then very fairly compare this vine of which we were only able to take a part, to happiness. And one of the ancient prophets bears his testimony in favour of my view of the matter, who speaking under divine inspiration has said, "The vineyard of the Lord Almighty is the house of Israel." [1098] (2.173) Now Israel is the mind inclined to the contemplation of God and of the world; for the name Israel is interpreted, "seeing God," and the abode of the mind is the whole soul; and this is the most sacred vineyard, bearing as its fruit the divine shoot, virtue: (2.174) thus thinking well (to eu phronein) is the derivation of the word joy (euphrosyneÂ), being a great and brilliant thing so that, says Moses, even God himself does not disdain to exhibit it; and most especially at that time when the human race is departing from its sins, and inclining and bending its steps towards justice, following of its own accord the laws and institutions of nature. (2.175) "For," says Moses, "the Lord thy God will return, that he may rejoice in thee for thy good as he rejoiced in thy fathers, if thou wilt hear his voice to keep all his commandments and his ordinances and his judgments which are written in the book of this Law." [1099] (2.176) Who could implant in man a desire for virtue and excellence, more strongly than is here done? Dost thou wish, says the scripture, O mind, that God should rejoice? Do thou rejoice in virtue thyself, and bring no costly offering, (for what need has God of anything of thine?) But, on the other hand, receive with joy all the good things which he bestows upon thee; (2.177) for he rejoices in giving, when they who receive are worthy of his grace; unless you think that those men who live blameably may be justly said to make God indignant and to excite his anger, but that those who live in a praiseworthy manner do not make him rejoice. (2.178) But there is nothing which gives so much pleasure to fathers and mothers, our mortal parents, as the virtues of their children, even though they may be in want of numbers of necessary things; And does not the excellence of these aforesaid persons in like manner rejoice the Creator of the universe, who is in no want of anything whatever? (2.179) Do thou therefore, O mind, having learnt how mighty a thing the anger of God is, and how great a good the joy of God is, do not do anything worthy to excite his anger to thy own destruction, but study only such things as may be the means of your pleasing God. (2.180) And you will find these actions not to be the making of long and unusual journeys, nor the passing over unnavigable seas, or wandering without stopping to take breath to the furthest boundaries of earth and sea: for good actions do not dwell at a distance and have not been banished beyond the confines of the habitable world, but, as Moses says, good is situated near you, and is planted along with you, being united to you in three necessary parts, in the heart, in the mouth, and in the hands: that is to say, in the mind, in the speech, and in the actions; since it is necessary to think and to say, and to do good things, which are made perfect by a union of good design, good execution, and good language.

XXVII

XXVII. (2.181) I say therefore to him whose occupation is to gratify one description of gluttony, the fondness for drinking, namely to the chief butler, "Why are you labouring hard, O unhappy man? For you think that you are preparing pleasant things to give delight, but in reality you are kindling a flame of folly and intemperance, and contributing great and abundant quantities of fuel to it." (2.182) But perhaps he may reply, do not blame me precipitately before you have considered my case; I was appointed to pour out wine, not indeed for a man who was endowed with temperance, and piety, and all the other virtues, but for a violent, and intemperate, and unjust master, one who was very proud in his impiety, and who dared once to say, "I do not know the Lord;" [1100] so that I very naturally studied what would afford him gratification: (2.183) and do not wonder that God is delighted with one thing, and the mind which is hostile to God, namely Pharaoh, with the contrary. Who then is the chief butler of God? The priest who offers libations to him, the truly great high priest, who, having received a draught of everlasting graces, offers himself in return, pouring in an entire libation full of unmixed wine. You see that there are differences between butlers in proportion to the differences existing between those whom they are waiting on; (2.184) on this account I, the butler of Pharaoh, who exerts his stiff-necked, and in all respects intemperate reason, in the direction of indulgences of his passions, am a eunuch, having had all the generative parts of my soul removed, and being compelled to migrate from the apartments of the men, and am a fugitive also from the women's chambers, inasmuch as I am neither male nor female; nor am I able to disseminate seed nor to receive it, being of an ambiguous nature, neither one thing nor the other; a mere false coin of human money, destitute of immortality, which is from time to time kept alive by the constant succession of children and offspring: being also excluded from the assembly and sacred meeting of the people, for it is expressly forbidden that any one who has suffered any injury or mutilation such as I have should enter in Thereto. [1101]

XXVIII

XXVIII. (2.185) But the high priest of whom we are speaking is a perfect man, the husband of a virgin (a most extraordinary statement), who has never been made a woman; but who on the contrary, has ceased to be influenced by the customs of women in regard to her connection with her Husband.[1102] And not only is this man competent to sow the seeds of unpolluted and virgin opinions, but he is also the father of sacred reasonings, (2.186) some of which are overseers and superintendents of the affairs of nature, such as Eleazar and Ithamar; others are ministers of the worship of God, earnestly occupied in kindling and burning up the flame of heaven; for, as they are always uttering discourses relating to holiness, they cause it to shine, bringing forth the most divine kind of piety like fire from a flint; (2.187) and the being who is at the same time the guide and father of those men is no insignificant part of the sacred assembly, but he is rather the person without whom the duly convened assembly of the parts of the soul could never be collected together at all; he is the president, the chairman, the creator of it, who, without the aid of any other being, is able by himself alone to consider and to do everything. (2.188) He, when taken in conjunction with others, is insignificant in point of number, but when he is looked at by himself he becomes numerous; he is a tribunal, an entire council, the whole people, a complete multitude, the entire race of mankind, or rather, if one is to speak the real truth, he is a sort of nature bordering on God, inferior indeed to him, but superior to man; (2.189) "for when," the scripture say, "the high priest goes into the Holy of Holies he will not be a Man."[1103] What then will he be if he is not a man? Will he be a God? I would not venture to say that (for the chief prophet, Moses, did receive the inheritance of this name while he was still in Egypt, being called "the god of Pharaoh;")[1104] nor again is he man, but he touches both these extremities as if he touched both the feet and the head.

XXIX

XXIX. (2.190) So now one kind of vine, which has been assigned as the portion of cheerfulness, and the intoxication which arises from it, namely unmingled goodness of counsel, and the cup-bearer too who drew the wine from the divine goblet, which God himself has filled with virtues up to the lip, has been explained; (2.191) but the other kind, that of folly, and grief, and drunkenness, is also already depicted in a fashion but in another character, by other expressions which are used in the greater canticle; "for," says the scripture, "their vine is of the vine of Sodom and their tendrils are of the vine of Gomorrah; their grapes are the grapes of gall; their bunches are full of bitterness itself. Their wine is the madness of dragons and the incurable fury of Asps."[1105] (2.192) You see here what great effects are produced by the drunkenness of folly: bitterness, an evil disposition, exceeding gall, excessive anger, implacability, a biting and treacherous disposition. The lawgiver most emphatically asserts the branch of the vine of folly to be in Sodom; and the name Sodom, being interpreted, means "blindness," or "barrenness;" since folly is a thing which is blind, and also barren of all good things; though, nevertheless, some people have been so greatly influenced by it as to measure, and weigh, and count everything with reference to themselves alone. (2.193) Gomorrah, being interpreted, means "measure;" but Moses conceived that God was the standard of weight, and measure, and number, in the universe, but he had not the same opinion of the human mind. And he shows this in the following passage, where he says, "There shall not be in thy sack one weight, and another weight, a great and a small; there shall not be in thy house one measure, and another measure, a great and a small; (2.194) thy weight shall be a true and just one." But a true and just measure is, to conceive that it is the only just God alone who measures and weighs everything, and who has circumscribed the nature of the universe with numbers, and limitations, and boundaries. But it is unjust and false to imagine that these things are regulated in accordance with the human mind. (2.195) But the eunuch and chief butler of Pharaoh, having beheld the plant generative of folly, namely, the vine, adds besides to his delineation there stocks, that he may signify the three extremities of error according to the three different times; for a root is equivalent to extremity.

XXX

XXX. (2.196) When, therefore, folly has overshadowed and occupied the whole soul, and when it has left no portion of it unoccupied or free, it not only compels it to commit such errors as are remediable, but such also as are irremediable. (2.197) Now those which admit of a remedy are set down as the easiest and the first; but those which are irremediable are altogether terrible, and are the last of all, being so far analogous to roots. (2.198) And as, in my notions, wisdom begins to benefit a man in small matters, and ends at last in the absolute perfection of all well-doing, so, in the same manner folly, constraining the soul from above and leading it away from instruction by small degrees, establishes it at

Philo Judaeus

last at a long distance from right reason, and finally leads it to the extreme point, and utterly overthrows it. (2.199) And the dream showed that after the roots appeared the vine flourished and put forth shoots and bore fruit; for, says the chief butler, "It was flourishing and bearing shoots, around which were bunches of Grapes."[1106] The foolish man is accustomed to display barrenness, and never to put forth even leaves, and, in fact, to be withered all his life; (2.200) for what could be a greater evil than folly flourishing and bearing fruit? But, says he, "the cup of Pharaoh," the vessel which is the receptacle of folly and drunkenness, and of the ceaseless intoxication of life, "is in my hand;" an expression equivalent to saying, depends upon my administration, and endeavours, and powers; for without my contrivances, the passion will not proceed rightly by its own efforts; (2.201) for as it is proper that the reins should be in the hands of the charioteer, and the rudder in the hands of the pilot--for this is the only way in which the course of the chariot and the voyage of the vessel can proceed successfully--so, also, the filling of the goblet with wine is in the hands and depends upon the power of him who by his art brings to perfection one of the two kinds of gluttony, namely, satiety of wine. (2.202) But why has he endured to boast in respect of a matter which deserved rather to be denied than to be confessed? Would it not have been better not to have confessed at all that he was a teacher of intemperance, and not to admit that he increased the excitement of the passions by wine in the case of the intemperate man, as being an inventor and producer of a luxurious, and debauched, and most disgraceful way of life. (2.203) Such, however, is the case. Folly boasts of those things which ought to be concealed; and in this present case it prides itself, not only on holding in its hands the receptacle of the intemperate soul, that is to say, the cup of wine, and in showing it to all men, but also in pressing out the grapes into it; that is to say, in making that which satisfies the passion, and bringing what is concealed to light. (2.204) For as children which require food, when they are about to receive the milk, squeeze and press out the breast of the nurse that feeds them, so likewise does the workman and cause of intemperance vigorously press the fountain from which the evil of abundance of wine pours forth, that he may derive food in a most agreeable manner from the drops which are squeezed out.

XXXI

XXXI. (2.205) Such a description then as I have here given may be applied to the man who is made frantic by the influence of unmixed wines, that he is a drunken, and foolish, and irremediable evil. We must now, in turn, investigate the character of the glutton, who is akin to the drunkard, and who is a sworn companion of all kinds of voracity and greediness, labouring, without any restraint, at the artificial gratification of his appetite. (2.206) And yet it does not require a great deal of care to arrive at his true character; for the dream which was seen is a representation of his likeness very closely resembling him; and when we have accurately examined him, let us look upon him as we would upon a representation in a mirror; (2.207) for "I thought," said the chief cook, "that I had three baskets of fine wheaten loaves upon my head." Now, using the word "head" in an allegorical manner, we mean by it the dominant part of the soul, that is, the mind, and we say that everything rests or depends upon that; for he once exclaimed concerning it, "All these things were in my charge." (2.208) Therefore when he had completed the preparation of these things which he had devised against the miserable belly, he displayed himself also, and, like a foolish man as he was, he was not ashamed to be weighed down with so great a burden, namely, the weight of three baskets; that is to say, with three portions of time. (2.209) For those who advocate the cause of pleasure affirm that it consists of three times, of the memory of past delights, and of the enjoyment of those that are present, and of the hope of what are to come; (2.210) so that the three baskets are likened unto the three portions of time, and the cakes upon the baskets to those circumstances which are suitable to each of the portions; to the recollection of past joys, to the enjoyment of present pleasures, to the hope of future delights. And he who carries all these things is likened unto the lover of pleasure, who has filled his faithless table, a table destitute of all hospitable and friendly salt, not with one kind of luxury only, but with almost every description and species of intemperance; (2.211) and this is enjoyed by king Pharaoh alone, as if he were sitting at a public banquet, and devoting himself to a dispersion, and scattering, and defeat, and destruction of temperance; for the name Pharaoh, being interpreted, means "dispersion." And it is magnificent and royal piece of conduct in him not to exult in the specious advantages of wisdom, but to pride himself on those pursuits of profligacy which it is unseemly to mention, wrecking himself on insatiable appetite and gluttony, and effeminacy of life. (2.212) Therefore the birds, that is to say, the chances which never could have been anticipated by conjecture, coming from outward quarters and hovering around him, will attack and kindle every thing like fire, and will destroy every thing with their all-devouring power, so that there is not a single fragment left to the bearer of the baskets for his enjoyment though he had hoped to proceed with his inventions and contrivances, for ever and ever carrying them on in a safe place, so that they could never be taken from him. (2.213) And thanks be to God who giveth the victory and who renders the labours of the man who is a slave to his passions, though ever so carefully carried out, still unproductive and useless, sending down winged natures in an invisible manner for their destruction and overthrow. Therefore, the mind, being deprived of those things which it had made for itself, having, as it were, its neck cut through, will be found headless and lifeless, and like those who are fixed to a cross, nailed as it were to the tree of hopeless and helpless ignorance. (2.214) For as long as none of these things come upon one which arrive suddenly and unexpectedly, then those acts which are directed to the enjoyment of pleasure appear to be successful; but when such evils descend upon them unexpectedly, they are overthrown, and their maker is destroyed with them.

XXXII

XXXII. (2.215) The dreams, therefore, of those men who divide those things which produce the taste according to every species of food, whether it be meat or drink, and such as is not necessary but superfluous, and sought only by the intemperate, have been sufficiently explained. But those of Pharaoh, who appears to exercise sovereignty over these men and over all the powers of the soul, must now be investigated if we would proceed in order and consistently with our plan. (2.216) Pharaoh says, "In my dream I thought that I was standing by the bank of a river, and seven oxen came up as it were out of the river, of eminent plumpness in their flesh, and beautiful to the view, and fed in the green marsh; and behold, seven other oxen came up out of the river after them, evil to look at and ill-favoured, and lean in their flesh, such that I never saw any leaner in all Egypt; (2.217) and the lean and ill-favoured oxen devoured the seven former oxen which were beautiful, and picked out, and they entered into their stomachs, and still their appearance remained illfavoured, as I have described it at first. (2.218) And when I had awoke I fell asleep again; and again I saw in my dream, and as it were seven ears of corn grew up on one stalk, full and beautiful. And seven other ears of corn also came up, lean and wind-beaten, close to them, and these last seven ears did swallow up the seven beautiful and full Ears." [1107] (2.219) You see now the preface of the lover of self who being easily moved, and changeable, and fickle, both in his body and soul, says, "I thought that I was standing," and did not consider that unchangeableness and steadiness belong to God alone, and to him who is dear to God. (2.220) And the most evident proof of the unchangeable power which exists in him is this world, which is always in the same place and in the same condition. And if the world is immovable how can the Creator of it be any thing but firm? In the second place the sacred scriptures are likewise most infallible witnesses; (2.221) for it is said in them, where the words are put into the mouth of God, "I stand here and there, before you were dwelling upon the rock, [1108] which is an expression equivalent to, Thus am I who am visible to you, and am here: and I am there and everywhere, filling all places, standing and abiding in the same condition, being unchangeable, before you or any one of the objects of creation had any existence, being beheld upon the highest and most ancient authority of power, from which the creation of all existing things was shed forth, and the stream of wisdom flowed; (2.222) "for I am he who brought the stream of water out of the solid Rock," [1109] is said in another place. And Moses also bears witness to the immutability of the Deity, where he says, "I saw the place where the God of Israel Stood;" [1110] intimating enigmatically that he is not given to change by speaking here of his standing, and of his being firmly established.

XXXIII

XXXIII. (2.223) But there is in the Deity such an excessive degree of stability and firmness, that he gave even to the most excellent natures a share of his durability as his most excellent possession: and presently afterwards he, the most ancient author of all things, namely God, says that he is about to erect firmly his covenant full of grace (and that means his law and his word) in the soul of the just man as on a solid foundation, which shall be an image in the likeness of God, when he says to Noah, "I will establish my covenant with Thee." [1111] (2.224) And besides this, he also indicates two other things, one that justice is in no respect different from the covenant of God, the other that other beings bestow gifts which are different from the persons who receive them; but God gives not only those gifts, but he gives also the very persons who receive them to themselves, for he has given me to myself, and every living being has he given to himself; for the expression, "I will establish my covenant with thee," is equivalent to, I will give thee to thyself. (2.225) And all those who are truly lovers of God desire eagerly to escape from the storm of multiplied affairs and business in which there is always tempestuous weather, and rough sea, and confusion, and to anchor in the calm and safe untroubled haven of virtue. (2.226) Do you not see what is said about the wise Abraham who "is standing before the Lord?" [1112] For when was it likely that the mind would be able to stand, no longer inclining to different sides like the balance in a scale, except when it is opposite to God, beholding him and being beheld by him? (2.227) For perfect absence of motion comes to it in two ways, either from beholding him with whom nothing can be compared, because he is not attracted by anything resembling himself, or from being beheld by him, because ... which he considered worthy, the ruler has assigned to himself alone as the most excellent of beings. And indeed a divine admonition was given in the following terms to Moses: "Stand thou here with Me," [1113] by which injunction both these things appear to be intimated, first, the fact that the good man is not moved, and secondly, the universal stability of the living God.

XXXIV

XXXIV. (2.228) For, in real truth, whatever is akin or near to God is appropriated by him, becoming steady and stationary by reason of his unchangeableness; and the mind, being at rest, well knows how great a blessing rest is, and admiring, its own beauty, it conceives that either it is assigned to God alone as his, or else to that intermediate nature which is between the mortal and the immortal race; (2.229) at all events, it says, "And I stood in the midst between the Lord and You,"[1114] not meaning by these words that he was standing on his own feet, but wishing to indicate that the mind of the wise man, being delivered from all storms and wars, and enjoying unruffled calm and profound peace, is superior indeed to man, but inferior to God. (2.230) For the ordinary human mind is influenced by opinion, and is thrown into confusion by any passing circumstances; but the other is blessed and happy, and free from all participation in evil. And the good man is on the borders, so that one may appropriately say that he is neither God nor man, but that he touches the extremities of both, being connected with the mortal race by his manhood, and with the immortal race by his virtue. (2.231) And there is something which closely resembles this in the passage of scripture concerning the high priest; "For when," says the scripture, "he goes into the holy of holies, he will not be a man till he has gone out Again." [1115] But if at that time he is not a man, it is clear that he is not God either, but a minister of God, belonging as to his mortal nature to creation, but as to his immortal nature to the uncreated God. (2.232) And he is placed in the middle class until he again goes forth among the things which belong to the body and to the flesh. And this is the order of things according to nature, when the mind, being entirely occupied with divine love, bends its course towards the temple of God, and approaches it with all possible earnestness and zeal, it becomes inspired, and forgets all other things, and forgets itself also. It remembers him alone, and depends on him alone, who is attended by it as by a body-guard, and who receives its ministrations, to whom it consecrates and offers up the sacred and untainted virtues. (2.233) But when the inspiration has ceased, and the excessive desire has relaxed, then it returns from divine things and becomes a man again, mixing with human affairs, which were awaiting him in the vestibule, that they might carry him off while gazing only on the things in them.

XXXV

XXXV. (2.234) Moses therefore describes the perfect man as being neither God nor man, but, as I said before, something on the border between uncreated and the perishable nature. Again, he classes him who is improving and advancing towards perfection in the region between the dead and the living, meaning by the "living" those persons who dwell with wisdom, and by "the dead" those who rejoice in folly; (2.235) for it is said with respect to Aaron, that "He stood between the dead and the living, and the plague was Stayed." [1116] For he who is making progress is not reckoned among those who are dead as to the life of virtue, inasmuch as he has a desire and admiration of what is honourable, nor among those who are living in extreme and perfect prosperity, for there is still something wanting to the end, but he touches both extremes; (2.236) on which account the expression, "the plague was stayed," is very properly used rather than "the plague ceased;" for in those who are perfect the things which break, and crush, and destroy the soul cease; but in those who are advancing towards perfection, they are only diminished, as if they were only cut short and checked.

XXXVI

XXXVI. (2.237) Since then all steadiness, and stability, and the abiding for ever in the same place unchangeably and immovably, is first of all seen in the living God, and next in the word of the living God, which he has called his covenant; and in the third place in the wise man, and in the fourth degree in him who is advancing towards perfection, what could induce the wicked mind, which is liable to all sorts of curses, to think that it is able to stand by itself, while it is in reality borne about as in a deluge, and dragged hither and thither by the incessant eddies of things flowing in through the dead and agitated body? (2.238) "For I thought," says the scripture, "that I was standing on the bank of the River:" [1117] and by the word river we say that speech is symbolically meant, since both these things are borne outward, and flow on with a vigourous and sustained speed. And the one is at one time filled up with a great abundance of water, and the other with a quantity of verbs and nouns, and at another time they are both empty and relaxed, and in a state of quiescence; (2.239) again, they are of use inasmuch as the one irrigates the fields, and the other fertilizes the souls of those who receive it. And at times they are injurious by reason of overflowing, as then the one deluges the land on its borders, and the other troubles and confuses the reason of those who do not attend to it. (2.240) Therefore speech is compared to a river, and the nature of speech is twofold, the one sort being better and the other worse; that is, the better kind which does good, and that of necessity is the worse kind which does harm; (2.241) and Moses has given most conspicuous examples of each kind to those who are able to see, for he says, "For a river goes out of Eden to water the Paradise, and from thence it is divided into four Branches:"[1118] (2.242) and by the name Eden he means the wisdom of the living God, and the interpretation of the name Eden is "delight," because I imagine wisdom is the delight of God, and God is the delight of wisdom, as it is said also in the Psalms, "Delight thou in the Lord." [1119] And the divine word, like a river, flows forth from wisdom as from a spring, in order to irrigate and fertilize the celestial and heavenly shoots and plants of such souls as love virtue, as if they were a paradise. (2.243) And this sacred word is divided into four beginnings, by which I mean it is portioned out into four virtues, each of which is a princess, for to be divided into beginnings, [1120] does not resemble divisions of place, but a kingdom, in order than any one, after having shown the virtues as boundaries, may immediately proceed to show the wise man who follows them to be king, being elected a such, not by men, but by the only free nature which cannot err, and which cannot be corrupted; (2.244) for those who behold the excellence of Abraham say unto him, "Thou art a king, sent from God among Us:" [1121] proposing as a maxim, for those who study philosophy, that the wise man alone is a ruler and a king, and that virtue is the only irresponsible authority and sovereignty.

XXXVII

XXXVII. (2.245) Accordingly, one of the followers of Moses, having compared this speech to a river, has said in the Psalms, "The river of God was filled with Water;" [1122] and it is absurd to give such a title to any of the rivers which flow upon the earth. But as it seems the psalmist is here speaking of the divine word, which is full of streams and wisdom, and which has no part of itself empty or desolate, or rather, as some one has said, which is diffused everywhere over the universe, and is raised up on high, on account of the continued and incessant rapidity of that ever-flowing spring. (2.246) There is also another expression in the Psalms, such as this, "The course of the river makes glad the city of God." [1123] What city? For the holy city, which exists at present, in which also the holy temple is established, at a great distance from any sea or river, so that it is clear, that the writer here means, figuratively, to speak of some other city than the visible city of God. (2.247) For, in good truth, the continual stream of the divine word, being borne on incessantly with rapidity and regularity, is diffused universally over everything, giving joy to all. (2.248) And in one sense he calls the world the city of God, as having received the whole cup of the divine draught, ... and being gladdened thereby, so as to have derived from it an imperishable joy, of which it cannot be deprived for ever. But in another sense he applies this title to the soul of the wise man, in which God is said also to walk, as if in a city, "For," says God, "I will walk in you, and I will be your God in You." [1124] (2.249) And who can pour over the happy soul which proffers its own reason as the most sacred cup, the holy goblets of true joy, except the cup-bearer of God, the master of the feast, the word? not differing from the draught itself, but being itself in an unmixed state, the pure delight and sweetness, and pouring forth, and joy, and ambrosial medicine of pleasure and happiness; if we too may, for a moment, employ the language of the poets.

XXXVIII

XXXVIII. (2.250) But that which is called by the Hebrews the city of God is Jerusalem, which name being interpreted means, "the sight of peace." So they do not look for the city of the living God in the region of the earth, for it is not made of wood or of stone, but seek it in the soul which is free from war, and which proposes to those who are endowed with acuteness of sight a contemplative and peaceful life; (2.251) since where could any find a more venerable and holy abode for God amid all existing things, than the mind fond of contemplation, which is eager to behold every thing and which does not, even in a dream, feel a wish for sedition or disturbance? (2.252) And again, the invisible spirit which is accustomed to converse with me in an unseen manner prompts me with a suggestion, and says, O my friend, you seem to be ignorant of an important and most desirable matter which I will explain to you completely; for I have also in a most seasonable manner explained many other things to you also. (2.253) Know, then, O excellent man, that God alone is the truest, and most real, and genuine peace, and that every created and perishable essence is continual war. For God is something voluntary, and mortal essence is necessity. Whoever, therefore, is able to forsake war, and necessity, and creation, and destruction, and to pass over to the uncreated being, to the immortal God, to the voluntary principle, and to peace, may justly be called the abode and city of God. (2.254) Do not, therefore, consider it a different thing whether you speak of the sight of peace or the sight of God, as they are the same thing;

because peace is not only the companion but also the chief of powers of the living God, which are distinguished by many names.

XXXIX

XXXIX. (2.255) And, moreover, he says to the wise Abraham, "that he will give him an inheritance of land from the river of Egypt to the great river, the river Euphrates," [1125] not meaning a portion of the land so much as a better portion in respect of our own selves. For our own body, and the passions which exist in it, and which are engendered by it, are likened to the river of Egypt, but the soul and the passions which are dear to that are likened to the river Euphrates. (2.256) And here a doctrine is laid down, at once most profitable to life and of the highest importance, that the good man has received for his inheritance the soul and the virtues of the soul: just as, on the contrary, the wicked man has received for his share the body and the vices of the body, and those which are engendered by the body. (2.257) And the expression "from," has a double sense. One, that by which the starting point from which it begins is included; the other that by which it is excluded. For when we say that from morning to evening there are twelve hours, or from the new moon to the end of the month there are thirty days, we are including in our enumeration both the first hour and the day of the new moon. And when any one says that such and such a field is three or four furlongs distant from the city, he clearly means to leave the city itself out of that measurement. (2.258) So that now, too, we must consider that the expression, "from the river of Egypt," is to be understood so as to include that river; for the writer intends to remove us to a distance from the things of the body which are seen to exist in a constant flow and course which is being destroyed and destroying, that so we may receive the inheritance of the soul with the imperishable virtues, which are, moreover, deserving of immortality. (2.259) Thus, therefore, by tracing it out diligently, we have found that praiseworthy speech is likened to a river; but speech which is deserving of blame is the very river of Egypt itself, untractable, unwilling to learn, as one may say in a word, lifeless speech; for which reason it is also changed into blood, [1126] as not being able to afford sustenance. For the speech of ignorance is not wholesome, and it is productive of bloodless and lifeless frogs, which utter only a novel and harsh sound, a noise painful to the ear. (2.260) And it is said, likewise, that all the fish in that river were destroyed. And by the fish are here figuratively meant the conceptions; for these things float about and exist in speech as in a river, resembling living things and filling the river with life. But in uninstructed speech all conceptions die; for it is not possible to find any thing intelligent in it, but only, as some one has said, some disorderly and unmusical voices of jackdaws.

XL

XL. (2.261) We have now then said enough on these subjects. But since he not only confesses that he saw in his dream, a standing and a river, but also the banks of a river, as his words are, "I thought that I was standing by the bank (cheilos) of the River." [1127] It must be desirable to say a few seasonable things also about the bank. (2.262) Now there appears to be two most necessary objects on account of which nature has adapted lips (cheileÂ) to all animals, and especially to men; one for the same of tranquillity, for they are the strongest bulwark and fortification of the voice; the other for the sake of distinctness, for it is through them that the stream of words issues forth. For when they are closed speech is checked; for it is impossible that it should be borne outward if they are not parted. (2.263) And by these means nature prepares and trains man for both objects, speech and silence, watching the appropriate time for each employment. As for instance, is anything said worth listening to? Then attend, raising no obstacle, in perfect quiet, according to the injunction of Moses, "Be silent and Hear." [1128] (2.264) For of those persons who mix themselves up with contentious discussions there is not one who can properly be considered as either speaking or listening; but this is only advantageous to him who is about to do so. (2.265) Again, when you see, amid the wars and disasters of life, the merciful hand of God and his favourable power held over you and standing in defence of you, be silent yourself; for that champion stands in no need of any assistance. And there are proofs of this fact recorded in the sacred writings; such, for instance, as the verse, "The Lord will fight for us, and ye shall be Silent." [1129] (2.266) And if you see the genuine offspring and the firstborn of Egypt destroyed, namely desire, and pleasures, and pain, and fear, and iniquity, and mirth, and intemperance, and all the other qualities which are similar and akin to these, then marvel and be silent, dreading the terrible power of God; (2.267) for, say the scriptures, "Not a dog shall move his tongue, nor shall anything, man or beast, utter a Sound;"[1130] which is equivalent to saying, It does not become either the impudent tongue to bark and curse--nor the man that is within us, that is to say, our dominant mind; nor the cattle-like beast which is within us, that is to say, the outward sense--to boast, when all the evil that was in us has been utterly destroyed, and when an ally from without comes of his own accord to hold his shield over us.

XLI

XLI. (2.268) But there are many occasions which are not well suited to silence: and if we go to the language of ordinary prose, of which we may again see memorials laid up, how did there, ever an unexpected participation in good take place to any one? It is well, therefore, to give thanks and to sing hymns in honour of him who bestowed it. (2.269) What, then, is the good? The passion which is attacking us is dead, and is thrown out on its face without burial. Let us not delay, but standing still, let us sing that most sacred and becoming hymn, feeling that we are command to say to all men, "Let us sing unto the Lord, for he has triumphed gloriously; the horse and his rider hath he thrown into the Sea." [1131] (2.270) But the rout and destruction of the passions is indeed a good, but not a perfect good; but the discovery of wisdom is a surpassing good, and when that is found all the people will sing harmonies and melodies, not with one kind of music only, but with every sort; (2.271) for then, says the scripture, "Israel sang this song at the Well;" [1132] that is to say, in triumph for the fact that knowledge, which had long been hidden but which was sought for, had at length been found by all men, though lying deep by nature; the duty of which was to irrigate the rational fields existing in the souls of those men who are fond of contemplation. (2.272) What, then, shall we say? When we bring home the legitimate fruit of the mind, does not the sacred scripture enjoin us to display in our reason, as in a sacred basket, the first fruits of our fertility; a specimen of the glorious flowers, and shoots, and fruits which the soul has brought forth, bidding us speak out distinctly, and to utter panegyrics on the God who brings things to perfection, and to say, "I have cleared away the things which were holy out of my house, and I have arranged them in the house of God:" [1133] appointing as stewards and guardians of them, men selected for their superior merit, and giving them the charge of these sacred things; (2.273) and these persons are Levites, proselytes, and orphans, and widows. But some are suppliants, some are emigrants and fugitives, some are persons widowed and destitute of all created things, but enrolled as belonging to God, the genuine husband and father of the soul which is inclined to worship.

XLII

XLII. (2.274) In this way, then, it is most proper both to speak and to be silent. But the wicked adopt an exactly contrary course; for they are admirers of a blamable kind of silence, and of an interpretation open to reproach, practising both lines of conduct to their own destruction and that of others. (2.275) But the greater part of their employment consists in saying what they ought not; for having opened their mouth and leaving it unbridled, like an unrestrained torrent, they allow their speech to run on indiscriminately, as the poet says, dragging on thousands of profitless sayings; (2.276) therefore those who have devoted themselves to the advocacy of pleasure and appetite, and every sort of excessive desire, building up irrational passion as a fortification against dominant reason, and preparing themselves for a contentious sort of discussion, have come at last to a regular dispute, hoping to be able to blind the race which is endowed with the faculty of sight, and to throw it down precipices, and into depths from which it will not be able at any future time to emerge. (2.277) But some have not only put themselves forward as rivals to human virtue, but have proceeded to such a pitch of folly as to oppose themselves also to divine virtue. Therefore Pharaoh, the king of the land of Egypt, is spoken of as the leader of the company which is devoted to the passions; for it is said to the prophet, "Behold, he is going forth to the river, and thou shalt stand in the way to meet him, on the bank of the River;" [1134] (2.278) for it is the peculiar characteristic of the wise man to go forth to the rapidity and continual pouring forth of the irrational passion; and it is also characteristic of one man to go forth of the irrational passion; and it is also characteristic of the wise man to oppose with exceeding vigour the arguments on behalf of pleasure and desire, not with his feet, but with his mind, firmly and immoveably, standing on the bank of the river; that is to say, on the mouth and on the tongue, which are the organs of speech. For standing firmly on these, he will be able to overturn and defeat the plausible specious arguments which advocate the cause of passion. (2.279) But the enemy of the race which is endowed with the power of seeing, is the people of Pharaoh, which never ceased attacking, and persecuting, and enslaving virtue, until ... it paid the penalty for the evils which it inflicted ... being overwhelmed in the sea of those iniquities ... which it excited ... So that that period exhibited an extraordinary sight, a victory which was in no doubt, and a joy greater than could have been hoped for. (2.280) On which account it is said, "And Israel saw the Egyptians dead upon the sea-Shore." [1135] Great indeed was the hand which fought for them, compelling those who had sharpened these organs against the truth to fall by the mouth, and lips, and speech, so that they who had taken up these weapons against others should perish by their own arms and not by those of others. (2.281) And this announces three most glorious things to the soul; one, the destruction of the passions of Egypt; another, that this has taken place in no other spot than near the salt and bitter springs, as if on the shore of the sea, by which sophistical reason, that enemy of virtue, is poured forth; and, lastly, the sight of the disaster. (2.282) For no glorious thing can be invisible, but should be brought to the light and brilliancy of the sun. For so also the contrary, namely evil, should be thrust into deep darkness, and should be accounted deserving of night. And it may indeed by chance happen to some one to behold this: but what is really good should be always beheld by more piercing eyes. And what is so good as that what is good should live, and what is evil should die?

XLIII

XLIII. (2.283) There were, therefore, three persons who uttered atrocious words which were to reach even to heaven; these men devoted themselves to studies against nature, or rather against their own souls, saying that this universe was the only thing which was perceptible to the outward senses, and visible, having never been created, and being never destined to be destroyed but being uncreated and imperishable, not requiring any superintendence, or care, or regulation, or management. (2.284) Afterwards piling up fresh attempts one upon another, they built up a doctrine which was not approved, and raised it to a height like a tower; for it is said, "And the whole earth spoke one Language," [1136] an inharmonious agreement of all the portions of the soul, for the purpose of overthrowing that which is the most comprehensive of all existing principles, namely, authority. (2.285) Therefore, a great and irresistable hand overthrew them when they were hoping to mount up even to heaven by their devices, for the purpose of destroying the everlasting kingdom; and it also dashed down the doctrine which they had built up; and the place is called confusion: (2.286) a very appropriate name for such an audacious and wicked attempt; for what can be more productive of confusion than anarchy? Are not houses which have no manager full of offences and disturbances? (2.287) And are not cities which are left unprovided with a king destroyed by the domination of the mob, the opposite evil to kingly power, and at the same time the greatest of all evils? And have not countries, and nations, and regions of the earth, the governments of which have been put down, lost all their ancient and great prosperity? (2.288) And why need I speak of matters of human history? For even the other species of animals, flocks of birds, and herds of terrestrial beasts, and shoals of aquatic creatures, never exist without some leader of their company; but they always desire and always pay attention to their own leader, as being the sole cause of the advantages they receive; at whose absence they are scattered and destroyed. (2.289) Do we suppose then, that in the case of earthly creatures, which are the most insignificant portion of the universe, authority is the cause of good things and anarchy the cause of evils, but that the world itself is not filled with extreme happiness by reason of the administration of God its king? (2.290) Therefore they have suffered punishment corresponding to their iniquities: for having polluted the sacred doctrine, they saw themselves polluted in like manner, all authority being taken away from among them; and being thrown themselves into confusion, but not having really caused any. But as long as they were left unpunished, being puffed up by insane pride, they sought to overthrow the authority of the universe by unholy speeches; and they set themselves up as rulers and kings, attributing the irresistible power of God to creatures which are perpetually coming to an end and being destroyed.

XLIV

XLIV. (2.291) Therefore these ridiculous men giving themselves tragic airs and using inflated language, are accustomed to speak thus: we are they who are leaders; we are kings; On us all things depend. Who, except ourselves, is the cause of good and of the contrary? To whom, except to us, can be doing well or ill be truly attributed? They talk nonsense too in another manner, saying, that all things depend upon an invisible power, which they fancy presides over all human and divine affairs in the whole world. (2.292) Uttering such insolent falsehoods as these, if after intoxication they have become sober, and have come to themselves again, and feel ashamed of the intoxication to which they have given way coming under the dominion of the external senses, and if they reproach themselves for the evil actions which they have been led on to commit by folly, giving ear to their new counsellor, which never flatters, and which cannot be corrupted, namely, repentance, having propitiated the merciful power of the living God by sacred hymns of repentance instead of profane songs, they will find entire forgiveness. (2.293) But if they are restive and obstinate for ever, and indulge in wanton behavior, as if they were independent, and free, and the rulers of others, then by a necessity which is deaf to all entreaties and implacable, they will learn to feel their own nothingness in all things both small and great; (2.294) for the driver who mounts upon them, putting a bridle, upon this world, as though it were a winged chariot, drawing back with main strength the reins which before were loose, and pressing the bits severely, will remind them by whip and spur of his authority as master, which they, like wicked servants, have forgotten by reason of the gentle and merciful temper of their manager; (2.295) for bad servants, looking upon the gentleness of masters as anarchy, fancy themselves entirely free from the power of any master at all, until their owner checks their great and increasing disease by applying punishment as a remedy. (2.296) For which reason the expression is used of "a lawless soul, which with its lips distinguishes well-doing and evil-doing, and then will subsequently announce its own Sin." [1137] What sayest thou, O soul, full of insolence? For dost thou know what real good or real evil, real justice or real holiness, are? or what is suited to what? (2.297) The knowledge of those things and the power of regulating them belongs to God alone, and to whoever is dear to him. And witness is borne to this assertion by the scripture in which it is said, "I will kill and I will cause to live; I will smite and I will Heal." [1138] (2.298) But the mind which was wise in its own conceit had not even a superficial dreaming intimation of the things placed above it; but, wretched that it was, it was so completely carried away by the wind of vain opinion that it swore that those things which it had erroneously imagined stood firmly and solidly. (2.299) If, therefore, the violence and convulsion of the disease begin to relax, the sparks of returning health becoming gradually re-kindled, will compel it at first to confess its error, that is to say, to reproach itself, and afterwards to become a suppliant at the altar, entreating with prayers, and supplications, and sacrifices, that it may only obtain pardon.

XLV

XLV. (2.300) After this who can fairly raise the question why the historian of the scriptures has spoken of the river of Egypt only as having banks and has made no such mention of the Euphrates or of any other of the sacred rivers; for here he says, "Thou shalt stand in the way to meet him by the bank of the river." (2.301) And yet perhaps some persons in a spirit of ridicule will say that it is not right to bring such matters as these forward for investigation, for that it rather displays a spirit of cavilling than does any good. But I imagine that such things, like sweetmeats, are prepared in the sacred scriptures, for the improvement of those who read them, and that we ought not to condemn the curiosity of those who investigate such matters, but that we should rather blame their indolence if they did not investigate them. (2.302) For our present discussion is not about the history of rivers but about ways of life, which are compared to the streams of rivers, running in opposite directions to one another. For the life of the good man consists in actions; but that of the wicked man is seen to consist only in words. And speech [...] in the tongue, and mouth, and lips, and [...] [1139]

Footnotes:

1075. Gen 37:7.
1076. there is an hiatus here, and there is a good deal of corruption about the beginning of this book.
1077. Gen 28:12.
1078. Gen 31:10.
1079. Lev 19:9.
1080. Deut 1:17.
1081. Num 6:2.
1082. Num 31:28.
1083. Gen 37:7.
1084. Num 11:4.
1085. Gen 37:33.
1086. Lev 10:6.
1087. Deut 25:12.
1088. Lev 2:1.
1089. Lev 23:10.
1090. Gen 37:7.
1091. Gen 37:8.
1092. Gen 50:19.
1093. Exod 13:19.
1094. Gen 37:9.
1095. Gen 40:16.
1096. Gen 40:9.
1097. Num 13:18.
1098. Isa 5:7.
1099. Deut 30:9.
1100. Exod 5:2.
1101. Deut 23:1.
1102. Gen 18:11.
1103. Lev 16:17.
1104. Exod 7:1.
1105. Deut 32:32.

1106. Gen 40:10.
1107. Gen 41:17.
1108. Exod 17:6.
1109. Deut 8:15.
1110. Exod 24:10.
1111. Gen 9:10.
1112. Gen 18:22.
1113. Deut 5:31.
1114. Deut 10:10.
1115. Lev 16:17.
1116. Num 16:48.
1117. Gen 41:17.
1118. Gen 2:10.
1119. Ps 36:4.
1120. there is an unavoidable obscurity in the translation here. The Greek word archai, which means beginnings, or principles, and also governments.
1121. Gen 23:6.
1122. Ps 65:10.
1123. Ps 45:5.
1124. Lev 26:12.
1125. Gen 15:18.
1126. Exod 7:17.
1127. Gen 41:17.
1128. Deut 27:19.
1129. Exod 14:14.
1130. Exod 11:7.
1131. Exod 15:1.
1132. Num 21:17.
1133. Deut 26:13.
1134. Exod 7:15.
1135. Exod 14:30.
1136. Gen 11:1.
1137. Lev 5:4.
1138. Deut 32:39.
1139. the rest of this treatise is lost.

ON ABRAHAM [1140]

I

I. (1) The sacred laws having been written in five books, the first is called and inscribed Genesis, deriving its title from the creation (genesis) of the world, which it contains at the beginning; although there are ten thousand other matters also introduced which refer to peace and to war, or to fertility and barrenness, or to hunger and plenty, or to the terrible destructions which have taken place on earth by the agency of fire and water; or, on the contrary, to the birth and rapid propagation of animals and plants in accordance with the admirable arrangement of the atmosphere, and the seasons of the year, and of men, some of whom lived in accordance with virtue, while others were associated with wickedness. (2) But since of these things some are portions of the world, and some are accidents, and since the world is the most perfect and complete of all things, he has normally assigned the whole book to that subject. We have then examined with all the accuracy that was in our power, in what manner the creation of the world was arranged in our previous treatises; (3) but since it is necessary, to be consistent with the regular order in which the sacred history proceeds to go on, now to investigate the laws, we will for the present postpone the particular laws which are copies as it were; and first of all examine the more general laws which are, as it were, the models of the others. (4) Now these are those men who have lived irreproachably and admirably, whose virtues are durably and permanently recorded, as on pillars in the sacred scriptures, not merely with the object of praising the men themselves, but also for the sake of exhorting those who read their history, and of leading them on to emulate their conduct; (5) for these men have been living and rational laws; and the lawgiver has magnified them for two reasons; first, because he was desirous to show that the injunctions which are thus given are not inconsistent with nature; and, secondly, that he might prove that it is not very difficult or laborious for those who wish to live according to the laws established in these books, since the earliest men easily and spontaneously obeyed the unwritten principle of legislation before any one of the particular laws were written down at all. So that a man may very properly say, that the written laws are nothing more than a memorial of the life of the ancients, tracing back in an antiquarian spirit, the actions and reasonings which they adopted; (6) for these first men, without ever having been followers or pupils of any one, and without ever having been taught by preceptors what they ought to do or say, but having embraced a line of conduct consistent with nature from attending to their own natural impulses, and from being prompted by an innate virtue, and looking upon nature herself to be, what in fact she is, the most ancient and duly established of laws, did in reality spend their whole lives in making laws, never of deliberate purpose doing anything open to reproach, and for their accidental errors propitiating God, and appeasing him by prayers and supplications, so as to procure for themselves the enjoyment of an entire life of virtue and prosperity, both in respect of their deliberate actions, and those which proceeded from no voluntary purpose.

II

II. (7) Since then the beginning of all participation in good things is hope, and since the soul devoted to virtue pioneers and opens this path as a plain and easy one, being anxious to attain to that which is really honourable, the sacred historian has named the first lover of hope, Enos, giving him the common name of the whole race as an especial favour. (8) For the Chaldaeans call man Enos; as if he were the only real man, who lived in expectation of good things, and who is established in good hopes; from which it is evident that they do not look upon the man devoid of hope as a man at all, but rather as an animal resembling a man, inasmuch as he is deprived of that most peculiar possession of the human soul, namely hope. (9) For which reason, being desirous to deliver an admirable panegyric on the hopeful man, the sacred historian tells us, first, that "he hoped in the father and creator of the Universe," [1141] and adds in a subsequent passage, "This is the book of the generation of Men," [1142] and of their fathers, and grandfathers who had existed previously; but he conceived that they were the ancestors of the mixed race, that is to say, of that purer and thoroughly sifted race which is the really rational one; (10) for, as the poet Homer, though the number of poets is beyond all calculation, is called "the poet" by way of distinction, and as the black [ink] with which we write is called "the black," though in point of fact everything which is not white is black; and as that archon at Athens is especially called "the archon," who is the archon eponymus and the chief of the nine archons, from whom the chronology is dated; so in the same manner the sacred historian calls him who indulges in hope, "a man," by way of pre-eminence, passing over in silence the rest of the multitude of human beings, as not being worthy to receive the same appellation. (11) And he has very properly called the first volume, the Book of the Generation of the Real Man, speaking with perfect correctness; because the man who is full of good hope is worthy of being described and remembered, not with such a memory as is given by a record in papers, which are hereafter to be destroyed by bookworms, but by that which exists in immortal nature, where the virtuous actions are regularly recorded. (12) If then any one were to reckon the generations, from the first man, who was made out of the earth, he will find him who, by the Chaldaeans is called Enos, and in the Greek language anthroÂpos (the man), to be the fourth in succession, (13) and in numbers the number four is honoured among other philosophers, who have studied and admired the incorporeal essences, appreciable only by the intellect, and especially by the all-wise Moses, who magnifies the number four, and says that it is "holy and Praiseworthy;"[1143] and the reasons for which this character has been given to it are mentioned in a former treatise. (14) And the man who is full of good hope is likewise holy and praiseworthy; as, on the contrary, he who has no hope is accursed and blameable, being always associated with fear, which is an evil counsellor in any emergency; for they say, that there is no one thing so hostile to another, as hope is to fear and fear to hope, and perhaps this may be correctly said, for both fear and hope are an expectation, but the one is an expectation of good things, and the other, on the contrary, of evil things; and the natures of good and evil are irreconcileable, and such as can never come together.

III

III. (15) What has now been said about hope is sufficient; and nature has placed her at the gates to be a sort of doorkeeper to the royal virtues within, which no one may approach who has not previously paid homage to hope. (16) Therefore the lawgivers, and the laws in every state on earth, labour with great diligence to fill the souls of free men with good hopes; but he who, without any recommendation and without being enjoined to be so, is nevertheless hopeful, has acquired this virtue by an unwritten, self-taught law, which nature has implanted in him. (17) That which is placed in the next rank after hope is repentance for errors committed, and improvement; in reference to which principle Moses mentions next in order to Enos, the man who changed from a worse system of life to a better, who is called among the Hebrews Enoch, but as the Greeks would say, "gracious," of whom the following statement is made, "that Enoch pleased God, and was not found, because God transported Him."[1144] (18) For transportation shows a change and alteration: and such a change is for the better, because it takes place through the providence of God; for every thing that is with God is in very case honourable and advantageous, since that which is destitute of any divine superintendence is useless and unprofitable. (19) And the expression, "he was not Found,"[1145] is very appropriately employed of him whose place was changed, either from the fact of his ancient blameable life being wiped out and effaced, and being no longer found, just as if it had never existed at all, or else because he whose place has been changed, and who is enrolled in a better class; is naturally difficult to be discovered. For wickedness is a very multiform and extensive thing, on which account it is known to many persons; but virtue is rare, so that it is not comprehended even by a few. (20) And besides, the bad man runs about through the market-place, and theatres, and courts of justice, and council halls, and assemblies, and every meeting and collection of men whatever, like one who lives with and for curiosity, letting loose his tongue in immoderate, and interminable, and indiscriminate conversation, confusing and disturbing every thing, mixing up what is true and what is false, what is unspeakable with what is public, private with public things, things profane with things sacred, what is ridiculous with what is excellent, from never having been instructed in what is the most excellent thing in season, namely silence. (21) And pricking up his ears, because of the abundance of his leisure, and his superfluous curiosity, and love of interference, he is eager to make himself acquainted with the business of other people, whether good or bad, so as at once to envy those who are prosperous, and to rejoice over those who are not so; for the bad man is by nature envious and a hater of all that is good, and a lover of all that is evil.

IV

IV. (22) But the good man, on the contrary, is a lover of that mode of life which is not troubled by business, and withdraws, and loves solitude, desiring to escape the notice of the many, not out of misanthropy, for he is a lover of mankind, if any one in the world is so, but because he eschews wickedness, which the chief multitude eagerly embraces, rejoicing at what it ought to mourn over, and grieving at what it is becoming rather to rejoice. (23) On which account the good man shuts himself up, and remains for the most part at home, scarcely going over his threshold, or if he does go out, for the sake of avoiding the crowds who come to visit him, he generally goes out of the city, and makes his abode in some country place, living more pleasantly with such companions as are the most virtuous of all mankind, whose bodies, indeed, time has dissolved, but whose virtues the records which are left of them keep alive, in poems and in prose, histories by which the soul is naturally improved and led on to perfection. (24) It is on this account that the sacred historian has said that the man whose place was changed was not found, inasmuch as he is difficult to find and hard to seek out. Therefore, such a man emigrates from ignorance to instruction, and from folly to wisdom and from cowardice to courage, and from impiety to piety; and, again, from devotion to pleasure to temperance, and from vaingloriousness to simplicity, qualities superior to all riches, and more valuable as a possession than any royal or imperial power. (25) For if one may speak the plain truth, that wealth which is not blind, but which is clear-sighted, is the abundance of virtues, which we must at once conclude to be the genuine and legitimate predominance of good in comparison of all other bastard and falsely named powers, and to be the just and lawful superior of them all. (26) But we must not be ignorant that repentance occupies the second place only, next after perfection, just as the change from sickness to convalescence is inferior to perfect uninterrupted health. Therefore, that which is continuous and perfect in virtues is very near divine power, but that condition which is improvement advancing in process of time is the peculiar blessing of a welldisposed soul, which does not continue in its childish pursuits, but by more vigorous thoughts and inclinations, such as really become a man, seeks a tranquil steadiness of soul, and which attains to it by its conception of what is good.

V

V. (27) For which reason the sacred historian very naturally classes the lover of God and the lover of virtue next in order to him who repents; and this man is in the language of the Hebrews called Noah, but in that of the Greeks, "rest," or "the just man," both being appellations very well suited to the wise man. That of "the just man" most evidently so, for nothing is better than justice, which is the chief among virtues, and which receives the highest honours like the most beautiful member of a company; and the appellation "rest" is likewise appropriate, since the opposite quality to rest is unnatural agitation, the cause of confusion, and tumults, and seditions, and wars, which the wicked pursue; while those who pay due honour to excellence cultivate a tranquil, and quiet, and stable, and peaceful life. (28) And in strict consistency with himself, the lawgiver also calls the seventh day "rest," which the Hebrews call "the sabbath;" not as some persons fancy, because after six days the multitude was refrained from its habitual employments, but because in real truth, the number seven is both in the world and in ourselves free from seditions and from wars, and is of all the numbers that which is the most averse to contention, and the greater lover of peace. (29) And a proof of what I have here asserted may be found in the powers which exist in us; for six of those powers, namely the five outward senses and uttered speech, stir up continued and ceaseless war, both by sea and land, some of them doing so from a desire for the objects of the outward senses, which if they cannot obtain they are grieved, and the last by divulging with unbridled mouth numbers of things which ought to be buried in silence. (30) But the seventh power is that which proceeds from the dominant mind, which is more glorious than the other six powers, and which has by pre-eminent vigour obtained the mastery over them all, and when that retires, choosing solitude, and its own society, and living by itself, as one that has no need of any other, and that is all-sufficient for itself, being then emancipated from the cares and troubles that are found in the human race, embraces a calm and tranquil life.

VI

VI. (31) And the lawgiver magnifies the lover of virtue in such a way, that even when he is given his genealogy, he does not trace himself as he usually does other persons, by giving a catalogue of his grandfathers and great grandfathers, and ancestors who are numbered as men and women, but he gives a list of certain virtues; and almost asserts in express words that there is no other house, or kindred, or country whatever to a wise man, except the virtues and the actions in accordance with virtues. "For these," says he, "are the generations of Noah; Noah was a just man, perfect in his generation, and one who pleased God." [1146] (32) But we must not be ignorant that when he says man here, he does not mean merely to use the common expressions for a rational mortal animal, but that he means to indicate in an eminent degree him who verifies the name, having driven away all the untameable and furious passions and brutal wickednesses of the soul; (33) and as a proof of this, after the word man he adds as an epithet, "the just," saying, "a just man," as if no unjust person were a man at all, but to speak more properly a beast in the likeness of a man, and as if he alone were a man who is an admirer of justice; (34) he also says that he was "perfect," intimating by this expression that he was possessed not of one virtue only but of all, and that being so possessed of them, he constantly exhibited every one of them according to his power and opportunities; (35) and finally crowning him like a wrestler who has gained a glorious victory, he honours him moreover with a most noble proclamation, saying that "he pleased God," (and what can there be in nature that is more excellent than this panegyric?) which is the most visible proof of excellence; for if they who displease God are miserable, those who please him are by all means happy.

VII

VII. (36) It is not then without great correctness that after he has praised the man as being possessed of such great virtues he adds, "and he was perfect in his generation." Showing that he was not perfect absolutely, but that he was good in comparison with the others who lived at that time; (37) for in a little time he will also speak of other wise men who were possessed of unconquerable and incomparable virtue, not merely if contrasted with the wicked, nor because they were better than the other men of their age, and as such were considered worthy of acceptance and pre-eminence, but because having received a well disposed nature, they preserved it without any error or change for the worse; not fleeing from evil habits, but never having once fallen into them, and being by deliberate purpose practicers of all virtuous actions and speeches, by which system they had adorned their life. (38) Those then are the most admirable of all men who have adopted free and noble inclinations, not in imitation of or by way of contrast to others, but from an inclination to genuine virtue and justice for its own sake; he also is to be admired who is superior to his own generation and his own age, and who is overcome by none of those things which the multitude follows; and he will be classed in the second rank, and nature will give to such men the best of her prizes; (39) and the second prize is of itself a great thing; for what is not a great and most desirable object which God offers to, and bestows upon men? And the greatest proof of this is to be found in the exceeding graces which this man attained to; (40) for as that time bore an abundant crop of injustice and impiety, and so every country, and nation, and city, and house, and every separate individual was full of wicked practices, all men of free will and of deliberate purpose, as if in an arena, living with one another for the first rank in iniquity, and strove with all possible zeal and rivalry, every one seeking to surpass his neighbour in the magnitude of his wickedness, and failing in nothing which might render life blameless and accursed.

VIII

VIII. (41) At whom God, being naturally indignant, and being angry that that which appeared to be the most excellent of animals, and which had been thought worthy of being reckoned akin to himself by reason of his participation in reason, when he ought to have practised virtue, devoted himself rather to wickedness, and to every species of vice, appointed a fitting punishment for them, and determined to destroy the whole race at that time existing by a deluge; and not only those who dwelt in the champain country and in the lower districts, (42) but those also who lived in the most lofty mountains, for the great deep, [1147] being raised to a height which it had never reached before, burst through its mouths with its whole collective impetuosity into the seas existing among us, and they overflowed and inundated all the islands and continents; and incessant floods of everlasting fountains, and of native rivers and torrents combined together, mingled with one another, and rising to a vast height, so as to surmount everything. (43) Nor indeed was the air tranquil, for a deep and unbroken cloud overspread the whole heaven, and there were fearful storms of wind, and roarings of thunder, and flashes of lightning, and rapid hurlings of thunderbolts, ceaseless storms of rain being poured forth, so that one might have thought that all the parts of the universe were hastening to dissolve themselves into the one element of the nature of water, until, while the water from above kept pouring down, and that below kept bursting up, the streams were raised to a height above everything, so that they not only overwhelmed and hid from sight all the plains and all the level ground, but even the tops of the highest mountains, (44) for every part of the earth was under water, so that it was wholly buried and carried away, and the world was mutilated of huge portions, and appeared in all its wholeness and integrity, fearful as it is to say or even to imagine such a thing, to be utterly crippled and destroyed. And likewise the air, with the exception of that small portion which is about the moon, was wholly obscured, being overcast by the violence and impetuosity of the water which overran all the region belonging to it with irresistible might. (45) Then were speedily destroyed all the crops and all the trees, for an unlimited quantity of water is as destructive to them as a scarcity, and innumerable flocks of animals, both tame and wild, perished at the same time; for it was natural when the most excellent race of all, that of man, had been destroyed, that none of the inferior races should be left, since they were only created to be slaves to his necessities, and to be in a manner subject to his authoritative commands as their master. (46) When such numbers then of such mighty evils had burst forth which that time poured out--for all the portions of the world, except the heaven itself, were moved in an unnatural manner--as if they were stricken with a terrible and deadly disease. And one house alone, that of the aforesaid just and God-loving man who had received the two highest of all gifts, was preserved; one gift being, as I have said already, the not being destroyed with all the rest of mankind, the other that of becoming himself, at a subsequent period, the founder of a new generation of mankind; for God thought him worthy to be both the end of our race and the beginning of it, the end of those men who lived before the deluge, and the beginning of those who lived after the deluge.

IX

IX. (47) Such was he who was the most virtuous of all the men of his age, and such were the rewards which were allotted to him which the holy scriptures enumerate; and the arrangement and classification of the aforesaid three, whether you call them men or dispositions of the soul, is very symmetrical, for the perfect man is entire from the beginning; but he who has his place changed is but half entire, having appropriated the earlier period of his life to wickedness, and the subsequent time to virtue to which he afterwards came over, and with which at that subsequent time he lived. But he who hopes, as his very name shows, has still a defect, for though he is always wishing for what is good, he is not as yet able to attain to it, but he is like those who are on a voyage, who while they are eager to reach the harbour, are still kept at sea without being able to anchor in port.

X

X. (48) I have now then explained the character of the first triad of those who desire virtue. There is also another more important company of which we must now proceed to speak, for the former resembles those branches of instruction which are allotted to the age of childhood, but this resembles rather the gymnastic exercises of athletic men, who are really preparing themselves for the sacred contests, who, despising all care of getting their body into proper condition, labour to bring about a healthy state of the soul, being desirous of that victory which is to be gained over the adverse passions. (49) The particulars then on which each individual differs from the other, though all are hastening to one and the same end, we will hereafter examine more minutely; but it is necessary not to pass over in silence what it seems desirable to premise concerning the whole three taken together. (50) It happens then that they are all three of one household and of one family, for the last of the three is the son of the middle one, and the grandson of the first; and they are all lovers of God, and beloved by God, loving the only God, and being loved in return by him who has chosen, as the holy scriptures tell us, by reason of the excess of their virtues in which they lived, to give them also a share of the same appellation as himself; (51) for having added his own peculiar name to their names he has united them together, appropriating to himself an appellation composed of the three names: "For," says God, "this is my everlasting name: I am the God of Abraham, and the God of Isaac, and the God of Jacob," [1148] using there the relative term instead of the absolute one; and this is very natural, for God stands in no need of a name. But though he does not stand in any such need, nevertheless he bestows his own title on the human race that they may have a refuge to which to betake themselves in supplications and prayers, and so may not be destitute of a good hope.

XI

XI. (52) This then is what appears to be said of these holy men; and it is indicative of a nature more remote from our knowledge than, and much superior to, that which exists in the objects of outward sense; for the sacred word appears thoroughly to investigate and to describe the different dispositions of the soul, being all of them good, the one aiming at what is good by means of instruction, the second by nature, the last by practice; for the first, who is named Abraham, is a symbol of that virtue which is derived from instruction; the intermediate Isaac is an emblem of natural virtue; the third, Jacob, of that virtue which is devoted to and derived from practice. (53) But we must not be ignorant that each of these men was endowed with all these powers, but that each derived his name from that one which predominated in him and mastered the others; for neither is it possible for instruction to be made perfect without natural endowments and practice, nor is nature able to arrive at the goal without instruction and practice, nor is practice unless it be founded on natural gifts and sound instruction. (54) Very appropriately, therefore, he has represented, as united by relationship, these three, which in name indeed are men, but in reality, as I have said before, virtues, nature, instruction, and practice, which men also call by another name, and entitle them the three graces (charites), either from the fact of God having bestowed (kecharisthai) on our race those three powers, in order to produce the perfection of life, or because they themselves have bestowed themselves on the rational soul as the most glorious of gifts, so that the eternal name, as set forth in the scriptures, may not be used in conjunction with three men, but rather with the aforesaid powers; (55) for the nature of mankind is mortal, but that of virtues is immortal; and it is more reasonable that the name of the everlasting God should be conjoined with what is immortal than with what is mortal, since what is immortal is akin to what is imperishable, but death is hostile to it.

XII

XII. (56) We must, however, not remain in ignorance that the sacred historian has represented the first man, him who was formed out of the earth as the father of all those who existed before the deluge; and him who, with his whole family, was the only person left out of so universal a destruction, because of his justice and his other excellencies and virtues, as the founder of the new race of men which was to flourish hereafter. And that venerable, and estimable, and glorious triad is comprehended by the sacred scriptures under one class, and called, "A royal priesthood, and a holy Nation."[1149] (57) And its name shows its power; for the nation is further called, in the language of the Hebrews, Israel, which name being interpreted means, "seeing God." But of sight, that which is exercised by means of the eyes is the most excellent of all the outward senses, since by that alone all the most beautiful of existing things are comprehended, the sun and the moon, and the whole heaven, and the whole world; but the sight of the soul which is exercised, through the medium of its dominant part excel all other powers of the soul, as much as the powers of the soul excel all other powers; and this is prudence, which is the sight of the mind. (58) But he to whose lot it falls, not only by means of his knowledge, to comprehend all the other things which exist in nature, but also to behold the Father and Creator of the universe, has advanced to the very summit of happiness. For there is nothing above God; and if any one, directing towards him the eye of the soul, has reached up to him, let him then pray for ability to remain and to stand firm before him; (59) for the roads which lead upwards to him are laborious and slow, but the descent down the declivity, being rather like a rapid dragging down than a gradual descent, is swift and easy. And there are many things urged downwards, in which there is no use whatever, when God having made the soul to depend on his own powers, drags it up towards himself with a more vigorous attraction.

XIII

XIII. (60) Let thus much, then, be said generally about the three persons, since it was absolutely necessary; but we must now proceed in regular order, to speak of those qualities in which each separate individual surpasses the others, beginning with him who is first mentioned. Now he, being an admirer of piety, the highest and greatest of all virtues, laboured earnestly to follow God, and to be obedient to the injunctions delivered by him, looking not only on those things as his commands which were signified to him by words and facts, but those also which were indicated by more express signs through the medium of nature, and which the truest of the outward senses comprehends before the uncertain and untrustworthy hearing can do so; (61) for if any one observes the arrangement which exists in nature, and the constitution according to which the world goes on, which is more excellent than any kind of reasoning, he learns, even though no one speaks to him, to study a course of life consistent with law and peace, looking to the example of good men. But the most manifest demonstrations of peace are those which the scriptures contain; and we must mention the first which also occurs the first in the order in which they are set down.

XIV

XIV. (62) He being impressed by an oracle by which he was commanded to leave his country, and his kindred, and his father's house, and to emigrate like a man returning from a foreign land to his own country, and not like one who was about to set out from his own land to settle in a foreign district, hastened eagerly on, thinking to do with promptness what he was commanded to do was equivalent to perfecting the matter. (63) And yet who else was it likely would be so undeviating and unchangeable as not to be won over by and as not to yield to the charms of one's relations and one's country? The love for which has in a manner--

of every individual, and even more, or at all events not less than the limbs united to the body have done. (64) And we have witnesses of this in the lawgivers who have enacted the second punishment next to death, namely, banishment, against those who are convicted of the most atrocious crimes: a punishment which indeed is not second to any, as it appears to me, if truth be the judge, but which is, in fact, much more grievous than death, since death is the end of all misfortunes, but banishment is not the end but the beginning of new calamities, inflicting instead of our death unaccompanied by pain ten thousand deaths with acute sensation. (65) Some men also, being engaged in traffic, do out of desire for gain sail over the sea, or being employed in some embassy, or being led by a desire to see the sights of foreign countries, or by a love for instruction, having various motives which attract them outwards and prevent their remaining where they are, some being led by a love of gain, others by the idea of being able to benefit their native city at its time of need in the most necessary and important particulars, others seeking to arrive at the knowledge of matters of which before they were ignorant, a knowledge which brings, at the same time, both delight and advantage to the soul. For men who have never travelled are to those who have, as blind men are to those who see clearly, are nevertheless anxious to behold their father's threshold and to salute it, and to embrace their acquaintances, and to enjoy the most delightful and wished-for sight of their relations and friends; and very often, seeing the affairs, for the sake of which they left their country, protracted, they have abandoned them, being influenced by that most powerful feeling of longing for a union with their kindred. (66) But this man with a few companions, or perhaps I might say by himself, as soon as he was commanded to do so, left his home, and set out on an expedition to a foreign country in his soul even before he started with his body, his regard for mortal things being overpowered by his love for heavenly things. (67) Therefore giving no consideration to anything whatever, neither to the men of his tribe, nor to those of his borough, nor to his fellow disciples, nor to his companions, nor those of his blood as sprung from the same father or the same mother, nor to his country, nor to his ancient habits, nor to the customs in which he had been brought up, nor to his mode of life and his mates, every one of which things has a seductive and almost irresistible attraction and power, he departed as speedily as possible, yielding to a free and unrestrained impulse, and first of all he quitted the land of the Chaldaeans, a prosperous district, and one which was greatly flourishing at that period, and went into the land of Charran, and from that, after no very distant interval, he departed to another place, which we will speak of hereafter, when we have first discussed the country of Charran.

XV

XV. (68) The aforesaid emigrations, if one is to be guided by the literal expressions of the scripture, were performed by a wise man; but if we look to the laws of allegory, by a soul devoted to virtue and busied in the search after the true God. (69) For the Chaldaeans were, above all nations, addicted to the study of astronomy, and attributed all events to the motions of the stars, by which they fancied that all the things in the world were regulated, and accordingly they magnified the visible essence by the powers which numbers and the analogies of numbers contain, taking no account of the invisible essence appreciable only by the intellect. But while they were busied in investigating the arrangement existing in them with reference to the periodical revolutions of the sun, and moon, and the other planets, and fixed-stars, and the changes of the seasons of the year, and the sympathy of the heavenly bodies with the things of the earth, they were led to imagine that the world itself was God, in their impious philosophy comparing the creature to the Creator. (70) The man who had been bred up in this doctrine, and who for a long time had studied the philosophy of the Chaldaeans, as if suddenly awakening from a deep slumber and opening the eye of the soul, and beginning to perceive a pure ray of light instead of profound darkness, followed the light, and saw what he had never see before, a certain governor and director of the world standing above it, and guiding his own work in a salutary manner, and exerting his care and power in behalf of all those parts of it which are worthy of divine superintendence. (71) In order, therefore, that he may the more firmly establish the sight which has thus been presented to him in his mind, the sacred word says to him, My good friend, great things are often made known by slight outlines, at which he who looks increases his imagination to an unlimited extent; therefore, having dismissed those who bend all their attention to the heavenly bodies, and discarding the Chaldaean science, rise up and depart for a short time from the greatest of cities, this world, to one which is smaller; for so you will be the better able to comprehend the nature of the Ruler of the universe. (72) It is for this reason that Abraham is said to have made this first migration from the country of the Chaldaeans into the land of Charran.

XVI

XVI. But Charran, in the Greek language, means "holes," which is a figurative emblem of the regions of our outward senses; by means of which, as by holes, each of those senses is able to look out so as to comprehend the objects which belong to it. (73) But, some one may say, what is the use of these holes, unless the invisible mind, like the exhibition of a puppet show, does from within prompt its own powers, which at one time losing and allowing to roam, and at another time holding back and restraining by force? He gives sometimes an harmonious motion, and sometimes perfect quiet to his puppets. And having this example at home, you will easily comprehend that being, the understanding of whom you are so anxious to arrive at; (74) unless, indeed, you fancy that the world is situated in you as the dominant part of you, which the whole common powers of the body obey, and which each of the outward senses follows; but that the world, the most beautiful, and greatest, and most perfect of works, of which everything else is but a part, is destitute of any king to hold it together, and to regulate it, and govern it in accordance with justice. And if it be invisible, wonder not at that, for neither can the mind which is in thee be perceived by the sight. (75) Any one who considers this, deriving his proofs not from a distance but close at hand, both from himself and from the circumstances around him, will clearly see that the world is not the first God, but that it is the work of the first God and Father of all things, who, being himself invisible, displays every thing, showing the nature of all things both small and great. (76) For he has not chosen to be beheld by the eyes of the body, perhaps because it was not consistent with holiness for what is mortal to touch what is everlasting, or perhaps because of the weakness of our sight; for it would never have been able to stand the rays which are poured forth from the living God, since it cannot even look straight at the rays of the sun.

XVII

XVII. (77) And the most visible proof of this migration in which the mind quitted astronomy and the doctrines of the Chaldaeans, is this. For it is said in the scriptures that the very moment that the wise man quitted his abode, "God appeared unto Abraham," [1150] to whom, therefore, it is plain that he was not visible before, when he was adhering to the studies of the Chaldaeans, and attending to the motions of the stars, not properly comprehending any nature whatever, which was well arranged and appreciable by the intellect only, apart from the world and the essence perceptible by the outward senses. (78) But after he changed his abode and went into another country he learnt of necessity that the world was subject, and not independent; not an absolute ruler, but governed by the great cause of all things who had created it, whom the mind then for the first time looked up and saw; (79) for previously a great mist was shed over it by the objects of the external senses, which she, having dissipated by fervent and vivid doctrines, was scarcely able, as if in clear fine weather, to perceive him who had previously been concealed and invisible. But he, by reason of his love for mankind, did not reject the soul which came to him, but went forward to meet it, and showed to it his own nature as far as it was possible that he who was looking at it could see it. (80) For which reason it is said, not that the wise man saw God but that God appeared to the wise man; for it was impossible for any one to comprehend by his own unassisted power the true living God, unless he himself displayed and revealed himself to him.

XVIII

XVIII. (81) And there is evidence in support of what has here been said to be derived from the change and alteration of his name: for he was anciently called Abram, but afterwards he was named Abraham: the alteration of sound being only that which proceeds from one single letter, alpha, being doubled, but the alteration revealing in effect an important fact and doctrine; (82) for the name Abram being interpreted means "sublime father;" but Abraham signifies, "the elect father of sound." The first name being expressive of the man who is called an astronomer, and one addicted to the contemplation of the sublime bodies in the sky, and who was versed in the doctrines of the Chaldaeans, and who took care of them as a father might take care of his children. (83) But the last name intimating the really wise man; for the latter name, by the word sound, intimates the uttered speech; and by the word father, the dominant mind. For the speech which is conceived within is naturally the father of that which is uttered, inasmuch as it is older than the latter, and as it also suggests what is to be said. And by the addition of the word elect his goodness is intimated. For the evil disposition is a random and confused one, but that which is elect is good, having been selected from all others by reason of its excellence. (84) Therefore, to him who is addicted to the contemplation of the sublime bodies of the sky there appears to be nothing whatever greater than the world; and therefore he refers the causes of all things that exist to the world. But the wise man, beholding with more accurate eyes that more perfect being that rules and governs all things, and is appreciable only by the intellect, to whom all things are subservient as to the master, and by whom every thing is directed, very often reproaches himself for his former way of life, and if he had lived the existence of a blind man, leaning upon objects perceptible by the outward senses, on things by their very nature worthless and unstable. (85) The second migration is again undertaken by the virtuous man under the influence of a sacred oracle, but this is no longer one from one city to another, but it is to a desolate country, in which he wandered about for a long time without being discontented at his wandering and at his unsettled condition, which necessarily arose from it. (86) And yet, what other man would not have been grieved, not only at departing from his own country but also at being driven away from every city into an inaccessible and impassable district? And what other man would have not turned back and returned to his former home, paying but little attention to his former hopes, but desiring to escape from his present perplexity, thinking it folly for the sake of uncertain advantages to undergo admitted evils? (87) But this man alone appears to have behaved in the contrary manner, thinking that life which was remote from the fellowship of many companions the most pleasant of all. And this is naturally the case; for those who seek and desire to find God, love that solitude which is dear to him, labouring for this as their dearest and primary object, to become like his blessed and happy nature. (88) Therefore, having now given both explanations, the literal one as concerning the man, and the allegorical one relating to the soul, we have shown that both the man and the mind are deserving of love; inasmuch as the one is obedient to the sacred oracles, and because of their influence submits to be torn away from things which it is hard to part; and the mind deserves to be loved because it has not submitted to be for ever deceived and to abide permanently with the essences perceptible by the outward senses, thinking the visible world the greatest and first of gods, but soaring upwards with its reason it has beheld another nature better than that which is visible, that, namely, which is appreciable only by the intellect; and also that being who is at the same time the Creator and ruler of both.

XIX

XIX. (89) These, then, are the first principles of the man who loves God, and they are followed by actions which do not deserve to be lightly esteemed. But the greatness of them is not evident to every one, but only to those who have tasted of virtue, and who are wont to look with ridicule upon the objects which are admired by the multitude, by reason of the greatness of the good things of the soul. (90) Therefore, God, having approved of his conduct which I have mentioned, presently rewarded the virtuous man with a great gift, inasmuch as he preserved sound and free from all pollution his marriage, which was in danger of being plotted against by a powerful and incontinent man. (91) And the cause of this man's design upon it arose from this beginning; there having been a barrenness and scarcity of crops for a long time, owing to a long and immoderate period of rain which prevailed at one time, and to a great drought and heat which ensued afterwards. The cities of Syria being oppressed by a long continuance of famine, became destitute of inhabitants, all of them being dispersed in different directions for the purpose of seeking food and providing themselves with necessaries. (92) Therefore, Abraham, hearing that there was unlimited abundance and plenty in Egypt, since the river there irrigated the fields with its inundations at the proper season, and since the winds by their salutary temperature brought up and nourished rich and heavy crops of corn, rose up with all his household to quit Syria and to go thither. (93) And he had a wife of a most excellent disposition, who was also the most beautiful of all the women of her time. The Egyptian magistrates, seeing her and admiring her exquisite form, for nothing ever escapes the notice of men in authority, gave information to the king. (94) And the king, sending for the woman and beholding her extreme beauty, gave but little heed to the dictates of modesty or to the laws which had been established with respect to the honour due to strangers, but yielding to his incontinent desires, conceived the intention in name, indeed, to marry her in lawful wedlock, but, in fact to seduce and defile her. (95) But she, being destitute of all succour, as being in a foreign land, before an incontinent and cruel-minded ruler (for her husband had no power to protect her, fearing the danger which impended over him from princes mightier than he), at last, with him, took refuge in the only alliance remaining to her, the protection of God. (96) And the merciful and gracious God, who takes compassion on the stranger, and who fights on behalf of those who are unjustly oppressed, inflicted in a moment painful sufferings and terrible chastisements on the king, filling his body and soul with all kinds of miseries difficult to be escaped or remedied, so that all his inclinations tending to pleasure were cut short, and, on the contrary, he was occupied with nothing but cares, seeking an alleviation from his endless and intolerable torments by which he was harrassed and tortured day and night; (97) and his whole household also received their share of his punishment, because none of them had felt any indignation at his lawless conduct, but had all consented to it, and had all but co-operated actively in his iniquity. (98) In this manner the chastity of the woman was preserved, and God condescended to display the excellence and piety of her husband, giving him the noblest reward, namely, his marriage free from all injury, and even from all insult, so as no longer to be in danger of being violated; a marriage which however was not intended to produce any limited number of sons and daughters--the most God-loving of all nations--and one which appears to me to have received the offices of priesthood and prophecy on behalf of the whole human race.

XX

XX. (99) I have heard men versed in natural philosophy interpreting this passage in an allegorical manner with no inconsiderable ingenuity and propriety; and their idea is, that the man here is a symbolical expression for the virtuous mind, conjecturing from the interpretation of his name that what is intended to be indicated is the virtuous disposition existing in the soul; and that by his wife is meant virtue, for the name of his wife is, in the Chaldaean language, Sarah, but in Greek "princess," because there is nothing more royal or more worthy of pre-eminence than virtue. (100) And the marriage in which pleasure unites people comprehends the connection of the bodies, but that which is brought about by wisdom is the union of reasonings which desire purification, and of the perfect virtues; and the two kinds of marriage here described are extremely opposite to one another; (101) for in the marriage of the bodies it is the male partner which sows the seed and the female which receives it, but in the union which takes place with regard to the soul it is quite the contrary, and it is virtue which appears to be there in the place of the woman, which sows good counsels, and virtuous speeches, and expositions of doctrines profitable to life; but the reason which is considered to be classed in the light of the man receives the sacred and divine seed, unless, indeed, there is any error in the names usually given; for certainly, in the grammatical view of the words, the word reason is masculine, and the word virtue has a feminine character. (102) But if any one, discarding the considerations of the names which tend to throw darkness over the subject, chooses to look at the plain facts without any disguise, he will know that virtue is masculine by nature, inasmuch as it puts things in motion, and arranges them, and suggests good conceptions of noble actions and speeches; but reason is feminine, inasmuch as it is put in motion by another, and is instructed and benefited, and, in short, is altogether the patient, as its passive state is its own safety.

XXI

XXI. (103) All men, therefore, even the most vile, in word honour and admire virture as far as appearance goes; but it is the virtuous alone who obey its injunctions; on which account the king of Egypt, who is a figurative representation of the mind devoted to the body, as if he were acting in a theatre, assumes the character of a pretended participation in temperance though being an intemperate man, and in continence though being an incontinent man, and in justice though an unjust man, and he invites justice to himself, being eager to obtain a good report from the multitude; (104) and the governor of the universe seeing this, for God alone has power to look into the soul, hates him and rejects him, and by the most cruel tests and powers convicts him of an utterly false disposition. But by what instruments are these tests carried out? Surely altogether by the parts of virtue which, whenever they enter, inflict great pain and severe wounds; for a torture is a deficiency of supply to that which is insatiable, and the torture of greediness is temperance; moreover, the man who is fond of glory is tortured while simplicity and humility are in the ascendent, and so is the unjust man when justice is extolled; (105) for it is impossible for two hostile natures to inhabit one soul, namely, for wickedness and virtue, for which reason, when they do come together, endless and irreconcilable seditions and wars are kindled between them; and yet this is the case though virtue is of a most peaceful disposition, and, as they say, is anxious whenever it is about to come to a contest of strength to make trial of its own powers first, so as only to contend if it has a prospect of being able to gain the victory; but if it finds its power unequal to the conflict, then it will never dare to descend into the arena at all, (106) for it is not disgraceful to wickedness to be defeated, inasmuch as ingloriousness is akin to it; but it would be a shameful thing for virtue, to which glory is the most appropriate and the most peculiarly belonging of all things, on which account it is natural for virtue either to secure the victory, or else to keep itself unconquered.

XXII

XXII. (107) It has been said then that the disposition of the Egyptians is inhospitable and intemperate; and the humanity of him who has been exposed to their conduct deserves admiration, for He [115] in the middle of the day beholding as it were three men travelling (and he did not perceive that they were in reality of a more divine nature), ran up and entreated them with great perseverance not to pass by his tent, but as was becoming to go in and receive the rites of hospitality: and they knowing the truth of the man not so much by what he said, as by his mind which they could look into, assented to his request without hesitation; (108) and being filled as to his soul with joy, he took every possible pains to make their extemporaneous reception worthy of them; and he said to his wife, "Hasten now, and make ready quickly three measures of fine meal," and he himself went forth among the herds of oxen, and brought forth a tender and well-fed heifer, and gave it to his servant; (109) and he having slain it, dressed it with all speed. For no one in the house of a wise man is ever slow to perform the duties of hospitality, but both women and men, and slaves and freemen, are most eager in the performance of all those duties towards strangers; (110) therefore, after having feasted, and being delighted, not so much with what was set before them, as with the good will of their entertainer, and with his excessive and unbounded zeal to please them, they bestow on him a reward beyond his expectation, the birth of a legitimate son in a short time, making him a promise which is to be confirmed by one the most excellent of the three; for it would have been inconsistent with philosophy for them all to speak together at the same moment, but it was desirous for all the rest to assent while one spoke. (111) Nevertheless he did not completely believe them even when they made him this promise, by reason of the incredible nature of the thing promised; for both he and his wife, through extreme old age, were so old as utterly to have abandoned all hope of offspring; (112) therefore the scriptures record that Abraham's wife, when she first heard what they were saying, laughed; and when they said afterwards, "Is anything impossible to God?" they were so ashamed that they denied that they had laughed; for Abraham knew that everything was possible to God, having almost learnt this doctrine as one may say from his cradle; (113) then for the first time he appears to me to have begun to entertain a different opinion of his guests from that which he conceived at first, and to have imagined that they were either some of the prophets or of the angels who had changed their spiritual and soul-like essence, and assumed the appearance of men.

XXIII

XXIII. (114) We have now then described the hospitable temper of the man, which was as it were a sort of addition to set off his greater virtue; but his virtue was piety towards God, concerning which we have spoken before, the most evident instance of which is to be found in his conduct now recorded towards the strangers; (115) but if any persons have fancied that house happy and blessed in which it has happened that wise men have stopped and abode, they should consider that they would not have done so, and would not even have looked into it at all, if they had seen any incurable disease in the souls of those who were therein, but I know not what excess of happiness and blessedness, I should say, existed in that house in which angels condescended to tarry and to receive the rites of hospitality from men, angels, those sacred and divine natures, the ministers and lieutenants of the mighty God, by means of whom, as of ambassadors, he announces whatever predictions he condescends to intimate to our race. (116) For how could they ever have endured to enter a human habitation at all, unless they had been certain that all the inhabitants within, like the well-managed and orderly crew of a ship, obeyed one signal only, namely, that of their master, as the sailors obey the command of the captain? And how would they ever have condescended to assume the appearance of guests and men feasted hospitably, if they had not thought that their entertainer was akin to them, and a fellow servant with them, bound to the service of the same master as themselves? We must think indeed that at their entrance all the parts of the house became improved and advanced in goodness, being breathed upon with a certain breeze of most perfect virtue. (117) And the entertainment was such as it was fitting that it should be, the persons who were being feasted displaying at the banquet their own simplicity towards that entertainer, and addressing him in a guileless manner, and all of them holding conversation suited to the occasion. (118) And it is a thing that deserves to be looked on as a prodigy, that though they did not drink they seemed to drink, and that though they did not eat they presented the appearance of persons eating. But this was all natural and consistent with what was going on. And the most miraculous circumstance of all was, that these beings who were incorporeal presented the appearance of a body in human form by reason of their favour to the virtuous man, for otherwise what need was there of all these miracles except for the purpose of giving the wise man the evidence of his external senses by means of a more distinct sight, because his character had not escaped the knowledge of the Father of the universe.

XXIV

XXIV. (119) This then is sufficient to say by way of a literal explanation of this account; we must now speak of that which may be given if the story be looked at as figurative and symbolical. The things which are expressed by the voice are the signs of those things which are conceived in the mind alone; when, therefore, the soul is shone upon by God as if at noonday, and when it is wholly and entirely filled with that light which is appreciable only by the intellect, and by being wholly surrounded with its brilliancy is free from all shade or darkness, it then perceives a threefold image of one subject, one image of the living God, and others of the other two, as if they were shadows irradiated by it. And some such thing as this happens to those who dwell in that light which is perceptible by the outward senses, for whether people are standing still or in motion, there is often a double shadow falling from them. (120) Let not any one then fancy that the word shadow is applied to God with perfect propriety. It is merely a catachrestical abuse of the name, by way of bringing before our eyes a more vivid representation of the matter intended to be intimated. (121) Since this is not the actual truth, but in order that one may when speaking keep as close to the truth as possible, the one in the middle is the Father of the universe, who in the sacred scriptures is called by his proper name, I am that I am; and the beings on each side are those most ancient powers which are always close to the living God, one of which is called his creative power, and the other his royal power. And the creative power is God, for it is by this that he made and arranged the universe; and the royal power is the Lord, for it is fitting that the Creator should lord it over and govern the creature. (122) Therefore, the middle person of the three, being attended by each of his powers as by body-guards, presents to the mind, which is endowed with the faculty of sight, a vision at one time of one being, and at another time of three; of one when the soul being completely purified, and having surmounted not only the multitudes of numbers, but also the number two, which is the neighbour of the unit, hastens onward to that idea which is devoid of all mixture, free from all combination, and by itself in need of nothing else whatever; and of three, when, not being as yet made perfect as to the important virtues, it is still seeking for initiation in those of less consequence, and is not able to attain to a comprehension of the living God by its own unassisted faculties without the aid of something else, but can only do so by judging of his deeds, whether as creator or as governor. (123) This then, as they say, is the second best thing; and it no less partakes in the opinion which is dear to and devoted to God. But the firstmentioned disposition has no such share, but is itself the very God-loving and God-beloved opinion itself, or rather it is truth which is older than opinion, and more valuable than any seeming. But we must now explain what is intimated by this statement in a more perspicuous manner.

XXV

XXV. (124) There are three different classes of human dispositions, each of which has received as its portion one of the aforesaid visions. The best of them has received that vision which is in the centre, the sight of the truly living God. The one which is next best has received that which is on the right hand, the sight of the beneficent power which has the name of God. And the third has the sight of that which is on the left hand, the governing power, which is called lord. (125) Therefore, the best dispositions cultivate that being who exists of himself, without the aid of any one else, being themselves attracted by nothing else, by reason of all their entire attention being directed to the honour of that one being. But of the other dispositions, some derive their existence and owe their being recognized by the father to his beneficent power; and others, again, owe it to his governing power. (126) My meaning in this statement is this:--Men when they perceive that, under the pretext of friendship, some persons come to them, being in reality only desirous to get what they can from them, look upon them with suspicion, and turn away from them, fearing their insincere, and flattering, and caressing behaviour, as very pernicious. (127) But God, inasmuch as he is not liable to any injury, gladly invites all men who choose, in any way whatever to honour him, to come unto him, not choosing altogether to reject any person whatever; and, in truth, he almost says in express words to those who have ears in the soul, "The most valuable prizes shall be offered to those who worship me for my own sake: (128) the second best to those who hope by their own efforts to be able to attain to good, or to find a means of escape from punishments. For even if the service of this latter class is mercenary and not wholly incorrupt, still it nevertheless revolves within the divine circumference, and does not stray beyond it. (129) But the rewards which shall be laid up for those who honour me for my own sake are rewards of affection; while those which are given to those who do so with a view to their own advantage are not given through affection, but because they are not looked upon as aliens. For I receive him who wishes to be a partaker of my beneficent power to a participation in my good things, and him who out of fear seeks to propitiate my governing and despotic power, I receive so far as to avert punishment from him. For I am not unaware that, in addition to these men not becoming worse, they will become better, by gradually arriving at a sincere and pure piety by their constant perseverance in serving me. (130) For even if the original dispositions, under the influence of which they originally endeavoured to please me, differ widely, still they must not be blamed, because they have in consequence only one aim and object, that of serving me." (131) But that which is seen is in reality a threefold appearance of one subject is plain, not only from the contemplation of the allegory, but also from that of the express words in which the allegory is couched. (132) For when the wise man entreats those persons who are in the guise of three travellers to come and lodge in his house, he speaks to them not as three persons, but as one, and says, "My lord, if I have found favour with thee, do not thou pass by thy Servant." [1152] For the expressions, "my lord," and "with thee," and "do not pass by," and others of the same kind, are all such as are naturally addressed to a single individual, but not to many. And when those persons, having been entertained in his house, address their entertainer in an affectionate manner, it is again one of them who promises that he by himself will be present, and will bestow on him the seed of a child of his own, speaking in the following words: "I will return again and visit thee again, according to the time of life, and Sarah thy wife shall have a Son." [1153]

XXVI

XXVI. (133) And what is signified by this is indicated in a most evident and careful manner by the events which ensued. The country of the Sodomites was a district of the land of Canaan, which the Syrians afterwards called Palestine, a country full of innumerable iniquities, and especially of gluttony and debauchery, and all the great and numerous pleasures of other kinds which have been built up by men as a fortress, on which account it had been already condemned by the Judge of the whole world. (134) And the cause of its excessive and immoderate intemperance was the unlimited abundance of supplies of all kinds which its inhabitants enjoyed. For the land was one with a deep soil, and well watered, and as such produced abundant crops of every kind of fruit every year. And he was a wise man and spoke truly who said--

*"The greatest cause of all iniquity
Is found in overmuch prosperity."*

(135) As men, being unable to bear discreetly a satiety of these things, get restive like cattle, and become stiff-necked, and discard the laws of nature, pursuing a great and intemperate indulgence of gluttony, and drinking, and unlawful connections; for not only did they go mad after women, and defile the marriage bed of others, but also those who were men lusted after one another, doing unseemly things, and not regarding or respecting their common nature, and though eager for children, they were convicted by having only an abortive offspring; but the conviction produced no advantage, since they were overcome by violent desire; (136) and so, by degrees, the men became accustomed to be treated like women, and in this way engendered among themselves the disease of females, and intolerable evil; for they not only, as to effeminacy and delicacy, became like women in their persons, but they made also their souls most ignoble, corrupting in this way the whole race of man, as far as depended on them. At all events, if the Greeks and barbarians were to have agreed together, and to have adopted the commerce of the citizens of this city, their cities one after another would have become desolate, as if they had been emptied by a pestilence.

XXVII

XXVII. (137) But God, having taken pity on mankind, as being a Saviour and full of love for mankind, increased, as far as possible, the natural desire of men and women for a connexion together, for the sake of producing children, and detesting the unnatural and unlawful commerce of the people of Sodom, he extinguished it, and destroyed those who were inclined to these things, and that not by any ordinary chastisement, but he inflicted on them an astonishing novelty, and unheard of rarity of vengeance; (138) for, on a sudden, he commanded the sky to become overclouded and to pour forth a mighty shower, not of rain but of fire; and as the flame poured down, with a resistless and unceasing violence, the fields were burnt up, and the meadows, and all the dense groves, and the thick marshes, and the impenetrable thickets; the plain too was consumed, and all the crop of wheat, and of everything else that was sown; and all the trees of the mountain district were burnt up, the trunks and the very roots being consumed. (139) And the folds for the cattle, and the houses of the men, and the walls, and all that was in any building, whether of private or public property, were all burnt. And in one day these populous cities became the tomb of their inhabitants, and the vast edifices of stone and timber became thin dust and ashes. (140) And when the flames had consumed everything that was visible and that existed on the face of the earth, they proceeded to burn even the earth itself, penetrating into its lowest recesses, and destroying all the vivifying powers which existed within it so as to produce a complete and everlasting barrenness, so that it should never again be able to bear fruit, or to put forth any verdure; and to this very day it is scorched up. For the fire of the lightning is what is most difficult to extinguish, and creeps on pervading everything, and smouldering. (141) And a most evident proof of this is to be found in what is seen to this day: for the smoke which is still emitted, and the sulphur which men dig up there, are a proof of the calamity which befell that country; while a most conspicuous proof of the ancient fertility of the land is left in one city, and in the land around it. For the city is very populous, and the land is fertile in grass and in corn, and in every kind of fruit, as a constant evidence of the punishment which was inflicted by the divine will on the rest of the country.

Philo Judaeus

XXVIII

XXVIII. (142) But I have not gone through all these particulars for the sake of showing the magnitude of that vast and novel calamity, but because I desired to prove that of the three beings who appeared to the wise Abraham in the guise of men, the scriptures only represent two as having come to the country which was subsequently destroyed for the purpose of destroying its inhabitants, since the third did not think fit to come for that purpose. (143) Inasmuch as he, according to my conception, was the true and living God, who thought it fitting that he being present should bestow good gifts by his own power, but that he should effect the opposite objects by the agency and service of his subordinate powers, so that he might be looked upon as the cause of good only, and of no evil whatever antecedently. (144) And kings too appear to me to imitate the divine nature in this particular, and to act in the same way, giving their favours in person, but inflicting their chastisements by the agency of others. (145) But since, of the two powers of God, one is a beneficent power and the other a chastising one, each of them, as is natural, is manifested to the country of the people of Sodom. Because of the five finest cities in it four were about to be destroyed by fire, and one was destined to be left unhurt and safe from every evil. For it was necessary that the calamities should be inflicted by the chastising power, and that the one which was to be saved should be saved by the beneficent power. (146) But since the portion which was saved was not endowed with entire and complete virtues, but was blessed with kindness by the power of the living God, it was deliberately accounted unworthy to have a sight of his presence afforded to it.

XXIX

XXIX. (147) This, then, is the open explanation which is to be given of this account, and which is to be addressed to the multitude. But there is another esoteric explanation to be reserved for the few who choose for the subjects of their investigation the dispositions of the soul, and not the forms of bodies; and this shall now be mentioned. The five cities of the land of Sodom are a figurative representation of the five outward senses which exist in us, the organs of the pleasures, by the instrumentality of which all the pleasures whether great or small are brought to perfection; (148) for we are pleased either when we behold the varieties of colours and forms, both in things inanimate and in those endowed with vitality, or when we hear melodious sounds, or again, we are delighted by the exercise of the faculty of taste in the things which relate to eating and drinking, or by that of the sense of smell in fragrant flavours and vapours, or in accordance with our faculty of touch when conversant with soft, or hot, or smooth things. (149) Now of these five outward senses there are three which have the greatest resemblance to the brute beasts and to slaves, namely the senses of taste, smell, and touch: as it is with reference to these that those species of beasts and cattle which are the most greedy and the most strongly inclined to sexual connections are the most vehemently excited. For all day and all night they are either glutting themselves insatiably with food, or else in a state of eagerness for sexual connection. (150) But there are two of these outward senses which have something philosophical and preeminent in them, namely, sight and hearing. But the ears are in some degree more slow and more effeminate than the eyes, since the latter go with promptness and courage to what is to be seen, and do not wait until the objects themselves are in motion, but go forward to meet them, and desire to move themselves so as to face them. But the sense of hearing inasmuch as that is slow and more effeminate, may be classed in the second rank, and the sense of seeing may be allowed an especial pre-eminence and privilege: for God has made this sense a sort of queen of the rest, placing it above them all, and stationing it as it were on a citadel, has made it of all the senses in the closest connection with the soul; (151) and any one may conjecture this from the common changes which take place in its essential organs; for when grief exists in the soul of man, the eyes are full of concern and melancholy; and on the other hand, when joy is in our heart the eyes smile and rejoice; and when fear gets the upper hand they are full of turbulent and disorderly confusion, and are subject to all kinds of irregular motions, and quiverings, and distortions. (152) Again, if anger occupies us, the sight becomes more fierce and bloodshot; and when we are considerating or deliberating, the eyes are tranquil and motionless, and almost as intent as the mind itself; just as at moments of the relaxation and indifference of the mind, the eyes are relaxed and indifferent; (153) when a friend approaches the feeling of goodwill towards him is proclaimed by a calm and serene look; on the other hand, if we meet with an enemy, the eyes give an early indication of the displeasure of the soul; when our mind is inspired by boldness, our eyes bound forward and are ready to start from our heads; when we are oppressed with feelings of shame or modesty, they are gentle and repressed. And, in short, we may say that the sight has been created to be an exact image of the soul, which is thus beautifully represented by it through the perfection of the Creator's skill, the eyes showing a visible representation of it, as in a mirror, since the soul has no visible nature in itself; (154) but it is not in this particular alone that the beauty of the eyes exceeds the rest of the outward senses, but also because the use of the other senses is interrupted during our waking moments; for we must not include in our statement the inactivity which results from sleep; for they are at rest whenever there is not some external object to put them in motion; but the energies of the eyes when they are open are continuous and uninterrupted, as the eyes are never satiated or wearied, but continue to operate in accordance with the connection which they have with the soul; (155) and the soul itself is everlastingly awake, and is in perpetual motion both night and day; but to the eyes, as being to a great degree partakers of the fleshly nature, a self sufficient gift was given, to be able to continue exercising their appropriate energies during one half of the entire period of life.

XXX

XXX. (156) But we must now proceed to speak of that which is the most necessary part of all, the advantage which we derive from the eyes. For it is to sight alone of the external senses that God has caused light to arise, which is both the most beautiful of all existing things, and is, moreover, the first thing which is pronounced in the sacred scriptures to be good. (157) Now the nature of light is twofold: for there is one light which proceeds from the fire which we use, a perishable light proceeding from a perishable material, and one which admits of being extinguished. But the other kind is inextinguishable and imperishable, descending to us from above heaven, as if every one of the stars was pouring down its beams upon us from an everlasting spring. And the sense of sight associates with each of these kinds of light, and through the medium of both of them does it approach the objects of sight so as to arrive at a most accurate comprehension of them. (158) Why now need we attempt to panegyrize the eyes further by a speech, when God has engraved their true praises on pillars erected in heaven, namely, the stars? For for what purpose were the rays of the sun, and the beams of the moon, and the light of all the other planets and fixed stars called into existence, except as fields for the energies of the eyes in their service of seeing? (159) On which account men, using the most excellent of all gifts, contemplate the things which exist in the world, the earth, the plants, the animals, the fruits of the earth, the seas, the effusion of waters springing from the earth and gushing forth in torrents and floods, and the varieties of fountains, some of which give forth cold and others hot water, and the nature of all things that exist in the air; and all the different species, of which we thus arrive at the knowledge, are innumerable and indescribable, and cannot be compromised in speech. And above all these things, the eyes can behold the heaven, which is truly a world created in another world, and it can also survey the beauties and divine images existing in heaven. Which now of the other external senses can boast that it has arrived at such a pitch of power as this?

XXXI

XXXI. (160) But now, dismissing the consideration of those of the outward senses which are in the stables, as it were, fattening up an animal which is born with us, namely, appetite, let us investigate the nature of that sense which receives speech, namely, hearing; the continued and vigorous, and most perfect course of which exists in the atmosphere which surrounds the earth, when the violence of the winds and the noise of thunder sound with a great dragging noise and terrible crash. (161) But the eyes in a single moment can reach from earth to heaven, and taking in the extremest boundaries of the universe, reaching at the same moment to the east and to the west, and to the north and to the south, so as to survey them all at once, drag the mind towards what is visible. (162) And the mind, at once receiving a similar impression, does not continue quiet, but being in perpetual motion, and never slumbering, receiving from the sight the power of observing the objects appreciable by the intellect, comes to consider whether these things which are brought visibly before it are uncreated, or whether they have derived their origin from creation; also, whether they are bounded or infinite. Again, whether there are many worlds or only one; also, whether there are five elements of the whole universe, or whether heaven and the heavenly bodies have a peculiar and separate nature of their own, having received a more divine conformation, differing from that of the rest of the world. (163) Again, by these means it considers if the world has been created, by whom it has been created, and who the creator is as to his essence or quality, and with what design he made it, and what he is doing now, and what his mode of existence or cause of life is; and all other such questions as the excellently-endowed mind when cohabiting with wisdom is accustomed to examine. (164) These, and similar subjects, belong to philosophers, from which it is plain that wisdom and philosophy have not derived their origin from anything else that exists in us except from that queen of the outward senses, the sight, which God saved alone of the region of the body when he destroyed the other four, because these last were slaves to the flesh and to the passions of the flesh; but the sight alone was able to raise its head and to look up, and to find other sources of delight far superior to those proceeding from the bodily pleasures, those, namely, that are derived from the contemplation of the world and the things in it. (165) Therefore it was appropriate for one of the five outward senses, namely, the sight, like one city in the Pentapolis, to receive an especial reward and honour, and to remain while the others were destroyed, because it is not only conversant with mortal objects as they are, but is able to forsake such, and to depart to the imperishable natures, and to rejoice in the sight of them. (166) On which account the holy scriptures very beautifully represent it as "a little city, and yet not a little One," [1154] describing the power of sight under this figure. For it is said to be little, inasmuch as it is but a small portion of the faculties which exist in us; and yet great, inasmuch as it desires great things, being eager to behold the entire heaven and the whole world.

XXXII

XXXII. (167) We have now, then, given a full explanation concerning the vision which appeared to Abraham, and concerning his celebrated and allglorious hospitality, in which the entertainer, who appeared to himself to be entertaining others was himself entertained; expounding every part of the passage with as much accuracy as we were able. But we must not pass over in silence the most important action of all, which is worthy of being listened to. For I was nearly saying that it is of more importance than all the actions of piety and religion put together. So we must say what seems to be reasonable concerning it. (168) A legitimate son is borne to the wise man by his wedded wife, a beloved and only son, very beautiful in his person, and very excellent in his disposition. For he was already beginning to display the more perfect exercises of his age, so that his father felt a most strong and vehement affection for him, not only from the impulse of natural regard, but also from the influence of deliberate opinion, from being, as it were, a judge of his character. (169) To him, then, being conscious of such a disposition, an oracular command suddenly comes, which was never expected, ordering him to sacrifice this son on a certain very lofty hill, distant three days' journey from the city. (170) And he, although attached to his child by an indescribable fondness, neither changed colour, nor wavered in his soul, but remained firm in an unyielding and unalterable purpose, as he was at first. And being wholly influenced by love towards God, he forcibly repressed all the names and charms of the natural relationship: and without mentioning the oracular command to any one of his household out of all his numerous body of servants, he took with him the two eldest, who were most thoroughly attached to their master, as if he were bent upon the celebration of some ordinary divine rite, and went forth with his son, making four in all. (171) And when, looking as it were from a watch-tower, he saw the appointed place afar off, he bade his servants remain there, and he gave his son the fire and the wood to carry, thinking it proper for the victim himself to be burdened with the materials for the sacrifice, a very light burden, for nothing is less troublesome than piety. (172) And as they proceeded onwards with equal speed, not marching more rapidly with their bodies than with their minds along that short road of which holiness is the end, they at last arrive at the appointed place. (173) And the father collected stones wherewith to build the altar; and when his son saw everything else prepared for the celebration of the sacrifice, but no animal, he looked to his father and said, "My father, behold the fire and the wood, but where is the victim for the burnt Sacrifice?" [1155] (174) Therefore, any other father, knowing what he was about to do, and being depressed in his soul, would have been thrown into confusion by his son's words, and being filled with tears, would, out of his excessive affliction, by his silence have betrayed what was about to be done; (175) but Abraham, betraying no alteration of voice, or countenance, or intention, looking at his son with steady eye, answered his question with a determination more steadily still, "My child," said he, "God will provide himself a victim for the burnt offering," although we are in a vast desert where perhaps you despair of such a thing as being found; but all things are possible to God, even all such things as are impossible and unintelligible to men. (176) And even while saying this, he seizes his son with all rapidity, and places him on the altar, and having taken his knife in his right hand, he raised it over him as if to slay him; but God the Saviour stopped the deed in the middle, interrupting him by a voice from heaven, by which he ordered him to stay his hand, and not to touch the child: calling the father by name twice, so as to turn him and divert him from his purpose, and forbid him to complete the sacrifice.

XXXIII

XXXIII. (177) And so Isaac is saved, God supplying a gift instead of him, and honouring him who was willing to make the offering in return for the piety which he had exhibited. But the action of the father, even though it was not ultimately given effect to, is nevertheless recorded and engraved as a complete and perfect sacrifice, not only in the sacred scriptures, but also in the middle of those who read them. (178) But to those who are fond of reviling and disparaging everything, and who are by their invariable habits accustomed to prefer blaming to praising the action which Abraham was enjoined to perform, it will not appear a great and admirable deed, as we imagine it to have been. (179) For such persons say that many other men, who have been very affectionate to their relations and very fond of their children, have given up their sons; some in order that they might be sacrificed for their country to deliver it either from war, or from drought, or from much rain, or from disease and pestilence; and others to satisfy the demands of some habitual religious observances, even though there may be no real piety in them. (180) At all events they say that some of the most celebrated men of the Greeks, not merely private individuals but kings also, caring but little for the children whom they have begotten, have, by means of their destruction secured safety to might and numerous forces and armies, arrayed together in an allied body, and have voluntarily slain them as if they had been enemies. (181) And also that barbarous nations have for many ages practised the sacrifice of their children as if it were a holy work and one looked upon with favour by God, whose wickedness is mentioned by the holy Moses. For he, blaming them for this pollution, says, that, "They burn their sons and their daughters to their Gods."[1156] (182) And they say that to this very day the Gymnosophists among the Indians, when that long or incurable disease, old age, begins to attack them, before it has got a firm hold of them, and while they might still last for many years, kindle a fire and burn themselves. And, moreover, when their husbands are already dead, they say that their wives rush cheerfully to the same funeral pile, and whilst living endure to be burnt along with their husbands' bodies. (183) One may well admire the exceeding courage of these women, who look thus contemptuously on death, and disdain it so exceedingly that they hasten and run impetuously towards it as if they were grasping immortality.

XXXIV

XXXIV. But why, say they, ought one to praise Abraham as the attempter of a wholly novel kind of conduct, when it is only what private men and kings, and even whole nations do at appropriate seasons? (184) But I will make the following reply to the envy and ill-temper of these men. Of those who sacrifice their children, some do so out of habit, as they say some of the barbarians do; others do it because they are unable by any other means to place on a good footing some desperate and important dangers threatening their cities and countries. And of these men, some have given up their children because they have been constrained by those more powerful than themselves: and others, out of a thirst for glory, and honour, and for renown at the present moment, and celebrity in all future ages. (185) Now those who sacrifice their children out of deference to custom, perform, in my opinion, no great exploit; for an inveterate custom is often as powerful as nature itself; so that it diminishes the terrible impression made by the action to be done, and makes even the most miserable and intolerable evils light to bear. (186) Again: surely, they who offer up their children out of fear deserve no praise; for praise is only given to voluntary good actions, but what is involuntary, is ascribed to other causes than the immediate actors--to the occasion, or to chance, or to compulsion from men. (187) Again, if any one, out of a desire for glory, abandons his son or his daughter; he would justly be blamed rather than praised; seeking acquire honour by the death of his dearest relations, while, even if he had glory, he ought rather to have risked the loss of it to secure the safety of his children. (188) We must investigate, therefore, whether Abraham was under the influence of any one of the aforesaid motives, custom, or love of glory, or fear, when he was about to sacrifice his son. Now Babylon and Mesopotamia, and the nation of the Chaldaeans, do not receive the custom of sacrificing their children; and these are the countries in which Abraham had been brought up and had lived most of his time; so that we cannot imagine that his sense of the misfortune that he was commanded to inflict upon himself was blunted by the frequency of such events. (189) Again, there was no fear from men which pressed upon him, for no one knew of this oracular command which had been given to him alone, nor was there any common calamity pressing upon the land in which he was living, such as could only be remedied by the destruction of his most excellent son. (190) May it not have been, however, from a desire to obtain praise from the multitude that he proceeded to this action? But what praise could be obtained in the desert, when there was no one likely to be present who could possibly say anything in his favour, and when even his two servants were left at a distance on purpose that he might not seem to be hunting after praise, or to be making a display by bringing witnesses with him to see the greatness of his devotion?

XXXV

XXXV. (191) Therefore putting a barrier on their unbridled and evil-speaking mouths, let them moderate that envy in themselves which hates everything that is good, and let them forbear to attack the virtues of men who have lived excellently, which they ought rather to reward and decorate with panegyric. And that this action of Abraham's was in reality one deserving of praise and of all love, it is easy to see from many circumstances. (192) In the first place, then, he laboured above all men to obey God, which is thought an excellent thing, and an especial object for all men's desire, by all right-minded persons, to such a degree, that he never omitted to perform anything which God commanded him, not even if it was full of arrogance and ingloriousness, or even of positive pain and misery; for which reason he also bore, in a most noble manner, and with the most unshaken fortitude, the command given to him respecting his son. (193) In the second place, though it was not the custom in the land in which he as living, as perhaps it is among some nations, to offer human sacrifices, and custom, by its frequency, often removes the horror felt at the first appearance of evils, he himself was about to be the first to set the example of a novel and most extraordinary deed, which I do not think that any human being would have brought himself to submit to, even if his soul had been made of iron or of adamant; for as some one has said, --

"Tis a hard task with nature to contend."

(194) In the second place, after he had become the father of this his only legitimate son, he, from the moment of his birth, cherished towards him all the genuine feelings of affection, which exceeds all modest love, and all the ties of friendship which have ever been celebrated in the world. (195) There was added also, this most forcible charm of all, that he had become the father of this son not in the prime of his life, but in his old age. For parents become to a certain degree insane in their affection for their children of their old age, either from the circumstance of their having been wishing for their birth a long time, or else because they have no longer any hope that they shall have any more; nature having taken her stand there as at the extreme and furthest limit. (196) Now there is nothing unnatural or extraordinary in devoting one child to God out of a numerous family, as a sort of first fruits of all one's children, while one still has pleasure in those who remain alive, who are no small comfort and alleviation of the grief felt for the one who is sacrificed. But the man who gives the only beloved son that he is possessed of performs an action beyond all powers of language to praise, as he is giving nothing to his own natural affection, but inclining with his whole will and heart to show his devotion to God. (197) Accordingly this is an extraordinary and almost unprecedented action which was done by Abraham. For other men, even if they have yielded up their children to be sacrificed on behalf of the safety of their native land or of their armies, have either remained at home themselves, or have kept at a distance from the altar of sacrifice; or at least, if they have been present they have averted their eyes, and left others to strike the blow which they have not endured to witness. (198) But this man, like a priest of sacrifice himself, did himself begin to perform the sacred rite, although he was a most affectionate father of a son who was in all respects most excellent. And, perhaps, according to the usual law and custom of burnt offerings he was intending to solemnise the rite by dividing his son limb by limb. And so he did not divide his feelings and allot one part of his regard to his son and another part to piety to God: but he devoted the whole soul, entire and undivided, to holiness; thinking but little of the kindred blood which flowed in the victim. (199) Now of all the circumstances which we have enumerated what is there which others have in common with Abraham? What is there which is not peculiar to him, and excellent beyond all power of language to praise? So that every one who is not struck by nature envious and a lover of evil must be struck with amazement and admiration for his excessive piety, even if he should not call at once to mind all the particulars on which I have been dwelling, but only some one of the whole number; for the conception of any one of these particulars is sufficient by a brief and faint outline to display the greatness and loftiness of the father's soul; though there is nothing petty in the action of the wise man.

XXXVI

XXXVI. (200) But the things which we have here been saying do not appear solely in the plain and explicit language of the text of the holy scriptures; but they appear, moreover, to exhibit a nature which is not so evident to the multitude, but which they who place the objects of the intellect above those perceptible by the outward senses, and who are able to appreciate them, recognise. And this nature is of the following description. (201) The victim who was about to be sacrificed is called in the Chaldaean language, Isaac; but if this name be translated into the Grecian language, it signifies, "laughter;" and this laughter is not understood to be that laughter of the body which is frequent in child sport, but is the result of settled happiness and rejoicing of the mind. (202) This kind of laughter the wise man is appropriately said to offer as a sacrifice to God; showing thus, by a figure, that to rejoice does properly belong to God alone. For the human race is subject to sorrow and to exceeding fear, from evils which are either present or expected, so that men are either grieved at unexpected evils actually pressing upon them, or are kept in suspense, and disquietude, and fear with respect to those which are impending. But the nature of God is free from grief, and exempt from fear, and enjoys the immunity from every kind of suffering, and is the only nature which possesses complete happiness and blessedness. (203) Now to the disposition which makes this confession in sincerity, God is merciful, and compassionate, and kind, driving envy to a distance from him; and to it he gives a gift in return, to the full extent of the power of the person benefited to receive it, and he all but gives such a person this oracular warning, saying, "I well know that the whole species of joy and rejoicing is the possession of no other being but me, who am the Father of the universe; (204) nevertheless, though it belongs to me, I have no objection to those who deserve it enjoying a share of it. But who can be deserving to do so, save he who obeys me and my will? for to this man it shall be given to feel as little grief as possible and as little fear as possible, proceeding along that road which is inaccessible to passions and vices, but which is frequented by excellence of soul and virtue." (205) And let no one fancy that that unmixed joy, which is without any alloy of sorrow, descends from heaven to the earth, but rather, that it is a combination of the two, that which is the better being predominant in the mixture; in the same manner as the light in heaven is unalloyed and free from any admixture of darkness, but in the sublunary atmosphere it is mingled with dark air. (206) For this reason, it seems to me to have been, that Sarah, [1157] the namesake of virtue, who had previously laughed, denied her laughter to the person who questioned her as to the cause of it, fearing lest she might be deprived of her rejoicing, as belonging to no created being, but to God alone; on which account the holy Word encouraged her, and said, "Be not afraid," thou hast laughed a genuine laugh, and thou hast a share in real joy; (207) for the Father has not permitted the race of mankind to be wholly devoured by griefs, and sorrows, and incurable anguish, but has mingled in their existence something of a better nature, thinking it fitting that the soul should sometimes enjoy rest and tranquillity; and he has also designed that the souls of wise men should be pleased and delighted for the greater portion of their existence with the contemplation of the soul.

XXXVII

XXXVII. (208) This is enough to say about the piety of the man, though there is a vast abundance of other things which might be brought forward in praise of it. We must also investigate his skill and wisdom as displayed towards his fellow men; for it belongs to the same character to be pious towards God and affectionate towards man; and both these qualities, of holiness towards God and justice towards man, are commonly seen in the same individual. Now it would take a long time to go through all the instances and actions which form this; but it is not out of place to record two or three. (209) Abraham, being rich above most men in abundance of gold and silver, and having numerous herds of cattle and flocks of sheep, and being equal in his affluence and abundance to any of the men of the country, or of the original inhabitants, who were the most wealthy, and being, in fact, richer than any sojourner could be expected to be, was never unpopular with any of the people among whom he was dwelling, but was continually praised and beloved by all who had any acquaintance with him; (210) and if, as is often the case, any contention or quarrel arose between his servants and retinue and those of others, he always endeavored to terminate it quietly by his gentle disposition, discarding and driving to a distance from his soul all quarrelsome, and turbulent, and disorderly things. (211) And there is no wonder, if he was such towards strangers, who might have agreed together and with a heavy and powerful hand have repelled him, if he had begun acts of violence, when he behaved with moderation towards those who were nearly related to him in blood, but very far removed from him in disposition, and who were desolate and isolated, and very inferior in wealth to himself, willingly allowing himself to be inferior to them in the very things in which he might have been superior; (212) for there was his brother's son, when he departed from his country, who went forth with him, an inconstant, variable, whimsical man, inclining now to one side and now to another; and at one time caressing him with friendly salutations, and at another, being restive and obstinate, by reason of the inequality of his disposition; (213) on which account his household also was a quarrelsome and turbulent one, as it had no one to correct it, and especially his shepherds were so, because they were removed to a great distance from their master. Accordingly, they, in their self-willed manner, behaving as if they claimed complete liberty, were always quarreling with the managers of the flocks of the wise Abraham, who yielded a great many points, because of the gentle disposition of their master; in consequence of which, the shepherds of his nephew turned to folly and to shameless audacity, and gave way to anger, cherishing illtemper, and exciting a spirit of irreconcilable enmity in their hearts, until they compelled those whom they injured to turn to their own defence; (214) and when a somewhat violent battle had taken place, the good Abraham, hearing of the attack made by his servants on the others, though only in self-defence, and knowing as he did that his own household was superior both in numbers and in power, would not allow the contest to be protracted till victory declared for his party, in order that he might not grieve his nephew by the defeat of his men; but standing between the two bodies of combatants, he, by his pacific speeches, reconciled the contending parties, and that not only for the moment, but for all future time too; (215) for he knew that if they continued to dwell together, and to abide in the same place, they would be always differing in opinion and quarrelling with one another, and continually raising up quarrels and wars with one another. In order that this might not be the case, he thought it desirable to abandon the custom of dwelling together, and to separate his habitation from that of his nephew. So, sending for his nephew, he gave him the choice of the better country, cheerfully agreeing himself to abandon whatever portion the other selected, as he should thus acquire the greatest of all gains, namely, peace; (216) and yet, what other man would ever have yielded in any point whatever to one weaker than himself, while he was stronger? and who that was able to gain the victory would ever have been willing to be defeated, without availing himself of his power? But this man alone placed the object of his desires, not in strength and superiority, but in a life free from dissension and blessed with tranquillity, as far as depended on himself; for which reason he appears the most admirable of all men.

XXXVIII

XXXVIII. (217) Since then this panegyric, if taken literally, is applied to Abraham as a man, and since the disposition of the soul is here intimated, it will be well for us to investigate that also, after the fashion of those men who go from the letter to the spirit of any statement. (218) Now there is an infinite variety of dispositions which arise from different circumstances and opportunities in every kind of action and event; but in this instance, we must distinguish between two characters, one of which is the elder and the other the younger. Now the elder of the two is that disposition which honours these things which are by nature principal and dominant; the younger is that which regards the things which are subject to others, and which are considered in the lowest rank. (219) Now the principal and more dominant things are wisdom, and temperance, and justice, and courage, and every description of virtue, and the actions in accordance with virtue; the younger things are wealth, and authority, and glory, and nobility, not real nobility, but that which the multitude think so, and all those other things which belong to the third class, next after the things of the soul, and the things of the body; the class which is in fact the last. (220) Each then of these dispositions has, as it were, flocks and herds. The one which desires external things has for its flocks, gold and silver, and all those things which are materials and furniture of wealth; and, moreover, arms, engines, triremes, armies of infantry and cavalry, and fleets of ships, and all kinds of provisions to procure domination, by which firm authority is secured. But the lover of excellence has for his flock the doctrines of each individual virtue, and its speculations respecting wisdom. (221) Moreover, there are overseers and superintendents of each of these flocks, just as there are shepherds to flocks of sheep. Of the flock of external things, the superintendents are those who are fond of money, those who are fond of glory, those who are eager for war, and all those who love authority over multitudes. And the managers of the flocks of things concerning the soul are all those who are lovers of virtue and of what is honourable, and who do not prefer spurious good things to genuine ones, but genuine to spurious good. (222) There is therefore a certain natural contest between them, inasmuch as they have no opinions in common with one another, but are always at variance and difference respecting the matter which has of all others the greatest influence in the maintenance of life as it should be, that is to say, the judgment of what things are truly good. (223) Now, for some time the soul was warred against by some enemy, and was full of this quarrelsome principle, inasmuch as it had not yet been completely pacified, but was still troubled by some passions and diseases which prevailed over sound reason. But from the time when it began to be more powerful, and with its superior force, to destroy the fortification of the opposite opinions, becoming elated and puffed up with pride, it in a most marvellous manner began to separate and detach the disposition in itself, which admires the external materials, and as if conversing with man, says to him, Thou art unable to dwell with--(224) it is impossible that thou shouldest be connected by alliance with--a lover, of wisdom and virtue. Come, then, and migrating from thy present abode, depart to a distance, since you have no communion with me, and, indeed, cannot possibly have any. For all the things which you conceive to be on the right he imagines to be on the left; and on the contrary, whatever you think is on the left, is looked upon by him as on the right.

XXXIX

XXXIX. (225) Therefore the virtuous man was not only peaceful and a lover of justice, but also a man of courage and of a warlike disposition; not for the sake of making war, for he was not of a contentious and quarrelsome character, but for the sake of a lasting peace for the future, which hitherto his adversaries had destroyed. (226) And the most convincing proof of this is to be found in what he did. Four great kings had received for their inheritance the eastern portion of the inhabited world; and they were obeyed by all the eastern nations, both on this and on the other side of the Euphrates. Now all the other parts remained unharassed by contentions, obeying the commands of these kings, and contributing their yearly taxes and tribute without seeking for any excuses; but the land of the inhabitants of Sodom alone before it was destroyed by the fire began to break the peace, having been designing to revolt for a long time. (227) For as it as a very rich country it was ruled by five kings, who had divided the cities and the land among them, though the district was not an extensive one, but fertile in corn and trees, and abounding in all kinds of fruit. What then their size gives to other cities, that the excellence of its soil gives to Sodom; on which account it had many princes for lovers who admire its beauty. (228) These, on all other occasions, had paid the appointed revenues to the collector of the taxes, honouring and at the same time fearing those more powerful sovereigns of whom they were the viceroys. But when they were completely sated with good things, and when, as is ordinarily the case, satiety had begotten insolence, they, cherishing a pride beyond their power! began at first to lift up their heads and to become restive. Then, like wicked servants, they set upon their masters, trusting more to their factious spirit than to their strength. (229) But their sovereigns, remembering their own nobleness and being fortified with superior power, went against them with great disdain, as if they would be able to defeat them by the mere cry of battle. And having engaged them in battle, they in a moment put some of them to flight, and others they slew in the flight, and so they destroyed their army to a man. And also they led away a vast multitude captive, which they distributed among themselves with much other booty. Moreover, they led away captive the brother's son of a wise Abraham, who had a little while before emigrated into one of the cities of the Pentapolis.

XL

XL. (230) This was communicated to Abraham by some one of those who escaped from the defeat of his countrymen, and it grieved him exceedingly, and he would not be quiet any longer, being much concerned at what had happened, and mourning more for him alive and in captivity than if he had heard that he had been killed. For he knew that death (teleuteÂ) as its very name imports, was the end (telos) of all living beings, and especially of the wicked, and that there are innumerable unexpected evils which lie, as it were, in ambush for the living. (231) But when he was preparing to pursue them for the purpose of delivering his brother's son, he found himself in want of allies, inasmuch as he himself was a stranger and a sojourner and as no one could dare to oppose the irresistible power of such mighty monarchs flushed with recent victory. (232) And he devised for himself a most novel alliance. For necessity is the mother of invention, and expedients are found in the most difficult circumstances when a man has set his heart on just and humane objects. For having collected together all his servants, and ordering the slaves whom he had purchased to remain at home (for he was afraid of desertion on their part), he assembled all his domestic servants, and divided them into centuries, and marched forward in their battalions; not, indeed, trusting to them, for his was still a most insignificant force, in comparison with that of the kings', but placing his confidence in the champion and defender of the just, namely in God. (233) Therefore putting forth all his exertions he hastened on, in nowise relaxing his speed, until, watching his opportunity, he fell upon the enemy by night, after they had supped, and when they were just on the point of betaking themselves to sleep. And some he slew in their beds, and those who were arrayed against him he utterly destroyed, and with great vigour he defeated them all, more by the courage of his soul than by the adequacy of his means. (234) And he did not cease from attacking them until he had utterly destroyed the hostile army with their kings, and slain them all to a man in front of their camp, and had brought back his brother's son after this splendid and most glorious victory, bringing back also as fair booty all their cavalry, and all the multitude of their beasts of burden, and a most enormous quantity of spoil. (235) And when the great high priest of the most high God beheld him returning and coming back loaded with trophies, in safety himself, with all his own force uninjured, for he had not lost one single man of all those who went out with him; marvelling at the greatness of the exploit, and, as was very natural, considering that he had never met with this success but through the favour of the divine wisdom and alliance, he raised his hands to heaven, and honoured him with prayers in his behalf, and offered up sacrifices of thanksgiving for his victory, and splendidly feasted all those who had had a share in the expedition; rejoicing and sympathising with him as if the success had been his own, and in reality it did greatly concern him. For as the proverb says:--

"All that befalls from friends we common call."

And much more are all instances of good fortune common to those whose main object it is to please God.

XLI

XLI. (236) These things, then, are what are contained in the plain words of the scriptures. But as many as are able to contemplate the facts related in them in their incorporeal and naked state, living rather in the soul than in the body, will say that of the nine kings the four are the powers of the four passions which exist within us, the passion of pleasure, of desire, of fear, and of grief; and that the other five kings are the outward senses, being equal in number, the sense of sight, of hearing, of smell, of taste, and of touch. (237) For these in some degree are sovereigns and rulers, having acquired a certain power over us, but not all to an equal extent; for the five are subordinate to the four, and are compelled to pay them taxes and tribute, such as are appointed by nature. (238) For it is from the things which we see, or hear, or smell, or taste, or touch, that pleasures, and pains, and fears, and desires arise; as there is no one of the passions which has any power to exist of itself, if it were not supplied by the materials furnished by the outward senses. (239) For it is in these things that their powers consist, either in figures and in colours, or in the faculty of speaking or hearing which depends on the voice, or in the flavours, or in odours, or by the subjects of touch, whether they are soft or hard, or rough, or smooth, or hot, or cold. For all these things are supplied to each of the passions by means of the outward senses. (240) And as long as the taxes beforementioned are paid, the alliance among the kings remains; but when they are no longer contributed, as they were before, then immediately do quarrels and wars arise. And this appears to happen when painful old age supervenes, in which none of the passions becomes weaker, but rather perhaps stronger than their ancient power; but the sight becomes dim, and the ears hard of hearing, and every one of the other outward senses more blunt, being no longer equally able as before to judge and decide accurately of every subject submitted to them, nor any longer to pay a tribute which will be equal to the number of the passions. So that it happened very naturally that they being thoroughly exhausted and laid prostrate by them were easily put to flight by the adverse passions; (241) and the statement that follows is in strict consistency with what might be naturally expected, namely, that of the five kings two fell into wells, and three took to flight. For touch and taste reach to the very deepest portions of the body, sending down into the entrails those things which are suitable for digestion; but the eyes and ears, and the smell, roaming abroad for the most part, escape the slavery of the body. (242) The good man--threatening to attack all of these, when he saw that those who had lately been friends and confederates were now in a state of disease, and that there was war instead of peace arising among the nine kingdoms, as the four kings were contending with the five for sovereignty and dominion--on a sudden, having watched his opportunity, attacked them; being desirous of the establishment of democracy in the soul, the most excellent of constitutions instead of tyrannies and absolute sovereignties, and wishing also to introduce law and justice instead of lawlessness and injustice, which had prevailed up to that time. (243) And what is here said is not a cunningly devised fable, but is rather one of the most completely true facts, which may be seen to be true in our own selves. For it very often happens that the outward senses observe a sort of confederacy which they have formed with the passions, supplying them with objects perceptible by the outward senses; and very often also, they raise contentions, no longer choosing to pay the tribute fairly due from them, or else being unable to do so, by reason of the presence of corrective reason; which when it has taken up its complete armour, namely, the virtues, and their doctrines and contemplations, which form an irresistible power, conquers all things in the most vigorous manner. For it is not lawful for perishable things to dwell with what is immortal. (244) Therefore the nine sovereignties of the four passions and the five outward senses are both perishable themselves and also the causes of mortality. But the truly sacred and divine word, which uses the virtues as a starting place, being placed in the number ten, that perfect number, when it descends into the contest and exerts that more vigorous power which it has in accordance with God, subdues by main force all the aforesaid powers.

XLII

XLII. (245) And at a subsequent period his wife dies, she who was most dear to his mind and most excellent in all respects, having given innumerable proofs of her affection towards her husband in leaving all her relations together with him; and in her unhesitating migration from her own country, and in her continued and uninterrupted wanderings in a foreign land, and in her endurance of want and scarcity, and in her accompanying him in his warlike expeditions. (246) For she was always with him at all times, and in all places, never being absent from any spot, or failing to share any of his fortune, being truly the partner of his life, and of all the circumstances of his life; judging it right equally to share all his good and evil fortune together with him. For she did not, as some persons do, shun any participation in his misfortunes, but lie in wait only for his prosperity, but with all cheerfulness took her share in both, as was fitting and becoming to a wedded wife.

XLIII

XLIII. (247) And though I might have many topics for panegyric on this woman, still I will only mention one, which shall be the most manifest possible proof of all the others. For she, being barren and childless, and fearing lest her husband's Godloving house might be left entirely destitute of offspring, came to her husband and spoke as follows:--(248) "We have now lived together a long time mutually pleasing each; but we have no children, which is the cause for which we ourselves came together, and for which also nature designed the original connection between husband and wife; nor indeed can there be any hope of your having any offspring by me, since I am now beyond the age of childbearing; (249)

do not you then suffer for my barrenness, and do not, out of your affection for me, while you are yourself able to still become a father, be hindered from being so. For I shall not feel any jealousy towards another woman whom you may marry, not for the gratification of irrational appetite, but in order to satisfy a necessary law of nature. (250) For which reason I will not delay to deck a new bride for you, that she may fulfil what is wanting on my part. And if the prayers which we will offer up for the birth of children be blessed with success, then the children which are born shall be your own legitimate children, but by adoption they shall be by all means mine. (251) "And that you may have no suspicion of any jealousy on my part, take, if you will, my own handmaid to wife; who is a slave indeed as to her body, but free and noble as to her mind; whose good qualities I have for a long time proved and experienced from the day when she was first introduced into my house, being an Egyptian by blood, and a Hebrew by deliberate choice. (252) We have great substance and abundant wealth, not like people who are sojourners. For even already we surpass the natives themselves in the brilliancy of our prosperity, but still we have no heir or successor, and that, too, though there might be one, if you would be guided by my advice." (253) But Abraham, marvelling more and more at the love of his wife for her husband thus continually being renewed and gaining fresh strength, and also at her spirit of forecast so desirous to provide for the future, takes to himself the handmaid who had been approved by her to the extent of having a son by her; though as those who give the most clear and probable account say he cohabited with her only till she became pregnant; and when she conceived, which she did after no long interval, he then desisted from all connection with her, by reason of his natural continence, and also of the honour in which he held his wife. (254) So then he speedily had a son by this handmaid, but at a very distant period after this he had also a legitimate son, after he and his wife had both despaired of any offspring from one another. The bounteous God having thus bestowed on them a reward for their excellence more perfect than their highest hopes.

XLIV

XLIV. (255) It is sufficient to mention this as a proof of the virtue of Abraham's wife. But the topics of praise of the wise man himself are more numerous, some of which I have lately enumerated. Moreover I will mention also one circumstance connected with the death of the wife, which ought not to be buried in silence. (256) For when Abraham had lost such a partner of his whole life, as our account has shown her to have been, and as the scriptures testify that she was, he still like a wrestler prevailed over the grief which attacked him and threatened to overwhelm his soul; strengthening and encouraging with great virtue and resolution, reason, the natural adversary of the passions, which indeed he had always taken as a counsellor during the whole of his life; but at this time above all others, he thought fit to be guided by it, when it was giving him the best and most expedient advice. (257) And the advice was this; not to afflict himself beyond all measure, as if he were stricken down with a novel and unprecedented calamity; nor, on the other hand, to give way to indifference, as if nothing had happened calculated to give him sorrow. But rather to choose the middle way in preference to either extreme; and to endeavour to grieve in a moderate degree; not being indignant at nature for having reclaimed what belonged to her as her due; and bearing what had befallen him with a mild and gentle spirit. (258) And there are evidences of these assertions to be seen in the holy scriptures; which it is impossible should be convicted of false witness, and they tell us that Abraham, having wept a short time over his wife's body, soon rose up from the corpse; thinking, as it should seem, that to mourn any longer would be inconsistent with that wisdom by which he had been taught that he was not to look upon death as the extinction of the soul, but rather as a separation and disjunction of it from the body, returning back to the region from whence it came; and it came, as is fully shown in the history of the creation of the world, from God. (259) But just as no man of moderation or sense would be indignant at having to repay a debt to a lender or to return a deposit to the man who had deposited it; so, in the same manner, he did not think it becoming to show impatience when nature reclaimed what belonged to her, but preferred to bear what was inevitable with cheerfulness. (260) And when the magistrates of that country came to sympathise with him in his sorrow, seeing none of the customary signs of woe which were usually exhibited in their land by mourners, no loud wailing or howling, no beating of the breast, no loud cries of men or women, but a steady, sober depression of spirits on the part of the whole household, they marvelled exceedingly, even though they had been previously full of astonishment and admiration at all the rest of the man's way of life. (261) And then, not concealing in their own minds their ideas of the greatness and beauty of his virtue, for it was all admirable, they approached him and addressed him thus:--"Thou art a king from God among Us." [1158] Speaking most truly, for all other kingdoms are established by man by means of wars, and military expeditions, and indescribable evils, which those persons who aim at power inflict mutually on one another, slaying one another, and raising up vast forces of infantry, and cavalry, and fleets. But the kingdom of the wise man is bestowed upon him by God; and the virtuous man receiving it is not the cause of evil to any one, but is rather the author to all his subjects of the acquisition and also of the use of good things, proclaiming to them peace and obedience to the law.

XLV

XLV. (262) There is also another praise of him recorded in his honour and testified to in the holy scriptures, which Moses has written, in which it is related of him that he believed in God; which is a statement brief indeed in words, but of great magnitude and importance to be confirmed in fact. (263) For on whom else can we believe? Are we to trust in authorities, or in glory and honour, or in abundance of wealth and noble birth, or in good health and a good condition of the senses and the mind, or in vigour of body and beauty of person? But in truth every kind of authority is unstable, as it has innumerable enemies lying it wait to attack it. And if in any instance it is firmly established, it is only so confirmed by innumerable evils and calamities which those who are in authority both inflict and suffer. (264) Again, honours and glory are most unstable, being tossed about among the indiscriminate inclinations and feeble language of careless and imprudent men; and even if they endure, their nature is not such as to produce any genuine good. (265) And as for riches and illustrious birth, those things sometimes fall to the lot of the most worthless men. And even if they should belong only to the virtuous, still they are but the praises of their ancestors and of fortune, and not of those who now possess them. (266) Nor, again, is it right for a man to pride himself on his personal advantages, in which other animals are superior to him. For what man is stronger or more vigorous than a bull among domestic animals, or than a lion among wild beasts? And what man is more sharp-sighted than a falcon or an eagle? And what man is so richly endowed with the sense of hearing as that stupidest of all animals, the ass? Also what man is more accurate in his sense of smell than a hound, who huntsmen say can trace out by means of his nose animals who are lying at a distance, and can run up to them with perfect correctness, and course, though he has not seen them; for what sight is to other animals that is the sense of smell to hounds and to all the dogs which pursue game. (267) Moreover, the greater part of the irrational animals enjoy excellent health, and are as far as possible entirely exempt from disease. And also in any competition in respect of beauty, some things which are even destitute of vitality, appear to me to surpass the elegance of either men or women ; as, for instance, images, and statues, and pictures, and in a word all the works of either the pictorial or plastic art which arrive at excellence in either branch, and which are the objects of study and desire both to Greeks and barbarians, who erect them in the most conspicuous places for the ornament of their cities.

XLVI

XLVI. (268) Therefore, the only real, and true, and lasting good is trust in God, the comfort of life, the fulfillment of all good hopes, the absence of all evils, and the attendant source of blessings, the repudiation of all unhappiness, the recognition of piety, the inheritance of all happiness, the improvement of the soul in every respect, as it thus relies for support on the cause of all things, who is able to do everything but who wills only to do what is best. (269) For as men who are going along a slippery road stumble and fall, but they who proceed by a dry, and level, and plain path, journey on without stumbling; so also those men who are conducting their soul through the road of bodily and external good things are only accustoming it to fall; for these things are full of stumbling and the most insecure of all. But they who by those speculations which are in accordance with virtue, hasten towards God, are guiding their souls in a safe and untroubled path. So that we may say with the most absolute truth, that the man who trusts in the good things of the body disbelieves in God, and that he who distributes them believes in him. (270) But not only do the holy scriptures bear witness to the faith of Abraham in the living God, which faith is the queen of all the virtues, but moreover he is the first man whom they speak of as an elder; though they were men who had preceded him who had lived three times as many years (or even more still) as he had, not one of whom is handed down to us as worthy of the appellation. And may we not say that this is in strict accordance with natural truth? For he who is really an elder is looked upon as such, not with reference to his length of time, but to the praiseworthiness of his life. (271) Those men, therefore, who have spent a long life in that existence which is in accordance with the body, apart from all virtue, we must call only long-lived children, having never been instructed in those branches of education which befit grey hairs. But the man who has been a lover of prudence, and wisdom, and faith in God, one may justly denominate an elder, forming his name by a slight change from the first. (272) For in real truth the wise man is the first man in the human race, being what a pilot is in a ship, a governor in a city, a general of war, the soul in the body, or the mind in the soul; or again, what the heaven is in the world, and what God is in the heaven. (273) And God, admiring this man for his faith (pistis) in him, giving him a pledge (pistis) in return, namely, a confirmation by an oath of the gifts which he had promised him; no longer conversing with him as God might with man, but as one friend with another. For he says, "By myself have I Sworn,"[1159] by him that is whose word is an oath, in order that Abraham's mind may be established still more firmly and immoveably than before. (274) Let the virtuous man both be and be called the younger and the last, since he only pursues such objects as may produce revolution and as are placed in the lowest rank. (275) Thus much is sufficient to say on this subject. But God, adding to the multitude and magnitude of the praises of the wise man one single thing as a crowning point, says that "this man fulfilled the divine law, and all the commandments of God," [1160] not having been taught to do so by written books, but in accordance with the unwritten law of his nature, being anxious to obey all healthful and salutary impulses. And what is the duty of man except most firmly to believe those things which God asserts? (276) Such is the life of the first author and founder of our nation; a man according to the law, as some persons think, but, as my argument has shown, one who is himself the unwritten law and justice of God.

Footnotes:

1140. Yonge's title, A Treatise on the Life of the Wise Man Made Perfect by Instruction or, On the Unwritten Law, That Is To Say, On Abraham.

1141. Gen 4:26.

1142. Gen 5:1.

1143. Lev 19:24.

1144. Gen 5:24.

1145. this is not the translation of the Bible which says "and Enoch walked with God, and he was not, for God took him."

1146. Gen 6:9.

1147. Gen 7:11.

1148. Exod 3:15.

1149. Exod 19:6.

1150. Gen 12:7.

1151. Gen 18:1, etc.

1152. Gen 18:3.

1153. Gen 18:10.

1154. Gen 19:20.

1155. Gen 22:7.

1156. Deut 12:31.

1157. Gen 18:15.

1158. Gen 23:6.

1159. Gen 15:6.

1160. Gen 26:5.

ON JOSEPH [1161]

I

I. (1) There are three different modes by which we proceed towards the most excellent end, namely, instruction, nature, and practice. There are also three persons, the oldest of the wise men who in the account given to us by Moses derive three names from these modes, whose lives I have now discussed, having examined the man who arrived at excellence in consequence of instruction, and him who was self-taught, and him who attained to the proposed end by practice. Accordingly, proceeding in regular order, I will now describe the life of the man occupied in civil affairs. And again, Moses has given us one of the patriarchs as deriving his name from this kind of life, in which he had been immersed from his earliest youth. (2) Now, this man began from the time he was seventeen years of age to be occupied with the consideration of the business of a shepherd, which corresponds to political business. On which account I think it is that the race of poets has been accustomed to call kings the shepherds of the people; for he who is skilful in the business of a shepherd will probably be also a most excellent king, having derived instruction in those matters which are deserving of inferior attention here to superintend a flock of those most excellent of all animals, namely, of men. (3) And just as attention to matters of hunting is indispensable to the man who is about to conduct a war or to govern an army, so in the same manner those who hope to have the government of a city will find the business of a shepherd very closely connected with them, since that is at is were a sort of prelude to any kind of government. (4) Therefore, as this man's father perceived in his son a very noble ability, and too great to be left in the obscurity of a private station, he admired him, and cultivated his talent, and loved him more than his other sons; because, too, he was the son of his old age, which last cause is one of the strongest incentives to affection possible. And like a man fond of virtue, he cherished and kindled the natural good disposition of his son by excessive and most diligent care and attention, in order that it might not only not be smothered, but might shine forth more brilliantly.

II

II. (5) But envy is at all times an adversary to great good fortune, and at this time it attacked a house which was prospering in all its parts, and divided it, setting all the brothers in enmity against one, who displayed an ill feeling on their own parts, sufficient to counterbalance the affection of his father, hating their brother as much as their father loved him; but they did not divulge their hatred by words, but kept it in their own bosoms, on which account it very naturally became more grievous and bitter; for passions which are repressed, and which are not allowed to evaporate in language, are more difficult to bear. (6) This man, therefore, indulging a disposition free from all guile and malice, and having no suspicion of the ill will which was secretly cherished against him by his brethren, having seen a dream of favourable import, related it to them, as if they were well affected towards him. "For," said he, "I thought that the time of harvest was arrived, and that we had all gone down to the plain to gather the crops, and had taken sickles in our hands to reap the harvest, and on a sudden my sheaf appeared to stand up, right, and to be raised up, and to erect itself; and I thought that your sheaves, as if at an appointed signal, ran up and fell down before it, and worshipped it with great Earnestness." [1162] (7) But they being men of acute intelligence, and shrewd in divining the nature of a matter thus intimated to them by means of a figure, with very felicitous conjectures, replied, "Dost thou think that thou shalt be king and lord over us? for this is what you are now intimating by this lying vision of yours." So their hatred was kindled against him more exceedingly than before, as it was continually receiving some fresh pretext for its increase. (8) And he, suspecting nothing, a few days afterwards saw another dream, still more astonishing than the former one, and again he related it to his brethren; for he thought that the sun, and the moon, and the eleven stars, all came and worshipped him, so that his father marvelling at what had thus happened, laid these events up in his mind, cherishing them, and considering within himself what was to happen. (9) But he reproved his son gravely, from a fear that he might be doing wrong in some respect, and said to him, "Shall I, and thy mother, and thy brethren, be able to fall down and worship thee? for by the sun you appear to indicate your father, and by the moon your mother, and by the eleven stars your eleven brethren? Let no such an idea ever come into your mind, O my son. But rather let all recollection of these visions which have appeared to you be forgotten, and let them pass from your mind; for to hope and expect a superiority over those of your family and kindred, is a detestable thing in my opinion, and I think, indeed, in that of every one else, who has an regard for equality and the principles of justice that subsist among kinsman." (10) But his father, being afraid lest from his meeting with his brothers there might arise some quarrel and disturbance with them, inasmuch as they bore ill will against him on account of the dreams which he had seen, sent them away to keep their flocks at a distance, but retained him at home till a fitting season, knowing that time is said to be a powerful physician for all the passions and diseases of the soul, and a remover of grief, and an extinguisher of anger, and a healer of fear; for it softens and mitigates everything, even such things as are, according to their own nature, hard to be cured. (11) But when he conjectured that no hatred was any longer abiding in their hearts he sent this his son forth to salute his brethren, and also to bring him word how they and their flocks of sheep were.

III

III. (12) This expedition of his was the origin both of great evils and also of great good, each of them being excessive beyond all expectation; for he, obeying the commands of his parents, went to visit his brethren; but they, seeing him coming towards them while at a great distance, conversed one with another, saying nothing of good omen, inasmuch as they did not choose even to call him by his name, but called him a dreamer, and a seer of visions, and such appellations as these. (13) And to such a height did they carry their rage that (I will not say all of them, but) the greater portion of them plotted his death; and designed, after having slain him, for the sake of not being detected, to throw him into a deep pit dug in the earth, for there are a great many such places in that district dug as receptacles for the rain water. (14) And they were very near incurring that most excessive pollution of fratricide, as they would have done if they had not been, though with difficulty, persuaded by the advice of their eldest brother, who counselled them not to meddle with such a pollution but merely to cast him into one of these pits, thinking then to contrive some means of saving him, so that when they had all departed he might send him back again to his father without having suffered any harm. And after they had agreed to this he came forward and saluted them; and they took him as though he had been an enemy, and stripped him of all his garments, and let him down into a vast pit, and then, having stained his cloak with the blood of a kid, they sent it to his father on the pretence that he had been slain by a wild beast.

IV

IV. (15) But on that day it happened by some chance that certain merchants who were accustomed to convey their merchandise from Arabia to Egypt were travelling that way, and so the eleven brethren drew Joseph up out of the pit and sold him to them; the one of them who was the fourth in respect of age instigating this contrivance; for in my opinion, he was afraid lest his brother might be treacherously slain by the others, who had conceived an irreconcilable hatred against him, and therefore he proposed that he should be sold, substituting slavery for death, the lighter evil for the greater. (16) But the eldest, for he was not present when he was sold, looking down into the pit, and not seeing him whom he had left there a short time before, cried out and lamented loudly, and rent his clothes, and tossed his hands up and down like a madman, and beat his breast and tore his hair, saying, (17) "What has become of him? Tell me, is he alive, or is he dead? If he is dead, show me his corpse that I may weep over his body, and so alleviate my grief. When I see him lying dead I shall be comforted; for why should we bear ill will to the dead? There is no envy excited against those who are out of sight. And if he is alive, to what country has he departed? (18) Where is he kept? for I am not, as he was, an object of suspicion, so as to be distrusted by you." And when they replied that he had been sold, and when they showed him the money which they had received for him, he said, "A fine trade, indeed, you have been driving? Let us divide the gain: let us wear crowns of victory after thus rivalling the slavedealers, and bearing off from them the prizes of iniquity; (19) we may well pride ourselves now that we have surpassed them in barbarity, for they indeed traffic in the liberty of strangers, but we in that of those who are most nearly related to and most dear to us. Surely here is newly contrived a great disgrace and a shame which will be known far and wide. Our fathers left behind them in every part of the world memorials of their virtue and excellence; we shall leave behind us the guilt of a charge of faithlessness and treacherous inhumanity which can never be effaced; for the reputation of extraordinary actions penetrates everywhere; those which are praiseworthy being admired, and those which are blameable meeting with blame and accusation. (20) In what manner now will our father receive the news of what has happened? You will now, as far as depends upon us, have made the life of him who has hitherto been wonderfully happy and fortunate, not worth living; which will he pity, the child who has been sold, for his slavery?

or those who have sold him, for their inhumanity? I am sure he will pity us much the most; since to do wrong is a more terrible evil than to suffer wrong, for the one has for an alleviation two consolations of the greatest influence, hope and pity; but the other is destitute of both these mitigations, and is more unfortunate in the judgment of every one. (21) But why do I mourn and bewail in this manner? It is better for me to be silent, lest I too should be treated in some terrible manner; for ye are most merciless men in your dispositions, and implacable; and the rage which was kindled in each of you is still furious and vehement."

V

V. (22) But when their father heard, not the truth indeed, that his son had been sold, but a falsehood that he was dead, and that he had been slain by wild beasts, he was smitten in his ears by the news that was reported to him, and in his eyes by what was shown to him (for they brought to him his son's coat rent and torn and defiled with quantities of blood); and being wholly bewildered by the exceeding greatness of the calamity, he lay for a long time without speaking, not being able even to lift up his head, the calamity overwhelming and completely prostrating him; (23) then suddenly pouring forth as it were a stream of tears with bitter lamentations, he bedewed his cheeks, and his chin, and his breast, and all the garments on his chest, saying at the same time such words as these, "It is not thy death that grieves me, O my son, but such a tomb as has fallen to your lot; for if you had been buried in your own land I should have been comforted; I would have cherished you, I would have tended you in sickness if you had died before me, I would have given you my last embrace, I would have closed your eyes, I would have wept over your dead body lying before me, I would have buried you sumptuously, I would have omitted none of the customary observances. (24) "Again, even if you had died in a foreign land, I should have said, nature has claimed what was due to, and what belonged to her; and therefore, O my mind, be not cast down; for living men have indeed their separate countries, but the whole earth is the grave of the dead; and all men are destined to a speedy death; for even the longest lived man is but short lived if compared with eternity; (25) but if it was necessary that he should die violently and by treachery, it would have been a lighter evil to me for him to have been slain by men, who would have laid out his corpse, and have pitied him so far as to scatter dust over him, and at least to have concealed his body; and even if they had been the most merciless of all people, what more could they have done than have thrown him out unburied, and so got rid of him? And then, perhaps, some one of the passers by on the road, standing by, and beholding him, and conceiving pity for our common nature, would have thought him worthy of some care, and of burial; but now, as the saying is, O my son, thou has become a feast, and a banquet for savage and carnivorous wild beasts, who will eat and devour thy bowels; (26) I am compelled to endure distresses which I never had imagined, I am without any cause practised in enduring many miseries; I am a wanderer, a stranger, a slave, living under compulsion, having even my very life plotted against by those whom it least became to do so. And I have seen many things, and I have heard many things, and I have suffered many things, all of which have been incurable evils, which however I have learnt to bear with moderation, so as not to yield to them. "But nothing has ever happened more intolerable than this misfortune which has now befallen me; which has consumed and destroyed all the vigour of my soul; (27) for what can be a greater or more pitiable calamity? The garment of my child has been brought to me, who am his father; but of him himself there is no portion brought, not a limb, not a small fragment, but he has been wholly and entirely destroyed and devoured, not being able even to receive burial; and it seems to me that even his garment would never have been sent to me at all if it had not been by the way of a reminder of my grief, and as a refreshment of my memory as to the sufferings which he endured, so as to afflict me with a never to be forgotten and never ending sorrow." He indeed bewailed his son in these terms; but the merchants sold his son in Egypt to one of the king's eunuchs who was his chief cook.

VI

VI. (28) It is worth while, however, after having thus explained the literal account given to us of these events, to proceed to explain also the figurative meaning concealed under that account; for we say that nearly all, or that at all events, the greater part of the history of the giving of the law is full of allegories; now the disposition which we have at present under consideration, is called by the Hebrews Joseph; but the name being interpreted in the Greek language means, "the addition of the Lord," a name most felicitously given, and most appropriate to the account given of the person so called; for the democratic constitution in vogue among states is an addition of nature which has sovereign authority over everything; (29) for this world is a sort of large state, and has one constitution, and one law, and the word of nature enjoins what one ought to do, and forbids what one ought not to do: but the cities themselves in their several situations are unlimited in number, and enjoy different constitutions, and laws which are not all the same; for there are different customs and established regulations found out and established in different nations; (30) and the cause of this the want of union, and participation existing not merely between the Greeks and the barbarians, or between the barbarians and the Greeks, but also between the different tribes of each of these respective nations. Then they, as it would seem, blaming those things which do not deserve blame, such as unexpected occurrences or opportunities, deficiency of crops, badness of soil, their own situation either as being by the sea-side, or inland, or insular, or on the continent, or anything of that sort, are silent as to the real truth. The real truth is their covetousness, their want of good faith towards and confidence in one another, on which account they have not been satisfied with the laws of nature, but have called those regulations, which have appeared to be for the common advantage of the agreeing and unanimous multitudes, laws, so that the individual constitutions do naturally appear rather in the light of additions to the one great general constitution of nature; (31) for the laws of individual cities are additions to the one right reason of nature; and so also the man who is occupied with political affairs is an addition to the man who lives in accordance with nature.

VII

VII. (32) And it is not without a particular and correct meaning that Joseph is said to have had a coat of many colours. For a political constitution is a many-coloured and multiform thing, admitting of an infinite variety of changes in its general appearance, in its affairs, in its moving causes, in the peculiar laws respecting strangers, in numberless differences respecting times and places. (33) For as the master of a ship collects together all the means which may tend to ensure him a favourable voyage with reference to and in dependency on the changes of the wind, not always guiding his vessel in one and the same way; and as a physician does not apply one and the same means of cure to every sick person, nor even to one person if his disease varies in its character, but watches the periods of its abatement, and of its intensity, and of its becoming full or empty, and the alterations of the causes of the sickness, and so varies his remedies as much as possible to secure the safety of his patient, applying one remedy at one time and another at another; (34) in the same manner I conceive that the man immersed in political affairs is of necessity a multiform man, assuming many different appearances, one in time of peace and another in time of war; and a different character according as those who are opposed to him are numerous or few in number, withstanding a small number with vigorous resolution, but using persuasion and gentle means towards a large body. And in some cases where there is much danger, still for the sake of the common advantage he will take the place of every one, and manage the business in hand by himself; in other cases, where it is merely a question of labour he will let others minister to him as his assistants. (35) It was appropriately said that the man was sold. For the haranguer of the people and the demagogue, mounting the tribunal, like slaves who are being sold and exposed to view, is a slave instead of a free man, by reason of the honours which he seems to be receiving, being led away by ten thousand masters? (36) The same person is also represented as having been torn by wild beasts; and vainglory, which lies in wait for a man, is an untameable wild beast, tearing and destroying all who give into it. And they who have been purchasers are likewise sellers; for there is one master only to the citizens who live in any city; but there is a multitude of masters, one succeeding another in a certain succession and regular order. But those who have been sold three times change their masters like bad slaves, not remaining with their original ones, by reason of the speedily satisfied irregularity of their dispositions, always thirsting after novelty.

VIII

VIII. (37) This is enough to say on this part of the subject. Accordingly, the young man, having been conducted into Egypt, and there, as has already been stated, having become the slave of a eunuch, gave in a few days such proofs of virtue and excellence of disposition, that he had authority over his fellow servants given to him, and the management of the whole household committed to his charge; for already his master had learnt by many circumstances to perceive that his servant in all his words and in all his actions was under the immediate direction of divine providence. (38) Accordingly, in consequence of this opinion of his purchaser, he was appointed superintendent of his house, apparently indeed by his master, but, in fact and reality, by nature herself, which procured for him the government of a mighty city, and nation, and country. For it was necessary that one who was destined to be a statesman should be previously practised and trained in the management of a single household; for a household is a city on a small and contracted scale, and the management of a household is a contracted kind of polity; so that a city may be called a large house, and the government of a city a widely spread economy. (39) And from these considerations we may see that the manager of a household and the governor of a state are identical, though the multitude and magnitude of the things committed to their charge may be different, as in the case too with the arts of painting and statuary; for the good statuary or painter, whether he is making many and colossal figures, or only few and those of a small size, is still the same person, and the art which he is practising is the same art.

IX

IX. (40) But while he is earning a very high reputation in the matters connected with the management of his master's house, he is plotted against by the wife of his master, because of the incontinent love which she had conceived for him; for she, being maddened by the beauty of the young man, and being unable to restrain the violence of her frenzy and passion, addressed a proposal of illicit intercourse to him; but he resisted it vigorously, and would not at all endure to approach her, by reason of the orderly and temperate disposition implanted in him by nature and habit. (41) But when she, inflaming and exciting her lawless desire, kept continually tempting him, and continually throwing herself in his way, and continually failing in her object, she at last, in the violence of her passion, had recourse to force, and seizing hold of his cloak dragged him vigorously toward the bed, her passion endowing her strength with greater vigour, as it often does strengthen even the weak. (42) But he, proving more powerful than even the alluring opportunity, uttered a cry becoming a free man, and worthy of his race, saying, What are you forcing me to? We, the descendants of the Hebrews, are guided by special customs and laws of our own; (43) in other nations the youths are permitted, after they are fourteen years of age, to use concubines and prostitutes, and women who make gain by their persons, without restraint. But among us a harlot is not allowed even to live, but death is appointed as a punishment for any one who adopts such a way of life. Therefore, before our lawful marriage we know nothing of any connection with any other woman, but, without ever having experienced any similar cohabitation, we approach our virgin brides as pure as themselves, proposing as the end of our marriage not pleasure but the offspring of legitimate children. (44) I, therefore, having kept myself pure to this day, will not begin now to transgress the law by adultery which is the greatest of all sins, when I ought rather, even if in past time I had lived in an irregular manner, and had been led away by the impulses of youth, and had imitated the licentiousness of the natives, still not to seek to pollute the marriage of another man, an offence which who is there would not avenge with blood? For though different nations differ in other points, still all agree in this alone, that all men think him worthy of ten thousand deaths who does so, and give up the man who is detected in adultery without trial to the husband who has detected him. (45) But you, pressing me thus to load myself with guilt, would add even a third pollution in my case, since you bid me not merely commit adultery, but also to violate my mistress and my master's wife, unless, indeed, this is to be looked upon as the reason for which I entered your house, that I might neglect the duties which a servant ought to perform, and get drunk, and become intoxicated with hopes fit for my master who has bought me, polluting his marriage, and his house and his family. (46) Nevertheless I am induced to honour him not merely as my master, but also as one who has before now been my benefactor. He has committed to my care the whole management of his household; there is nothing whatever, be it great or small, which is withdrawn from my superintendence, except you who are his wife. In return for these kindnesses is it fitting for me to requite him with such an action as you recommend to me? I will rather, as becomes me, endeavour with honourable service to requite the kindness of which he has set me the example, and which is due him. (47) He, being my master, has made me, who was a captive and a slave, a free man and a citizen by his great goodness, as far at least as depended on him; and shall I, who am a slave, compare myself to my master as if he were a stranger and a captive? And with what disposition can I commit this unholy action? and with what face can I be impudent enough to look upon him? The consciousness of guilt which I shall have contracted will not suffer me to look him in the face, even if I should be able to be undiscovered, but in fact I shall never escape detection, for there are innumerable witnesses of all the things which are done privily who may not be silent. (48) I forbear to say that, even if no one else should know it, or being privy to it should not divulge it, still I nevertheless shall be a witness against myself by my complexion, by my look, by my voice, as I said a little while ago, being convicted by my own conscience; and if no one else informs against me, shall I not fear nor respect, justice the assessor of God, and the overlooker of all human actions?

X

X. (49) He put all these arguments together and philosophised in this way till she ceased to importune him; for the desires are powerful, to cast in the shade even the most powerful of the outward senses, which he, being aware of, fled from them, leaving his garment in her hands, as she had seized hold of him. (50) This circumstance gave her an opportunity to contrive a story, and to invent a plausible tale against the young man, by means of which she might revenge herself on him; for when her husband came from the public assembly, she, pretending to play the part of a modest and orderly woman, even among the intemperate habits by which she was surrounded, said to him, with excessive indignation, "You brought a servant into us, a slave of the Hebrews, who had not only corrupted his soul, since you, in a simple manner without due inquiry, committed your household to him, but has even dared to assault my body. (51) For he was not contented with seducing only his fellow servants, inasmuch as he has become a most lascivious and debauched man, but he has attempted to defile even me, his mistress, and to use force to me; and the proofs of his insane lust are visible and clear; for when, having been very ill-treated by him, I cried out, calling to my aid assistants from within; he fled, from fear of being apprehended." (52) And showing his garment, she appeared to give a proof of the truth of what she said; and his master thinking that it was true, ordered his officers to conduct the man to prison, erring in two most important points: first, that without giving him any time to defend himself, he, without a trial, condemned one who had done no wrong, as if he had committed the greatest crimes; secondly, because the garment which the woman displayed as having been left behind by the young man, was indeed a proof of violence, but not of that which he had committed, but rather of that which had been offered to him, and of the fortitude with which he endured it from the woman; for if he had been offering violence, it was probable that he might have laid hold of the garment of his mistress; but it was owing to his having had violence offered to him that he was deprived of his own. (53) But perhaps he should be pardoned for his excessive ignorance, inasmuch as he lived chiefly in the cook's house, being filled with blood, and smoke, and ashes, his reasoning having no opportunity to become tranquillised and to enjoy leisure in itself, because it was confused still more, or, at all events, not less than the body.

XI

XI. (54) I have already sketched out three characters of the man immersed in civil business; that of him who is occupied as a shepherd, that of the regulator of a house, and that of the man possessed of fortitude: and we have now discussed the two first of these sufficiently. But the temperate man is no less connected with the regulation of political affairs than those two are; (55) for temperance is a beneficial and saving thing for all the affairs of life; and in affairs of state it is most especially so, as those who wish to understand the matter may learn from numerous and easily obtained proofs. (56) For who is there who does not know that great calamities have befallen nations, and districts, and whole countries all over the world, both by land and sea, in consequence of intemperance; for the most numerous and most serious wars have been kindled on account of love, and adultery, and the wiles of women; by which the most numerous and most excellent portion of both of the Grecian and barbarian race has been destroyed, and the youth of the cities has perished. (57) And of the consequences of intemperance, are domestic seditions, and wars, and evils upon evils in unutterable number. It is plain that the consequences of temperance, are stability, and peace, and the acquisition and enjoyment of perfect blessing.

XII

XII. (58) It is worth while, however, to proceed in regular order, and by this course to exhibit what is intended to be intimated by this figurative history. The man who brought this servant of whom we are speaking is said to have been a eunuch; very naturally, for the multitude which purchases the services of a man skilful in affairs of state is truly a eunuch, having in appearance, indeed, the organs of generation, but being deprived of all the power requisite for generating; just as those persons who have a confused sight though they have eyes, are nevertheless deprived of the active use of them, inasmuch as they are not able to see clearly. (59) What, then, is the resemblance of eunuchs to the multitude? That the multitude too is unable to generate wisdom, but that it studies virtue; for when a multitude of men, brought promiscuously together from all quarters and of different races, meets in the same place, what is said indeed may be proper and becoming, but what is intended and what is done is quite contrary; since the multitude embraces what is spurious in preference to what is genuine, because it is carried away by false opinion, and has not studied what is truly honourable. (60) On which account (though it seems a most unnatural thing), a wife is represented as cohabiting with this eunuch; for the multitudes court desire, as a man courts a woman; for the sake of which it says and does everything, making it its counsellor in everything which should and should not be spoken, trifling or important, being not at all accustomed to attend to considerations of calm wisdom; (61) therefore the sacred historian very appropriately calls him the chief cook. For a cook studies nothing beyond the insatiable and immoderate pleasures of the belly, in the same manner the multitude, which is occupied with public affairs, studies only those pleasures and allurements which are conveyed by means of the hearing, by which the energies of the mind are relaxed, as one may say the nerves of the soul are in a manner loosened. (62)

And who is there who is not aware of the great quarrel which exists between physicians and cooks; since the first exert all their diligence and ingenuity in preparing things which are salutary, even if they are not pleasant; but the others, on the contrary, prepare only what is pleasant, disregarding what is advantageous? (63) Therefore, the laws which exist among a people and those who govern in accordance with the laws resemble physicians, and so also do those counsellors and judges who have a regard to the common safety and security of the state, and who use no flattery to the people. But the chief body of the younger men resembles cooks; for their object is not to supply what will be beneficial to the people, but only to contrive for the present moment to reap gratification.

XIII

XIII. (64) And the desire of the multitude, like an incontinent woman, loves the man who is experienced in state affairs, and says to him: Go forth, my good man, unto the multitude among which you are dwelling, and forget all your own individual disposition, and the pursuits, and discourses, and actions in which you have been brought up. And be guided by me, and attend to me, and do every thing which is agreeable to me; (65) for I cannot endure any thing that is austere and obstinate, and foolishly fond of truth, and pertinaciously adhering to justice, which puts on an air of importance and dignity on all occasions, which yields in no point, and never proposes to itself any object but plain expediency, without any thought of gratifying the hearers. (66) And do you not know the innumerable calumnies which some persons load you with, uttering them to my husband and your master, the multitude; for up to this time you appear to me to have been behaving like a free man, and you seem not at all to know that you are the slave of a very tyrannical master. But if you had understood that independence of action belongs to a free man, but obedience to the orders of others to a slave, you would then, laying aside your self-willed obstinancy, have learnt to look upon me who am his wife, being desire, and to do every thing with a reference to my gratification, by which means you yourself also will receive the greatest pleasure.

XIV

XIV. (67) But the statesman is not in reality ignorant that the people has the authority of a master, but still he will not admit that he himself is its slave, but looks upon himself as free, and as entitled to consider mainly the gratification of the soul. And he will say in plain words: I have not learnt to be slave to the will of the populace, nor will I ever study such a practice, but being desirous to attain to the government and administration of the city like a good steward or wellintentioned father, I will save it in a guileless and honourable manner, without any hostile character. (68) And while I cherish these sentiments I shall be open to examination, concealing nothing, and not hiding any thing like a thief, but keeping my conscience clear as in the light of the sun and of day; for the truth is the light. And I shall fear none of the evils with which they menace me, not even if they threaten me with death; for hypocrisy is in my eyes a more grievous evil than death. (69) And why should I encounter what I look upon in such a light? For even if the populace be a despot, am I therefore a slave, I who am born of as noble ancestors as any one in the world, entitled to be enrolled as a free citizen in the greatest and most admirable state in the whole world? (70) For as I am not influenced by gifts, nor by exhortations, nor by a love of honours, nor by a desire of power, nor by insolence, nor by a desire of seeming different from what I am, nor by intemperance, nor by cowardice, nor by injustice, nor by any other motive partaking of either passion or wickedness; what can, then, be the dominion of what I have need to fear? (71) Surely it can only be the dominion of men. But they claim authority, indeed, over my body, but none at all over me; for I estimate myself by the more excellent part of myself, namely, by the mind in accordance with which I have determined to live, thinking but little of my mortal body, which sticks to me like a limpet, and even if it is injured by something or other, I shall not be grieved at having got rid of cruel masters and mistresses who are settled within, inasmuch as I shall have escaped the most formidable necessity. (72) If, therefore, it shall be necessary for me to act as a judge, I will decide, neither adhering to any rich man for the sake of his riches, nor gratifying a poor man by reason of my compassion for his misfortunes, but putting out of sight the rank and outward circumstances of those respecting whom I am to judge, I will honestly pronounce in favour of what shall appear to me to be just. (73) And if I am called to counsel I will bring forward such opinions as shall appear to me to be for the common advantage, even though they may not be palatable. And if I am a member of the assembly, leaving flattering speeches to others, I will adopt only such as are advantageous and salutary, reproving, admonishing, correcting, and studying not a frantic and insane license of speech, but a sober freedom. (74) And if any one dislikes improvement, let such a one find fault with parents, and guardians, and teachers, and with all who have the care of youth, because they reprove their own children, or their orphan wards, or their pupils, and sometimes even beat them; and yet they are not to be accused of evil speaking, nor of insolent violence, but on the contrary, they must be looked upon as friends and real well-wishers; (75) for it would be utterly unworthy for me who am experienced in affairs of state, and who have all the interests of the people entrusted to me in discussions respecting what is for the advantage of the commonwealth to behave worse than a man would who has studied the art of a physician; (76) for he would not in the least regard the brilliant position or the accredited good fortune of his patient, nor whether he is of noble birth or of large fortune, nor whether he is the most renowned monarch or tyrant of all his contemporaries, but would attend to one object alone, that, namely, of preserving his health to the best of his power. And if it should be necessary to use excision or cautery, he, though a subject, or as some might say a slave, would cut or burn his governor or his master. (77) But I, who have got for my patient not one man but a whole city sick with those more grievous diseases which the kindred desires have brought upon it, what ought I to do? Shall I, abandoning all idea of what will be of general advantage to the whole state seek to please the ears of this or that man with an ungentleman-like and thoroughly slavish flattery? I would rather choose to die than to speak merely with the object of gratifying the ear, and to conceal the truth, disregarding all thought of what is really advantageous. (78) "Now then," as the tragedian says:

> "Now then let fire, let biting steel come on;
> Burn, scorch my flesh, and glut your appetite
> Drinking my dark, warm blood; for here I swear
> Sooner shall those bright stars which deck the heaven
> Descend beneath the earth, the earth itself
> Soar upwards to the sky, than servile words
> Of flattery creep from out my mouth to thee."

(79) But the people, when it is the master, cannot endure a statesman of so masculine a spirit, and one who keeps so completely aloof from the passions, from pleasure, from fear, from grief, from desire; but it arrests its well-wisher and friend, and punishes him as an enemy, in doing which it first of all inflicts upon itself the most grievous of all punishments, namely, ignorance; in consequence of which state it does not itself learn that lesson which is the most beautiful and profitable of all, namely, obedience to its governor, from which the knowledge how to govern subsequently springs.

XV

XV. (80) Having now discussed this matter at sufficient length, let us see what follows next. The young man, having been calumniated to his master by his master's wife, who was in love with him, and who had invented against him the accusation to which she herself was liable, is not allowed to make any defence, but is led away to prison. And while he was in prison he displayed such exceeding virtue that even the most abandoned persons there marvelled and were amazed, and looked upon it as an alleviation of their calamities to have found such a man as the averter of evil from them. (81) And of the cruelty and inhumanity of which gaolers are full there is no one who is ignorant. For they are both by nature pitiless, and also by constant practice they are made more and more brutal, and increase in ferocity day by day, never seeing, or saying, or doing any good thing, but committing only acts of violence and barbarity. (82) For as men who have very strongly knit bodies, when besides their natural strength they add to it the practice of wrestlers, becomes stronger still, and acquire an irresistible power and a surpassing perfection of body, so in the same manner when an untameable and implacable nature adds habit to its natural ferocity, it becomes inaccessible to, and immovable by any kind of pity or any single respectable or humane feeling. (83) And as those who associate with good men are improved in their disposition by such association, rejoicing in the pleasant and good persons with whom they are living; so also do they who are living with the wicked take the impression of their wicked ways; for habit is a very powerful thing to put a force upon nature, and to make it resemble itself. (84) now keepers of prisons live among thieves and robbers, and housebreakers, and men of insolence and violence, and murderers, and adulterers, and plunderers of temples, from every one of whom they contract some wickedness, and collect a sort of contribution: and from their manifold mixture, make up one thoroughly confused and wholly polluted iniquity.

XVI

XVI. (85) Nevertheless, even such a man as this was propitiated by the virtue of this young man, and not only gave him liberty and security, but even entrusted to him a share of authority over all the prisoners; so that in word, indeed, and as far as the title went, he continued to be the gaoler; but in reality he has made over all the active part of the work to the young man, in consequence of which conduct of his the prisoners were benefited in no slight degree. (86) Accordingly they no longer thought fit to call the place a prison, but a house of correction: for instead of tortures and punishments which they had previously undergone night and day, being beaten and bound with chains, and suffering every imaginable kind of ill-treatment; they were now admonished with the language and doctrines of philosophy, and also by the life and conduct of their teacher, which was more effective than any discourse in the world; (87) for he, by placing his own life full of temperance and every kind of virtue before them, as a picture and wellconstructed model of virtue, changed even those who had appeared to be utterly incurable, so that the long diseases of their souls now got a respite, since they were afflicting themselves for what they had hitherto done, and were repenting of it, and uttering such expressions as these, "Where was there all this good formerly which we originally failed to find? For behold! now it shines forth to such a degree that we are ashamed to face it, seeing our deformity in it as in a looking-glass."

XVII

XVII. (88) While they then were being improved in this manner two of the king's eunuchs are brought into the prison; the one being his chief butler, and the other his chief baker, having been accused and condemned for malversation in the offices committed to their charge. And Joseph took the same care of them that he took of the others, praying that he might be able to make all those who were entrusted to his care in no respect inferior to irreproachable persons. (89) And when no long period had elapsed, he went to visit his prisoners on one occasion, when he saw these eunuchs more full of perplexity, and more downcast than they had been before; and conjecturing from their excessive grief that some strange event had befallen them, he inquired the reason of their sorrow. (90) And when they answered him, that they were full of distress and perplexity because they had seen dreams, and because there was no one who could interpret them to them, he said "Be of good cheer, and relate them to me; for so, if God will, you shall be led to understand them; for he is willing to reveal, to those who are desirous of the truth, those things which are concealed in darkness." (91) Then the chief butler spoke first, and said, "I thought that a great vine grew up, having three roots, and one very vigorous trunk, and flourishing, and bearing bunches of grapes as if in the height of autumn, and when the grapes became dark and ripe I picked the bunches, and squeezed the grapes into the king's cup, in order to convey to my sovereign a sufficient quantity of unmixed wine." (92) And Joseph, pausing for awhile, said, "Thy vision announces good fortune to thee, and a recovery of thy former situation; for the three roots of the vine signify figuratively three days, after which the king will remember thee, and will send for thee from hence, and will pardon thee, and will permit thee to resume the former rank, and shalt again pour him out wine for confirmation of thy authority, and shalt give the cup into thy master's hand." And the chief butler rejoiced when he heard these things.

XVIII

XVIII. (93) And the chief baker, gladly receiving this interpretation, and rejoicing in the idea that he too had seen a favourable dream (though his dream was of a very contrary character), being deceived by the fair hopes which were held out to the other, spoke as follows:"And I, too, fancied that I was carrying a basket, and that I was holding three baskets full of cakes upon my head. And the upper basket was full of all sorts of cakes which the king was accustomed to eat; and there were in it confections and delicacies of all kinds imaginable for the king's food: and the birds flew down and took them from off my head, and devoured them insatiably till they had eaten them all up; and none of the things which I had so skilfully prepared were left." (94) But Joseph replied, "I wish that the vision had not appeared to you, or that, if any one would speak of it, he had done so at a distance, so that I might not have heard him, and that his account had been given out of the reach of my ears, for I disliked to be a messenger of evil: for I sympathise with those who are in distress, being greatly grieved at what befalls them by reason of my own humanity. (95) But since interpreters of dreams are bound to speak the truth, since they are interpreters of the divine oracles, and prophets of the divine will, I will explain your dream to you, and conceal nothing; for to speak truly is in every case the best thing, and is, moreover, the most holy of all holy speeches. (96) "The three baskets are a symbol of three days: and after three days the king will command you to be crucified, and your head to be cut off, and the birds will fly down and feast upon your flesh, until you are wholly devoured." (97) And the chief baker, as was natural, was confused at this, and cast down greatly, expecting the fate which was thus denounced against him, and being full of misery in his mind. But when the three days had passed, the king's birth-day came, on which all the natives of the country made an assembly and a feast, and especially those in the king's palace. (98) Therefore, while the magistrates were feasting, and while all the household and all the servants were revelling as in a public banquet, the king, remembering his eunuchs who were in prison, commanded them to be brought; and when he had seen them he confirmed the interpretation of their dreams which Joseph had given, ordering one of them to be crucified, and to have his head cut off, and restoring to the other the office which he had formerly enjoyed.

XIX

XIX. (99) But the chief butler, after he was released, forgot him who had foretold his release to him, and who had alleviated all the misfortunes which had befallen him, perhaps, indeed, because every ungrateful man is forgetful of benefits, and perhaps, too, because of the providence of God, who designed that the prosperity of the young man should not be owing to man, but rather to himself; (100) for after two years he, by means of a dream, and by two visions, predicted to the king the good and evil which was about to happen to his land, each of the visions indicating the same thing, so as to produce a firmer belief in them. (101) For he thought that seven oxen were coming slowly up out of the river, fat and very well fleshed, beautiful to look upon, and that they began to feed by the river; after which seven others, equal in number, destitute of flesh in a strange degree, and very lean, came up, exceedingly ill-favoured, and they too fed alongside of the others. Then, on a sudden, the better oxen were devoured by the inferior ones, and yet those who ate them were in none, not even in the very slightest degree, increased in bulk in their bodies, but were still leaner than before, or at all events, not less lean; (102) and when he had awakened and gone to sleep a second time, he had a second vision appear to him; for he thought that seven ears of wheat sprang up from one root, equal in magnitude, and that they grew and flourished, and rose up to a height with great vigour; and then that seven other ears, thin and weak, grew up near them, and the root with good ears was devoured by the weak ears when they too had grown up. (103) Seeing this sight he remained sleepless all the rest of the night, for cares stinging and wounding him kept him awake, and at dawn he sent for the sophists and related his dream; (104) and as none of them was able, by any probable conjectures, to trace out the truth, the chief butler came forward and said, "O master, there is a hope that you may find the man whom you are seeking; for when I and the chief baker had done evil against you you ordered us to be committed to prison; and in that prison there was a servant of the chief cook, a Hebrew, to whom both the chief baker and I related some dreams which had appeared to us, and he answered them with such felicity and accuracy of interpretation, that all that he foretold to either of us came to pass, the punishment to the chief baker, which was appointed to him, and I found you favourable and merciful to me."

XX

XX. (105) Therefore the king hearing these things, orders men to go in haste and summon the young man before him; but they having cut his hair, for the hair, both of his head and of his beard, had grown very long while he was kept in prison, and having given him a splendid garment instead of a sordid one, and having adorned him in other ways, led him before the king; (106) who, perceiving from his appearance that he was a free-born and noble man (for there are certain outward characteristics which are stamped upon the persons of some people whom one sees, which are not visible to all, but only to such as have very clear-sighted eyes in their mind), said, "My soul forebodes that my dreams will not be altogether permanently hidden in uncertainty; for this young man exhibits an appearance of wisdom, by which he will be able to reveal the truth, and, as it were, dissipate the darkness by light, and the ignorance of the sophists at our court by his knowledge," And then he related to him his dream. (107) But Joseph, without being at all dismayed at the rank and majesty of the speaker, conversed with him rather as a king with a subject than like a subject with a king, using freedom of speech, though mingled with respect, and he said: "God has shown you before what he is about to do in your country. Do not imagine that the two visions which have appeared to thee are two different dreams; they are but one and the reduplication of them is not superfluous, but is intended to produce the conviction of a firmer belief; (108) for the seven fat oxen, and the seven flourishing and vigorous ears of corn, show seven years of great fertility and plenty; and the seven lean and ill-favoured oxen which came up after the fat ones, and the seven withered and shrivelled ears of corn, denote seven other years of famine; (109) therefore the first period of seven years thus denoted will arrive first, having great and abundant fertility of crops, in which the river will every year overflow all the land of Egypt with inundations, and all the plains, as if they had never been irrigated or fertilised before. "And after these years there will come a period of seven years entirely contrary to them bringing with it a terrible want and scarcity of necessary things, during which time the river will not overflow, nor will the earth be fertilised, so that it will forget its former prosperity, and so that all that was left from the former abundance of the crops will be consumed. (110) "This then is the interpretation of the dreams which have appeared to you. But there is something divine which prompts me and communicates some suggestions to me which may be salutary in this disease; and the most terrible disease of all cities and countries is famine, which must be checked or mitigated to some degree that it may not be so exceedingly strong as to devour the inhabitants; (111) how then can it be mitigated? That which shall be more than sufficient of the crop in the seven years, during which the plenty lasts, after having taken so much as is adequate to the nourishment of the people, and that will be perhaps a fifth part, must be stored up in granaries in the cities and villages, not removing the crops to any great distance, but storing them in the countries to which they belong, and keeping them there for the relief of the people who dwell in each district; (112) and it will be well to bring together the crop with the sheaves, not thrashing it out, nor winnowing, nor sifting it at all, for four reasons. "First of all, because if it is thus protected by the straw it will remain uninjured a longer time; secondly, in order that every year the people may be reminded of the former period of plenty while they are threshing and winnowing; for the imitation of the former real blessings is calculated to produce a second pleasure; (113) thirdly, in order to prevent any exact calculation of the quantity stored up, as, while the crop is in the ear and in the sheaf, it is of uncertain amount and not easily to be described; that so the hearts of the people of the land may not faint beforehand at the consumption of what has been treasured up, but may use with cheerfulness the nourishment of the corn which is thus provided for them, (for hope is of all things the most strengthening), and so many to a certain extent feel relief in the bitter disease of scarcity; fourthly, because in this way fodder may also be provided for the cattle, as the straw and the chaff derived from the threshing of the wheat will be of use to them in this way. (114) And you must appoint a man to superintend all these measures, of great prudence, and great acuteness, and well approved in all matters, who may be able without incurring hatred or envy to do all that I have here described in a proper manner, without giving to the multitude any reason to suspect the impending famine; for it would be a sad thing for them to anticipate their distress, and so to faint in their souls through despair; (115) and if any one should inquire the reason of all this being done, the superintendent may say that, as in peace it is right to provide things that may be necessary in war, so also it is desirable in years of plenty to provide against want; and that wars and famine are in their nature uncertain, and in short so are all the different events which befell men unexpectedly at different times; for which therefore it is necessary to be prepared; and not when such things have befallen one, then to seek a remedy when it is no longer of any avail."

XXI

XXI. (116) And when the king had heard these words, and had seen that the interpretation of the dreams did thus with felicity and accuracy of conjecture arrive at the truth, and that the advice which the young man gave appeared to be of exceeding use in the way of providing against the uncertainty of the future, he ordered those who were about him to approach nearer so that they might hear what he said; and then he spoke as follows: Can we, O men, find any man equal to this man who has the spirit of God resting on him? (117) And when they all praised his words, and raised their voices in accordance with them, he looked upon Joseph as he was standing before him and said: The man whom you advise me to seek out is near at hand; the wise and intelligent man whom we have need of is at no great distance; you yourself are he whom, in accordance with our recommendation, we ought to seek for, for you do not appear to me to have been inspired by anything short of God himself, when you said what you have now said to me. Go then, and take the superintendence of my household and the government of all Egypt; (118) and no one will blame my indifference or easiness, as if I were yielding to indolence and selfish love of ease, under this calamity so difficult to be remedied; for great natures are often tested without requiring a long time for their examination, compelling men by their intrinsic weight and power to be rapid, and to discard all delay in receiving them, and some affairs do not admit to any delay or procrastination when the occasions compel us to necessary promptness of action. (119) After speaking thus, Pharaoh appointed Joseph his lieutenant in the kingdom, or rather, if one is to speak the exact truth, actual king, leaving to himself only the name of kingly power; but in reality yielding up the whole sovereignty to him, and behaving in every respect so as to confer honour on the young man. (120) Therefore he gave him a royal seal, and a sacred robe, and a golden circlet to go round his neck, and he made him to ride in the second chariot which he had, and commanded him in that state to go round the city, a herald also going round with him, and announcing his appointment to those who were ignorant of it. (121) Moreover, he changed his name with reference to his interpretation of dreams, giving him an appellation according to the language of the country, and he gave him for his wife the most beautiful and noble of all the women of Egypt, the daughter of the priest of the sun. These things happened when Joseph was about thirty years of age. (122) And such is the end of pious persons; for, even if they stumble they do not wholly fall, but rise again after an interval, and are re-established in a firm and solid manner, so as not to be completed prostrated. (123) For who would ever have expected that in one day the same man would become a master from having been a slave, and from having been a prisoner would rise up the most illustrious of men, and that the under turnkey of the keeper of the prison would become the king's lieutenant, and that he would dwell in the king's palace instead of in the gaol, having the highest honour in the whole land instead of being held in the greatest disrepute? (124) Nevertheless these things really did come to pass, and similar things often will come to pass when it seems good to God. Only let there be one single spark of excellence and virtue implanted in the soul, and that must some day or other be fanned into a flame and shine forth.

XXII

XXII. (125) But since we have prospered to ourselves to give not only an explanation of the literal account given to us, but also of its more figurative meaning, we must say what is necessary to be said concerning that also. Perhaps now some persons of rash and inconsiderate dispositions will laugh; nevertheless, I will speak without concealing anything. And I will say that the statesman is at all times an interpreter of dreams, not classing him by this statement among the charlatans and vain chatterers, and men who put forth sophistical pretences by way of making money, or among those who profess the explanation of visions which have appeared to persons in their sleep in the hope of acquiring gain; but I mean that the statesman is accustomed to interpret accurately the great, and common, and universal general dreams, not only of sleeping but also of waking persons. (126) And this dream, to speak the truth, is the life of man; for as in the visions which appear to us in sleep, which seeing we do not see, and hearing we do not hear, and tasting and touching we do not either taste or touch, and speaking we do not speak, and walking we do not walk, and while appearing to exert other motions or to win other positions we are not in reality in any such motions or positions; but they are mere empty fancies without any truth in them of the mind which fancies to itself a sketch, and makes to itself a representation of things which are not, as if they were; and in like manner the fancies which occur to waking people resemble the dreams of sleepers. They have come, they have departed; they have appeared, they have disappeared; before they could be scarcely comprehended they have flown away. (127) And let every one who dreams in this way inquire within himself and he will find a proof of these things within, and without any proofs from me he will know the truth of what I say, especially if he happens to be at all an old man. He was at one time an infant, and after that a child, and then a boy, and then a youth, and subsequently a young man, and then a man, and last of all an old man, (128) but he was not all these things at the same time. Did not the infant disappear before the child, and the child before the boy, and the boy before the youth, and the youth before the young man, and the young man before the full-grown man, and the man in the prime of life before the old man? and did not old age disappear in death? (129) Perhaps, also, every one of the different ages of life yields in vigour to the one which comes next to it, and so dies before its time, nature by these means teaching us not to fear the death which comes upon all men, inasmuch as we have found it easy to bear the previous deaths, the death that is of the infant, and that of the child, and that of the boy, and that of the youth, and that of the young man, and that of the full grown man, not one of whom exist any longer when old age has arrived.

XXIII

XXIII. (130) And are not all the other things, relating to the body, dreams? Is not beauty an ephemeral thing, wasting away almost before it comes to its prime? And is not health an unsure thing by reason of the wickednesses which lie in wait to upset it? Again, is not strength a thing easily destroyed by diseases arising from innumerable causes? and is not the accuracy of all our outward senses easily overturned by the entrance of any vicious humour? (131) As to external things, who is there who is ignorant of the uncertainty of them? In one day vast riches have often come absolutely to nothing. Numbers of persons who have been of the highest consideration, and who have enjoyed the highest honours that the earth affords, have come into disrepute from causes which they neglected or despised. The most mighty powers and authority of kings have been overthrown, and have disappeared in a very brief moment of time. (132) There is an example to testify to the truth of my argument in Dionysius, who lived at Corinth, who had been tyrant of Sicily, and who, after he was expelled from his dominions, took refuge in Corinth; and though he had been so mighty a sovereign, became a schoolmaster. (133) There is another witness to the same point in Croesus, the king of Lydia, the wealthiest of all monarchs, who, having conceived the hope of destroying the kingdom of the Persians, not only lost all his men, but was taken prisoner, and was at the point of being burnt alive. (134) And there are witnesses of dreams not only among men, but also among cities, and nations, and countries; Greece is such, and the region of the barbarians, and inhabitants of continents, and islanders, and Europe and Asia, and the west, and the east; for absolutely nothing whatever has ever remained in its original condition; but everything has in every particular been subject to change. (135) Egypt had once the supreme authority over many nations, but now it is a slave. The Macedonians at one time were so flourishing and powerful that they had obtained the supreme dominion over the whole world; but now they pay yearly tribute, which is levied on them by their masters, to the collectors of the revenue. (136) Where is the house of the Ptolemies, and the glory of all the individual successors of Alexander which at one time shone over all the bounds both of earth and sea? Where is the liberty of so many independent nations and cities? On the other hand, where is the slavery of those which were subject to them? Did not the Persians at one time reign over the Parthians? and do not the Parthians now, through the changes of human affairs, and through the extraordinary and total alterations which are continually taking place, rule over the Persians? (137) Some persons flatter themselves with ideas of long and interminable prosperity; but they find that their good fortune is only the beginning of great calamities; and hastening forward as if to an inheritance of good things, they find instead, terrible reverses; and on the contrary it has often happened, that when they have expected evil fortune they have met with good. (138) Athletes, who have prided themselves on their personal good condition, and power, and vigour of body, and who have hoped to obtain an indisputable victory, have often been either refused permission to contend for the prize at all, not having been approved of, or else, after they have descended into the arena, they have been defeated; while others who have despaired of arriving even at the second honours, have been crowned with the garland of victory, and have carried off the first prize. (139) Again, some persons setting sail in the summer (for that is the seas for fair voyages) have been shipwrecked; while others, who have expected to be overwhelmed by reason of being forced to put to sea, have reached their harbour uninjured, without having even incurred any danger. As some merchants hasten forward as if to confessed gain, being ignorant of the losses which are awaiting them; while others who have anticipated losses, have in effect met with great profits"(140) so very uncertain is fortune on either side, whether for good or evil; and human affairs are as it were, weighed in a scale, being lightened or depressed according as the weights in each scale are unequal. And a terrible indistinctness and dense darkness is spread over human affairs. And we wander about as if in a deep sleep, without being able to arrive at anything with perfect accuracy of reasoning, or to seize hold of anything with a firm and retentive grasp; for all things are like shadows and phantoms. (141) And as in processions, what comes first passes by quickly and escapes the sight; and as in torrents, the stream which is hurried by outruns, by its swiftness and rapidity, the comprehension of man, so likewise do the affairs of life, being rapidly borne onwards, and passing by swiftly, appear indeed; to be stationary, but in fact, do not stand still a moment, but are continually being dragged onwards. (142) And men awake too, who, as far as the uncertain character of their comprehensions goes, are in no respect different from people asleep, deceiving themselves, think themselves competent to contemplate the nature of things with reasoning powers which cannot err; in whose case every one of their external senses is a hindrance to knowledge, being hurried by spectacles, and by peculiarities of flavours or odours, to which they incline, and by which they are perverted, and in consequence of which they prevent any part of the soul from being in a sound state, and from advancing without stumbling as if along a level road. And humble pride, and great littleness, and all other similar states which are made up of inequality and anomaly, compel men to walk in a sort of giddiness, and create great dizziness and perplexity.

XXIV

XXIV. (143) Since, then, life is full of all this irregularity, and confusion, and indistinctness, it is necessary that the statesman as well as the philosopher should approach the science of the interpretation of dreams, so as to understand the dreams and visions which appear by day to people who believe themselves to be awake, being guided by probable conjectures and rational probabilities, and in this way he must explain each separate one, and show that such and such a thing is honourable, another disgraceful, that this is good or that is bad; that this thing is just, that thing is on the contrary unjust; and so on in the same way with respect to prudence, and courage, and piety, and holiness, and expediency, and usefulness; and in like manner of the opposite things, with respect to what was not useful nor reasonable, what was ignoble, impious, unholy, inexpedient, pernicious, and selfish. (144) Moreover, he warns you in this way: is this something belonging to another? do not covet it. Is it your own? use it as not using it. Have you great abundance? share it with others; for the beauty of riches is not in the purse, but in the power it gives one to succour those who are in need. Have you but little? do not envy those who have much; no one will pity a poor man who is always envious. Are you in high reputation, and are you held in much honour? be not insolent on that account. Are you lowly in your fortunes? still let not your spirit be depressed. Does everything succeed with you according to your wish? fear a change. Do you often stumble? hope for good fortune hereafter; for the change of human affairs are apt to be in a direction opposite to the course they have formerly taken. (145) The moon and the sun, indeed, and the whole of the heaven have clearness bright and distinct, inasmuch as all things are alike which exist permanently in the heaven; and as they are all measured by the rules of truth itself, in harmonious order and in the most admirable agreement. But as for earthly things, which are full of great disorder and confusion, they are inharmonious and discordant, to speak with perfect correctness, so that dense darkness has overtaken some of them, while others resemble the most brilliant light, or rather they are themselves the clearest and purest of light. (146) If, therefore, any one should wish to look closely into the nature of things, he will find that heaven is everlasting day, free from all participation in night or in any kind of shade, inasmuch as it is surrounded uninterruptedly by a brilliant display of inextinguishable and unadulterated light. (147) And in the same proportion as among us those who are awake are superior to those who are asleep, so also in the universal world the things of heaven are superior to the things of earth; since the one enjoys an everlasting wakefulness which knows no sleep, on account of its energies which never stray, and never stumble, and which proceed rightly and successfully in every thing; while the others are oppressed by sleep, and if they wake up for a short time they are again pulled down and buried in slumber; because they are unable to look steadfastly and correctly at any thing with their souls, but are always straying and stumbling. For they are overshadowed by false opinions, by which they are compelled to submit to dreams, and are always behind the real truth, and are unable to comprehend any thing with a firm and tenacious grasp.

XXV

XXV. (148) Moreover, Joseph is figuratively said to have been mounted upon the second best chariot which the king had, for the following reason. The statesman stands in the second rank next to the king; for he is not a private individual nor a king, but some one on the confines between the two. Being indeed superior to a private individual, and inferior in respect of authority to an absolute and independent king, having the people for his king; on behalf of whom he had determined to do every thing with a pure and perfectly guileless good faith; (149) and he is borne as it were on high in a well-built chariot, being lifted on high both by the things committed to his charge and by the people, and especially so when he contains in his mind every thing, whether small or great, without any one ever opposing or resisting him, but all being cheerfully governed by him under God to their own safety like sailors enjoying a fair voyage. And the ring which the king gives him is the most manifest proof of confidence which the people, his king, places in the statesman, and also of that trust with which the statesman relies on the people which is as powerful as a king. (150) And the golden circlet round his neck appears to indicate figuratively both high reputation and punishment at the same moment. For as long as all the affairs which concern the administration of the state proceed prosperously as far as he is concerned, he is proud, and is looked upon with veneration, and is honoured by the multitudes. But the moment that any unforeseeen mishap occurs to him, not indeed intended, for such error deserves reproach, but arising from pure chance, which always deserves pardon, he is not the less dragged downwards by the ornament around his neck, and is humbled, his master all but saying to him in plain words, "I, indeed, gave you this circlet to be around thy neck, to be both an ornament while my affairs were going on well, and a halter when they were proceeding unfavourably."

XXVI

XXVI. (151) Moreover, I have also heard people discussing this passage with great apparent accuracy in a more figurative manner and according to quite a different interpretation. And their notion of it is this. They say that the king of Egypt means our mind: the governor of the region of the body in every individual in us, and who like a king claims the supreme power. (152) And by him when he has become devoted to the service of the body three objects are especially laboured at as being accounted worthy of exceeding care, namely, meat, and sweetmeats, and drinkables. With reference to which fact he also employs three persons to superintend the objects aforesaid, his chief baker, and his chief butler, and his chief cook. The one of whom presides over those things which relating to eating, the second over those things which belong to drinking, and the last to those sweetenings and sauces which belong to the confections. (153) And they are all eunuchs; because the man who is devoted to pleasure is barren and unproductive of every thing which is most necessary, such as modesty, temperance, continence, justice, and every kind of virtue. For there is no one thing so hostile to another as pleasure is to virtue, for the sake of which most people neglect all those matters which alone it is worth while to attend to, gratifying their unrestrained appetites, and submitting to all the commands which they impose upon them. (154) Therefore, the chief cook is not committed to prison at all, nor does he fall into any misfortune, because his sauces and sweetenings are not among the things which are very necessary, not being pleasures but only provocations to pleasure, such as are easily extinguished. But of the two who are occupied in the employment of the miserable belly, the chief baker and the chief butler, since eating and drinking are of all the thing which are useful to life those which have the greatest power to keep the being together, and those who have the management of those things, if they bestow great care upon them, do very justly obtain praise; while, if they neglect them, they are thought worthy of anger or punishment. (155) But there is a difference in their punishments, because the need of the two things is different; that of food being the most indispensable, but that of wine not being very useful; for men can live without any wine, using only the pure drink of spring water. (156) On which account there is a reconciliation made with, and pardon bestowed upon, the chief butler, as upon one who has erred in the least important particular. But the offences of the chief baker admit of no reconciliation and of no forgiveness, but incur an anger which leads to death, as he has been guilty of wrong in the most necessary matters; for want of food is followed by death. On which account he who has erred on these points very appropriately is put to death by hanging, suffering an evil similar to that which he has inflicted; for he also has hanged, and suffocated, and stretched out the famishing man by means of hunger.

XXVII

XXVII. (157) This is enough to say on this subject. Accordingly Joseph, being appointed the king's lieutenant, and having undertaken the government and superintendence of the whole of Egypt, went forth in order to become acquainted with all the natives, and investigated all the laws that were established in the different cities, and caused a great affection for himself to arise in the breasts of those who saw him, not only because of the services which he conferred upon every one of them, but also by the unspeakable and unrivalled graces of his appearance and by the courtesy with which he associated with them. (158) But when, in accordance with the interpretation of the dreams, the first seven years of fertility arrived, he collected one-fifth of the produce every year by means of his subordinate officers and others who were employed under him in the public offices, and by this means he collected such a vast quantity of sheaves of corn as no one recollected has having ever existed at any previous time. And the most evident proof of this is that they could not possibly be counted, even although thousands and thousands of persons were occupied in the task, whose sole business it was to devote all their energies to count them. (159) And when these seven years had passed, during which the plain of Egypt was fertile, the famine began, which, as it proceeded and increased, was not confined to Egypt; for as it became diffused, and from time to time extended, so as to be always comprehending fresh cities and countries in succession, it reached to the farthest borders of the land, both in the eastern and western direction, so as to reach at last over the whole world all around. (160) Accordingly, it is said that no general pestilence ever extended so widely, not even that which the sons of the physicians call "the creeping pestilence;" for that also attacks all parts at once, and proceeding onwards rapidly like fire, utterly and completely devours the whole mass of the ulcerated body. (161) Accordingly, they selected the men of the highest reputation in every district, and sent them into Egypt to procure corn; for already the prudence of the young man was celebrated in all quarters, who had thus provided abundant food against a time of necessity. (162) And he at first commanded all the treasure-houses to be opened, calculating that he should make the people more cheerful when they had beheld the store that was provided, and that in some degree he should be feeding their souls rather than their bodies on good hopes. After that, by means of those to whom the office of regulating the distribution of corn was committed, he sold it to all who wished to buy, keeping a constant eye on the future, and seeing that what was impending even more clearly than the present.

XXVIII

XXVIII. (163) And at this crisis, his father also, [1163] since his necessary food had by this time become scarce, not being aware of the good fortune of his son, sent ten of his sons to buy food, keeping the youngest at home, who was the uterine and own brother of the king's lieutenant. (164) And they, when they had arrived in Egypt, met their brother as if he were a stranger, and being amazed at the dignity with which they beheld him surrounded, they addressed him with prostration according to the ancient fashion, the dreams now receiving confirmation and fulfilment. (165) And he, when he beheld those who had sold him, immediately recognised them all, though he was not in the least recognised by any one of them himself, since God was not yet willing to reveal the truth on account of some necessary causes which at that time it was better should be buried in silence; and therefore he either altered the countenance of their brother who governed the country, so as to give him a more dignified appearance, or else he perverted the accurate judgment of the mind of those who beheld him. (166) But he acted not like a young man who, being the lieutenant and magistrate invested with such extensive powers, and having attained to the authority next to that of the king himself, to whom the east and west looked up, and elated with the pride of manhood and the vastness of his authority, might now that the opportunity of revenge had presented itself, have shown his remembrance of the ill-treatment which he had received; but he bore what happened with self-restraint, and governed his own soul, and with great prudence feigned a perfect ignorance of and strangeness to them, and both by his looks, and by his voice, and by all the rest of his behaviour he pretended to be displeased at them. He said to them, "My men, you say nothing peaceful; but some one of the king's enemies has sent you forth as spies, and you, performing a base service for him, have expected to escape detection. But nothing that is done treacherously does escape detection, even if it be enveloped in profound darkness." (167) And when they endeavoured to make excuses for themselves, they argued that he was accusing them of what had never taken place, for that they had not come from a hostile people, and that they were not themselves imbued with any unfriendly feelings toward the people of the country, and that they could never have been induced to undertake such an office as that of spies, for that they were by nature men of peace, and that they had learnt, almost from their childhood, from a most holy, and pious, and religious father, to honour stability and tranquillity; and that their father was a man who had had twelve sons, the youngest of whom, as he was not yet of an age to bear a long journey, was remaining at home, while we, whom you see here are ten more, and the remaining is not.

XXIX

XXIX. When he heard this, and heard those who had sold him all speak of him as dead, what think you did Joseph feel in his soul? (168) for even if he did not utter the feelings which then encompassed him, still they unquestionably were burning within his breast, and exciting, and kindling strange emotions within him; nevertheless, with deep wisdom and humanity does he address them, saying, "If, in good truth, you have not come hither to spy the land, then, in order to prove your good faith to me, remain here some short period, and write a letter and send for your youngest brother, and let him come to you; (169) or if, for your father's sake, you are anxious to depart, lest he perchance may be alarmed at your protracted absence, in that case depart all the rest of you, but let one of you remain behind as a hostage, until you return again with your youngest brother; and if you do not obey, then the most terrible death shall be your punishment." (170) He then threatened them in this manner, looking sternly at them, and giving them every sign of violent anger, as far as appearances could go, and so he left them. But they, being full of consciousness and depression, afflicted themselves for their former treachery towards their brother, saying, "That wickedness which we committed is the cause of all our present evils, since justice, which takes the regulation of all human affairs, is now contriving some punishment for us; for having been quiet for a short time it is now awakened, displaying its nature, which is at all times relentless and implacable towards those who are deserving of punishment, and how can we deny that we are deserving of it? (171) We in a merciless manner disregarded our brother when he besought us and supplicated us, though he had done no wrong, but had only, in the fulness of his natural affection, related to us, as to his nearest relations, the visions which had appeared to him in sleep; for which cause we, the most brutal and savage of men, became enraged, and committed (for we must not now deny the truth) most impious actions; (172) therefore let us now expect to suffer these things and even worse, we who, though we are almost the only men in the whole world who are called noble by birth, by reason of the exceeding virtues of our fathers, and grandfathers, and ancestors, have nevertheless disgraced our kindred, hastening to cover ourselves with notorious infamy." (173) But the eldest of the brethren, who also at the very beginning had opposed them when they were originally concocting their treachery, said to them, "Repentance is useless after the thing has been done; I exhorted you, I entreated you, pointing out to you how enormous the impiety you were meditating was, I begged you not to indulge your passion; but though you ought to have assented to me, you yielded to your own inconsiderate folly; (174) therefore, we now are reaping the fruit of your self-will and impiety, and now the treachery which we exercised towards him is required at our hands; and he who requires it is not man, but either God, or reason, or the law of God."

XXX

XXX. (175) The brother whom they had sold heard them conversing in this manner without saying anything himself, as he had hitherto spoken to them by an interpreter. And being overcome by his feelings, he was unable to restrain his tears, and turned away that he might not be seen by them, and pouring forth hot and incessant tears, and so, having relieved himself for a short time, he wiped his eyes and returned to them, and commanded the second in age of the brothers to be bound in the sight of them all, since he, as it were, corresponded to himself, who was the youngest but one; for in a large number the second corresponds to the last but one, as the first does to the last. (176) Perhaps, too, he bound him because the greatest share of the guilt belonged to him, as he was almost the original author of the plot against him, and as it was he who excited the others to the enmity which they displayed against him; for if he had arrayed himself on the side of the eldest when he gave his merciful and humane counsel, being younger than he, but older than all the rest, perhaps, and indeed most probably, the iniquity would have been checked, in consequence of those who had the highest rank and honour agreeing and co-operating together in the matter, which fact would have carried great weight with it; (177) but now, he, departing from the merciful and more excellent side of the question, went over to the unmerciful and cruel one, and putting himself forward as the leader of it, he in this way encouraged those who were inclined to join him in his audacious action, so that they unshrinkingly carried out their nefarious purpose. This is the reason why he appears to me to have been selected from the whole body for the purpose of being bound. (178) But the others now prepared for their return home, since the governor of the country had given charge to the officers to whom the sale of the wheat was entrusted to fill all the bags of his brothers, as though they had been strangers, and privily to replace in the mouths of their sacks the money which they had brought, without mentioning to any one that they had so restored it; and in the third place, to give them also abundant food which might be sufficient, and more than sufficient for them, on the way, in order that the corn which they had bought might be conveyed undiminished to their father. (179) But while they were on their way, and expressing, as was natural, their compassion for their brother who was in prison, and being equally grieved also for their father's sake at this second calamity which he was to hear of, his flourishing family of children being thus diminished and curtailed at every journey, and saying that he would never believe that he was kept in prison, because those who had been once stricken with misfortune are always dreading a repetition of the same calamity, evening overtook them, and having relieved their beasts of their burdens, they lightened them, but received themselves heavier anxiety than ever in their minds; for in times of rest to the body, the mind receives the impression made by unexpected events more readily, so as to be very severely weighed down and oppressed by them.

XXXI

XXXI. (180) For one of them, having opened one of the sacks, saw in the mouth of it his purse full of money; and when he had counted it, he found the whole price which he had paid down for the corn restored to him; and being amazed, he brought it to his brothers; and they, not imagining that it was meant as a favour to them, but rather, suspecting that it was a plot against them, were in great despondency (181) and wishing to examine all their sacks, set off again for fear of being pursued, and made all imaginable speed, almost, as one may say, running without stopping to take breath, and so they completed a journey which should have taken many days, in a short time. (182) Then, one after another embracing their father, with copious tears, they all clung to him, and kissed him; and while he returned their embraces, although his soul speedily began to forebode some new calamity, for while they were thus approaching and saluting him he perceived the absence of the son who was left behind, and in his own mind blamed him for his slowness in being behind the others; for he was looking at them as they came in, being anxious to behold the number of his children complete. (183) But when no one from without came in besides, they, seeing that he was in a state of agitated suspense, said, "O my father! doubt is worse than even the certain knowledge of unexpected calamities; for when one is certainly apprised of such, one may discover a road to safety: but ignorance and doubt are the cause of error and perplexity; listen then, to the sad story which we have to tell, but which still must be told. (184) "The brother whom you sent along with us to buy corn, and who has not returned with us, is alive; for we must release you from the more terrible apprehension that he may be dead; but he is alive, and is remaining in Egypt with the governor of the country, who, whether it be from any false accusation which has been laid against us, or from any suspicion which he has himself conceived, charged us with being spies. (185) And when we said all that the time would allow us to say in our defence, and mentioned you as being our father, and the brothers who were not of our company, one of them being dead, and the other remaining with you, who we said tarried behind at home on account of his age, inasmuch as he was still a child, making known and revealing to him all the circumstances of our family by reason of our absence of all suspicion, we availed nothing; but he said, that the only proof that could be given him of our truth and honesty would be the coming of our youngest brother to see him; for which reason he also detained the second of us, as a pledge and surety for his coming. (186) Therefore his command is most grievous to us. But the occasion is also more imperious than even his command, which we must necessarily submit to from our want of necessaries, since Egypt is the only country which can supply us, who are thus oppressed by famine, with necessary food."

XXXII

XXXII. (187) But he, groaning most bitterly, said, "Whom shall I lament first? the youngest but one, who was not the last, but the first to encounter the series of disasters which has befallen our family? or the second, on whom the second evil has fallen, namely, captivity, which is only inferior in misery to death? or the youngest, who is now to undertake that most detestable journey, since go he must, without being warned by the calamities which have befallen his brethren? and I, torn to pieces as to all my limbs and all my parts (for children are the limbs of their parents), am in danger of becoming utterly childless who was so short a time ago accounted happy in the number and excellence of my children." (188) But the eldest replied, "I gave you my two sons as hostages, the only children that I have, slay them if I bring not back again to you, safe and sound, the brother whom you entrust to my hand, and who, by his visit to Egypt, will effect two things of the greatest importance for us; first, he will give a most evident proof that we are not spies and enemies; and, secondly, he will enable us to recover our brother, whom we have left in captivity." (189) But as his father was much grieved and said that he did not know what to do, because while he had but two sons of one mother, one of them was now dead, and the other was left desolate and almost alone, so that he dreaded the journey, and though alive would die from fear before he could accomplish it, from a recollection of those fearful events which his elder brother had encountered; while he was speaking thus, the brethren put forward as their spokesman him who was the boldest among them, and by nature inclined to take the lead, and who was eloquent in speech, and he said what seemed good to them all; (190) for they agreed, as their necessary food was falling short, for the corn which they had previously bought was now exhausted, and as the famine was again pressing upon and overwhelming them, to go for more in one united body, but not to go at all if the youngest still remained behind; because the governor of the country had forbidden them to appear before him without him. (191) And their father, calculating like a wise man that it was better to expose one son to the uncertain and doubtful danger of the future, than to encounter the certain loss of so large a family, which the whole house must endure if they continued to be overwhelmed by the present scarcity, that most incurable of diseases, says to them, (192) "But if the necessity which presses upon us is more powerful than my wishes, we must yield: for perhaps, perhaps I say, nature may be devising something better which she does not choose as yet to reveal to our minds. (193) Depart, therefore, taking with you your youngest brother as you have determined; but do not go in the same manner as ye went before. For formerly you had only need of money to buy corn, since no one knew you, and since you had not at that time suffered any intolerable calamity. But now you require presents also; for three reasons. First of all, to propitiate the governor and dispenser of corn, to whom you say that you are known. Secondly, in order that so you may the more speedily recover him who is held in captivity, by thus paying down a large ransom for him. And thirdly, for the sake of as far as possible removing any idea of your being spies. (194) Therefore, taking presents of all that our land supplies, offer them to the man as a kind of first fruits, and take double money, both that which you paid before, for perhaps it was restored to you through the oversight of some one, and also another sum sufficient to buy corn; (195) and take with you also my prayer, which we offer to God our Saviour, that you who are strangers may go acceptably to the natives of the country, and that you may return in safety, giving back to your father those necessary pledges, his children, and bringing back the brother whom you have left in bondage, and also the youngest, as yet unacquainted with trouble, whom you are now taking with you." And so they took their departure and hastened towards Egypt.

XXXIII

XXXIII. (196) Then a few days afterwards they arrived in Egypt, and when the governor of the country saw them he was greatly pleased, and ordered the steward of his house to prepare a sumptuous dinner, and to bring the men in that they might partake of his salt and of his table. (197) And when they were brought in to dinner they were in a state of great suspense, as not knowing what would be done with them, and were in confusion, suspecting that they might perhaps have a false accusation of theft brought against them on the ground of their having taken away the price of the corn that they had bought and which they had found in their sacks, as if they had done so wilfully. So then they came up to the steward of the house, and made a defence on a subject on which no one ventured to accuse them, purging their consciences, and, at the same time, displaying the money which they had brought back and offering to return it. (198) But he cheered them with favourable and humane language, saying, "There is no one so impious as to found a false accusation on the graces of God, who is all-merciful. He it is who has rained treasures into your sacks, giving you not only food but also riches out of his abundant store." (199) So they being comforted, then arranged in order the presents which they had brought from home to display them to the governor. And when the master of the house came in they offered them to him. (200) And when he had inquired of them how they were, and whether their father, of whom they had previously spoken, was still alive, they answered nothing concerning themselves, but concerning their father they replied that he was alive and well. And when he had prayed for him, and addressed them in the most favourable and God-fearing manner, looking upon his brother by the same mother, when he saw him he could not restrain his tears, but being now overcome by his feelings, he turned himself about before he made himself known to them, and going out on a pretext as if some urgent cause compelled him (for it was not a favourable opportunity for him to tell them the truth), he wept in a secret chamber of his house and poured forth abundance of tears.

XXXIV

XXXIV. (201) Then when he had washed his hands he restrained his sorrow by the power of reason, and coming back again he feasted the strangers, returning to them the brother who had come with them before, and who had been kept as a hostage for the appearance of the youngest. And with them there also feasted others of the nobles of the Egyptians. (202) And the manner of their entertainment was to each party in accordance with their national customs, since Joseph thought it wrong to overturn ancient laws, and especially at a banquet where the pleasures should be more numerous than the annoyances. (203) And as he commanded them all to sit down in order according to their age, as the men had not yet learnt the fashion of lying down on occasions of banqueting, they marvelled to see whether the Egyptians would adopt the same habits as the Hebrews, having a regard to regular order, and knowing how to distinguish between the honours due to the eldest and the youngest. (204) Perhaps, too, they thought this man who manages all the common business of the house, because the country has hitherto been less refined in matters relating to eating, has now not only introduced regularity and good order into great matters, by which the affairs of peace and war are accustomed to be brought to a successful issue, but also into those things which are usually accounted of less importance, most of which, indeed, refer mainly to amusement. For the object of banquets is cheerfulness, and they do not at all allow the guests to be too solemn and austere-looking. (205) While they were praising the arrangements of the feast in this quiet way, tables are brought indeed, of no great costliness or luxury, as, by reason of the famine, their host did not think it proper to revel too much amid the distresses of others; and they, like men of sense and understanding, praised this part of his conduct also, because he had thus avoided an unseemly magnificence, which is a thing calculated to provoke envy, saying that he was maintaining the character at the same time of one who sympathised with the needy, and also of a liberal entertainer, placing himself between the two, and avoiding all cause for blaming him in either particular. (206) Therefore his preparations for the entertainment escaped all ill-will being suited to the time, and what was wanting was made up by continual cheerfulness, and by pledging one another in wine, and by good wishes, and by exhortations to eat what there was, which to persons of gentlemen-like and accomplished minds was more pleasant than all the sumptuous dishes and liquors which men fond of eating and of epicurism provide for eating and drinking, which are in reality deserving of no serious care, but by which they do in truth display their littlemindedness with great pomp.

XXXV

XXXV. (207) And on the next day he sent, the first thing in the morning, for the steward of his household, and commanded him to fill all the sacks of the men which they had brought with them with corn, and a second time to put back in the mouths of their sacks the price which they had brought with them, and to put in the sack of the youngest the most beautiful of his silver cups out of which he himself was accustomed to drink; (208) and he cheerfully did as he was commanded, taking care that no one was a witness of his actions. And they, not knowing any of the things which had been done thus secretly, departed, rejoicing in all the good fortune which had befallen them beyond all their expectations; (209) for what they had expected was this, to have a false accusation laid against them, as if they had stolen the money which has been restored to them, and never to recover their brother whom they had left as a hostage, and perhaps also, besides that, to lose their youngest brother who would be seized upon by force by the man who had been so determined that he should be brought. (210) But what has happened to them was better than their most sanguine prayers, since, in addition to having no false accusations laid against them, they had also been admitted to the bread and salt of the governor, which among all men is a token of genuine friendship, and had also recovered their brother without having received any injury, without having had recourse to the intercession and entreaty of any mediator, and were also taking back their youngest brother in safety to their father, having escaped all suspicion of being spies, and bearing with them an abundant quantity of food, and having good and well-founded hopes for the future, for they thought that even if necessary food was repeatedly to fail them, they should never again themselves be in exceeding want as before, but might return joyfully to the governor of the country as to a friend and not a stranger.

XXXVI

XXXVI. (211) But while they were feeling disposed in this way, and revolving such thoughts in their souls, a sudden and unexpected confusion came upon them, for the steward of the household, being commanded to do so, ran after them as if to attack them, bringing with him a vast multitude of servants, waving his hands, and making signs to them to stop, (212) and then coming up to them out of breath he said, "You have now set the seal to all the accusations that have been brought against you; you have returned evil for good, and turned back upon the same road of iniquity as before; you have not only stolen and carried off the price of the corn, but you have committed even a greater offence than that, for wickedness which has obtained forgiveness gets more shameless; (213) you, you very grateful and very peaceful men, have stolen the most beautiful and most valuable drinking cup belonging to my master, the very cup in which he pledged you; you who did not even know what was meant by the name of spy, and who brought back double money to restore that which you had previously paid and professed to have found in your sacks,"a trick, as it should seem, and a bait to enable you to catch and snare a more valuable prize; but wickedness does not always prosper, but though always endeavoring to escape notice it is detected." (214) While he was running on in this way against them they stood motionless and speechless, those most grievous of all evils, sorrow and fear, falling upon them thus suddenly, so that they were unable even to open their mouths, for the advent of unexpected evils makes even those who are eloquent actually speechless; (215) but at length they recovered themselves, and lest they should seem to be silent, because they were selfconvicted by their own consciences, they spoke and said, "How shall we reply and defend ourselves, and to whom? for you who are our accuser are going to be our judge also; you, who even if others had accused us ought to have been our advocate from the experience that you have already had of us. The money which on the former occasion we found replaced in our sacks, we brought back again in order to restore it, though no one had convicted us of having received it again, and do you suppose that after that we became so completely changed as to requite our entertainer with injury and theft? This was not so; and never let it enter your mind that we have done any such thing; (216) but whichever of us brethren is found to have the cup let him die the death; for if any such wicked deed has been done there are many reasons why we should suffer death in atonement of it; in the first place, because covetousness and a desire for the property of others is a most wicked thing; secondly, because to attempt to injure those who have done one good is a most impious action; thirdly, because for men who are proud of the nobility of their birth to dare to destroy the reputation of their ancestors by scandalous actions of their own is a most shameful disgrace; and since if any one of us has stolen the cup of the governor he is liable to all these reproaches, let him die as one who has performed actions worthy of ten thousand deaths."

XXXVII

XXXVII. (217) And while speaking thus they unloose the burdens from off their beasts and take them down, and encourage the steward with all diligence to search them, and to look for the cup, and he, not being unaware that it was lying in the sack of the youngest, inasmuch as he himself had secretly placed it there, behaved cunningly, and began with the eldest, and so went on in regular order, taking them according to their ages, and searching, while each willingly brought forward his sack and displayed its contents, till he came to the last, in whose possession the sought-for cup was found, so that they all when they saw it lifted up their voices, and lamented, and rent their clothes, groaning heavily, and shedding tears, and before his execution bewailing their brother while he was still alive, and bewailing also their father no less than him, because he had foretold the calamities which would happen to his son, on which account he was unwilling to permit their brother to travel with them when they wished him to do so. (218) And being downcast and confused they returned back by the same road to the city, being quite overwhelmed at what had happened, and looking at what had taken place as a plot, and not suspecting their brother of covetousness. Then when they were brought before the governor of the country they displayed their real affection and brotherly love with genuine feeling, (219) for falling altogether at his knees as if they were all liable to be punished for the theft, a wickedness too great to be mentioned, they all wept over him, and besought him, and gave themselves up to him, and offered to submit to voluntary slavery, and called him their master, speaking of themselves as foreign captives, as slaves, as bought with a price, and omitting no name whatever indicative of the most complete slavery; (220) but he, wishing to try them still more, addressed them in a most angry manner, and with the greatest possible severity, and said to them, "May I never be guilty of such an action as to condemn such a number to captivity for the sin of one, for how can it be right to summon those persons to share in a punishment who have had no share in the commission of the offence? Let him alone be punished, since he alone has committed the crime. (221) I know therefore that by your laws you condemn the man who has been found guilty of theft to be put to death in front of the city; but I, wishing to act in all respects in a gentle and most merciful manner, will mitigate the punishment, and adjudge him to slavery instead of to death."

XXXVIII

XXXVIII. (222) And when they were grieved at his threat, and wholly overwhelmed at the false accusations brought against them, the fourth in age, and he was one of a daring character, combined with modesty, and full of true courage, inasmuch as he had studied freedom of speech without impudence, came forward and said, "I entreat you, O master! not to give way to your passion; nor, because you are placed in the rank next to the king, to be in a hurry to condemn us before you have heard our defence. (223) When on our former journey hither, you inquired of us concerning our brother and our father, we answered you: Our father was an old man, aged, not more because of the power of time, than because of his uninterrupted misfortunes, by which he had been constantly exercised like a wrestler, and has passed his whole life amid labours and calamities hard to be borne. "And our brother is very young, a mere child, loved beyond all measure by his father, since he is the son of his old age, and because also he had but him and one other child by the same mother, and this one alone is left, since the elder died a violent death. (224) And when you commanded us to bring our brother hither, and threatened us that, if he did not come, you would not permit us to come into your sight, we departed in great depression of spirits; and with difficulty, when we had arrived at home, did we declare the commands which we had received from you to our father. (225) And he at first wholly refused, being greatly alarmed for the child; but as necessary food was becoming scarce, and as not one of us dared to come hither to buy food without our youngest brother, by reason of your vehement commands; he was at last, with difficulty, persuaded to send him with us, blaming us bitterly for having confessed that we had another brother, and pitying himself very much for being about to be separated from him; for he is but a child and wholly ignorant of business, and not only of business in a foreign land, but even of such as is transacted in his own city. (226) "How, then, shall we approach our father who is under the influence of such feelings? And with what eyes shall we be able to behold him without this his youngest son? He will die most miserably if he only hears that his son has not returned; and then all those who delight in hatred and in evil-speaking, and who rejoice in such misfortunes of their neighbours, will call us murderers and parricides, (227) and the greater part of the accusation will fall upon me; for I promised my father to give him up many things, confessing that I received my brother as a pledge, which I was to restore whenever he was re-claimed from me. And how shall I be able to restore him unless you are prevailed upon to show us mercy? I entreat you, then, to have pity on the old man, and to give a thought to the evils by which he will be grieved, if he does not receive back again him whom he has unwisely entrusted to my hands. (228) "Nevertheless, do you exact punishment for the injuries which you imagine to have been done to you; and that punishment I will volunteer to submit to. Set me down as your slave from this day forth. I will cheerfully undergo the fate of those who have been just bought, if you will only be willing to let the child go free; (229) and not only shall you, if you will give him his liberty, receive thanks from him and me, but also from him who is not present, but who will then be relieved from his anxiety, the father of these men here, and of all the family; for we are all your suppliants, having fled for succour to your right hand, and may we never fail to obtain it. (230) "Let, then, compassion for the age of the old man seize your heart, who during his whole life has constantly devoted himself to the labours of virtue. He has brought all the cities of Syria to receive him, and to submit to his authority, and to do him honour; even though he guides himself by foreign customs and laws very different from them, and although he is in all respects very unlike the natives of the land. But the excellence of his life, and the consistency and uniformity of his actions with his words, and of his words with his actions, have prevailed, so that he has been able to win over those who, out of regard for their national customs, were not at first well-disposed towards him. (231) You will do him such a favour that it will not be possible for him to receive a greater. For what can be a more valuable gift to a father, than to allow him to receive back a son of whose safety he has despaired?"

XXXIX

XXXIX. (232) But all this conduct was but an experiment, just as the former circumstances had been too, because the governor of the country was desirous to see what kind of good-will they had towards him who was his brother by the same mother. For he had been afraid that they felt some kind of natural dislike towards him, as children of a stepmother often do to the family of a previous wife of their father, who may have been held in equal honours by him. (233) It was with this view that he both reproached them as spies and inquired about their family, for the sake of knowing whether his brother was still alive, or whether he had been put out of the way by treachery. And he retained one while he allowed the rest to depart, after they had agreed to bring back their youngest brother with them, whom he desired to see above all things, and so to be relieved of his bitter and grievous sorrow on his account. (234) And when he arrived, and when he beheld his brother, he was then in a slight degree relieved from his anxiety, and he invited them to an entertainment, and while he was feasting them he regaled his own brother by the same mother with more costly viands and luxuries than the rest, looking carefully at every one of them, and judging from their countenances whether there was any envy secretly cherished in their hearts. (235) And when he saw them all cheerful, and all eager, and earnest for the honour of the youngest, conjecturing now by two strong proofs that there was no hatred smouldering beneath, he devised a third mode of trial likewise, bringing a charge against their youngest brother, that he appeared to have committed a theft; for this was likely to be the clearest possible proof of the disposition of each of them and of the affection which they bore to their brother, who was thus falsely accused. (236) From all which circumstances he now clearly saw that his mother's offspring was not looked upon with hostile feelings and was not plotted against, and he also received a very probable impression respecting the events which had befallen himself, and learnt to think that he had suffered what he had, not so much because of the treachery of his brethren, as though the direction of the providence of God who sees things afar off, and who beholds the future no less than the present.

XL

XL. (237) After this he had recourse to a reconciliation and agreement with his brethren, being influenced by his own affectionate disposition, and from his desire to cause no shame to his brethren, and to give no cause of reproach against them because of their conduct towards him, he did not choose that any of the Egyptians should be present on the occasion of his first making himself known to them. (238) But he ordered all the servants to leave the apartment, and suddenly pouring forth a stream of tears, and signing to them with his right hand to approach nearer to him, that no one else might be able by chance even to hear any thing that passed, he said unto them, "I, being about to reveal a matter which had long been kept in the shade, and which has appeared to be hidden by the long lapse of time, do now by myself disclose it to you by yourselves. I myself am that brother whom you sold to go into Egypt, I whom you now behold standing here." (239) And when they were all amazed at seeing him beyond all their expectation, and were greatly agitated, and, as if under the influence of some violent attraction, cast their eyes down to the ground, and stood motionless, mute, and speechless, he said, "Be not cast down; I give you complete forgiveness for all the things which you have done to me. Do not think that you want any one else as a mediator. (240) I, of my own absolute power and of my own voluntary inclination, come of my own accord to an agreement with you; being guided by two especial signs, first, by my piety towards my father, to whom I owe a great deal of gratitude, and also, secondly, by my own natural humanity, which I feel towards all men, and especially towards those of my own blood. (241) "And I think that it was not you, but God, who was the author of the events which happened to me, because he desired that I should be the servant and minister of his grace and gifts which he thought fit to bestow on the human race in the time of their greatest necessity. (242) And in the very outset you may receive a proof of what I say in the things which you see. I am the governor of all the land of Egypt, and the honours which I enjoy are next to those of the king himself, and the aged monarch honours me, though I am only a young man, as if I were his father; and I am honoured and obeyed not only by the people of the country but also by numerous other nations, whether they are subject to Egypt or independent; for they all have need of me, the governor of the land, by reason of their present scarcity. (243) For silver and gold, and what is still more necessary than either of these things, namely, food, is all stored up in my treasure-houses alone, and it is I who distribute and dispense what they want for their unavoidable necessities to each individual, so that nothing is wanting either for food or for the satisfying of their natural wants. (244) "And I have not detailed all this to you from a wish to exalt myself or to give myself airs, but that you may know that it is no one of you or any man whatsoever that has been the cause of my being first a slave and afterwards a prisoner. For on one occasion a false accusation was brought against me, and I was thrown into prison. But he who changed that extremity of calamity and misfortune into the highest and most complete good fortune was God, with whom all things are possible. (245) 'since these then, are my opinions, do not fear any longer, but discard all your sorrow and anxiety, and change to a joyful cheerfulness; and it will be well for you to hasten to your father, and to be the first to take him the good news of my being found, for reports are quick in penetrating everywhere."

XLI

XLI. (246) So they one after another began to pour forth praises of him without ceasing, and panegyrized him with unmodified encomium, each relating some different circumstance to his credit, one extolling his forgiving spirit, another his affection towards his family, and another his acuteness; and the whole company of them extolled his piety, and attributed to God the happy end to which everything had been brought, and being no longer melancholy or out of humour at the unexpected events which befell them, on their first arrival or at their original difficulties; (247) they also praised his excessive patience and fortitude, combined with modesty, when he, who had experienced such vicissitudes of fortune, neither when he was a slave, allowed himself to say a single word to the injury of his brothers, as having sold him, nor, when he was led away to prison, did he in his despondency say a single word that he should not have said, nor, though he remained there a long time, as prisoners usually do, did he, as is so much the custom, compare his misfortunes with those of his fellow prisoners so as to reveal anything, (248) but kept silence as if he had no knowledge of the cause of the events that had happened to him. Nor again, when he was interpreting the dreams either to the eunuch or to the king, which was a favourable occasion for relating his own story, did he ever say a word about his own nobility of birth, nor yet when he was appointed lieutenant of the king, and received the superintendence and government of the whole of Egypt, even with the view of not being thought an ignoble and obscure person, but one who was really descended of noble ancestors, not a slave by nature, but one who had been exposed to intolerable treachery, and calamities at the hands of persons from whom he was least entitled to expect it. (249) Moreover in addition to all this, great praise was bestowed on his affability and courtesy; for being acquainted with the insolence and rudeness of other governors, they marvelled at the absence of pretence and display which they saw in him, and they admired his kindness too, who, though the moment that he beheld them after their first journey he might have put them to death, or on the last occasion either, merely by refusing to supply them with food when oppressed with hunger, was not content with not punishing them, but even gave them necessary food gratuitously as though they had been persons worthy of favour, ordering the price they had paid to be restored to them: (250) and all the circumstances of their treachery towards him, and of their selling him, were so wholly concealed from, and unknown to any one, that the magistrates of the Egyptians sympathised with him in his joy, as if this was the first occasion of the brothers of the governor having arrived; moreover they invited them to hospitality, and made haste to relate their arrival to the king, and everything everywhere was full of joy, no less than would have been the case if the plain had suddenly become fertile, and the famine had changed into abundance.

XLII

XLII. (251) But the king, when he heard that Joseph had a father and a numerous family, advised him to press his father to remove into Egypt with all his house, promising to give them the most fertile district in Egypt on their arrival. Therefore Joseph gave his brothers chariots, and waggons, and a great multitude of beasts of burden, loaded with all necessary things, and a number of servants, that they might conduct his father into Egypt in safety. (252) But when they arrived at home, and told their father their story about their brother, which was so apparently incredible and beyond all his hopes, he did not much believe them; for even though those who brought the account were trustworthy, still the greatness and extraordinary character of the circumstances which they reported, did not allow him to believe them easily: (253) but when the old man saw the vast preparation, and the supplies of all necessary things, at such a time, in such abundance, corresponding to the good fortune of his son which they were reporting to him, he praised God that he had made complete that part of his house which seemed to be deficient; (254) but his joy immediately begat fear again in his soul, respecting his departure from his natural laws and customs; for he knew that youth is by nature prone to fall, and that in foreign nations there is great indulgence given to error; and especially in the country of Egypt, a land in a state of utter blindness respecting the true God, in consequence of their making created and mortal things into gods. Moreover, the addition of riches and glory is a snare to weak minds, and he also recollected that he had been left to himself, as no one had gone forth out of his father's house with him to keep him in the right way, but he had been left solitary and destitute of all good instructions, and might therefore be supposed to be ready to change and adopt their foreign customs. (255) Therefore, when that Being who alone is able to behold the invisible soul, saw him in this frame of mind, he took pity on him and appearing unto him by night while he was lying asleep, said unto him, "Fear nothing about your departure into Egypt; I myself will guide you on your way, and will give you a safe and pleasant journey; and I will restore you your long lamented son, who was once many years ago believed by you to have died, but who is not only alive, but is even governor of all that mighty country." So Jacob, being filled with good hopes, rose up in the morning with joy, and hastened on his way; (256) and when his son heard that he was near, for scouts and watchers who were placed along the road gave him notice of everything, he went with speed to meet his father when he was at no great distance from the borders of the land; and they met one another near the city, which is called the city of heroes, and they fell into one another's arms placing their heads on each other's necks, and soaking their garments with tears, and satisfying themselves abundantly with long enduring embraces, and unwillingly at last loosing one another, they proceeded to the palace. (257) And when the king beheld them he was amazed at the dignity of Jacob's appearance, and he received and saluted him not as the father of his lieutenant but as his own, with all possible respect and honour; and after showing him not only all the ordinary but also many extraordinary marks of respect, he gave him a most excellent district of land of the greatest fertility; and hearing that his sons were skilful breeders of cattle, having great substance in flocks and herds, he appointed them overseers of all his own flocks and herds, and committed to their charge his goats, and his oxen, and his sheep, and all his innumerable animals of every kind.

XLIII

XLIII. (258) And the young man, Joseph, displayed such excessive good faith and honesty in all his dealings, that though the time and the circumstances of the time gave him innumerable opportunities of making money, so that he might, in a short period, have become the richest man of that age or kingdom, he still so truly honoured genuine riches before illegitimate wealth, and the treasure which sees rather than that which is blind, that he stored up all the silver and gold which he collected as the price of the corn in the king's treasury, not appropriating a single drachm of it to his own use, but being satisfied with nothing beyond the gifts which the king bestowed on him voluntarily, in acknowledgment of his services. (259) And in this manner he governed Egypt, and other countries also with it, and other nations, while oppressed with the famine, in a manner too admirable for any description to do it justice, distributing food to all in a proper manner, and looking, not only at the present advantage, but also at what would be of future benefit: (260) therefore, when the seventh year of the scarcity arrived, he sent for the farmers (for there was now a prospect of fertility and abundance), and gave them barley and wheat for seed, taking care that no one should appropriate what he gave for other purposes, but should sow what he received in the fields, to which end he selected men of honesty and virtue as overseers and superintendents, who were to take care that the sowing was properly performed. (261) And when a long time after the famine his father died, his brothers were filled with secret misgivings, and feared lest now he should remember the evil that they had done to him, and should retaliate upon them and afflict them, and so they came to him and besought him earnestly, bringing with them their wives and children. (262) And he wept and said, "The occasion indeed is a natural one, to fill with secret apprehension those who have done intolerable things, and who are convicted more by their own consciences than by anything else; for the death of our father has revived in you the ancient fear which you entertained before our reconciliation, that I had merely bestowed pardon on you for the sake of not grieving our father; but I do not change my disposition with the changes of time, nor, after I have agreed to a reconciliation and forgiveness, will I ever do anything inconsistent with such agreement; (263) for I have not been postponing revenge and watching for opportunities to wreak it, but I once for all gave you immunity from all punishment, being influenced partly by feelings of respect for my father, for I must speak in plain truth, and partly by natural necessary affection for you. (264) "But if I did every thing that was merciful and humane for my father's sake while he was alive, I will also adhere to it now that he is dead. But in my real opinion no good man ever dies, but such will live for ever and ever, without growing old, in an immortal nature which is no longer bound up in the necessities of the body. (265) And why should I remember only that father who was created and born? We have also the uncreated, immortal, everlasting God for our father, who sees all things and hears all people, even when silent, and who always sees even those things which lie hidden in the recesses of the mind, and whom I look upon and invoke as a witness of my sincere reconciliation; (266) for "I am (and do not you be astonished at my words), I am in the place of God," [1164] who has changed your evil designs against me so as to bring forth from them an abundance of good things. Be ye therefore fearless, and know that for the future you shall enjoy still better fortune than hitherto you have while our father was still alive."

XLIV

XLIV. (267) Having encouraged his brethren with these words he confirmed his promises still more by actions, leaving out nothing which could show his care for his brethren. And after the famine, when the inhabitants were now full of joy at the fertility and prosperity of the country he was honoured by all men, who thus recompensed him for the benefits which they had received from him in the season of their despair. (268) And the report of him became noised abroad, and filled all the cities with his glory and reputation. And he lived a hundred and ten years, and then died at a good old age, having enjoyed the greatest perfection of beauty, and wisdom, and eloquence of speech. (269) The beauty of his person is testified to by the violent love with which he inflamed the wife of the eunuch; his wisdom by the evenness of his conduct in the indescribable variety of circumstances that attended the whole of his life, by which he wrought regularity among things that were irregular, and harmony among things that were discordant. His eloquence of speech is displayed in his interpretation of the dreams, in his affability in ordinary conversation, and by the persuasion which followed his words; in consequence of which his subjects all obeyed him cheerfully and voluntarily, rather than from any compulsion. (270) Of these hundred and ten years he spent seventeen, till the expiration of his boyhood, in his father's house; and thirteen he passed amid unforeseen events, being plotted against, and sold, and becoming a slave, and having false accusations brought against him, and being thrown into prison; and the remaining eighty years he spent in authority and in all manner of prosperity, being the most excellent manager and administrator both of scarcity and plenty, and the most competent of all men to manage affairs under either complexion of circumstances.

Footnotes:

1161. Yonge's title, A Treatise of the Life of a Man Occupied with Affairs of State, or On Joseph.
1162. Gen 37:7.
1163. Gen 42:1.
1164. Gen 50:19.

ON THE LIFE OF MOSES, I

I

I. (1) I have conceived the idea of writing the life of Moses, who, according to the account of some persons, was the lawgiver of the Jews, but according to others only an interpreter of the sacred laws, the greatest and most perfect man that ever lived, having a desire to make his character fully known to those who ought not to remain in ignorance respecting him, (2) for the glory of the laws which he left behind him has reached over the whole world, and has penetrated to the very furthest limits of the universe; and those who do really and truly understand him are not many, perhaps partly out of envy, or else from the disposition so common to many persons of resisting the commands which are delivered by lawgivers in different states, since the historians who have flourished among the Greeks have not chosen to think him worthy of mention, (3) the greater part of whom have both in their poems and also in their prose writings, disparaged or defaced the powers which they have received through education, composing comedies and works full of Sybaritish profligacy and licentiousness to their everlasting shame, while they ought rather to have employed their natural endowments and abilities in preserving a record of virtuous men and praiseworthy lives, so that honourable actions, whether ancient or modern, might not be buried in silence, and thus have all recollection of them lost, while they might shine gloriously if duly celebrated; and that they might not themselves have seemed to pass by more appropriate subjects, and to prefer such as were unworthy of being mentioned at all, while they were eager to give a specious appearance to infamous actions, so as to secure notoriety for disgraceful deeds. (4) But I disregard the envious disposition of these men, and shall proceed to narrate the events which befell him, having learnt them both from those sacred scriptures which he has left as marvellous memorials of his wisdom, and having also heard many things from the elders of my nation, for I have continually connected together what I have heard with what I have read, and in this way I look upon it that I am acquainted with the history of his life more accurately than other people.

II

II. (5) And I will begin first with that with which it is necessary to begin. Moses was by birth a Hebrew, but he was born, and brought up, and educated in Egypt, his ancestors having migrated into Egypt with all their families on account of the long famine which oppressed Babylon and all the adjacent countries; for they were in search of food, and Egypt was a champaign country blessed with a rich soil, and very productive of every thing which the nature of man requires, and especially of corn and wheat, (6) for the river of that country at the height of summer, when they say that all other rivers which are derived from winter torrents and from springs in the ground are smaller, rises and increases, and overflows so as to irrigate all the lands, and make them one vast lake. And so the land, without having any need of rain, supplies every year an unlimited abundance of every kind of good food, unless sometimes the anger of God interrupts this abundance by reason of the excessive impiety of the inhabitants. (7) And his father and mother were among the most excellent persons of their time, and though they were of the same time, still they were induced to unite themselves together more from an unanimity of feeling than because they were related in blood; and Moses is the seventh generation in succession from the original settler in the country who was the founder of the whole race of the Jews.

III

III. (8) And he was thought worthy of being bred up in the royal palace, the cause of which circumstance was as follows. The king of the country, inasmuch as the nation of the Hebrews kept continually increasing in numbers, fearing lest gradually the settlers should become more numerous than the original inhabitants, and being more powerful should set upon them and subdue them by force, and make themselves their masters, conceived the idea of destroying their strength by impious devices, and ordered that of all the children that were born the females only should be brought up (since a woman, by reason of the weakness of her nature, is disinclined to and unfitted for war), and that all the male children should be destroyed, that the population of their cities might not be increased, since a power which consists of a number of men is a fortress difficult to take and difficult to Destroy. [1166] (9) Accordingly as the child Moses, as soon as he was born, displayed a more beautiful and noble form than usual, his parents resolved, as far as was in their power, to disregard the proclamations of the tyrant. Accordingly they say that for three months continuously they kept him at home, feeding him on milk, without its coming to the knowledge of the multitude; (10) but when, as is commonly the case in monarchies, some persons discovered what was kept secret and in darkness, of those persons who are always eager to bring any new report to the king, his parents being afraid lest while seeking to secure the safety of one individual, they who were many might become involved in his destruction, with many tears exposed their child on the banks of the river, and departed groaning and lamenting, pitying themselves for the necessity which had fallen upon them, and calling themselves the slayers and murderers of their child, and commiserating the infant too for his destruction, which they had hoped to avert. (11) Then, as was natural for people involved in a miserable misfortune, they accused themselves as having brought a heavier affliction on themselves than they need have done. "For why," said they, "did we not expose him at the first moment of his birth?" For people in general do not look upon one who has not lived long enough to partake of salutary food as a human being at all. "But we, in our superfluous affection, have nourished him these three entire months, causing ourselves by such conduct more abundant grief, and inflicting upon him a heavier punishment, in order that he, having at last attained to a great capacity for feeling pleasures and pains, should at last perish in the perception of the most grievous evils."

IV

IV. (12) And so they departed in ignorance of the future, being wholly overwhelmed with sad misery; but the sister of the infant who was thus exposed, being still a maiden, out of the vehemence of her fraternal affection, stood a little way off watching to see what would happen, and all the events which concerned him appear to me to have taken place in accordance with the providence of God, who watched over the infant. (13) Now the king of the country had an only daughter, whom he tenderly loved, and they say that she, although she had been married a long time, had never had any children, and therefore, as was natural, was very desirous of children, and especially of male offspring, which should succeed to the noble inheritance of her father's prosperity and imperial authority, which was otherwise in danger of being lost, since the king had no other grandsons. (14) And as she was always desponding and lamenting, so especially on that particular day was she overcome by the weight of her anxiety, that, though it was her ordinary custom to stay in doors and never to pass over the threshold of her house, yet now she went forth with her handmaidens down to the river, where the infant was lying. And there, as she was about to indulge in a bath and purification in the thickest part of the marsh, she beheld the child, and commanded her handmaidens to bring him to her. (15) Then, after she had surveyed him from head to foot, and admired his elegant form and healthy vigorous appearance, and saw that he was crying, she had compassion on him, her soul being already moved within her by maternal feelings of affection as if he had been her own child. And when she knew that the infant belonged to one of the Hebrews who was afraid because of the commandment of the king, she herself conceived the idea of rearing him up, and took counsel with herself on the subject, thinking that it was not safe to bring him at once into the palace; (16) and while she was still hesitating, the sister of the infant, who was still looking out, conjecturing her hesitation from what she beheld, ran up and asked her whether she would like that the child should be brought up at the breast by some one of the Hebrew women who had been lately delivered; (17) and as she said that she wished that she would do so, the maiden went and fetched her own mother and that of the infant, as if she had been a stranger, who with great readiness and willingness cheerfully promised to take the child and bring him up, pretending to be tempted by the reward to be paid, the providence of God thus making the original bringing up of the child to accord with the genuine course of nature. Then she gave him a name, calling him Moses with great propriety, because she had received him out of the water, for the Egyptians call water "mos."

V

V. (18) But when the child began to grow and increase, he was weaned, not in accordance with the time of his age, but earlier than usual; and then his mother, who was also his nurse, came to bring him back to the princess who had given him to her, inasmuch as he no longer required to be fed on milk, and as he was now a fine and noble child to look upon. (19) And when the king's daughter saw that he was more perfect than could have been expected at his age, and when from his appearance she conceived greater good will than ever towards him, she adopted him as her son, having first put in practice all sorts of contrivances to increase the apparent bulk of her belly, so that he might be looked upon as her own genuine child, and not as a supposititious one; but God easily brings to pass whatever he is inclined to effect, however difficult it may be to bring to a successful issue. (20) Therefore the child being now thought worthy of a royal education and a royal attendance, was not, like a mere child, long delighted with toys and objects of laughter and amusement, even though those who had undertaken the care of him allowed him holidays and times for relaxation, and never behaved in any stern or morose way to him; but he himself exhibited a modest and dignified deportment in all his words and gestures, attending diligently to every lesson of every kind which could tend to the improvement of his mind. (21) And immediately he had all kinds of masters, one after another, some coming of their own accord from the neighbouring countries and the different districts of Egypt, and some being even procured from Greece by the temptation of large presents. But in a short time he surpassed all their knowledge, anticipating all their lessons by the excellent natural endowments of his own genius; so that everything in his case appeared to be a ecollecting rather than a learning, while he himself also, without any teacher, comprehended by his instinctive genius many difficult subjects; (22) for great abilities cut out for themselves many new roads to knowledge. And just as vigorous and healthy bodies which are active and quick in motion in all their parts, release their trainers from much care, giving them little or no trouble and anxiety, and as trees which are of a good sort, and which have a natural good growth, give no trouble to their cultivators, but grow finely and improve of themselves, so in the same manner the well disposed soul, going forward to meet the lessons which are imparted to it, is improved in reality by itself rather than by its teachers, and taking hold of some beginning or principle of knowledge, bounds, as the proverb has it, like a horse over the plain. (23) Accordingly he speedily learnt arithmetic, and geometry, and the whole science of rhythm and harmony and metre, and the whole of music, by means of the use of musical instruments, and by lectures on the different arts, and by explanations of each topic; and lessons on these subjects were given him by Egyptian philosophers, who also taught him the philosophy which is contained in symbols, which they exhibit in those sacred characters of hieroglyphics, as they are called, and also that philosophy which is conversant about that respect which they pay to animals which they invest with the honours due to God. And all the other branches of the encyclical education he learnt from Greeks; and the philosophers from the adjacent countries taught him Assyrian literature and the knowledge of the heavenly bodies so much studied by the Chaldaeans. (24) And this knowledge he derived also from the Egyptians, who study mathematics above all things, and he learnt with great accuracy the state of that art among both the Chaldaeans and Egyptians, making himself acquainted with the points in which they agree with and differ from each other--making himself master of all their disputes without encouraging any disputatious disposition in himself--but seeking the plain truth, since his mind was unable to admit any falsehood, as those are accustomed to do who contend violently for one particular side of a question; and who advocate any doctrine which is set before them, whatever it may be, not inquiring whether it deserves to be supported, but acting in the same manner as those lawyers who defend a cause for pay, and are wholly indifferent to the justice of their cause.

VI

VI. (25) And when he had passed the boundaries of the age of infancy he began to exercise his intellect; not, as some people do, letting his youthful passions roam at large without restraint, although in him they had ten thousand incentives by reason of the abundant means for the gratification of them which royal places supply; but he behaved with temperance and fortitude, as though he had bound them with reins, and thus he restrained their onward impetuosity by force. (26) And he tamed, and appeased, and brought under due command every one of the other passions which are naturally and as far as they are themselves concerned frantic, and violent, and unmanageable. And if any one of them at all excited itself and endeavoured to get free from restraint he administered severe punishment to it, reproving it with severity of language; and, in short, he repressed all the principal impulses and most violent affections of the soul, and kept guard over them as over a restive horse, fearing lest they might break all bounds and get beyond the power of reason which ought to be their guide to restrain them, and so throw everything everywhere into confusion. For these passions are the causes of all good and of all evil; of good when they submit to the authority of dominant reason, and of evil when they break out of bounds and scorn all government and restraint. (27) Very naturally, therefore, those who associated with him and every one who was acquainted with him marvelled at him, being astonished as at a novel spectacle, and inquiring what kind of mind it was that had its abode in his body, and that was set up in it like an image in a shrine; whether it was a human mind or a divine intellect, or something combined of the two; because he had nothing in him resembling the many, but had gone beyond them all and was elevated to a more sublime height. (28) For he never provided his stomach with any luxuries beyond those necessary tributes which nature has appointed to be paid to it, and as to the pleasures of the organs below the stomach he paid no attention to them at all, except as far as the object of having legitimate children was concerned. (29) And being in a most eminent degree a practiser of abstinence and self-denial, and being above all men inclined to ridicule a life of effeminacy and luxury (for he desired to live for his soul alone, and not for his body), he exhibited the doctrines of philosophy in all his daily actions, saying precisely what he thought, and performing such actions only as were consistent with his words, so as to exhibit a perfect harmony between his language and his life, so that as his words were such also was his life, and as his life was such likewise was his language, like people who are playing together in tune on a musical instrument. (30) Therefore men in general, even if the slightest breeze of prosperity does only blow their way for a moment, become puffed up and give themselves great airs, becoming insolent to all those who are in a lower condition than themselves, and calling them dregs of the earth, and annoyances, and sources of trouble, and burdens of the earth, and all sorts of names of that kind, as if they had been thoroughly able to establish the undeviating character of their prosperity on a solid foundation, though, very likely, they will not remain in the same condition even till tomorrow. (31) for there is nothing more inconstant than fortune, which tosses human affairs up and down like dice. Often has a single day thrown down the man who was previously placed on an eminence, and raised the lowly man on high. And while men see these events continually taking place, and though they are well assured of the fact, still they overlook their relations and friends, and transgress the laws according to which they were born and brought up; and they overturn their national hereditary customs to which no just blame whatever is attached, dwelling in a foreign land, and by reason of their cordial reception of the customs among which they are living, no longer remembering a single one of their ancient usages.

VII

VII. (32) But Moses, having now reached the very highest point of human good fortune, and being looked upon as the grandson of this mighty king, and being almost considered in the expectations of all men as the future inheritor of his grandfather's kingdom, and being always addressed as the young prince, still felt a desire for and admiration of the education of his kinsmen and ancestors, considering all the things which were thought good among those who had adopted him as spurious, even though they might, in consequence of the present state of affairs, have a brilliant appearance; and those things which were thought good by his natural parents, even though they might be for a short time somewhat obscure, at all events akin to himself and genuine good things. (33) Accordingly, like an uncorrupt judge both of his real parents and of those who had adopted him, he cherished towards the one a good will and an ardent affection, and he displayed gratitude towards the others in requital of the kindness which he had received at their hands, and he would have displayed the same throughout his whole life if he had not beheld a great and novel iniquity wrought in the country by the king; (34) for, as I have said before, the Jews were strangers in Egypt, the founders of their race having migrated from Babylon and the upper satrapies in the time of the famine, by reason of their want of food, and come and settled in Egypt, and having in a manner taken refuge like suppliants in the country as in a sacred asylum, fleeing for protection to the good faith of the king and the compassion of the inhabitants; (35) for strangers, in my opinion, should be looked upon as refugees, and as the suppliants of those who receive them in their country; and, besides, being suppliants, these men were likewise sojourners in the land, and friends desiring to be admitted to equal honours with the citizens, and neighbours differing but little in their character from original natives. (36) The men, therefore, who had left their homes and come into Egypt, as if they were to dwell in that land as in a second country in perfect security, the king of the country reduced to slavery, and, as if he had taken them prisoners by the laws of war, or had bought them from masters in whose house they had been bred, he oppressed them and treated them as slaves, though they were not only free men, but also strangers, and suppliants, and sojourners, having no respect for nor any awe of God, who presides over the rights of free men, and of strangers, and of suppliants, and of hospitality, and who beholds all such actions as his. (37) Then he laid commands on them beyond their power to fulfil, imposing on them labour after labour; and, when they fainted from weakness, the sword came upon them. He appointed overseers over their works, the most pitiless and inhuman of men, who pardoned and made allowance for no one, and whom they from the circumstances and from their behaviour called persecutors of work. (38) And they wrought with clay, some of them fashioning it into bricks, and others collecting straw from all quarters, for straw is the bond which binds bricks together; while others, again, had the task allotted to them of building up houses, and walls, and gates, and cutting trenches, bearing wood themselves day and night without interruption, having no rest or respite, and not even being allowed time so much as to sleep, but being compelled to perform all the works not only of workmen but also of journeymen, so that in a short time their bodies failed them, their souls having already fainted beneath their afflictions. (39) And so they died, one after another, as if smitten by a pestilential destruction, and then their taskmasters threw their bodies away unburied beyond the borders of the land, not suffering their kinsmen or their friends to sprinkle even a little dust on their corpses, nor to weep over those who had thus miserably perished; but, like impious men as they were, they threatened to extend their despotism over the passions of the soul (that cannot be enslaved, and which are nearly the only things which nature has made completely free), oppressing them with the intolerable weight of a necessity beyond their powers.

VIII

VIII. (40) At all these events Moses was greatly grieved and indignant, not being able either to chastise the unjust oppressors of his people nor to assist those who were oppressed, but he gave them all the assistance that was in his power, by words, recommending their overseers to treat them with moderation, and to relax and abate somewhat of the oppressive nature of their commands, and exhorting the oppressed who were labouring thus to bear their present distresses with a noble spirit and to be men in their minds, and not to let their souls faint as well as their bodies, but to hope for good fortune after their present adversity; (41) for that all things in this world have a tendency to change to the opposite, cloudy weather to fine, violent gales to calm and absence of wind, storms and heavy billows at sea to fair weather and an unruffled surface of the water; and much more are human affairs likely to change, inasmuch as they are more unstable than anything. (42) By using these charms, as it were, like a good physician, he thought he should be able to alleviate their afflictions, although they were most grievous. But whenever their distress abated, then again their taskmasters returned and oppressed them with increased severity, always after the respite adding some new evil which should be even more intolerable than their previous sufferings; (43) for some of their overseers were very savage and furious men, being, as to their cruelty, not at all different from poisonous serpents or carnivorous beasts--wild beasts in human form--being clothed with the form of a human body so as to give an appearance of gentleness in order to deceive and catch their victim, but in reality being harder than iron or adamant. (44) One of these men, then, the most violent of them, when, in addition to yielding nothing of his purpose, he was even exasperated at the exhortations of Moses and rendered more savage by them, beating those who did not labour with energy and unremittingly at the work which was imposed upon them, and insulting them and subjecting them to every kind of ill-treatment, so as even to be the death of many, Moses slew, thinking the deed a pious action; and, indeed, it was a pious action to destroy one who only lived for the destruction of others. (45) When the king heard of this action he was very indignant, thinking it an intolerable thing, not for one man to be dead, or for another to have killed him, whether justly or unjustly, but for his grandson not to agree with him, and not to look upon his friends or his enemies as his own, but to hate persons whom the king loved, and to love persons whom the king looked upon as outcasts, and to pity those whom he regarded with unchangeable and implacable aversion.

IX

IX. (46) But when the Egyptian authorities had once got an opportunity of attacking the young man, having already reason for looking upon him with suspicion (for they well knew that he would hereafter bear them ill-will for their evil practices, and would revenge himself on them when he had an opportunity) they poured in, at all times and from all quarters, thousands and thousands of calumnies into the willing ears of his grandfather, so that they even implanted in his mind an apprehension that Moses was plotting to deprive him of his kingdom, saying to him: "He will strip you of your crown. He has no humble designs or notions. He is continually seeking to busy himself in what does not concern him, and to acquire some additional power. He is eager for the kingdom before his time. He caresses some people; he threatens others; he kills others without a trial; he hates all those who are the best affected towards you. Why do you delay? Why do you not cut short all his designs and machinations? Delay on the part of those against whom they are plotting is of the greatest advantage to those who wish to attack them." (47) As they urged these arguments to the king he retreated to the contiguous country of Arabia, where it was safe to abide, entreating God that he would deliver his countrymen from inextricable calamities, and would worthily chastise their oppressors who omitted no circumstance of insolence and tyranny, and would double his joy by allowing him to behold the accomplishment of both these prayers. And God heard his prayers, looking favourably on his disposition, so devoted to what is good, and so hostile to what is evil, and not long after he pronounced his decision upon the affairs of that land as became a God. (48) But while he was preparing to display the decision which he was about to pronounce, Moses was devoting himself to all the labours of virtue, having a teacher within himself, virtuous reason, by whom he had been trained to the most virtuous pursuits of life, and had learnt to apply himself to the contemplation and practice of virtue and to the continual study of the doctrines of philosophy, which he easily and thoroughly comprehended in his soul, and committed to memory in such a manner as never to forget them; and, moreover, he made all his own actions, which were intrinsically praiseworthy, to harmonise with them, desiring not to seem wise and good, but in truth and reality to be so, because he made the right reason of nature his only aim; which is, in fact, the only first principle and fountain of all the virtues. (49) Any one else, perhaps, fleeing from the implacable fury of the king, and coming now for the first time into a foreign land, when he had not as yet associated with or learnt the customs of the natives, and not knowing with any accuracy the objects in which they delighted or which they regarded with aversion, would have been desirous to enjoy tranquillity and to live in obscurity, escaping the notice of men in general; or else, if he had wished to come forward in public, he would have endeavoured by all means to propitiate the powerful men and those in the highest authority in the country by persevering attentions, as men from whom some advantage or assistance might be expected, if any pursuers should come after him and endeavour to drag him away by force. (50) But this man proceeded by the path which was the exact opposite of that which was the probable one for him to take, following the healthy impulses of his soul, and not allowing any one of them to be impeded in its progress. On which account, at times, with the fervour of youth, he attempted things beyond his existing strength; looking upon justice as an irresistible power, by which he was encouraged so as to go spontaneously to the assistance of the weaker side.

X

X. (51) I will also mention one action which was done by him at that time, even although it may be but a trifling one in appearance, but still it proceeded from a lofty spirit. The Arabs are great breeders of cattle, and they all feed their flocks together, not merely men, but also women, and youths, and maidens with them, and this, too, not merely in the obscurer classes and lower ranks of life, but also among the most eminent persons of the nation. (52) Now there were seven damsels, whose father was the priest, and they all came to a certain fountain leading their flocks, and having loosened their vessels and let them down by thongs they succeeded one another in drawing up the water, so as for them all to have an equal share in the work; and in this way they cheerfully and rapidly filled the troughs which were at hand. (53) And when other shepherds came up they disregarded the weakness of the damsels and endeavoured to drive them away with their flocks, and then brought their own herds to the drink that was prepared, desiring to reap the fruits of the labour of others. (54) But Moses, seeing what was done, for he was at no great distance, hastened and ran up; and, when he had come near to them, he said: "Will not you desist from behaving thus unjustly, thinking this solitary place a fitting field for the exercise of your covetousness? Are you not ashamed to have such cowardly arms and hands? You are long-haired people, female flesh, and not men. The damsels behave like vigorous youths, hesitating about nothing that they ought to do; but you, young men, are now behaving lazily, like girls. (55) Will you not depart? Will you not be off and give place to those who arrived first, to whom the water belongs, and who are entitled to it; when you ought rather to have drawn water for them, that so they might have had it in greater abundance? And are you, on the contrary, endeavouring to take away from them what they themselves have got ready? "But I swear, by the celestial eye of justice, which sees what is done even in the most solitary places, that you shall not take it from them. (56) And at all events, now justice has sent me and appointed me to bring them assistance who never expected such an officer; for I am an ally to these damsels who are thus injured by violence, and I come with a might which you evil-doers and covetous people cannot face, but you shall feel it wounding you in an invisible manner, if you do not change your ways." (57) He said this; and they, being alarmed at his words, since while he was speaking he appeared inspired, and his appearance became changed, so that he looked like a prophet, and fearing lest he might be uttering divine oracles and predictions, they obeyed and became submissive, and brought back the flock of the maidens to the troughs, first of all removing their own cattle.

XI

XI. (58) So the damsels went home exceedingly delighted, and they related all that had happened to them beyond their hopes, so that they wished their father with an earnest desire to see the stranger. At all events he blamed them for their ingratitude, speaking as follows: "What were ye about, that ye let him go, when you ought at once to have brought him hither, and to have entreated him to come if he declined? Or when did you see any inhospitality in me? Or do you expect never again to fall into difficulties? Those who are forgetful of services must needs lack defenders, but nevertheless hasten after him, for as yet the error which you have committed may be repaired; and go with haste and invite him first of all to a hospitable reception, and then endeavour to requite his service, for great thanks are due to him." (59) So they made haste, and went after him, and overtook him at no great distance from the fountain; and when they had delivered their father's message to him, they persuaded him to return home with them. And their father was at once greatly struck by his appearance, and soon afterwards he learnt to admire his wisdom, for great natures are very easily discovered, and do not require a length of time to be appreciated, and so he gave him the most beautiful of his daughters to be his wife, conjecturing by that one action of his how completely good and excellent he was, and testifying that what is good is the only thing which deserves to be loved, and that it does not require any external recommendation, but bears in itself proofs by which it may be known and understood. (60) And after his marriage, Moses took his father-in-law's herds and tended them, being thus instructed in the lessons proper to qualify him for becoming the leader of a people, for the business of a shepherd is a preparation for the office of a king to any one who is destined to preside over that most manageable of all flocks, mankind, just as hunting is a good training-school for men of warlike dispositions; for they who are practising with a view to learning the management of an army, previously study the science of hunting, brute animals being as some raw material exposed to their attacks in order for them to practise the art of commanding on each occasion of war or of peace, (61) for the pursuit of wild beasts is a training-school of strategy to be developed against enemies, and the care and management of tame animals is a royal training for the government of subjects; for which reason kings are called shepherds of their people, not by way of reproach, but as a most especial and pre-eminent honour. (62) And it appears to me, who have examined the matter not with any reference to the opinions of the many, but solely with regard to truth (and he may laugh who pleases), that that man alone can be a perfect king who is well skilled in the art of the shepherd, being thus instructed as to more important matters by experience of the inferior animals; for it is impossible for great things to be brought to perfection before small ones.

XII

XII. (63) Therefore Moses, having become the most skilful herdsman of his time, and the most prudent provider of all the necessary things for his flock, and of all things which tended to their advantage, because he never delayed or hesitated, but exerted a voluntary and spontaneous cheerfulness in all things necessary for the animals under his charge, (64) saw his flocks increase with great joy and guileless good faith, so that he soon incurred the envy of the other herdsmen, who saw nothing in their own flocks resembling the condition of his; but they thought themselves well off if they continued as before, while the flock of Moses would have been thought to be falling off if it had not improved, every day, by reason of the vast augmentations that it was in the habit of receiving in beauty from its high condition and fatness, and in number from the prolific character of the females, and the wholesome way in which it was fed and managed. (65) And when Moses was leading his flock into a situation full of good water and good grass, where there was also a great deal of herbage especially suitable for sheep, he came upon a certain grove in a valley, where he saw a most marvellous sight. There was a bush or briar, a very thorny plant, and very weak and supple. This bush was on a sudden set in a blaze without any one applying any fire to it, and being entirely enveloped from the root to the topmost branch by the abundant flame, as though it had proceeded from some fountain showering fire over it, it nevertheless remained whole without being consumed, like some impassible essence, and not as if it were striking the natural fuel for fire, but rather as if it were taking the fire for its own fuel. (66) And in the middle of the flame there was seen a certain very beautiful form, not resembling any visible thing, a most Godlike image, emitting a light more brilliant than fire, which any one might have imagined to be the image of the living God. But let it be called an angel, because it merely related (dieÂngelleto) the events which were about to happen in a silence more distinct than any voice by reason of the marvellous sight which was thus exhibited. (67) For the burning bush was a symbol of the oppressed people, and the burning fire was a symbol of the oppressors; and the circumstance of the burning bush not being consumed was an emblem of the fact that the people thus oppressed would not be destroyed by those who were attacking them, but that their hostility would be unsuccessful and fruitless to the one party, and the fact of their being plotted against would fail to be injurious to the others. The angel, again, was the emblem of the providence of God, who mitigates circumstances which appear very formidable, so as to produce from them great tranquillity beyond the hopes or expectation of any one.

XIII

XIII. (68) But we must now accurately investigate the comparison here made. The briar, as has been already said, is a most weak and supple plant, yet it is not without thorns, so that it wounds one if one only touches it. Nor was it consumed by fire, which is naturally destructive, but on the contrary it was preserved by it, and in addition to not being consumed, it continued just as it was before, and without undergoing any change whatever itself, acquired additional brilliancy. (69) All these circumstances are an allegory to intimate the suggestions given by the other notions which at that time prevailed, almost crying out in plain words to persons in affliction, "Do not faint; your weakness if your strength, which shall pierce and wound innumerable hosts. You shall be saved rather than destroyed, by those who are desirous to destroy your whole race against their will, so that you shall not be overwhelmed by the evils with which they will afflict you, but when your enemies think most surely that they are destroying you, then you shall most brilliantly shine out in glory." (70) Again, the fire, which is a destructive essence, convicting the men of cruel dispositions, says, Be not elated so as to rely on your own strength; be admonished rather when you see irresistible powers destroyed. The consuming power of flame is itself consumed like firewood, and the wood, which is by its intrinsic nature capable of being burnt, burns other things visibly like fire.

XIV

XIV. (71) God, having shown this prodigious and miraculous sight to Moses, gave him, in this way, a most visible lesson as to the events which are about to be accomplished; and he begins to exhort him, by divine admonitions and predictions, to apply himself to the government of his nation, as one who was to be not only the author of its freedom, but also its leader in its migration from Egypt, which should take place at no distant period; promising to be present with him as his coadjutor in every thing. (72) For says God, "I myself have had compassion for a long time on them while ill-treated and subjected to insolence hard to be borne, while there was no man to lighten their sufferings, nor to pity their calamities; for I have seen them all, each individual privately and the whole nation, with one accord turning to address supplications and prayer to me, and hoping for assistance from me. And I am by nature merciful, and propitious to all sincere suppliants. (73) But go thou to the king of the country, without fearing any thing whatever; for the former king is dead from whom you fled for fear of his plotting against thee. And another king now governs the land, who has no ill-will against thee on account of any thing, and who has taken the elders of the nation into his council; tell him that the whole nation is called forth by me, by my divine oracle, that in accordance with the customs of their ancestors they may depart three days' journey out of the country, and there may sacrifice unto me." (74) But Moses, not being ignorant that even his own countrymen would distrust his word, and also that every one else would do so, said, "If then they ask what is the name of him who sent thee, and if I know not what to reply to them, shall I not seem to be deceiving them?" (75) And God said, "At first say unto them, I am that I am, that when they have learnt that there is a difference between him that is and him that is not, they may be further taught that there is no name whatever that can properly be assigned to me, who am the only being to whom existence belongs. (76) And if, inasmuch as they are weak in their natural abilities, they shall inquire further about my appellation, tell them not only this one fact that I am God, but also that I am the God of those men who have derived their names from virtue, that I am the God of Abraham, and the God of Isaac, and the God of Jacob, one of whom is the rule of that wisdom which is derived from teaching, another of natural wisdom, and the third of that which is derived from practice. And if they are still distrustful they shall be taught by these tokens, and then they shall change their dispositions, seeing such signs as no man has hitherto either seen or heard." (77) Now the tokens were as follows. The rod which Moses held in his hand God ordered him to throw down on the ground; and immediately it received life, and crawled along, and speedily became the most powerful of all the animals which want feet, namely an immense serpent, complete in all its parts. And when Moses retreated from the beast, and out of fear was on the point of taking to flight, he was called back again; and when God laid his commands upon him, and inspired him with courage, he laid hold of it by the tail; (78) and the serpent, though still crawling onwards, stopped at his touch, and being stretched out at its full length again returned to its original elements and because the same rod as before, so that Moses marvelled at both the changes, not knowing which was the most wonderful; as he was unable to decide between them, his soul being overwhelmed with these appearances of equal strangeness. (79) This now was the first sign. The second miraculous token was afforded to him at no great distance of time. God commanded him to put one of his hands in his bosom and hide it there, and a moment afterwards to draw it out again. And when he had done what he was commanded, his hand in a moment appeared whiter than snow. Again, when he had put his hand a second time into his bosom, and had a second time drawn it forth, it returned to its original complexion, and resumed its proper appearance. (80) These two lessons he was taught in solitude, when he was alone with God, like a pupil alone with his master, and having about him the instruments with which these wonders were worked, namely, his hand and his rod, with which indeed he walked along the road. (81) But the third he could not carry about with him, nor could he be instructed as to that beforehand; but it was destined to astonish him not less than the others, deriving the origin of its existence from Egypt. And this was its character. God said, "The water of the river, as much as you can take up in your hand and pour upon the ground shall be dark blood, being both in colour and in power transformed with a complete transformation." (82) And, as was natural, this also appeared credible to Moses, not merely by reason of the truth-telling nature of the speaker but also because of the marvels that had already been shown to him, with respect to his hand and to his rod. (83) But though he believed the words of God, nevertheless he tried to avoid the office to which God was appointing him, urging that he was a man of a weak voice, and slow of speech, and not eloquent, and especially so ever since he had heard God himself speaking. For judging the greatest human eloquence to be mere speechlessness in comparison with the truth, and being also prudent and cautious by nature, he shrunk from the undertaking, thinking such great matters proper for proud and bold men and not for him. And he entreated God to choose some one else who would be able easily to accomplish all the commands which he thus laid upon him. (84) But he approved of his modesty, and said, "Art thou ignorant who it is that giveth to man a mouth, and who has formed his windpipe and his tongue, and all the apparatus of the articulate voice? I am he. Therefore, fear thou nothing. For when I approve, every thing will become articulate and clear, and will change for the better, and improve; so that no one shall hinder thee, but the stream of thy words shall flow forth in a rapid and smooth current as if from a pure fountain. And if there is any need of an interpreter, thou shalt have thy brother, who will be a subordinate mouthpiece for thee, that he may utter to the multitude the words which he receives from thee, while thou utterest to him the words that thou receivest from God."

XV

XV. (85) Having heard these things (for it as not at all safe or free from danger to oppose the commands of God), he departed and proceeded with his wife and children by the road leading to Egypt, on which he met with his brother and persuaded him to accompany him, announcing to him the oracular commands which he had received from God. And his brother's soul was already wrought up to obedience by divine providence, so that he, without hesitation, agreed to his proposal and readily followed him. (86) And when they thus arrived in Egypt with one mind and soul, they first of all collected together the elders of the nation in a secret place, and there they laid the commands of God before them, and told them how God had conceived pity and compassion for them, promised them freedom and a departure from thence to a better country, promising also that he himself would be their guide on their road. (87) And after these events, they take courage now to converse with the king with respect to sending forth their people from his territories that they might sacrifice to God; for they said, "That it was necessary that their national sacrifices should be accomplished in the wilderness, inasmuch as they were not performed in the same manner as the sacred rites of other nations, but according to a system and law removed from the ordinary course, on account of the special peculiarities of their habits." (88) But the monarch, who from his cradle had had his soul filled with all the arrogance of his ancestors, and who had no notion in the world of any God appreciable only by the intellect apart from those objects which are visible to the sight, answered them with insolence, saying, "Who is it whom I am to obey? I know not this new Lord of whom you are speaking. I will not let the nation go to be disobedient and headstrong under pretence of fasts and sacrifices." (89) And then, like a man of cruel and passionate disposition and implacable in his anger, he commanded the overseers of the works to oppress them still more, because they had previously given them some relaxation and leisure, saying that, it was from this relaxation and leisure, that their forming designs of feasting and sacrifice had arisen; for that men who were in great straits did not think of these things, but only those whose life had been spent in much east and luxury. (90) Therefore the Jews had now to endure more terrible afflictions than before, and were indignant at Moses and his brother as deceivers, and accused them, sometimes secretly and sometimes openly, and charged them with impiety in appearing to have spoken falsely against God; and accordingly Moses began to exhibit the marvellous wonders which he had been previously taught, thinking that thus he should be able to bring over those who saw them from their former incredulity to believe all that he said. (91) And this exhibition of prodigies was carefully displayed before the king and magistrates of the Egyptians.

XVI

XVI. Therefore, when all the powerful men of the state were assembled round the king, the brother of Moses taking his rod, and shaking it in a very remarkable and demonstrative manner, threw it on the ground, and it immediately became a serpent. And all those who were standing around saw it, and marvelled and, in alarm and terror, withdrew, and fled. (92) But all the sophists and magicians who were present said, "Why are you thus alarmed? we also are not unpractised in such tricks as these, and we are skilled in an art which can produce similar effects." And then each of them threw down the rod which he held in his hand, and so there was a multitude of serpents which went crawling about that rod which had first been changed. (93) And that serpent, with the excess of his power, raised himself up on high, and dilated his chest, and opened his mouth, and with the violent impulse of an attractive drawing in of his breath, drew them all towards him as if he had surrounded a large cast of fishes in a net cast around them, and then, when he had swallowed them all, he returned to his original nature of a stick. (94) So now the marvellous sight thus exhibited to them wrought a fear in the soul of every one of these wicked and malicious men, so that they no longer fancied that what was done was the trick or artifice of men, devised merely for deceit; but they saw that it was a more divine power which was the cause of these things, to which all things are easy. (95) But when by the evident might of what was done they were compelled to confess this, they still were not the less audacious, clinging to their original inhumanity and impiety as to some inalienable virtue, and not pitying those who were unjustly enslaved, nor doing any such things as they were commanded by the word of God. And though God himself had declared his will to them by demonstrations clearer than any verbal commands, namely, by signs and wonders, still they required a yet more severe impression to be made upon them, and it was necessary for him to rise up against them with still greater power; and accordingly, those foolish men, whom reason and command could not influence, are corrected by a series of afflictions: and ten punishments were inflicted on the land; (96) so that the number of the chastisements might be complete which was inflicted upon those who had completed their sins; and the punishment far transcended all ordinary visitations.

XVII

XVII. For the elements of the universe, earth, water, air, and fire, of which the world was made, were all by the command of God, brought into a state of hostility against them, so that the country of those impious men was destroyed, in order to exhibit the height of the authority which God wielded, who had also fashioned those same elements at the creation of the universe, so as to secure its safety, and who could change them all whenever he pleased, to effect the destruction of impious men. (97) And he divided his punishments, entrusting three, those which proceeded from those elements which are composed of more solid parts, namely, earth and water, from which all the corporeal distinctive realities are perfected, to the brother of Moses. An equal number, those which proceeded from the elements which are the most prolific of life, namely, air and fire, he committed to Moses himself alone. One, the seventh, he entrusted to both in common; the other three, to make up the whole number of ten, he reserved for himself. (98) And first of all he began to bring on the plagues derived from water; for as the Egyptians used to honour the water in an especial degree, thinking that it was the first principle of the creation of the universe, he thought it fitting to summon that first to the affliction and correction of those who thus honoured it. (99) What then happened no long time after the events I have already mentioned? The brother of Moses, by the divine command, smote with his rod upon the river, and immediately, throughout its whole course, from Ethiopia down to the sea, it is changed into blood and simultaneously with its change, all the lakes, and ditches, and fountains, and wells, and spring, and every particle of water in all Egypt, was changed into blood, so that, for want of drink, they digged round about the banks of the river, but the streams that came up were like veins of the body in a hoemorrhage, and spirted up channels of blood like springs, no transparent water being seen anywhere. (100) And all the different kinds of fish died, inasmuch as all the vivifying power of the river was changed to a destructive power, so that everything was everywhere filled with foetid odours, from such vast number of bodies putrifying all together. Moreover, a great number of men perished from thirst, and their bodies lay in heaps in the roads, since their relations had not strength to convey those who had died to the tombs; (101) for this evil lasted seven days, until the Egyptians entreated Moses, and Moses entreated God, to show pity on those who were thus perishing. And God, being merciful in his nature, changed the blood back again to wholesome water, restoring to the river its pristine clear and vivifying streams.

XVIII

XVIII. (102) But again, after a brief respite, the Egyptians returned to the same cruelty and carelessness as before, as if either justice had been utterly banished from among men, or as if those who had endured one punishment were not wont to be chastised a second time; but when they suffered they were taught like young children, not to despise those who corrected them; for the punishment which followed, on the track of the last, was slow indeed to come, while they were also slow, but when they hastened to do wrong, it ran after them and overtook them. (103) For again, the brother of Moses, being ordered to do so, stretched out his hand and held his rod over all the canals, and lakes, and marches; and at the holding forth of his rod, so immense a multitude of frogs came up, that not only the market-place, and all the spots open to the air, were filled with them, but likewise all the stables for cattle, the houses, and all the temples, and every building, public or private, as if nature had designed to send forth one race of aquatic animals into the opposite region of earth, to form a colony there, for the opposite region to water is earth. (104) Inasmuch then as they could not go out of doors, because all the passages were blocked up, and could not remain in-doors, for the frogs had already occupied all the recesses, and had crawled up to the very highest parts of the houses, they were now in the very greatest distress, and in complete despair of safety. (105) Again, therefore, they have recourse to the same means of escape by entreating Moses, and the king now promised to permit the Hebrews to depart, and they propitiated God with prayers. And when God consented, some of the frogs at once returned into the river, and there were also heaps of those which died in the roads, and the people also brought loads of them out of their houses, on account of the intolerable stench which proceeded from them, and the smell from their dead carcases, in such numbers, went up to heaven, especially as frogs, even while alive, cause great annoyance to the outward senses.

XIX

XIX. (106) And when they had a little recovered from this punishment, then, like wrestlers at the games, who have recovered fresh strength after a struggle, that so they may contend again with renewed vigour, they again returned to their original wickedness, forgetting the evils which they had already experienced. (107) And when God had put an end to the punishments which were to proceed out of the water, he brought up others out of the land, still employing the same minister of punishment; and he now, in obedience to the command which he received, smote the ground with his rod, and an abundance of lice was poured out everywhere, and it extended like a cloud, and covered the whole of Egypt. (108) And that little animal, even though it is very small, is exceedingly annoying; for not only does it spoil the appearance, creating unseemly and injurious itchings, but it also penetrates into the inmost parts, entering in at the nostrils and ears? And it flies into the eyes and injures the pupils, unless one takes great care; and what care could be taken against so extensive a plague, especially when it was God who was inflicting the punishment? (109) And perhaps some one may here ask why God punished the land with such insignificant and generally despised animals, omitting bears, and lions, and leopards, and the other races of wild beasts who devour human flesh; and if he did not send these, at least, he might have sent Egyptian asps, the bites of which have naturally the power to cause death instantly. (110) But if such a man really does not know, let him learn, first of all, that God was desirous rather to admonish the Egyptians than to destroy them: for if he had designed to destroy them utterly once for all, he would not have employed animals to be, as it were, his coadjutors in the work of destruction, but rather such heaven-sent afflictions as famine and pestilence; (111) and in the second place, let him also learn a lesson which is necessary to be learnt, and applicable to every condition and age of life; and what is the lesson? This; that men, when they make war, seek out the most mighty powers to gain them over to their alliance, such as shall make amends for their own want of power: but God, who is the supreme and mightiest of all powers, having need of no assistant, if ever he desires to use any instruments as it were for the punishments which he desires to inflict, does not choose the most mighty or the greatest things as his ministers, since he takes but little heed of their capacity, but he uses insignificant and small agents, which he renders irresistible and invincible powers, and by their means he chastises those who do wrong, as he does in this instance, (112) for what can be more insignificant than a louse? And yet it was so powerful that all Egypt fainted under the host of them, and was compelled to cry out, that "this is the anger of God." For all the earth put together, from one end to the other, could not withstand the hand of God, no nor all the universe.

XX

XX. (113) Such then were the chastisements which were inflicted by the agency of the brother of Moses. But those in which Moses himself was the minister, and from what parts of nature they were derived, must be next considered. Now next after the earth and the water, the air and the heaven, which are the purest portions of the essences of the universe, succeeded them as the medium of the correction of the Egyptians: and of this correction Moses was the minister; (114) and first of all he began to operate upon the air. For Egypt almost alone, if you except those countries which lie to the south of the equator, never is subject to that one of the seasons of the year which is called winter, perhaps, as some say, from the fact of its not being at any great distance from the torrid zone, since the essence of fire flows from that quarter in an invisible manner, and scorches everything all around, or perhaps it is because the river overflows at the time of the summer solstice, and so consumes all the clouds before they can collect for winter; (115) for the river begins to rise at the beginning of the summer, and to fall towards the end of summer; during which period the etesian gales increase in violence blowing from a direction opposite to the mouths of the Nile, and by which it is prevented from flowing freely into the sea, and by the violence of which winds, the sea itself is also raised to a considerable height, and erects vast waves like a long wall, and so the river is agitated within the country. And then when the two streams meet together, the river descending from its sources above, and the waters which ought to escape abroad being turned back by the beating of the sea, and not being able to extend their breadth, for the banks on each side of the river confine its streams, the river, as is natural, rises to a height, and breaks its bounds; (116) perhaps also it does so because it was superfluous for winter to occur in Egypt; for the object for which showers of rain are usually serviceable, is in this instance provided for by the river which overflows the fields, and turns them into one vast lake, to make them productive of the annual crops; (117) but nature does not expend her powers to no purpose when they are not wanted, so as to provide rain for a land which does not require it, but it rejoices in the variety and diversity of scientific operations, and arranges the harmony of the universe from a number of opposite qualities. And for this reason it supplies the benefits which are derivable from water, to some countries, by bestowing it on them from above, namely from heaven, and to others it gives it from below by means of springs and rivers; (118) though then the land was thus arranged, and enjoyed spring during the winter solstice, and since it is only the parts along the seacoasts that are ever moistened with a few drops of rain, and since the country beyond Memphis, where the palace of the king of Egypt is, does never even see snow at all; now, on the contrary, the air suddenly assumed a new appearance, so that all the things which are seen in the most stormy and wintry countries, come upon it all together; abundance of rain, and torrents of dense and ceaseless hail, and heavy winds met together and beat against one another with violence; and the clouds burst, and there were incessant lightnings, and thunders, and continued roarings, and flashes which made a most wonderful and fearful appearance. For though the lightning and the thunderbolts penetrated and descended through the hail, being quite a contrary substance, still they did not melt it, nor were the flashes extinguished by it, but they remained as they were before, and ran up and down in long lines, and even preserved the hail. (119) And not only did the excessive violence of the storm drive all the inhabitants to excessive despair, but the unprecedented character of the visitation tended likewise to the same point. For they believed, as was indeed the case, that all these novel and fearful calamities were caused by the divine anger, the air having assumed a novel appearance, such as it had never worn before, to the destruction and overthrow of all trees and fruits, by which also great numbers of animals were destroyed, some in consequence of the exceeding cold, others though the weight of the hail which fell upon them, as if they had been stoned, while some again were destroyed by the fire of the lightning. And some remained half consumed, bearing the marks of the wounds caused by the thunderbolts, for the admonition and warning of all who saw them.

XXI

XXI. (120) And when this evil had abated, and when the king and his court had again resumed their confidence, Moses stretched forth his rod into the air, at the command of God. And then a south wind of an uncommon violence set in, which increased in intensity and vehemence the whole of that day and night, being of itself a very great affliction; for it is a drying wind, causing headaches, and terrible to bear, calculated to cause grief, and terror, and perplexity in Egypt above all countries, inasmuch as it lies to the south, in which part of the heaven the revolutions of the light-giving stars take place, so that whenever that wind is set in motion, the light of the sun and its fire is driven in that direction and scorches up every thing. (121) And with this wind a countless number of animals was brought over the land, animals destroying all plants, locusts, which devoured every thing incessantly like a stream, consuming all that the thunderstorms and the hail had left, so that there was not a green shoot seen any longer in all that vast country. (122) And then at length the men in authority came, though late, to an accurate perception of the evils that had come upon them, and came and said to the king, "How long wilt thou refuse to permit the men to depart? Dost thou not understand, from what has already taken place, that Egypt is destroyed?" And he agreed to all they said, yielding as far as appearances went at least; but again, when the evil was abated at the prayer of Moses, the wind came from the sea side, and took up the locusts and scattered them. (123) And when they had been completely dispersed, and when the king was again obstinate respecting the allowing the nation to depart, a greater evil than the former ones was descended upon him. For while it was bright daylight, on a sudden, a thick darkness overspread the land, as if an eclipse of the sun more complete than any common one had taken place. And it continued with a long series of clouds and impenetrable density, all the course of the sun's rays being cut off by the massive thickness of the veil which was interposed, so that day did not at all differ from night. For what indeed did it resemble, but one very long night equal in length to three days and an equal number of nights? (124) And at this time they say that some persons threw themselves on their beds, and did not venture to rise up, and that some, when any of the necessities of nature overtook them, could only move with difficulty by feeling their way along the walls or whatever else they could lay hold of, like so many blind men; for even the light of the fire lit for necessary uses was either extinguished by the violence of the storm, or else it was made invisible and overwhelmed by the density of the darkness, so that that most indispensable of all the external senses, namely, sight, though unimpaired, was deprived of its office, not being able to discern any thing, and all the other senses were overthrown like subjects, the leader having fallen down. (125) For neither was any one able to speak or to hear, nor could any one venture to take food, but they lay themselves down in quiet and hunger, not exercising any of the outward senses, but being wholly overwhelmed by the affliction, till Moses again had compassion on them, and besought God in their behalf. And he restored fine weather, and produced light instead of darkness, and day instead of night.

XXII

XXII. (126) Such, they say, were the punishments inflicted by the agency of Moses alone, the plague, namely, of hail and thunderstorms, the plague of locusts, and the plague of darkness, which rejected every imaginable description of light. Then he himself and his brother brought on one together, which I shall proceed to relate. (127) At the command of God they both took up ashes from the furnace in their hands, which Moses on his part sprinkled in the air. Then a dust arose on a sudden, and produced a terrible, and most painful, and incurable ulceration over the whole skin both of man and of the brute beasts; and immediately their bodies became swollen with the pustules, having blisters all over them full of matter which any one might have supposed were burning underneath and ready to burst; (128) and the men were, as was natural, oppressed with pain and excessive agony from the ulceration and inflammation, and they suffered in their souls even more than in their bodies, being wholly exhausted with anguish. For there was one vast uninterrupted sore to be seen from head to foot, those which covered any particular part of any separate limb spreading so as to become confused into one huge ulcer; until again, at the supplication of the lawgiver, which he made on behalf of the sufferers, the disease became more tolerable. (129) Therefore, in this instance the two brothers afforded the Egyptians this warning in unison, and very properly; the brother of Moses acting by means of the dust which rose up, since to him had been committed the superintendence of the things which proceeded from the earth; and Moses, by means of the air which was thus changed for the affliction of the inhabitants, and his ministrations were assigned to the afflictions to be cause by the air and by the heaven.

XXIII

XXIII. (130) The remaining punishments are three in number, and they were inflicted by God himself without any agency or ministration of man, each of which I will now proceed to relate as well I can. The first is that which was inflicted by means of that animal which is the boldest in all nature, namely, the dog-fly (kynomuia) which those person who invent names have named with great propriety (for they were wise men); combining the name of the appellation of the most impudent of all animals, a fly and a dog, the one being the boldest of all terrestrial, and the other the boldest of all flying, animals. For they approach and run up fearlessly, and if any one drives them away, they still resist and renew their attack, so as never to yield until they are sated with blood and flesh. (131) And so the dog-fly, having derived boldness from both these animals, is a biting and treacherous creature; for it shoots in from a distance with a whizzing sound like an arrow; and when it has reached its mark it sticks very closely with great force. (132) But at this time its attack was prompted by God, so that its treachery and hostility were redoubled, since it not only displayed all its own natural covetousness, but also all that eagerness which it derived from the divine providence which went it forth, and armed it and excited it to acts of valour against the natives. (133) And after the dog-fly there followed another punishment unconnected with any human agency, namely, the mortality among the cattle; for all the herds of oxen, and flocks of goats, and vast flocks of sheep, and all the beasts of burden, and all other domestic animals of every kind died in one day in a body, as if by some agreement or at some given signal; foreshowing the destruction of human beings which was about to take place a short time afterwards as in a pestilential disease; for the sudden destruction of irrational animals is said to be an ordinary prelude to pestilential diseases.

XXIV

XXIV. (134) After which the tenth and last punishment came, exceeding in terror all that had gone before, namely, the death of the Egyptians themselves. Not of them all, for God had not decreed to make the whole country desolate, but only to correct it. Nor even of the greatest number of the men and women of every age all together, but he permitted the rest to live, and only passed sentence of death on all the first-born, beginning with the eldest of the king's sons, and ceasing with the first-born son of the most obscure grinder at the mill; (135) for, about midnight, all those children who had been the first to address their fathers and their mothers, and who had also been the first to be addressed by them as their sons, though they were in good health and in full vigour of body, all, without any apparent cause, were suddenly slain in the flower of their youth; and they say that there was not a single house in the whole land which was exempt from the visitation. (136) But at dawn of day, as was natural, when every one beheld his nearest and dearest relatives unexpectedly dead, with whom up to the evening before they had lived in one home and at one table, being overwhelmed with the most bitter grief, filled every place with lamentation. So that it came to pass, on account of the universality of the calamity, as all men were weeping altogether with one accord, that there was but one universal sound of wailing heard over the whole land from one end to the other. (137) And, for a while, they remained in their houses, no one being aware of the misfortune which had befallen his neighbour, but lamenting only for his individual loss. But when any one went out of doors and learnt the misfortunes of others also, he at once felt a double sorrow, grieving for the common calamity, in addition to his own private misfortune, a greater and more grievous sorrow being thus added to the lesser and lighter one, so that every one felt deprived of all hope of consolation. For who was likely to comfort another when he himself stood in need of the same consolation? (138) But, as is usual in such circumstances, men thinking that the present evils were the beginning of greater ones, and being filled with fear lest those who were still living should also be destroyed, ran weeping to the king's palace, and rent their clothes, and cried out against the sovereign, as the cause of all the terrible evils that had befallen them. (139) "For if," said they, "immediately when Moses at the beginning first came to him he had allowed his nation to depart, we should never have experienced any one of the miseries that have befallen us at all. But he yielded to his natural obstinacy and haughtiness, and so we have reaped the ready reward of his unreasonable contentiousness." Then one man encouraged another to drive the Jewish people with all speed out of the whole country, and not to allow them to remain one day, or rather one single hour, looking upon every moment that they abode among them as an irremediable calamity.

XXV

XXV. (140) So they, being now driven out of the land and pursued, coming at last to a proper notion of their own nobility and worth, ventured upon a deed of daring such as became the free to dare, as men who were not forgetful of the iniquitous plots that had been laid against them; (141) for they carried off abundant booty, which they themselves collected, by means of the hatred in which they were held, and some of it they carried themselves, submitting to heavy burdens, and some they placed upon their beasts of burden, not in order to gratify any love of money, or, as any usurer might say, because they coveted their neighbours' goods. (How should they do so?) But, first of all, because they were thus receiving the necessary wages from those whom they had served for so long a time; and, secondly, because they had a right to afflict those at whose hands they had suffered wrong with afflictions slighter than, and by no means equal to, what they had endured. For how can the deprivation of money and treasures be equivalent to the loss of liberty? on behalf of which those who are in possession of their senses dare not only to cast away all their property, but even to venture their lives? (142) So they now prospered in both particulars: whether in that they received wages as it in price, which they now exacted from unwilling paymasters, who for a long period had not paid them at all; and, also, as if they were at war, they looked upon it as fitting to carry off the treasures of the enemy, according to the laws of conquerors; for it was the Egyptians who had set the example of acts of injustice, having, as I said before, enslaved foreigners and suppliants, as if they had been prisoners taken in war. And so they now, when an opportunity offered, avenged themselves without any preparation of arms, justice itself holding a shield over them, and stretching forth its hand to help them.

XXVI

XXVI. (143) Such, then, were the afflictions and punishments by which Egypt was corrected; not one of which ever touched the Hebrews, although they were dwelling in the same cities and villages, and even houses, as the Egyptians, and touching the same earth and water, and air and fire, which are all component parts of nature, and which it is impossible to escape from. And this is the most extraordinary and almost incredible thing, that, by the very same events happening in the same place and at the same time, one people was destroyed and the other people was preserved. (144) The river was changed into blood, but not to the Hebrews; for when these latter went to draw water from it, it underwent another change and became drinkable. Frogs went up from the water upon the land, and filled all the market-places, and stables, and dwelling-houses; but they retreated from before the Hebrews alone, as if they had been able to distinguish between the two nations, and to know which people it was proper should be punished and which should be treated in the opposite manner. (145) No lice, no dog-flies, no locusts, which greatly injured the plants, and the fruits, and the animals, and the human beings, ever descended upon the Hebrews. Those unceasing storms of rain and hail, and thunder and lightning, which continued so uninterruptedly, never reached them; they never felt, no not even in their dreams, that most terrible ulceration which caused the Egyptians so much suffering; when that most dense darkness descended upon the others, they were living in bright daylight, a brilliancy as of noon-day shining all around them; when, among the Egyptians, all the first-born were slain, not one of the Hebrews died; for it was not likely, since even that destruction of such countless flocks and herds of cattle never carried off or injured a single flock or a single beats belonging to the Hebrews. (146) And it seems to me that if any one had been present to see all that happened at that time, he would not have conceived any other idea than that the Hebrews were there as spectators of the miseries which the other nation was enduring; and, not only that, but that they were also there for the purpose of being taught that most beautiful and beneficial of all lessons, namely, piety. For a distinction could otherwise have never been made so decidedly between the good and the bad, giving destruction to the one and salvation to the other.

XXVII

XXVII. (147) And of those who now went forth out of Egypt and left their abodes in that country, the men of age to bear arms were more than six hundred thousand men, and the other multitude of elders, and children, and women were so great that it was not easy to calculate it. Moreover, there also went forth with them a mixed multitude of promiscuous persons collected from all quarters, and servants, like an illegitimate crowd with a body of genuine citizens. Among these were those who had been born to Hebrew fathers by Egyptian women, and who were enrolled as members of their father's race. And, also, all those who had admired the decent piety of the men, and therefore joined them; and some, also, who had come over to them, having learnt the right way, by reason of the magnitude and multitude of the incessant punishments which had been inflicted on their own countrymen. (148) Of all these men, Moses was elected the leader; receiving the authority and sovereignty over them, not having gained it like some men who have forced their way to power and supremacy by force of arms and intrigue, and by armies of cavalry and infantry, and by powerful fleets, but having been appointed for the sake of his virtue and excellence and that benevolence towards all men which he was always feeling and exhibiting; and, also, because God, who loves virtue, and piety, and excellence, gave him his authority as a well-deserved reward. (149) For, as he had abandoned the chief authority in Egypt, which he might have had as the grandson of the reigning king, on account of the iniquities which were being perpetrated in that country, and by reason of his nobleness of soul and of the greatness of his spirit, and the natural detestation of wickedness, scorning and rejecting all the hopes which he might have conceived from those who had adopted him, it seemed good to the Ruler and Governor of the universe to recompense him with the sovereign authority over a more populous and more powerful nation, which he was about to take to himself out of all other nations and to consecrate to the priesthood, that it might for ever offer up prayers for the whole universal race of mankind, for the sake of averting evil from them and procuring them a participation in blessings. (150) And when he had received this authority, he did not show anxiety, as some persons do, to increase the power of his own family, and promote his sons (for he had two) to any great dignity, so as to make them at the present time partakers in, and subsequently successors to, his sovereignty; for as he always cherished a pure and guileless disposition in all things both small and great, he now subdued his natural love and affection for his children, like an honest judge, making these feelings subordinate to his own incorruptible reason; (151) for he kept one most invariable object always steadily before him, namely, that of benefiting those who were subjected to his authority, and of doing everything both in word and deed, with a view to their advantage, never omitting any opportunity of doing anything that might tend to their prosperity. (152) Therefore he alone of all the persons who have ever enjoyed supreme authority, neither accumulated treasures of silver and gold, nor levied taxes, nor acquired possession of houses, or property, or cattle, or servants of his household, or revenues, or anything else which has reference to magnificence and superfluity, although he might have acquired an unlimited abundance of them all. (153) But as he thought it a token of poverty of soul to be anxious about material wealth, he despised it as a blind thing, but he honoured the far-sighted wealth of nature, and was as great an admirer as any one in the world of that kind of riches, as he showed himself to be in his clothes, and in his food, and in his whole system and manner of life, not indulging in any theatrical affectation of pomp and magnificence, but cultivating the simplicity and unpretending affable plainness of a private individual, but a sumptuousness which was truly royal, in those things which it is becoming for a ruler to desire and to abound in; (154) and these things are, temperance, and fortitude, and continence, and presence of mind, and acuteness, and knowledge, and industry, and patience under evil, and contempt of pleasure, and justice, and exhortations to virtue and blame, and lawful punishment of offenders, and, on the contrary, praise and honour to those who did well in accordance with law.

XXVIII

XXVIII. (155) Therefore, as he had utterly discarded all desire of gain and of those riches which are held in the highest repute among men, God honoured him, and gave him instead the greatest and most perfect wealth; and this is the Wealth [1167] of all the earth and sea, and of all the rivers, and of all the other elements, and all combinations whatever; for having judged him deserving of being made a partaker with himself in the portion which he had reserved for himself, he gave him the whole world as a possession suitable for his heir: (156) therefore, every one of the elements obeyed him as its master, changing the power which it had by nature and submitting to his commands. And perhaps there was nothing wonderful in this; for if it be true according to the proverb, --

"That all the property of friends is common;"

and if the prophet was truly called the friend of God, then it follows that he would naturally partake of God himself and of all his possessions as far as he had need; (157) for God possesses everything and is in need of nothing; but the good man has nothing which is properly his own, no, not even himself, but he has a share granted to him of the treasures of God as far as he is able to partake of them. And this is natural enough; for he is a citizen of the world; on which account he is not spoken of as to be enrolled as a citizen of any particular city in the habitable world, since he very appropriately has for his inheritance not a portion of a district, but the whole world. (158) What more shall I say? Has he not also enjoyed an even greater communion with the Father and Creator of the universe, being thought unworthy of being called by the same appellation? For he also was called the god and king of the whole nation, and he is said to have entered into the darkness where God was; that is to say, into the invisible, and shapeless, and incorporeal world, the essence, which is the model of all existing things, where he beheld things invisible to mortal nature; for, having brought himself and his own life into the middle, as an excellently wrought picture, he established himself as a most beautiful and Godlike work, to be a model for all those who were inclined to imitate him. (159) And happy are they who have been able to take, or have even diligently laboured to take, a faithful copy of this excellence in their own souls; for let the mind, above all other parts, take the perfect appearance of virtue, and if that cannot be, at all events let it feel an unhesitating and unvarying desire to acquire that appearance; (160) for, indeed, there is no one who does not know that men in a lowly condition are imitators of men of high reputation, and that what they see, these last chiefly desire, towards that do they also direct their own inclinations and endeavours. Therefore, when the chief of a nation begins to indulge in luxury and to turn aside to a delicate and effeminate life, then the whole of his subjects, or very nearly the whole, carry their desire for indulging the appetites of the belly and the parts below the belly beyond all reasonable bounds, except that there may be some persons who, through the natural goodness of their disposition, have a soul far removed from treachery, being rather merciful and kind. (161) If, on the other hand, the chief of a people adopts a more austere and dignified course of life, then even those of his subjects, who are inclined to be very incontinent, change and become temperate, hastening, either out of fear or out of shame, to give him an idea that they are devoted to the same pursuits and inclinations that he is; and, in fact, the lower orders will never, no, nor will mad men even, reject the customs and habits of their superiors: (162) but, perhaps, since Moses was also destined to be the lawgiver of his nation, he was himself long previously, through the providence of God, a living and reasonable law, since that providence appointed him to the lawgiver, when as yet he knew nothing of his appointment.

XXIX

XXIX. (163) When then he received the supreme authority, with the good will of all his subjects, God himself being the regulator and approver of all his actions, he conducted his people as a colony into Phoenicia, and into the hollow Syria (Coele-syria), and Palestine, which was at that time called the land of the Canaanites, the borders of which country were three days' journey distant from Egypt. (164) Then he led them forward, not by the shortest road, partly because he was afraid lest the inhabitants should come out to meet and to resist him in his march, from fear of being overthrown and enslaved by such a multitude, and so, if a war arose, they might be again driven back into Egypt, falling from one enemy to another, and being driven by their new foes upon their ancient tyrants, and so become a sport and a laughingstock to the Egyptians, and have to endure greater and more grievous hardships than before. He was also desirous, by leading them through a desolate and extensive country, to prove them, and see how obedient they would be when they were not surrounded by any abundance of necessaries, but were but scantily provided and nearly in actual want. (165) Therefore, turning aside from the direct road he found an oblique path, and thinking that it must extend as far as the Red Sea, he began to march by that road, and, they say, that a most portentous miracle happened at that time, a prodigy of nature, which no one anywhere recollects to have ever happened before; (166) for a cloud, fashioned into the form of a vast pillar, went before the multitude by day, giving forth a light like that of the sun, but by night it displayed a fiery blaze, in order that the Hebrews might not wander on their journey, but might follow the guidance of their leader along the road, without any deviation. Perhaps, indeed, this was one of the ministers of the mighty King, an unseen messenger, a guide of the way enveloped in this cloud, whom it was not lawful for men to behold with the eyes of the body.

XXX

XXX. (167) But when the king of Egypt saw them proceeding along a pathless track, as he fancied, and marching through a rough and untrodden wilderness, he was delighted with the blunder they were making respecting their line of march, thinking that now they were hemmed in, having no way of escape whatever. And, as he repented of having let them go, he determined to pursue them, thinking that he should either subdue the multitude by fear, and so reduce them a second time to slavery, or else that if they resisted he should slay them all from the children upwards. (168) Accordingly, he took all his force of cavalry, and his darters, and his slingers, and his equestrian archers, and all the rest of his light-armed troops, and he gave his commanders six hundred of the finest of his scythe-bearing chariots, that with all becoming dignity and display they might pursue these men, and join in the expedition and so suing all possible speed, he sallied forth after them and hastened and pressed on the march, wishing to come upon them suddenly before they had any expectation of him. For an unexpected evil is at all times more grievous than one which has been looked for, in proportion as that which has been despised finds it easier to make a formidable attack than that which has been regarded with care. (169) The king, therefore, with these ideas, pursued after the Hebrews, thinking that he should subdue them by the mere shout of battle. And, when he overtook them, they were already encamped along the shore of the Red Sea. And they were just about to go to breakfast, when, at first, a mighty sound reached them, as was natural from such a host of men and beasts of burden all proceeding on with great haste, so that they all ran out of their tents to look round, and stood on tip-toes to see and hear what was the matter. Then, a short time afterwards, the army of the enemy came in sight as it rose over a hill, all in arms, and ready arranged in line of battle.

XXXI

XXXI. (170) And the Hebrews, being terrified at this extraordinary and unexpected danger, and not being well prepared for defence, because of a scarcity of defensive armour and of weapons (for they had not marched out for war, but to found a colony), and not being able to escape, for behind was the sea, and in front was the enemy, and on each side a vast and pathless wilderness, reviled against Moses, and, being dismayed at the magnitude of the evils that threatened them, began, as is very common in such calamities, to blame their governors, and said: (171) "Because there were no graves in Egypt in which we could be buried after we were dead, have you brought us out hither to kill and bury us here? Or, is not even slavery a lighter evil than death? Having allured the multitude with the hope of liberty, you have caused them to incur a still more grievous danger than slavery, namely, the risk of the loss of life. (172) Did you not know our simplicity, and the bitterness and cruel anger of the Egyptians? Do you not see the magnitude of the evils which surround us, and from which we cannot escape? What are we to do? Are we, unarmed, to fight against men in complete armour? or shall we flee now that we are hemmed in as by nets cast all around us by our pitiless enemies--hemmed in by pathless deserts and impassable seas? Or, even, if the sea was navigable, how are we to get any vessels to cross over it?" (173) Moses, when he heard these complaints, pardoned his people, but remembered the oracles of God. And, at the same time, he so divided and distributed his mind and his speech, that with the one he associated invisibly with God, in order that God might deliver him from otherwise inextricable calamities; and, with the other, he encouraged and comforted those who cried out to him, saying: "Do not faint and despair. God does not deliver in the same way that man does. (174) Why do you only trust such means of deliverance as seem probable and likely? God, when he comes as an assistant, stands in need of no adventitious preparations. It is his peculiar attribute to find a path amid inextricable perplexities. What is impossible to every created being is possible and easy to him above." (175) Thus he spoke to them while yet standing still. But after a short time he became inspired by God, and being full of the divine spirit and under the influence of that spirit which was accustomed to enter into him, he prophesied and animated them thus: "This army which you behold so splendidly equipped with arms, you shall no more see arrayed against you; for it shall fall, utterly and completely overthrown, so that not a relic shall be seen any more upon the earth, and that not at any distance of time, but this very next night."

XXXII

XXXII. (176) He then spoke thus. But when the sun had set, immediately a most violent south wind set in and began to blow, under the influence of which the sea retreated; for, as it was accustomed to ebb and flow, on this occasion it was driven back much further towards the shore, and drawn up in a heap as if into a ravine or a whirlpool. And no stars were visible, but a dense and black cloud covered the whole of the heaven, so that the night became totally dark, to the consternation of the pursuers. (177)

And Moses, at the command of God, smote the sea with his staff. And it was broken and divided into two parts, and one of the divisions at the part where it was broken off, was raised to a height and mounted up, and being thus consolidated like a strong wall, stood quiet and unshaken; and the portion behind the Hebrews was also contracted and raised in, and prevented from proceeding forwards, as if it were held back by invisible reins. And the intermediate space, where the fracture had taken place, was dried up and became a broad, and level, and easy road. When Moses beheld this he marvelled and rejoiced; and, being filled with joy, he encouraged his followers and exhorted them to march forward with all possible speed. (178) And when they were about to pass over, a most extraordinary prodigy was seen; for the cloud, which had been their guide, and which during all the rest of the period of their march had gone in front of them, now turned back and placed itself at the back of the multitude to guard their rear; and, being situated between the pursuers and the pursued, it guided the one party so as to keep them with safety and perfect freedom from danger, and it checked and embarrassed the others, who were hastening on to pursue them. And, when the Egyptians saw this, they were entirely filled with disorder and confusion, and through their consternation they threw all their ranks into disorder, falling upon one another and endeavouring to flee, when there was no advantage to be derived from flight. (179) For, at the first appearance of morning, the Hebrews passed over by a dry path, with their wives, and families, and infant children. But the portions of the sea which were rolled up and consolidated on each side overwhelmed the Egyptians with their horses and chariots, the tide being brought back by a strong north wind and poured over them, and coming upon them with vast waves and overpowering billows, so that there was not even a torchbearer left to carry the news of this sudden disaster back to Egypt. (180) Then the Hebrews, being amazed at this great and wonderful event, gained a victory which they had never hoped for without bloodshed or loss; and, seeing the instantaneous and complete destruction of the enemy, formed two choruses, one of men and the other of women, on the sea shore, and sang hymns of gratitude to God, Moses leading the song of the men, and his sister that of the women; for these two persons were the leaders of the choruses.

XXXIII

XXXIII. (181) And when they had departed from the sea they went on for some time travelling, and no longer feeling any apprehension of their enemies. But when water failed them, so that for three days they had nothing to drink, they were again reduced to despondency by thirst, and again began to blame their fate as if they had not enjoyed any good fortune previously; for it always happens that the presence of an existing and present evil takes away the recollection of the pleasure which was caused by former good. (182) At last, when they beheld some fountains, they ran up full of joy with the idea that they were going to drink, being deceived by ignorance of the truth; for the springs were bitter. Then when they had tasted them they were bowed down by the unexpected disappointment, and fainted, and yielded both in body and soul, lamenting not so much for themselves as for their helpless children, whom they could not endure without tears to behold imploring drink; (183) and some of those who were of more careless dispositions, and of no settled notions of piety, blamed all that had gone before, as if it had turned out not so as to do them any good, but rather so as to lead them to a suffering of more grievous calamities than ever; saying that it was better for them to die, not only once but three times over, by the hands of their enemies, than to perish with thirst; for they affirmed that a quick and painless departure from life did in no respect differ from freedom from death in the opinion of wise men, but that that was real death which was slow and accompanied by pain; that what was fearful was not to be dead but only to be dying. (184) When they were lamenting and bewailing themselves in this manner, Moses again besought God, who knew the weakness of all creatures, and especially of men, and the necessary wants of the body which depends for its existence on food, and which is enslaved by those severe taskmistresses, eating and drinking, to pardon his desponding people, and to relieve their want of everything, and that too not after a long interval of time, but by a prompt and undeferred liberality, since by reason of the natural impotency of their mortal nature, they required a very speedy measure of assistance and deliverance. (185) But he, by his bountiful and merciful power, anticipated their wishes, sending forth and opening the watchful, anxious eye of the soul of his suppliant, and showed him a piece of wood which he bade him take up and throw into the water, which indeed had been made by nature with such a power for that purpose, and which perhaps had a quality which was previously unknown, or perhaps was then first endowed with it, for the purpose of effecting the service which it was then about to perform: (186) and when he had done that which he was commanded to do, the fountains became changed and sweet and drinkable, so that no one was able to recognise the fact of their having been bitter previously, because there was not the slightest trace or spark of their ancient bitterness left to excite the recollection.

XXXIV

XXXIV. (187) And so having appeased their thirst with double pleasure, since the blessing of enjoyment when it comes beyond one's hopes delights one still more, and having also replenished their ewers, they departed as from a feast, as if they had been entertained at a luxurious banquet, and as if they were intoxicated not with the drunkenness which proceeds from wine, but with a sober joy which they had imbibed purely, while pledging and being pledged by the piety of the ruler who was leading them; (188) and so they arrive at a second halting place, well supplied with water, and well shaded with trees, called Aileem, irrigated with twelve fountains, near which were young and vigorous trunks of palm trees to the number of seventy, a visible indication and token of good to the whole nation, to all who were gifted with a clear-sighted intellect. (189) For the nation itself was divided into twelve tribes, each of which, if pious and religious, would be looked upon in the light of a fountain, since piety is continually pouring forth everlasting and unceasing springs of virtuous actions. And the elders and chiefs of the whole nation were seventy in number, being therefore very naturally likened to palm trees which are the most excellent of all trees, being both most beautiful to behold, and bearing the most exquisite fruit, which has also its vitality and power of existence, not buried in the roots like other trees, but situated high up like the heart of a man, and lodged in the centre of its highest branches, by which it is attended and guarded like a queen as it really is, they being spread all round it. (190) And the intellect too of those persons who have tasted of holiness has a similar nature; for it has learned to look upwards and to soar on high, and is continually keeping its eye fixed on sublime objects, and investigating divine things, and ridiculing, and scorning all earthly beauty, thinking the last only toys, and divine things the only real and proper objects worthy of its attention.

XXXV

XXXV. (191) But after these events only a short time elapsed, when they became oppressed by famine through the scarcity of provisions, as if one necessary thing after another was to foil them in succession: for thirst and hunger are very cruel and terrible mistresses, and having portioned out the afflictions between them, attacked them by turns; and it so fell out that when the first calamity was relaxed the second came on, which was most intolerable to those who had to bear it, inasmuch as having only just fancied that they were delivered from thirst, they now found another evil, namely famine, lying in ambush to attack them; (192) and not only was their present scarcity terrible, but they were also in despair as to the supply of necessary food for the future; for when they saw the vast and extensive desert around them, so utterly unproductive of any kind of crop, their hearts sank within them. For all around were rugged and precipitous rocks, or else a salt and brackish plain, and stony mountains, or deep sands reaching up and forming mountains of inaccessible height; and moreover there was no river, neither winter torrent nor ever-flowing stream; there were no springs, no plant growing from seed, no tree whether for fruit or timber, no animal whether flying or terrestrial, except some few poisonous reptiles born for the destruction of mankind, and serpents, and scorpions. (193) So then the Hebrews, remembering the plenty and luxury which they had enjoyed in Egypt, and the abundance of all things which was bestowed upon them there, and contrasting it with the universal want of all things which they were now experiencing, were grieved and indignant, and talked the matter over with one another, saying:-- "We left our former abodes and emigrated, from a hope of freedom, happy only in the promises of our leader; as far as his actions go, we are of all men the most miserable. (194) What will be the end of this long and interminable journey? Everyone else, whether sailing over the sea or marching on foot, has some limit before him at which he will eventually arrive; some being bound for marts and harbours, others for some city or country; but we alone have nothing to look forward to but a pathless desert, and a difficult journey, and terrible hopelessness, and despair; for as we advance, the desert lies before us like an ever open, vast, and pathless sea which widens and increases every day. (195) But Moses having raised our expectations, and puffed us up with fine speeches, and filled our ears with vain hopes, racks our bodies with hunger and does not give us even necessary food. He has deceived this vast multitude with the name of a settlement in a colony; having first of all led us out of an inhabited country into an uninhabitable district, and now sending us down to the shades below, which is the last journey of life."

XXXVI

XXXVI. (196) Moses, being reviled in this way, was nevertheless not so much grieved at their accusations which they brought against himself, as at the inconstancy of their own resolutions and minds. For though they had already experienced an infinite number of blessings which had befallen them unexpectedly and out of the ordinary course of affairs, they ought, in his opinion, not to have allowed themselves to be led away by any specious or plausible complaints, but to have trusted in him, as they had already received the clearest possible proofs that he spoke truly about everything. (197) But again, when he came to take into consideration the want of food, than which there is no more terrible evil which can afflict mankind, he pardoned them, knowing that the multitude is by nature inconstant and always moved by present circumstances, which cause it to forget what has gone before, and despair of the future. (198) Therefore, as they were all in the extremity of suffering, and expecting the most fearful misery which they fancied was lying in ambush for them and close at hand, God, partly by reason of his natural love and compassion for man, and partly because he desired to honour the commander whom he had appointed to govern them, and still more to show his great piety and holiness in all matters whether visible or invisible, pitied them and relieved their distress. (199) Therefore he now devised an entirely new kind of benefit, that they, being taught by manifest signs and displays of his power, might feel reverence for him, and learn for the future not to be impatient if anything turned out contrary to their wishes, but to endure present evils with fortitude, in the expectation of future blessings. (200) What then happened? The very next day, about sun-rise, a dense and abundant dew fell in a circle all round about the camp, which rained down upon it gently and quietly in an unusual and unprecedented shower; not water, nor hail, nor snow, nor ice, for these are the things which the changes of the clouds produce in the winter season; but what was now rained down upon them was a very small and light grain, like millet, which, by reason of its incessant fall, rested in heaps before the camp, a most extraordinary sight. And the Hebrews marvelled at it, and inquired of the commander what this rain was, which no man had ever seen before, and for what it was sent. (201) And he was inspired, and full of the spirit of prophecy, and spoke to them as follows: "A fertile plain has been granted to mortal men, which they cut up into furrows, and plough, and sow, and do everything else which relates to agriculture, providing the yearly fruits so as to enjoy abundance of necessary food. But it is not one portion only of the universe, but the whole world that belongs to God, and all its parts obey their master, supplying everything which he desires that they should supply. (202) Now therefore, it has seemed good to him that the air should produce food instead of water, since the earth has often brought forth rain; for when the river in Egypt every year overflows with inundations and irrigates all the fields, what else is that but a rain which is showered up from below?" (203) That other would have been indeed a most surprising fact if it had stopped there; but now he wrought wonders with still more surprising circumstances; for all the population bringing vessels one after another, collected what fell, some putting them upon beasts of burden, others loading themselves and taking them on their shoulders, being prudently eager to provide themselves with necessary food for a longer time. (204) But it was something that would bear to be stored up and dispensed gradually, since God is accustomed always to give his gifts fresh. Accordingly, they now prepared enough for their immediate necessities and present use, and ate it with pleasure. But of what was left till the next day they found not a morsel unhurt, but it was all changed and fetid, and full of little animals of the kind which usually cause putrefaction. So this they naturally threw away, but they found fresh quantities of it ready for food, so that it fell out that this food was carried down every day with the dew. (205) But the holy seventh day had an especial honour; for, as it is not permitted to do anything whatever on that day (and it is expressly commanded that men are then to abstain from every work, great or little), so that they were not able to collect food that day, instead of food for one day, God rained upon them a double quantity, and ordered them to collect what shall be food enough for two days. And what was then collected remained sound, no portion of it becoming spoiled as it had before.

XXXVII

XXXVII. (206) I will also relate a circumstance which is more marvellous than even this one; for, though they were travelling for forty years, yet during all this long period of time they had an abundant supply of all necessary things in their appointed order, as is the case in clubs and messes which are regularly measured out with a view to the distribution of what is required by each individual. And, at the same time, they learnt the value of that long-wished for day; (207) for, having inquired for a long time what the day of the creation of the world as, the day on which the universe was completely finished, and, having received this question from their fathers and their ancestors undecided, they at last, though with great difficulty, did ascertain it, not being taught only by the sacred scriptures, but also by a certain proof which was very distinct; for, as that portion of the manna (as has been already said) which was more than was wanted on the other days of the week was spoiled, still that portion which was rained down on the day before the seventh not only did not change its nature, but was dispensed in a twofold quantity. (208) And the use was as follows. At dawn they collected what had been showered down, and then they ground or pounded it; and then they roasted it and made every sweet food of it, like honey cheesecake, and so they ate it, without requiring any exceeding skill on the part of the preparers of the food. (209) But they also had no scarcity of, nor any great distance to go for, the means of making life even luxurious, as if they had been in a populous and productive land, since God had determined out of his great abundance to supply them with plenty of all things which they required even in the wilderness; for, in the evenings, there was an uninterrupted cloud of quails borne to them from the sea, which overshadowed the whole camp, flying very near the ground so as to be easily caught. Therefore, the Hebrews, taking them and preparing them as each individual liked, enjoyed the most exquisite meat, pleasing themselves and varying their food with this necessary and delicious addition.

XXXVIII

XXXVIII. (210) Accordingly, they had a great abundance of these birds, as they never failed. But, a second time, a terrible scarcity of water came upon them and afflicted them; and, as they again speedily began to despair of their safety, Moses, taking his sacred rod with which he had wrought the signs in Egypt, being inspired by God, smote the precipitous rock. (211) And the rock being struck this seasonable blow, whether it was that there was a spring previously concealed beneath it, or whether water was then for the first time conveyed into it by invisible channels pouring in all together and being forced out with violence, at all events the rock, I say, was cleft open by the force of the blow and poured forth water in a stream, so that it not only then furnished a relief from thirst, but also supplied for a long time an abundance of drink for so many myriads of people. For they filled all their water vessels, as they had done before, from the fountains which were bitter by nature, but which, by divine providence, were changed to sweet water. (212) And, if any one disbelieves these facts, he neither knows God nor has he ever sought to know him; for, if he had, he would have instantly known, he would have known and surely comprehended, that all these unexpected and extraordinary things are the amusement of God; looking at the things which are really great and deserving of serious attention, namely, the creation of the heaven, and the revolutions of the planets and fixed stars, and the shining of light--of the light of the sun by day and that of the moon by night--and the position of the earth in the most centre spot of the universe, and the vast dominions of the different continents and islands, and the innumerable varieties of animals and plants, and the effusion of the sea, and the rapid courses of the ever-flowing rivers and winter mountain torrents, and the streams of everlasting springs, some of which pour forth cold and others hot water, and the various changes and alterations of the air and climate, and the different seasons of the year, and an infinite number of other beautiful objects. (213) And the whole of a man's life would be too short if he wished to enumerate all the separate instances of such things, or even to detail fully all that is to be seen in one complete portion of the world; aye, if he were to be the most longlived man that has ever been seen. But all these things, though they are in truth really wonderful, are despised by us by reason of our familiarity with them. But the things to which we are not accustomed, even though they may be unimportant, still make an impression upon us from our love of novelty, while we yield to strange ideas concerning them.

XXXIX

XXXIX. (214) And now, as they had gone over a vast tract of land previously untravelled, there appeared some boundaries of habitable country and some suburbs, as it were, of the land to which they were proceeding, and the Phoenicians inhabited it. But they, hoping that a tranquil and peaceable life would now be permitted to them, were deceived in their expectation; (215) for the king of the country, being afraid lest he might be destroyed, roused up all the youth of his cities, and collected an army, and went forth to meet them to keep them from his borders. And if they attempted to force their way, he showed that he would proceed to repel them with all his forces, his army being fresh, and now for the first time levied and marshalled for battle, while the Hebrews were wearied and worn out with their long travelling and with the scarcity of meat and drink which had in turns oppressed them. (216) But when Moses had learnt from his scouts that the army of the enemy was marshalled at no great distance, he chose out those men who were in the flower of their youth, and appointed one of his subordinate officers, named Joshua, to be their general, while he himself went to procure a more powerful alliance; for, having purified himself with the customary purification, he rode up with speed to a neighbouring hill, and there he besought God to hold his shield over the Hebrews and to give them the victory and the mastery, as he had delivered them before from more formidable dangers and from other evils, not only dissipating the calamities with which they were threatened at the hands of men, but also all those which the transformation of the elements so wonderfully caused in the land of Egypt, and from those which the long scarcity inflicted upon them in their travels. (217) And just as the two armies were about to engage in battle, a most marvellous miracle took place with respect to his hands; for they became by turns lighter and heavier. Then, whenever they were lighter, so that he could hold them up on high, the alliance between God and his people was strengthened, and waxed mighty, and became more glorious. But whenever his hands sank down the enemy prevailed, God showing thus by a figure that the earth and all the extremities of it were the appropriate inheritance of the one party, and the most sacred air the inheritance of the other. And as the heaven is in every respect supreme to and superior over the earth, so also shall the nation which has heaven for its inheritance be superior to their enemies. (218) For some time, then, his hands, like the balances in a scale, were by turns light, and by turns descended as being heavy; and, during this period, the battle was undecided. But, on a sudden, they became quite devoid of weight, using their fingers as if they were wings, and so they were raised to a lofty height, like winged birds who traverse the heaven, and they continued at this height until the Hebrews had gained an unquestionable victory, their enemies being slain to a man from the youth upward, and suffering with justice what they had endeavoured to inflict on others, contrary to what was befitting. (219) Then Moses erected an altar, which from the circumstances that had taken place he named the refuge of God, on which he offered sacrifices in honour of his victory, and poured forth prayers of gratitude to God.

XL

XL. (220) After this battle he considered that it was proper to reconnoitre the country into which the nation was being led as a colony (and it was now the second year that they had been travelling), not wishing that his followers should (as is often the case) change their designs out of ignorance, but that they should learn by accurate report, what the nature of the country really was, availing themselves of the positive knowledge of the inhabitants, and should then consider what was best to be done; (221) and accordingly he chose out twelve men, to correspond in number to the twelve tribes, one out of each tribe to be the leader of it, selecting the most approved men, with reference to their excellence, in order that no quarrels might arise from any one party being better or worse off than another, but that they might all, by the agency of those to whom the matter was entrusted, be equally instructed as to the state of affairs among the inhabitants, if only the spies who were sent out brought a true report. (222) And when he had selected the men he spoke to them as follows: "The inheritance which is before us is the prize of those labours and dangers which we have endured hitherto, and are still enduring, and let us not lose the hope of these things, we who are thus conducting a most populous nation to a new settlement. But the knowledge of the places, and of the men, and of the circumstances, is most useful, just as ignorance of these particulars is most injurious. (223) We have therefore appointed you as spies, that we, by your eyes and by your intellects, may see the state of things there; ye, therefore, must be the ears and eyes of all these myriads of people, that thus they may arrive at an accurate comprehension of what is indispensable to be known. (224) "Now what we wish to know consists of three points; the number of the inhabitants, and the strength of their cities, whether they are planted in favourable situations, whether they are strongly built and fortified, or the contrary. As to the country, we wish to know whether it has a deep and rich soil, whether it is good to bear all kinds of fruits, both of such plants as are raised from seed and of fruit-trees; or whether, on the contrary, it has a shallow soil; that so we may be prepared against the power and numbers of the inhabitants with equal forces, and against the fortified state of buildings and cities by means of engines and machines, for the destruction of cities. "And it is indispensable to understand the nature of the country, and whether it is a good land or not; for to encounter voluntary dangers for a poor and bad land is an act of folly; (225) and our weapons, and our engines, and all our power, consist solely in our trust and confidence in God. Having this preparation we will yield to no danger or fear, for this is sufficient with great superfluity of power to subdue otherwise invincible strength, which relies only on bodily vigour and on armies, and on courage, and skill, and numbers; since to that too we owe it, that even in a vast wilderness we have full supplies of everything, as if we were in well-stocked cities; (226) and the time in which it is most easy to come to a proper understanding of the good qualities of the land is the spring, the season which is now present; for in the season of spring what has been sown is coming to perfection, and the natures of the trees are beginning to propagate themselves further. It will be better, therefore, for you to enter the land now, and to remain till the middle of the summer, and to bring back with you fruits, as samples of what is to be procured from a prosperous and fertile country."

XLI

XLI. (227) When they had received these orders, they went forth to spy out the land, being conducted on their way by the whole multitude who feared lest they might be taken prisoners and so be put to death, and lest in that way two great evils might happen to them, namely, the slaughter of the men who were the eye of each tribe, and also ignorance of what was being done by their enemies who were plotting against them, the knowledge of which was most desirable. (228) So, taking with them scouts to examine the road and guides to show them the way, they accompanied them at their first setting out. And when they approached the borders of the country they ran up to the highest mountain of all those in that district, and from thence they surveyed the land, part of which was an extensive champaign district, fertile in barley, and wheat, and herbage; and the mountain region was not less productive of vines, and all kinds of other trees, and rich in every kind of timber, full of dense thickets, and girdled by rivers and fountains so as to be abundantly well watered, so that even from the foot of the mountain district to the highest summit of the hills themselves, the whole region was covered closely with a net-work of shady trees, and more especially the lower ridges, and the deep valleys and glens. (229) They also surveyed all the strongest cities, looking upon them in two points of view; first, with reference to their advantages of situation, and also to the strength of their fortification; also, when they inquired respecting the inhabitants, they saw that they were very numerous indeed, and giants of exceeding tallness with absolutely gigantic bodies, both as to their magnitude and their strength. (230) When they had seen thus much they waited to get a more accurate knowledge of everything: for first impressions are not trustworthy, but require the slow confirmation of time. They also took great care to gather specimens of the productions of the land, though they were not as yet ripe and solid, but only just beginning to be properly coloured, that they might show them to all the multitude, for which reason they selected such as would not be easily spoiled; (231) but what above all things astonished them was the fruit of the vines, for the branches were of unrivalled sizes, stretching along all the young shoots and branches in a way that seemed almost incredible. Therefore, having cut off one branch, and having suspended it on a stick by the middle, the ends of which they gave to two young men, placing one on one side and one on the other, and others succeeding them as bearers of it as the former bearers got tired, for the weight was very great, they carried it so, the whole body of the spies not at all agreeing with respect to some points of necessary importance.

XLII

XLII. (232) Accordingly, there were a great many contest between them even before they returned to the camp, but not very serious ones, in order that there might not be seditions between them from any of them adhering very contentiously to his own opinion, or from different persons giving different accounts, but they became more violent after their return; (233) for some of them brought back formidable stories of the strength of the different cities, and the great populousness and opulence of each of them, exaggerating and making the most of everything in their description so as to cause excessive consternation among their hearers; while others, on the contrary, disparaged and made light of all that they saw, and exhorted their fellow countrymen not to faint but to persevere in their design of colonising that country, as they would subdue the natives with a mere shout; for that no city whatever would be able to resist the onset of so mighty a power attacking it with its united force, but would be overwhelmed with its might and submit at once. Moreover, each of the spies infused into the souls of his hearers some portion of his own spirit, the cowardly spreading cowardice, and the indomitable and bold diffusing confidence united with sanguine hope. (234) But these last made but a fifth part of those who were frightened out of their senses, while they, on the other hand, were five times as numerous as the high-spirited; and the small number of those who displayed any courage, is often beaten down by the vast number of those who behaved in a cowardly manner, as they say was the case at this time also; for they who maintained the better side of the question were only two, while those who made the contrary report were ten; and these last so entirely prevailed over the two former, that they led away the whole multitude after them, alienating them from the two, and binding them wholly to themselves. (235) But about the country itself they all brought back the same report with perfect unanimity, praising the beauty both of the champaign and of the mountainous district. But then they further cried out, "But what is the advantage to us of those good things which belong to others, when they are guarded by a mighty force, so that they can never be taken from their owners?" And so, attacking the two who brought the opposite report, they were very near stoning them, preferring to hear pleasant rather than useful things, and also preferring deceit to truth. (236) At which their leader was indignant, and he was also at the same time afraid lest some heaven-inflicted evil might descend upon them, since they so obstinately persisted in despairing and in disbelieving the word of God, which indeed took place. For of the spies, the ten who brought back cowardly tiding all perished by a pestilential disease, with those of the multitude who united in their feelings of despondency, and only the two who had agreed and counselled the people not to fear but to persevere in the plan of the colony were saved, because they were obedient to the word of God, on which account they received the especial honour of not being involved in the destruction of the others.

XLIII

XLIII. (237) This was the reason why they did not arrive sooner in the land which they went forth to colonize; for though they might, in the second year after their departure from Egypt, have conquered all the cities in Syria, and divided the inheritance amongst themselves, still they turned aside from the direct and short road, and wandered about, using one long, and difficult, and pathless line of march after another, so as to be incessantly toiling both in soul and body, and enduring the necessary and deserved punishment of their excessive impiety; (238) accordingly, for eight and thirty years more, after the two years which I have already mentioned as having elapsed, the life of a complete generation of mankind did they wander up and down, traversing the pathless wilderness; and at last in the fortieth year, they with difficulty came to the borders of the country which they had reached so many years before. (239) And at the entrance to this country there dwelt other tribes akin to themselves, who they thought would cheerfully join them in the war against their neighbours, and would co-operate in everything necessary for the establishment of the colony; and if they hesitated to do that, they thought that at all events they would range themselves on neither side, but would preserve a strict neutrality, holding up their hands; (240) for in fact the ancestors of both nations, both of the Hebrews and of those who dwelt on the skirts of the country, were brethren descended from the same father and the same mother, and moreover were twins; for it was from two brothers, who had thus increased with numerous descendants, and had enjoyed a great productiveness of offspring, that each of their families had grown into a vast and numerous Nation.[1168] But one of these nations had clung to its original abodes; but the other, as has been already mentioned, having migrated to Egypt by reason of the famine, at this subsequent period was now returning, (241) and one of the two preserved its respect for its kindred though it had been for such a length of time separated from it, still having a regard for those who no longer preserved any one of their ancestral customs, but who had in every respect departed from their ancient habits and constitutions, thinking that it became those who claimed to be of civilised natures, to give and yield something to the name of relationship. (242) But the other utterly overturned all notions of friendship and affection, giving in to fierce, and unfriendly, and irreconcilable dispositions, and language, and counsels, and actions; and thus keeping alive the ill-will of their original ancestor to his brother; for the first founder of their race, though he had himself given up his birthright to his brother, yet a short time afterwards endeavoured to assert his claim to what he had abandoned voluntarily, violating his agreement, and he sought to slay his brother, threatening him with death if he did not surrender what he had purchased. And now the whole nation after the interval of so many generations, renewed the ancient enmity between one individual and another. (243) Therefore Moses, the leader of the Hebrews, although he might with one single effort, aye with the mere shout of his army, have subdued the whole nation, still, by reason of the aforesaid relationship did not think fit to do so; but desired only to use the road through their country, promising that he would in every respect observe the treaties between them, and not despoil them of territory, or cattle, or of any booty, that he would even pay a price for water if there should be a scarcity of drink, and for anything else that they might require to buy, as not being supplied with it; but they violently rejected their peaceful invitations, threatening them with war, if they heard of their crossing over their borders or even of their setting foot upon them.

XLIV

XLIV. (244) But as the Hebrews received their answer with great indignation, and prepared at once to oppose them, Moses stood in a place from whence he would be well heard, and said, "O men, your indignation is reasonable and just; for though we, in a peaceable disposition, have made them good and friendly offers, they have made us an evil reply out of their evil and perverse disposition. (245) But it does not follow that because they deserve to pay the penalty for their cruelty, therefore it is desirable for us to proceed to take vengeance upon them, by reason of the honour due to our own nation, that we may show that in this particular we are good and different from wicked men, inasmuch as we consider not only whether such and such persons deserve to be punished, but whether also it is proper that they should receive their punishment from us." (246) On this he turned aside and led his army by another road, since he knew that all the roads in that district were surrounded with garrisons, by those who were not in danger of receiving any injury, but who were out of envy and jealousy would not allow them to proceed by the shortest road; (247) and this was the most manifest proof of their sorrow, which they felt in consequence of the nation having obtained their liberty, namely when they rejoiced when they were enduring that bitter slavery of theirs in Egypt; for it follows of necessity that those men to whom the good fortune of their neighbours causes grief, do also rejoice at their evil fortune, even if they do not admit that they do so; (248) for they had already related to their neighbours, as to persons in accordance with themselves, and cherishing the same thoughts, all the misfortunes and also all the agreeable pieces of good fortune which had happened to them, not knowing that they had proceeded to a great degree of iniquity, and that they were full of unfriendly, and hostile, and malicious thoughts towards them, so that they were like to grieve at their good fortune, but to rejoice at any thing of a contrary tendency. (249) But when their malevolence was fully revealed, the Hebrews were nevertheless restrained from coming to open war with them by their ruler, who thus displayed two most excellent qualities at the same time; namely prudence and a compassionate disposition; for to take care that no evil should happen to any one is the part of wisdom, and not to be willing even to repel one's own kinsmen is a proof of a humane disposition.

XLV

XLV. (250) Therefore he passed by the cities of these nations; but a certain king of the neighbouring country, Canaan by name, when his spies reported to him that the army of the Hebrews, which was making in his direction was at no great distance, thinking that it was in a state of confusion and disorder, and that he should be able easily to conquer it if he were to attack it at once, proceeded forth with the youth of his nation well armed and equipped, and marched with all speed, and put the van of their host to flight as soon as he encountered them, inasmuch as they were not arrayed or prepared for battle; and having taken many prisoners, and being elated at the prosperity beyond his hopes which he had met with, he marched on thinking that he should defeat all the others also. (251) But the Hebrews, for they were not dismayed at the defeat of their advanced guard, but had rather derived even more confidence than they had felt before, being eager also to make amends by their eagerness for battle for the loss of those of their number who had been taken prisoners, exhorted one another not to faint nor to yield. "Let us rise up," said they; "let us at once invade their land. Let us show that we are in no wise alarmed or depressed, by our vigour in action and our confidence. The end is very often judged of by the beginning. Let us seize the keys of the country and strike terror into the inhabitants as deriving prosperity from cities, and inflicting upon them in return the want of necessary things which we bring with us out of the wilderness." (252) And they, at the same time, exhorted one another often with these words, and likewise began to dedicate to God, as the first fruits of the land, the cities of the king and all the citizens of each city. And he accepted their views and inspired the Hebrews with courage, and prepared the army of the enemy to be defeated. (253) Accordingly, the Hebrews defeated them with mighty power, and fulfilled the agreement of gratitude which they had made, not appropriating to themselves the slightest portion of the booty. And they dedicated to God the cities with all the men and treasures that were in them, and, from what had thus taken place, they called the whole country an offering to God; (254) for, as every pious man offers unto God the first fruits of the fruits of the year, which he collects from his own possessions, so in the same manner did the Hebrews dedicate the whole nation of this mighty country into which they had come as settlers, and that great spoil, the kingdom which they had so speedily subdued, as a sort of first-fruit of their colony; for they did not think it consistent with piety to distribute the land among themselves, or to inherit the cities, before they had offered up to God the first fruits of that country and of those cities.

XLVI

XLVI. (255) A short time afterwards, having found a copious spring of water which supplied drink to all the multitude, and the spring was in a well and on the borders of the country, drawing it up and drinking it as though it had been not water but pure wine, they were refreshed in their souls, and those among the people who loved God established choruses and dances in a circle around the well, out of their cheerfulness and joy, and sang a new song to God, the possessor and giver of their inheritance and the real leader of their colony, because now at the first moment of their coming forth from the direction in which they had so long been dwelling in to the inhabited land which they were ordained to possess, they had found abundant drink, and therefore they thought it right not to pass this spring by without due honour. (256) For this well had been originally cut not by the hands of private individuals, but of kings, who had laboured in rivalry of one another, as the tale went, not only in the discovery of the water, but likewise in the digging of the well, in order that by its magnificence it might be seen to be a royal work, and that the power and magnanimity of those who built it might appear from the beginning. (257) And Moses, rejoicing at the unexpected blessings which from time to time were presenting themselves to him, advanced further, dividing the youth of his people into the vanguard and the rearguard, and placing the old men, and the women, and the children in the centre, that they might be protected by those who were thus at each extremity, in the case of their having to encounter any force of the enemy either in front or behind.

XLVII

XLVII. (258) A few days afterwards he entered the country of the Amorites, and sent ambassadors to the king, whose name was Sihon, exhorting him to the same measures to which he had previously invited his kinsman. But he not only replied to these ambassadors when they came with great insolence, but he very nearly put them to death, and would have done so if the law with respect to ambassadors had not hindered him; but he did collect an army and made against them, thinking that he should immediately be able to subdue them in war. (259) But when he encountered them he then found that he had to fight not men who had no experience or practice in the art of war, but men skilful in all warfare and truly invincible, who only a short time before had done many and important valiant achievements, displaying great personal valour, and great wisdom, and excellence of sense and virtue. Owing to which qualities they subdued these their enemies with great ease and defeated them with great loss, but they took no part of the spoil, desiring to dedicate to God the first booty which they gained; (260) and, on this occasion, they guarded their own camp vigorously, and then, with one accord and with equally concerted preparation, rushed forward in opposition to the enemy as he advanced and charged them, availing themselves of the invincible alliance of the just God, in consequence of which they had the greatest boldness, and became cheerful and sanguine combatants. (261) And the proof of this was clear; there was no need of any second battle, but the first was also the only one, and in it the whole power of the enemy was frustrated for ever. And it was utterly overthrown, and immediately it disappeared for ever. (262) And about the same time the cities were both empty and full; empty of their ancient inhabitants, and full of those who now succeeded to their dominions over them. In the same manner, also, the stables of cattle in the fields, being made desolate, received instead men who were in all respects better than their former masters.

XLVIII

XLVIII. (263) This war struck all the Asiatic nations with terrible consternation, and especially all those who were near the borders of the Amorites, inasmuch as they looked upon the dangers as being nearer to themselves. Accordingly, one of the neighbouring kings, by name Balak, who ruled over a large and thickly inhabited country of the east, before he met them in battle, feeling great distrust of his own power, did not think fit to meet them in close combat, being desirous to avoid carrying on a war of extermination by open arms; but he had recourse to inquiries and divination, thinking that by some kind of ruse or other he might be able to overthrow the irresistible power of the Hebrews. (264) Now there was a man at that time very celebrated for his skill in divination, dwelling in Mesopotamia, who was initiated in every branch of the soothsayers' art. And he was celebrated and renowned above all men for his experience as a diviner and prophet, as he had in many instances foretold to many people incredible and most important events; (265) for, on one occasion, he had predicted heavy rain to one nation at the height of summer; to another he had foretold a drought and burning heat in the middle of winter. Others he had forewarned of a dearth which should follow a season of abundance; and, on the other hand, plenty after famine. In some instances he had predicted the inundations of rivers; or, on the contrary, their falling greatly and becoming dried up; and the departure of pestilential diseases, and ten thousand other things. From all which he had obtained a name of wide celebrity, as he was believed to have foreseen them all, and so he had attained to great renown and his glory had spread everywhere and was continually increasing. (266) So this man, Balak, now sent some of his companions, entreating him to come to him, and he gave him some presents at once, and he promised to give him others also, explaining to him the necessity which he was in, on account of which he had sent for him. But he did not treat the messengers with any noble or consistent disposition, but with great courtesy and civility evaded their request, as if he were one of the most celebrated prophets, and as such was accustomed to do nothing whatever without first consulting the oracle, and so he declined, saying that the Deity would not permit him to go with them. (267) So the messengers returned back to the king, without having succeeded in their errand. And immediately other messengers of the highest rank in the whole land were sent on the same business, bringing with them more abundant presents of money, and promising still more ample rewards than the former ambassadors had promised. (268) And Balaam, being allured by the gifts which were already proffered to him, and also by the hopes for the future which they held out to him, and being influenced also by the rank of those who invited him, began to yield, again alleging the commands of the Deity as his excuse, but no longer with sincerity. Accordingly, on the next day he prepared for his departure, relating some dreams by which he said he had been influenced, affirming that he had been compelled by their manifest visions not to remain, but to follow the ambassadors.

XLIX

XLIX. (269) But when he was on his road a very manifest sign met him in the way, showing him plainly that the purpose for which he was travelling was displeasing to God, and ill-omened; for the beast on which he was riding, while proceeding onwards in the straight road, at first stopped suddenly, (270) then, as if some one was forcibly resisting it, or standing in front and driving it back by force, it retreated, moving first to the right and then to the left, and could not stand still, but kept moving, first to one side and then to the other, as if it had been under the influence of wine and intoxication; and though it was repeatedly beaten, it disregarded the blows, so that it very nearly threw its rider, and though he stuck on did still hurt him considerably; (271) for close on each side of the path there were walls and strong fences; therefore, when the beast in its violent motions struck heavily against the walls, the owner had his knee, and leg, and foot pressed and crushed, and was a good deal lacerated. (272) The truth is, that there was, as it seems, a divine vision, which, as the beast, on which the diviner was seeking, saw at a great distance as it was coming towards him, and it was frightened at it; but the man did not see it, which was a proof of his insensibility, for he was thus shown to be inferior to a brute beast in the power of sight, at a time when he was boasting that he could see, not only the whole world, but also the Creator of the world. (273) Accordingly, having after some time seen the angel opposing him, not because he was desiring to see so astonishing a spectacle, but that he might become acquainted with his own insignificance and nothingness, he betook himself to supplications and prayers, entreating to be pardoned, on the ground that he had acted as he had done out of ignorance, and had not sinned of deliberate purpose. (274) Then, as he said that he ought to return back again, he asked of the vision which appeared to him, whether he should go back again to his own house; but the angel beholding his insincerity, and being indignant at it (for what need was there for him to ask questions in a matter which was so evident, which had its answer plain in itself, and which did not require any more positive information by means of words, unless a person's ears are more to be trusted than his eyes, and words than things), said, "Go on in the journey in which you have set out, for you shall do no good to those who have sent for you, and you must say what I prompt you, without any thoughts of your own, finding utterance, as I will guide the organs of your speech in the way that shall be just and expedient, for I will direct your words, predicting all that shall happen through the agency of your tongue, though you yourself understand nothing of it.

L

L. (275) But when the king heard that he was now near at hand, he went forth with his guards to meet him; and when they met at first there were, as was natural, greetings and salutations, and then a brief reproof of his tardiness and of his not having come more readily. After this there were feastings and costly entertainments, and all those other things which are usually prepared on the occasion of the reception of strangers, everything with royal magnificence being prepared, so as to give an exaggerated idea of the power and glory of the king. (276) The next day at the rising of the sun, Balak took the prophet and led him up to a high hill, where it also happened that a pillar had been erected to some deity which the natives of the country had been accustomed to worship; and from thence there was seen a portion of the camp of the Hebrews, which was shown to the magician from this point, as if from a watch tower. (277) And he when he beheld it said: "Do thou, O king, build here seven altars, and offer upon every one of them a bullock and a ram. And I will turn aside and inquire of God what I am to say." So, having gone forth, immediately he became inspired, the prophetic spirit having entered into him, which drove all his artificial system of divination and cunning out of his soul; for it was not possible that holy inspiration should dwell in the same abode with magic. Then, returning back to the king, and beholding the sacrifices and the altars flaming, he became like the interpreter of some other being who was prompting his words, (278) and spoke in prophetic strain as follows: "Balak has sent for me from Mesopotamia, having caused me to take a long journey from the east, that he might chastise the Hebrews by means of curses. But in what manner shall I be able to curse those who have not been cursed by God? For I shall behold them with my eyes from the loftiest mountains, and I shall see them with my mind; and I shall never be able to injure the people which shall dwell alone, not being numbered among the other nations, not in accordance with the inheritance of any particular places, or any apportionment of lands, but by reason of the peculiar nature of their remarkable customs, as they will never mingle with any other nation so as to depart from their national and ancestral ways. (279) Who has ever discovered with accuracy the first origin of the birth of these people? Their bodies, indeed, may have been fashioned according to human means of propagation; but their souls have been brought forth by divine agency, wherefore they are nearly related to God. May my soul die as to the death of the body, that it may be remembered among the souls of the righteous, such as the souls of these men are."

LI

LI. (280) When Balak heard these words he was grieved within himself; and after he had stopped speaking, not being able to contain his sorrow, he said: "You were invited hither to curse my enemies, and are you not ashamed to offer up prayers for their good? I must, without knowing it, have been deceiving myself, thinking you a friend; who were, on the contrary, without my being aware of it, enrolled among the ranks of the enemy, as is now plain. Perhaps, too, you made all the delay in coming to me by reason of the regard for them, which you were secretly cherishing in your soul, and your secret dislike to me and to my people; for, as the old proverb says, what is apparent affords the best means of judging of what is not visible." (281) But Balaam, his moment of inspiration being now past, replied: "I am exposed in this to a most unjust charge, and am undeservedly accused; for I am saying nothing of my own, but whatever the Deity prompts me to say. And this is not the first time that I have said and that you have heard this, but I declared it on the former occasion when you sent the ambassadors, to whom I made the same answer." (282) But as the king thought either that the prophet was deceiving him, or that the Deity might change his mind, and the consequence of a change of place might alter the firmness of his decision, he led him off to another spot, where, from an exceedingly long, and high, and distant hill, he might be able to show him a part of the army of his enemies. Then, again, he built seven altars and sacrificed the same number of victims that he had sacrificed at first, and sent the prophet to look for favourable omens and predictions. (283) And he, as soon as he was by himself, was again suddenly filled by divine inspiration, and, without at all understanding the words which he uttered, spoke everything that was put into his mouth, prophesying in the following manner:--"Rise up and listen, O king! prick up thy ears and hear. God is not able to speak falsely as if he were a man, nor does he change his purpose like the son of man. When he has once spoken, does he not abide by his word? For he will say nothing at all which shall not be completely brought to pass, since his word is also his deed. I, indeed, have been brought hither to bless this nation, and not to curse it. (284) There shall be no labour or distress among the Hebrews. God visibly holds his shield over them, who also dissipated the violence of the Egyptian attacks, leading forth all these myriads of people as one man. Therefore they disregarded auguries and every other part of the prophetic art, trusting to the one sole Governor of the world alone. And I see the people rising up like a young lion, and exulting as a lion. He shall feast on the prey, and for drink he shall drink the blood of the wounded; and, when he is satisfied, he shall not turn to sleep, but he shall be awake and sing the song of victory."

LII

LII. (285) But Balak, being very indignant at finding that all the assistance which he expected to derive from divination was turning out contrary to his hopes, said: "O man, neither curse them at all, nor bless them at all; for silence, which is free from danger, is better than unpleasant speeches." And when he had said this, as if he had forgotten what he had said, owing to the inconstancy of his mind, he led the prophet to another place, from which he could show him a part of the Hebrew army; and again he invited him to curse them. (286) But the prophet, as being even more wicked than the king, although he had always replied to the accusations which were brought against him with one true excuse, namely, that he was saying nothing out of his own head, but was only interpreting the words of another, being himself carried away and inspired, when he ought no longer to have accompanied him but to have gone away home, ran forward even more eagerly than his conductor, although in his secret thoughts he was oppressed by a heavy feeling of evil, yet still desired in his mind to curse this people, though he was forbidden to do so with his mouth. (287) So, coming to a mountain greater than any of those on which he had stood before, and which reached a very long way, he bade the king perform the same sacrifices as before, again building seven altars, and again offering up fourteen victims, on each altar two, a bullock and a ram. And he himself did no longer, according to his usual custom, go to seek for divination and auguries, since he much loathed his art, looking upon it as a picture which had become defaced through age, and had been obscured, and lost its felicity of conjecture. But he now, though with difficulty, understood the fact that the designs of the king, who had hired him, did not correspond with the will of God. (288) Therefore, turning to the wilderness, he saw the Hebrews encamped in their tribes, and he saw their numbers and their array, and admired it as being like the order of a city rather than of a camp, and, becoming inspired, he again spoke. (289) What, then, said the man who saw truly, who in his sleep saw a clear vision of God with the ever open and sleepless eyes of his soul? "How goodly are thy abodes, O army of Hebrews; they tents are shady as groves, as a paradise on the bank of a river, as a cedar by the waters. (290) A man shall hereafter come forth out of thee who shall rule over many nations, and his kingdom shall increase every day and be raised up to heaven. This people hath God for its guide all the way from Egypt, who leads on their multitude in one line. (291) Therefore they shall devour many nations of their enemies, and they shall take all their fat as far as their very marrow, and shall destroy their enemies with their far-shooting arrows. He shall lie down to rest like a lion, and like a lion's whelp, fearing no one, but showing great contempt for every one, and causing fear to all other nations. Miserable is he who shall stir up and rouse him to anger. Blessed are they that bless thee, and cursed are they that curse thee."

LIII

LIII. (292) And the king, being very indignant at these words, said: "Having been invited hither to curse my enemies, you have now prayed for and blessed them these three times. Fly, therefore, quickly, passion is a hasty affection, lest I be compelled to do something more violent than usual. (293) Of what a vast amount of money, O most foolish of men, of how many presents, and of how much renown, and celebrity, and glory, hast thou deprived thyself in thy madness! Now you will return to thy home from a foreign land, bearing with thee no good thing, but only reproaches and (as it seems likely) great disgrace, being ridiculed and despised for that knowledge on which you formerly so greatly prided yourself." (294) And Balaam replied: "All that I have hitherto uttered have been oracles and words of God; but what I am going to say are merely the suggestions of my own mind: and taking him by the right hand, he, while they two were alone, gave him advice, by the adoption of which he might, as far as possible, guard against the power of his enemies, accusing himself of the most enormous crimes. For why, some one may perhaps say, do you thus retire into solitude and give counsel suggesting things contrary to the oracles of God, unless indeed that your counsels are more powerful than his decrees?"

LIV

LIV. (295) Come, then, let us examine into his fine recommendations, and see how cunningly they were contrived with reference to the most certain defeat of those who had hitherto always been able to conquer. As he knew that the only way by which the Hebrews could be subdued was by leading them to violate the law, he endeavoured to seduce them by means of debauchery and intemperance, that mighty evil, to the still greater crime of impiety, putting pleasure before them as a bait; (296) for, said he, "O king! the women of the country surpass all other women in beauty, and there are no means by which a man is more easily subdued than by the beauty of a woman; therefore, if you enjoin the most beautiful of them to grant their favours to them and to prostitute themselves to them, they will allure and overcome the youth of your enemies. (297) But you must warn them not to surrender their beauty to those who desire them with too great facility and too speedily, for resistance and coyness will stimulate the passions and excite them more, and will kindle a more impetuous desire; and so, being wholly subdued by their appetites, they will endure to do and to suffer anything. (298) "And let any damsel who is thus prepared for the sport resist, and say, wantonly, to a lover who is thus influenced, "It is not fitting for you to enjoy my society till you have first abandoned your native habits, and have changed, and learnt to honour the same practices that I do. And I must have a conspicuous proof of your real change, which I can only have by your consenting to join me in the same sacrifices and libations which I use, and which we may then offer together at the same images and statues, and other erections in honour of my gods. (299) And the lover being, as it were, taken in the net of her manifold and multiform snares, not being able to resist her beauty and seductive conversation, will become wholly subdued in his reason, and, like a miserable man, will obey all the commands which she lays upon him, and will en enrolled as the salve of passion."

LV

LV. (300) This, then, was the advice which Balaam gave to Balak. And he, thinking that what he said to him did not want sense, repealed the law against adulteries, and having abrogated all the enactments which had been established against seduction and harlotry, as if they had never been enacted at all, exhorted the women to admit to their favours, without any restraint, every man whom they chose. (301) Accordingly, when licence was thus given, they brought over a multitude of young men, having already long before this seduced their minds, and having by their tricks and allurements perverted them to impiety; until Phinehas, the son of the chief priest, being exceedingly indignant at all that was taking place (for it appeared to him to be a most scandalous thing for his countrymen to give up at one time both their bodies and souls--their bodies to pleasure, and their souls to transgression of the law, and to works of wickedness), undertook a bold and impetuous action, such as was becoming to a young, and grave, and virtuous man. (302) For when he saw a man of his nation sacrificing with and then entering into the tent of a harlot, and that too without casting his eyes down on the ground and seeking to avoid the notice of the multitude, but making a display of his licentiousness with shameless boldness, and giving himself airs as if he were about to engage in a creditable action, and one deserving of smiles--

Philo Judaeus

Phinehas, I say, being very indignant and being filled with a just anger, ran in, and while they were still lying on the bed, slew both the lover and the harlot, cutting them in two pieces in the middle, because they thus indulged in illicit connections. (303) When some persons of those who admired temperance, and chastity, and piety, saw this example, they, at the command of Moses, imitated it, and slew all their own relations and friends, even to a man, who had sacrificed to idols made with hands, and thus they effaced the stain which was defiling the nation by this implacable revenge which they thus wreaked on those who had set the example of wrong doing, and so saved the rest, who made a clear defence of themselves, demonstrating their own piety, showing no compassion on any one of those who were justly condemned to death, and not passing over their offences out of pity, but looking upon those who slew them as pure from all sin. Therefore they did not allow any escape whatever to those who sinned in this way, and such conduct is the truest praise; (304) and they say that twenty-four thousand men were slain in one day, the common pollution, which was defiling the whole army, being thus at once got rid of. And when the works of purification were thus accomplished, Moses began to seek how he might give an honour worthy of him who had displayed such permanent excellence to the son of the chief priest, who was the first who hastened to inflict chastisement on the offenders. But God was beforehand with him, giving to Phinehas, by means of his holy word, the greatest of all good things, namely, peace, which no man is able to bestow; and also, in addition to this peace, he gave him the perpetual possession of the priesthood, an inheritance to his family, which could not be taken from it.

LVI

LVI. (305) But when none of the civil and intestine evils remained any longer, but when all the men who were suspected of having either forsaken the ways of their ancestors or of treachery had perished, it appeared to be a most favourable opportunity for making an expedition against Balak, a man who had both planned to do, and had also executed an innumerable host of evil deeds, since he had planned them through the agency of the prophet, who he hoped would be able, by means of his curses, to destroy the power of the Hebrews, and who had executed his purpose by the agency of the licentiousness and incontinence of the women, who destroyed the bodies of those who associated with them by debauchery, and their souls by impiety. (306) Therefore Moses did not think fit to carry on war against him with his whole army, knowing that superfluous numbers are apt to meet with disaster in consequence of those very numbers; and also, at the same time, thinking it useful to have stations of reserve, to be assistants to those of their allies who appeared likely to fail; but he selected a thousand picked men of the youth of the nation, selected man by man, out of each tribe, twelve thousand in all, for that was the number of the tribes, and he appointed Phinehas to be the commander in the war, as he had already given proof of the happy daring which becomes a general; and after he had offered up sacrifices of good omen, he sent forth his warriors, and encouraged them in the following words:--(307) "The present contest is not one for dominion or sovereignty, nor is it waged for the sake of acquiring the property of others, though these are the objects for which alone, or almost invariably, wars take place; but this war is undertaken in the cause of piety and holiness, from which the enemy has alienated our relations and friends, being the causes of bitter destruction to those who have been brought under their yoke. (308) It is therefore absurd for us to be the slayers of our own countrymen, for having offended against the law, and to spare our enemies, who have violated it in a much worse degree, and to slay, with every circumstance of violence, those who were only learning and beginning to sin, but to leave those who taught them to do so unpunished, who are, in reality, the guilty causes of all that has taken place, and of all the evils which our countrymen have either done or suffered."

LVII

LVII. (309) Therefore being nerved by these exhortations, and being kindled and filled with noble courage which was indeed in their souls already, they went forth to that contest with invincible spirit as to a certain victory; and when they engaged with the enemy, they displayed such incredible vigour and courage that they slew all their enemies, and returned themselves unhurt, every one of them, not one of their number having been slain or even wounded. (310) Any one who did not know what had taken place, might have supposed, when he saw them returning, that they were coming in, not from war and from a pitched battle, but rather from a display and field-day of exercise under arms, such as often take place in time of peace; and these fielddays are days of exercise and practice, while the men train themselves among friends to attack their enemies. (311) Therefore they destroyed all their cities, razing them to the ground or else burning them, so that no one could tell that any cities had ever been inhabited in that land. And they led away a perfectly incalculable number of prisoners, of whom they chose to slay all the full-grown men and women, the men because they had set the example of wicked counsels and actions, and the women because they had beguiled the youth of the Hebrews, becoming the causes to them of incontinence and impiety, and at the last of death; but they pardoned all the young male children and all the virgins, their tender age procuring them forgiveness; (312) and as they had taken a vast booty from the king's palace, and from private houses, and also from the dwellings of all kinds in the open country (for there was not less booty in the country places than in the cities), they came to the camp, laden with all the wealth which they had taken from the enemy. (313) And Moses praised Phinehas their general, and those who had served under him for their good success, and also because they had not been covetous of their own advantage, running after booty and thinking of nothing, but appropriating the spoil to themselves, but because they had brought it all into the common stock, so that they who had staid behind in the tents might share in the booty; and he ordered those men to remain outside the camp for some days, and the high priest he commanded to purify both the men themselves, and those of their allies who had returned from fighting by their side, of bloodshed; (314) for even though the slaughter of the enemies of one's country is according to law, still he who kills a man, even though justly and in self-defence, and because he has been attacked, still appears to be guilty of blood by reason of his supreme and common relationship to a common father; on which account those who had slain enemies were in need of rites of purification, to cleanse them from what was looked upon as a pollution.

LVIII

LVIII. (315) However, after no long lapse of time he divided the booty among those who had taken a part in the expedition, and they were but a small number, giving one half among those who had remained inactive at home, and the other half to those who were still in the camp; for he looked upon it as just and equitable to give the share of the advantages gained, to those who had shared in the contest, if not with their souls, at all events with their bodies; for as the spectators were not inferior to the actual combatants in their zeal, they were inferior only in point of time and in respect of their being anticipated. (316) And as the smaller body had received each a larger share of the booty, by reason of their having been the foremost in encountering danger, and the larger body had received each a smaller share, by reason of their having remained at home; it appeared indispensable that they should consecrate the first fruits of the whole of the booty; those therefore who had remained at home brought a fiftieth, and those who had been actually engaged in the war, brought and contributed a five hundredth part; and of ten first fruits Moses commanded that portion which came from those who had borne a part in the expedition, to be given to the high priest, and that portion which came from those who had remained in the camp, to the keepers of the temple whose name were the Levites. (317) And the captains of thousands, and centurions, and all the rest of the multitude of commanders of battalions and companies willingly contributed special first fruits, as an offering for their own safety, and that of those who had gone out to war, and for the victory which had been gained in a manner beyond all hope, giving up all the golden ornaments which had fallen to the lot of each individual, in the apportionment of the booty, and the most costly vessels, of which the material was gold. All which things Moses took, and, admiring the piety of those who contributed them, dedicated them in the consecrated tabernacle as a memorial of the gratitude of the men; and the division of the first fruits was very beautiful; (318) those which had been given by the men who had borne their share in the war, he distributed among the keepers of the temple as among men who had only displayed one half of virtue, namely eagerness without action; but the first fruits of those who had warred and fought, who had encountered danger with their bodies and lives, and thus had displayed perfect and complete excellence, he allotted to him who presided over the keepers of the temple, namely to the high priest; and the first fruits of the captains, as being the offerings of chiefs and rulers, he allotted to the great ruler of all, namely to God.

LIX

LIX. (319) All these wars were carried on and brought to an end before the Hebrews had crossed Jordan, the river of the country, being wars against the inhabitants of the country on the other side of Jordan, which was a rich and fertile land, in which there was a large champaign fertile in corn, and also very productive of herbage and fodder for cattle; (320) and when the two tribes who were occupied in feeding cattle saw this country, the two tribes being a sixth part of the whole Hebrew host, they besought Moses to permit them to take their inheritance in that district, where in fact they were already settled; for they said that the place was very suitable for cattle to be kept, and fed, and bred in, inasmuch as it was well watered and full of good herbage, and as it produced spontaneously abundant grass for the feeding of sheep. (321) But as he thought that they claimed a sort of right, by some kind of pre-eminence, to receive their share and the honours due to them before their time, or else that they preferred this petition by reason of their being unwilling to encounter the wars which were impending, as there were still many kings who were making ready to attack them, and who were the possessors of all the country inside the river, he was very indignant at their request, and answered them in anger, and said, (322) "Shall you then sit here and enjoy leisure, and yield to indolence at so improper a time? and shall the wars which still threaten us, afflict all your countrymen, and your relations, and your friends, and shall the prizes be given to you alone, as if you had all contributed to the success? And shall battles and wars, and distresses, and the most extreme dangers await others? (323) But it is not just that you should enjoy peace, and the blessings that flow from peace, and that the rest should endure wars and all the other indescribable evils which they bring with them, and that the whole should only be looked upon as an adjunct of a part; while, on the contrary, it is for the sake of the whole that the parts are thought worthy of any inheritance at all. (324) Ye are all entitled to equal honour, ye are one race, ye have the same fathers, one house, ye have the same customs, a community of laws, and an infinite number of other things, every one of which binds your kindred closer together, and cements your mutual good will; why then when you are thought worthy of equal shares of the most important and most necessary things, do you show a covetous spirit in the division of the lands, as if you were rulers despising your subjects as masters looking disdainfully on your slaves?" (325) You ought to have derived instruction from the afflictions of others; for it is the part of wise men not to wait till misfortunes come upon themselves. But now, though you have domestic examples in your own fathers, who went and spied out this land, and in the calamities which befell them, and all who participated in their despondency (for they all perished except two), and when, therefore, you ought to take care and avoid resembling them in any respect whatever, still, foolish-minded men that ye are, ye are imitating their cowardice, as if by such conduct you would be more strongly fortified against capture; and you check and damp the eagerness of those who are desirous to display their manhood and valour, relaxing and depressing their spirits; (326) therefore, while you are hastening to do wrong, you are also hastening to incur punishment. For justice is always a long time before it can be put in motion, but when it is once put in motion it makes great haste and speedily overtakes those who flee from it. (327) When, therefore, all our enemies are destroyed, and when there is no other war which can be expected or feared as impending, and when all those in our present alliance have been, on examination, found to be without reproach nor liable to any charge of desertion or treachery, or of any misconduct which could possibly tend to our defeat, but shall be seen to have endured steadfastly from the beginning to the end, with their bodily exertion and with all eagerness of mind, and when the whole country is cleared of those who have previously inherited it, then rewards and prizes for valour shall be given to all the tribes with perfect fairness.

LX

LX. (328) So they, bearing this rebuke with moderation, as being genuine sons of a very kindly disposed father (for they knew that Moses was not a man to behave insolently because of his power and authority, but one who cared for all of them, and honoured justice and equality, and who hated wickedness, not so as to reproach or insult the wicked, but so as to be constantly endeavouring by admonition and correction to improve those who were susceptible of improvement), said to him, "Very naturally you are indignant, if you imagine that we now are anxious to desert the alliance and to obtain our allotments before the proper time; (329) but you must know that we are not alarmed at any undertaking that calls for valorous and virtuous exertion, even though it may be most laborious. And we judge that the task of virtue is to obey you who are such a brave and wise ruler, and not to fear to encounter dangers, and to be willing to bear our share in all future expeditions until all our business is brought to a fortunate conclusion. (330) "We, therefore, as we have agreed before, will remain in our ranks and cross over Jordan in complete armour, giving no soldier any excuse for lagging behind. But our infant children, and our daughters, and wives, and mothers, and the bulk of our cattle, shall, if you have no objection, be left behind, after we have made houses for our children and wives, and stables for our cattle that they may not be exposed to any incursion of the enemy, and so suffer injury from being taken in unwalled and unprotected dwellings." (331) And Moses answered with a mild look and even still gentler voice, "If you speak the truth and behave honestly, the allotments which you have asked for shall remain assured to you. Leave behind you now, as you desire, your wives and children, and flocks and herds, and go yourselves across Jordan in your ranks with the rest of the soldiers in full armour, arrayed for battle, as if you were prepared to fight at once, if it should be needful. (332) And hereafter when all our enemies are destroyed, and when, peace being established, we have made ourselves masters of the whole country, and have begun to divide it among ourselves, then you also shall return to your families to enjoy the good things which belong to you, and to possess the region which you have selected." (333) When Moses had said this, and given them this promise, they were filled with cheerfulness and joy, and established their families in safety as well as their flocks and herds in wellfortified and impregnable strongholds, the greater part of which were artificial. And taking their arms they marched forth more cheerfully than any of the rest of the allied forces, as if they alone had been going to fight, or at all events to fight in the first ranks as the champions of the whole army, for he who has received any gift beforehand is more eager in the cause in which he is engaged, since he thinks

The Works of Philo Judaeus: Volume II

that he is repaying a necessary debt, and not giving a free gift. (334) I have now, then, given an account of what was done by Moses while invested with kingly power. I must now proceed to relate in order all the actions which he performed in accordance with virtue, and also successfully as a chief priest, and also in his character as a lawgiver; for he also exercised these two powers as very closely connected with his kingly authority.

Footnotes:

1165. Yonge's full title, A Treatise on the Life of Moses, that is to say, On the Theology and Prophetic Office of Moses, Book I.

1166. the similitude of this passage to Sir William Jones' Ode is very remarkable: "What constitutes a state."

1167. the text here is very corrupt.

1168. the brothers are Jacob and Esau, Jacob being the father of the Israelites and Esau of the Edomites.

ON THE LIFE OF MOSES, II [1169]

I

I. (1) The first volume of this treatise relates to the subject of the birth and bringing up of Moses, and also of his education and of his government of his people, which he governed not merely irreproachably, but in so exceedingly praiseworthy a manner; and also of all the affairs, which took place in Egypt, and in the travels and journeyings of the nation, and of the events which happened with respect to their crossing the Red Sea and in the desert, which surpass all power of description; and, moreover, of all the labours which he conducted to a successful issue, and of the inheritances which he distributed in portions to his soldiers. But the book which we are now about to compose relates to the affairs which follow those others in due order, and bear a certain correspondence and connection with them. (2) For some persons say, and not without some reason and propriety, that this is the only way by which cities can be expected to advance in improvement, if either the kings cultivate philosophy, or if philosophers exercise the kingly power. But Moses will be seen not only to have displayed all these powers--I mean the genius of the philosopher and of the king--in an extraordinary degree at the same time, but three other powers likewise, one of which is conversant about legislation, the second about the way of discharging the duties of high priest, and the last about the prophetic office; (3) and it is on these subjects that I have now been constrained to choose to enlarge; for I conceive that all these things have fitly been united in him, inasmuch as in accordance with the providential will of God he was both a king and a lawgiver, and a high priest and a prophet, and because in each office he displayed the most eminent wisdom and virtue. We must now show how it is that every thing is fitly united in him. (4) It becomes a king to command what ought to be done, and to forbid what ought not to be done; but the commanding what ought to be done, and the prohibition of what ought not to be done, belongs especially to the law, so that the king is at once a living law, and the law is a just king. (5) But a king and a lawgiver ought to pay attention not only to human things, but also to divine ones, for the affairs of neither kings nor subjects go on well except by the intervention of divine providence; on which account it was necessary that such a man as Moses should enjoy the first priesthood, in order that he might with perfectly conducted sacrifices, and with a perfect knowledge of the proper way to serve God, entreat for a deliverance from evil and for a participation in good, both for himself and for the people whom he was governing, from the merciful God who listens favourably to prayers. (6) But since there is an infinite variety of both human and divine circumstances which are unknown both to king, and lawgiver, and chief priest, for a man is no less a created and mortal being from having all these offices, or because he is clothed with such a vast and boundless inheritance of honour and happiness, he was also of necessity invested with the gift of prophecy, in order that he might through the providence of God learn all those things which he was unable to comprehend by his own reason; for what the mind is unable to attain to, that prophecy masters. (7) Therefore the connection of these four powers is beautiful and harmonious, for being all connected together and united one to another, they unite in concert, receiving and imparting a reciprocity of benefits from and to one another, imitating the virgin graces with whom it is an immutable law of their nature that they cannot be disunited, with respect to whom one might fairly say, what is habitually said of the virtues, that he who has one has them all.

II

II. (8) And first of all we must speak of the matters which relate to his character and conduct as a lawgiver. I am not ignorant that the man who desires to be an excellent and perfect lawgiver ought to exercise all the virtues in their complete integrity and perfection, since in the houses of his nation some are near relations and some distant, but still they are all related to one another. And in like manner we must look upon some of the virtues as connected more closely with some matters, and on others as being more removed from them. (9) Now these four qualities are closely connected with and related to the legislative power, namely, humility, the love of justice, the love of virtue, and the hatred of iniquity; for every individual who has any desire for exercising his talents as a lawgiver is under the influence of each of these feelings. It is the province of humanity to prepare for adoption such opinions as will benefit the common weal, and to teach the advantages which will proceed from them. It is the part of justice to point out how we ought to honour equality, and to assign to every man his due according to his deserts. It is the part of the love of virtue to embrace those things which are by nature good, and to give to every one who deserves them facilities without limit for the most unrestrained enjoyment of happiness. It is also the province of the hatred of iniquity to reject all those who dishonour virtue, and to look upon them as common enemies of the human race. (10) Therefore it is a very great thing if it has fallen to the lot of any one to arrive at any one of the qualities before mentioned, and it is a marvellous thing, as it should seem, for any one man to have been able to grasp them all, which in fact Moses appears to have been the only person who has ever done, having given a very clear description of the aforesaid virtues in the commandments which he established. (11) And those who are well versed in the sacred scriptures know this, for if he had not had these principles innate within him he would never have compiled those scriptures at the promptings of God. And he gave to those who were worthy to use them the most admirable of all possessions, namely, faithful copies and imitations of the original examples which were consecrated and enshrined in the soul, which became the laws which he revealed and established, displaying in the clearest manner the virtues which I have enumerated and described above.

III

III. (12) But that he himself is the most admirable of all the lawgivers who have ever lived in any country either among the Greeks or among the barbarians, and that his are the most admirable of all laws, and truly divine, omitting no one particular which they ought to comprehend, there is the clearest proof possible in this fact, the laws of other lawgivers, (13) if any one examines them by his reason, he will find to be put in motion in an innumerable multitude of pretexts, either because of wars, or of tyrannies, or of some other unexpected events which come upon nations through the various alterations and innovations of fortune; and very often luxury, abounding in all kind of superfluity and unbounded extravagance, has overturned laws, from the multitude not being able to bear unlimited prosperity, but having a tendency to become insolent through satiety, and insolence is in opposition to law. (14) But the enactments of this lawgiver are firm, not shaken by commotions, not liable to alteration, but stamped as it were with the seal of nature herself, and they remain firm and lasting from the day on which they were first promulgated to the present one, and there may well be a hope that they will remain to all future time, as being immortal, as long as the sun and the moon, and the whole heaven and the whole world shall endure. (15) At all events, though the nation of the Hebrews experienced so many changes both in the direction of prosperity and of the opposite destiny, no one, no not even the very smallest and most unimportant of all his commandments was changed, since every one, as it seems, honoured their venerable and godlike character; (16) and what neither famine, nor pestilence, nor war, nor sovereign, nor tyrant, nor the rise of any passions or evil feelings against either soul or body, nor any other evil, whether inflicted by God or deriving its rise from men, ever dissolved, can surely never be looked upon by us in any other light than as objects of all admiration, and beyond all powers of description in respect of their excellence.

IV

IV. (17) But this is not so entirely wonderful, although it may fairly by itself be considered a thing of great intrinsic importance, that his laws were kept securely and immutably from all time; but this is more wonderful by far, as it seems, that not only the Jews, but that also almost every other nation, and especially those who make the greatest account of virtue, have dedicated themselves to embrace and honour them, for they have received this especial honour above all other codes of laws, which is not given to any other code. (18) And a proof of this is to be found in the fact that of all the cities in Greece and in the territory of the barbarians, if one may so say, speaking generally, there is not one single city which pays any respect to the laws of another state. In fact, a city scarcely adheres to its own laws with any constancy for ever, but continually modifies them, and adapts them to the changes of times and circumstances. (19) The Athenians rejected the customs and laws of the Lacedaemonians, and so did the Lacedaemonians repudiate the laws of the Athenians. Nor, again, in the countries of the barbarians do the Egyptians keep the laws of the Scythians, nor do the Scythians keep the laws of the Egyptians; nor, in short, do those who live in Asia attend to the laws which obtain in Europe, nor do the inhabitants of Europe respect the laws of the Asiatic nations. And, in short, it is very nearly an universal rule, from the rising of the sun to its extreme west, that every country, and nation, and city, is alienated from the laws and customs of foreign nations and states, and that they think that they are adding to the estimation in which they hold their own laws by despising those in use among other nations. (20) But this is not the case with our laws which Moses has given to us; for they lead after them and influence all nations, barbarians, and Greeks, the inhabitants of continents and islands, the eastern nations and the western,

Philo Judaeus

Europe and Asia; in short, the whole habitable world from one extremity to the other. (21) For what man is there who does not honour that sacred seventh day, granting in consequence a relief and relaxation from labour, for himself and for all those who are near to him, and that not to free men only, but also to slaves, and even to beasts of burden; (22) for the holiday extends even to every description of animal, and to every beast whatever which performs service to man, like slaves obeying their natural master, and it affects even every species of plant and tree; for there is no shoot, and no branch, and no leaf even which it is allowed to cut or to pluck on that day, nor any fruit which it is lawful to gather; but everything is at liberty and in safety on that day, and enjoys, as it were, perfect freedom, no one ever touching them, in obedience to a universal proclamation. (23) Again, who is there who does not pay all due respect and honour to that which is called "the fast," and especially to that great yearly one which is of a more austere and venerable character than the ordinary solemnity at the full moon? on which, indeed, much pure wine is drunk, and costly entertainments are provided, and everything which relates to eating and drinking is supplied in the most unlimited profusion, by which the insatiable pleasures of the belly are inflamed and increased. (24) But on this fast it is not lawful to take any food or any drink, in order that no bodily passion may at all disturb or hinder the pure operations of the mind; but these passions are wont to be generated by fulness and satiety, so that at this time men feast, propitiating the Father of the universe with holy prayers, by which they are accustomed to solicit pardon for their former sins, and the acquisition and enjoyment of new blessings.

V

V. (25) And that beauty and dignity of the legislation of Moses is honoured not among the Jews only, but also by all other nations, is plain, both from what has been already said and from what I am about to state. (26) In olden time the laws were written in the Chaldaean language, and for a long time they remained in the same condition as at first, not changing their language as long as their beauty had not made them known to other nations; (27) but when, from the daily and uninterrupted respect shown to them by those to whom they had been given, and from their ceaseless observance of their ordinances, other nations also obtained an understanding of them, their reputation spread over all lands; for what was really good, even though it may through envy be overshadowed for a short time, still in time shines again through the intrinsic excellence of its nature. Some persons, thinking it a scandalous thing that these laws should only be known among one half portion of the human race, namely, among the barbarians, and that the Greek nation should be wholly and entirely ignorant of them, turned their attention to their translation. (28) And since this undertaking was an important one, tending to the general advantage, not only of private persons, but also of rulers, of whom the number was not great, it was entrusted to kings and to the most illustrious of all kings. (29) Ptolemy, surnamed Philadelphus, was the third in succession after Alexander, the monarch who subdued Egypt; and he was, in all virtues which can be displayed in government, the most excellent sovereign, not only of all those of his time, but of all that ever lived; so that even now, after the lapse of so many generations, his fame is still celebrated, as having left many instances and monuments of his magnanimity in the cities and districts of his kingdom, so that even now it is come to be a sort of proverbial expression to call excessive magnificence, and zeal, for honour and splendour in preparation, Philadelphian, from his name; (30) and, in a word, the whole family of the Ptolemies was exceedingly eminent and conspicuous above all other royal families, and among the Ptolemies, Philadelphus was the most illustrious; for all the rest put together scarcely did as many glorious and praiseworthy actions as this one king did by himself, being, as it were, the leader of the herd, and in a manner the head of all the kings.

VI

VI. (31) He, then, being a sovereign of this character, and having conceived a great admiration for and love of the legislation of Moses, conceived the idea of having our laws translated into the Greek language; and immediately he sent out ambassadors to the high-priest and king of Judea, for they were the same person. (32) And having explained his wishes, and having requested him to pick him out a number of men, of perfect fitness for the task, who should translate the law, the high-priest, as was natural, being greatly pleased, and thinking that the king had only felt the inclination to undertake a work of such a character from having been influenced by the providence of God, considered, and with great care selected the most respectable of the Hebrews whom he had about him, who in addition to their knowledge of their national scriptures, had also been well instructed in Grecian literature, and cheerfully sent them. (33) And when they arrived at the king's court they were hospitably received by the king; and while they feasted, they in return feasted their entertainer with witty and virtuous conversation; for he made experiment of the wisdom of each individual among them, putting to them a succession of new and extraordinary questions; and they, since the time did not allow of their being prolix in their answers, replied with great propriety and fidelity as if they were delivering apophthegms which they had already prepared. (34) So when they had won his approval, they immediately began to fulfil the objects for which that honourable embassy had been sent; and considering among themselves how important the affair was, to translate laws which had been divinely given by direct inspiration, since they were not able either to take away anything, or to add anything, or to alter anything, but were bound to preserve the original form and character of the whole composition, they looked out for the most completely purified place of all the spots on the outside of the city. For the places within the walls, as being filled with all kinds of animals, were held in suspicion by them by reason of the diseases and deaths of some, and the accursed actions of those who were in health. (35) The island of Pharos lies in front of Alexandria, the neck of which runs out like a sort of tongue towards the city, being surrounded with water of no great depth, but chiefly with shoals and shallow water, so that the great noise and roaring from the beating of the waves is kept at a considerable distance, and so mitigated. (36) They judged this place to be the most suitable of all the spots in the neighbourhood for them to enjoy quiet and tranquillity in, so that they might associate with the laws alone in their minds; and there they remained, and having taken the sacred scriptures, they lifted up them and their hands also to heaven, entreating of God that they might not fail in their object. And he assented to their prayers, that the greater part, or indeed the universal race of mankind might be benefited, by using these philosophical and entirely beautiful commandments for the correction of their lives.

VII

VII. (37) Therefore, being settled in a secret place, and nothing even being present with them except the elements of nature, the earth, the water, the air, and the heaven, concerning the creation of which they were going in the first place to explain the sacred account; for the account of the creation of the world is the beginning of the law; they, like men inspired, prophesied, not one saying one thing and another another, but every one of them employed the self-same nouns and verbs, as if some unseen prompter had suggested all their language to them. (38) And yet who is there who does not know that every language, and the Greek language above all others, is rich in a variety of words, and that it is possible to vary a sentence and to paraphrase the same idea, so as to set it forth in a great variety of manners, adapting many different forms of expression to it at different times. But this, they say, did not happen at all in the case of this translation of the law, but that, in every case, exactly corresponding Greek words were employed to translate literally the appropriate Chaldaic words, being adapted with exceeding propriety to the matters which were to be explained; (39) for just as I suppose the things which are proved in geometry and logic do not admit any variety of explanation, but the proposition which was set forth from the beginning remains unaltered, in like manner I conceive did these men find words precisely and literally corresponding to the things, which words were alone, or in the greatest possible degree, destined to explain with clearness and force the matters which it was desired to reveal. (40) And there is a very evident proof of this; for if Chaldaeans were to learn the Greek language, and if Greeks were to learn Chaldaean, and if each were to meet with those scriptures in both languages, namely, the Chaldaic and the translated version, they would admire and reverence them both as sisters, or rather as one and the same both in their facts and in their language; considering these translators not mere interpreters but hierophants and prophets to whom it had been granted it their honest and guileless minds to go along with the most pure spirit of Moses. (41) On which account, even to this very day, there is every year a solemn assembly held and a festival celebrated in the island of Pharos, to which not only the Jews but a great number of persons of other nations sail across, reverencing the place in which the first light of interpretation shone forth, and thanking God for that ancient piece of beneficence which was always young and fresh. (42) And after the prayers and the giving of thanks some of them pitched their tents on the shore, and some of them lay down without any tents in the open air on the sand of the shore, and feasted with their relations and friends, thinking the shore at that time a more beautiful abode than the furniture of the king's palace. (43) In this way those admirable, and incomparable, and most desirable laws were made known to all people, whether private individuals or kings, and this too at a period when the nation had not been prosperous for a long time. And it is generally the case that a cloud is thrown over the affairs of those who are not flourishing, so that but little is known of them; (44) and then, if they make any fresh start and begin to improve, how great is the increase of their renown and glory? I think that in that case every nation, abandoning all their own individual customs, and utterly disregarding their national laws, would change and come over to the honour of such a people only; for their laws shining in connection with, and simultaneously with, the prosperity of the nation, will obscure all others, just as the rising sun obscures the stars.

VIII

VIII. (45) Now what has been here said is quite sufficient for the abundant praise of Moses as a lawgiver. But there is another more extensive praise which his own holy writings themselves contain, and it is to them that we must now turn for the purpose of exhibiting the virtue of him who compiled them. (46) Now these writings of Moses may be divided into several parts; one of which is the historical part, another is occupied with commands and prohibitions, respecting which part we will speak at some other time when we have first of all accurately examined that part which comes first in the order of our division. (47) Again, the historical part may be subdivided into the account of the creation of the world, and the genealogical part. And the genealogical part, or the history of the different families, may be divided into the accounts of the punishment of the wicked, and of the honours bestowed on the just; we must also explain on what account it was that he began his history of the giving of the law with these particulars, and placed the commandments and prohibitions in the second order; (48) for he was not like any ordinary compiler of history, studying to leave behind him records of ancient transactions as memorials to future ages for the mere sake of affording pleasure without any advantage; but he traced back the most ancient events from the beginning of the world, commencing with the creation of the universe, in order to make known two most necessary principles. First, that the same being was the father and creator of the world, and likewise the lawgiver of truth; secondly, that the man who adhered to these laws, and clung closely to a connection with and obedience to nature, would live in a manner corresponding to the arrangement of the universe with a perfect harmony and union, between his words and his actions and between his actions and his words.

IX

IX. (49) Now of all other lawgivers, some the moment that they have promulgated positive commands as to what it is right to do and what it is right not to do, proceed to appoint punishments for those who transgress those laws; but others, who appear to have proceeded on a better plan, have not begun in this manner, but, having first of all built and established their city in accordance with reason, have then adapted to this city which they have built, that constitution which they have considered the best adapted and most akin to it, and have confirmed this constitution by the giving of laws. (50) But he, thinking the first of the two courses above mentioned to be tyrannical and despotic, as indeed it is, namely, that of laying positive commands on persons as if they were not free men but slaves, without offering them any alleviation; and that the second course was better indeed, but was not entirely to be commended, must appear to all judges to be superior in each of the above considerations. (51) For both in his commandments and also in his prohibitions he suggests and recommends rather than commands, endeavouring with many prefaces and perorations to suggest the greater part of the precepts that he desires to enforce, desiring rather to allure men to virtue than to drive them to it, and looking upon the foundation and beginning of a city made with hands, which he has made the commencement of his work a commencement beneath the dignity of his laws, looking rather with the most accurate eye of his mind at the importance and beauty of his whole legislative system, and thinking it too excellent and too divine to be limited as it were by any circle of things on earth; and therefore he has related the creation of that great metropolis, the world, thinking his laws the most fruitful image and likeness of the constitution of the whole world.

X

X. (52) At all events if any one were inclined to examine with accuracy the powers of each individual and particular law, he will find them all aiming at the harmony of the universe, and corresponding to the law of eternal nature: (53) on which account those men who have had unbounded prosperity bestowed upon them, and all things tending to the production of health of body, and riches, and glory, and all other external parts of good fortune, but who have rejected virtue, and have chosen crafty wickedness, and all others kinds of vice, not through compulsion, but of their own spontaneous free will, looking upon that which is the greatest of all evils as the greatest possible advantage, he looks upon as enemies not of mankind only, but of the entire heaven and world, and says that they are awaiting, not any ordinary punishments, but new and extraordinary ones, which that constant assessor of God, justice, who detests wickedness, invents and inflicts terribly upon them, turning against them the most powerful elements of the universe, water and fire, so that at appointed times some are destroyed by deluges, others are burnt with fire, and perish in that manner. (54) The seas were raised up, and the rivers both such as flow everlastingly, and the winter torrents were swollen and washed away, and carried off all the cities in the plain; and those in the mountain country were destroyed by incessant and irresistible impetuosity of rain, ceasing neither by day nor by night, (55) and when at a subsequent period the race of mankind had again increased from those who had been spared, and had become very numerous, since the succeeding generations did not take the calamities which had befallen their ancestors as a lesson to teach themselves wisdom and moderation, but turned to acts of intemperance and became studiers of evil practices, God determined to destroy them with fire. (56) Therefore on this occasion, as the holy scriptures tell us, thunderbolts fell from heaven, and burnt up those wicked men and their cities; and even to this day there are seen in Syria monuments of the unprecedented destruction that fell upon them, in the ruins, and ashes, and sulphur, and smoke, and dusky flame which still is sent up from the ground as of a fire smouldering beneath; (57) and in this way it came to pass that those wicked men were punished with the aforesaid chastisements, while those who were eminent for virtue and piety were well off, receiving rewards worthy of their virtue. (58) But when the whole of that district was thus burnt, inhabitants and all, by the impetuous rush of the heavenly fire, one single man in the country, a sojourner, was preserved by the providence of God because he had never shared in the transgressions of the natives, though sojourners in general were in the habit of adopting the customs of the foreign nations, among which they might be settled, for the sake of their own safety, since, if they despised them, they might be in danger from the inhabitants of the land. And yet this man had not attained to any perfection of wisdom, so as to be thought worthy of such an honour by reason of the perfect excellence of his nature; but he was spared only because he did not join the multitude who were inclined to luxury and effeminacy, and who pursued every kind of pleasure and indulged every kind of appetite, gratifying them abundantly, and inflaming them as one might inflame fire by heaping upon it plenty of rough fuel.

XI

XI. (59) But in the great deluge I may almost say that the whole of the human race was destroyed, while the history tells us that the house of Noah alone was preserved free from all evil, inasmuch as the father and governor of the house was a man who had never committed any intentional or voluntary wickedness. And it is worth while to relate the manner of his preservation as the sacred scriptures deliver it to us, both on account of the extraordinary character of it, and also that it may lead to an improvement in our own dispositions and lives. (60) For he, being considered a fit man, not only to be exempted from the common calamity which was to overwhelm the world, but also to be himself the beginning of a second generation of men, in obedience to the divine commands which were conveyed to him by the word of God, built a most enormous fabric of wood, three hundred cubits in length, and fifty in width, and thirty in height, and having prepared a number of connected chambers within it, both on the ground floor and in the upper story, the whole building consisting of three, and in some parts of four stories, and having prepared food, brought into it some of every description of animals, beasts and also birds, both male and female, in order to preserve a means of propagating the different species in the times that should come hereafter; (61) for he knew that the nature of God was merciful, and that even if the subordinate species were destroyed, still there would be a germ in the entire genus which should be safe from destruction, for the sake of preserving a similitude to those animals which had hitherto existed, and of preventing anything that had been deliberately called into existence from being utterly destroyed.

XII

XII. On which account everything was now made obedient to Noah; and even beasts, which up to that time had been savage, became gentle, and being tamed, followed him as their shepherd and superintendent; (62) and after they had all entered into the ark, if any one had beheld the entire collection, he would not have been wrong if he had said that it was a representation of the whole earth, containing, as it did, every kind of animal, of which the whole earth had previously produced innumerable species, and will hereafter produce such again. (63) And what was expected happened at no long period after; for the evil abated, and the destruction caused by the deluge was diminished every day, the rain being checked, and the water which had been spread over the whole earth, being partly dried up by the flame of the sun, and partly returning into the chasms and rivers, and other channels and receptacles in the earth; for, as if God had issued a command to that effect, every nature received back, as a necessary repayment of a loan, what it had lent, that is, every sea, and fountain, and river, received back their waters; and every stream returned into its appropriate channel. (64) But after the purification, in this way, of all the things beneath the moon, the earth being thus washed and appearing new again, and such as it appeared to be when it was at first created, along with the entire universe, Noah came forth out of his wooden edifice, himself and his wife, and his sons and their wives, and with his family there came forth likewise, in one company, all the races of animals which had gone in with them, in order to the generation and propagation of similar creatures in future. (65) These are the rewards and honours for pre-eminent excellence given to good men, by means of which, not only did they themselves and their families obtain safety, having escaped from the greatest dangers which were thus aimed against all men all over the earth, by the change in the character of the elements; but they became also the founders of a new generation, and the chiefs of a second period of the world, being left behind as sparks of the most excellent kind of creatures, namely, of men, man having received the supremacy over all earthly creatures whatsoever, being a kind of copy of the powers of God, a visible image of his invisible nature, a created image of an uncreated and immortal Original. [1170]

XIII

XIII. (66) We have already, then, gone through two parts of the life of Moses, discussing his character in his capacity of a king and of a lawgiver. We must now consider him in a third light, as fulfilling the office of the priesthood. Now this man, Moses, practised beyond all other men that which is the most important and most indispensable virtue in a chief priest, namely, piety, partly because he was endowed with most admirable natural qualities; and philosophy, receiving his nature like a fertile field, cultivated and improved it by the contemplation of excellent and beautiful doctrines, and did not dismiss it until all the fruits of virtue were brought to perfection in him, in respect of words and actions. (67) Therefore he, with a few other men, was dear to God and devoted to God, being inspired by heavenly love, and honouring the Father of the universe above all things, and being in return honoured by him in a particular manner. And it was an honour well adapted to the wise man to be allowed to serve the true and living God. Now the priesthood has for its duty the service of God. Of this honour, then, Moses was thought worthy, than which there is no greater honour in the whole world, being instructed by the sacred oracles of God in everything that related to the sacred offices and ministrations.

XIV

XIV. (68) But, in the first place, before assuming that office, it was necessary for him to purify not only his soul but also his body, so that it should be connected with and defiled by no passion, but should be pure from everything which is of a mortal nature, from all meat and drink, and from all connection with women. (69) And this last thing, indeed, he had despised for a long time, and almost from the first moment that he began to prophesy and to feel a divine inspiration, thinking that it was proper that he should at all times be ready to give his whole attention to the commands of God. And how he neglected all meat and drink for forty days together, evidently because he had more excellent food than that in those contemplations with which he was inspired from above from heaven, by which also he was improved in the first instance in his mind, and, secondly, in his body, through his soul, increasing in strength and health both of body and soul, so that those who saw him afterwards could not believe that he was the same person. (70) For, having gone up into the loftiest and most sacred mountain in that district in accordance with the divine commands, a mountain which was very difficult of access and very hard to ascend, he is said to have remained there all that time without eating any of that food even which is necessary for life; and, as I said before, he descended again forty days afterwards, being much more beautiful in his face than when he went up, so that those who saw him wondered and were amazed, and could no longer endure to look upon him with their eyes, inasmuch as his countenance shone like the light of the sun.

XV

XV. (71) And while he was still abiding in the mountain he was initiated in the sacred will of God, being instructed in all the most important matters which relate to his priesthood, those which come first in order being the commands of God respecting the building of a temple and all its furniture. (72) If, then, they had already occupied the country into which they were migrating, it would have been necessary for them to have erected a most magnificent temple of the most costly stone in some place unincumbered with wood, and to have built vast walls around it, and abundant and wellfurnished houses for the keepers of the temple, calling the place itself the holy city. (73) But, as they were still wandering in the wilderness, it was more suitable for people who had as yet no settled habitation to have a moveable temple, that so, in all their journeyings, and military expeditions, and encampments, they might be able to offer up sacrifices, and might not feel the want of any of the things which related to their holy ministrations, and which those who dwell in cities require to have. (74) Therefore Moses now determined to build a tabernacle, a most holy edifice, the furniture of which he was instructed how to supply by precise commands from God, given to him while he was on the mount, contemplating with his soul the incorporeal patterns of bodies which were about to be made perfect, in due similitude to which he was bound to make the furniture, that it might be an imitation perceptible by the outward senses of an archetypal sketch and pattern, appreciable only by the intellect; (75) for it was suitable and consistent for the task of preparing and furnishing the temple to be entrusted to the real high priest, that he might with all due perfection and propriety make all his ministrations in the performance of his sacred duties correspond to the works which he was now to make.

XVI

XVI. (76) Therefore the general form of the model was stamped upon the mind of the prophet, being accurately painted and fashioned beforehand invisibly without any materials, in species which were not apparent to the eye; and the completion of the work was made in the similitude of the model, the maker giving an accurate representation of the impression in material substances corresponding to each part of the model, (77) and the fashion of the building was as follows. There were eight and forty pillars of cedar, which is the most incorruptible of all woods, cut out of solid trunks of great beauty, and they were all veneered with gold of great thickness. Then under each pillar there were placed two silver pedestals to support it, and on the top of each was placed one golden capital; (78) and of these pillars the architect arranged forty along the length of the tabernacle, one half of them, or twenty, on each side, placing nothing between them, but arranging them and uniting them all in regular order, and close together, so that they might present the appearance of one solid wall; and he ranged the other eight along the inner breadth, placing six in the middle space, and two at the extreme corners, one on each side at the right and left of the centre. Again, at the entrance he placed four others, like the first in all other respects except that they had only one pedestal instead of two, as those opposite to them had, and behind them he placed five more on the outside differing only in the pedestals, for the pedestals of these last were made of brass. (79) So that all the pillars of the tabernacle taken together, besides the two at the corners which could not be seen, were fifty-five in number, all conspicuous, being the number made by the addition of all the numbers from the unit to the complete and perfect decade. (80) And if any were inclined to count those five pillars of the outer vestibule in the open air separately, as being in the outer court as it was called, there will then be left that most holy number of fifty, being the power of a rectangular triangle, which is the foundation of the creation of the universe, and is here entirely completed by the pillars inside the tabernacle; there being first of all forty, twenty on either side, and those in the middle being six, without counting those which were out of sight and concealed at the corners, and those opposite to the entrance, from which the veil was suspended, being four; (81) and the reason for which I reckon the other five with the first fifty, and again why I separate them from the fifty, I will now explain. The number five is the number of the external senses, and the external sense in man at one time inclines towards external things, and at another time comes back again upon the mind, being as it were a kind of handmaid of the laws of its nature; on which account it is that the architect has here allotted a central position to the five pillars, for those which are inside of them leant towards the innermost shrine of the tabernacle, which under a symbol is appreciable only by the intellect; and the outermost pillars, which are in the open air, and in the outer courtyard, and which are also perceptible by the external senses, (82) in reference to which fact it is that they are said to have differed from the others only in the pedestals, for they were made of brass. But since the mind is the principal thing in us, having an authority over the external senses, and since that which is an object of the external senses is the extremity, and as it were the pedestal or foundation of it, the architect has likened the mind to gold, and the object of the external sense to brass. (83) And these are the measures of the pillars, they are ten cubits in length, and five cubits and a half in width, in order that the tabernacle may be seen to be of equal dimensions in all its parts.

XVII

XVII. (84) Moreover the architect surrounded the tabernacle with very beautiful woven work of all kinds, employing work of hyacinth colour, and purple, and scarlet, and fine linen for the tapestry; for he caused to be wrought ten cloths, which in the sacred scriptures he has called curtains, of the kinds which I have just mentioned, every one of them being eight and twenty cubits in length, and extending four cubits in width, in order that the complete number of the decade, and also the number four, which is the essence of the decade, and also the number twenty-eight, which is likewise a perfect number, being equal to its parts; and also the number forty, the most prolific and productive of all numbers, in which number they say that man was fashioned in the workshop of nature. (85) Therefore the eight and twenty cubits of the curtains have this distribution: there are ten along the roof, for that is the width of the tabernacle, and the rest are placed along the sides, on each side nine, which are extended so as to cover and conceal the pillars, one cubit from the floor being left uncovered in order that the beautiful and holy looking embroidery might not be dragged. (86) And of the forty which are included in the calculation and made up of the width of the ten curtains, the length takes thirty, for such is the length of the tabernacle, and the chamber behind takes nine. And the remaining one is in the outer vestibule, that it may be the bond to unite the whole circumference. (87) And the outer vestibule is overshadowed by the veil; and the curtains themselves are nearly the same as veils, not only because they cover the roof and the walls, but also because they are woven and embroidered by the same figures, and with hyacinth colour, and purple, and scarlet, and fine linen. And the veil, and that thing, too, which was called the covering, was made of the same things. That which was within was placed along the five pillars, that the innermost shrine might be concealed; and that which was outside being placed along the five pillars, that no one of those who were not holy men might be able from any secret or distant place to behold the holy rites and ceremonies.

XVIII

XVIII. (88) Moreover, he chose the materials of this embroidery, selecting with great care what was most excellent out of an infinite quantity, choosing materials equal in number to the elements of which the world was made, and having a direct relation to them; the elements being the earth and the water, and the air and the fire. For the fine flax is produced from the earth, and the purple from the water, and the hyacinth colour is compared to the air (for, by nature, it is black), and the scarlet is likened to fire, because each is of a red colour; for it followed of necessity that those who were preparing a temple made by hands for the Father and Ruler of the universe must take essences similar to those of which he made the universe itself. (89) Therefore the tabernacle was built in the manner that has been here described, like a holy temple. And all around it a sacred precinct extended a hundred cubits in length and fifty cubits in width, having pillars all placed at an equal distance of five cubits from one another, so that there were in all sixty pillars; and they were divided so that forty were placed along the length and twenty along the breadth of the tabernacle, one half on each side. (90) And the material of which the pillars were composed was cedar within, and on the surface without silver; and the pedestals of all of them were made of brass, and the height was equal to five cubits. For it seemed to the architect to be proper to make the height of what was called the hall equal to one half of the entire length, that so the tabernacle might appear to be elevated to double its real height. And there were thin curtains fitted to the pillars along their entire length and breadth, resembling so many sails, in order that no one might be able to enter in who was not pure.

XIX

XIX. (91) And the situation was as follows. In the middle was placed a tent, being in length thirty cubits and in width ten cubits, including the depth of the pillars. And it was distant from the centre space by three intervals of equal distance, two being at the sides and one along the back chamber. And the interval between was by measurement twenty cubits. But along the vestibule, as was natural, by reason of the number of those who entered, the distance between them was increased and extended to fifty cubits and more; for in this way the hundred pillars of the hall were intended to be made up, twenty being along the chamber behind, and those which the tent contained, thirty in number, being included in the same calculation with the fifty at the entrances; (92) for the outer vestibule of the tabernacle was placed as a sort of boundary in the middle of the two fifties, the one, I mean, towards the east where the entrance was, and the other being on the west, in which direction the length of the tabernacle and the surrounding wall behind was. (93) Moreover, another outer vestibule, of great size and exceeding beauty, was made at the beginning of the entrance into the hall, by means of four pillars, along which was stretched the embroidered curtain in the same manner as the inner curtains were stretched along the tabernacle, and wrought also of similar materials; (94) and with this there were also many sacred vessels made, an ark, and a candlestick, and a table, and an altar of incense, and an altar of sacrifice. Now, the altar of sacrifice was placed in the open air, right opposite to the entrances of the tabernacle, being distant from it just so far as was necessary to give the ministering officers room to perform the sacrifices that were offered up every day.

XX

XX. (95) But the ark was in the innermost shrine, in the inaccessible holy of holies, behind curtains; being gilded in a most costly and magnificent manner within and without, the covering of which was like to that which is called in the sacred scriptures the mercy-seat. (96) Its length and width are accurately described, but its depth is not mentioned, being chiefly compared to and resembling a geometrical superficies; so that it appears to be an emblem, if looked at physically, of the merciful power of God; and, if regarded in a moral point of view, of a certain intellect spontaneously propitious to itself, which is especially desirous to contract and destroy, by means of the love of simplicity united with knowledge, that vain opinion which raises itself up to an unreasonable height and puffs itself up without any grounds. (97) But the ark is the depository of the laws, for in that are placed the holy oracles of God, which were given to Moses; and the covering of the ark, which is called the mercy-seat, is a foundation for two winged creatures to rest upon, which are called, in the native language of the Hebrews, cherubim, but as the Greeks would translate the word, vast knowledge and science. (98) Now some persons say, that these cherubim are the symbols of the two hemispheres, placed opposite to and fronting one another, the one beneath the earth and the other above the earth, for the whole heaven is endowed with wings. (99) But I myself should say, that what is here represented under a figure are the two most ancient and supreme powers of the divine God, namely, his creative and his kingly power; and his creative power is called God; according to which he arranged, and created, and adorned this universe, and his kingly power is called Lord, by which he rules over the beings whom he has created, and governs them with justice and firmness; (100) for he, being the only true living God, is also really the Creator of the world; since he brought things which had no existence into being; and he is also a king by nature, because no one can rule over beings that have been created more justly than he who created them.

XXI

XXI. (101) And in the space between the five pillars and the four pillars, is that space which is, properly speaking, the space before the temple, being cut off by two curtains of woven work, the inner one of which is called the veil, and the outer one is called the covering: and the remaining three vessels, of those which I have enumerated, were placed as follows:--The altar of incense was placed in the middle, between earth and water, as a symbol of gratitude, which it was fitting should be offered up, on account of the things that had been done for the Hebrews on both these elements, for these elements have had the central situation of the world allotted to them. (102) The candlestick was placed on the southern side of the tabernacle, since by it the maker intimates, in a figurative manner, the motions of the stars which give light; for the sun, and the moon, and the rest of the stars, being all at a great distance from the northern parts of the universe, make all their revolutions in the south. And from this candlestick there proceeded six branches, three on each side, projecting from the candlestick in the centre, so as altogether to complete the number of seven; (103) and in all the seven there were seven candles and seven lights, being symbols of those seven stars which are called planets by those men who are versed in natural philosophy; for the sun, like the candlestick, being placed in the middle of the other six, in the fourth rank, gives light to the three planets which are above him, and to those of equal number which are below him, adapting to circumstances the musical and truly divine instrument.

XXII

XXII. (104) And the table, on which bread and salt are laid, was placed on the northern side, since it is the north which is the most productive of winds, and because too all nourishment proceeds from heaven and earth, the one giving rain, and the other bringing to perfection all seeds by means of the irrigation of water; (105) for the symbols of heaven and earth are placed side by side, as the holy scripture shows, the candlestick being the symbol of heaven, and that which is truly called the altar of incense, on which all the fumigatory offerings are made, being the emblem of the things of earth. (106) But it became usual to call the altar which was in the open air the altar of sacrifice, as being that which preserved and took care of the sacrifices; intimating, figuratively, the consuming power of these things, and not the lambs and different parts of the victims which were offered, and which were naturally calculated to be destroyed by fire, but the intention of him who offered them; (107) for if the man who made the offerings was foolish and ignorant, the sacrifices were no sacrifices, the victims were not sacred or hallowed, the prayers were ill-omened, and liable to be answered by utter destruction, for even when they appear to be received, they produce no remission of sins but only a reminding of them. (108) But if the man who offers the sacrifice be bold and just, then the sacrifice remains firm, even if the flesh of the victim be consumed, or rather, I might say, even if no victim be offered up at all; for what can be a real and true sacrifice but the piety of a soul which loves God? The gratitude of which is blessed with immortality, and without being recorded in writing is engraved on a pillar in the mind of God, being made equally everlasting with the sun, and moon, and the universal world.

XXIII

XXIII. (109) After these things the architect of the tabernacle next prepared a sacred dress for him who was to be appointed high priest, having in its embroidery a most exceedingly beautiful and admirable work; and the robe was two-fold; one part of which was called the under-robe, and the other the robe over the shoulders. (110) Now the under-robe was of a more simple form and character, for it was entirely of hyacinthine colours, except the lowest and exterior portions, and these were ornamented with golden pomegranates, and bells, and wreaths of flowers; (111) but the robe over the shoulders or mantle was a most beautiful and skilful work, and was made with most perfect skill of all the aforesaid kinds of material, of hyacinth colour, and purple, and fine linen, and scarlet, gold thread being entwined and embroidered in it. For the leaves were divided into fine hairs, and woven in with every thread, (112) and on the collar stones were fitted in, two being costly emeralds of exceeding value, on which the names of the patriarchs of the tribes were engraved, six on each, making twelve in all; and on the breast were twelve other precious stones, differing in colour like seals, in four rows of three stones each, and these were fitted in what was called the logeum (113) and the logeum was made square and double, as a sort of foundation, that it mighty bear on it, as an image, two virtues, manifestation and truth; and the whole was fastened to the mantle by fine golden chains, and fastened to it so that it might never get loose; (114) and a golden leaf was wrought like a crown, having four names engraved on it which may only be mentioned or heard by holy men having their ears and their tongues purified by wisdom, and by no one else at all in any place whatever. (115) And this holy prophet Moses calls the name, a name of four letters, making them perhaps symbols of the primary numbers, the unit, the number two, the number three, the number four: since all things are comprised in the number four, namely, a point, and a line, and a superficies, and a solid, and the measures of all things, and the most excellent symphonies of music, and the diatessaron in the sesquitertial proportion, and the chord in fifths, in the ratio of one and a half to one, and the diapason in the double ratio, and the double diapason in the fourfold ratio. Moreover, the number four has an innumerable list of other virtues likewise, the greater part of which we have discussed with accuracy in our dissertation on numbers. (116) And in it there was a mitre, in order that the leaf might not touch the head; and there was also a cidaris made, for the kings of the eastern countries are accustomed to use a cidaris, instead of a diadem.

XXIV

XXIV. (117) Such, then, is the dress of the high priest. But we must not omit to mention the signification which it conceals beneath both in its whole and in its parts. In its whole it is a copy and representation of the world; and the parts are a representation of the separate parts of the world. (118) And we must begin with the long robe reaching down to the feet of the wearer. This tunic is wholly of the colour of a hyacinth, so as to be a representation of the air; for by nature the air is black, and in a measure it reaches down from the highest parts to the feet, being stretched from the parts about the moon, as far as the extremities of the earth, and being diffused everywhere. On which account also, the tunic reaches from the chest to the feet, and is spread over the whole body, (119) and unto it there is attached a fringe of pomegranates round the ankles, and flowers, and bells. Now the flowers are an emblem of the earth; for it is from the earth that all flowers spring and bloom; but the pomegranates (rhoiskoi) are a symbol of water, since, indeed, they derive their name from the flowing (rhysis) of water, being very appropriately named; and the bells are the emblem of the concord and harmony that exist between these things; for neither is the earth without the water, nor the water without the earthly substance, sufficient for the production of anything; but that can only be effected by the meeting and combination of both. (120) And the place itself is the most distinct possible evidence of what is here meant to be expressed; for as the pomegranates, and the flowers, and the bells, are placed in the hem of the garment which reaches to the feet, so likewise the things of which they are the symbols, namely, the earth and water, have had the lowest position in the world assigned to them, and being in strict accord with the harmony of the universe, they display their own particular powers in definite periods of time and suitable seasons. (121) Now of the three elements, out of which and in which all the different kinds of things which are perceptible by the outward senses and perishable are formed, namely, the air, the water and the earth, the garment which reached down to the feet in conjunction with the ornaments which were attached to that part of it which was about the ankles have been plainly shown to be appropriate symbols; for as the tunic is one, and as the aforesaid three elements are all of one species, since they all have all their revolutions and changes beneath the moon, and as to the garment there attached the pomegranates, and the flowers; so also in certain manner the earth and the water may be said to be attached to and suspended from the air, for the air is their chariot. (122) And our argument will be able to bring forth twenty probable reasons that the mantle over the shoulders is an emblem of heaven. For in the first place, the two emeralds on the shoulderblades, which are two round stones, are, in the opinion of some persons who have studied the subject, emblems of those stars which are the rulers of night and day, namely, the sun and moon; or rather, as one might argue with more correctness and a nearer approach to truth, they are the emblems of the two hemispheres; for, like those two stones, the portion below the earth and that over the earth are both equal, and neither of them is by nature adapted to be either increased or diminished like the moon. (123) And the colour of the stars is an additional evidence in favour of my view; for to the glance of the eye the appearance of the heaven does resemble an emerald; and it follows necessarily that six names are engraved on each of the stones, because each of the hemispheres cuts the zodiac in two parts, and in this way comprehends within itself six animals. (124) Then the twelve stones on the breast, which are not like one another in colour, and which are divided into four rows of three stones in each, what else can they be emblems of, except of the circle of the zodiac? For that also is divided into four parts, each consisting of three animals, by which divisions it makes up the seasons of the year, spring, summer, autumn, and winter, distinguishing the four changes, the two solstices, and the two equinoxes, each of which has its limit of three signs of this zodiac, by the revolutions of the sun, according to that unchangeable, and most lasting, and really divine ratio which exists in numbers; (125) on which account they attached it to that which is with great propriety called the logeum. For all the changes of the year and the seasons are arranged by well-defined, and stated, and firm reason; and, though this seems a most extraordinary and incredible thing, by their seasonable changes they display their undeviating and everlasting permanence and durability. (126) And it is said with great correctness, and exceeding beauty also, that the twelve stones all differ in their colour, and that no one of them resembles the other; for also in the zodiac each animal produces that colour which is akin to and belongs to itself, both in the air, and in the earth, and in the water; and it produces it likewise in all the affections which move them, and in all kinds of animals and of plants.

XXV

XXV. (127) And this logeum is described as double with great correctness; for reason is double, both in the universe and also in the nature of mankind, in the universe there is that reason which is conversant about incorporeal species which are like patterns as it were, from which that world which is perceptible only by the intellect was made, and also that which is concerned with the visible objects of sight, which are copies and imitations of those species above mentioned, of which the world which is perceptible by the outward senses was made. Again, in man there is one reason which is kept back, and another which finds vent in utterance: and the one is, as it were, a spring, and the other (that which is uttered) flows from it; and the place of the one is the dominant part, that is, the mind; but the place of the one which finds vent in utterance is the tongue, and the mouth, and all the rest of the organs of the voice. (128) And the architect assigned a quadrangular form to the logeum, intimating under an exceedingly beautiful figure, that both the reason of nature, and also that of man, ought to penetrate everywhere, and ought never to waver in any case; in reference to which, it is that he has also assigned to it the two virtues that have been already enumerated, manifestation and truth; for the reason of nature is true, and calculated to make manifest, and to explain everything; and the reason of the wise man, imitating that other reason, ought naturally, and appropriately to be completely sincere, honouring truth, and not obscuring anything through envy, the knowledge of which can benefit those to whom it would be explained; (129) not but what he has also assigned their two appropriate virtues to those two kinds of reason which exist in each of us, namely, that which is uttered and that which is kept concealed in the mind; for it is suitable to the mind that it should admit of no error or falsehood, and to explanation that it should not hinder anything that can conduce to the most accurate manifestation. (130) Therefore there is no advantage in reason which expends itself in dignified and pompous language, about things which are good and desirable, unless it is followed by consistent practice of suitable actions; on which account the architect has affixed the logeum to the robe which is worn over the shoulder, in order that it may never get loose, as he does not approve of the language being separated from the actions; for he puts forth the shoulder as the emblem of energy and action.

XXVI

XXVI. (131) Such then are the figurative meanings which he desires to indicate by the sacred vestments of the high priest; and instead of a diadem he represents a cidaris on the head, because he thinks it right that the man who is consecrated to God, as his high priest, should, during the time of his exercising his office be superior to all men, not only to all private individuals, but even to all kings; (132) and above this cidaris is a golden leaf, on which an engraving of four letters was impressed; by which letters they say that the name of the living God is indicated, since it is not possible that anything that it in existence, should exist without God being invoked; for it is his goodness and his power combined with mercy that is the harmony and uniter of all things. (133) The high priest, then, being equipped in this way, is properly prepared for the performance of all sacred ceremonies, that, whenever he enters the temple to offer up the prayers and sacrifices in use among his nation, all the world may likewise enter in with him, by means of the imitations of it which he bears about him, the garment reaching to his feet, being the imitation of the air, the pomegranate of the water, the flowery hem of the earth, and the scarlet dye of his robe being the emblem of fire; also, the mantle over his shoulders being a representation of heaven itself; the two hemispheres being further indicated by the round emeralds on the shoulder-blades, on each of which were engraved six characters equivalent to six signs of the zodiac; the twelve stones arranged on the breast in four rows of three stones each, namely the logeum, being also an emblem of that reason which holds together and regulates the universe. (134) For it was indispensable that the man who was consecrated to the Father of the world, should have as a paraclete, his son, the being most perfect in all virtue, to procure forgiveness of sins, and a supply of unlimited blessings; (135) perhaps, also, he is thus giving a previous warning to the servant of God, even if he is unable to make himself worthy of the Creator, of the world, at least to labour incessantly to make himself worthy of the world itself; the image of which he is clothed in, in a manner that binds him from the time that he puts it on, to bear about the pattern of it in his mind, so that he shall be in a manner changed from the nature of a man into the nature of the world, and, if one may say so (and one may by all means and at all times speak the plain truth in sincerity), become a little world himself.

XXVII

XXVII. (136) Again, outside the outer vestibule, at the entrance, is a brazen laver; the architect having not taken any mere raw material for the manufacture of it, as is very common, but having employed on its formation vessels which had been constructed with great care for other purposes; and which the women contributed with all imaginable zeal and eagerness, in rivalry of one another, competing with the men themselves in piety, having determined to enter upon a glorious contest, and to the utmost extent of their power to exert themselves so as not to fall short of their holiness. (137) For though no one enjoined them to do so, they, of their own spontaneous zeal and earnestness, contributed the mirrors with which they had been accustomed to deck and set off their beauty, as the most becoming first fruits of their modesty, and of the purity of their married life, and as one may say of the beauty of their souls. (138) The maker then thought it well to accept these offerings, and to melt them down, and to make nothing except the laver of them, in order that the priests who were about to enter the temple might be supplied from it, with water of purification for the purpose of performing the sacred ministrations which were appointed for them; washing their feet most especially, and their hands, as a symbol of their irreproachable life, and of a course of conduct which makes itself pure in all kinds of praiseworthy actions, proceeding not along the rough road of wickedness which one may more properly call no road at all, but keeping straight along the level and direct path of virtue. (139) Let him remember, says he, let him who is about to be sprinkled with the water of purification from this laver, remember that the materials of which this vessel was composed were mirrors, that he himself may look into his own mind as into a mirror; and if there is perceptible in it any deformity arising from some agitation unconnected with reason or from any pleasure which would excite us, and raise us up in hostility to reason, or from any pain which might mislead us and turn us from our purpose of proceeding by the straight road, or from any desire alluring us and even dragging us by force to the pursuit of present pleasures, he seeks to relieve and cure that, desiring only that beauty which is genuine and unadulterated. (140) For the beauty of the body consists in symmetry of parts, and in a good complexion, and a healthy firmness of flesh, having also but a short period during which it is in its prime; but the beauty of the mind consists in a harmony of doctrines and a perfect accord of virtues, which do not fade away or become impaired by lapse of time, but as long as they endure at all are constantly acquiring fresh vigour and renewed youth, being set off by the preeminent complexion of truth, and the agreement of its words with its actions, and of its actions with its words, and also of its designs with both.

XXVIII

XXVIII. (141) And when he had been taught the patterns of the sacred tabernacle, and had in turn himself taught those who were gifted with acute comprehension, and well-qualified by nature for the comprehension and execution of those works, which it was indispensably necessary should be made; then, as was natural, when the temple had been built and finished, it was fitting also, that most suitable persons should be appointed as priests, and should be instructed in what manner it was proper for them to offer up their sacrifices, and perform their sacred ministrations. (142) Accordingly, Moses selected his brother, choosing him out of all men, because of his superior virtue, to be high priest, and his sons he appointed priests, not giving precedence to his own family, but to the piety and holiness which he perceived to exist in those men; and what is the clearest proof of this is, that he did not think either of his sons worthy of this honour (and he had two); while he must inevitably have appointed both of them, if he had attached any importance to love for his family; (143) and he appointed them with the unanimous consent of the whole nation, as the sacred scriptures have recorded, which was a most novel mode of proceeding, and one especially worthy of being mentioned; and, in the first place, he washed them all over with the most pure and vivifying water of the fountain; and then he gave them their sacred vestments, giving to his brother the robe which reached down to his feet, and the mantle which covered the shoulders, as a sort of breast-plate, being an embroidered robe, adorned with all kinds of figures, and a representation of the universe. And to all his nephews he gave linen tunics, and girdles, and trowsers; (144) the girdles, in order that the wearers might be unimpeded and ready for all their sacred ministrations, were fastened up tight round the loose waists of the tunics; and the breeches, that nothing which ought to be hidden might be visible, especially when they were going up to the altar, or coming down from the high place, and doing everything with earnestness and celerity. (145) For if their equipment had not been so accurately attended to for the sake of guarding against the uncertain future, and for the sake of providing for an energetic promptness in the sacred ministrations, the men would have appeared naked, not being able to preserve the becoming order necessary to holy men dedicated to the service of God.

XXIX

XXIX. (146) And when he had thus furnished them with proper vestments, he took very fragrant ointment, which had been made by the skill of the perfumer, and first of all he anointed the altar in the open air, and the laver, sprinkling it with the perfume seven times; after that he anointed the tabernacle and every one of the sacred vessels, the ark, and the candlestick, and the altar of incense, and the table, and the censers, and the vials, and all the other things which were either necessary or useful for the sacrifices; and last of all bringing the high priest close to himself, he anointed his head with abundant quantities of oil. (147) When he had done all this, he then, in strict accordance with what was holy, commanded a heifer and two rams to be brought; the one that he might sacrifice it for the remission of sins, intimating by a figure that to sin is congenital with every created being, however good it may be, inasmuch as it is created, and that therefore it is indispensable that God should be propitiated in its behalf by means of prayers and sacrifices, that he may not be provoked to chastise it. (148) And of the rams, one he required for a whole burnt-offering of gratitude for the successful arrangement of all those things, of which every individual has such a share as is suited to him, deriving benefit from all the elements, enjoying the earth for his abode and in respect of the nourishment which is derived from it; the water for drinking, and washing, and sailing on; the air for breathing and for the comprehension of those things which are the objects of our outward senses (since the air is the medium in which they all are exerted), and for the seasons of the year; enjoying fire both of that kind which is used for cooking food and for warming one's self, and also that heavenly kind which is serviceable for light and for all the objects of sight. (149) The other ram he employed for the complete accomplishment of the purification of the priests, which he appropriately called the ram of perfection, since the priests were intended to exercise their office in teaching proper and convenient rites and ceremonies to the servants and ministers of God. (150) And he took the blood, and with some of it he poured a libation all round the altar, and part he took, holding a vial under it to catch it, and with it he anointed three parts of the body of the initiated priests, the tip of the ear, the extremity of the hand, and the extremity of the foot, all on the right side, signifying by this action that the perfect man must be pure in every word and action, and in his whole life, for it is the hearing which judges of his words, and the hand is the symbol of action, and the foot of the way in which a man walks in life; (151) and since each of these members is an extremity of the body, and is likewise on the right side, we must imagine that it is here indicated by a figure that improvement in every thing is to be arrived at by a certain dexterity, being a portion of supreme felicity, and being the true aim in life, which a man must necessarily labour to attain, and to which he ought to refer all his actions, aiming at them in his life, as in the practice of archery men aim at a target.

XXX

XXX. (152) Accordingly, he first of all anointed the three parts before mentioned of the bodies of the priests with the unmixed blood of one of the victims, that, namely, which was called the ram of perfection; and afterwards, taking some of the blood which was upon the altar, being the blood of all the victims mingled together, and some also of the unguent which has already been mentioned, which the ointment makers had prepared, and mixing some of the oil with the mingled blood of the different victims, he sprinkled some upon the priests and upon their garments, with the intention that they should have a share not only in that purity which was external and in the open air, but also of that which was in the inmost shrine, since they were about to minister within the temple. And all the things within the temple were anointed with oil. (153) And when they had brought forward other sacrifices in addition to the former ones, partly the priests sacrificing for themselves, and partly the elders sacrificing on behalf of the whole nation, then Moses entered into the tabernacle, leading his brother by the hand (and it was the eighth and last day of the festival, for the seven previous days had been devoted to the initiation of the hierophants), he now initiated both him and his nephews. And when he had entered in he taught him as a learned teacher might instruct an ignorant pupil, in what way the high priest ought to perform the ministrations which are performed inside the temple. (154) Then, when they had both come out and held up their hands in front of their head, they, with a pure and holy mind, offered up such prayers as were suitable and becoming for the nation. And while they were still praying a most marvellous prodigy happened; for from out of the inmost shrine, whether it was a portion of the purest possible aether, or whether the air, according to some natural change of the elements, had become dissolved with fire, on a sudden a body of flame shone forth, and with impetuous violence descended on the altar and consumed all that was thereon, with the view, as I imagine, of showing in the clearest manner that none of the things which had been done had been done without the especial providence of God. (155) For it was natural that an especial honour should be assigned to the holy place, not only by means of those things in which men are the workmen employed, but also by that purest of all essences, fire, in order that the ordinary fire which is used by men might not touch the altar; perhaps by reason of its being defiled by ten thousand impurities. (156) For it is concerned not only with irrational animals when they are roasted or boiled for the unjust appeasing of our miserable bellies, but also in the case of men who are slain by hostile attack, not merely in a small body of three or four, but in numerous hosts. (157) At all events, before now, arrows charged with fire have been aimed at vast naval fleets and have burnt them; and fire has destroyed whole cities, which have blazed away till they have been consumed down to their very foundations and reduced to ashes, so that no trace whatever has remained of their former situation. (158) It appears to me that this was the reason for which God rejected from his sacred altar the fire which is applied to common uses, as being defiled; and that, instead of it, he rained down celestial flame from heaven, in order to make a distinction between holy and profane things, and to separate the things belonging to man from the things belonging to God; for it was fitting that a more incorruptible essence of fire than that which served the common purposes of life should be set apart for sacrifices.

XXXI

XXXI. (159) And as many sacrifices were of necessity offered up every day, and especially on all days of solemn assembly and festival, both on behalf of each individual separately and in common for the whole nation, for innumerable and various reasons, inasmuch as the nation was very populous and very pious, there was a need also of a multitude of keepers of the temple for the sacred and subordinate ministrations. (160) And, again, the election of these officers was conducted in a novel and not in the ordinary manner. God chose out one of the twelve tribes, having selected it for its superior excellence, and appointed that to furnish the keepers of the temple, giving it rewards and peculiar honours in return for its pious acting. And the action which it had to perform was of this kind. (161) When Moses had gone up into the neighbouring mountain and had remained several days alone with God, the fickle-minded among the people, thinking that his absence was a favourable opportunity, as if they had no longer any ruler at all, rushed unrestrainedly to impiety, and, forgetting the holiness of the living God, became eager imitators of the Egyptian inventions. (162) Then, having made a golden calf in imitation of that which appeared to be the most sacred animal in that district, they offered up unholy sacrifices, and instituted blasphemous dances, and sang hymns which differed in no respect from dirges, and, being filled with strong wine, gave themselves up to a twofold intoxication, the intoxication of wine and that of folly, revelling and devoting the night to feasting, and, having no foresight as to the future, they spent their time in pleasant sins, though justice had her eye upon them, who saw them while they would not see, and decided what punishments they deserved. (163) But when the continued outcries in the camp, from men collected in numerous and dense crowds, reached over a great distance, so that the sound penetrated even to the summit of the mountain, Moses, hearing the uproar, was in great perplexity, as being at the same time a devout worshipper of God and a friend to mankind, not being able to bring his mind to quit the society of God with whom he was conversing, and in which he, being alone with him, was conferring with him by himself, nor, on the other hand, could he be indifferent to the multitude thus full of anarchy and wickedness; (164) for he recognised the tumult, since he was a very shrewd man at conjecturing, from inarticulate sounds of no distinct meaning, the passions of the soul which were inaccessible to and out of the reach of the conjectures of others, because he perceived at once that the noise proceeded partly from intoxication, since intemperance had produced satiety and a disposition to insult the law. (165) And being drawn both ways, and under strong attraction in both directions, he fluctuated this way and that way, and did not know what he ought to do; and while he was considering the matter the following command was given to him. "Go down quickly; descend from this place, the people have turned with haste to lawlessness, having fashioned a god made with hand sin the form of a bull, they are falling down before that which is no god, and sacrificing unto him, forgetting all the things that they have seen, and all that they have heard, which might lead them to piety." (166) So Moses, being amazed, and being also constrained by this command, believes those incredible events, and springs down to be a mediator and reconciler; not however, in a moment, for first of all he addressed supplications and prayers on behalf of his nation to God, entreating God that he would pardon these their sins; then, this governor of and intercessor for his people, having appeased the Ruler of the universe, went down at the same time rejoicing and feeling sorrowful; he rejoiced indeed that God had admitted his supplication, but he was full of anxiety and depression, being greatly indignant at the lawless transgression of the multitude.

XXXII

XXXII. (167) And when he came into the middle of the camp, and marvelled at the sudden way in which the multitude had forsaken all their ancient habits, and at the vast amount of falsehood which they had embraced instead of truth, he, seeing that the disease had not extended among them all, but that some were still sound, and still cherished a disposition which loathed wickedness; wishing to distinguish those who were incurable from those who felt indignation at what had taken place, and to know also whether any of those who had offended repented them of their sin, caused a proclamation to be made; and it was indeed a shrewd test of the inclination of each individual, to see how he was disposed to holiness, or to the contrary. (168) "Whoever," said he, "is on the side of the Lord, let him come to me." It was but a brief sentence which he thus uttered, but the meaning concealed under it was important; for what was intimated by his words was the following sense: "If any one does not think anything whatever that is made by hands, or anything that is created, a god, but believes that there is one ruler of the universe only, let him come to me." (169) Now of the others, some resisted by reason of the admiration which they had conceived for the Egyptian pride, and they did not attend to what he said; others wanted courage to come nearer to him, perhaps out of fear of punishment; or else perhaps they dreaded punishment at the hand of Moses, or a rising up against them on the part of the people; for the multitude invariably attack those who do not share in their frenzy. (170) But that single tribe of the whole number which was called the tribe of Levi, when they heard the proclamation, as if by one preconcerted agreement, ran with great haste, displaying their earnestness by their promptness and rapidity, and proving the keenness of the desire of their soul for piety; (171) and, when Moses saw them rushing forward as if starting from the goal in a race, he said, "Surely it is not with your bodies alone that you are hastening to come unto me, but you shall soon bear witness with your minds to your eagerness; let every one of you take a sword, and slay those men who have done things worthy of ten thousand deaths, who have forsaken the true God, and made for themselves false gods, of perishable and created substances, calling them by the name which belongs only to the uncreated and everlasting God; let every one, I say, slay those men, whether it be his own kinsmen or his friends, looking upon nothing to be either friendship or kindred but the holy fellowship of good men." (172) And the tribe of Levi, outrunning his command with the most eager readiness, since they were already alienated from those men in their minds, almost from the first moment that they beheld the beginning of their lawless iniquity, killed them all to a man, to the number of three thousand, though they had been but a short time before their dearest friends; and as the corpses were lying in the middle of the place of the assembly of the people, the multitude beholding them pitied them, and fearing the still fervid, and angry, and indignant disposition of those who had slain them, reproved them out of fear; (173) but Moses, gladly approving of their exceeding virtue, devised in their favour and confirmed to them an honour which was appropriate to their exploit, for it was fitting that those who had undertaken a voluntary war for the sake of the honour of God, and who had carried it out successfully in a short time, should be thought worthy to receive the priesthood and charge of officiating in his service.

XXXIII

XXXIII. (174) But, since there is not one order only of consecrated priests, but since to some of them the charge is committed of attending to all the prayers, and sacrifices, and other most sacred ceremonies, being allowed to enter into the inmost and most holy shrine; while others are not permitted to do any of these things, but have the duty of taking care of and guarding the temple and all that is therein, both day and night, whom some call keepers of the temple; a sedition arose respecting the precedency in honour, which was to many persons in many ways the cause of infinite evils, and it broke out now from the keepers of the temple attacking the priests, and endeavouring to deprive them of the honour which belonged to them; and they thought that they should be able easily to succeed in their object, since they were many times more numerous than the others. (175) But for the sake of not appearing to be planning any innovations of their own heads, they persuaded also the eldest of the twelve tribes to embrace their opinions, which last tribe was followed by many of the more fickle of the populace, as thinking it entitled to the precedence and to the principal share of authority over the whole host. (176) Moses now knew that a great plot was in agitation against him; for he had appointed his brother high priest in accordance with the will of God, which had been declared to him. And now false accusations were brought against him, as if he had falsified the oracles of God, and as if he had done so and made the appointment by reason of his family affection and goodwill towards his brother. (177) And he, being very naturally grieved at this, inasmuch as he was not only distrusted by such accusations while exhibiting his own good faith in a most genuine manner, but he was also grieved at those actions of his being calumniated which had for their object the honour of God, and which were of such a nature as to deserve by themselves that even such a man who had in other respects shown an insincere disposition should be looked upon as behaving in this case with truth; for truth is the invariable attendant of God. But he did not think fit to give any explanation by words respecting his appointment of his brother, knowing that it was difficult to endeavour to persuade those who were previously possessed by contrary opinions to change their minds; but he besought God to give the people a visible demonstration that he had in no respect behaved with dishonesty respecting the appointment to the priesthood. (178) And he, therefore, commanded that twelve rods should be taken, so as to be equal in number to the tribes of the nation; and he commanded further that the names of the other patriarchs of the tribes should be written on eleven of the rods, but on the remaining one the name of his brother, the high priest, and then that they should all be carried into the temple as far as the inmost shrine; and the officer who did what he had been commanded waited in expectation to see the result. (179) And on the next day, in obedience to a command from God, he went into the temple, while all the people were standing around, and brought out the rods, the others differing in no respect from the state in which they were when they were put in; but the one on which the name of his brother was written had undergone a miraculous change; for like a fine plant it suddenly put forth shoots all over, and was weighed down with the abundance of its crop of fruit.

XXXIV

XXXIV. (180) And the fruit were almonds, which is a fruit of a different character from any other. For in most fruit, such as grapes, olives, and apples, the seed and the eatable part differ from one another, and being different are separated as to their position, for the eatable part is outside, and the seed is shut up within; but in the case of this fruit the seed and the eatable part are the same, both of them being comprised in one species, and their position is one and the same, being without strongly protected and fortified with a twofold fence, consisting partly of a very thick bark, and partly of what appears in no respect short of a wooden case, (181) by which perfect virtue is figuratively indicated. For as in the almond the beginning and the end are the same, the beginning as far as it is seed, and the end as far as it is fruit; so also is it the case with the virtues; for each one of them is at the same time both beginning and end, a beginning, because it proceeds not from any other power, but from itself; and an end, because the life in accordance with nature hastens towards it. (182) This is one reason; and another is also mentioned, more clear and emphatic than the former; for the part of the almond which looks like bark is bitter, but that which lies inside the bark, like a wooden case, is very hard and impenetrable, so that the fruit, being enclosed in these two coverings, is not very easily to be got at. (183) This is an emblem of the soul which is inclined to the practice of meditation, from which he thinks it is proper to turn it to virtue by showing it that it is necessary first of all to encounter danger. But labour is a bitter, and distasteful, and harsh thing, from which good is produced, for the sake of which one must not yield to effeminate indolence; (184) for he who seeks to avoid labour is also avoiding good. And he, again, who encounters what is disagreeable to be borne with fortitude and manly perseverance, is taking the best road to happiness; for it is not the nature of virtue to abide with those who are given up to delicacy and luxury, and who have become effeminate in their souls, and whose bodies are enervated by the incessant luxury which they practise every day; but it is subdued by such conduct, and determined to change its abode, having first of all arranged its departure so as to depart to, and abide with, the ruler of right reason. (185) But, if I must tell the truth, the most sacred company of prudence, and temperance, and courage, and justice seeks the society of those who practise virtue, and of those who admire a life of austerity and rigid duty, devoting themselves to fortitude and self-denial, with wise economy and abstinence; by means of which virtues the most powerful of all the principles within us, namely, reason, improves and attains to a state of perfect health and vigour, overthrowing the violent attacks of the body, which the moderate use of wine, and epicurism, and licentiousness, and other insatiable appetites excite against it, engendering a fulness of flesh which is the direct enemy of shrewdness and wisdom. (186) Moreover, it is said, that of all the trees that are accustomed to blossom in the spring, the almond is the first to flourish, bringing as it were good tidings of abundance of fruit; and that afterwards it is the last to lose its leaves, extending the yearly old age of its verdure to the longest period; in each of which particulars it is an emblem of the tribe of the priesthood, as Moses intimates under the figure of this tree that this tribe shall be the first of the whole human race to flourish, and likewise the last; as long as it shall please God to liken our life to the revolutions of the spring, destroying covetousness that most treacherous of passions, and the fountain of all unhappiness.

XXXV

XXXV. (187) Since, therefore, I have now stated that in the absolutely perfect governor there ought to be four things, royal power, the legislative disposition, and the priesthood, and the prophetic office (in order that by his legislative disposition he may command such things as are right to be done, and forbid such things as are not proper to be done, and that by his priesthood he may arrange not only all human but likewise all divine things; and that by his prophetic office he may predict those things which cannot be comprehended by reason): having fully discussed the first three, and having shown that Moses as a most excellent king, and lawgiver, and high priest, I come in the last place to show that he was also the most illustrious of prophets. (188) I am not unaware then that all the things which are written in the sacred books are oracles delivered by him; and I will set forth what more peculiarly concerns him, when I have first mentioned this one point, namely, that of the sacred oracles some are represented as delivered in the person of God by his interpreter, the divine prophet, while others are put in the form of question and answer, and others are delivered by Moses in his own character as a divinely-prompted lawgiver possessed by divine inspiration. (189) Therefore, all the earliest oracles are manifestations of the whole of the divine virtues, and especially of that merciful and bounteous character by means of which he trains all men to virtue, and especially the race which is devoted to his service, to which he lays open the road leading to happiness. (190) The second class have a sort of admixture and communication in them, the prophet asking information on the subjects as to which he is in difficulty, and God answering him and instructing him. The third sort are attributed to the lawgiver, God having given him a share of his prescient power, by means of which he will be able to foretell the future. (191) Therefore, we must for the present pass by the first; for they are too great to be adequately praised by any man, as, indeed, they could scarcely be panegyrised worthily by the heaven itself and the nature of the universe; and they are also uttered by the mouth, as it were, of an interpreter. But interpretation and prophecy differ from one another. And concerning the second kind I will at once endeavour to explain the truth, connecting with them the third species also, in which the inspired character of the speaker is shown, according to which it is that he is most especially and appropriately looked upon as a prophet.

XXXVI

XXXVI. (192) And we must here begin with the promise. There are four places where the oracles are given by way of question and answer, being contained in the exposition of the law, and having a mixed character. For, first, the prophet feels inspiration and asks questions, and then the father prophesies to him, giving him a share of his discourse and replies. And the first case where this occurs is one which would have irritated, not only Moses, who was the most holy and pious man that ever lived, but even any one who had only had a slight taste of piety. (193) A certain man, illegitimately born of two unequal parents, namely, an Egyptian father and a Jewish mother, and who disregarded the national and hereditary customs which he had learnt from her, as it is reported, inclined to the Egyptian impiety, being seized with admiration for the ungodly practices of the men of that nation; (194) for the Egyptians, almost alone of all men, set up the earth as a rival of the heaven considering the former as entitled to honours equal with those of the gods, and giving the latter no especial honour, just as if it were proper to pay respect to the extremities of a country rather than to the king's palace. For in the world the heaven is the most holy temple, and the further extremity is the earth; though this too is in itself worthy of being regarded with honour; but if it is brought into comparison with the air, is as far inferior to it as light is to darkness, or night to day, or corruption to immortality, or a mortal to God. (195) For, since that country is not irrigated by rain as all other lands are, but by the inundations of the river which is accustomed every year to overflow its banks; the Egyptians, in their impious reason, make a god of the Nile, as if it were a copy and a rival of heaven, and use pompous language about the virtue of their country.

XXXVII

XXXVII. (196) Accordingly, this man of mixed race, having had a quarrel with some one of the consecrated and well-instructed house of Israel, becoming carried away by his anger, and unable to restrain himself, and being also an admirer and follower of the impiety of the Egyptians, extended his impiety from earth to heaven, cursing it with his accursed, and polluted, and defiled soul, and with his wicked tongue, and with the whole power of all his vocal organs in the superfluity of his ungodliness; though it ought to be blessed and praised, not by all men, indeed, but only by those who are most virtuous and pious, as having received perfect purification. (197) Wherefore Moses, marvelling at his insanity and at the extravagance of his audacity, although he was filled with a noble impetuosity and indignation, and desired to slay the man with his own hand, nevertheless feared lest he should be inflicting on him too light a punishment; for he conceived that no man could possibly devise any punishment adequate to such enormous impiety. (198) And since it followed of necessity that a man who did not worship God could not honour his father either, or his mother, or his country, or his benefactors, this man, in addition to not reverencing them, dared to speak ill of them. And then what extravagance of wickedness did he fall short of? And yet evil-speaking, if compared with cursing, is the lighter evil of the two. But when intemperate language and an unbridled tongue are subservient to lawless folly, then inevitably and invariably some iniquitous conduct must follow. (199) O man! does any one curse God? What other god can he invoke to ratify and confirm his curse? Is it not plain that he must invoke God to give effect to his curses against himself? Away with such profane and impious ideas! It would be well to cleanse that miserable soul which has been insulted by the voice, and which has sued the ears for ministers, keeping the external senses blind. (200) And was not either the tongue of the man who uttered such impiety loosened, or the ears of him who was destined to hear such things closed up? unless, indeed, that was done in consequence of some providential arrangement of justice, which does not think that either any extraordinary good or that any enormous evil ought to be kept in darkness, but that such should be revealed in order to the most complete manifestation of virtue or vice, so that it may adjudge the one to be worthy of acceptance and the other of punishment. (201) On this account Moses ordered the man to be thrown into prison and bound with chains; and then he addressed propitiatory prayers to God, begging him to be merciful to the necessities of the external senses (by means of which we both see what it is not proper to see, and hear what it is not lawful to hear), and to point out what the author of such a strange and unprecedented blasphemy and impiety ought to suffer. (202) And God commanded him to be stoned, considering, as I imagine, the punishment of stoning to be a suitable and appropriate one for a man who had a stony and hardened heart, and wishing at the same time that all his fellow countrymen should have a share in inflicting punishment on him, as he knew that they were very indignant and eager to slay him; and the only punishment which so many myriads of men could possibly join in was that which was inflicted by throwing stones. (203) But after the punishment of this impious murderer, a new commandment was enacted, which had never before been thought worthy of being reduced to writing; but unexpected innovations cause new laws to be devised for the repression of their evils. At all events, the following law was immediately introduced: "Whoever curses God shall be guilty of sin, and whoever names the name of the Lord shall Die." [1171] (204) Well done, O all-wise man! You alone have drunk of the cup of unalloyed wisdom. You have seen that it was worse to name God than even to curse him; for you would never have treated lightly a man who had committed the heaviest of all impieties, and inflicted the heaviest punishment possible on those who committed the slightest faults; but you fixed death, which is the very greatest punishment imaginable, as the penalty for the man who appeared to have committed the heaviest crime.

XXXVIII

XXXVIII. (205) But, as it seems, he is not now speaking of that God who was the first being who had any existence, and the Father of the universe, but of those who are accounted gods in the different cities; and they are falsely called gods, being only made by the arts of painters and sculptors, for the whole inhabited world is full of statues and images, and erections of that kind, of whom it is necessary however to abstain from speaking ill, in order that no one of the disciples of Moses may ever become accustomed at all to treat the appellation of God with disrespect; for that name is always most deserving to obtain the victory, and is especially worthy of love. (206) But if any one were, I will not say to blaspheme against the Lord of gods and men, but were even to dare to utter his name unseasonably, he must endure the punishment of death; (207) for those persons who have a proper respect for their parents do not lightly bring forward the names of their parents, though they are but mortal, but they avoid using their proper names by reason of the reverence which they bear them, and call them rather by the titles indicating their natural relationship, that is, father and mother, by which names they at once intimate the unsurpassable benefits which they have received at their hands, and their own grateful disposition. (208) Therefore these men must not be thought worthy of pardon who out of volubility of tongue have spoken unseasonably, and being too free of their words have repeated carelessly the most holy and divine name of God.

XXXIX

XXXIX. (209) Moreover, in accordance with the honour due to the Creator of the universe, the prophet hallowed the sacred seventh day, beholding with eyes of more acute sight than those of mortals its pre-eminent beauty, which had already been deeply impressed on the heaven and the whole universal world, and had been borne about as an image by nature itself in her own bosom; (210) for first of all Moses found that day destitute of any mother, and devoid of all participation in the female generation, being born of the Father alone without any propagation by means of seed, and being born without any conception on the part of any mother. And then he beheld not only this, that it was very beautiful and destitute of any mother, neither being born of corruption nor liable to corruption; and then, in the third place, he by further inquiry discovered that it was the birthday of the world, which the heaven keeps as a festival, and the earth and all the things in and on the earth keep as a festival, rejoicing and delighting in the all-harmonious number of seven, and in the sabbath day. (211) For this reason the all-great Moses thought fit that all who were enrolled in his sacred polity should follow the laws of nature and meet in a solemn assembly, passing the time in cheerful joy and relaxation, abstaining from all work, and from all arts which have a tendency to the production of anything; and from all business which is connected with the seeking of the means of living, and that they should keep a complete truce, abstaining from all laborious and fatiguing thought and care, and devoting their leisure, not as some persons scoffingly assert, to sports, or exhibitions of actors and dancers, for the sake of which those who run madly after theatrical amusements suffer disasters and even encounter miserable deaths, and for the sake of these the most dominant and influential of the outward senses, sight and hearing, make the soul, which should be the heavenly nature, the slave of these senses. (212) But, giving up their time wholly to the study of philosophy, not of that sort of philosophy which wordcatchers and sophists, seek to reduce to a system, selling doctrines and reasonings as they would any other vendible thing in the market. Men who (O you earth and sun!) employ philosophy against philosophy, and yet never wear a blush on their countenance; but who, applying themselves to the kindred philosophy, which they make up of these component parts, namely, of intention, and words, and actions, all united into one species, in order to the acquisition and enjoyment of happiness. (213) Now some one disregarding this injunction, even while he yet had the sacred words of God respecting the holy seventh day still ringing in his ears, which God had uttered without the intervention of the prophet, and, what is the most wonderful thing of all, by a visible voice which affected the eyes of those who were present even more than their ears, went forth through the middle of the camp to pick up sticks, well knowing that all the people in the camp were perfectly quiet and doing nothing, and even while he was committing the iniquity was seen and detected, all disguise being impossible; (214) for some persons, having gone forth out of the gates to some quiet spot, that they might pray in some retired and peaceful place, seeing a most unholy spectacle, namely this man carrying a faggot of sticks, and being very indignant, were about to put him to death; but reasoning with themselves they restrained the violence of their wrath, that they might not appear, as they were only private persons, to chastise any one rather than the magistrates, and that too uncondemned; though indeed in other respects the transgression was manifest and undeniable, wishing also that no pollution arising from an execution, even though most righteously inflicted, should defile the sacred day. But they apprehended him, and led him away to the magistrate, with whom the priests were sitting as assessors; and the whole multitude collected together to hear the trial; (215) for it was invariably the custom, as it was desirable on other days also, but especially on the seventh day, as I have already explained, to discuss matters of philosophy; the ruler of the people beginning the explanation, and teaching the multitude what they ought to do and to say, and the populace listening so as to improve in virtue, and being made better both in their moral character and in their conduct through life; (216) in accordance with which custom, even to this day, the Jews hold philosophical discussions on the seventh day, disputing about their national philosophy, and devoting that day to the knowledge and consideration of the subjects of natural philosophy; for as for their houses of prayer in the different cities, what are they, but schools of wisdom, and courage, and temperance, and justice, and piety, and holiness, and every virtue, by which human and divine things are appreciated, and placed upon a proper footing?

XL

XL. (217) On this day, then, the man who had done this deed of impiety was led away to prison; and Moses being at a loss what ought to be done to the man (for he knew that he had committed a crime worthy of death, but did not know what was the most suitable manner for the punishment to be inflicted upon him), came with his invisible soul to the invisible judgment seat, and asked of that Judge who heareth everything before it is related to him what his sentence was. (218) And that Judge delivered his sentence that the man ought to die, and in no other way than being stoned, since in his case, as in that of the criminal mentioned above, his mind had been changed to a dumb stone, and he had committed the most complete of offences, in which nearly every other sin is comprised which can be committed against the laws enacted respecting the reverence due to the seventh day. (219) Why so? Because, not only mere handicraft trades, but also nearly all other acts and businesses, and especially all such as have reference to any providing of or seeking for the means of life, are either carried on by means of fire themselves, or, at all events, not without those instruments which are made by fire. On which account Moses, in many places, forbids any one to handle a fire on the sabbath day, inasmuch as that is the most primary and efficient source of things and the most ancient and important work; and if that is reduced to a state of tranquillity, he thought that it would be probable that all particular works would be at a stand-still likewise. (220) And wood is the material of fire, so that a man who is picking up wood is committing a crime which is akin to and nearly connected with that of burning fire, doubling his transgression, in fact, partly in that he was collecting what it was commanded should remain unmoved, and partly that what he was collecting was that which is the material of fire, the beginning of all arts.

XLI

XLI. (221) Therefore both those instances which I have mentioned comprise the punishments of wicked men, appointed and confirmed by question and answer. And there are two other instances, not of the same, but of a different character; the one of which has reference to the succession of an inheritance; the other, as far at least as it appears to me, to a sacrifice which was performed at an unseemly time. And we must first discuss the latter of the two. (222) Moses puts down the beginning of the vernal equinox as the first month of the year, attributing the chief honour, not as some persons do to the periodical revolutions of the year in regard of time, but rather to the graces and beauties of nature which it has caused to shine upon men; for it is through the bounty of nature that the seeds which are sown to produce the necessary food of mankind are brought to perfection. And the fruit of trees in their prime, which is second in importance only to the necessary crops, is engendered by the same power, and as being second in importance it also ripens late; for we always find in nature that those things which are not very necessary are second to those which are indispensable. (223) Now wheat and barley are among the things which are very necessary; as, likewise, are all the other species of food, without which it is impossible to live. But oil, and wine, and almonds are not among necessaries, since men often live without them to the very extremity of old age, extending their life over a number of years. (224) Accordingly, in this month, about the fourteenth day of the month, when the orb of the moon is usually about to become full, the public universal feast of the passover is celebrated, which in the Chaldaic language is called pascha; at which festival not only do private individuals bring victims to the altar and the priests sacrifice them, but also, by a particular ordinance of this law, the whole nation is consecrated and officiates in offering sacrifice; every separate individual on this occasion bringing forward and offering up with his own hands the sacrifice due on his own behalf. (225) Therefore all the rest of the people rejoiced and was of joyful countenance, every one thinking that he himself was honoured by this participation in the priesthood. But the others passed the time of the festival amid tears and groans, their own relations having lately died, whom they were now mourning for, and were overwhelmed with a two fold sorrow, having, in addition to their grief for their relations who were slain, the pain also which arose from being deprived of the pleasure and honour which accrue from the offering up of sacrifice, as they were not purified or cleansed on that day, inasmuch as their mourning had not yet lasted beyond the appointed and legitimate period of lamentation. (226) These men coming, after the assembly was over, to the ruler of the people, being full of melancholy and depression, related to him what had happened, namely, "that the recent death of their relations was an unavoidable affliction to which they could not help yielding, and that it was a further grief that, on that account, they were unable to bear their share in the sacrifice of the passover. (227) And then they besought him that they too might make their offerings no less than the others, and that the misfortune which had befallen them in the death of their kinsmen might not be reckoned against them as an iniquity of theirs, so as to produce them punishment instead of compassion; for that they thought that they were worse off than even the people who were dead, since these last had, indeed, no sense of the grievous privation, but they who continued live would appear to die the death perceptible to the outward sense."

XLII

XLII. (228) When he heard this he saw that the justification which they alleged was not inconsistent with reason and truth, and that the excuse which they alleged for not having previously offered their sacrifice was founded in necessity, and that they were entitled to merciful consideration. And while he as wavering in his opinion, and inclining this way and that way as if in the balance of a scale, for compassion and justice inclined him one way, and on the other side the law of the sacrifice of the passover weighed him down, in which the first month and the fourteenth day of the month are appointed for the offering of the sacrifice; accordingly, Moses, being perplexed and balancing between consent and refusal, besought God to decide the question and to announce his decision to him by an oracular command. (229) And God listened to his entreaty and gave him an oracle bearing not only on the circumstances which had taken place, but on all such as should hereafter happen with reference to the same subject, if people should ever again find themselves in a similar case. He likewise, out of the abundance of his providence, gave further and general directions with respect to other individuals who at any time, for one reason or other, should be unable to offer up their sacrifice with the whole of the rest of the nation. (230) We must now, therefore, proceed to relate the oracular commands which were thus given by God with reference to these Cases. [1172] He says, "The mourning for a relation is a necessary sorrow to those who are related by blood, and it is not set down as a piece of guilty indifference. (231) As long, therefore, as it lasts, until the time that is appointed by law for it to cease, let the man be repelled from the sacred precincts, which must be kept pure, not only from all intentional pollution, but likewise from all such as is involuntary. But when the legal time for mourning is expired, then let the mourners be no longer deprived of an equal share in the performance of the sacrifices, that those who are alive may not become an adjunct to those who are dead. And let them, as if they were in a second class, come again in the second month, on the fourteenth day of the month, and let them sacrifice in the same manner as the former sacrificers, and let them adopt the sacrifice in the same way as they did, in a similar manner and under similar rules." (232) Also, let the same regulations be observed with respect to those who are hindered, not by mourning, but by a distant journey, from offering up their sacrifice in common with and at the same time with the whole nation. "For those who are travelling in a foreign land, or dwelling in some other country, do no wrong, so as to deserve to be deprived of equal honour with the rest, especially since one country will not contain the entire nation by reason of its great numbers, but has sent out colonies in every direction."

XLIII

XLIII. (233) Having now, then, given this account of those who were too late to sacrifice the festival of the passover with the rest of the nation by reason of some unexpected circumstances, but who were desirous to fulfil the duty which had thus been omitted, even though late, still in the necessary manner, I now proceed to the last injunction relating to the succession to inheritances; that being, in like manner, of a mixed character, and consisting of question and answer. (234) There was a certain man, named Shalpaath, a man of high character and of a distinguished tribe. He had four daughters, but not a single son. And after the death of their father the daughters, being afraid that they should be deprived of their father's inheritance, because the allotments of such inheritances were given to the male heirs, came to the ruler of the people with the modesty befitting maidens, not because they were eager for riches, but because they desired to preserve the name and reputation of their father. (235) And they said to Moses, "Our father is dead; and he died without having been mixed up in any of those seditions in which it has happened that so many thousands have been slain; but he was a cultivator of a life free from trouble and notoriety; unless, indeed, it is to be considered as a crime that he was without male offspring. And we are now here orphans in appearance, but in real fact desiring to find a father in you; for a lawful ruler is as closely connected with his subjects as a Father." [1173] (236) And Moses marvelled at the wisdom of the maidens, and at their affection for their father, nevertheless he hesitated, being biased in some degree by other thoughts in accordance with which it seemed proper for men to divide the inheritances among themselves, that so they might receive the due reward of their military services and of the wars which they had gone through. But nature, which has given to woman protection from all such contests, does likewise by so doing plainly deprive them of their right to a share in what is put forward as a reward for encountering them. (237) On which account the mind of Moses was very naturally in a state of indecision, and was dragged different ways, so that Moses laid his perplexities before God, whom he knew to be the only being who could with true and unerring judgment decide such delicate differences with a complete display of truth and justice. (238) But the Creator of the universe, the Father of the world, who holds together earth and heaven, and the water and the air, and everything which is composed of any one of these things, and who rules the whole world, the King of gods and men, did not think it unbecoming for him to take upon himself the part of arbitrator respecting these orphan maidens.

Philo Judaeus

And, as arbitrator, he, in my opinion, did more for them than if he had been merely a judge of the law, inasmuch as he is merciful and beneficent, and has filled all things everywhere with his beneficent power for he gave great praise to the maidens. (239) O! Master how can any one sing your praises adequately, with what mouth, with what tongue, with what organisation of voice? Can the stars become a chorus and pour forth any melody which shall be worthy of the subject? Even if the whole of the heaven were to be dissolved into voice, would it be able to recount even a portion of your virtues? "Very rightly," says God, "have the daughters of Shalpaath spoken." (240) Who is there who can fail to perceive how great a praise this is when God bears witness in their favour? Come, now, ye who are violent; ye, who give yourselves airs because of your virtuous actions; ye, who hold up your hands higher than nature justifies, and who raise your eyebrows; ye, among whom the widowhood of woman is a cause for laughter, though it is a most pitiable evil; and in whose thoughts the desolation of orphan children is ridiculed even more shamefully than the distress before mentioned. (241) So now, seeing that those who appeared in such a low and unfortunate condition were not marked by God among the neglected and obscure, though all the kingdoms of the whole habitable world are the most insignificant portion of his dominion, because the whole circumference and space of the world is but the extremity of his works, learn a necessary lesson from this fact. (242) But Moses, having praised the conversation of the maidens, did not either leave them without their due honour and reward, nor yet, on the other hand, did he raise them to an equal degree of honour with the men on whom the brunt of the war falls; but to the latter he allotted the inheritances as the prizes which belonged to them as a reward for the gallant exploits which they had performed. But the former he thought worthy of grace and kindness, not of reward; as he showed most plainly by the expressions which he used, speaking of "gifts" and "presents," but not of "requital" or "recompense." For the one form of language is suited to those who receive what they have a right to, and the other belongs to those who are treated with gratuitous favour.

XLIV

XLIV. (243) And having given his divine directions respecting the petitions which the orphan maidens had preferred, he proceeds to lay down a more general law concerning the succession to inheritances, summoning the sons in the first instance to the sharing of the paternal property; and, if there should be no sons, then the daughters in the second place, to whom he says that it is proper to attach the inheritance as an external and adventitious ornament, but not as a possession belonging to and rightly connected with them; for that which is attached to anything has no actual relationship to that which is adorned by it, inasmuch as it is devoid of all harmony and union with it. (244) And, after the daughters, then he invites the brothers to share it in the third place; and, in the fourth place, he assigns the property to the uncles on the father's side, showing under this figure that the fathers might, if alive be the heirs of their sons. For it is a very foolish idea to imagine that when he allots the inheritance of the nephew to his father's brother, out of a regard to his relationship to his father, he has excluded the father himself from the succession. (245) But since the law permits the property of parents to be inherited by the children, but does not allow the parents themselves to inherit, he has abstained from any express mention of the subject as one to be deprecated and of evil omen, in order that the father and mother might not seem to receive any gain from the inconsolable affliction of the loss of children dying prematurely; but he indirectly intimated their right to be invited to such an inheritance when he conceded it to the uncles, in order that in this way he might attain the best objects of cultivating propriety and of avoiding the improper alienation of the estate. And, after the uncles, the fifth class of inheritors was to be composed of the nearest relations, to the first of whom he invariably assigns the inheritance.

XLV

XLV. (246) Having now, as I was forced to do, gone through the entire account of those sacred commands referring to a mixed possession of an inheritance, I shall now proceed to show the oracles which were divinely given by the inspiration of the prophet; for this was a subject which I promised to explain. Now the beginning of his divine inspiration, which was also the commencement of prosperity to his nation, arose when he was sent out of Egypt to dwell as a settler in the cities of Syria, with many thousands of his countrymen; (247) for both men and women, having accomplished together a long and desolate journey through the wilderness, destitute of any beaten road, at last arrived at the sea which is called the Red Sea. Then, as was natural, they were in great perplexity, neither being able to cross over by reason of their want of vessels, nor thinking it safe to return back by the way by which they had come. (248) And while they were all in this state of mind, a still greater evil was impending over them; for the king of the Egyptians, having collected a power which was far from contemptible, a vast army of cavalry and infantry, sallied forth in pursuit of them, and made haste to overtake them, that he might avenge himself on them for the departure which he had been compelled by undeniable communications from God to permit them to take. But, as it should seem, the disposition of wicked men is unstable, so that, like any thing in a lightly-balanced scale, it inclines on very slight causes to different directions at different times. (249) So now, the Hebrews being intercepted between their enemies and the sea, despaired of their safety, some looking on the most miserable death as a blessing to be prayed for; and others thinking it better to perish by the agency of the parts of nature than to become a laughing-stock to their enemies, were inclined to throw themselves into the sea; and now, being laden with heavy burdens, they sat down on the sea shore, that when they saw the enemy near they might more readily leap into the sea. (250) For now, by reason of the necessity which environed them, and from which they saw no means of extricating themselves, they were in great agitation, being full of expectation of a miserable death.

XLVI

XLVI. But when the prophet saw that the whole nation was now enclosed like a shoal of fish, and in great consternation, he no longer remained master of himself, but became inspired, and prophesied as follows:--(251) "The fear is necessary, and the terror is inevitable, and the danger is great; in front of us is the widely open sea, there is no retreat to which we can flee, we have no vessels, behind are the phalanxes of the enemy ready to attack us, which march on and pursue us, never stopping to take breath. Where shall any one turn? Which way can any one look to escape? Every thing from every quarter has unexpectedly become hostile to us, the sea, the land, men, and the elements of nature. (252) But be ye of good cheer; do not faint; stand still without wavering in your minds; await the invincible assistance of God; it will be present immediately of its own accord; it will fight in our behalf without being seen. Before now you have often had experience of it, defending you in an invisible manner. I see it now preparing to take part in the contest; casting halters round the necks of the enemy, who are now, as if violently dragged onward, going down into the depths of the sea like lead. You now see them while still alive; but I conceive the idea of them as dead. And this very day you yourselves shall also behold them Dead." [1174] (253) He then now said these things to them, things greater than any hopes that could have been formed. And they very speedily experienced in the real facts the truth of his divine words; for what he thus predicted by means of the power divinely given to him, came to pass in a manner more marvellous than can be well expressed. The sea was broken asunder, each portion retired back, there was a consolidation of the waves along each brokenoff fragment throughout the whole breadth and depth, so that the waves stood up like the strongest walls; and there was a straight line cut of a road thus miraculously made, which was a path for the Hebrews between the congealed waters, (254) so that the whole nation without any danger passed on foot through the sea, as if on a dry road and on a stony soil; for the sand was dried up, and its usually fine grains were now united into one compact substance. Then, also, there was a rush onwards of their enemies pursuing them, without stopped to take breath, hastening to their own destruction, and a driving forward of the cloud that guarded the rear of the Hebrews, on which there was a certain divine appearance of fire emitting a brilliant blaze, and a reflux of the sea, which up to that moment had been cut in two parts and stood asunder, and a sudden returning of the part which had been cut off and dried up into its original channel, (255) and an utter destruction of the enemy, whom the walls the sea, which had been congealed and which now turned back again, overwhelmed, and the sea pouring down and hurrying into what had just been a road, as if into some deep ravine, washed away every thing, and there was evidence of the completeness of the destruction in the bodies which floated on the waters, and which strewed the surface of the sea; and a great agitation of the waves, by which all the dead were cast up into a heap on the opposite shore, becoming a necessary spectacle to those who had been delivered, and to whom it had been granted not merely to escape from their dangers, but also to behold their enemies punished, in a manner too marvellous for description, by no human but by a divine power. (256) For this mercy Moses very naturally honoured his Benefactor with hymns of gratitude. For having divided the host into two choruses, one of men and one of women, he himself became the leader of that of the men, and appointed his sister to be the chief of that of the women, that they might sing hymns to their father and Creator, joining in harmonies responsive to one another, by a combination of dispositions and melody, the former being eager to offer the same requital for the mercies which they had received, and the latter consisting of a symphony of the deep male with the high female voices, for the tones of men are deep and those of women are high; and when there is a perfect and harmonious combination of the two a most delightful and thoroughly harmonious melody is effected. (257) And he persuaded all those myriads of men and women to be of one mind, and to sing in concert the same hymn at the same time in praise of those marvellous and mighty works which they had beheld, and which I have been just now relating. At which the prophet rejoicing, and seeing also the exceeding joy of his nation, and being himself too unable to contain his delight, began the song. And they who heard him being divided into two choruses, sang with him, taking the words which he uttered.

XLVII

XLVII. (258) This is the beginning and preface of the prophecies of Moses under the influence of inspiration. After this he prophesied about the first and most necessary of all things, namely, food, which the earth did not produce, for it was barren and unfruitful; and the heaven rained down not once only, but every day for forty years, before the dawn of day, an ethereal fruit under the form of a dew very like millet seed. (259) And Moses, when he saw it, commanded them to collect it; and being full of inspiration, said: "You must believe in God, inasmuch as you have already had experience of his mercies and benefits in matters beyond all your hopes. This food may not be treasured up or laid up in garners. Let no one leave any portion of it till the morning." (260) When they heard this, some of those who had no firm piety, thinking perhaps that what was now said to them was not an oracle from God, but merely the advice of their leader, left some till the next day. And it putrified, and at first filled all the camp around with its foul smell, and then it turned to worms, the origin of which always is from corruption. (261) And Moses, when he saw this, was naturally indignant with those who were thus disobedient; for how could he help being so, when those who had beheld such numerous and great actions which could not possibly be perverted into mere fictitious and well contrived appearances, but which had been easily accomplished by the divine providence, did not only doubt, but even absolutely disbelieved, and were the hardest of all man to be convinced? (262) But the Father established the oracle of his prophet by two most conspicuous manifestations, the one of which he gave immediately by the destruction of what had been left, and by the evil stench which arose, and by the change of it into worms, the vilest of animals; and the other demonstration he afforded subsequently, for that which was over and above after that which had been collected by the multitude, was always melted away by the beams of the sun, and consumed, and destroyed in that manner.

XLVIII

XLVIII. (263) He gave a second instance of his prophetical inspiration not long afterwards in the oracle which he delivered about the sacred seventh day. For though it had had a natural precedence over all other days, not only from the time that the world was created, but even before the origination of the heaven and all the objects perceptible to the outward senses, men still knew it not, perhaps because, by reason of the continued and uninterrupted destructions which had taken place by water and fire, succeeding generations had not been able to receive from former ones any traditions of the arrangement and order which had been established in the connection of preceding times, which, as it was not known, Moses, now being inspired, declared to his people in an oracle which was borne testimony to by a visible sign from heaven. (264) And the sign was this. A small portion of food descended from the air on the previous days, but a double portion on the day before the seventh day. And on the previous days, if any portion was left it became liquefied and melted away, until it was entirely changed into dew, and so consumed; but on this day it endured no alteration, but remained in the same state as before, and when this was reported to him, and beheld by him, Moses did not so much conjecture as receive the impulse of divine inspiration under which he prophesied of the seventh day. (265) I omit to mention that all such conjectures are akin to prophecy; for the mind could never make such correct and felicitous conjectures, unless it were a divine spirit which guided their feet into the way of truth; (266) and the miraculous nature of the sign was shown, not merely in the fact of the food being double in quantity, nor in that of its remaining unimpaired, contrary to the usual customs, but in both these circumstances taking place on the sixth day, from the day on which this food first began to be supplied from heaven, from which day the most sacred number of seven begun to be counted, so that if any one reckons he will find that this heavenly food was given in exact correspondence with the arrangement instituted at the creation of the world. For God began to create the world on the first day of a week of six days: and he began to rain down the food which has just been mentioned on the same first day; (267) and the two images are alike; for as he produced that most perfect work, the world, bringing it out of non-existence into existence, so in the same manner did he produce plenty in the wilderness, changing the elements with reference to the pressing necessity, that, instead of the earth, the air might bestow food without labour, and without trouble, to those who had no opportunity of providing themselves with food at their leisure. (268) After this he delivered to the people a third oracle of the most marvellous nature, namely that on the seventh day the air would not afford the accustomed food, and that not the very slightest portion would fall upon the earth, as it did on other days; (269) and this turned out to be the case in point of fact; for he delivered this prediction on the day before; but some of those who were unstable in their dispositions, went forth to collect it, and being deceived in their expectations, returned unsuccessful, reproaching themselves for their unbelief, and calling the prophet the only true prophet, the only one who knew the will of God, and the only one who had any foreknowledge of what was uncertain and future.

XLIX

XLIX. (270) Such then are the predictions which he delivered, under the influence of inspiration, respecting the food which came down from heaven; but he also delivered others in succession of great necessity, though they appeared to resemble recommendations rather than actual oracles; one of which is that prediction, which he delivered respecting their greatest abandonment of their national customs, of which I have already spoken, when they made a golden calf in imitation of the Egyptian worship and folly, and established dances and prepared an altar, and offered up sacrifices, forgetful of the true God and discarding the noble disposition of their ancestors, which had been increased by piety and holiness, (271) at which Moses as very indignant, first of all, at all the people having thus suddenly become blind, which but a short time before had been the most sharp-sighted of all nations; and secondly, at a vain invention of fable being able to extinguish such exceeding brilliancy of truth, which even the sun in its eclipse or the whole company of the stars could never darken; for it is comprehended by its own light, appreciable by the intellect and incorporeal, in comparison of which the light, which is perceptible by the external senses, is like night if compared to day. (272) And, moved by this cause, he no longer continued as before, but leaped as it were out of his former appearance and disposition, and became inspired, and said, "Who is there who has not consented to this error, and who has not given sanction to what ought not to be sanctioned? Let all such come over to Me." [1175] (273) And when one tribe had come over to him, and not less with their minds than with their bodies, who indeed had some time before been eager for the slaughter of the impious and wicked doers, and who had sought for a leader and chief of their host who would justly point out to them the opportunity and proper manner of repressing their wickedness; then he, seeing that they were enraged and full of good confidence and courage, was inspired still more than before, and said, "Let every one of you take a sword, and go swiftly through the whole army, and slay not only strangers, but also those who are nearest and dearest to him of his own friends and relations, attacking them all, judging his action to be a most holy one, as being in the defence of truth and of the honour due to God, to fight for which, and to be the champion of which objects, is the lightest of labours." (274) So they rushed forth with a shout, and slew three thousand, especially those who were the leaders of this impiety, and not only were excused themselves from having had any participation in the wicked boldness of the others, but were also enrolled among the most noble of valiant men, and were thought worthy of an honour and reward most appropriate to their action, to wit the priesthood. For it was inevitable that those men should be ministers of holiness, who had shown themselves valiant in defence of it, and had warred bravely as its champions.

L

L. (275) I have also another still more marvellous and prodigy-like oracle to report, which indeed I have mentioned before, when I was relating the circumstances of the high priesthood of the prophet, one which he himself uttered when fully inspired by the divine spirit, and which received its accomplishment at no long period afterwards, but at the very moment that it was delivered. (276) There were two classes of ministrations concerning the temple; the higher one belonging to the priests, and the lower one to the keepers of the temple; and there were at this time three priests, but many thousand keepers of the temple. (277) These men, being puffed up at the exceeding greatness of their own numbers, despised the scanty numbers of the priests; and so they concerted two impious attempts at the same time, the one of which was the destruction of those who were superior to them, and the other was the promotion of the inferior body, the subjects as it were attacking the leaders, to the confusion and overthrow of that most excellent and most beneficial thing for the people, namely order. (278) Then, joining together and assembling in one place, they cried out upon the prophet as if he had given the priesthood to his brother, and to his nephews, out of consideration for their relationship to him, and had given a false account of their appointment, as if it had not taken place under the direction of divine providence, as we have represented. (279) And Moses, being vexed and grieved beyond measure at these things, although he was the meekest and mildest of men, was not so excited to a just anger by his disposition, which hated iniquity, that he besought God to reject their sacrifice. Not because there was any chance of that most righteous Judge receiving the unholy offerings of wicked men, but because the soul of the man who loved God could not be silent for his part, so eager was it that the wicked should not prosper, but should always fail in their purpose; (280) and while he was still boiling over and inflamed with anger by this lawful indignation he became inspired, and changed into a prophet, and uttered the following oracles. "Apostacy is an evil thing, but these faithless men shall be taught, not only by words but also by actions; they shall, by personal suffering, learn my truth and good faith, since they would not learn it by ordinary instruction; (281) and this shall be discerned in the end of their life: for it they receive the ordinary death according to nature, then I have invented these oracles; but if they experience a new and unprecedented destruction, then my truth will be testified to; for I see chasms of the earth opening against them, and widened to the greatest extent, and numbers of men perishing in them, dragged down into the gulf with all their kindred, and their very houses swallowed up, and the men going down alive into hell." (282) And when he ceased speaking the earth was cloven asunder, being shaken by an earthquake, and it was burst open, especially where the tents of those wicked men were so that they were all swallowed up together, and so hidden from sight. For the parts which were rent asunder came together again as soon as the purpose for which they had been divided was accomplished. (283) And a little after this thunderbolts fell on a sudden from heaven, and slew two hundred men, the leaders of this sedition, and destroyed them all together, not leaving any portion of their bodies to receive burial. (284) And the rapid and unintermittent character of the punishment, and the magnitude of each infliction, rendered the piety of the prophet conspicuous and universally celebrated, as he thus brought God forward as a witness of the truth of his oracular denunciations. (285) We must also not overlook this circumstance, that both earth and heaven, which are the first principles of the universe, bore their share in the punishment of these wicked men, for they had rooted their wickedness in the earth, and extended it up to the sky, raising it to that vast height, (286) on which account each of the elements contributed its part to their chastisement, the earth, so as to drag down and swallow up those who were at that time weighing it down, bursting asunder and dividing; and the heaven, by tearing up and destroying them, raining down a mighty storm of much fire, a most novel kind of rain, and the end was the same, (287) both to those who were swallowed up by the earth and to those who were destroyed by the thunderbolts, for neither of them were seen any more; the one body being concealed by the earth, the chasm being united again and meeting as before, so as to make solid ground; and the other people being consumed entirely by the fire of the thunderbolts.

LI

LI. (288) And some time afterwards, when he was about to depart from hence to heaven, to take up his abode there, and leaving this mortal life to become immortal, having been summoned by the Father, who now changed him, having previously been a double being, composed of soul and body, into the nature of a single body, transforming him wholly and entirely into a most sun-like mind; he then, being wholly possessed by inspiration, does not seem any longer to have prophesied comprehensively to the whole nation altogether, but to have predicted to each tribe separately what would happen to each of them, and to their future generations, some of which things have already come to pass, and some are still expected, because the accomplishment of those predictions which have been fulfilled is the clearest testimony to the future. (289) For it was very appropriate that those who were different in the circumstances of their birth and in the mothers, from whom they were descended, should differ also in the variety of their designs and counsels, and also in the excessive diversity of their pursuits in life, and should therefore have for their inheritance, as it were, a different distribution of oracles and predictions. (290) These things, therefore, are wonderful; and most wonderful of all is the end of his sacred writings, which is to the whole book of the law what the head is to an animal. (291) For when he was now on the point of being taken away, and was standing at the very starting-place, as it were, that he might fly away and complete his journey to heaven, he was once more inspired and filled with the Holy Spirit, and while still alive, he prophesied admirably what should happen to himself after his death, relating, that is, how he had died when he was not as yet dead, and how he was buried without any one being present so as to know of his tomb, because in fact he was entombed not by mortal hands, but by immortal powers, so that he was not placed in the tomb of his forefathers, having met with particular grace which no man ever saw; and mentioning further how the whole nation mourned for him with tears a whole month, displaying the individual and general sorrow on account of his unspeakable benevolence towards each individual and towards the whole collective host, and of the wisdom with which he had ruled them. (292) Such was the life and such was the death of the king, and lawgiver, and high priest, and prophet, Moses, as it is recorded in the sacred scriptures.

Footnotes:

1169. Yonge's full title, A Treatise on the Life of Moses, that is to say, On the Theology and Prophetic Office of Moses, Book II.

1170. Yonge's translation includes a separate treatise title at this point: On the Life of Moses, That Is to Say, On the Theology and Prophetic Office of Moses, Book III. Accordingly, his next paragraph begins with roman numeral I (= XIII in the Loeb). Yonge's "treatise" concludes with number XXXIX (= LI in the Loeb). The publisher has elected to follow the Loeb numbering.

1171. Lev 24:15.

The Works of Philo Judaeus: Volume II
1172. Num 9:10.
1173. Num 27:4.
1174. Exod 15:1.
1175. Exod 32:26.

THE DECALOGUE [1176]

I

I. (1) I have in my former treatises set forth the lives of Moses and the other wise men down to his time, whom the sacred scriptures point out as the founders and leaders of our nation, and as its unwritten laws; I will now, as seems pointed out by the natural order of my subject, proceed to describe accurately the character of those laws which are recorded in writing, not omitting any allegorical meaning which may perchance be concealed beneath the plain language, from that natural love of more recondite and laborious knowledge which is accustomed to seek for what is obscure before, and in preference to, what is evident. (2) And to those who raise the question why the lawgiver gave his laws not in cities but in the deep desert, we must say, in the first place, that the generality of cities are full of unspeakable evils, and of acts of audacious impiety towards the Deity, and of injustice on the part of the citizens to one another; (3) for there is nothing which is wholly free from alloy, what is spurious getting the better of what is genuine, and what is plausible of what is true; which things in their nature are false, but which suggest plausible imaginations to the engendering of deceit in cities; (4) from whence also that most designing of all things, namely pride, is implanted, which some persons admire and worship, dignifying and making much of vain opinions, with golden crowns and purple robes, and numbers of servants and chariots, on which those men who are looked upon as fortunate and happy are borne aloft, sometimes harnessing mules or horses to their chariots, and sometimes even men, who bear their burdens on their necks, through the excess of the insolence of their masters, weighed down in soul even before they faint in body.

II

II. (5) Pride is also the cause of many other evils, such as insolence, arrogance, and impiety. And these are the beginnings of foreign and civil wars, allowing nothing whatever to rest in peace in any part, whether it be public or private, by sea or by land. (6) And why need I mention the offences of such men against one another? For even divine things are neglected by pride, even though they are generally thought to be entitled to the highest honour. And what honour can there be where there is not truth also which has an honourable name and reality, since falsehood, on the other hand, is by nature devoid of honour; (7) and the neglect of divine things is evident to those who see clearly; for they, having fashioned an infinite variety of appearances by the arts of painting and sculpture, have surrounded them with temples and shrines, and have erected altars, and adorned them with images and statues, and erections of that kind, giving celestial honours to all sorts of inanimate things, (8) and these men the sacred scriptures very felicitously liken to men born of a harlot. For as these men are inscribed as the children of all the lovers whom their mothers have had and call their fathers, from ignorance of the one who is by nature their real father, so also these men in cities, not knowing the truly and really existing and true God, have made deities of an innumerable host of false gods. (9) Then, as different beings were treated with divine honours by different nations, the diversity of opinions respecting the Supreme Being, begot also disputes about all kinds of other subjects; and it was from having a regard to these facts in the first place that Moses decided on giving his laws outside of the city. (10) He also considered this point, in the second place, that it is indispensable that the soul of the man who is about to receive sacred laws should be thoroughly cleansed and purified from all stains, however difficult to be washed out, which the promiscuous multitude of mixed men from all quarters has impregnated cities with; (11) and this is impossible to be effected unless the man dwells apart; and even then it cannot be done in a moment, but only at a much later period, when the impressions of ancient transgressions, originally deeply imprinted, have become by little and little fainter, and gradually become more and more dim, and at last totally effaced; (12) in this manner those who are skilful in the art of medicine, save their patients; for they do not think it advisable to give food before they have removed the causes of their diseases; for while the diseases remain, food is useless, being the pernicious materials of their sufferings.

III

III. (13) Very naturally therefore, having led his people from the injurious associations prevailing in the cities, into the desert, that he might purify their souls from their offences he begun to bring them food for their minds; and what could this food be but divine laws and reasonings? (14) The third cause is this; as men who set out on a long voyage do not when they have embarked on board ship, and started from the harbour, then begin for the first time to prepare their masts, and cables, and rudders, but, while still remaining on the land, they make ready everything which can conduce to the success of their voyage; so in the same manner Moses did not think it fit that his people, after they had received their inheritances, and settled as inhabitants of their cities, should then seek laws in accordance with which they were to regulate their cities, but that, having previously prepared laws and constitutions, and being trained in those regulations, by which nations can be governed with safety, they should then be settled in their cities, being prepared at once to use the just regulations which were already prepared for them, in unanimity and a complete participation in and proper distribution of those things which were fitting for each person.

IV

IV. (15) And some persons say that there is also a fourth cause which is not inconsistent with, but as near as possible to the truth; for that, as it was necessary that a conviction should be implanted in the minds of men that these laws were not the inventions of men, but the most indubitable oracles of God, he on that account, led the people as far as possible from the cities into the deep wilderness, which was barren not only of all fruits that admitted of cultivation, (16) but even of wholesome water, in order that, when after having found themselves in want of necessary food, and expecting to be destroyed by hunger and thirst, they should on a sudden find themselves amid abundance of all necessary things, spontaneously springing up around them; the heaven itself raining down upon them food called manna, and as a seasoning delicacy to that meat an abundance of quails from the air; and the bitter water being sweetened so as to become drinkable, and the precipitous rock pouring forth springs of sweet water; then they might no longer look back upon the Nile with wonder, nor be in doubt as to whether those laws were the laws of God, having received a most manifest proof of the fact from the supplies by which they now found their scarcity relieved beyond all their previous expectations; (17) for they would see that he, who had given them a sufficiency of the means of life was now also giving them a means which should contribute to their living well; accordingly, to live at all required meat and drink which they found, though they had never prepared them; and towards living well, and in accordance with nature and decorum, they required laws and enactments, by which they were likely to be improved in their minds.

V

V. (18) These are the causes which may be advanced by probable conjecture, to explain the question which is raised on this point; for the true causes God alone knows. But having said what is fitting concerning these matters, I shall now proceed in regular order to discuss the laws themselves with accuracy and precision: first of all of necessity, mentioning this point, that of his laws God himself, without having need of any one else, thought fit to promulgate some by himself alone, and some he promulgated by the agency of his prophet Moses, whom he selected, by reason of his pre-eminent excellence, out of all men, as the most suitable man to be the interpreter of his will. (19) Now those which he delivered in his own person by himself alone, are both laws in general, and also the heads of particular laws; and those which he promulgated by the agency of his prophet are all referred to those others; (20) and I will explain each kind as well as I can.

VI

VI. And first of all, I will speak of those which rather resemble heads of laws, of which in the first place one must at once admire the number, inasmuch as they are completed in the perfect number of the decade, which contains every variety of number, both those which are even, and those which are odd, and those which are even-odd; [1177] the even numbers being such as two, the odd numbers such as three, the even-odd such as five, it also comprehends all the varieties of the multiplication of numbers, and of those numbers which contain a whole number and a fraction, and of those which contain several fractional parts; (21) it comprehends likewise all the proportions; the arithmetical, which exceeds and it exceeded by an equal number: as in the case of the numbers one, and two, and three; and the geometrical, according to which, as the proportion of the first number is to the second, the same is the ratio of the second to the third, as is the case in the numbers one, two and four; and also in multiplication, which double, or treble, or in short multiply figures to any extent; also in those which are half as much again as the numbers first spoken of, or one third greater, and so on. It also contains the harmonic proportion, in accordance with which that number which is in the middle between two extremities, is exceeded by the one, and exceeds the other by an equal part; as is the case with the numbers three, four, and six. (22) The decade also contains the visible peculiar properties of the triangles, and squares, and other polygonal figures; also the peculiar properties of symphonic ratios, that of the diatessaron in proportion exceeding by one fourth, as is the ratio of four to three; that of fifths exceeding in the ratio of half as much again, as is the case with the proportion of three to two. Also, that of the diapason, where the proportion is precisely twofold, as is the ratio of two to one, or that of the double diapason, where the proportion is fourfold, as in the ratio of eight to two. (23) And it is in reference to this fact that the first philosophers appear to me to have affixed the names to things which they have given them. For they were wise men, and therefore they very speciously called the number ten the decade (teÂn dekada), as being that which received every thing (holsanei dechada ousan), from receiving (tou dechesthai) and containing every kind of number, and ratio connected with number, and every proportion, and harmony, and symphony.

VII

VII. (24) Moreover, at all events, in addition to what has been already said, any one may reasonably admire the decade for the following reason, that it contains within itself a nature which is at the same time devoid of intervals and capable of containing them. Now that nature which has no connection with intervals is beheld in a point alone; but that which is capable of containing intervals is beheld under three appearances, a line, and a superficies, and a solid. (25) For that which is bounded by two points is a line; and that which has two dimensions or intervals is a superficies, the line being extended by the addition of breadth; and that which has three intervals is a solid, length and breadth having taken to themselves the addition of depth. And with these three nature is content; for she has not engendered more intervals or dimensions than these three. (26) And the archetypal numbers, which are the models of these three are, of the point the limit, of the line the number two, and of the superficies the number three, and of the solid the number four; the combination of which, that is to say of one, and two, and three, and four completes the decade, which displays other beauties also in addition to those which are visible. (27) For one may almost say that the whole infinity of numbers is measured by this one, because the boundaries which make it up are four, namely, one, two, three, and four; and an equal number of boundaries, corresponding to them in equal proportions, make up the number of a hundred out of decades; for ten, and twenty, and thirty, and forty produce a hundred. And in the same way one may produce the number of a thousand from hundreds, and that of a myriad from thousands. (28) And the unit, and the decade, and the century, and the thousand, are the four boundaries which generate the decade, which last number, besides what has been already said, displays also other differences of numbers, both the first, which is measured by the unit alone, of which an instance is found in the numbers three, or five, or seven; and the square which is the fourth power, which is an equally equal number. Also the cube, which is the eighth power, which is equally equal equally, and also the perfect number, the number six, which is made equal to its component parts, three, and two, and one.

VIII

VIII. (29) But what is the use now of enumerating the excellencies of the decade, which are infinite in number; treating our most important task as one of no importance, which is, indeed, of itself most all-sufficient, and worthy material for the study of those who devote themselves to mathematics? The other points we must pass over for the present; but perhaps it may not be out of place to mention one by way of example; (30) for those who have devoted themselves to the doctrines of philosophy say that what are called the categories in nature are ten only in number, --quality, essence, quantity, relation, action, passion, possession, condition, and those two without which nothing can exist, time and place. (31) For there is nothing which is devoid of participation in these things; as, for instance, I partake of essence, borrowing of each one of the elements of which the whole world was made, that is to say, of earth and water, and air and fire, what is sufficient for my own existence. I also partake of quality, inasmuch as I am a man; and of quantity, inasmuch as I am a man of such and such a size. I also partake of relation, when any one is on my right hand or on my left. Again, I am in action when I rub or burn any thing. I am in passion when I am cut or rubbed by any one else. I am discerned as a possessor, when I am clothed or equipped with anything. And I am seen in condition, when sitting still or lying down. And I am altogether in time and place, since not one of all the categories just mentioned can exist without both these things.

IX

IX. (32) This, then, may be enough to say on these subjects; but it is necessary now to connect with these things what I am about to say, namely, that it was the Father of the universe who delivered these ten maxims, or oracles, or laws and enactments, as they truly are, to the whole assembled nation of men and women altogether. Did he then do so, uttering himself some kind of voice? Away! let not such an idea ever enter your mind; for God is not like a man, in need of a mouth, and of a tongue, and of a windpipe, (33) but as it seems to me, he at that time wrought a most conspicuous and evidently holy miracle, commanding an invisible sound to be created in the air, more marvellous than all the instruments that ever existed, attuned to perfect harmonies; and that not an inanimate one, nor yet, on the other hand, one that at all resembled any nature composed of soul and body; but rather it was a rational soul filled with clearness and distinctness, which fashioned the air and stretched it out and changed it into a kind of flaming fire, and so sounded forth so loud and articulate a voice like a breath passing through a trumpet, so that those who were at a great distance appeared to hear equally with those who were nearest to it. (34) For the voices of men, when they are spread over a very long distance, do naturally become weaker and weaker, so that those who are at a distance from them cannot arrive at a clear comprehension of them, but their understanding is gradually dimmed by the extension of the sound over a larger space, since the organs also by which it is extended are perishable. (35) But the power of God, breathing forth vigorously, aroused and excited a new kind of miraculous voice, and diffusing its sound in every direction, made the end more conspicuous at a distance than the beginning, implanting in the soul of each individual another hearing much superior to that which exists through the medium of the ears. For the one, being in some degree a slower kind of external sense, remains in a state of inactivity until it is struck by the air, and so put in motion. But the sense of the inspired mind outstrips that, going forth with the most rapid motion to meet what is said.

X

X. (36) This, then, may be enough to say about the divine voice. But a person may very reasonably raise the question on what account it happened, when there were so vast a number of myriads of men collected into one place that Moses chose to deliver each of the ten commandments in such a form as if they had been addressed not to many persons but to one, saying:--

Thou shalt not commit adultery.
Thou shalt not steal.
Thou shalt not Kill. [1178]

And giving the other commandments in the same form. (37) We must say, therefore that he is desirous here to teach that most excellent lesson to those who read the sacred scriptures, that each separate individual by himself when he is an observer of the law and obedient to God, is of equal estimation with a whole nation, be it ever so populous, or I might rather say, with all the nations upon earth. And if I were to think fit I might proceed further and say, with all the world; (38) because in another passage of the scriptures God, praising a certain just man, says, "I am thy God."[1179] But the same being was also the God of the world; so that all those who are subject to him are arranged according to the same classification, and, if they be equally pleasing to the supreme Governor of them all, they partake of an equal acceptance and honour. (39) And, secondly, we must say that any one addressing himself to an assembly in common as to a multitude is not bound to speak as if he were conversing with a single individual, but sometimes he commands or forbids a thing in a particular manner in such a way that whatever he commands does at once appear requisite to be done by every one who hears him, and does also seem to be commanded to the whole collective multitude together; for the man who receives an admonition as if addressed to himself personally is more inclined to obey it; but he who hears it as if it were only directed to him in common with others is, to a certain degree, rendered deaf to it, making the multitude a kind of veil and excuse for his obstinacy. (40) A third view of the question is, that no king or tyrant may ever despise an obscure private individual, from being full of insolence and haughty pride; but that such an one, coming as a pupil to the school of the sacred laws, may relax his eyebrows, unlearning his self-opinionativeness, and yielding rather to true reason. (41) For if the uncreated, and immortal, and everlasting God, who is in need of nothing and who is the maker of the universe, and the benefactor and King of kings, and God of gods, cannot endure to overlook even the meanest of human beings, but has thought even such worthy of being banqueted in sacred oracles and laws, as if he were about to give him a lovefeast, and to prepare for him alone a banquet for the refreshing and expanding of his soul instructed in the divine will and in the manner in which the great ceremonies ought to be performed, how can it be right for me, who am a mere mortal, to hold my head up high and to allow myself to be puffed up, behaving with insolence to my equals whose fortunes may, perhaps, not be equal to mine, but whose relationship to me is equal and complete, inasmuch as they are set down as the children of one mother, the common nature of all men? (42) I will, therefore, behave myself in an affable, and courteous, and conciliatory manner to all men, even if I should obtain the dominion over the whole earth and the whole sea, and especially to those who are in the greatest difficulties and of the least reputation, and who are destitute of all assistance from kindred of their own, to those who are orphaned of either or of both their parents, to women who have experienced widowhood, and to old men who have either never had any children at all, or who have lost at an early age those who have been born to them; (43) for, inasmuch as I myself am a man, I will not think it right to cherish a pompous and tragedian-like dignity of manner, but I will keep myself within my nature, not transgressing its boundaries, but accustoming my mind to bear human events with complacency and equanimity. Not only because of the unforeseen changes by which things of one character assume a different appearance, both in the case of those in prosperity and of those who are in adversity, but also because it is becoming, even if prosperity were to remain unaltered and unshaken that a man should not forget himself. For these reasons it appears to me to have been that God expressed his oracular commandments in the singular number, as if they were directed to a single individual.

XI

XI. (44) And, moreover, as was natural, he filled the whole place with miraculous signs and works, with noises of thunder too great for the hearing to support, and with the most radiant brilliancy of flashes of lightning, and with the sound of an invisible trumpet extending to a great distance, and with the march of a cloud, which, like a pillar, had its foundation fixed firmly on the earth, but raised the rest of its body even to the height of heaven; and, last of all, by the impetuosity of a heavenly fire, which overshadowed everything around with a dense smoke. For it was fitting that, when the power of God came among them, none of the parts of the world should be quiet, but that everything should be put in motion to minister to his service. (45) And the people stood by, having kept themselves clean from all connection with women, and having abstained from all pleasures, except those which arise from a participation in necessary food, having been purifying themselves with baths and ablutions for three days, and having washed their garments and being all clothed in the purest white robes, and standing on tiptoe and pricking up their ears, in compliance with the exhortations of Moses, who had forewarned them to prepare for the solemn assembly; for he knew that such would take place, when he, having been summoned up alone, gave forth the prophetic commands of God. (46) And a voice sounded forth from out of the midst of the fire which had flowed from heaven, a most marvellous and awful voice, the flame being endowed with articulate speech in a language familiar to the hearers, which expressed its words with such clearness and distinctness that the people seemed rather to be seeing than hearing it. (47) And the law testifies to the accuracy of my statement, where it is written, "And all the people beheld the voice most evidently." For the truth is that the voice of men is calculated to be heard; but that of God to be really and truly seen. Why is this? Because all that God says are not words, but actions which the eyes determine on before the ears. (48) It is, therefore, with great beauty, and also with a proper sense of what is consistent with the dignity of God, that the voice is said to have come forth out of the fire; for the oracles of God are accurately understood and tested like gold by the fire. (49) And God also intimates to us something of this kind by a figure. Since the property of fire is partly to give light, and partly to burn, those who think fit to show themselves obedient to the sacred commands shall live for ever and ever as in a light which is never darkened, having his laws themselves as stars giving light in their soul. But all those who are stubborn and disobedient are for ever inflamed, and burnt, and consumed by their internal appetites, which, like flame, will destroy all the life of those who possess them.

XII

XII. (50) These, then, were the things which it was necessary to explain beforehand. But now we must turn to the commands themselves, and investigate everything which is marked by especial importance or difference in them. Now God divided them, being ten, as they are, into two tables of five each, which he engraved on two pillars. And the first five have the precedence and pre-eminence in honour; but the second five have an inferior place assigned to them. But both the tables are beautiful and advantageous to life, opening to men wrought and level roads kept within limits by one end, so as to secure the unwavering and secure progress of that soul which is continually desiring what is most excellent. (51) Now the most excellent five were of this character, they related to the monarchial principle on which the world is governed; to images and statues, and in short to all erections of any kind made by hand; to the duty of not taking the name of God in vain; to that of keeping the holy seventh day in a manner worthy of its holiness; to paying honour to parents both separately to each, and commonly to both. So that of the one table the beginning is the God and Father and Creator of the universe; and the end are one's parents, who imitate his nature, and so generate the particular individuals. And the other table of five contains all the prohibitions against adulteries, and murder, and theft, and false witness, and covetousness. (52) But we must consider, with all the accuracy possible, each of these oracles separately, not looking upon any one of them as superfluous. Now the best beginning of all living beings is God, and of all virtues, piety. And we must, therefore, speak of these two principles in the first place. There is an error of no small importance which has taken possession of the greater portion of mankind concerning a subject which was likely by itself, or, at least, above all other subjects, to have been fixed with the greatest correctness and truth in the mind of every one; (53) for some nations have made divinities of the four elements, earth and water, and air and fire. Others, of the sun and moon, and of the other planets and fixed stars. Others, again, of the whole world. And they have all invented different appellations, all of them false, for these false gods put out of sight that most supreme and most ancient of all, the Creator, the ruler of the great city, the general of the invincible army, the pilot who always guides everything to its preservation; (54) for they call the earth Proserpine, and Ceres, and Pluto. And the sea they call Neptune, inventing besides a number of marine deities as subservient to him, and vast companies of attendants, both male and female. The air they call Juno; fire, Vulcan; and the sun, Apollo; the moon, Diana; and the evening star, Venus; Lucifer, they call Mercury; (55) and to every one of the stars they have affixed names and given them to the inventors of fables, who have woven together cleverly-contrived imaginations to deceive the ear, and have appeared to have been themselves the ingenious inventors of these names thus given. (56) Again, in their descriptions, they divided the heaven into two parts, each one hemisphere, the one being above the earth and the other under the earth, which they called the Dioscuri; [1180] inventing, besides, a marvellous story concerning their living on alternate days. (57) For, as the heaven is everlasting revolving, in a circle without any cessation or interruption, it follows of necessity that each of the hemispheres must every day be in a different position from that which it was in the day before, everything being turned upside down as far as appearance goes, at least; for, in point of fact, there is no such thing as any uppermost or undermost in a spherical figure. And this expression is only used with reference to our own formation and position; that which is over our head being called uppermost, and that which is in the opposite direction being called undermost. (58) Accordingly, to one who understands how to apply himself to philosophy in a genuine, honest spirit, and who lays claim to a guiltless and pure piety, God gives that most beautiful and holy commandment, that he shall not believe that any one of the parts of the world is its own master, for it has been created; and the fact of having been created implies a liability to destruction, even though the thing created may be made immortal by the providence of the Creator; and there was a time once when it had no existence, but it is impiety to say that there was a previous time when God did not exist, and that he was born at some time, and that he does not endure for ever.

XIII

XIII. (59) But some persons indulge in such foolish notions respecting their judgments on these points, that they not only look upon the things which have been mentioned above as gods, but as each separate one of them as the greatest and first of gods, either because they are really ignorant of the true living God, from their nature being uninstructed, or else because they have no desire to learn, because they believe that there is no cause of things invisible, and appreciable only by the intellect, apart from the objects of the external senses, and this too, though the most distinct possible proof is close at hand; (60) for though, as it is owing to the soul that they live, and form designs, and do everything which is done in human life, they nevertheless have never been able to behold their soul with their eyes, nor would they be able if they were to strive with all imaginable eagerness, wishing to see it as the most beautiful possible of all images or appearances, from a sight of which they might, by a sort of comparison, derive a notion of the uncreated and everlasting God, who rules and guides the whole world in such a way as to secure its preservation, being himself invisible. (61) As, therefore, if any one were to assign the honours of the great king to his satraps and viceroys, he would appear to be not only the most ignorant and senseless of men, but also the most fool-hardy, giving to slaves what belongs to the master; in the same manner, let the man who honours the Creator, with the same honours as those with which he regards the creature, know that he is of all men the most foolish and the most unjust, in giving equal things to unequal persons, and that too not in such a way as to do honour to the inferior, but only to take it from the superior. (62) There are again some who exceed in impiety, not giving the Creator and the creature even equal honour, but assigning to the latter all honour, and respect, and reverence, and to the former nothing at all, not thinking him worthy of even the common respect of being recollected; for they forget him whom alone they should recollect, aiming, like demented and miserable men as they are, at attaining to an intentional forgetfulness. (63) Some men again are so possessed with an insolent and free-spoken madness, that they make an open display of the impiety which dwells in their hearts, and venture to blaspheme the Deity, whetting an evil-speaking tongue, and desiring, at the same time, to vex the pious, who immediately feel an indescribable and irreconcilable affliction, which enters in at their ears and pervades the whole soul; for this is the great engine of impious men, by which alone they bridle those who love God, as they think it better at the moment to preserve silence, for the sake of not provoking their wickedness further.

XIV

XIV. (64) Let us, therefore, reject all such impious dishonesty, and not worship those who are our brothers by nature, even though they may have received a purer and more immortal essence than ourselves (for all created things are brothers to one another, inasmuch as they are created; since the Father of them all is one, the Creator of the universe); but let us rather, with our mind and reason, and with all our strength, gird ourselves up vigorously and energetically to the service of that Being who is uncreated and everlasting, and the maker of the universe, never shrinking or turning aside from it, nor yielding to a desire of pleasing the multitude, by which even those who might be saved are often destroyed. (65) Let us, therefore, fix deeply in ourselves this first commandment as the most sacred of all commandments, to think that there is but one God, the most highest, and to honour him alone; and let not the polytheistical doctrine ever even touch the ears of any man who is accustomed to seek for the truth, with purity and sincerity of heart; (66) for those who are ministers and servants of the sun, and of the moon, and of all the host of heaven, or of it in all its integrity or of its principal parts, are in grievous error; (how can they fail to be, when they honour the subjects instead of the prince?) but still they sin less grievously than the others, who have fashioned stocks, and stones, and silver, and gold, and similar materials according to their own pleasure, making images, and statues, and all kinds of other things wrought by the hand; the workmanship in which, whether by statuary, or painter, or artisan, has done great injury to the life of man, having filled the whole habitable world. (67) For they have cut away the most beautiful support of the soul, namely the proper conception of the ever-living God; and therefore, like ships without ballast, they are tossed about in every direction for ever, being borne in every direction, so as never once to reach the haven, and never to be able to anchor firmly in truth, being blind respecting that which is worth seeing, and the only object as to which it is absolutely necessary to be sharp-sighted; (68) and such men appear to me to have a more miserable life than those who are deprived of their bodily sight; for these latter have either been injured without their own consent, or else have endured some terrible disease of the eyes, or else have been plotted against by their enemies; but those others by their own deliberate intention, have not only dimmed the eye of their soul, but have even chosen utterly to discard it; (69) on which account pity is bestowed on the one class as unfortunate, but the other class are justly punished as being wicked, who in conjunction with others have not chosen to recognize that fact which even an infant child would understand, namely, that the Creator is better than the creature; for he is both more ancient in point of time, and is also in a manner the father of that which he has made. He is also superior in power, for the agent is more glorious than the patient. (70) And though it would be proper, if they had not committed sins, to deify the painters and statuaries themselves with exceeding honours, they have left them in obscurity, giving them no advantage, but have looked upon the figures which have been made, or the pictures which have been painted by them, as gods; (71) and these artists have often grown old in poverty and obscurity, dying, worn out by incessant misfortunes, while the things which they have fabricated, are made splendid with purple, and gold, and all sorts of costly splendour which wealth can furnish, and are worshipped not only by freemen but even by men of noble birth, and of the greatest personal strength and beauty. For the race of priests is scrutinised with the greatest rigour and minuteness, to see whether they are without blemish, and to see whether the whole combination of the parts of their bodies is entire and perfect; (72) and these are not the worst points of all, bad as they are: but this is entirely intolerable, for I have known before now, some of the very men who have made the things, praying and sacrificing to the very things which have been made by them, when it would have been more to their purpose to worship either of their own hands, or, if they feared the reproach of self-conceit, and therefore did not choose to do that, at all events to worship their anvils, and hammers, and graving tools, and compasses, and other instruments, by means of which the materials have been fashioned into shape.

XV

XV. (73) And yet it is well for us, speaking with all proper freedom, to say to those who have shown themselves so devoid of sense; "My good men, the best of all prayers, and the end, and proper object of happiness, is to attain to a likeness to God. (74) Do you therefore pray to become like those erections of yours, that so you may reap the most supreme happiness, neither seeing with your eyes, nor hearing with your ears, nor respiring, nor smelling with your nostrils, nor speaking, nor tasting with your mouth, nor taking, nor giving, nor doing anything with your hands, nor walking with your feet, nor doing anything at all with any one of your members, but being as it were confined and guarded in the temple, as if in a prison, and day and night continually imbibing the steam from the sacrifices offered up; for this is the only one good thing which can be attributed to any kind of building or erection." (75) But I think that when they hear these things, they will be indignant, as if they were listening not to prayers, but to curses, and that they will take refuge in such defence as chance may furnish them with, bringing retaliatory accusations; which may be the greatest proof of the manifest and undesirable impiety of those men, who look upon those beings as gods, to whom they themselves would never wish to have their own natures assimilated.

XVI

XVI. (76) Let no one therefore of those beings who are endowed with souls, worship any thing that is devoid of a soul; for it would be one of the most absurd things possible for the works of nature to be diverted to the service of those things which are made by hand; and against Egypt, not only is that common accusation brought, to which the whole country is liable, but another charge also, which is of a more special character, and with great fitness; for besides falling down to statues, and images they have also introduced irrational animals, to the honours due to the gods, such as bulls, and rams, and goats, inventing some prodigious fiction with regard to each of them; (77) and as to these particular animals, they have indeed some reason for what they do, for they are the most domestic, and the most useful to life. The bull, as a plougher, draws furrows for the reception of the seed, and is again the most powerful of all animals to thresh the corn out when it is necessary to purify it of the chaff; the ram gives us the most beautiful garments for the coverings of our persons; for if our bodies were naked, they would easily be destroyed either through heat, or though intense cold, caused at one time by the blaze of the sun, and at another by the cooling of the air. (78) But as it is they go beyond these animals, and select the most fierce, and untameable of all wild animals, honouring lions, and crocodiles, and of reptiles the poisonous asp, with temples, and sacred precincts, and sacrifices, and assemblies in their honour, and solemn processions, and things of that kind. For if they were to seek out in both elements, among all the things given to man for his use by God, searching through earth and water, they would never find any animal on the land more savage than the lion, or any aquatic animal more fierce than the crocodile, both which creatures they honour and worship; (79) they have also deified many other animals, dogs, ichneumons, wolves, birds, ibises, and hawks, and even fish, taking sometimes the whole, and sometimes only a part; and what can be more ridiculous than this Conduct? [1181] (80) And, accordingly, the first foreigners who arrived in Egypt were quite worn out with laughing at and ridiculing these superstitions, till their minds had become impregnated with the conceit of the natives; but all those who have tasted of right instruction, are amazed and struck with consternation, at their system of ennobling things which are not noble, and pity those who give into it, thinking the men, as is very natural, more miserable than even the objects which they honour, since they in their souls are changed into those very animals, so as to appear to be merely brutes in human form, now returning to their original nature. (81) Therefore, God, removing out of his sacred legislation all such impious deification of undeserving objects, has invited men to the honour of the one true and living God; not indeed that he has any need himself to be honoured; for being all-sufficient for himself, he has no need of any one else; but he has done so, because he wished to lead the race of mankind, hitherto wandering about in trackless deserts, into a road from which they should not stray, that so by following nature it might find the best and end of all things, namely, the knowledge of the true and living God, who is the first and most perfect of all good things; from whom, as from a fountain, all particular blessings are showered upon the world, and upon the things are people in it.

XVII

XVII. (82) Having now spoken of the second commandment to the best of our ability, let us proceed to investigate the one which follows with accuracy, as is pointed out by the order in which they come. The next commandment is, "not to take the name of God in vain." Now the principle on which this order or arrangement proceeds is very plain to those who are gifted with acute mental vision; for the name is always subsequent in order to the subject of which it is the name; being like the shadow which follows the body. (83) Having, therefore, previously spoken of the existence of God, and also of the honour to be paid to the everlasting God; he then, following the natural order of connection proceeds to command what is becoming in respect of his name; for the errors of men with respect to this point are manifold and various, and assume many different characters. (84) That being which is the most beautiful, and the most beneficial to human life, and suitable to rational nature, swears not itself, because truth on every point is so innate within him that his bare word is accounted an oath. Next to not swearing at all, the second best thing is to keep one's oath; for by the mere fact of swearing at all, the swearer shows that there is some suspicion of his not being trustworthy. (85) Let a man, therefore, be dilatory, and slow if there is any chance that by delay he may be able to avoid the necessity of taking an oath at all; but if necessity compels him to swear, then he must consider with no superficial attention, every one of the subjects, or parts of the subject, before him; for it is not a matter of slight importance, though from its frequency it is not regarded as it ought to be. (86) For an oath is the calling of God to give his testimony concerning the matters which are in doubt; and it is a most impious thing to invoke God to be witness to a lie. Come now, if you please, and with your reason look into the mind of the man who is about to swear to a falsehood; and you will see that it is not tranquil, but full of disorder and confusion, accusing itself, and enduring all kinds of insolence and evil speaking; (87) for the conscience which dwells in, and never leaves the soul of each individual, not being accustomed to admit into itself any wicked thing, preserves its own nature always such as to hate evil, and to love virtue, being itself at the same time an accuser and a judge; being roused as an accuser it blames, impeaches, and is hostile; and again as a judge it teaches, admonishes, and recommends the accused to change his ways, and if he be able to persuade him, he is with joy reconciled to him, but if he be not able to do so, then he wages an endless and implacable war against him, never quitting him neither by day, nor by night, but pricking him, and inflicting incurable wounds on him, until he destroys his miserable and accursed life.

XVIII

XVIII. (88) "What sayest thou?" I should say to the perjured man, "will you dare to go to any one of your own acquaintances and say, My friend, come and bear witness for me that you have seen and heard, and been present at a whole catalogue of things which you have neither seen, nor heard? I think not; for that would be an act of incurable insanity; (89) with what face can you while sober, and while appearing to be master of yourself look upon your friend, and say, By reason of our acquaintance and companionship, act unjustly, violate the law, commit impiety for my sake; for it is plain that if he heard such a request, he would quickly renounce that companionship which you now believe to exist, reproaching himself for having ever had any friendship at all with a man of such a character as you, and would flee from you, as from a savage, and maddened, wild beast. (90) "Will you then, without shame call upon God, the father and sovereign of the world, to give his testimony in favour of those things, to witness which you will not venture even to bring your friend? And if you do so, will you do it knowing that he sees everything and hears everything, or not knowing this fact? (91) If you know it not you are an atheist, and atheism is the beginning of all iniquity, and, in addition to your atheism, you are also adding the wickedness of an oath, by swearing by him who in your opinion is not attending to you, nor paying any regard to human affairs. But if you are well assured that he does exert his providence in respect of such matters, still you are not free from the charge of excessive impiety, saying to God, if not with your mouth and tongue, still at all events with your conscience: Bear false witness for me, aid me in my wickedness, assist me in my impiety. I have but one hope of preserving a fair reputation among men, namely by concealing the truth; be thou wicked for another's sake, you who are the better, for the sake of one who is worse; you who are God, the most excellent of all beings, for the sake of a man, and that too a wicked one.

XIX

XIX. (92) But there are also some people who, without any idea of acquiring gain, do from a bad habit incessantly and inconsiderately swear upon every occasion, even when there is nothing at all about which any doubt is raised, as if they were desirous to fill up the deficiency of their argument with oaths, as if it would not be better to cut their conversation short, or I might rather say to utter nothing at all, but to preserve entire silence, for from a frequency of oaths arises a habit of perjury and impiety. (93) On which account the man who is going to take an oath ought to investigate everything with care and exceeding accuracy, considering whether the subject is of serious importance, and whether it has really taken place, and whether, if it has, he has comprehended it properly; and considering himself, also, whether he is pure in soul, and body, and tongue, having the first free from all violation of the law, the second from all defilement, and the last from all blasphemy. For it is an impiety for any disgraceful words to be uttered by that mouth by which the most sacred name is also mentioned. (94) Let him also consider whether the place and the time are suitable; for before now I have known some persons, in profane and impure places (in which it is not fitting that mention should be made of either their father or their mother, or of even any old man among their kindred who may have lived a virtuous life), swearing, and stringing together whole sentences full of oaths, using the name of God with all the variety of titles which belong to him, when they should not, out of sheer impiety. (95) And let him who pays but little heed to what has been said here know, in the first place, that he is impure and defiled; and, in the second place, that the most terrible punishments are constantly lying in wait for him; that justice who keeps her eye upon all human affairs, being implacable and inflexible towards all enormities of such a character; and, when she does not think fit to inflict her punishments at once, still exacting satisfaction with abundant usury whenever the opportunity seems to offer in combination with the general advantage.

XX

XX. (96) The fourth commandment has reference to the sacred seventh day, that it may be passed in a sacred and holy manner. Now some states keep the holy festival only once in the month, counting from the new moon, as a day sacred to God; but the nation of the Jews keep every seventh day regularly, after each interval of six days; (97) and there is an account of events recorded in the history of the creation of the world, comprising a sufficient relation of the cause of this ordinance; for the sacred historian says, that the world was created in six days, and that on the seventh day God desisted from his works, and began to contemplate what he had so beautifully created; (98) therefore, he commanded the beings also who were destined to live in this state, to imitate God in this particular also, as well as in all others, applying themselves to their works for six days, but desisting from them and philosophising on the seventh day, and devoting their leisure to the contemplation of the things of nature, and considering whether in the preceding six days they have done anything which has not been holy, bringing their conduct before the judgment-seat of the soul, and subjecting it to a scrutiny, and making themselves give an account of all the things which they have said or done; the laws sitting by as assessors and joint inquirers, in order to the correcting of such errors as have been committed through carelessness, and to the guarding against any similar offences being hereafter repeated. (99) But God, on one occasion, employed the six days for the completion of the world, though he had no need of any length of time for such a purpose; but each man, as partaking of a mortal nature, and as being in need of ten thousand things for the unavoidable necessities of life, ought not to hesitate, even to the end of his life, to provide himself with all requisites, always allowing himself an interval of rest on the sacred seventh day. (100) Is it not a most beautiful recommendation, and one most admirably adapted to the perfecting of, and leading man to, every virtue, and above all to piety? The commandment, in effect says: Always imitate God; let that one period of seven days in which God created the world, be to you a complete example of the way in which you are to obey the law, and an all-sufficient model for your actions. Moreover, the seventh day is also an example from which you may learn the propriety of studying philosophy; as on that day, it is said, God beheld the works which he had made; so that you also may yourself contemplate the works of nature, and all the separate circumstances which contribute towards happiness. (101) Let us not pass by such a model of the most excellent ways of life, the practical and the contemplative; but let us always keep our eyes fixed upon it, and stamp a visible image and representation of it on our own minds, making our mortal nature resemble, as far as possible, his immortal one, in respect of saying and doing what is proper. And in what sense it is said that the world was made by God in six days, who never wants time at all to make anything, has been already explained in other passages where we have treated of allegories.

XXI

XXI. (102) Now, those who have applied themselves to mathematical studies, fully explain the precedence and pre-eminence to which the number seven is entitled among all existing things, tracing it out with great care and exceeding minuteness and accuracy; for among numbers seven is the virgin number, the nature which has no mother, that which is most nearly related to the unit, the foundation of all numbers; the idea of the planets, just as the unit is of the immovable sphere; for of the unit and the number seven consists the incorporeal heaven, the model of the visible heaven, and the heaven is made up of indivisible and divisible nature. (103) Now, indivisible nature has assigned to it the first, and highest, and immovable circumference, which the unit inspects and overlooks; but the divisible nature has received that circumference which is inferior both in power and in arrangement, which the number seven inspects, which, being divided into six parts, has produced what are called the seven planets; (104) not indeed that any of the heavenly bodies do really wander (peplaneÂtai), inasmuch as they all enjoy a divine, and happy, and blessed nature, to all of which characteristics a freedom from wandering is most closely akin: at all events, they always preserve a kind of identity in a constantly similar motion, and pass a long eternity without ever admitting any change or variation whatever. But because they revolve in a manner contrary to the indivisible and outermost sphere, they have been named planets (planeÎtes), though without any strict propriety, by men speaking at random, who have by such language attributed their own propensity to wander to the heavenly bodies, which, in fact, never quit that position in the divine lamp in which they have been originally placed. (105) For all these reasons, and more besides, the number seven is honoured. But there is no one cause on account of which it has received its precedence so completely, as because it is by its means that the Creator and Father of the universe is most especially made manifest; for the mind beholds God in this as in a mirror, acting, and creating the world, and managing the whole universe.

XXII

XXII. (106) And after this commandment relating to the seventh day he gives the fifth, which concerns the honour to be paid to parents, giving it a position on the confines of the two tables of five commandments each; for being the concluding one of the first table, in which the most sacred duties to the Deity are enjoined, it has also some connection with the second table which comprehends the obligations towards our fellow creatures; (107) and the cause of this, I imagine, is as follows: The nature of one's parents appears to be something on the confines between immortal and mortal essences. Of mortal essence, on account of their relationship to men and also to other animals, and likewise of the perishable nature of the body. And of immortal essence, by reason of the similarity of the act of generation to God the Father of the universe. (108) But it has often happened that men have attached themselves to one of these divisions, and have seemed to neglect the other; for being filled with a sincere love for piety, they have renounced all other occupations and considerations, and have devoted the whole of their lives to the service of God. (109) But they who have thought that beyond their duties to their fellow men there was no such thing as goodness, have clung solely to their fellowship with and to the society of men, and, being wholly occupied by a love of the society of men, have invited all men to an equal participation in all their good things, labouring at the same time to the best of their power to alleviate all their disasters. (110) Now, one may properly call both these latter, these philanthropic men, and also the former class, the lovers of God, but half perfect in virtue; for those only are perfect who have a good reputation in both points: but those who do not attend to their duties towards men so as to rejoice with them at their common blessings, or to grieve with them at events of a contrary character, and who yet do not devote themselves to piety and holiness towards God, may be thought to have changed into the nature of wild beasts, the very preeminence among whom, in point of ferocity, those are entitled to who neglect their parents, being hostile to both the divisions of virtue above mentioned, namely, piety towards God, and their duty towards men.

XXIII

XXIII. (111) Let them, then, not be ignorant that they are convicted before the two tribunals which are the only ones which exist in nature, of impiety as regards their duty towards God, as not worshipping those who have introduced beings who do not exist into existence, and who, in this respect, have imitated God; and as regards their duty towards men, of misanthropy and cruelty. (112) For to whom else will those men do good who neglect their nearest relations and those who have bestowed the greatest gifts upon them, some of which are of so great a character that they do not admit of any requital? For how can he who has been begotten by a parent, in requital again beget his parents, since nature has bestowed on parents this especial endowment in respect of their children, which can never be requited or recompensed? On which account it is becoming to a man to feel exceeding indignation when people, because they are unable to make a full return for the benefits which they have received, do not choose to make the very slightest; (113) to whom I might say, with perfect propriety, that wild beasts even must be made tame towards men; and, indeed, I have frequently known instances of lions being domesticated, and bears and leopards, and made gentle, not only to those who feed them, by reason of their gratitude for necessaries, but also to others, on account, in my opinion, of their resemblance to their feeders. For it is always well that what is worse should follow what is better, from a hope of deriving improvement; (114) but in this case I shall be constrained to use an entirely opposite language. You who are men, are imitators of some wild beasts. Even the beasts have learnt and know how to requite with service those who have done them service. Dogs who keep the house will defend their masters, and encounter death for their sakes when any danger suddenly overtakes them. And they say that the dogs employed among flocks of sheep will fight on behalf of the flocks, and endure till they either obtain the victory or meet with death, for the sake of protecting the shepherds themselves from injury. (115) Is it not then the most shameful of all shameful things for a man, in respect of the requital of favours, to be left behind by a dog, for that being, which of all others is the most gentle, to be outrun by the most audacious of beasts? But if we will not be taught by the land animals, let us go across to the nature of the winged birds which traverse the air, and learn what we have need of from them. (116) In the case of storks the old birds remain in their nests because they are unable to fly; but their children, I had very nearly said, traverse the whole of earth and sea, and from all quarters provide their parents with what is necessary for them. (117) And so they, living in a tranquillity worthy of their time of life, enjoy all abundance, and pass their old age in luxury; while their children make light of all the hardships they undergo to furnish them with the means of support, under the influence both of piety and also of the expectation that they also in their old age will receive the same treatment from their descendants; and so they now discharge the indispensable debt which they owe their parents, knowing that in proper time, they will themselves receive what they are now bestowing. And there are also others who are unable to support themselves, for children are no more able to do so at the commencement of their existence, than their parents are at the end of their lives. On which account the children, having while young been fed in accordance with the spontaneous promptings of nature, now with joy do in return support the old age of their parents. (118) Is it not right, then, after these examples, that men who neglect their parents should cover their faces from shame, and reproach themselves for disregarding those things which they ought to have cared for alone, or in preference to any thing else whatever? And this too, when they would not have been so much conferring benefits as requiting them? For the children have nothing of their own which does not belong to the parents, who have either bestowed it upon them from their own substance, or have enabled them to acquire it by supplying them with the means. (119) And have then these men within the borders of their souls piety and holiness, the chiefs of all the virtues? No; rather they have driven them beyond their borders, and forced them into exile; for parents are the servants of God for the propagation of children, and he who dishonours the servant dishonours also the master. (120) But some persons, who are rather audacious, magnify the title of parents, saying that the father and mother are evident gods, inasmuch as they imitate the uncreated God in their production of living animals, limiting, however, their assertion in this way, that the one is the God of the whole world, but the others only of those children whom they have begotten. And it is impossible that the invisible God can be piously worshipped by those people who behave with impiety towards those who are visible and near to them.

XXIV

XXIV. (121) Having then now philosophized in this manner about the honour to be paid to parents, he closes the one and more divine table of the first five commandments. And being about to promulgate the second which contains the prohibitions of those offences which are committed against men, he begins with adultery, looking upon this as the greatest of all violations of the law; (122) for, in the first place, it has for its source the love of pleasure, which enervates the bodies of those who indulge in it, and relaxes the tone of the soul, and destroys the essences of it, consuming every thing that it touches, like unquenchable fire, and leaving nothing which affects human life uninjured, (123) inasmuch as it not only persuades the adulterer to commit iniquity, but also teaches him to join others in wickedness, making an association in things in which there ought to be no such participation. For when this violent passion seizes on a man it is impossible for the appetites to arrive at the accomplishment of their object by one person alone, but it is indispensable that two should share in the action, the one taking the place of the teacher, and the other that of the pupil, for the complete confirmation of those most disgraceful evils, intemperance and licentiousness. (124) Nor can one allege as an excuse that it is only the body of the woman who is committing adultery that is corrupted, but, if one must tell the truth, even before the corruption of the body the soul is accustomed to alienation from virtue, being taught in every way to repudiate and to hate its husband. (125) And it would be a less grievous evil if this hatred were displayed without disguise; for it is easiest to guard against what is plainly seen. But at present it is with difficulty suspected, and difficult of detection, being concealed by cunning and wicked arts, and at times it assumes the contrary appearance of love and affection, by means of its trickery and deceit. (126) Accordingly, adultery exhibits the destruction of three houses by its means; that of the house of the man who sustains the violation of all the vows which were made to him at his marriage, and the loss of all the hopes of legitimate children, of which he is now deprived; and two others, namely, the house of the adulterer, and that of his wife. For each of these is filled with insolence, and dishonour, and the most excessive disgrace. (127) And if their connections and families are very numerous, then by reason of their intermarriages and the mutual connections formed with different houses the iniquity and injury will proceed and infect the whole city all around. (128) Moreover, the doubt as to the legitimacy of the children is a most terrible evil. For if the wife be not chaste, it is quite a matter of doubt and uncertainty to what father the children belong. And then, if the matter remain undiscovered, the children of adultery enter unjustly into the classification of legitimate children, and make a race spurious to which they have no pretensions to belong, and receive an inheritance which in appearance indeed is their own patrimony, but which in reality has no connection with them. (129) And then the adulterer, behaving with insolence and pluming himself upon his iniquity in having propagated an offspring full of reproach, when he has satiated his appetites will depart, leaving the object behind him, and turning into ridicule the ignorance that exists of the unholy wickedness which he has committed, on the part of the man against whom he has sinned. And the husband, like a blind man, knowing nothing of what has been going on in his own house, will be compelled to nourish and to cherish as his own the offspring sprung from his greatest enemies. (130) And it is plain that if such a wickedness takes place, the most miserable of all persons must be the wretched children, who have done no wrong themselves, and who cannot be assigned to either family, neither to that of the husband of the adulteress, nor to that of the adulterer. (131) Since, then, illicit cohabitation produces such great calamities, adultery is very naturally a detestable thing hated by God, and has been set down as the first of all transgressions.

XXV

XXV. (132) The second commandment of this second table is to do no murder. For nature, having produced man as a gregarious and sociable creature, and the most easily domesticated of all animals, has invited it to a fellowship of opinion and partnership, giving him reason, as a means to lead to a harmony and admixture of dispositions. And he who slays any man must not be ignorant that he is overturning the laws and ordinances of nature, which have been beautifully established for the common advantage of all men. (133) Moreover, let him be aware that he is liable to the charge of sacrilege as having plundered the most sacred of all the possessions of God; for what is a more venerable or more sublime offering to God than man? For gold, and silver, and precious stones, and all such other valuable materials, are only an inanimate ornament of inanimate erections; (134) but man, who is the most excellent of all animals, in respect of that predominant part that is in him, namely, his soul, is also most closely related to the heaven, which is the purest of all things in its essence, and as the common language of the multitude affirms, to the Father of the world, inasmuch as he has received mind, which is of all the things that are upon the earth the closest copy and most faithful representation of the everlasting and blessed idea.

XXVI

XXVI. (135) The third commandment of the second table of five is not to steal. For he who keeps continually gaping after the property of others is the common enemy of the city, since, as far as his inclination goes, he would deprive all men of their property; and in respect of his power he actually does deprive some, because his covetousness is extended to the greatest imaginable length, and because his impotence, coming too late after it, is contracted into a small space, and can scarcely extend so as to overtake more than a few. (136) Therefore as many robbers as have the strength to do so plunder whole cities, paying no attention to the punishments with which they are threatened, because they appear to themselves to be superior to the laws. These are those men who are oligarchical in their natures, who have set their hearts on tyrannies and absolute power, who commit enormous thefts, concealing their robbery, as it is in reality, under the specious and imposing names of authority and supremacy. (137) Let every one then learn from his earliest infancy, never privily to steal anything that belongs to any one else, not even though it may be the merest trifle, because the habit, when it becomes inveterate, is more powerful than nature; and small things, if they are not checked, increase and grow, becoming gradually greater and greater till they reach a formidable magnitude.

XXVII

XXVII. (138) And after he has forbidden stealing he proceeds in regular order to prohibit bearing false witness, knowing that those who bear false witness are liable to many great accusations, and in short to every kind of terrible charge; for in the first place they are corrupting that holy thing, truth, than which there is no more sacred possession among men, which like the sun sheds a light upon all things, so that not one of them may be kept in darkness; (139) and in the second place, in addition to speaking falsely, they also as it were envelop facts in night and dense darkness, and they co-operate with those who offend, and they join in attacking those who are injured by others, affirming that they positively know and have completely comprehended what they in reality have not seen nor heard, and of which they know nothing. (140) Moreover, they also commit a third violation of the law, which is more grievous than either of those which have been mentioned before; for, when there is a scarcity of demonstrations, either by reasons or by letters, then those who have questions in dispute betake themselves to witnesses, whose words are rules to the judges concerning those matters on which they are to deliver their opinion; for it is necessary for the judges to attend to them alone, when there is nothing else existing which can contribute to proof in the matter in question; from which it arises that those who are borne down by evidence in this way meet with injustice when they might have won their cause, and that those who attend to the false witnesses are recorded as unjust and illegal judges, instead of just and legal ones. (141) Moreover, this kind of crafty wickedness outstrips all other offences in its impiety; for it is not customary for judges to decide without being sworn, but rather after having taken the most fearful oaths, which those men transgress who deceive others, more than they do who are deceived by them, since the error of the one is not intentional, but the others do deliberately plot against them, and do of malice aforethought sin, persuading those in whose power it is to give the decisive vote to err, not knowing what they do, so that things which deserve no chastisement meet with punishment and loss.

XXVIII

XXVIII. (142) Last of all, the divine legislator prohibits covetousness, knowing that desire is a thing fond of revolution and of plotting against others; for all the passions of the soul are formidable, exciting and agitating it contrary to nature, and not permitting it to remain in a healthy state, but of all such passions the worst is desire. On which account each of the other passions, coming in from without and attacking the soul from external points, appears to be involuntary; but this desire alone derives its origin from ourselves, and is wholly voluntary. (143) But what is it that I am saying? The appearance and idea of a present good, or of one that is accounted such, rouses up and excites the soul which was previously in a state of tranquillity, and raises it to a high degree of elation, like a light suddenly flashing before the eyes; and this passion of the soul is called pleasure. (144) But the contrary to good is evil, which, when it forces its way in, and inflicts a mortal wound, immediately fills the soul against its will with depression and despondency; and the name of the passion is sorrow. (145) But when the evil presses upon the soul, when it has not as yet taken up its habitation in it, but when it is only impending, being about to come and to agitate it, it sends before it agitation and suspense, as express messengers, to fill the soul with alarm; and this passion is denominated fear. (146) And when any one, having conceived an idea of some good which is not present, hastens to lay hold of it, he then drives his soul forward to a great distance, and extending it in the greatest possible degree, from his anxiety to attain the object of his desires, he is stretched as it were upon the rack, being anxious to lay hold of the thing, but being unable to reach it, and being in the same condition with those who are pursuing people who are running away, following with an inferior speed, but with unrivalled eagerness. (147) And something of the same kind appears to happen, also, with respect to the external senses; for very frequently the eyes, hastening to come to the comprehension of something which is removed to a great distance, strain themselves, exerting themselves to the very fullest extent of and even beyond their power, are unsuccessful, and grow dim in the empty space between themselves and their object, wholly failing in attaining to an accurate knowledge of the subject before them, and moreover impairing and injuring their sight by the exceeding intensity of their efforts and steady gaze. (148) And, again, sometimes when an indistinct noise is borne towards us from a long distance, the ears are excited, and feeling as it were a fair breeze, are eager and hasten to approach nearer to it if possible, from a desire that the sound should be distinctly apprehended by the sense of hearing. (149) But the noise, for it is still obscure as it seems, strikes the ear but faintly, not giving forth any more distinct tone by which it may be understood, so that the desire of comprehending it, being unsuccessful and unsatisfied, is excited more and more, the desire causing a Tantalus-like kind of punishment. For Tantalus, whenever he seemed about to lay his hands on any of the objects which he desired, was invariably disappointed, and the man who is overcome by desire, being always thirsting for what is not present, is never satisfied, wallowing about among vain appetites, (150) like those diseases which would creep over the whole body, if they were not checked by excision or cautery, and which would overrun and seize upon the whole composition of the body, not leaving a single part in a sound state; in like manner, unless discourse in accordance with philosophy did not, like a good physician, check the influx of appetite, all the affairs of life would of necessity be set in motion in a manner contrary to nature; for there is nothing exempt from such an affliction, nothing which can escape the dominion of passion, but, when once it has obtained immunity and license, it devours everything and becomes by itself everything in every part. (151) Perhaps it is a piece of folly to make a long speech upon matters which are so manifest, as to which there is no individual and no city that is ignorant, that they are not only every day, but even every hour, as one may say, supplying a visible proof of the truth of my assertion. Is the love of money, or of women, or of glory, or of any one of the other efficient causes of pleasure, the origin of slight and ordinary evils? (152) Is it not owing to this passion that relationships are broken asunder, and change the good will which originates in nature into an irreconcilable enmity? And are not great countries and populous kingdoms made desolate by domestic seditions, through such causes? And are not earth and sea continually filled with novel and terrible calamities by naval battles and military expeditions for the same reason? (153) For, both among the Greeks and barbarians, the wars between one another, and between their own different tribes, which have been so celebrated by tragedians, have all flowed from one source, namely, desire of money, or glory, or pleasure; for it is on such subjects as these that the race of mankind goes mad.

XXIX

XXIX. (154) However, enough of these matters. Still we must not be ignorant of this fact either, that the ten commandments are the heads of all the particular and special laws which are recorded throughout all the history of the giving of the law related in the sacred scriptures. (155) The first law is the fountain of all those concerning the government of one supreme Ruler, and they show that there is one first cause of the world, one Ruler and King, who guides and governs the universe in such a way as conduces to its preservation, having banished from the pure essence of heaven all oligarchy and aristocracy, those treacherous forms of government which arise among wicked men, as the offspring of disorder and covetousness. (156) And the second commandment is the summary of all those laws which can possibly be enacted, about all the things made by hands, such as images and statues, and, in short, erections of any kind, of which the painters' and statuaries' arts are pernicious creators, for that commandment forbids such images to be made, and prohibits the cleaving to any of the fabulous inventions about the marriage of gods and the birth of gods, and the number of indescribable and painful calamities which are represented to have ensued from both such circumstances. (157) By the third commandment he restrains people from taking oaths, and limits the objects for which one may swear, defining when and where it may be lawful, and who may swear, and how the swearer ought to be disposed, both in his soul and body, and many other minute particulars, concerning those who keep their oaths, and the contrary.

XXX

XXX. (158) And the fourth commandment, the one about the seventh day, we must not look upon in any other light than as a summary of all the laws relating to festivals, and of all the purificatory rites enjoined to be observed on each of them. But the service appointed for them was one of holy ablutions, and prayers deserving to be heard, and perfect sacrifices. (159) And in speaking of the seventh here, I mean both that which is combined with the number six, the most generative of all numbers, and also that which, without being combined with the number six, is added to it, being made to resemble the unit, each of which numbers is reckoned among the festivals; for the lawgiver refers to the term, the sacred festival of the new moon, which the people give notice of with trumpets, and the day of fasting, on which abstinence from all meats and drinks is enjoined, which the Hebrews call, in their native language, pascha, on which the whole nation sacrifices, each individual among them, not waiting for the priests, since on this occasion the law has given, for one especial day in every year, a priesthood to the whole nation, so that each private individual slays his own victim on this day. (160) And also the day on which is offered the sheaf of corn, as an offering of gratitude for the fertility and productiveness of the plain, as exhibited in the fulness of the ears of corn. And the day of pentecost, which is numbered from this day by seven portions of seven days, in which it is the custom to offer up loaves, which are truly called the loaves of the first fruits, since, in fact, they are the first fruits of the productions and crops of eatable grain, which God has given to mankind, as the most tractable of all his creatures. (161) But to the seventh day of the week he has assigned the greatest festivals, those of the longest duration, at the periods of the equinox both vernal and autumnal in each year; appointing two festivals for these two epochs, each lasting seven days; the one which takes place in the spring being for the perfection of what is being sown, and the one which falls in autumn being a feast of thanksgiving for the bringing home of all the fruits which the trees have produced. And seven days have very appropriately been appointed to the seventh month of each equinox, so that each month might receive an especial honour of one sacred day of festival, for the purpose of refreshing and cheering the mind with its holiday. (162) There are also other laws brought forward, enacted with great wisdom and excellence, conducing to the production of gentleness and fellowship among men, and inviting them to simplicity and equality; of these some have reference to that which is called the sabbatical year, in which it is expressly commanded that the people shall leave the whole land uncultivated, neither sowing, nor ploughing, nor preserving the trees, nor doing any other of the works which relate to agriculture; (163) for God thought the land, both the champaign and the mountainous country, after it had been labouring for six years in the production of crops, and the yearly yielding of its expected fruits, worthy of some relaxation, for the sake of recovering its breath as it were, and that, becoming free again, if one may say so, it might exert the spontaneous riches of its own nature. (164) There are also other laws about the fiftieth year, in which what has been enumerated above is performed in the most complete manner; and, what is the most important thing of all, the restitution is made of the different portions of land to those families which originally received them, a transaction full of humanity and equity.

XXXI

XXXI. (165) And the fifth commandment, that about the honour due to parents, conceals under its brief expression, many very important and necessary laws, some enacted as applicable to old and young men, some as bearing on the relations existing between rulers and subjects, others concerning benefactors and those who have received benefits, others affecting slaves and masters; (166) for parents belong to the superior class of all these divisions just mentioned, the class, I mean, of elders, of rulers, of benefactors, and of masters; and children are in the inferior class, in which are ranked the younger people, the subjects, those who have received benefits, and slaves. (167) There are also many other commandments given, some to the young, admonishing them to receive gladly the admonitions of old age; others to the old, bidding them take care of the young; some to subjects, enjoining them to show obedience to their rulers; others to the rulers, commanding them to consult for the advantage of those who are under their authority; some to those who have received benefits, recommending them a requital of the favours which have been conferred on them; others to those who have set the example of beneficence, bidding them not to exact a strict restitution as if they were usurers; some to servants, encouraging them to show an affectionate service towards their masters, others to the masters recommending them to practise that gentleness and mildness towards their slaves, by which the inequality of their respective conditions is in some degree equalised.

XXXII

XXXII. (168) The first table of five, then, is completed in these commandments, exhibiting a comprehensive character; but of the special and particular laws the number is very great. Of the second table, the first commandment is that against adulterers, under which many other commands are conveyed by implication, such as that against seducers, that against practisers of unnatural crimes, that against all who live in debauchery, that against all men who indulge in illicit and incontinent connections; (169) but the lawgiver has set down all the different species of such intemperance, not for the sake of exhibiting its manifold, and diverse, and ever-changing varieties, but in order to cause those who live in an unseemly manner to show most evident signs of depression and shame, drinking in with their ears all the reproaches heaped together which they incur, and which may well make them blush. (170) The second brief commandment, the prohibition of slaying men, is that under which are implied all those necessary and most universally advantageous laws, relating to acts of violence, to insults, to assaults, to wounds, to mutilation. (171) The third, that which forbids stealing, is the one under cover of which are enacted all the regulations which have been laid down, respecting the repudiation of debts, and those who deny what has been deposited with them, and who form unhallowed partnerships, and indulge in shameless acts of rapine, and, in short, in any kind of covetousness by which some person are induced, either openly or secretly to appropriate the possessions of others. (172) The fourth, that which is concerning the duty of not bearing false witness, is one under which many other prohibitions are conveyed, such as that of not deceiving, of not bringing false accusations, of not co-operating with those who are committing sin, of not making a pretence of good faith a cloak for faithlessness; for all which objects suitable laws have been enacted. (173) The fifth is that which cuts off desire, the fountain of all iniquity, from which flow all the most unlawful actions, whether of individuals or of states, whether important or trivial, whether sacred or profane, whether they relate to one's life and soul, or to what are called external things; for, as I have said before, nothing ever escapes desire, but, like a fire in a wood, it proceeds onward, consuming and destroying everything; (174) and there are a great many subordinate sins, which are prohibited likewise under this commandment, for the sake of correcting those persons who cheerfully receive admonitions, and of chastising those stubborn people who devote their whole lives to the indulgence of passion.

XXXIII

XXXIII. (175) I have now spoken in this manner, at sufficient length, concerning the second table of five commandments, which make up the whole number of ten, which God himself promulgated with the dignity befitting their holy character; for it was suitable to his own nature to promulgate in his own person the heads and principles of all particular laws, but to send forth the particular and special laws by the most perfect of the prophets, whom he selected for his preeminent excellence, and filled with his divine spirit, and then appointed to be the interpreter of his holy oracles. (176) After having explained these matters, let us now proceed to relate the cause for which God, having pronounced these ten commandments or laws, in simple injunctions and prohibitions, appointed no punishment for those who should violate them, as lawgivers usually do. The reason is this: he was God, and being so he was at once the good Lord, the cause of good alone, and of no evil; (177) therefore, thinking it most appropriate to his own nature to deliver saving commands unalloyed, and partaking of no punishment, so that no one yielding to a foolish counsellor might accidentally choose what is best, but might do so from wise consideration and of his own deliberate purpose, he did not think fit to give his oracles to mankind in connection with any denunciation of punishment; not because he meant to give immunity to transgressors, but because he knew that justice was sitting by him, and surveying all human affairs, and that she would never rest, as being by nature a hater of evil and looking upon the chastisement of sinners as her own most appropriate task. (178) For it is proper for all the ministers and lieutenants of God, just as for generals in war, to put in practice severe punishments against those deserters, who forsake the ranks of the just one; but it becomes the great King, that general safety should be ascribed to him, as preserving the universe in peace, and giving at all times, to all people, in all riches and abundance, all the blessings of peace: for, in truth, God is the president of peace, but his subordinate ministers are the chiefs of war.

Footnotes:

1176. Yonge's title, A Treatise Concerning the Ten Commandments, Which Are the Heads of the Law.

1177. Liddell and Scott explain this as meaning such even numbers as become odd when divided, as 2, 6, 10, 14, etc.

1178. Exod 20:13.

1179. Gen 17:1.

1180. dios kouroi. Sons of Jupiter, i.e., Castor and Pollux. The Gemini or Twins of the Zodiac. The story of their living and dying on alternate days is alluded to by Virgil, Aen. 6.121, where Aeneas says (as it is translated by Dryden)--"If Pollux, off'ring his alternate life, / Could free his brother; and can daily go / By turns aloft, by turns descend below."

1181. this was one of the things which especially excited the ridicule of the Romans. Juvenal says, Sat. 15.1, (as it is translated by Gifford)--"Who knows not to what monstrous gods, my friend, / The mad inhabitants of Egypt bend? / The snake devouring ibis, these enshrine / Those think the crocodile alone divine; / Others, where Thebes' vast ruins strew the ground / And shattered Memnon yields a magic sound, / Set up a glittering brute of uncouth shape, / And bow before the image of an ape! / Thousands regard the hound with holy fear, / Not one Diana."

THE SPECIAL LAWS, I [1182]

I

I. (1) The genera and heads of all special laws, which are called "the ten commandments," have been discussed with accuracy in the former treatise. We must now proceed to consider the particular commands as we read them in the subsequent passages of the holy scriptures; and we will begin with that which is turned into ridicule by people in general. (2) The ordinance of circumcision of the parts of generation is ridiculed, though it is an act which is practised to no slight degree among other nations also, and most especially by the Egyptians, who appear to me to be the most populous of all nations, and the most abounding in all kinds of wisdom. (3) In consequence of which it would be most fitting for men to discard childish ridicule, and to investigate the real causes of the ordinance with more prudence and dignity, considering the reasons why the custom has prevailed, and not being precipitate, so as without examination to condemn the folly of mighty nations, recollecting that it is not probable that so many myriads should be circumcised in every generation, mutilating the bodies of themselves and of their nearest relations, in a manner which is accompanied with severe pain, without adequate cause; but that there are many reasons which might encourage men to persevere and continue a custom which has been introduced by previous generations, and that these are from reasons of the greatest weight and importance. (4) First of all, that it is a preventive of a painful disease, and of an affliction difficult to be cured, which they call a carbuncle; [1183] because, I imagine, when it becomes inflamed it burns; from which fact it has derived that appellation. And this disease is very apt to be engendered among those who have not undergone the rite of circumcision. (5) Secondly, it secures the cleanliness of the whole body in a way that is suited to the people consecrated to God; with which object the Egyptian priests, being extravagant in their case, shave the whole of their bodies; for some of these evils which ought to be got rid of are collected in and lodge under the hair and the prepuce. (6) Thirdly, there is the resemblance of the part that is circumcised to the heart; for both parts are prepared for the sake of generation; for the breath contained within the heart is generative of thoughts, and the generative organ itself is productive of living beings. Therefore, the men of old thought it right to make the evident and visible organ, by which the objects of the outward senses are generated, resemble that invisible and superior part, by means of which ideas are formed. (7) The fourth, and most important, is that which relates to the provision thus made for prolificness; for it is said that the seminal fluid proceeds in its path easily, neither being at all scattered, nor flowing on its passage into what may be called the bags of the prepuce. On which account those nations which practise circumcision are the most prolific and the most populous.

II

II. (8) These considerations have come to our ears, having been discussed of old among men of divine spirit and wisdom, who have interpreted the writings of Moses in no superficial or careless manner. But, besides what has been already said, I also look upon circumcision to be a symbol of two things of the most indispensable importance. (9) First of all, it is a symbol of the excision of the pleasures which delude the mind; for since, of all the delights which pleasure can afford, the association of man with woman is the most exquisite, it seemed good to the lawgivers to mutilate the organ which ministers to such connections; by which rite they signified figuratively the excision of all superfluous and excessive pleasure, not, indeed, of one only, but of all others whatever, though that one which is the most imperious of all. (10) The second thing is, that it is a symbol of a man's knowing himself, and discarding that terrible disease, the vain opinion of the soul; for some men, like good statuaries, have boasted that they can make that most beautiful animal, man; and, being puffed up with arrogance, have deified themselves, hiding from sight the true cause of the creation of all things namely, God, although they might have corrected that error from a consideration of other persons among whom they live; (11) for there are among them many men who have no children, and many barren women whose connections lead to nothing, so that they grow old in childlessness. We must therefore eradicate evil opinions from the mind, and all other ideas which are not devoted to God. This, then, is enough to say on these subjects. (12) But we must now turn to the special and particular laws; and first of all to those which relate to those people by whom it is well to be governed, those which have been enacted concerning Monarchy.[1184]

III

III. (13) Some persons have conceived that the sun, and the moon, and the other stars are independent gods, to whom they have attributed the causes of all things that exist. But Moses was well aware that the world was created, and was like a very large city, having rulers and subjects in it; the rulers being all the bodies which are in heaven, such as planets and fixed stars; (14) and the subjects being all the natures beneath the moon, hovering in the air and adjacent to the earth. But that the rulers aforesaid are not independent and absolute, but are the viceroys of one supreme Being, the Father of all, in imitation of whom they administer with propriety and success the charge committed to their care, as he also presides over all created things in strict accordance with justice and with law. Others, on the contrary, who have not discovered the supreme Governor, who thus rules everything, have attributed the causes of the different things which exist in the world to the subordinate powers, as if they had brought them to pass by their own independent act. (15) But the most sacred lawgiver changes their ignorance into knowledge, speaking in the following manner: "Thou shalt not, when thou seest the sun, and the moon, and the stars, and all the host of heaven, be led astray and fall down and worship Them."[1185] With great felicity and propriety has he here called the reception of these bodies as gods, an error; (16) for they who see that the different seasons of the year owe their existence to the advances and retreats of the sun, in which periods also the generation of animals, and plants, and fruits, are perfected according to well-defined times, and who see also that the moon is the servant and successor of the sun, taking that care and superintendence of the world by night which the sun takes by day; and also that the other stars, in accordance with their sympathy with things on earth, labour continually and do ten thousand things which contribute to the duration of the existing state of things, have been led into an inextricable error, imagining that these bodies are the only gods. (17) But if they had taken pains to travel along the straight and true road, they would soon have known that just as the outward sense is the subordinate minister of the mind, so in the same manner all the objects of the outward senses are servants of that which is appreciable only by intellect, being well contented if they can attain to the second place in honour. (18) But it is altogether ridiculous to imagine that the mind, which is the smallest thing in us, being in fact invisible, is the ruler of those organs which belong to the external senses, but that the greatest and most perfect ruler of the whole universe is not the King of kings; that the being who sees, is not the ruler of those who do not see. (19) We must, therefore, look on all those bodies in the heaven, which the outward sense regards as gods, not as independent rulers, since they are assigned the work of lieutenants, being by their intrinsic nature responsible to a higher power, but by reason of their virtue not actually called to render in an account of their doings. (20) So that, transcending all visible essence by means of our reason, let us press forward to the honour of that everlasting and invisible Being who can be comprehended and appreciated by the mind alone; who is not only the God of all gods, whether appreciable only by the intellect or visible to the outward senses, but is also the creator of them all. And if any one gives up the service due to the everlasting and uncreated God, transferring it to any more modern and created being, let him be set down as mad and as liable to the charge of the greatest impiety.

IV

IV. (21) But there are some persons who have given gold and silver to sculptors and statuaries, as people able to fashion gods for them. And they, taking the lifeless materials and using a mortal model, have (which is a most extraordinary thing) made gods, as far as appearance went, and have built temples and erected altars, and dedicated them to them, honouring them with excessive pains and diligence, with sacrifices and processions, and all kinds of other sacred ceremonies and purifications; the priests and priestesses exciting themselves to the very extremity of their power to extend this kind of pride and vanity. (22) To whom the Father of the universe thus speaks, saying: "You shall not make to yourselves gods of silver and Gold;"[1186] all but teaching them in express words, "You shall not make to yourselves any gods whatever of this or of any other material, nor shall you worship anything made with hands," being forbidden expressly with respect to the two most excellent materials; for silver and gold are esteemed the most honourable of all materials. (23) And, besides this distinct prohibition, there is another meaning which appears to me to be intended to be figuratively conveyed under these words, which is one of very great influence as contributing to the formation of the moral character, and which convicts in no slight degree those who are covetous of money and who seek to procure silver and gold from all quarters, and when they have acquired it treasure it up, as though it were some divine image, in their inmost shrines, looking upon it as the cause of all good things and of all happiness. (24) And all the poor men that are possessed of that terrible disease, the love of money, but who, from not having any riches of their own which they can think worthy of their attention, fix their admiration on the wealth of their neighbours, and, for the purpose of offering adoration to it, come the first thing in the morning to the houses of those who have abundance, as if they were noble temples at which they were going to offer prayers, and to entreat blessings from their owners as if from the gods. (25) And to these men, Moses says, in another passage, "You shall not follow images, and you shall not make to yourselves molten Gods." [1187] Teaching them, by figurative language, that it is not right to pay such honours to wealth as one would pay to the gods; for those celebrated materials of wealth, silver and gold, are made to be used, which, however, the multitude follows, looking upon them as the only causes of wealth which is proverbially called blind, and the especial sources of happiness. (26) These are the things which Moses calls idols, resembling shadows and phantoms, and having about them nothing strong, or trustworthy, or lasting; for they are tossed about like the unstable wind, and are subject to all kinds of variations and changes. And the greatest possible proof of this is that, when people have not at all expected it, it suddenly has descended upon them; and, again, when they fancied that they had taken firm hold of it, it has flown away. And when, indeed, it is present, then images appear as in a mirror, deceiving the outward senses and imposing upon them with traps, and appearing as if they would last for a long time, while in reality they do not endure. (27) And why need I explain how unstable the wealth and pride of men are, which vain opinions decorate with showy colours? For, before now, some men have existed who have affirmed that all other animals and plants, of which there is any birth or any decay, are in one continual and incessant state of transition, and that the external sense of this transition is somewhat indistinct, inasmuch as the swiftness of nature surpasses the very quickest and most precise glance of the vision.

V

V. (28) But not only are wealth, and glory, and all other such things, mere phantoms and unsubstantial images, but also all the other deceits which the inventors of fables have devised, puffing themselves up by reason of their ingenuity, while they have been raising a fortification of false opinion in opposition to the truth, bringing in God as if by some theatrical machine, in order to prevent the everlasting and only true existing God from being consigned to oblivion, are so likewise. But such men have adapted their falsehood to melodies, and rhythm, and metres, with a reference to what is persuasive, thinking that by these means they should easily cajole all who read their works. (29) Not but what they have also joined to themselves the arts of statuary and painting as copartners in their system of deceit, in order that, bringing over the spectators by well-fabricated appearances of colours, and forms, and distinctive qualities, and having won over by their allurements those principal outward senses of sight and hearing, the one by the exquisite beauty of lifeless forms, and the other by a poetical harmony of numbers--they may ravish the unstable soul and render it feeble, and deprive it of any settled foundation. (30) On this account, Moses, being well aware that pride had by that time advanced to a very high pitch of power, and that it was well guarded by the greater part of mankind, and that too not from compulsion but of their own accord, and fearing lest those men who are admirers of uncorrupted and genuine piety may be carried away as by a torrent, stamped a deep impression on the minds of men, engraving piety on them, in order that the impression he thus made might not become confused or weakened, so as at last to become wholly effaced by time. And he is constantly prophesying and telling his people that there is one God, the creator and maker of the universe; and at other time he teaches them that he is the Lord of all created things, since all that is firm, and solid, and really stable and sure, is by nature so framed as to be connected with him alone. (31) And it is said in the scriptures that, "Those that are attached to the living God do all Live." [1188] Is not this, then, a thrice happy life, a thrice blessed existence, to be contented with performing due service to the most venerable Cause of all things, and not to think fit to serve his subordinate ministers and door-keepers in preference to the King himself? And this life is an immortal one, and is recorded as one of great duration in the pillars of nature. And it is inevitably necessary that these writings should last to all eternity with the world itself.

VI

VI. (32) But the Father and Ruler of the universe is a being whose character it is difficult to arrive at by conjecture and hard to comprehend; but still we must not on that account shrink from an investigation of it. Now, in the investigations which are made into the nature of God, there are two things of the greatest importance, about which the intellect of the man who devotes himself to philosophy in a genuine spirit is perplexed. One is, whether there is any Deity at all? this question arises from the atheism (which is the greatest of all vices) of those men who study philosophy. The other question is, supposing there to be a God, what he is as to his essence? Now the former question it is not very difficult to determine; but the second is not only difficult, but perhaps impossible. We must, however, consider both these matters. (33) It has invariably happened that the works which they have made have been, in some degree, the proofs of the character of the workmen; for who is there who, when he looks upon statues or pictures, does not at once form an idea of the statuary or painter himself? And who, when he beholds a garment, or a ship, or a house, does not in a moment conceive a notion of the weaver, or shipbuilder, or architect, who has made them? And if any one comes into a well-ordered city, in which all parts of the constitution are exceedingly well arranged and regulated, what other idea will he entertain but that this city is governed by wise and virtuous rulers? (34) He, therefore, who comes into that which is truly the greatest of cities, namely, this world, and who beholds all the land, both the mountain and the champaign district full of animals, and plants, and the streams of rivers, both overflowing and depending on the wintry floods, and the steady flow of the sea, and the admirable temperature of the air, and the varieties and regular revolutions of the seasons of the year; and then too the sun and moon, the rulers of day and night, and the revolutions and regular motions of all the other planets and fixed stars, and of the whole heaven; would he not naturally, or I should rather say, of necessity, conceive a notion of the Father, and creator, and governor of all this system; (35) for there is no artificial work whatever which exists of its own accord? And the world is the most artificial and skilfully made of all works, as if it had been put together by some one who was altogether accomplished and most perfect in knowledge. It is in this way that we have received an idea of the existence of God.

VII

VII. (36) Again, even if it is very difficult to ascertain and very hard properly to comprehend, we must still, as far as it is possible, investigate the nature of his essence; for there is no employment more excellent than that of searching out the nature of the true God, even though the discovery may transcend all human ability, since the very desire and endeavour to comprehend it is able by itself to furnish indescribable pleasures and delights. (37) And the witnesses of this fact are those who have not merely tasted philosophy with their outermost lips, but who have abundantly feasted on its reasonings and its doctrines; for the reasoning of these men, being raised on high far above the earth, roams in the air, and soaring aloft with the sun, and moon, and all the firmament of heaven, being eager to behold all the things that exist therein, finds its power of vision somewhat indistinct from a vast quantity of unalloyed light being poured over it, so that the eye of his soul becomes dazzled and confused by the splendour. (38) But he does not on that account faint and renounce the task which he has undertaken, but goes on with invincible determination towards the sight which he considers attainable, as if he were a competitor at the games, and were striving for the second prize, though he has missed the first. And guess and conjecture are inferior to true perception, as are all those notions which are classed under the description of reasonable and plausible opinions. (39) Though, therefore, we do not know and cannot accurately ascertain what each of the stars is as to its pure and real essence, still we are eager to investigate the subject, delighting in probable reasonings, because of the fondness for learning which is implanted in our nature. (40) And so in the same way, though we cannot attain to a distinct conception of the truly living God, we still ought not to renounce the task of investigating his character, because even if we fail to make the discovery, the very search itself is intrinsically useful and an object of deserved ambition; since no one ever blames the eyes of the body because they are unable to look upon the sun itself, and therefore shrink from the brilliancy which is poured upon them from its beams, and therefore look down upon the earth, shrinking from the extreme brilliancy of the rays of the sun.

VIII

VIII. (41) Which that interpreter of the divine word, Moses, the man most beloved by God, having a regard to, besought God and said, "Show me thyself"--all but urging him, and crying out in loud and distinct words--"that thou hast a real being and existence the whole world is my teacher, assuring me of the fact and instructing me as a son might of the existence of his father, or the work of the existence of the workman. But, though I am very desirous to know what thou art as to thy essence, I can find no one who is able to explain to me anything relating to this branch of learning in any part of the universe whatever. (42) On which account, I beg and entreat of thee to receive the supplication of a man who is thy suppliant and devoted to God's service, and desirous to serve thee alone; for as the light is not known by the agency of anything else, but is itself its own manifestation, so also thou must alone be able to manifest thyself. For which reason I hope to receive pardon, if, from want of any one to teach me, I am so bold as to flee to thee, desiring to receive instruction from thyself." (43) But God replied, "I receive, indeed, your eagerness, inasmuch as it is praiseworthy; but the request which you make is not fitting to be granted to any created being. And I only bestow such gifts as are appropriate to him who receives them; for it is not possible for a man to receive all that it is easy for me to give. On which account I give to him who is deserving of my favour all the gifts which he is able to receive. (44) But not only is the nature of mankind, but even the whole heaven and the whole world is unable to attain to an adequate comprehension of me. So know yourself, and be not carried away with impulses and desires beyond your power; and let not a desire of unattainable objects carry you away and keep you in suspense. For you shall not lack anything which may be possessed by you." (45) When Moses heard this he betook himself to a second supplication, and said, "I am persuaded by thy explanations that I should not have been able to receive the visible appearance of thy form. But I beseech thee that I may, at all events, behold the glory that is around thee. And I look upon thy glory to be the powers which attend thee as thy guards, the comprehension of which having escaped me up to the present time, worketh in me no slight desire of a thorough understanding of it." (46) But God replied and said, "The powers which you seek to behold are altogether invisible, and appreciable only by the intellect; since I myself am invisible and only appreciable by the intellect. And what I call appreciable only by the intellect are not those which are already comprehended by the mind, but those which, even if they could be so comprehended, are still such that the outward senses could not at all attain to them, but only the very purest intellect. (47) And though they are by nature incomprehensible in their essence, still they show a kind of impression or copy of their energy and operation; as seals among you, when any wax or similar kind of material is applied to them, make an innumerable quantity of figures and impressions, without being impaired as to any portion of themselves, but still remaining unaltered and as they were before; so also you must conceive that the powers which are around me invest those things which have no distinctive qualities with such qualities, and those which have no forms with precise forms, and that without having any portion of their own everlasting nature dismembered or weakened. (48) And some of your race, speaking with sufficient correctness, call them ideas (ideai), since they give a peculiar character (idiopoiousi) to every existing thing, arranging what had previously no order, and limiting, and defining, and fashioning what was before destitute of all limitation, and defination, and fashion; and, in short, in all respects changing what was bad into a better condition. (49) "Do not, then, ever expect to be able to comprehend me nor any one of my powers, in respect of our essence. But, as I have said, I willingly and cheerfully grant unto you such things as you may receive. And this gift is to call you to the beholding of the world and all the things that are in it, which must be comprehended, not indeed by the eyes of the body, but by the sleepless vision of the soul. (50) The desire of wisdom alone is continual and incessant, and it fills all its pupils and disciples with famous and most beautiful doctrines." When Moses heard this he did not cease from his desire, but he still burned with a longing for the understanding of invisible things. [...] [1189]

IX

IX. (51) And he receives all persons of a similar character and disposition, whether they were originally born so, or whether they have become so through any change of conduct, having become better people, and as such entitled to be ranked in a superior class; approving of the one body because they have not defaced their nobility of birth, and of the other because they have thought fit to alter their lives so as to come over to nobleness of conduct. And these last he calls proselytes (proseÂlytous), from the fact of their having come over (proseleÎlythenai) to a new and Godfearing constitution, learning to disregard the fabulous inventions of other nations, and clinging to unalloyed truth. (52) Accordingly, having given equal rank and honour to all those who come over, and having granted to them the same favours that were bestowed on the native Jews, he recommends those who are ennobled by truth not only to treat them with respect, but even with especial friendship and excessive benevolence. And is not this a reasonable recommendation? What he says is this. "Those men, who have left their country, and their friends, and their relations for the sake of virtue and holiness, ought not to be left destitute of some other cities, and houses, and friends, but there ought to be places of refuge always ready for those who come over to religion; for the most effectual allurement and the most indissoluble bond of affectionate good will is the mutual honouring of the one God." (53) Moreover, he also enjoins his people that, after they have given the proselytes an equal share in all their laws, and privileges, and immunities, on their forsaking the pride of their fathers and forefathers, they must not give a license to their jealous language and unbridled tongues, blaspheming those beings whom the other body looks upon as gods, lest the proselytes should be exasperated at such treatment, and in return utter impious language against the true and holy God; for from ignorance of the difference between them, and by reason of their having from their infancy learnt to look upon what was false as if it had been true, and having been bred up with it, they would be likely to err. (54) And there are some of the Gentiles, who, not attending to the honour due to the one God alone, deserve to be punished with extreme severity of punishment, as having forsaken the most important classification of piety and holiness, and as having chosen darkness in preference to the most brilliant light, and having rendered their own intellect blind when it might have seen clearly. (55) And it is well that a charge should be given to all those who have any admiration for virtue to inflict all such punishment out of hand without any delay, not bringing them before either any judgment seat, or any council, or any bench of magistrates, but giving vent to their own disposition which hates evil and loves God, so as to chastise the impious with implacable rigour, looking upon themselves as everything for the time being, counsellors, and judges, and generals, and members of the assembly, and accusers, and witnesses, and laws, and the people; that so, since there is no conceivable hindrance, they may with all their company put themselves forward fearlessly to fight as the champions of holiness.

X

X. (56) There is, in the history of the law, a record of one man who ventured on this exploit of noble daring, for when he saw some men connecting themselves with foreign women, and by reason of their allurements neglecting all their national customs and laws, and practising fabulous ceremonies, he was seized with a sudden enthusiasm in the presence of the whole multitude; and driving away all those on each side who were collected to see the sight, he slew one man who was so daring as to put himself forward as the leader and chief of this transgression of the law (for the impious deed had been already displayed and made a public exhibition of), and while he was openly performing sacrifices to images and unholy idols, he, I say, without being influenced by any fear, slew him, together with the woman who was with him; the one on account of his inclination to learn those things which it would have been more advantageous for him not to have learnt, and the woman because she was his preceptress in evil. (57) This action being done of a sudden, in the warm impetuosity of the moment, admonished a vast multitude of those who were prepared to commit similar follies; therefore God, having praised this virtuous exploit done in this manner, out of a voluntary and spontaneous zeal, recompensed the doer with two rewards, namely, peace and the priesthood. With the one, because he judged him who had thus voluntarily encountered a contest for the sake of the honour of his God worthy to enjoy a life safe from war; and with the other, because the priesthood is the most fitting honour for a pious man, who professes an eagerness for the service of the Father of all, to serve whom is not only better than all freedom, but even than royal authority. (58) But some men have gone to such a pitch of extravagant madness, that they have left themselves no retreat or way to repentance, but hasten onwards to the slavery and service of images made by hands, confessing it in distinct characters, not written on paper, as is the custom in the case of slaves, but branding the characters deep on their persons with a burning iron, in order that they may remain ineffacebly, for these things are not dimmed or weakened by time.

XI

XI. (59) And the most sacred Moses appears to have preserved the same object and intention in all other cases whatever, being a lover and also a teacher of truth, which he desires to stamp and to impress upon all his disciples, expelling all false opinions, and compelling them to settle far from their minds. (60) At all events, knowing that the act of divination co-operates in no slight degree with the errors of the lives of the multitude, so as to lead them out of the right way, he did not suffer his disciples to use any species of it whatever, but drove all who paid it any observance far from his everlasting constitution, and banished all sacrificers and purifiers, and augurs, and soothsayers, and enchanters, and men who applied themselves to the art of prophesying from sounds; (61) for all these men are but guessers at what is probable and likely, at different times adopting different notions from the same appearances, because the subjects of their art have no stable and constant character, and because the intellect has never devised any accurate test by which those opinions which are approved may be examined. (62) And all these things are but the furniture of impiety. How so? Because he who attends to them, and who allows himself to be influenced by them, disregards the cause of all things, looking upon those things alone as the causes of all things, whether good or evil; and he does not perceive that he is making all the cares of life to depend upon the most unstable supports, upon the motion of birds and feathers in the air, in this and that direction; and upon the paths of reptiles, crawling along the ground, which creep forth out of their holes in quest of food; and even upon entrails, and blood, and dead corpses, which, the moment that they are deprived of life, fall to pieces and become confused; and being deprived of their original nature which belonged to them, are changed, and subjected to a transformation for the worse. (63) For he thinks it right, that the man who is legally enrolled as a citizen of his constitution must be perfect, not indeed in those things in which the multitude is educated, such as divination, and augury, and plausible conjectures, but in the observances due to God, which have nothing doubtful or uncertain about them, but only indubitable and naked truth. (64) And since there is implanted in all men a desire of the knowledge of future events, and as, on account of this desire, they have recourse to sacrifices and to other species of divination, as if by these means they would be able to search out and discover the truth (but these things are, in reality, full of indistinctness and uncertainty, and are continually being convicted by themselves). He, with great energy, forbids his disciples to apply themselves to such sources of knowledge; and he says, that if they are truly pious they shall not be deprived of a proper knowledge of the future; (65) but that some other Prophet[1190] will appear to them on a sudden, inspired like himself, who will preach and prophesy among them, saying nothing of his own (for he who is truly possessed and inspired, even when he speaks, is unable to comprehend what he is himself saying), but that all the words that he should utter would proceed from him as if another was prompting him; for the prophets are interpreters of God, who is only using their voices as instruments, in order to explain what he chooses. Having now then said this, and other things like this, concerning the proper idea to be entertained of the one real, and true, and living God; he proceeds to express in what manner one ought to pay him the honours that are his Due. [1191]

XII

XII. (66) We ought to look upon the universal world as the highest and truest temple of God, having for its most holy place that most sacred part of the essence of all existing things, namely, the heaven; and for ornaments, the stars; and for priests, the subordinate ministers of his power, namely, the angels, incorporeal souls, not beings compounded of irrational and rational natures, such as our bodies are, but such as have the irrational parts wholly cut out, being absolutely and wholly intellectual, pure reasonings, resembling the unit. (67) But the other temple is made with hands; for it was desirable not to cut short the impulses of men who were eager to bring in contributions for the objects of piety, and desirous either to show their gratitude by sacrifices for such good fortune as had befallen them, or else to implore pardon and forgiveness for whatever errors they might have committed. He moreover foresaw that there could not be any great number of temples built either in many different places, or in the same place, thinking it fitting that as God is one, his temple also should be one. (68) In the next place, he does not permit those who desire to perform sacrifices in their own houses to do so, but he orders all men to rise up, even from the furthest boundaries of the earth, and to come to this temple, by which command he is at the same time testing their dispositions most severely; for he who was not about to offer sacrifice in a pure and holy spirit would never endure to quit his country, and his friends, and relations, and emigrate into a distant land, but would be likely, being under the influence of a more powerful attraction than that towards piety, to continue attached to the society of his most intimate friends and relations as portions of himself, to which he was most closely attached. (69) And the most evident proof of this may be found in the events which actually took place. For innumerable companies of men from a countless variety of cities, some by land and some by sea, from east and from west, from the north and from the south, came to the temple at every festival, as if to some common refuge and safe asylum from the troubles of this most busy and painful life, seeking to find tranquillity, and to procure a remission of and respite from those cares by which from their earliest infancy they had been hampered and weighed down, (70) and so, by getting breath as it were, to pass a brief time in cheerful festivities, being filled with good hopes and enjoying the leisure of that most important and necessary vacation which consists in forming a friendship with those hitherto unknown, but now initiated by boldness and a desire to honour God, and forming a combination of actions and a union of dispositions so as to join in sacrifices and libations to the most complete confirmation of mutual good will.

XIII

XIII. (71) Of this temple the outer circuit, being the most extensive both in length and width, was fortified by fortifications adorned in a most costly manner. And each of them is a double portico, built and adorned with the finest materials of wood and stone, and with abundant supplies of all kinds, and with the greatest skill of the workmen, and the most diligent care on the part of the superintendants. But the inner circuits were less extensive, and the fashion of their building and adorning was more simple. (72) And in the centre was the temple itself, beautiful beyond all possible description, as one may conjecture from what is now seen around on the outside; for what is innermost is invisible to every human creature except the high priest alone, and even he is enjoined only to enter that holy place once in each year. Everything then is invisible. For he carries in a brasier full of coals and frankincense; and then, when a great smoke proceeds from it, as is natural, and when everything all around is enveloped in it, then the sight of men is clouded, and checked, and prevented from penetrating in, being wholly unable to pierce the cloud. (73) But, being very large and very lofty, although built in a very low situation, it is not inferior to any of the greatest mountains around. The buildings of it are of most exceeding beauty and magnificence, so as to be universal objects of admiration to all who behold them, and especially to all foreigners who travel to those parts, and who, comparing them with their own public edifices, marvel both at the beauty and sumptuousness of this one. (74) But there is no grove of plantation in the space which surrounds it, in accordance with the prohibitions of the law, which for many reasons forbid this. In the first place, because a building which is truly a temple does not aim at pleasure and seductive allurements, but at a rigid and austere sanctity. Secondly, because it is not proper that those things which conduce to the verdure of trees should be introduced, such as the dung of irrational animals and of men. Thirdly, because those trees which do not admit of cultivation are of no use, but are as the poets say, the burden of the earth; while those which do admit of cultivation, and which are productive of wholesome fruit, draw off the attention of the fickle-minded from the thoughts of the respect due to the holy place itself, and to the ceremonies in which they are engaged. (75) And besides these reasons, shady places and dense thickets are places of refuge for evil doers, since by their enveloping them in darkness they give them safety and enable them, as from an ambuscade, suddenly to fall upon any whom they choose to attack. But wide spaces, open and uncovered in every direction, where there is nothing which can hinder the sight, are the most suitable for the distinct sight of all those who enter and remain in the temple.

XIV

XIV. (76) But the temple has for its revenues not only portions of land, but also other possessions of much greater extent and importance, which will never be destroyed or diminished; for as long as the race of mankind shall last, the revenues likewise of the temple will always be preserved, being coeval in their duration with the universal world. (77) For it is commanded that all men shall every year bring their first fruits to the temple, from twenty years old and upwards; and this contribution is called their ransom. On which account they bring in the first fruits with exceeding cheerfulness, being joyful and delighted, inasmuch as simultaneously with their making the offering they are sure to find either a relaxation from slavery, or a relief from disease, and to receive in all respects a most sure freedom and safety for the future. (78) And since the nation is the most numerous of all peoples, it follows naturally that the first fruits contributed by them must also be most abundant. Accordingly there is in almost every city a storehouse for the sacred things to which it is customary for the people to come and there to deposit their first fruits, and at certain seasons there are sacred ambassadors selected on account of their virtue, who convey the offerings to the temple. And the most eminent men of each tribe are elected to this office, that they may conduct the hopes of each individual safe to their destination; for in the lawful offering of the first fruits are the hopes of the pious.

XV

XV. (79) Now there are twelve tribes of the nation, and one of them having been selected from the others for its excellence has received the priesthood, receiving this honour as a reward for its virtue, and fidelity, and its devout soul, which it displayed when the multitude appeared to be running into sin, following the foolish choices of some persons who persuaded their countrymen to imitate the vanity of the Egyptians, and the pride of the nations of the land, who had invented fables about irrational animals, and especially about bulls, making gods of them. For this tribe did of its own accord go forth and slay all the leaders of this apostacy from the youth upwards, in which they appeared to have done a holy action, encountering thus a contest and a labour for the sake of piety.

XVI

XVI. (80) Now these are the laws which relate to the priests. It is enjoined that the priest shall be entire and unmutilated, having no blemish on his body, no part being deficient, either naturally or through mutilation; and on the other hand, nothing having been superfluous either from his birth or having grown out subsequently from disease; his skin, also, must never have changed from leprosy, or wild lichen, or scab, or any other eruption or breaking out; all which things appear to me to be designed to be symbols of the purity of his soul. (81) For if it was necessary to examine the mortal body of the priest that it ought not be imperfect through any misfortune, much more was it necessary to look into his immortal soul, which they say is fashioned in the form of the living God. Now the image of God is the Word, by which all the world was made. (82) And after enjoining that the priest is to be of pure blood, and sprung from fathers of noble birth, and that he must be perfect in body and soul, laws are enacted also respecting the garments which the priest must wear when he is about to offer the sacred sacrifices and to perform the sacred ceremonies. (83) And this dress is a linen tunic and a girdle, the latter to cover those parts which must not be displayed in their nakedness near the altar of sacrifice. And the tunic is for the sake of promptness in performing the requisite ministrations; for they are but lightly clad, only in their tunics, when they bring their victims, and the libations, and the other requisite offerings for sacrifice, being apparelled so as to admit of unhesitating celerity. (84) But the high priest is commanded to wear a similar dress when he goes into the holy of holies to offer incense, because linen is not made of any animal that dies, as woollen garments are. He is also commanded to wear another robe also, having very beautiful embroidery and ornament upon it, so that it may seem to be a copy and representation of the world. And the description of the ornament is a clear proof of this; (85) for in the first place the whole of the round robe is of hyacinthine colour, a tunic reaching to the feet, being an emblem of the air, since the air also is by nature black, and in a manner may be said to be reaching to the feet, as it is extended from above from the regions about the moon, to the lowest places of the earth. (86) Next there was a woven garment in the form of a breastplate upon it, and this was a symbol of the heaven; for on the points of the shoulders are two emerald stones of most exceeding value, one on one side and one on the other, each perfectly round and single on each side, as emblems of the hemispheres, one of which is above the earth and the other under the earth. (87) Then on his chest there are twelve precious stones of different colours, arranged in four rows of three stones in each row, being fashioned so as an emblem of the zodiac. For the zodiac also consists of twelve animals, and so divides the four seasons of the year, allotting three animals to each season. (88) And the whole place is very correctly called the logeum (logeion), since every thing in heaven has been created and arranged in accordance with right reason (logois) and proportion; for there is absolutely nothing there which is devoid of reason. And on the logeum he embroiders two woven pieces of cloth, calling the one manifestation and the other truth. (89) And by the one which he calls truth he expresses figuratively that it is absolutely impossible for falsehood to enter any part of heaven, but that it is entirely banished to the parts around the earth, dwelling among the souls of impious men. And by that which he calls manifestation he implies that the natures in heaven make manifest every thing that takes place among us, which of themselves would be perfectly and universally unknown. (90) And the clearest proof of this is that if there were no light, and if the sun did not shine, it would be impossible for the indescribable variety of qualities of bodies to be seen, and for all the manifold differences of colours and forms to be distinguished from one another. And what else could exhibit to us the days and the nights, and the months and the years, and in short the divisions of time, but the harmonious and inconceivable revolutions of the sun, and moon, and other stars? (91) And what could exhibit the true nature of number, except those same bodies just mentioned in accordance with the observation of the combination of the parts of time? And what else could have cut the paths through the ocean and through such numerous and vast seas, and shown them to navigators, except the changes and periodical appearances of the stars? And wise men have observed, (92) also, an innumerable quantity of other circumstances, and have recorded them, conjecturing from the heavenly bodies the advent of calm weather and of violent storms, and the fertility or barrenness of crops, and the mild or violently hot summers, and whether the winters will be severe or spring-like, whether there will be droughts or abundance of rain, whether the flocks and trees will be fruitful, or on the contrary barren, and all such matters as these. For the signs of every thing on earth are engraved and firmly fixed in heaven.

XVII

XVII. (93) And besides this, golden pomegranates are attached to the lower parts of the tunic, reaching to the feet, and bells and borders embroidered with flowers. And these things are the emblems of earth and of water; the flowers are the emblems of the earth, inasmuch as it is out of it that they all rise and derive strength to bloom. And the Pomegranates [1192] as above mentioned are the emblems of water, being so named from the flowing of the stream. And the harmony, and concord, and unison of sound of the different parts of the world is betokened by the bells. (94) And the arrangement is a very excellent one; for the upper garment, on which the stones are placed, which is called the breast-plate, is a representation of heaven, because the heaven also is the highest of all things. And the tunic that reaches to the feet is in every part of a hyacinthine colour, since the air also is black, and is placed in the second classification next in honour to the heaven. And the embroidered flowers and pomegranates are on the hem, because the earth and water have been assigned the lowest situation in the universe. (95) This is the arrangement of the sacred dress of the high priest, being a representation of the universe, a marvellous work to be beheld or to be contemplated. For it has an appearance thoroughly calculated to excite astonishment, such as no embroidered work conceived by man ever was for variety and costly magnificence; (96) and it also attracts the intellect of philosophers to examine its different parts. For God intends that the high priest should in the first place have a visible representation of the universe about him, in order that from the continual sight of it he may be reminded to make his own life worthy of the nature of the universe, and secondly, in order that the whole world may co-operate with him in the performance of his sacred rites. And it is exceedingly becoming that the man who is consecrated to the service of the Father of the world should also bring his son to the service of him who has begotten him. (97) There is also a third symbol contained in this sacred dress, which it is important not to pass over in silence. For the priests of other deities are accustomed to offer up prayers and sacrifices solely for their own relations, and friends, and fellow citizens. But the high priest of the Jews offers them up not only on behalf of the whole race of mankind, but also on behalf of the different parts of nature, of the earth, of water, of air, and of fire; and pours forth his prayers and thanksgivings for them all, looking upon the world (as indeed it really is) as his country, for which, therefore, he is accustomed to implore and propitiate its governor by supplications and prayers, beseeching him to give a portion of his own merciful and humane nature to the things which he has created.

XVIII

XVIII. (98) After he has given these precepts, he issues additional commandments, and orders him, whenever he approaches the altar and touches the sacrifices, at the time when it is appointed for him to perform his sacred ministrations, not to drink wine or any other strong drink, on account of four most important reasons, hesitation, and forgetfulness, and sleep, and folly. (99) For the intemperate man relaxes the powers of his body, and renders his limbs more slow of motion, and makes his whole body more inclined to hesitation, and compels it by force to become drowsy. And he also relaxes the energies of his soul, and so becomes the cause to it of forgetfulness and folly. But in the case of abstemious men all the parts of the body are lighter, and as such more active and moveable, and the outer senses are more pure and unalloyed, and the mind is gifted with a more acute sight, so that it is able to see things beforehand, and never forgets what it has previously seen; (100) in short, therefore, we must look upon the use of wine to be a most unprofitable thing for all the purposes of life, inasmuch as by it the soul is weighed down, the outward senses are dimmed, and the body is enervated. For it does not leave any one of our faculties free and unembarrassed, but is a hindrance to every one of them, so as to impede its attaining that object to which it is by nature fitted. But in sacred ceremonies and holy rites the mischief is most grievous of all, in proportion as it is worse and more intolerable to sin with respect to God than with respect to man. On which account it probably is that it is commanded to the priest to offer up sacrifices without wine, in order to make a difference and distinction between sacred and profane things, and pure and impure things, and lawful and unlawful things.

XIX

XIX. (101) But since the priest was a man before he was a priest, and since he is of necessity desirous to indulge the appetites which prompt him to seek for the connections of love, he procures for him a marriage with a pure virgin, and one who is born of pure parents, and grandfathers, and great-grandfathers, selected for their excellency with reference both to their virtue and to their noble birth. (102) For God does not allow him even to look upon a harlot, or a profane body or soul, or upon any one who, having put away her pursuit of gain, now wears an elegant and modest appearance, because such a one is unholy in respect of her former profession and way of life; though in other respects she may be looked upon as honourable, by reason of her having purified herself of her former evil courses. For repentance for past sins is a thing to be praised; and no one else need be forbidden to marry her, only let her not come near a priest. For the especial property of the priesthood is justice and purity, which from the first beginning of its creation to the end, seeks a concord utterly irreproachable. (103) For it would be mere folly that some men should be excluded from the priesthood by reason of the scars which exist on their bodies from ancient wounds, which are the emblem of misfortune indeed, but not of wickedness; but that those persons who, not at all out of necessity but from their own deliberate choice, have made a market of their beauty, when at last they slowly repent, should at once after leaving their lovers become united to priests, and should come from brothels and be admitted into the sacred precincts. For the scars and impressions of their old offences remain not the less in the souls of those who repent. (104) On which account it is wisely and truly said in another passage, that "One may not bring the hire of a harlot into the Temple." [1193] And yet the money is not in itself liable to any reproach, except by reason of the woman who received it, and the action for which it was given to her. How then could one possibly admit those women to consort with priests whose very money is looked upon as profane and base, even though as to its material and stamp it may be good and lawful money?

XX

XX. (105) The regulations, therefore, are laid down with precision in this manner for the high priest, so that he is not allowed either to marry a widow, nor one who is left desolate after the death of the man to whom she has been espoused, nor one who has been divorced from a husband who is still alive, in order that the sacred seed may be sown for the first time in a field which is hitherto untrodden and pure, and that his offspring may have no admixture of the blood of any other house. And in the second place, in order that the pair coming together with souls which have as yet known no defilement or perversion, may easily form their dispositions and characters in a virtuous manner. For the minds of virgins are easily attracted and drawn over to virtue, being exceedingly ready to be taught. (106) But the woman who has had experience of another husband is very naturally less inclined to obedience and to instruction, inasmuch as she has not a soul perfectly pure, like thoroughly smooth wax, so as to receive distinctly the doctrines which are to be impressed upon it, but one which is to a certain degree rough from the impressions which have been already stamped upon it, which are difficult to be effaced, and so remain, and do not easily receive any other impression, or if they do they render it confused by the irregularity of their own surface. (107) Let the high priest, therefore, take a pure virgin to be his wife; I say a virgin, meaning not only one with whom no other man has even been connected, but one in connection with whom no other man has ever been named in reference to the agreement of marriage, even though her body may be pure.

XXI

XXI. (108) But besides this, injunctions are given to the particular and inferior priests concerning their marriages, which are the very same in most points, which are given to those who have the supreme priesthood. But they are permitted with impunity to marry not only maidens but widows also; not, indeed, all widows, but those whose husbands are dead. For the law thinks it fitting to remove all quarrels and disputes from the life of the priests. And if they had husbands living there very likely might be disputes from the jealousy which is caused by the love of men for women. But when the first husband is dead, then with him the hostility which could be felt towards the second husband dies also. (109) And even on other accounts he might have thought that the high priest ought to be of superior purity and holiness, as in other matters so also in the connection of marriage, and on this account it may have been that God only allowed the high priest to marry a virgin. But to the priests of the second rank he remitted something of the rigour of his regulations concerning the connection with women, permitting them to marry women who have made trials of other husbands.

XXII

XXII. (110) And besides these commands, he also defined precisely the family of the women who might be married by the high priest, commanding him to marry not merely a woman who was a virgin, but also one who was a priestess, the daughter of a priest, that so both bridegroom and bride might be of one house, and in a manner of one blood, so as to display a most lasting harmony and union of disposition during the whole of their lives. (111) The others also were permitted to marry women who were not the daughters of priests, partly because their purificatory sacrifices are of but small importance, and partly because he was not willing entirely to disunite and separate the whole nation from the order of the priesthood; for which reason he did not prevent the other priests from making intermarriages with any of their countrywomen, as that is relationship in the second degree; for sons-in-law are in the place of sons to their fathersin-law, and fathers-in-law instead of fathers to their sons-in-law.

XXIII

XXIII. (112) These, then, are the ordinances which were established respecting marriage, and respecting what greatly resembles marriage, the procreation of children. But since destruction follows creation, Moses also gave the priests laws relating to death, [1194] commanding them not to permit themselves to be defiled in respect of all people whatsoever, who might happen to die, and who might be connected with them through some bond of friendship, or distant relationship: but allowing them to mourn for six classes only, their fathers or their mothers, their sons of their daughters, their brothers or their sisters, provided that these last were virgins; (113) but the high priest he absolutely forbade to mourn in any case whatever; and may we not say that this was rightly done? For as to the ministrations which belong to the other priests, one individual can perform them instead of another, so that, even if some be in mourning, still none of the usual observances need be omitted; but there is no one besides the high priest himself, who is permitted to perform his duties instead of him; for which reason, he must always be kept free from all defilement, never touching any dead body, in order that, being always ready to offer up prayers and sacrifices on behalf of the whole world at suitable seasons, he may continue to fulfil the duties of his office without hindrance. (114) And otherwise too, besides this consideration, the man who has been assigned to God, and who has become the leader of his sacred band of worshippers, ought to be disconnected with, and alienated from, all things of creation, not being so much the slave of the love of either parents, or children, or brothers, as either to omit or to delay any one of those holy actions, which it is by all means better should be done at once; (115) and God commands the high priest neither to rend his clothes over his very nearest relations when they die, nor to take from his head the ensign of the priesthood, nor in short to depart from the holy place on any plea of mourning, that, showing proper respect to the place, and to the sacred ornaments with which he himself is crowned, he may show himself superior to pity, and pass the whole of his life exempt from all sorrow. (116) For the law designs that he should be the partaker of a nature superior to that of man; inasmuch as he approaches more nearly to that of the Deity; being, if one must say the plain truth, on the borders between the two, in order that men may propitiate God by some mediator, and that God may have some subordinate minister by whom he may offer and give his mercies and kindnesses to mankind.

XXIV

XXIV. (117) After he has said this, he immediately proceeds to lay down laws, concerning those who are to use the first fruits, "If therefore, any One," [1195] says he, "should mutilate the priests as to their eyes, or their feet, or any part of their bodies, or if he should have received any blemish, let him not partake of the sacred ministrations by reason of the defects which exist in him, but still let him enjoy those honours which are common to all the priests, because of his irreproachable nobility of birth." (118) "Moreover, if any leprosies break out and attack him or if any one of the priests he afflicted with any flux, let him not touch the sacred table, nor any of the duties which are set apart for his race, until the flux stop, or the leprosy change, so that he become again resembling the complexion of sound Flesh." [1196] (119) And, if any priest do by any chance whatever touch anything that is unclean, or if he should have impure dreams by night, as is very often apt to be the case, let him during all that day touch nothing that has been consecrated, but let him wash himself and the ensuing evening, and after that let him not be hindered from touching them. (120) And let the sojourner in the priest's house, and the hireling, be prevented from approaching the first fruits; the sojourner, because it is not every one who is a neighbour who shares a man's hearth and eats at his table; [1197] for there is reason to fear that some such person may cast away what is hallowed, using as a cloak for his impiety the pretence of some unseasonable humanity; for one might not give all men a share of all things, but only of such as are adapted to those who are to receive them; otherwise, that which is the most beautiful and most beneficial of all the things in this life, namely order, will be wasted away and destroyed by that which is the most mischievous of all things, namely, confusion. (121) For if in merchant vessels the sailors were to receive an equal share with the pilot of the ship, and if in ships of war the rowers and the mariners were to receive an equal share with the captain, and if in military camps the cavalry of the line were to receive an equal share with their officers, the heavy armed infantry with their colonels, and the colonels with the generals; again, if in cities the parties before the court were to be placed on the same footing with the judges, the committeemen with the ministers, and in short private individuals with the magistrates, there would be incessant troubles and seditions, and the equality in words would produce inequality in fact; for it is an unequal measure to give equal honour to persons who are unequal in rank or desert; and inequality is the root of all evil. (122) On which account one must not give the honours of the priests to sojourners, just as one must not give them to any one else, who in that case, because of their proximity, would be meddling with what they have no business; for the honour does not belong to the house, but to the race.

XXV

XXV. (123) In like manner, no one must give this sacred honour to a hireling, as his wages, or as a recompense for his service; for sometimes he who receives it being unholy will employ it for illegitimate purposes, making the honours due to purity of birth common, and profaning all the sacred ceremonies and observances relating to the temple; (124) on which account the law altogether forbids any foreigner to partake in any degree of the holy things, even if he be a man of the noblest birth among the natives of the land, and irreproachable as respects both men and women, in order that the sacred honours may not be adulterated, but may remain carefully guarded in the family of the priests; (125) for it would be absurd that the sacrifices and holy ordinances, and all the other sacred observances pertaining to the altar, should be entrusted not to all men but to the priests alone; but that the rewards for the performance of those things should be common and liable to fall to the share of any chance persons, as if it were reasonable that the priests should be worn out with labours and toils, and nightly and daily cares, but that the rewards for such pains should be common and open to those who do nothing. (126) But, he proceeds, let the priest who is his master give to the slave who is born in his house, and to him who has been purchased with money, a share of meat and drink from the first fruits. In the first place, because the master is the only source of supply to the servant, and the inheritance of the master are the sacred offices of humanity, by which the slave must necessarily be supported. (127) In the second place, because it is by all means necessary that they should not do what is to be done unwillingly; and servants, even though we may not like it, since they are always about us and living with us, preparing meat, and drink, and delicacies for their masters beforehand, and standing at their tables, and carrying away the fragments that are left, even though they may not take any openly, will at all events secretly appropriate some of the victuals, being compelled by necessity to steal, so that instead of one injury (if indeed it is an injury to their masters that they should be supported at their expense), they are compelled to add a second to it, namely, theft; in order that, like thieves, they may enjoy what has been consecrated by their masters who live irreproachably themselves; which is the most unreasonable thing possible. (128) Thirdly, one ought to take this also into consideration, that share of the first fruits will not be neglected merely because they are distributed to the servants, through their fear of their masters; for this is sufficient to stop their mouths, preventing the arrogance of such persons from showing itself.

XXVI

XXVI. (129) Having said thus much he proceeds next to put forth a law full of humanity. If, says he, the daughter of a priest, having married a man who is not a priest, becomes a widow by the death of her husband, or if she be left childless while he is still alive, let her return again to her father's house, to receive her share of the first fruits which she enjoyed when she was a virgin;[1198] for in some degree and in effect she is now also a virgin, since she has neither husband nor children, and has no other refuge but her father; (130) but if she has sons or daughters, then the mother must of necessity be classed with the children; and the sons and daughters, being ranked as of the family of their father, draw their mother also with them into his House.[1199]

XXVII

XXVII. (131) The law did not allot any share of the land to the priests, in order that they like others might derive revenues from the land, and so possess a sufficiency of necessary things; but admitting them to an excessive degree of honour, he said that God was their inheritance, having a reference to the things offered to God; for the sake of two objects, both that of doing them the highest honour, since they are thus made partners in those things which are offered up by pious men, out of gratitude to God; and also in order that they might have no business about which to trouble themselves except the offices of religion, as they would have had, if they were forced to take care of their inheritance. And the following are the rewards and preeminent honours which he assigns to them; (132) in the first place, that the necessary food for their support shall at all times be provided for them without any labour or toil of their own; for God commands those who are making bread, to take of all the fat and of all the dough, a loaf as first fruits for the use of the priests, making thus, by this legitimate instruction, a provision for those men who put aside these first fruits, proceeding in the way that leads to piety; (133) for being accustomed at all times to offer first fruits of the necessary food, they will thus have an everlasting recollection of God, than which it is impossible to imagine a greater blessing; and it follows of necessity, that the first fruits offered by the most populous of nations must be very plentiful, so that even the very poorest of the priests, must, in respect of his abundance of all necessary food, appear to be very wealthy. (134) In the second place, he commands the nation also to give them the first fruits of their other possessions; a portion of wine out of each winepress; and of wheat and barley from each threshing floor. And in like manner they were to have a share of oil from all; the olive trees, and of eatable fruit from all the fruit trees, in order that they might not pass a squalid existence, having only barely enough of necessary food to support life, but that they might have sufficient for a certain degree of comfort and luxury, and so live cheerfully on abundant means, with all becoming ornament and refinement. (135) The third honour allotted to them is an assignment of all the first-born males, of all kinds of land animals which are born for the service and use of mankind; for these are the things which God commands to be given to the men consecrated to the priesthood; the offspring of oxen, and sheep, and goats, namely calves, and lambs, and kids, inasmuch as they both are and are considered clean, both for the purposes of eating and of sacrifice, but he orders that money shall be given as a ransom for the young of other animals, such as horses, and asses and camels, and similar beasts, without disparaging their real value; (136) and the supplies thus afforded them are very great; for the people of this nation breed sheep, and cattle, and flocks of all kinds above all other peoples, separating them with great care into flocks of goats, and herds of oxen, and flocks of sheep, and a vast quantity of other troops of animals of all kinds. (137) Moreover the law, going beyond all these enactments in their favour, commands the people to bring them the first fruits, not only of all their possessions of every description, but also of their own lives and bodies; for the children are separable portions of their parents as one may say; but if one must tell the plain truth, they are inseparable as being of kindred blood, [...] [1200] and being bound to them by the allurements of united good will, and by the indissoluble bonds of nature. (138) But nevertheless, he consecrates also their own first-born male children after the fashion of other first fruits, as a sort of thanks-offering for fertility, and a number of children both existing and hoped for, and wishing at the same time that their marriages should be not only free from all blame, but even very deserving of praise, the first fruit arising from which is consecrated to God; and keeping this in their minds, both husbands and wives ought to cling to modesty, and to attend to their household concerns, and to cherish unanimity, agreeing with one another, so that what is called a communion and partnership may be so in solid truth, not only in word, but likewise in deed. (139) And with reference to the dedication of the first-born male children, in order that the parents may not be separated from their children, nor the children from their parents, he values the first fruits of them himself at a fixed price in money ordering everyone both poor and rich to contribute an equal sum, not having any reference to the ability of the contributors, nor to the vigour or beauty of the children who were born; but considering how much even a very poor man might be able to give; (140) for since the birth of children happens equally to the most noble and to the most obscure persons of the race, he thought it just to enact that their contribution should also be equal, aiming, as I have already said, particularly to fix a sum which should be in the power of everyone to give.

XXVIII

XXVIII. (141) After this he also appointed another source of revenue of no insignificant importance for the priests, bidding them to take the first fruits of every one of the revenues of the nation namely, the first fruits of the corn, and wine, and oil, and even of the produce of all the cattle, of the flocks of sheep, and herds of oxen, and flocks of goats, and of all other animals of all kinds; and how great an abundance of these animals there must be, any one may conjecture from the vast populousness of the nation; (142) from all which circumstances it is plain that the law invests the priests with the dignity and honour that belongs to kings; since he commands contributions from every description of possession to be given to them as to rulers; (143) and they are accordingly given to them in a manner quite contrary to that in which cities usually furnish them to their rulers; for cities usually furnish them under compulsion, and with great unwillingness and lamentation, looking upon the collectors of the taxes as common enemies and destroyers, and making all kinds of different excuses at different times, and neglecting all laws and ordinances, and with all this jumbling and evasion do they contribute the taxes and payments which are levied on them. (144) But the men of this nation contribute their payments to the priests with joy and cheerfulness, anticipating the collectors, and cutting short the time allowed for making the contributions, and thinking that they are themselves receiving rather than giving; and so with words of blessing and thankfulness, they all, both men and women, bring their offerings at each of the seasons of the year, with a spontaneous cheerfulness, and readiness, and zeal, beyond all description.

XXIX

XXIX. (145) And these things are assigned to the priests from the possessions of each individual, but there are also often especial revenues set apart for them exceedingly suitable for the priests, which are derived from the sacrifices which are offered up; for it is commanded that two portions from two limbs of every victim shall be given to the priests, the arm from the limb on the right side, and the fat from the chest; for the one is a symbol of strength and manly vigour, and of every lawful action in giving, and taking, and acting: and the other is an emblem of human gentleness as far as the angry passions are concerned; (146) for it is said that these passions have their abode in the chest, since nature has assigned them the breast for their home as the most suitable place; around which as around a garrison she has thrown, in order more effectually to secure them from being taken, a very strong fence which is called the chest, which she has made of many continuous and very strong bones, binding it firmly with nerves which cannot be broken. (147) But from the victims which are sacrificed away from the altar, in order to be eaten, it is commanded that three portions should be given to the priest, an arm, and a jaw-bone, and that which is called the paunch; the arm for the reason which has been mentioned a short time ago; the jaw-bone as a first fruit of that most important of all the members of the body, namely the head, and also of uttered speech, for the stream of speech could not flow out without the motion of these jaws; for they being Agitated [1201] (and it is very likely from this, that they have derived their name), when they are struck by the tongue, all the organisation of the voice sounds simultaneously; (148) and the paunch is a kind of excrescence of the belly. And the belly is a kind of stable of that irrational animal the appetite, which, being irrigated by much wine-bibbing and gluttony, is continually washed with incessant provision of meat and drink, and like a swine is delighted while wallowing in the mire; in reference to which fact, a very suitable place indeed has been assigned to that intemperate and most unseemly beast, namely, the place to which all the superfluities are conveyed. (149) And the opposite to desire is temperance, which one must endeavour, and labour, and take pains by every contrivance imaginable to acquire, as the very greatest blessing and most perfect benefit both to an individual and to the state. (150) Appetite therefore, being a profane, and impure, and unholy thing, is driven beyond the territories of virtue, and is banished as it ought to be; but temperance, being a pure and unblemished virtue, neglecting everything which relates to eating and drinking, and boasting itself as superior to the pleasures of the belly, may be allowed to approach the sacred altars, bringing forward as it does the excrescence of the body, as a memorial that it may be reminded to despise all insatiability and gluttony, and all those things which excite the appetites to this pitch.

XXX

XXX. (151) And beyond all these things he also orders that the priests who minister the offering of the sacrifices, shall receive the skins of the whole burnt offerings (and they amount to an unspeakable number, this being no slight gift, but one of the most exceeding value and importance), from which circumstances it is plain, that although he has not given to the priesthood a portion of land as its inheritance, in the same manner that he has to others, he has yet assigned to them a more honourable and more untroubled share than any other tribe, granting them the first fruits of every description of sacrifice and offering. (152) And to prevent anyone of those who give the offerings, from reproaching those who receive them, he commands that the first fruits should first of all be carried into the temple, and then orders that the priests shall take them out of the temple; for it was suitable to the nature of God, that those who had received kindness in all the circumstances of life, should bring the first fruits as thank-offering, and then that he, as a being who was in want of nothing, should with all dignity and honour bestow them on the servants and ministers who attend on the service of the temple; for to appear to receive these things not from men, but from the great Benefactor of all men, appears to be receiving a gift which has in it no alloy of sadness.

XXXI

XXXI. (153) Since, then, these honours are put forth for them, if any of the priests are in any difficulty while living virtuously and irreproachably, they are at once accusers of us as disregarding the law, even though they may not utter a word. For if we were to obey the commands which we have received, and if we were to take care to give the first fruits as we are commanded, they would not only have abundance of all necessary things, but would also be filled with all kinds of supplies calculated for enabling them to live in refinement and luxury. (154) And if ever at any subsequent time the tribe of the priests is found to be blessed with a great abundance of all the necessaries and luxuries of life, this will be a great proof of their common holiness, and of their accurate observance of the laws and ordinances in every particular. But the neglect of some persons (for it is not safe to blame every one) is the cause of poverty to those who have been dedicated to God, and, if one must tell the truth, to the men themselves also. (155) For to violate the law is injurious to those who offend, even though it may be an attractive course for a short time; but to obey the ordinances of nature is most beneficial, even if at the time it may wear a painful appearance and may show no pleasant character.

XXXII

XXXII. (156) Having given all these supplies and revenues to the priests, he did not neglect those either who were in the second rank of the priesthood; and these are the keepers of the temple, of whom some are placed at the doors, at the very entrance of the temple, as door-keepers; and others are within, in the vestibule of the temple, in order that no one who ought not to do so might enter it, either deliberately or by accident. Others, again, stand all around, having had the times of their watches assigned to them by lot, so as to watch by turns night and day, some being day watchmen and others night watchmen. Others, again, had charge of the porticoes and of the courts in the open air, and carried out all the rubbish, taking care of the cleanliness of the temple, and the tenths were assigned as the wages of all these men; for these tenths are the share of the keepers of the temple. (157) At all events the law did not permit those who received them to make use of them, until they had again offered up as first fruits other tenths as if from their own private property, and before they had given these to the priests of the superior rank, for then it permitted them to enjoy them, but before that time it would not allow it. (158) Moreover, the law allotted to them fortyeight cities, and in every city, suburbs, extending two hundred cubits all round, for the pasture of their cattle, and for the other necessary purposes of which cities have need. But of these cities, six were set apart, some on the near side, and some on the further side of Jordan, three on each side, as cities of refuge for those who had committed unintentional murder. (159) For as it was not consistent with holiness for one who had by any means whatever become the cause of death to any human being to come within the sacred precincts, using the temple as a place of refuge and as an asylum, Moses gave a sort of inferior sanctity to the cities above mentioned, allowing them to give great security, by reason of the privileges and honours conferred upon the inhabitants, who were to be justified in protecting their suppliants if any superior power endeavoured to bring force against them, not by warlike preparations, but by rank, and dignity, and honour, which they had from the laws by reason of the venerable character of the priesthood. (160) But the fugitive, when he has once got within the borders of the city to which he has fled for refuge, must be kept close within it, because of the avengers waiting for him on the outside, being the relations by blood of the man who has been slain, and who, out of regret for their kinsman, even if he has been slain by one who did not intend to do so, are still eager for the blood of him who slew him, their individual and private grief overpowering their accurate notions of what is right. And should he go forth from the city, let him know that he is going forth to undoubted destruction; for he will not escape the notice of any one of the slain man's relations, by whom he will at once be taken in nets and toils, and so he will perish. (161) And the limit of his banishment shall be the life of the high priest; and when he is dead, he shall be pardoned and return to his own city. Moses, having promulgated these and similar laws about the priests, proceeds to enact others concerning animals, as to what beasts are suitable for Sacrifice. [1202]

XXXIII

XXXIII. (162) Or the creatures which are fit to be offered as sacrifices, some are land animals, and some are such as fly through the air. Passing over, therefore, the infinite varieties of birds, God chose only two classes out of them all, the turtledove and the pigeon; because the pigeon is by nature the most gentle of all those birds which are domesticated and gregarious, and the turtle-dove the most gentle of those which love solitude. (163) Also, passing over the innumerable troops of land animals, whose very numbers it is not easy to ascertain, he selected these especially as the best--the oxen, and sheep, and goats; for these are the most gentle and the most manageable of all animals. At all events, great herds of oxen, and numerous flocks of goats and sheep, are easily driven by any one, not merely by any man, but by any little child, when they go forth to pasture, and in the same way they are brought back to their folds in good order when the time comes. (164) And of this gentleness, there are many other proofs, and the most evident are these: that they all feed on herbage, and that no one of them is carnivorous, and that they have neither crooked talons, nor any projecting tusks or teeth whatever; for the back parts of the upper jaw do not hold teeth, but all the incisor teeth are deficient in them: (165) and, besides these facts, they are of all animals the most useful to man. Rams are the most useful for the necessary covering of the body; oxen, for ploughing the ground and preparing the arable land for seed, and for the growth of the crops that shall hereafter come to be threshed out, in order that men may partake of and enjoy food; and the hair and fleeces of goats, where one is woven, or the other sewn together, make movable tents for travellers, and especially for men engaged in military expeditions, whom their necessities constantly compel to abide outside of the city in the open air.

XXXIV

XXXIV. (166) And the victims must be whole and entire, without any blemish on any part of their bodies, unmutilated, perfect in every part, and without spot or defect of any kind. At all events, so great is the caution used with respect not only to those who offer the sacrifices, but also to the victims which are offered, that the most eminent of the priests are carefully selected to examine whether they have any blemishes or not, and scrutinise them from head to foot, inspecting not only those parts which are easily visible, but all those which are more out of sight, such as the belly and the thighs, lest any slight imperfection should escape notice. (167) And the accuracy and minuteness of the investigation is directed not so much on account of the victims themselves, as in order that those who offer them should be irreproachable; for God designed to teach the Jews by these figures, whenever they went up to the altars, when there to pray or to give thanks, never to bring with them any weakness or evil passion in their soul, but to endeavour to make it wholly and entirely bright and clean, without any blemish, so that God might not turn away with aversion from the sight of it.

XXXV

XXXV. (168) And since, of the sacrifices to be offered, some are on behalf of the whole nation, and indeed, if one should tell the real truth, in behalf of all mankind, while others are only in behalf of each individual who has chosen to offer them; we must speak first of all of those which are for the common welfare of the whole nation, and the regulations with respect to this kind of sacrifice are of a marvellous nature. (169) For some of them are offered up every day, and some on the days of the new moon, and at the festivals of the full moon; others on days of fasting; and others at three different occasions of festival. Accordingly, it is commanded that every day the priests should offer up two lambs, one at the dawn of day, and the other in the evening; each of them being a sacrifice of thanksgiving; the one for the kindnesses which have been bestowed during the day, and the other for the mercies which have been vouchsafed in the night, which God is incessantly and uninterruptedly pouring upon the race of men. (170) And on the seventh day he doubles the number of victims to be offered, giving equal honour to equal things, inasmuch as he looks upon the seventh day as equal in dignity to eternity, since he has recorded it as being the birthday of the whole world. On which account he has thought fit to make the sacrifice to be offered on the seventh day, equal to the continuation of what is usually sacrificed in one day. (171) Moreover, the most fragrant of all incenses are offered up twice every day in the fire, being burnt within the veil, both when the sun rises and sets, before the morning and after the evening sacrifice, so that the sacrifices of blood display our gratitude for ourselves as being composed of blood, but the offerings of incense show our thankfulness for the dominant part within us, our rational spirit, which was fashioned after the archetypal model of the divine image. (172) And loaves are placed on the seventh day on the sacred table, being equal in number to the months of the year, twelve loaves, arranged in two rows of six each, in accordance with the arrangement of the equinoxes; for there are two equinoxes every year, the vernal and the autumnal, which are each reckoned by periods of six months. At the vernal equinox all the seeds sown in the ground begin to ripen; about which time, also, the trees begin to put forth their fruit. And by the autumnal one the fruit of the trees has arrived at a perfect ripeness; and at this period, again, is the beginning of seed time. Thus nature, going through a long course of time, showers gifts after gifts upon the race of man, the symbols of which are the two sixes of loaves thus placed on the table. (173) And these loaves, also, do figuratively intimate that most useful of all virtues, temperance; which is attended by frugality, and economy, and moderation as so many bodyguards, on account of the pernicious attacks which intemperance and covetousness prepare to make upon it. For, to a lover of wisdom, a loaf is a sufficient nourishment, keeping the bodies free from disease, and the intellect sound, and healthy, and sober. (174) But high seasonings, and cheesecakes, and sweetmeats, and all the other delicacies which the superfluous skill of confectioners and cooks concoct to cajole the illiterate, and unphilosophical, and most slavish of all the outward senses, namely, taste, which is never influenced by any noble sight, or by any perceptible lesson, but only by desire to indulge the appetites of the miserable belly, constantly engenders incurable diseases both in the body and the mind. (175) And with the loaves there is also placed on the table frankincense and salt. The one as a symbol that there is no sweetmeat more fragrant and wholesome than economy and temperance, if wisdom is to be the judge; while salt is an emblem of the duration of all things (for salt preserves everything over which it is sprinkled), and also of sufficient seasoning. (176) I know that those men who devote themselves wholly to drinking parties and banquets, and who care only for costly entertainments, will make a mock at these things and turn them into ridicule, miserable slaves as they are of birds, and fishes, and meat, and all such nonsense as that, and not being able to taste of true freedom, not even in a dream. And all such men are to be disregarded and despised by those who seek to live in accordance with the will of God, in a manner pleasing to the true and living God; who, having learnt to despise the pleasures of the flesh, pursue the delights and luxuries of the mind, having exercised themselves in the contemplation of the objects of Nature. [1203] (177) After he had ordered these things concerning the seventh day, he said that for the new moons it is necessary to offer ten whole burntofferings in all: two young bulls, one ram, seven lambs. For since the month is perfect in which the moon makes its way through its cycle, he thought that a perfect number of animals should be Sacrificed. [1204] (178) The number ten is the completely perfect number which he most appropriately assigned to the animals which have been mentioned: the two young bulls since there are two motions of the moon as it continually runs its double-course—"the motion of waxing until full moon and the motion of waning until its conjunction with the sun; one ram since there is one principle of reason by which the moon waxes and wanes in equal intervals, both as it increases and diminishes in illumination; the seven lambs because it receives the perfect shapes in periods of seven days—"the half-moon in the first seven day period after its conjunction with the sun, full moon in the second; and when it makes its return again, the first is to half-moon, then it ceases at its conjunction with the sun. (179) With the sacrificial victims he ordered that the finest wheaten flour mixed with oil be offered and wine in stipulated amounts for drink-offerings. The reason is that even these are brought to maturity by the orbits of the moon in the annual seasons, especially as the moon helps to ripen fruits; wheat and wine and oil—"the most helpful substances for life and the most essential for use by humans—"are suitably dedicated together with all sacrifices. (180) For the feast which begins the sacred Month [1205] double sacrifices are fitly offered since the reason for it is double: one, since it is the new moon; the other, since it is the feast which begins the sacred month. Regarding the fact that it is the new moon it is distinctly stated that sacrifices equal to the other new moons are to be sacrificed. Regarding the fact that it is the feast which begins the sacred month, the gifts are doubled apart from the young bulls. For one rather than two is offered since the judge has thought it correct to use the indivisible nature of the number one instead of the divisible number two at the beginning of the year. (181) In the first season--he calls springtime and its equinox the first season--he ordered that a feast which is called "the feast of unleavened bread" be celebrated for seven days and declared that every day was equal in honor in religious services. For he commanded that each day ten whole burnt offerings should be sacrificed just as they are for the new moons, making the total number of whole burnt offerings apart from those dealing with the trespass offerings seventy. (182) For he thought that the same reason governed the relation of the new moon to the month which governed the relation of the seven days of the feast to the equinox that took place in the seventh month. As a result he declared sacred both the beginning of each month and the beginning, consisting of the same number of days as the new moons, of the aggregate seven months. (183) In the middle of spring the harvest takes place during which season thank offerings are offered to God from the field because it has produced fruit in abundance and the crops are being harvested. This feast is the most publicly celebrated feast and is called "the feast of the first produce," named etymologically from the circumstance that the first of the produce, the first fruits, are dedicated at that time. (184) We are ordered to offer two young bulls as sacrifices, one ram, and seven lambs-- these ten are sacred whole burnt offerings--and in addition, two lambs as meat for the priests which he calls "lambs of preservation" since food is preserved for humans out of multiple and varied circumstances. For destructive forces frequently occur: some by heavy rains, some by droughts, some by other unspeakably great changes in nature; and again, some are humanly produced through the invasion of enemies who attempt to lay waste their neighbors' land. (185) Suitably then, the preservation offerings are offered to the one who has dispersed all plots as thank offerings. They are offered with loaves which, after the people have brought them to the altar and lifted them up to heaven, they give to the priests along with the meat of the sacrifice of preservation for a most appropriate sacred feast. (186) When the third season takes place in the seventh month at the autumnal equinox, at the beginning of the month, the feast which begins the sacred month named "the feast of trumpets" and which was discussed earlier is celebrated. On the tenth day the fast takes place which they take seriously--not only those who are zealous about piety and holiness, but even those who do nothing religious the rest of the time. For all are astounded, overcome with the sacredness of it; in fact, at that time the worse compete with the better in selfcontrol and virtue. (187) The reputation of the day is due to two reasons: one that it is a feast and the other that it is purification and escape from sins for which amnesty has been given by the favors of the gracious God who has assigned the same honor to repentance that he has to not committing a single Sin.[1206] (188) Therefore he declared that since it was a feast the sacrifices should be the same number as those of the feast which begins the sacred month: a young bull, a ram, and seven lambs. In this way he mixed the number one with the number seven and lined the end up with the beginning, for the number seven has been appointed the end of things and the number one the beginning. He added three sacrifices since it was for purification. For he ordered that two hegoats and a ram be offered. Then he said that it was necessary to offer the ram as a whole burnt offering, but to cast lots for the he-goats. The hegoat selected by lot for God must be sacrificed, but the other was to be sent out into a pathless and inaccessible desolate place carrying on himself the curses of those who had committed offenses, but who were purified by changes for the better and who have washed themselves from their old lawlessness with a new sense of loyalty to the law. (189) On the fifteenth day, at full moon, the feast which is called "the feast of booths" is celebrated for which the supplies of the sacrifices are more numerous. For during seven days, seventy young bulls, fourteen rams and ninety-eight lambs are sacrificed--all animals as whole burnt offerings. We are ordered to consider the eighth day sacred, a day which I must deal with carefully when the entire account of the feasts is thoroughly examined. On this day as many sacrifices are offered as on the feast which begins the sacred month. (190) The sacrifices which are whole burnt offerings and are joint offerings on behalf of the nation or--to speak more accurately--on behalf of the entire race of humanity have been addressed to the best of my ability. However, a he-goat accompanies the whole burnt offerings on each day of the feast. He is called "concerning sins" and is sacrificed for the forgiveness of sins. His meat is Distributed [1207] to the priests for food. (191) What is the reason for this? Is it because a feast is a time of good cheer, and undeceiving and true good cheer is good sense firmly established in the soul, and this unwavering good sense is impossible to receive without a cure from sins and cutting off of the passions? For it would be out of place if each of the animals of the whole burnt offerings is sacrificed only when it is found undamaged and unhurt, but the mind of the sacrificer has not been purified in every way and cleansed by making use of washings and lustrations which the right reason of nature pours into God-loving souls through healthy and uncorrupt ears. (192) In addition the following ought to be said. These festal and holiday rests have in the past often opened up countless avenues to sins. For unmixed beverage and luxurious diets with excessive drinking arouse the insatiable desires of the stomach and also kindle the desires of the parts beneath the stomach. As these desires both flow and stream out in every way, they produce a surge of unspeakable evils using the fearless stimulant of the feast as a refuge to avoid suffering anything. (193) Knowing these things, he did not allow them to celebrate a feast in the same way as other peoples, but at the very time of good cheer he first commanded that they purify themselves by bridling the impulses of pleasure. Then he summoned them into the temple for participation in hymns and prayers and sacrifices so that both from the place and from the things seen and said through the most powerful of senses, sight and hearing, they might come to love self-control and piety. Last of all, he reminded them not to sin through the sacrifice for sin. For the one who is asking for amnesty for the sins he has committed is not so dominated by evil that at the very time he is asking for release from old wrongs he should begin other new ones.

XXXVI

XXXVI. (194) After the lawgiver has given these commands with reference to these subjects, he begins to distinguish between the different kinds of sacrifices, and he divides the victims into three classes. The most important of which he makes a whole burnt offering; the next an offering for preservation; the last, a sin-offering. And then he adapts suitable ceremonies and rites to each, aiming, in no inadequate manner, at what is at the same time decorous and holy. (195) And the distinction which he makes is one of great beauty and propriety, having a close connection and a sort of natural kindred with the things themselves; for if any one were to wish to examine minutely the causes for which it seemed good to the first men to betake themselves at the same time to sacrifices to show their gratitude, and also to supplications, he will find two most especial reasons for this conduct. Firstly, that it conduces to the honour of God, which ought to be aimed at not for the sake of any other reason, but for itself alone, as being both honourable and necessary; and, secondly, for the benefits which have been poured upon the sacrificers themselves, as has been said before. And the benefit they derive is also twofold, being both an admission to a share of good things and a deliverance from evils. (196) Therefore the law has assigned the whole burnt offering as a sacrifice adequate to that honour which is suited to God, and which belongs to God alone, enjoining that what is offered to the allperfect and absolute God must be itself entire and perfect, having no taint of mortal selfishness in it. But that sacrifice which is offered for the sake of men, since its appearance admits of distinction, the law has distinguished also, appointing it to be a sacrifice for the participation in blessings which mankind has enjoined, and calling it a thank-offering for their preservation. And for the deliverance from evils it has allotted the sacrifice called a sin-offering, so that these are very appropriately their sacrifices for these causes; (197) the whole burntoffering being sacrificed for God himself alone, who must be honoured for his own sake, and not for that of any other being or thing; and the others for our sake; the thank-offering for our preservation, for the safety and amelioration of human affairs; and the sin-offering for the cure of those offences which the soul has committed.

XXXVII

XXXVII. (198) And we must now enumerate the laws which have been enacted respecting each sacrifice, making our commencement with that which is the most excellent. Now, the most excellent sacrifice is the whole burnt-offering. The law says, "In the first place the victim shall be a male, carefully selected for its excellence from all the animals which are fit for sacrifice, a calf, or a lamb, or a kid. And then let him who brings it wash his hands, and lay his hands on the head of the victim. (199) And after this let some one of the priests take the victim and sacrifice it, and let another hold a bowl under it, and, having caught some of the blood, let him go all around the altar and sprinkle it with the blood, and let him flay the victim and divide it into large pieces, having washed its entrails and its feet. And then let the whole victim be given to the fire of the altar of God, [1208] having become many things instead of one, and one instead of many." (200) These things, then, are comprehended in express words of command. But there is another meaning figuratively concealed under the enigmatical expressions. And the words employed are visible symbols of what is invisible and uncertain. Now the victim which is to be sacrificed as a whole burnt offering must be a male, because a male is both more akin to domination than a female and more nearly related to the efficient cause; for the female is imperfect, subject, seen more as the passive than as the active partner. (201) And since the elements of which our soul consists are two in number, the rational and the irrational part, the rational part belongs to the male sex, being the inheritance of intellect and reason; but the irrational part belongs to the sex of woman, which is the lot also of the outward senses. And the mind is in every respect superior to the outward sense, as the man is to the woman; who, when he is without blemish and purified with the proper purifications, namely, the perfect virtues, is himself the most holy sacrifice, being wholly and in all respects pleasing to God. (202) Again, the hands which are laid upon the head of the victim are a most manifest symbol of irreproachable actions, and of a life which does nothing which is open to accusation, but which in all respects is passed in a manner consistent with the laws and ordinances of nature; (203) for the law, in the first place, desires that the mind of the man who is offering the sacrifice shall be made holy by being exercised in good and advantageous doctrines; and, in the second place, that his life shall consist of most virtuous actions, so that, in conjunction with the imposition of hands, the man may speak freely out of his cleanly conscience, and may say, (204) "These hands have never received any gift as a bribe to commit an unjust action, nor any division of what has been obtained by rapine or by covetousness, nor have they shed innocent blood. nor have they wrought mutilation, nor works of insolence, nor acts of violence, nor have they inflicted any wounds; nor, in fact, have they performed any action whatever which is liable to accusation or to reproach, but have been ministers in everything which is honourable and advantageous, and which is honoured by wisdom, or by the laws, or by honourable and virtuous men."

XXXVIII

XXXVIII. (205) And the blood is poured out in a circle all round the altar, because a circle is the most complete of all figures, and also in order that no part whatever may be left empty and unoccupied by the libation of life; for, to speak properly, the blood is the libation of the life. Therefore the law here symbolically teaches us that the mind, which is always performing its dances in a circle, is by every description of words, and intentions, and actions which it adopts, always showing its desire to please God. (206) And it is commanded that the belly and the feet shall be washed, which command is a figurative and very expressive one; for, by the belly it is figuratively meant to be signified that it is desirable that the appetites shall be purified, which are full of stains, and intoxication, and drunkenness, being thus a most pernicious evil, existing, and concocted, and exercised to the great injury of the life of mankind. (207) And by the command that the feet of the victim should be washed, it is figuratively shown that we must no longer walk upon the earth, but soar aloft and traverse the air. For the soul of the man who is devoted to God, being eager for truth, springs upward and mounts from earth to heaven; and, being borne on wings, traverses the expanse of the air, being eager to be classed with and to move in concert with the sun, and moon, and all the rest of the most sacred and most harmonious company of the stars, under the immediate command and government of God, who has a kingly authority without any rival, and of which he can never be deprived, in accordance with which he justly governs the universe. (208) And the division of the animal into limbs shows plainly that all things are but one, or that they are derived from one, and dissolved into one; which some persons have called satiety and also want, while others have called it combustion and arrangement: combustion, in accordance with the supreme power of God, who rules all other things in the world; and arrangement, according to the equality of the four elements which they all mutually allow to one another. (209) And when I have been investigating these matters, this has appeared to me to be a probable conjecture; the soul which honours the living God, ought for that very reason to honour him not inconsiderately nor ignorantly, but with knowledge and reason; and the reasoning which we indulge in respecting God admits of division and partition, according to each of the divine faculties and excellencies; for God is both all good, and is also the maker and creator of the universe; and he also created it having a foreknowledge of what would take place, and being its preserver and most blessed benefactor, full of every kind of happiness; all which circumstances have in themselves a most dignified and praiseworthy character, both separately and when looked at in conjunction with their kindred qualities; (210) and we must speak in the same way of other matters. When you wish to give thanks to God with your mind, and to assert your gratitude for the creation of the world, give him thanks for the creation of it as a whole, and of all its separate parts in their integrity, as if for the limbs of a most perfect animal; and by the parts I mean, for instance, the heaven, and the sun, and the moon, and the fixed stars; and secondly the earth, and the animals, and plants which spring from it; and next the seas and rivers, whether naturally springing from the ground or swollen by rain as winter torrents, and all the things in them: and lastly, the air and all the changes that take place in it; for winter, and summer, and spring, and autumn, being the seasons of the year, and being all of great service to mankind, are what we may call affections of the air for the preservation of all these things that are beneath the moon. (211) And if ever you give thanks for men and their fortunes, do not do so only for the race taken generally, but you shall give thanks also for the species and most important parts of the race, such as men and women, Greeks and barbarians, men on the continent, and those who have their habitation in the islands; and if you are giving thanks for one individual, do not divide your thankfulness in expression into gratitude for minute trifles and inconsiderable matters, but take in your view the most comprehensive circumstances, first of all, his body and his soul, of which he consists, and then his speech, and his mind, and his outward senses; for such gratitude cannot of itself be unworthy of being listened to by God, when uttered, for each of these particulars.

XXXIX

XXXIX. (212) These things are enough for us to say respecting the sacrifice of the whole burntoffering. We must now proceed in due order to consider that offering which is called the sacrifice for preservation; for with respect to this one it is a matter of consequence whether the victim be male or female; and when it is slain, these three parts are especially selected for the altar, the fat, and the lobe of the liver, and the two kidneys; and all the other parts are left to make a feast for the sacrificer; (213) and we must consider with great accuracy the reason why these portions of the entrails are in this case looked upon as sacred, and not pass this point by carelessly. Often when I have been considering this matter in my own mind, and investigating all these commandments, I have doubted why the law selected the lobe of the liver, and the kidneys, and the fat, as the first fruits of the animals thus sacrificed; and did not choose the heart or the brain, though the dominant part of the man resides in one of these parts; (214) and I think also that many other persons who read the sacred scriptures with their mind, rather than merely with their eyes, will ask the same question. If therefore they, when they have considered the matter, can find any more probable reason, they will be benefiting both themselves and us; but if they cannot, let them consider the cause which has been discovered by us, and see whether it will stand the test; and this is it. The dominant power alone of all those that exist in us is able to restrain our natural folly, and injustice, and cowardice, and our other vices, and does restrain them; and the abode of this dominant power is one or other of the aforesaid portions of us, that is, it is either the brain or the heart; (215) therefore the sacred commandment has thought fit that one should not bring to the altar of God, by means of which a remission and complete pardon of all sins and transgressions is procured, that vessel from which the mind having at one time been abiding in it, has gone forth on the trackless road of injustice and impiety, having turned out of the way which leads to virtue and excellence; for it would be folly to suppose that sacrifices were not to procure a forgetfulness of offences, but were to act as a reminder of them. This it is which appears to me to be the reason why neither of those two parts, which are of supreme importance, namely, the brain or the heart, is brought to the altar; (216) and the parts which are commanded to be brought have a very suitable reason why they should be; the fat is brought because it is the richest part, and that which guards the entrails; for it envelops them and makes them to flourish, and benefits them by the softness of its touch. And the kidneys are commanded to be selected on account of the adjacent parts and the organs of generation, which they, as they dwell near them, do, like good neighbours, assist and co-operate with, in order that the seed of nature may prosper without anything in its vicinity being any obstacle to it; for they are channels resembling blood, by which that part of the purification of the superfluities of the body which is moist is separated from the body; and the testicles are near by which the seed is irrigated. And the lobe of the liver is the first fruit of the most important of the entrails, by means of which the food is digested, and being conveyed into the stomach is diffused through all the veins, and so conduces to the durability of the whole body; (217) for the stomach, lying close to the gullet which swallows the food, receives it as soon after it has first been chewed by the teeth and been made smooth, and so digests it; and the body again receives it from the stomach and performs the second part of the service required, to which indeed it has been destined by nature, giving forth a juice to aid in liquefying the food; and there are tow pipes like channels in the belly, which pour forth chyle into the liver, through the two channels which are originally placed in it. (218) And the liver has a twofold power, a secretive one, and also a power of making blood. Now the secretive power secretes everything which is hard and difficult to be digested, and removes it into the adjacent vessels of gall; and the other power turns all that portion of the food which is pure and properly strained, by the means of its own innate flame, into life-like vivifying blood; and presses it into the heart, from which, as has been already said, it is conveyed through the veins and by these channels is diffused through the whole body to which it becomes the nourishment. (219) We must also add to what has been here said, that the nature of the liver being a lofty character and very smooth, by reason of its smoothness is looked upon as a very transparent mirror, so that when the mind, retreating from the cares of the day (while the body is lying relaxed in sleep, and while no one of the outward senses is any hindrance or impediment), begins to roll itself about, and to consider the objects of its thought by itself without any interruption, looking into the liver as into a mirror, it then sees, very clearly and without any alloy, every one of the proper objects of the intellect, and looking round upon all vain idols, and seeing that no disgrace can accrue to it, but taking care to avoid that and to choose the contrary, and being contented and pleased with all that it sees, it by dreams obtains a prophetic sight of the future.

XL

XL. (220) And there are two days only during which God permits the nation to make use of the sacrifice for preservation, enjoining them to carve nothing of it till the third day, on many accounts, first of all, because all the things which are ever placed on the sacred table, ought to be made use of in due season, while the users take care that they shall suffer no deterioration from the lapse of time; but the nature of meat that has been kept is very apt to become putrid, even though it may have been seasoned in the cooking; (221) secondly, because it is fitting that the sacrifices should not be stored up for food, but should be openly exposed, so as to afford a meal to all who are in need of it, for the sacrifice when once placed on the altar, is no longer the property of the person who has offered it, but belongs to that Being to whom the victim is sacrificed, who, being a beneficent and bounteous God, makes the whole company of those who offer the sacrifice, partakers at the altar and messmates, only admonishing them not to look upon it as their own feast, for they are but stewards of the feast, and not the entertainers; and the entertainer is the man to whom all the preparation belongs, which it is not lawful to conceal while preferring parsimony and illiberal meanness to humanity which is a noble virtue. (222) Lastly, this command was given because it so happens that the sacrifice for preservation is offered up for two things, the soul and the body, to each of which the lawgiver has assigned one day for feasting on the meats, for it was becoming that a number of days should be allotted for this purpose equal to the number of those parts in us which were designed to be sacred; so that in the first day we should, together with our eating of the food, receive a recollection of the salvation of our souls; and on the second day be reminded of the sound health of our bodies. (223) And since there is no third object which is naturally appointed as one that should receive preservation, he has, with all possible strictness, forbidden the use of those meats being reserved to the third day, commanding that if it should so happen that, out of ignorance or forgetfulness, any portion was left, it should be consumed with fire; and he declares that the man who has merely tasted of it is blameable, saying to him, "Though thinking that you were sacrificing, O foolish man, you have not sacrificed; I have not accepted the unholy, unconsecrated, profane, unclean meats which you have roasted, O gluttonous man; never, even in a dream, having a proper idea of sacrifice."

XLI

XLI. (224) To this species of sacrifice for preservation that other sacrifice also belongs, which is called the sacrifice of praise, and which rests on the following Principle. [1209] The man who has never fallen into any unexpected disaster whatever, neither as to his body nor as to his external circumstances, but who has passed a tranquil and peaceful life, living in happiness and prosperity, being free from all calamity and all mishap, steering through the long voyage of life in calmness and serenity of circumstances, good fortune always blowing upon the stern of his vessel, is, of necessity, bound to requite God, who has been the pilot of his voyage, who has bestowed upon him untroubled salvation and unalloyed benefits, and, in short, all sorts of blessings unmingled with any evil, with hymns, and songs, an prayers, and also with sacrifices, and all other imaginable tokens of gratitude in a holy manner; all which things taken together have received the one comprehensive name of praise. (225) This sacrifice the lawgiver has not commanded to be spread like the one before mentioned over two days, [1210] but he has confined it to one only, in order that these men, who meet with ready benefits freely poured upon them, may offer up their requital freely and without any delay.

XLII

XLII. (226) This is sufficient to say on these subjects. We must now proceed, in due order, to consider the third sacrifice, which is called the sinoffering. This is varied in many ways, both in respect to the persons and to the description of victims offered; in respect of persons, that is, of the high priest, and of the whole nation, and of the ruler in his turn, and of the private individual; in respect of the victim offered, whether it be a calf, or a kid, or a she-goat, or a lamb. (227) Also there is a distinction made, which is very necessary, as to whether they are voluntary or involuntary, with reference to those who, after they have erred, change for the better, confessing that they have sinned, and reproaching themselves for the offences that they have committed, and turning, for the future, to an irreproachable way of life. (228) The sins therefore of the high priest, and of the whole nation, are atoned for by animals of equal value, for the priest is commanded to offer up a calf for each. The sins of the ruler are atoned for by an inferior animal, but still a male, for a kid is the appointed victim. The sins of the private individual by a victim of an inferior species, for it is a female, not a male, a she-goat, that is sacrificed; (229) for it was fitting that a ruler should be ranked above a private individual, even in his performance of sacred ceremonies also: but the nation is superior to the ruler, since the whole must, at all times, be superior to the part. But the high priest is accounted worthy of the same honour as the whole nation, in respect of purification and of entreating a forgiveness of his sins from the merciful power of God. And he receives an equality of honour, not so much as it appears for his own sake, as because he is a servant of the nation, offering up a common thank-offering for them all in his most sacred prayers and most holy sacrifices. (230) And the commandment given respecting these matters is one of great dignity and admirable solemnity. "If," says the law, "the high priest have sinned unintentionally," and then it adds, "so that the people has sinned too," all but affirming in express words that the true high priest, not the one incorrectly called so, has no participation in sin; and if ever he stumble, this will happen to him, not for his own sake, but for the common errors of the nation, and this error is not incurable, but is one which easily admits of a remedy. (231) When, therefore, the calf has been sacrificed, the lawgiver commands the sacrificer to sprinkle some of the blood with his finger seven times in front of the veil which is before the holy of holies, within the former veil, in which place the sacred vessels are placed; and after that to smear and anoint the four horns of the altar, for it is square; and to pour out the rest of the blood at the foot of the altar, which is in the open air. (232) And to this altar they are commanded to bring three things, the fat, and the lobe of the liver, and the two kidneys, in accordance with the commandment given with reference to the sacrifice for preservation; but the skin and the flesh, and all the rest of the body of the calf, from the head to the feet, with the entrails, they are commanded to carry out and to turn in an open place, to which the sacred ashes from the altar have been conveyed. The lawgiver also gives the same command with respect to the whole nation when it has sinned. (233) But if any ruler has sinned he makes his purification with a kid, [1211] as I have said before; and if a private individual has sinned, he must offer a she-goat or a lamb; and for the ruler he appoints a male victim, but to the private individual a female, making all his other injunctions the same in both cases, to anoint the horns of the altar in the open air with blood, to bring the fat and the lobe of the liver, and the two kidneys, and to give the rest of the victim to the priests to eat.

XLIII

XLIII. (234) But since, of offences some are committed against men, and some against holy and sacred things; he has hitherto been speaking with reference to those which are unintentionally committed against men; but for the purification of such as have been committed against sacred things he commands a ram to be offered up, after the offender has first paid the value of the thing to which the offence related, adding one fifth to the exact value. (235) And after having put forth these and similar enactments with reference to sins committed unintentionally, he proceeds to lay down rules respecting intentional offences. "If any one," says the law, "shall speak falsely concerning a partnership, or about a deposit, or about a theft, or about the finding of something which another has lost, and being suspected and having had an oath proposed to him, shall swear, and when he appears to have escaped all conviction at the hands of this accusers, shall himself become his own accuser, being convicted by his own conscience residing within, and shall reproach himself for the things which he has denied, and as to which he has sworn falsely, and shall come and openly confess the sin which he has committed, and implore pardon; (236) then pardon shall be given to such a man, who shows the truth of his repentance, not by promises but by works, by restoring the deposit which he has received, and by giving up the things which he has stolen or found, or of which in short he has in any way deprived his neighbour, paying also in addition one fifth of the value, as an atonement for the evil which he had Done." [1212] (237) And then, after he has appeased the man who had been injured, the law proceeds to say, "After this let him go also into the temple, to implore remission of the sins which he has committed, taking with him an irreproachable mediator, namely, that conviction of the soul which has delivered him from his incurable calamity, curing him of the disease which would cause death, and wholly changing and bringing him to good health." And it orders that he should sacrifice a ram, and this victim is expressly mentioned, as it is in the case of the man who has offended in respect of the holy things; (238) for the law speaks of an unintentional offence in the matter of holy things as of equal importance with an intentional sin in respect of men; if we may not indeed say that this also is holy, since an oath is added to it, which, as having been taken for an unjust cause, it has corrected by an alteration for the better. (239) And we must take notice that the parts of the victim slain as a sin-offering which are placed upon the altar, are the same as those which are taken from the sacrifice for preservation, namely the lobe of the liver, and the fat, and the kidneys; for in a manner we may speak also of the man who repents as being preserved, since he is cured of a disease of the soul, which is worse than the diseases of the body; (240) but the other parts of the animal are assigned to be eaten in a different manner; and the difference consists in three things; in the place, and time, and in those who receive It. [1213] Now the place is the temple; the time is one day instead of two; and the persons who partake of it are the priests, and the male servants of the priests, but not the men who offer the sacrifice. (241) Therefore the law does not permit the sacrifice to be brought out of the temple, with the intent that, if the man who repents has committed any previous offence also, he may not now be overwhelmed by envious and malicious men, with foolish dispositions and unbridled tongues, always lying in wait for reproach and false accusation; but it must be eaten in the sacred precincts, within which the purification has taken place.

XLIV

XLIV. (242) And the law orders the priests to feast on what is offered in the sacrifice for many reasons; first of all, that by this command it may do honour to him who has offered the sacrifice, for the dignity of those who eat of the feast is an honour to those who furnish it; secondly, that they may believe the more firmly that those men who feel repentance for their sins do really have God propitious to them, for he would never have invited his servants and ministers to a participation in such a banquet, if his forgiveness of those who provided it had not been complete; and thirdly, because it is not lawful for any one of the priests to bear a part in the sacred ceremonies who is not perfect, for they are rejected for the slightest blemish. (243) And God comforts those who have ceased to travel by the road of wickedness, as if they now, by means of the race of the priesthood, had received a pure purpose of life for the future, and had been sent forth so as to obtain an equal share of honour with the priests. And it is for this reason that the victim sacrificed as a sin-offering is consumed in one day, because men ought to delay to sin, being always slow and reluctant to approach it, but to exert all possible haste and promptness in doing well. (244) But the sacrifices offered up for the sins of the high priest, or for those of the whole nation, are not prepared to be eaten at all, but are burnt to ashes, and the ashes are sacred as has been said; for there is no one who is superior to the high priest or to the whole nation, or who can as such be an intercessor for them, as to the sins which they have committed. (245) Very naturally, therefore, is the meat of this sacrifice ordered to be consumed by fire, in imitation of the whole burnt offerings, and this to the honour of those who offer it; not because the sacred judgments of God are given with reference to the rank of those who come before his tribunal, but because the offences committed by men of pre-eminent virtue and real holiness are accounted of a character nearly akin to the good actions of others; (246) for as a deep and fertile soil, even if it at times yields a bad crop, still bears more and better fruit than one which is naturally unproductive, so in the same manner it happens that the barrenness of virtuous and God-fearing men is more full of excellence than the best actions which ordinary people perform by chance; for these men cannot intentionally endure to do anything blameable.

XLV

XLV. (247) Having given these commandments about every description of sacrifice in its turn, namely, about the burnt offering, and the sacrifice for preservation, and the sin-offering, he adds another kind of offering common to all the three, in order to show that they are friendly and connected with one another; and this combination of them all is called the great vow; (248) and why it received this appellation we must now proceed to say. When any persons offer first fruits from any portion of their possessions, wheat, or barley, or oil, or wine, or the best of their fruits, or the firstborn males of their flocks and herds, they do so actually dedicating those first fruits which proceed from what is clean, but paying a price as the value of what is unclean; and when they have no longer any materials left in which they can display their piety, they then consecrate and offer up themselves, displaying an unspeakable holiness, and a most superabundant excess of a God-loving disposition, on which account such a dedication is fitly called the great vow; for every man is his own greatest and most valuable possession, and this even he now gives up and abandons. (249) And when a man has vowed this vow the law gives him the following command; first of all, to touch no unmixed wine, nor any wine that is made of the grape, nor to drink any other strong drink whatever, to the destruction of his reason, considering that during this period his reason also is dedicated to God; for all which could tend to drunkenness is forbidden to those of the priests who are employed in the sacred ministrations, they being commanded to quench their thirst with water; (250) in the second place they are commanded not to show their heads, giving thus a visible sign to all who see them that they are not debasing the pure coinage of their vow; thirdly, they are commanded to keep their body pure and undefiled, so as not even to approach their parents if they are dead, nor their brothers; piety overcoming the natural good will and affection towards their relations and dearest friends, and it is both honourable and expedient that piety should at all times prevail.

XLVI

XLVI. (251) But when the appointed time for their being Released [1214] from this vow has arrived, the law then commands the man who has dedicated himself to bring three animals to procure his release from his vow, a male lamb, and a female lamb, and a ram; the one for a burnt offering, the second for a sin-offering, and the ram as a sacrifice for preservation; (252) for in some sense the man who has made such a vow resembles all these things. He resembles the sacrifice of the entire burnt offering, because he is dedicating to his preserver not only a portion of the first fruits of other things, but also of his own self. And he resembles the sin-offering, inasmuch as he is a man; for there is no one born, however perfect he may be, who can wholly avoid the commission of sin. He resembles also the offering for preservation, inasmuch as he has recorded that God the saviour is the cause of his preservation, and does not ascribe it to any physician or to any power of his; for those who have been born themselves, and who are liable to infirmity, are not competent to bestow health even on themselves. Medicine does not benefit all persons, nor does it always benefit the same persons; but there are times even when it does them great injury, since its power depends on different things, both on the thing itself and also on those persons who use it. (253) And a great impression is made on me by the fact that of three animals offered up in these different sacrifices, there is no one of a different species from the others, but they are every one of the same kind, a ram, and a male lamb, and a female lamb; for God wishes, as I said a little while ago, by this commandment to point out that the three kinds of sacrifice are nearly connected with and akin to one another; because, both the man who repents is saved, and the man who is saved from the diseases of the soul repents, and because both of them hasten with eagerness to attain to an entire and perfect disposition, of which the sacrifice of the whole burnt-offering is a symbol. (254) But since the man has begun to offer himself as his first fruits, and since it is not lawful for the sacred altar to be polluted with human blood, but yet it was by all means necessary that a portion should be consecrated, he has taken care to take a portion, which, being taken, should cause neither pain nor defilement; for he has cut Off [1215] the hair of the head, the superfluities of the natural body, as if they were the superfluous branches of a tree, and he has committed them to the fire on which the meat of the sacrifice offered for preservation will be suitably prepared, [1216] in order that some portion of the man who has made the vow, which it is not lawful to place upon the altar, may still at all events be combined with the sacrifice, burning the fuel of the sacred flame.

XLVII

XLVII. (255) These sacred fires are common to all the rest of the people. But it was fitting that the priests also should offer up something on the altar as first fruits, not thinking that the services and sacred ministrations to which they have been appointed have secured them an exemption from such duties. And the first fruits suitable for the priests to offer do not come from anything containing blood, but from the purest portion of human food; (256) for the fine wheaten flour is their continual offering; a tenth part of a sacred measure every day; one half of which is offered up in the morning, and one half in the evening, having been soaked in oil, so that no portion of it can be left for food; for the command of God is, that all the sacrifices of the priests shall be wholly burnt, and that no portion of them shall be allotted for food. Having now, then, to the best of our ability, discussed the matters relating to the sacrifices, we will proceed in due order to speak concerning those who offer Them. [1217]

XLVIII

XLVIII. (257) The law chooses that a person who brings a sacrifice shall be pure, both in body and soul; --pure in soul from all passions, and diseases, and vices, which can be displayed either in word or deed; and pure in body from all such things as a body is usually defiled by. (258) And it has appointed a burning purification for both these things; for the soul, by means of the animals which are duly fit for sacrifices; and for the body, by ablutions and sprinklings; concerning which we will speak presently; for it is fit to assign the pre-eminence in honour in every point to the superior and dominant part of the qualities existing in us, namely, to the soul. (259) What, then, is the mode of purifying the soul? "Look," says the law, "take care that the victim which thou bringest to the altar is perfect, wholly without participation in any kind of blemish, selected from many on account of its excellence, by the uncorrupted judgments of the priests, and by their most acute sight, and by their continual practice derived from being exercised in the examination of faultless victims. For if you do not see this with your eyes more than with your reason, you will not wash off all the imperfections and stains which you have imprinted on your whole life, partly in consequence of unexpected events, and partly by deliberate purpose; (260) for you will find that this exceeding accuracy of investigation into the animals, figuratively signifies the amelioration of your own disposition and conduct; for the law was not established for the sake of irrational animals, but for that of those who have intellect and reason." So that the real object taken care of is not the condition of the victims sacrificed in order that they may have no blemish, but that of the sacrificers that they may not be defiled by any unlawful passion. (261) The body then, as I have already said, he purifies with ablutions and bespringklings, and does not allow a person after he has once washed and sprinkled himself, at once to enter within the sacred precincts, but bids him wait outside for seven days, and to be besprinkled twice, on the third day and on the seventh day; and after this it commands him to wash himself once more, and then it admits him to enter the sacred precincts and to share in the sacred ministrations.

XLIX

XLIX. (262) We must consider what great prudence and philosophical wisdom is displayed in this law; for nearly all other persons are besprinkled with pure water, generally in the sea, some in rivers, and others again in vessels of water which they draw from fountains. But Moses, having previously prepared ashes which had been left from the sacred fire (and in what manner shall be explained hereafter), appointed that it should be right to take some of them and to put them in a vessel, and then to pour water upon them, and then, dipping some branches of hyssop in the mixture of ashes and water, to sprinkle it over those who were to be purified. (263) And the cause of this proceeding may very probably be said to be this:--The lawgiver's intention is that those who approach the service of the living God should first of all know themselves and their own essence. For how can the man who does not know himself ever comprehend the supreme and all-excelling power of God? (264) Therefore, our bodily essence is earth and water, of which he reminds us by this purification, conceiving that this result--namely, to know one's self, and to know also of what one is composed, of what utterly valueless substances mere ashes and water are--is of itself the most beneficial purification. (265) For when a man is aware of this he will at once reject all vain and treacherous conceit, and, discarding haughtiness and pride, he will seek to become pleasing to God, and to conciliate the merciful power of that Being who hates arrogance. For it is said somewhere with great beauty, "He that exhibits over proud words or actions offends not men alone but God also, the maker of equality and of every thing else that is most excellent." (266) Therefore, to us who are amazed and excited by this sprinkling the very elements themselves, earth and water, may almost be said to utter distinct words, and to say plainly, we are the essence of your bodies; nature having mixed us together, divine art has fashioned us into the figure of a man. Being made of us when you were born, you will again be dissolved into us when you come to die; for it is not the nature of any thing to be destroyed so as to become non-existent; but the end brings it back to those elements from which its beginnings come.

L

L. (267) But now it is necessary to fulfil our promise and to explain the peculiar propriety involved in this use of ashes. For they are not merely the ashes of wood which has been consumed by fire, but also of an animal particularly suited for this kind of purification. (268) For the law Orders [1218] that a red heifer, which has never been brought under the yoke, shall be sacrificed outside of the city, and that the high priest, taking some of the blood, shall seven times sprinkle with it all the things in front of the temple, and then shall burn the whole animal, with its hide and flesh, and with the belly full of all the entrails. And when the flame begins to pour down, then it commands that these three things shall be thrown into the middle of it, a stick of cedar, a stick of hyssop, and a bunch of saffron; and then, when the fire is wholly extinguished, it commands that some man who is clean shall collect the ashes, and shall again place them outside of the city in some open place. (269) And what figurative meanings he conceals under these orders as symbols, we have accurately explained in another treatise, in which we have discussed the allegories. It is necessary, therefore, for those who are about to go into the temple to partake of the sacrifice, to be cleansed as to their bodies and as to their souls before their bodies. For the soul is the mistress and the queen, and is superior in every thing, as having received a more divine nature. And the things which cleanse the mind are wisdom and the doctrines of wisdom, which lead to the contemplation of the world and the things in it; and the sacred chorus of the rest of the virtues, and honourable and very praiseworthy actions in accordance with the virtues. (270) Let the man, therefore, who is adorned with these qualities go forth in cheerful confidence to the temple which most nearly belongs to him, the most excellent of all abodes to offer himself as a sacrifice. But let him in whom covetousness and a desire of unjust things dwell and display themselves, cover his head and be silent, checking his shameless folly and his excessive impudence, in those matters in which caution is profitable; for the temple of the truly living God may not be approached by unholy sacrifices. (271) I should say to such a man: My good man, God is not pleased even though a man bring hecatombs to his altar; for he possesses all things as his own, and stands in need of nothing. But he delights in minds which love God, and in men who practise holiness, from whom he gladly receives cakes and barley, and the very cheapest things, as if they were the most valuable in preference to such as are most costly. (272) And even if they bring nothing else, still when they bring themselves, the most perfect completeness of virtue and excellence, they are offering the most excellent of all sacrifices, honouring God, their Benefactor and Saviour, with hymns and thanksgivings; the former uttered by the organs of the voice, and the latter without the agency of the tongue or mouth, the worshippers making their exclamations and invocations with their soul alone, and only appreciable by the intellect, and there is but one ear, namely, that of the Deity which hears them. For the hearing of men does not extend so far as to be sensible of them.

LI

LI. (273) And that this statement is true, and not mine but that of nature, is testified to a certain degree by the evident nature of the thing itself, which affords a manifest proof which none can deny who do not cleave to credulity out of a contentious disposition. It is testified also by the law which commands two altars to be prepared, differing both as to the materials of which they are made, as to the places in which they are erected, and as to the purposes to which they are applied; (274) for one is made of stones, carefully selected so to fit one another, and unhewn, and it is erected in the open air, near the steps of the temple, and it is for the purpose of sacrificing victims which contain blood in them. And the other is made of gold, and is erected in the inner part of the temple, within the first veil, and may not be seen by any other human being except those of the priests who keep themselves pure, and it is for the purpose of offering incense upon; (275) from which it is plain that God looks upon even the smallest offering of frankincense by a holy man as more valuable than ten thousand beasts which may be sacrificed by one who is not thoroughly virtuous. For in proportion, I imagine, as gold is more valuable than stones, and as the things within the inner temple are more holy than those without, in the same proportion is the gratitude displayed by offerings of incense superior to that displayed by the sacrifice of victims full of blood, (276) on which account the altar of incense is honoured not only in the costliness of its materials, and in the manner of its erection, and in its situation, but also in the fact that it ministers every day before any thing else to the thanksgivings to be paid to God. For the law does not permit the priest to offer the sacrifice of the whole burnt offering outside before he has offered incense within at the earliest Dawn. [1219] (277) And this command is a symbol of nothing else but of the fact that in the eyes of God it is not the number of things sacrificed that is accounted valuable, but the purity of the rational spirit of the sacrificer. Unless, indeed, one can suppose that a judge who is anxious to pronounce a holy judgment will never receive gifts from any of those whose conduct comes before his tribunal, or that, if he does receive such presents, he will be liable to an accusation of corruption; and that a good man will not receive gifts from a wicked person, not even though he may be poor and the other rich, and he himself perhaps in actual want of what he would so receive; and yet that God can be corrupted by bribes, who is most all-sufficient for himself and who has no need of any thing created; who, being himself the first and most perfect good thing, the everlasting fountain of wisdom, and justice, and of every virtue, rejects the gifts of the wicked. (278) And is not the man who would offer such gifts the most shameless of all men, if he offers a portion of the things which he has acquired by doing injury, or by rapine, or by false denial, or by robbery, to God as if he were a partner in his wickedness? O most miserable of all men! I should say to such a man, "You must be expecting one of two things. Either that you will be able to pass undetected, or that you will be discovered. (279) Therefore, if you expect to be able to pass undetected, you are ignorant of the power of God, by which he at the same time sees everything and hears everything. And if you think that you will be discovered, you are most audacious in (when you ought rather to endeavour to conceal the wicked actions which you have committed) bringing forward to light specimens of all your iniquitous deeds, and giving yourself airs, and dividing the fruits of them with God, bringing him unholy first fruits. And have you not considered this, that the law does not admit of lawlessness, nor does the light of the sun admit of darkness; but God is the archetypal model of all laws, and the sun, which can be appreciated only by the intellect, is the archetypal model of that which is visible to the senses, bringing forth from its invisible fountains visible light to afford to him who sees." Moreover, there are other commandments relating to the Altar. [1220] (280) This injunction also is very admirably and properly set down in the sacred tablets of the law, that the wages of a harlot are not to be received into the temple, and inasmuch as she has earned them by selling her beauty, having chosen a most infamous life for the sake of shameful gain; (281) but if the gifts which proceed from a woman who has lived as a concubine are unholy, how can those be different which proceed from a soul which is deriled in the same manner, which has voluntarily abandoned itself to shame and to the lowest infamy, to drunkenness and gluttony, and covetousness and ambition, and love of pleasure, and to innumerable other kinds of passions, and diseases, and wickednesses? For what time can be long enough to efface those defilements, I indeed do not know. (282) Very often in truth time has put an end to the occupation of a harlot, since, when women have outlived their beauty, no one any longer approaches them, their prime having withered away like that of some flowers; and what length of time can ever transform the harlotry of the soul which from its youth has been trained in early and habitual incontinence, so as to bring it over to good order? No time could do this, but God alone, to whom all things are possible, even those which among us are impossible. (283) Accordingly, the man who is about to offer a sacrifice ought to examine and see, not whether the victim is without blemish, but whether his mind is sound, and entire, and perfect. Let him likewise investigate the causes for which he is about to offer the sacrifice; for it must be as an expression of thankfulness for kindnesses which have been shown to him, or else of supplication for the permanence of his present blessings, or for the acquisition of some future good, or else to avert some evil either present or expected; for all which objects he should labour to bring his reason into a state of good health and sanity; (284) for if he is giving thanks for benefits conferred upon him, he must take care not to behave like an ungrateful man, becoming wicked, for the benefits are conferred on a virtuous man; or if his object be to secure the permanence of his present prosperity and happiness, and to be enabled to look forward to such for the future, he must still show himself worthy of his good fortune, and behave virtuously; or if he is asking to escape from evils, let him not commit actions deserving of correction and punishment.

LII

LII. (285) The law says, "A fire shall be kept burning on the altar which shall never be extinguished, but shall be kept burning for Ever." [1221] I think with great reason and propriety; for, since the graces of God are everlasting, and unceasing, and uninterrupted, which we now enjoy day and night, and since the symbol of gratitude is the sacred flame, it is fitting that it should be kindled, and that it should remain unextinguished for ever. (286) And, perhaps, the lawgiver designed by this command to connect the old with the new sacrifices, and to unite the two by the duration and presence of the same fire by which all such sacrifices are consecrated, in order to demonstrate the fact that all perfect sacrifices consisted in thanksgiving, although, according to the diversity of the occasions on which they are offered, more victims are offered at one time and fewer at another. (287) But some are verbal symbols of things appreciable only by the intellect, and the mystical meaning which is concealed beneath them must be investigated by those who are eager for truth in accordance with the rules of allegory. The altar of God is the grateful soul of the wise man, being compounded of perfect numbers undivided and indivisible; for no part of virtue is useless. (288) On this soul the sacred fire is continually kept burning, preserved with care and unextinguishable. But the light of the mind is wisdom; as, on the contrary, the darkness of the soul is folly. For what the light discernible by the outward senses is to the eyes, that is knowledge to reason with a view to the contemplation of incorporeal things discernible only by the intellect, the light of which is continually shining and never extinguished.

LIII

LIII. (289) After this the law says, "On every offering you shall add Salt." [1222] By which injunction, as I have said before, he figuratively implies a duration for ever; for salt is calculated to preserve bodies, being placed in the second rank as inferior only to the soul; for as the soul is the cause of bodies not being destroyed, so likewise is salt, which keeps them together in the greatest degree, and to some extent makes them immortal. (290) On which account the law calls the altar thysiasteÃrion, giving it a peculiar name of especial honour, from its preserving (diateÌreoÌ) the sacrifices (tas thysias) in a proper manner, and this too though the flesh is consumed by fire; so as to afford the most evident proof possible that God looks not upon the victims as forming the real sacrifice, but on the mind and willingness of him who offers them, that so the durability and firmness of the altar may be ensured by virtue. (291) Moreover, it also ordains that every sacrifice shall be offered up without any leaven or honey, not thinking it fit that either of these things should be brought to the altar. The honey, perhaps, because the bee which collects it is not a clean animal, inasmuch as it derives its birth, as the story goes, from the putrefaction and corruption of dead oxen, [1223] just as wasps spring from the bodies of horses. (292) Or else this may be forbidden as a figurative declaration that all superfluous pleasure is unholy, making, indeed, the things which are eaten sweet to the taste, but inflicting bitter pains difficult to be cured at a subsequent period, by which the soul must of necessity be agitated and thrown into confusion, not being able to settle on any sure resting place. (293) And leaven is forbidden on account of the rising which it causes; this prohibition again having a figurative meaning, intimating that no one who comes to the altar ought at all to allow himself to be elated, being puffed up by insolence; but that such persons may keep their eyes fixed on the greatness of God, and so obtain a proper conception of the weakness of all created beings, even if they be very prosperous; and that so cherishing correct notions they may correct the arrogant lofiness of their minds, and discard all treacherous self-conceit. (294) But if the Creator and maker of the universe, who has no need of anything which he has created, not looking at the exceeding greatness of his own power and at his own authority, but at your weakness, gives you a share of his own merciful power, supplying the deficiencies with which you are overwhelmed, how do you think it fitting that you should behave towards men who are akin to you by nature, and who are springing from the same elements with yourself, when you have brought nothing into the world, not even yourself? (295) For, my fine fellow, you came naked into the world, and you shall leave it again naked, having received the interval between your birth and death as a loan from God; during which what ought you to do rather than take care to live in communion and harmony with your fellow creatures, studying equality, and humanity, and virtue, repudiating unequal, and unjust, and irreconcilable unsociable wickedness, which makes that animal which is by nature the most gentle of all, namely, man, a cruel and untractable monster?

LIV

LIV. (296) Again, the law commands that candles shall be kept burning from evening until Morning [1224] on the sacred candlesticks within the veil, on many accounts. One of which is that the holy places may be kept illuminated without any interruption after the cessation of the light of day, being always kept free from any participation in darkness, just as the stars themselves are, for they too, when the sun sets, exhibit their own light, never forsaking the place which was originally appointed for them in the world. (297) Secondly, in order that by night, also, a rite akin to and closely resembling the sacrifices by day may be performed so as to give pleasures to God, and that no time or occasion fit for offering thanksgiving may ever be left out, which is a duty most suitable and natural for night; for it is not improper to call the blaze of the most sacred light in the innermost shrine itself a sacrifice. (298) The third, which is a reason of the very greatest importance, is this. Since we are not only well treated while we are awake, but also when we are asleep, inasmuch as the mighty God gives sleep as a great assistance to the human race, for the benefit of both their bodies and souls, of their bodies as being by it relieved of the labours of the day, and of their souls as being lightened by it of all their cares, and being restored to themselves after all the disorder and confusion caused by the outward senses, and as being then enabled to retire within and commune with themselves, the law has very properly thought fit to make a distinction of the actions of thanksgiving, so that sacrifices may be made on behalf of those who are awake by means of the victims which are offered, and on behalf of those who are asleep, and of those who are benefited by sleep, by the lighting of the sacred candles.

LV

LV. (299) These, then, and other commandments like them, are those which are established for the purpose of promoting piety, by express injunctions and prohibitions. But those which are in accordance with philosophical suggestions and recommendations must be explained in this manner; for the lawgiver, in effect, says, "God, O mind of man! demands nothing of you which is either oppressive, or uncertain, or difficult, but only such things as are very simple and easy. (300) And these are, to love him as your benefactor; and if you fail to do so, at all events, to fear him as your Governor and Lord, and to enter zealously upon all the paths which may please him, and to serve him in no careless or superficial manner, but with one's whole soul thoroughly filled as it ought to be with God-loving sentiments, and to cleave to his commandments, and to honour justice, by all which means the world itself continues constantly in the same nature without ever changing, and all other things which are contained in the world have a tendency towards improvement, such as the sun and the moon, and the whole multitude of the rest of the stars, and the entire heaven. But the mountains of the earth are elevated to the greatest possible height, and the champaign country, like other fusible essences, is spread over a body of wide extent, and the sea also changes so as to become united with sweet waters, and the rains also become in their turn similar to the sea. Therefore every one of those things is still fixed within the same boundaries as those within which it was originally created, when it was first disposed of in regular order. But you shall be better, living quite irreproachably. (301) And what of all these things is either grievous or laborious? You are not compelled to pass over unnavigable seas; or, when tossed about by the billows of the middle of winter and the force of contrary winds, to wander about the sea in every direction; or to travel on foot over rough and pathless byeways, always being in dread of the haunts of robbers, or of the attacks of wild beasts; or to watch all night to protect your walls in the open air, while the enemy are lying in ambush for you, and threatening you with the very extremity of danger. Come, now, let no unpleasant topics be brought up in pleasant circumstances. We must use words of good omen with reference to such advantageous matters. (302) It is only necessary for the mind to consent and everything will be ready. Are you not aware that both that heaven which is invisible to the outward senses, and that likewise which is appreciable only by the intellect, belongs to God: the heaven of heavens as we may call it; and again, that the earth and all that is in it, and the whole world, both that which is visible and that which is invisible and incorporeal, being a model of the real heaven?

LVI

LVI. (303) But, nevertheless, he selected out of the whole race of mankind those who were really men for their superior excellence; and he elected them and thought them worthy of the highest possible honour, calling them to the service of himself, to that everlasting fountain of all that is good; from which he has showered forth other virtues, drawing forth, at the same time, for our enjoyment, combined with the greatest possible advantage, a drink contributing more than ever nectar, or at all events not less, to make those who drink of it immortal. (304) But those men are to be pitied, and are altogether miserable, who have never banquetted on the labours of virtue; and they have remained to the end the most miserable of all men who have been always ignorant of the taste of moral excellence, when it was in their power to have feasted on and luxuriated among justice and equality. But these men are uncircumcised in their hearts, as the law expresses it, and by reason of the hardness of their hearts they are stubborn, resisting and breaking their traces in a restive manner; (305) whom the Lord reproves, saying, "Be ye circumcised as to your hard-Heartedness;" [1225] that means, "do ye eradicate the overbearing character of your dominant part, which the immoderate impulses of the passing hour have sown and caused to grow within you, and which the wicked husbandman of the soul, folly, planted. (306) Again, it says, "Let not your necks be Stiff," [1226] that is to say, let not your mind be unbending and self-willed, and let it not admit into itself that most blameable ignorance of excessive perverseness. But discarding obstinacy and moroseness of nature as an enemy, let it change so as to become gentle, and inclined to obey the laws of nature. (307) Do you not see that the most important and greatest of all the powers of the living God are his beneficent and his punishing power? And his beneficent power is called God, since it is by means of this that he made and arranged the universe. And the other, or punishing power, is called Lord, on which his sovereignty over the universe depends. And God is God, not only of men, but also of gods; and he is mighty, being truly strong and truly Powerful. [1227]

LVII

LVII. (308) But, nevertheless, though he is so great in excellence and in power, he feels pity and compassion for all those who are most completely sunk in want and distress, not considering it beneath his dignity to be the judge in the causes of proselytes, and orphans, and widows, and disregarding kings and tyrants, and men in high commands, and honouring the humility of those men above mentioned, I mean the proselytes, with precedence, on this account. (309) These men, having forsaken their country and their national customs in which they were bred up, which, however, were full of the inventions of falsehood and pride, becoming genuine lovers of truth, have come over to piety; and becoming in all worthiness suppliants and servants of the true and living God, they very properly receive a precedence which they have deserved, having found the reward of their fleeing to God in the assistance which they now receive from him. (310) And in the case of orphans and widows, since they have been deprived of their natural protectors, the one class having lost their parents, and the others their husbands, they have no refuge whatever to which they can flee, no aid which they can hope for from man, being utterly destitute; on which account they are not deprived of the greatest hope of all, the hope of relief from God, who, because of his merciful character, does not refuse to provide and to care for persons so wholly desolate. (311) "Let then," says the law, "God alone be thy boast, and thy greater Glory," [1228] And do not pride thyself either on thy wealth, or on thy glory, or on the beauty of thy person, or on thy strength, or on anything of the same kind as the objects at which foolish empty-headed persons are apt to be elated; considering that, in the first place, these things have no connection at all with the nature of good, and secondly, that they are liable to rapid changes, fading away in a manner before they have time to flourish permanently. (312) And let us cling to the custom of addressing our supplications to him, and let us not, after we have subdued our enemies, imitate their impiety in those matters of conduct in which they fancy that they are acting piously, burning their sons and their daughters to their gods, not, indeed, that it is the custom of all the barbarians to burn their children. (313) For they are not become so perfectly savage in their natures as to endure in time of peace to treat their nearest and dearest relatives as they would scarcely treat their irreconcilable enemies in time of war. But that they do in reality inflame and corrupt the souls of the children of whom they are the parents from the very moment that they are out of their swaddling clothes; not imprinting on their minds, while they are still tender, any true opinions respecting the one only and truly living God. Let us not then be overcome by, and fall down before, and yield to their good fortune as if they had prevailed by reason of their piety. (314) For present prosperity is given to many persons for a snare, being only a bait to be followed by excessive and incurable evils. And it is very likely that even men who are unworthy may be allowed to be successful, not for their own sakes, but in order that we who act impiously may be more vehemently grieved and pained, who having been born in a God-fearing city, and having been bred up in laws which would imbue men with every virtue, and having been instructed from our earliest youth in all such pursuits as are most honourable to men, neglect them all, and cling only to such practices as deserve to be neglected, considering all good things as subjects for amusement, and looking upon things fit only for sport as seriously good.

LVIII

LVIII. (315) And if, indeed, any one assuming the name and appearance of a prophet, [1229] appearing to be inspired and possessed by the Holy Spirit, were to seek to lead the people to the worship of those who are accounted gods in the different cities, it would not be fitting for the people to attend to him being deceived by the name of a prophet. For such an one is an impostor and not a prophet, since he has been inventing speeches and oracles full of falsehood, (316) even though a brother, or a son, or a daughter, or a wife, or a steward, or a firm friend, or any one else who seems to be well-intentioned towards one should seek to lead one in a similar course; exhorting one to be cheerful among the multitude, and to approach the same temples and to adopt the same sacrifices; but such an one should be punished as a public and common enemy, and we should think but little of any relationship, and one should relate his recommendations to all the lovers of piety, who with all speed and without any delay would hasten to inflict punishment on the impious man, judging it a virtuous action to be zealous for his execution. (317) For we should acknowledge only one relationship, and one bond of friendship, namely, a mutual zeal for the service of God, and a desire to say and do everything that is consistent with piety. And these bonds which are called relationships of blood, being derived from one's ancestors, and those connections which are derived from intermarriages and from other similar causes, must all be renounced, if they do not all hasten to the same end, namely, the honour of God which is the one indissoluble bond of all united good will. For such men will lay claim to a more venerable and sacred kind of relationship; (318) and the law confirms my assertion, where it says that those who do what is pleasing to nature and virtuous are the sons of God, for it says, "Ye are the sons of the Lord your God," [1230] inasmuch as you will be thought worthy of his providence and care in your behalf as though he were your father. And that care is as much superior to that which is shown by a man's own parents, as I imagine the being who takes it is superior to them.

LIX

LIX. (319) In addition to this the lawgiver also entirely removes out of his sacred code of laws all ordinances respecting initiations, and mysteries, and all such trickery and buffoonery; not choosing that men who are brought up in such a constitution as that which he was giving should be busied about such matters, and, placing their dependence on mystic enchantments, should be led to neglect the truth, and to pursue those objects which have very naturally received night and darkness for their portion, passing over the things which are worthy of light and of day. Let no one, therefore, of the disciples or followers of Moses either be initiated himself into any mysterious rites of worship, or initiate any one else; for both the act of learning and that of teaching such initiations is an impiety of no slight order. (320) For if these things are virtuous, and honourable, and profitable, why do ye, O ye men who are initiated, shut yourselves up in dense darkness, and limit your benefits to just three or four men, when you might bring down the advantages which you have to bestow into the middle of the market place, and benefit all men; so that every one might without hindrance partake of a better and more fortunate life? (321) for envy is never found in conjunction with virtue. Let men who do injurious things be put to shame, and seeking hiding places and recesses in the earth, and deep darkness, hide themselves, concealing their lawless iniquity from sight, so that no one may behold it. But to those who do such things as are for the common advantage, let there be freedom of speech, and let them go by day through the middle of the market place where they will meet with the most numerous crowds, to display their own manner of life in the pure sun, and to do good to the assembled multitudes by means of the principal of the outward senses, giving them to see those things the sight of which is most delightful and most impressive, and hearing and feasting upon salutary speeches which are accustomed to delight the minds even of those men who are not utterly illiterate. (322) Do you not see that nature has concealed none of those works which are deservedly celebrated and honourable, but has exhibited openly the stars and the whole of heaven, so as to cause the sight pleasure, and to excite a desire for philosophy, and she also displays her seas, and fountains, and rivers, and the excellencies of the atmosphere, and the beautiful adaptation of the winds to the various seasons of the year, and of plants, and of animals, and, moreover, the innumerable species of fruits, for the use and enjoyment of men? (323) Would it not have been right, then, for you, following her example and design, to give to those who are worthy of it all things that are necessary for their advantage? But now it very often happens that no good men at all are initiated by them, but that sometimes robbers, and wreckers, and companies of debauched and polluted women are, when they have given money enough to those who initiate them, and who reveal to them the mysteries which they call sacred. But let all such men be driven away and expelled from that city, and denied all share in that constitution, in which honour and truth are reverenced for their own sake. And this is enough to say on this subject.

LX

LX. (324) But the law, being most especially an interpreter of equal communion, and of courteous humanity among men, has preserved the honour and dignity of each virtue; not permitting any one who is incurably sunk in vice to flee to them, but rejecting all such persons and repelling them to a distance. (325) Therefore, as it was aware that no inconsiderable number of wicked men are often mingled in these assemblies, and escape notice by reason of the crowds collected there, in order to prevent that from being the case in this instance, he previously excludes all who are unworthy from the sacred assembly, beginning in the first instance with those who are afflicted with the disease of effeminacy, men-women, who, having adulterated the coinage of nature, are willingly driven into the appearance and treatment of licentious women. He also banishes all those who have suffered any injury or mutilation in their most important members, and those who, seeking to preserve the flower of their beauty so that it may not speedily wither away, have altered the impression of their natural manly appearance into the resemblance of a woman. (326) The law also excludes not only all harlots, but also those who being born of a harlot bear about them the disgrace of their mother, because their original birth and origin have been adulterated. (327) For this passage (if there is any passage at all in the whole scripture which does so) admits of an allegorical interpretation; for there is not one description only of impious and unholy men, but there are many and different. For some persons affirm that the incorporeal ideas are only an empty name, having no participation in any real fact, removing the most important of all essences from the list of existing things, though it is in fact the archetypal model of all things which are the distinctive qualities of essence, in accordance with which each thing is assigned to its proper species and limited to its proper dimensions. (328) The sacred pillars of the law call all these men broken; for such an injury as is implied by that term leaves a man destitute of all distinctive quality and species, and what is so broken is nothing else, to speak the strict truth, than mere shapeless material. Thus, the doctrine which takes away species throws every thing into confusion, and moreover brings back that want of proper form which existed before the elements were reduced into proper order. (329) And what can be more absurd than this? For it is out of that essence that God created every thing, without indeed touching it himself, for it was not lawful for the all-wise and all-blessed God to touch materials which were all misshapen and confused, but he created them by the agency of his incorporeal powers, of which the proper name is "ideas," which he so exerted that every genus received its proper form. But this opinion has created great irregularity and confusion. For when it takes away the things by means of which the distinctive qualities exist, it at the same time takes away the distinctive qualities themselves. (330) But other persons, as if they were engaged in a contest of wickedness, being anxious to carry off the prizes of victory, go beyond all others in impiety, joining to their denial of the ideas a negative also of the being of God, as if he had no real existence but were only spoken of for the sake of what is beneficial to men. Others, again, out of fear of that Being who appears to be present everywhere and to see every thing, are barren of wisdom, but devoted to the maintenance of that which is the greatest of all wickednesses, namely impiety. (331) There is also a third class, who have entered on the contrary path, guiding a multitude of men and women, of old and young, filling the world with arguments in favour of a multiplicity of rulers, in order by such means to eradicate all notions of the one and truly living God from the minds of men. (332) These are they who are symbolically called by the law the sons of a harlot. For as mothers who are harlots do not know who is the real father of their children, and cannot register him accurately, but have many, or I might almost say all men, their lovers and associates, the same is the case with those who are ignorant of the one true God. For, inventing a great number whom they falsely call gods, they are blinded as to the most important of all existing things which they ought to have thoroughly learnt, if not alone, at all events as the first and greatest of all things from their earliest childhood; for what can be a more honourable thing to learn than the knowledge of the true and living God?

LXI

LXI. (333) The law also excludes a fourth class, and a fifth, both hastening to the same end, but not with the same intention; for, as they are both followers of the same great evil, self-will, they have divided between them the whole soul as a kind of common inheritance, consisting of a rational and an irrational part; and the one class has appropriate the rational part, which is the mind, and the other the irrational part which is again subdivided into the outward senses; (334) therefore, the champions of the mind attribute to it the predominance in and supreme authority over all human affairs, and affirm that it is able to preserve all past things in its recollection, and to comprehend all present things with great vigour, and to divine the future by probable conjecture; (335) for this is the faculty which sowed and planted all the fertile soil in both the mountainous and champaign districts of the earth, and which invented agriculture, the most useful of all sciences for human life. This also is the faculty which surveyed the heaven, and by a proper contemplation of it made the earth accessible to ships by an ingenuity beyond all powers of description; (336) this, also invented letters, and music, and the whole range of encyclical instruction, and brought them to perfection. This also, is the parent of that greatest of all good things, philosophy, and by means of its different parts it has benefited human life, proceeding by the logical portion of it to an infallible interpretation of difficulties, and by its moral part to a correction of the manners and dispositions of men; and by its physical division to the knowledge of the heaven and the world. And they have also collected and assembled many other praises of the mind on which they dwell, having a continual reference to the species already mentioned, about which we have not at the present time leisure to occupy ourselves.

LXII

LXII. (337) But the champions of the outward senses extol their praises, also, with great energy and magnificence; enumerating in their discourse all the wants which are supplied by their means, and they say that two of them are the causes of living; smell and taste; and two of living well, seeing and hearing; (338) therefore, by means of taste the nourishment derived from food is conveyed into the system, and by means of the nostrils the air on which every living thing depends; for this also is a continual food, which nourishes and preserves men, not only while they are awake, but also while they are asleep. And the proof of this is clear; for if the passage of the breath be obstructed for even the shortest period, to such a degree as wholly to cut off the air which is intended by nature to be conveyed into the system from without, inevitable death will of necessity ensue. (339) Again, of the more philosophical of the outward senses by means of which the living well is produced, the power of sight beholds the light which is the most beautiful of all essences, and by means of the light it beholds all other things, the sun, the moon, the stars, the heaven, the earth, the sea, the innumerable varieties of plants and animals, and in short all bodies, and shapes, and odours, and magnitudes whatever, the sight of which has given birth to excessive wisdom, and has begotten a great desire for knowledge. (340) And even without reckoning the advantage derived from these things; sight also affords us the greatest benefits in respect of the power of distinguishing one's relatives and strangers, and friends, and avoiding what is injurious and choosing what is beneficial. Now each of the other parts of the body has been created with reference to appropriate uses, which are of great importance, as, for instance, the feet were made for walking, and for all the other uses to which the legs can be applied; again, the hands were created for the purpose of doing, or giving, or taking anything; and the eyes, as a sort of universal good, afford both to the hands and feet, and to all the other parts of the body the cause of being able to act or move rightly; (341) and that this is the case is most unerringly demonstrated by the evidence of those who have suffered any mutilation in these members, who cannot in real truth be said to have either feet or hands, and who by the reality of their condition prove the correctness of their name, which they say that men of old gave them not so much by way of reproach as out of compassion, calling them impotent, out of surprise at what they see. (342) Again, hearing is the thing by which melodies and rhythm, and all parts and divisions of music are distinguished; for song and speech are salutary and wholesome medicines, the one charming the passions and the inharmonious qualities within us by its rhythm, and our unmelodious qualities by its melodies, and bridling our immoderate vehemence by its fixed measures; (343) and each of those parts of it are various and multiform, as the musicians and poets do testify, whom we must believe; and speech, checking and cutting short all the impulses which lead to wickedness, and healing those who are under the dominion of folly and misery, and strengthening those who are inclined to yield in a cowardly manner, and subduing those who resist more obstinately, becomes thus the cause of the greatest advantages.

LXIII

LXIII. (344) The advocates of the mind and of the outward senses, having put these arguments together, make gods of both of them, the one deifying the first, and the other the last; both classes out of their self-will and self-conceit forgetting the truly living God. On which account the lawgiver very naturally excludes them all from the sacred assembly, calling those who would take away the ideas, broken in the stones, and those too who are utterly atheistical, to whom he has given the appropriate name of eunuchs; and those who are the teachers of an opposite system of theogony, whom he calls the sons of a harlot; and besides all these classes he excludes also the self-willed and self-conceited, some of whom have deified reason, and others have called each separate one of the outward senses gods. For all these men are hastening to the same end, even though they are not all influenced by the same intentions. (345) But we who are the followers and disciples of the prophet Moses, will never abandon our investigation into the nature of the true God; looking upon the knowledge of him as the true end of happiness; and thinking that the true everlasting life, as the law says, [1231] is to live in obedience to and worship of God; in which precept it gives us a most important and philosophical lesson; for in real truth those who are atheists are dead as to their souls, but those who are marshalled in the ranks of the true living God, as his servants, enjoy an everlasting Life. [1232]

Footnotes:

1182. Yonge's title, A Treatise on Circumcision.

1183. the Greek word is anthrax, which also signifies a coal. The Latin, from which our carbuncle is derived, carbunculus, a diminutive of carbo, which also means a coal.

1184. Yonge's translation includes a separate treatise title at this point: On Monarchy, Book I. Accordingly, his next paragraph begins with roman numeral I (= III in Loeb). Yonge's "treatise" concludes with number IX (= XI in the Loeb). The publisher has elected to follow the Loeb numbering.

1185. Deut 4:19.

1186. Exod 20:20.

1187. Lev 19:4.

1188. Deut 4:4.

1189. Mangey thinks that there is a considerable hiatus here. What follows relates to the regulations respecting proselytes, which as the text stands is in no way connected with what has gone before about the worship of God.

1190. this prophecy, Deut 18:18, is always looked upon as one of the most remarkable of the early prophecies of our Saviour.

1191. Yonge's translation includes a separate treatise title at this point: On the Monarchy, Book II. Accordingly, his next paragraph begins with roman numeral I (= XII in the Loeb). Yonge's "treatise" concludes with number XV (= XXVI in the Loeb). The publisher has elected to follow the Loeb numbering.

1192. the Greek for a pomegranate is rhoia, or rhoiskos, which Philo imagines to be derived from rheoÂ, "to flow."

1193. Deut 23:18.

1194. Lev 23:1.

1195. Lev 21:17.

1196. Lev 22:4.

1197. Lev 22:10.

1198. Lev 22:12.

1199. Yonge's translation includes a separate treatise title at this point: On the Question: What the Rewards and Honours Are Which Belong to the Priests. Accordingly, his next paragraph begins with roman numeral I (= XVII in the Loeb). Yonge's "treatise" concludes with number VI (= XXXII in the Loeb). The publisher has elected to follow the Loeb numbering.

1200. the above passage is quite unintelligible in the Greek, and is given up by Mangey as irremediably corrupt.

1201. the Greek word here used is seioÂ, and the word used for jawbone is siagoÌn, which Philo appears to think may be derived from seioÌ.

1202. Yonge's translation includes a separate treatise title at this point: On Animals Fit for Sacrifice, or On Victims. Accordingly, his next paragraph begins with roman numeral I (= XXXIII in the Loeb). Yonge's "treatise" concludes with number XV (= XLVII in the Loeb). The publisher has elected to follow the Loeb numbering.

1203. sections 177-193 were omitted in Yonge's translation because the edition on which Yonge based his translation, Mangey, lacked this material. These sections have been newly translated for this edition.

1204. an alternative would be to understand teleion as a predicate adjective and supply an einai which would mean "that the number of animals to be sacrificed should be perfect." The absence of a definite article before "perfect number" suggests the translation in the text is preferable.

1205. the exact meaning of ieromeÂnia is unclear. The best explanation of the term was suggested by a scholiast on Pindar Nem. 3.2 who explained that the beginnings of months were sacred (A. B. Drachmann, Scholia Vetera in Pindari Carmina [3 vols., Leipzig: B. G. Teubner, 1903-27] 3:42). Thus understood to be Philo's designation for the feast day which opens the sacred month, it is here consistently translated "the feast which begins the sacred month."

1206. L. Cohn emended meÌden to meÌde in order to avoid the notion of sinlessness in the text. The translation follows the MSS since they offer the more difficult reading and this is a rhetorical statement designed to commend repentance, not make an observation on human perfection.

1207. although S. Daniel included a negative in her edition (PAPM 24)--[ouk] aponemetai ("is not distributed")--in order to harmonize this statement with 1.232 and 1.244, this translation has followed the more difficult reading.

1208. Lev 1:3.

1209. Lev 19:1.
1210. Lev 7:5.
1211. Lev 4:22.
1212. Lev 5:20.
1213. Lev 6:9.
1214. Num 6:14.
1215. Num 6:18.
1216. Lev 6:13.
1217. Yonge's translation includes a separate treatise title at this point: On Those Who Offer Sacrifice. Accordingly, his next paragraph begins with roman numeral I (= XLVIII in the Loeb). Yonge's "treatise" concludes with number XVI (= LXIII in the Loeb). The publisher has elected to follow the Loeb numbering.
1218. Num 19:1.
1219. Exod 30:8.
1220. Yonge's translation places sections 280-284 after what is section 345 in the Loeb and makes them part of a new treatise entitled On the Commandment that the Wages of a Harlot Are Not To Be Received in the Sacred Treasury. The sections are included here in their proper place.
1221. Lev 6:9.
1222. Lev 2:13.
1223. this refers to the same idea so beautifully expressed by Virgil, Georgie 4.548 (as it is translated by Dryden)--"His mother's precepts he performs with care; / The temple visits and adores with prayer; / Four altars raises; from his herd he culls, / For slaughter, four the fairest of his bulls; / Four heifers from his female store he took, / All fair and all unknowing of the yoke, / Nine mornings thence with sacrifice and prayers, / The powers atoned, he to the grove repairs. / Behold a prodigy! for from within / The broken vowels and the bloated skin, / A buzzing noise of bees his ears alarms: / Straight issue through the sides assembling swarms, / Dark as a cloud they make a wheeling flight, / Then on a neighbouring tree, descending light: / Like a large cluster of black grapes they show, / And make a large dependance from the bough."
1224. Lev 24:2.
1225. Deut 10:16.
1226. Deut 10:18.
1227. Deut 10:17.
1228. Deut 10:21.
1229. Deut 13:1.
1230. Deut 14:1.
1231. Deut 4:4.
1232. Yonge's translation includes a separate treatise title at this point: On the Commandment that the Wages of a Harlot Are Not To Be Received in the Sacred Treasury. The first three paragraphs of this "treatise" are actually sections 280-284 of The Special Laws, I which have been relocated to their proper positon. The remainder of the "treatise" more correctly belongs to On the Sacrifices of Abel and Cain 1.21-33 and have been relocated accordingly.

THE SPECIAL LAWS, II [1233]

I

I. (1) In the treatise preceding this one we have discussed with accuracy two articles of the ten commandments, that which relates to not thinking that any other beings are absolute gods, except God himself; and the other which enjoins us not to worship as God any object made with hands. And we also spoke of the laws which relate specially to each of these points. But we will now proceed to discuss the three which come next in the regular order, again adapting suitable special laws to each. (2) And the first of these other commandments is not to take the name of God in vain; for the word of the virtuous man, says the law, shall be his oath, firm, unchangeable, which cannot lie, founded steadfastly on truth. And even if particular necessities shall compel him to swear, then he should make the witness to his oath the health or happy old age of his father or mother, if they are alive; or their memory, if they are dead. And, indeed, a man's parents are the copies and imitations of divine power, since they have brought people who had no existence into existence. (3) One person is recorded in the law, one of the patriarchs of the race, and one of those most especially admired for his wisdom, "as swearing by the face of his father," for the benefit, I imagine, of all those who might live afterwards, and with the object of giving necessary instruction, so that posterity might honour their parents in the proper manner, loving them as benefactors and respecting them as rulers appointed by nature, and might therefore not rashly invoke the name of God. (4) And these men also deserve to be praised who, when they are compelled to swear, by their slowness, and delay, and evasion, cause fear not only to those who see them, but to those also who invite them to take an oath; for when they do pronounce the oath they are accustomed to say only thus much, "By the--;" or, "No, by the--;" without any further addition, giving an emphasis to these words by the mutilation of the usual form, but without uttering the express oath. (5) However, if a man must swear and is so inclined, let him add, if he pleases, not indeed the highest name of all, and the most important cause of all things, but the earth, the sun, the stars, the heaven, the universal world; for these things are all most worthy of being named, and are more ancient than our own birth, and, moreover, they never grow old, lasting for ever and ever, in accordance with the will of their Creator.

II

II. (6) And some men display such easiness and indifference on the subject, that, passing over all created things, they dare in their ordinary conversation to rise up to the Creator and Father of the universe, without stopping to consider the place in which they are, whether it be profane or sacred; or the time, whether it be suitable; or themselves, whether they are pure in body and soul; or the business, whether it be important; or the occasion, whether it is necessary; but (as the proverb says), they pollute everything with unwashed feet, as if it were decent, since nature has bestowed a tongue upon them, for them to let it loose unrestrained and unbridled to approach objects which it is impious to approach. (7) When they ought rather to employ that most excellent of all the organs by which voice and speech (the most useful things in human life, and the causes of all communion among men) are made distinct and articulate, in a manner to contribute to the honour, and dignity, and blessing of the great Cause of all things. (8) But now, out of their excessive impiety, they use the most awful names in speaking of the most unimportant matters, and heaping one appellation upon another in a perfect crowd they feel no shame, thinking that by the frequency and number of their uninterrupted oaths they will attain to the object which they desire, being very foolish to think so; for a great number of oaths is no proof of credibility, but rather of a man's not deserving to be believed in the opinion of men of sense and wisdom.

III

III. (9) But if any one being compelled to swear, swears by anything whatever in a manner which the law does not forbid, let him exert himself with all his strength and by every means in his power to give effect to his oath, interposing no hindrance to prevent the accomplishment of the matter thus ratified, especially if neither implacable anger or frenzied love, or unrestrained appetites agitate the mind, so that it does not know what is said or done, but if the oath has been taken with sober reason and deliberate purpose. (10) For what is better than to speak with perfect truth throughout one's whole life, and to prove this by the evidence of God himself? For an oath is nothing else but the testimony of God invoked in a matter which is a subject of doubt, and to invoke God to witness a statement which is not true is the most impious of all things. (11) For a man who does this, is all but saying in plain words (even though he hold his peace), "I am using thee as a veil for my iniquity; do thou co-operate with me, who am ashamed to appear openly to be behaving unjustly. For though I am doing wrong, I am anxious not to be accounted wicked, but thou canst be indifferent to thy reputation with the multitude, having no regard to being well spoken of." But to say or imagine such things as these is most impious, for not only would God, who is free from all participation in wickedness, but even any father or any stranger, provided he were not utterly devoid of all virtue, would be indignant if he were addressed in such a way as this. (12) A man, therefore, as I have said, must be sure and give effect to all oaths which are taken for honourable and desirable objects, for the due establishment of private or public objects of importance, under the guidance of wisdom, and justice, and holiness.

IV

IV. And in this description of oaths those most lawful vows are included which are offered up in consequence of an abundance of blessings, either present or expected; but if any vows are made for contrary objects, it is not holy to ratify them, (13) for there are some men who swear, if chance so prompts them, to commit theft, or sacrilege, or adultery, or rape, or to inflict wounds or slaughter, or any similar acts of wickedness, and who perform them without any delay, making an excuse that they must keep their oaths, as if it were not better and more acceptable to God to do no iniquity, than to perform such a vow and oath as that. The national laws and ancient ordinances of every people are established for the sake of justice and of every virtue, and what else are laws and ordinances but the sacred words of nature having an authority and power in themselves, so that they differ in no respect from oaths? (14) And let every man who commits wicked actions because he is so bound by an oath, beware that he is not keeping his oath, but that he is rather violating one which is worthy of great care and attention to preserve it, which sets a seal as it were to what is honourable and just, for he is adding wickedness to wickedness, adding lawless actions to oaths taken on improper occasions, which had better have been buried in silence. (15) Let such a man, therefore, abstain from committing iniquity, and seek to propitiate God, that he may grant to him the mercy of that humane power which is innate in him, so as to pardon him for the oaths which he took in his folly. For it is incurable madness and insanity to take upon himself twofold evils, when he might put off one half of the burden of them. (16) But there are some men who, out of the excess of their wicked hatred of their species, being naturally unsociable and inhuman, or else being constrained by anger as by a hard mistress, think to confirm the savageness of their natural disposition by an oath, swearing that they will not admit this man or that man to sit at the same table with them, or to come under the same roof; or, again, that they will not give any assistance to such an one, or that they will not receive any from him as long as he lives. And sometimes even after the death of their enemy, they keep up their irreconcileable enmity, not allowing their friends to give the customary honours even to their dead bodies when in the grave. (17) I would recommend to such men, as to those I have mentioned before, to seek to propitiate the mercy of God by prayers and sacrifices, that so they may find some cure for the diseases of their souls which no man is competent to heal.

V

V. (18) But there are other persons, also, boastful, puffed up with pride and arrogance, who, being insatiably greedy of glory, are determined to obey none of the precepts which point to that most beneficial virtue, frugality; but even if any one exhorts them to it, in order to induce them to shake off the obstinate impetuosity of the appetites, they look upon all their admonitions as insults, and drive their course on headlong to every kind of effeminate luxury, despising those who seek to correct them, and making a joke of and turning into ridicule all the honourable and advantageous recommendations of wisdom. (19) And if such men happen to be in such circumstances as to have any abundance and superfluity of the means of living, they declare with positive oaths that they will indulge in all imaginable expense for the use and enjoyment of costly luxury. For instance, a man who has lately come into the enjoyment of considerable riches, embraces a prodigal and extravagant course of life; and when some old man, some relation perhaps, or some friend of his father, comes and admonishes him, exhorting him to alter his ways and to come over to a more honourable and strict behaviour, he is indignant beyond all measure at the advice, and being obstinate in his contentious disposition, swears that as long as he has the means and resources necessary for supplying his wants he will not practise any single way which leads to economy or moderation, neither in the city nor in the country, neither when travelling by sea nor by land, but that he will at all times and in all places show how rich and liberal he is; but as it seems to me such conduct as this is not so much a display of riches as of insolence and intemperance. (20) And yet many men who have before now been placed in situations of great authority, and even many who now are so, though they have most abundant resources of all kinds, and enormous riches, wealth continually and uninterruptedly flowing upon them as if from some unceasing spring, do nevertheless at times turn to the same things which we poor men use, to earthenware cups, and small cheap loaves, and olives, or cheese, or vegetables, for a seasoning to their dinners; and in the summer put on a girdle and a linen garment, and in winter any whole and stout cloak, and for sleep use a bed made on the ground, discarding gladly couches made of ivory or wrought in tortoiseshell and gold, and coverlets of various embroidery, and rich clothes and purple dyes, and the luxury of sweet and elaborate confectionery, and costly viands; (21) and the reason of this conduct is not merely that they have a virtuous and abstemious disposition by nature, but also that they have enjoyed a good education from their earliest youth, which has taught them to honour what belongs to man rather than what belongs to authority, which also taking up its settled abode in the soul, I may almost say reminds it every day of its humanity, drawing it down from lofty and arrogant thoughts, and reducing it within due bounds, and correcting whatever is unequal by the introduction of equality. (22) Therefore such men fill their cities with vigour and abundance, and with good laws and peace, depriving them of no good thing whatever, but providing them with all requisite blessings in the most unlimited and unsparing manner; for this conduct and actions of this sort are the achievements of men of real nobility, and of men who may truly be called governors. (23) But the actions of men newly become rich, of men who by some blunder of fortune have arrived at great wealth, who have no notion, not even in their dreams, of wealth which is genuine and truly endowed with sight, which consists of the perfect virtues, and of actions in accordance with such virtues, but who stumble against that wealth which is blind, leaning upon which, and therefore of necessity missing the right road, they turn into one which is no road at all, admiring objects which deserve no honour at all, and ridiculing things that are honourable by nature; men whom the word of God reproves and reproaches in no moderate degree for introducing oaths on unfitting occasions; for such men are difficult to purify and difficult to cure, so as not to be thought deserving pardon even by God, who is all-merciful by nature.

VI

VI. (24) But the law takes away from virgins and from married women the power of making vows independently, pronouncing the parents of the one class, and the husbands of the other, their lords; and with reference to any confirmation or disavowal of their oaths, declaring that that power belongs in the one case to the father, and in the other to the husband. And very reasonably, for the one class by reason of their youth are not aware of the importance of oaths, so that they stand in need of the advice of others to judge for them; while the other class do often out of easiness of disposition take oaths which are not for the interest of their husbands, on which account the law invests the husbands and fathers with authority either to ratify their oaths or to declare them void. (25) And let not widows swear inconsiderately, for they have no one who can beg them off from the effect of their oaths; neither husbands, from whom they are now separated, nor fathers, whose houses they have quitted when they departed from home on the occasion of their marriage, since it is unavoidable that their oaths must stand as being confirmed through the absence of any one to take care of the interests of the swearers. (26) But if any one knows that any one else is violating his oath, and does not inform against him, or convict him, being influenced by friendship, or respect, or fear, rather than by piety, he shall be liable to the same punishment as the perjured person; [1234] for assenting to one who does wrong differs in no respect from doing wrong one's self. (27) And punishment is inflicted on perjured persons in some cases by God and in others by men; but those punishments which proceed from God are the most fearful and the most severe, for God shows no mercy to men who commit such impiety as that, but allows them to remain for ever unpurified, and in my opinion with great justice and propriety, for the man who despises such important matters cannot complain if he is despised in his turn, receiving a fate equal to his actions. (28) But the punishments which are inflicted by men are of various characters, being death, or scourging; [1235] those men who are more excellent and more strict in their piety inflicting death on such offenders, but those who are of milder dispositions scourging them with rods publicly in the sight of all men; and to men who are not of abject and slavish dispositions scourging is a punishment not inferior in terror to death.

VII

VII. (29) These then are the ordinances contained in the express language of these commandments; but there is also an allegorical meaning concealed beneath, which we must extract by a careful consideration of the figurative expressions used. We must be aware, therefore, that the correct principles of nature recognise the power both of the father and of the husband as equal, but still in different respects. The power of the husband exists because of his sowing the seed of the virtues in the soul, as in a fertile field; that of the father arises from its being his natural office to implant good counsels in the minds of his children, and to stimulate them to honourable and virtuous actions; and because, when he has done so, he cherishes them with salutary doctrines, which education and wisdom supply; (30) and the mind is compared at one time to a virgin, and at another to a woman who is a widow, and again to one who is still united to a husband. It is compared to a virgin, when it preserves itself pure, and undefiled, free from the influence of pleasures and appetites, and likewise of pains and fears, treacherous passions, and then the father who begot it retains the regulation of it; and her principle, as in the case of a virtuous woman, she now being united to pure reason, in accordance with virtue, will exert a proper care to defend her, implanting in her, like a husband, the most excellent conceptions. (31) But the soul which is deprived of the wisdom and guardianship of a parent, and of the union of right reason, being widowed of her most excellent defences, and abandoned by wisdom, if it has chosen a life open to reproach, must be bound by its own conduct, not having reason in accordance with wisdom to act as intercessor, to relieve her of the consequences of her sins, neither has a husband living with her, nor as a father who has begotten her.

VIII

VIII. (32) But in the case of those persons who have vowed not merely their own property or some part of it, but also their own selves, the law has affixed a price to their vows, not having a regard to their beauty, or their importance, or to any thing of that kind, but with reference to the number of the individuals separating the men from the women, and the infants from those who are full grown. (33) For the law Ordains [1236] that from twenty years of age to sixty the price of a man shall be two hundred drachmas of solid silver money, and of a woman a hundred and twenty drachmas. And from five years of age to twenty, the price of a male child is eighty, and of a female child forty drachmas. And from infancy to five years old, the price of a male is twenty; of a female child, twelve Drachmas. [1237] And in the case of men who have lived beyond sixty years of age, the ransom of the old men is sixty, and of the old women forty drachmas. (34) And the law has regulated this ransom with reference to the same age both in men and women on account of three most important considerations. First of all, because the importance of their vow is equal and similar, whether it be made by a person of great or of little importance. Secondly, because it is fitting that those who have made a vow should not be exposed to the treatment of slaves; for they are valued at a high or at a low price, according to the good condition and beauty of their bodies, or the contrary. Thirdly, which, indeed, is the most important consideration of all, because inequality is valued among men, but equality is honoured by God.

IX

IX. (35) These are the ordinances established in respect of men, but about animals the following commands are given. If any one shall set apart any beast; if it be a clean beast of any one of the three classes which are appropriate to sacrifice, such as an ox, or a sheep, or a goat, he shall surely sacrifice it, not substituting either a worse animal for a better, or a better for a worse. For God does not take delight in the fleshiness of fatness of animals, but in the blameless disposition of the man who has vowed it. But if he should make a substitution, then he must sacrifice two instead of one; both the one which he had originally vowed, and the one which he wished to substitute for it. (36) But if any one vows one of the unclean animals, let him bring it to the most venerable of the priests; and let him value it, not exaggerating its price, but adding to its exact value one-fifth, in order that if it should be necessary to sacrifice an animal that is clean instead of it, the sacrifice may not fall short of its proper value. And this is ordained also for the sake of causing the man who has vowed it to feel grieved at having made an inconsiderate vow, having vowed an animal which is not clean, looking upon it, in my opinion, for the moment as clean, being led away by error of mind through some passion. (37) And if the thing which he has vowed be his house, again he must have the priest for a valuer. But those who may chance to buy it shall not pay an equal ransom for it; but if the man who has vowed it chooses to ransom it, he shall pay its price and a fifth besides, punishing his own rashness and impetuous desire for his two faults, his rashness for making the vow, and his impetuous desire for wishing for things back again which he had before abandoned. But if any one else brings it he shall not pay more than its value. (38) And let not the man who has made the vow make any long delay either in the accomplishment of his vow or in procuring a proper valuation to be made of it. For it is absurd to attempt to make strict covenants with men, but to look upon agreements made with God who has no need of any thing, and who has no deficiency of any thing as unnecessary to be observed, while those who do so are by their delays and slowness convicting themselves of the greatest of offences, namely, of a neglect of him whose service they ought to look upon as the beginning and end of all happiness. This is enough to say of oaths and Vows.[1238]

X

X. (39) The next commandment is that concerning the sacred seventh day, in which are comprehended an infinite number of most important festivals. For instance, there is the release of those men who by nature were free, but who, through some unforeseen necessity of the times, have become slaves, which release takes place every seventh year. Again, there is the humanity of creditors towards their debtors, as they forgive their countrymen their debts every seventh year. Also there is the rest given to the fertile ground, whether it be in the champaign or in the mountainous country, which also takes place every seventh year. Moreover, there are those ordinances which are established respecting the fiftieth year. And of all these things the bare narration (without looking to any inner and figurative signification) is sufficient to lead those who are well disposed to perfect virtue, and to make even those who are obstinate and stubborn in their dispositions more docile and tractable. (40) Now we have already spoken at some length about the virtue of the number seven, explaining what a nature it has in reference to the number ten; and also what a connection it has to the decade itself, and also to the number four, which is the foundation and the source of the decade. And now, having been compounded in regular order from the unit, it in regular order produces the perfect number twenty-eight; being multiplied according to a regular proportion equal in all its parts, it makes at last both a cube and a square. I also showed how there is an infinite number of beauties which may be extracted from a careful contemplation of it, on which we have not at present time to dilate. But we must examine every one of the special matters which are before us as comprehended in this one, beginning with the first. The first matter to be considered is that of the Festivals.[1239]

XI

XI. (41) Now there are ten festivals in number, as the law sets them down.

The first is that which any one will perhaps be astonished to hear called a festival. This festival is every day.

The second festival is the seventh day, which the Hebrews in their native language call the sabbath.

The third is that which comes after the conjunction, which happens on the day of the new moon in each month.

The fourth is that of the passover which is called the passover.

The fifth is the first fruits of the corn--the sacred sheaf.

The sixth is the feast of unleavened bread, after which that festival is celebrated, which is really

The seventh day of seventh days.

The eighth is the festival of the sacred moon, or the feast of trumpets.

The ninth is the fast.

The tenth is the feast of tabernacles, which is the last of all the annual festivals, ending so as to make the perfect number of ten. We must now begin with the first festival.

THE FIRST FESTIVAL

XII

XII. (42) The law sets down every day as a festival, adapting itself to an irreproachable life, as if men continually obeyed nature and her injunctions. And if wickedness did not prosper, subduing by their predominant influence all those reasonings about what things might be expedient, which they have driven out of the soul of each individual, but if all the powers of the virtues remained in all respects unsubdued, then the whole time from a man's birth to his death would be one uninterrupted festival, and all houses and every city would pass their time in continual fearlessness and peace, being full of every imaginable blessing, enjoying perfect tranquillity. (43) But, as it is at present, covetousness and the system of mutual hostility and retaliation with which both men and women are continually forming designs against one another, and even against themselves, have destroyed the continuity of cheerfulness and happiness. And the proof of what I have just asserted is visible to all men; (44) for all those men, whether among the Greeks or among the barbarians, who are practisers of wisdom, living in a blameless and irreproachable manner, determining not to do any injustice, nor even to retaliate it when done to them, shunning all association with busy-bodies, in all the cities which they inhabit, avoid all courts of justice, and council halls, and market-places, and places of assembly, and, in short, every spot where any band or company of precipitate headstrong men is collected, (45) admiring, as it were, a life of peace and tranquillity, being the most devoted contemplators of nature and of all the things in it. Investigating earth and sea, and the air, and the heaven, and all the different natures in each of them; dwelling, if one may so say, in their minds, at least, with the moon, and the sun, and the whole company of the rest of the stars, both planets and fixed stars. Having their bodies, indeed, firmly planted on the earth, but having their souls furnished with wings, in order that thus hovering in the air they may closely survey all the powers above, looking upon them as in reality the most excellent of cosmopolites, who consider the whole world as their native city, and all the devotees of wisdom as their fellow citizens, virtue herself having enrolled them as such, to whom it has been entrusted to frame a constitution for their common city.

XIII

XIII. (46) Being, therefore, full of all kinds of excellence, and being accustomed to disregard all those good things which affect the body and external circumstances, and being inured to look upon things indifferent as really indifferent, and being armed by study against the pleasures and appetites, and, in short, being always labouring to raise themselves above the passions, and being instructed to exert all their power to pull down the fortification which those appetites have built up, and being insensible to any impression which the attacks of fortune might make upon them, because they have previously estimated the power of its attacks in their anticipations (for anticipation makes even those things light which would be most terrible if unexpected), their minds in this manner calculating that nothing that happens is wholly strange, but having a kind of faint perception of everything as old and in some degree blunted. These men, being very naturally rendered cheerful by their virtues, pass the whole of their lives as a festival. (47) These men, however, are therefore but a small number, kindling in their different cities a sort of spark of wisdom, in order that virtue may not become utterly extinguished, and so be entirely extirpated from our race. (48) But if men everywhere agreed with this small number, and became, as nature originally designed that they should, all blameless and irreproachable, lovers of wisdom, delighting in all that is virtuous and honourable, and thinking that and that alone good, and looking on everything else as subordinate and slaves, as if they themselves were the masters of them, then all the cities would be full of happiness, being wholly free from all the things which are the causes of pain or fear, and full of all those which produce joy and cheerfulness. So that no time would ever cease to be the time of a happy life, but that the whole circle of the year would be one festival.

XIV

XIV. (49) Wherefore, if truth were to be the judge, no wicked or worthless man can pass a time of festival, no not even for the briefest period, inasmuch as he must be continually pained by the consciousness of his own iniquities, even though, with his soul, and his voice, and his countenance, he may pretend to smile; for how can a man who is full of the most evil counsels, and who lives with folly, have any period of genuine joy? A man who is in every respect unfortunate and miserable, in his tongue, and his belly, and all his other members, (50) since he uses the first for the utterance of things which ought to be secret and buried in silence, and the second he fills full of abundance of strong wine and immoderate quantities of food out of gluttony, and the rest of his members he uses for the indulgence of unlawful desires and illicit connections, not only seeking to violate the marriage bed of others, but lusting unnaturally, and seeking to deface the manly character of the nature of man, and to change it into a womanlike appearance, for the sake of the gratification of his own polluted and accursed passions. (51) On which account the all-great Moses, seeing the pre-eminence of the beauty of that which is the real festival, looked upon it as too perfect for human nature and dedicated it to God himself, speaking thus, in these very words: "The feast of the Lord." [1240] (52) In considering the melancholy and fearful condition of the human race, and how full it is of innumerable evils, which the covetousness of the soul begets, which the defects of the body produce, and which all the inequalities of the soul inflict upon us, and which the retaliations of those among whom we live, both doing and suffering innumerable evils, are continually causing us, he then wondered whether any one being tossed about in such a sea of troubles, some brought on deliberately and others unintentionally, and never being able to rest in peace nor to cast anchor in the safe haven of a life free from danger, could by any possibility really keep a feast, not one in name, but one which should really be so, enjoying himself and being happy in the contemplation of the world and all the things in it, and in obedience to nature, and in a perfect harmony between his words and his actions, between his actions and his words. (53) On which account he necessarily said that the feasts belonged to God alone; for he alone is happy and blessed, having no participation in any evil whatever, but being full of all perfect blessings. Or rather, if one is to say the exact truth, being himself the good, who has showered all particular good things over the heaven and earth. (54) In reference to which fact, a certain pre-eminently virtuous mind among the people of old, [1241] when all its passions were tranquil, smiled, being full of and completely penetrated with joy, and reasoning with itself whether perhaps to rejoice was not a peculiar attribute of God, and whether it might not itself miss this joy by pursuing what are thought delights by men, was timorous, and denied the laughter of her soul until she was comforted. (55) For the merciful God lightened her fear, bidding her by his holy word confess that she did laugh, in order to teach us that the creature is not wholly and entirely deprived of joy; but that joy is unmingled and the purest of all which can receive nothing of an opposite nature, the chosen peculiar joy of God. But the joy which flows from that is a mingled one, being alloyed, being that of a man who is already wise, and who has received as the most valuable gift possible such a mixture as that in which the pleasant are far more numerous than the unpleasant ingredients. And this is enough to say on this subject.

THE SECOND FESTIVAL

XV

XV. (56) But after this continued and uninterrupted festival which thus lasts through all time, there is another celebrated, namely, that of the sacred seventh day after each recurring interval of six days, which some have denominated the virgin, looking at its exceeding sanctity and purity. And others have called the motherless, as being produced by the Father of the universe alone, as a specimen of the male kind unconnected with the sex of women; for the number seven is a most brave and valiant number, well adapted by nature for government and authority. Some, again, have called it the occasion, forming their conjectures of that part of its essence which is appreciable only by the intellect, from the objects intelligible to their outward senses. (57) For whatever is best among the objects of the external senses, the things by means of which the seasons of the year and the revolutions of time are brought to perfection in their appointed order, partake of the number seven. I mean that there are seven planets; that the stars of the Bear are seven, that the Pleiads are seven, and the revolutions of the moon when increasing and waning, and the orderly well-regulated circuits of the other bodies, the beauty of which exceeds all description. (58) But Moses, from a most honourable cause, called it consummation and perfection; attributing to the number six the origination of all the parts of the world, and to the number seven their perfection; for the number six is an oddeven number, being composed of twice three, having the odd number for the male and the even number for the female, from the union of which, production takes place in accordance with the unalterable laws of nature. (59) But the number seven is free from all such commixture, and is, if one must speak plainly, the light of the number six; for what the number six engendered, that the number seven displayed when brought to perfection. In reference to which fact it may properly be called the birthday of the world, as the day in which the work of the Father, being exhibited as perfect with all its parts perfect, was commanded to rest and abstain from all works. (60) Not that the law is the adviser of idleness, for it is always accustoming its followers to submit to hardships, and training them to labour, and it hates those who desire to be indolent and idle; at all events, it expressly commands us to labour diligently for six days, [1242] but in order to give some remission from uninterrupted and incessant toil, it refreshes the body with seasons of moderate relaxation exactly measured out, so as to renew it again for fresh works. For those who take breath in this way, I am speaking not merely about private individuals but even about athletes, collect fresh strength, and with more vigorous power, without any shrinking and with great endurance, encounter everything that must be done. (61) And the works meant are those enjoined by precepts and doctrines in accordance with virtue. And in the day he exhorts us to apply ourselves to philosophy, improving our souls and the dominant part of us, our mind. (62) Accordingly, on the seventh day there are spread before the people in every city innumerable lessons of prudence, and temperance, and courage, and justice, and all other virtues; during the giving of which the common people sit down, keeping silence and pricking up their ears, with all possible attention, from their thirst for wholesome instruction; but some of those who are very learned explain to them what is of great importance and use, lessons by which the whole of their lives may be improved. (63) And there are, as we may say, two most especially important heads of all the innumerable particular lessons and doctrines; the regulating of one's conduct towards God by the rules of piety and holiness, and of one's conduct towards men by the rules of humanity and justice; each of which is subdivided into a great number of subordinate ideas, all praiseworthy. (64) From which considerations it is plain that Moses does not leave those persons at any time idle who submit to be guided by his sacred admonitions; but since we are composed of both soul and body, he has allotted to the body such work as is suited to it, and to the soul also such tasks as are good for that. And he has taken care that the one shall succeed the other, so that while the body is labouring the soul may be at rest, and when the body is enjoying relaxation the soul may be labouring; and so the best lives with the contemplative and the active life, succeed to one another in regular alternations. The active life having received the number six, according to the service appointed for the body; and the contemplative life the number seven, as tending to knowledge and to the perfecting of the intellect.

XVI

XVI. (65) It is forbidden also on this day to kindle a fire, as being the beginning and seed of all the business of life; since without fire it is not possible to make any of the things which are indispensably necessary for life, so that men in the absence of one single element, the highest and most ancient of all, are cut off from all works and employments of arts, especially from all handicraft trades, and also from all particular services. (66) But it seems likely that it was on account of those who were less obedient, and who were the least inclined to attend to what was done, that Moses gave additional laws, besides, thinking it right, not only that those who were free should abstain from all works on the seventh day, but also that their servants and handmaids should have a respite from their tasks, proclaiming a day of freedom to them also after every space of six days, in order to teach both classes this most admirable lesson; (67) so that the masters should be accustomed to do some things with their own hands, not waiting for the services and ministrations of their servants, in order that if any unforeseen necessities came upon them, according to the changes which take place in human affairs, they might not, from being wholly unaccustomed to do anything for themselves, faint at what they had to do; but, finding the different parts of the body active and handy, might work with ease and cheerfulness; and teaching the servants not to despair of better prospects, but having a relaxation every six days as a kind of spark and kindling of freedom, to look forward to a complete relaxation hereafter, if they continued faithful and attached to their masters. (68) And from the occurrence of the free men at times submitting to the tasks of servants, and of the servants enjoying a respite and holiday, it will arise that the life of mankind advances in improvement towards perfect virtue, from their being thus reminded of the principles of equality, and repaying each other with necessary services, both those of high and those of obscure rank. (69) But the law has given a relaxation, not to servants only on the seventh day, but also to the cattle. And yet by nature the servants are born free; for no man is by nature a slave. But other animals are expressly made for the use and service of man, and are therefore ranked as slaves; but, nevertheless, those that ought to bear burdens, and to endure toil and labour on behalf of their owners, do all find a respite on the seventh day. (70) And why need I mention other particulars? The ox, the animal who is born for the most important and most useful of all the purposes of life, namely, for the plough, when the earth is already prepared for seed; and again, when the sheaves are brought into the barn, for threshing in order to the purification of the crop, is on this day unharnessed, keeping as a festival that day which is the birthday of the year. And thus its holiness pervades every thing and affects every creature.

XVII

XVII. (71) And Moses thinks the number seven worthy of such reverence that even all other things which at all partake of it are honoured by him; at all events, on every seventh year he ordains a remission of debts, assisting the poor, and inviting the rich to humanity;[1243] that so they, from their abundance, giving to those that are in want, may also look forward to receiving services from them in the case of any disaster happening to them. For the accidents of human life are numerous, and life is not always anchored on the same bottom, but is apt to change like the fickle wind which blows in different directions at different times. (72) It is well, therefore, that the kindness shown by the creditors should extend to all the debtors. But since all men are not naturally inclined to magnanimity, but some men are the slaves of money, or perhaps not very rich, the law has appointed that they should contribute what will not inconvenience them when parted with. (73) For while it does not permit them to lend on usury to their fellow countrymen, it has allowed them to receive interest from foreigners; calling the former, with great felicity of expression, their brothers, in order to prevent any one's grudging to give of his possessions to those who are as if by nature joint inheritors with themselves; but those who are not their fellow countrymen are called strangers, as is very natural. For the being a stranger shows that a person has no right to a participation in any thing, unless, indeed, any one out of an excess of virtue should treat even those in the conditions of strangers as kindred and related, from having been bred up under a virtuous state of things, and under virtuous laws which look upon what is virtuous alone as good. (74)

Philo Judaeus

But the action of lending on usury is blameable; for a man who lends on usury has not abundant means of living, but is clearly in some want; and he does so as being compelled to add the interest to his principal in order to subsist, and so he at last becomes of necessity very poor; and while he thinks that he is deriving advantage he is in reality injured, just as foolish animals are when they are deceived by a present bait. (75) But I should say to such persons, "O you who lend on usury, why do you seek to disguise your unsociable disposition by an apparent pretence of good fellowship? And why do you in words, indeed, pretend to be a humane and considerate person, while in your actions you exhibit a want of humanity and a terrible hardness of heart, exacting more than you gave, and sometimes even doubling your original loan, so as to make the poor man an absolute beggar? (76) Therefore no one sympathises with you in your distress, when, having endeavoured to obtain more, you fail to do so, and besides lose even what you had before. But, on the contrary, all men are glad of your misfortunes, calling you a usurer, and a skinflint, and all kinds of names like those, looking on you as one who lies in wait for human misfortunes, and who esteems the misfortunes of others his own prosperity." (77) But, as some have said, wickedness is a most laborious thing; and he who lends on usury is blind, not seeing the time of repayment, in which he will scarcely, or perhaps not at all, receive the things which in his covetousness he had hoped to gain. (78) Let such a man pay the penalty of his avaricious disposition, not recovering back what he has expended, so as to make a gain of the misfortunes of men, deriving a revenue from unbecoming sources. But let the debtors be thought worthy of a humanity enjoined by the law, not paying back their loans and usurious interest upon them, but paying back merely the original sum lent. For again, at a proper season, they will give the same assistance to those who have aided them, requiting those who set the example of kindness with equal services.

XVIII

XVIII. (79) After having given these commandments, Moses proceeds in regular order to establish a law full of all gentleness and humanity. "If," says this law, "one of thy brethren be sold to thee, let him serve thee for six years; and in the seventh year let him be set free without any Payment," [1244] (80) Here again Moses calls their fellow countrymen their brothers, implanting in the soul of the owner by this appellation an idea of relationship to his servant, that he may not neglect him as a stranger, towards whom he has no bond of goodwill. But that, yielding to a feeling of affection for him as a relation, in consequence of the lesson which the holy scripture thus suggests, he may not feel indignant when his servant is about to recover his freedom. (81) For it has come to pass that such men are called slaves (douloi), but they are in reality only servants (theÂtes), serving their masters for the sake of their necessities. And even though they had a thousand times over given their masters absolute power and authority over them, (82) still their masters ought to be gentle to them, considering these beautiful injunctions of the law. O man, he is a hireling who is called a slave, and he also is a man, having a most sublime relationship to you, inasmuch as he is of the same nation as yourself; and perhaps he is even of the same tribe and the same borough as yourself, and is now reduced to this condition through want. (83) Do you, therefore, casting out of your soul that treacherous evil, insolence, behave to him as if he were a hireling, giving some things and receiving others. And so he will, with all energy and cheerfulness perform the services due to you, at all times and in all places, never delaying, but by his speed and willingness anticipating your commands. And do you, in return, provide him with food and raiment, and take all other necessary care of him; not yoking him to the plough like a brute beast, and not oppressing him with heavy burdens beyond his power to bear, nor treating him with insolence, nor reducing him to painful despondency by threats and infliction of punishment; but giving him proper relaxation and well-regulated periods of rest; for the precept, "Let nothing be too much," applies to every case, and especially to the conduct of masters to their servants. (84) Therefore, when he has served you for a very sufficient time, for six years, then, when the most sacred number, the seventh year is about to arrive, let him who is free by nature depart in freedom; and grant him this kindness without hesitating as to your part, my good man, but joyfully, because you have now an opportunity of doing a service to that most excellent of all animals, man, in the most important of all matters; for there is no blessing to a slave greater than freedom. (85) Do you, therefore, set him free joyfully; and, moreover, make him a present from your own property, from each portion of your possessions, giving to him who has served you faithfully means to support himself on his journey. For it will tend to your credit if he does not leave your house in poverty but having a plentiful supply for all his necessities, so that he may not again, through want, fall into his previous calamity, namely, slavery, being compelled through want of his daily food to sell himself, and so your kindness will be lost. This, then, is enough to say about the poor.

XIX

XIX. (86) In the next place Moses commands the people to leave the land fallow and untilled every seventh year, for many reasons; [1245] first of all, that they may honour the number seven, or each period of days, and months, and years; for every seventh day is sacred, which is called by the Hebrews the sabbath; and the seventh month in every year has the greatest of the festivals allotted to it, so that very naturally the seventh year also has a share of the veneration paid to this number, and receives especial honour. (87) And the second reason is this, "Be not," says the lawgiver, "wholly devoted to gain, but even willingly submit to some loss," that so you may bear with the more indifference involuntary calamity if it should ever fall upon you, and not grieve and despond, as if at some new and strange occurrence; for there are some rich men so unfortunate in their dispositions, as, when want comes upon them, to groan and despond no less than they might do if they were deprived of all their substance. (88) But of the followers of Moses, all who are true disciples, being practised in good laws, are accustomed, from their earliest age, to bear want with patience, by the custom of leaving their fertile land fallow; and being also taught magnanimity, and one may almost say, to let slip out of their hands, from deliberate intention, revenues of admitted certainty. (89) The third reason appears to me to be thus, which is intimated in a somewhat figurative manner, namely, to show that it does not become any one whatever to weigh down and oppress men with burdens; for if one is to allow a period of rest to the portions of the earth which cannot by nature have any share in the feelings of pleasure or of pain, how much the more must men be entitled to a similar relaxation, who have not only these outward senses, which are common to the brute beasts, but also the especial gift of reason, by which the painful feelings which arise from toil and fatigue, are more vividly imprinted on their imaginations? (90) Cease, therefore, ye who are called masters, from imposing harsh and intolerable commands on your slaves, which break the strength of the body by their compulsion, and compel the soul to faint even before the bodies; (91) for there is no objection to your exerting a moderate degree of authority, giving orders by which you will receive the services to which you are entitled, and in consequence of which your servants will cheerfully do what they are desired; and then they will discharge their duties but for a short period, as if early exhausted, and, if one must say the truth, brought by their labours to old age before their time; but like athletes, preserving their youthful vigour for a long time, who do not become fat and corpulent, but who are accustomed, by exertion and sweat, to train themselves, so as to be able to acquire the things which are necessary and useful for life. (92) Moreover let the governors of cities cease to oppress them with continual and excessive taxes and tributes, filling their own stores with money, and in preserving as a treasure the illiberal vices which defile their whole lives; (93) for they do, on purpose, select as collectors of their revenues the most pitiless of men, persons full of all kinds of inhumanity, giving them abundant opportunity for the exercise of their covetousness; and they, in addition to their own innate severity of temper, receiving free license from the commands of their masters, and having determined to do everything so as to please them, practise all the harshest measures which they can imagine, having no notion of gentleness or humanity, not even in their dreams; (94) therefore they throw everything into disorder and confusion, levying their exactions, not only on the possessions of the citizens, but also on their persons, with insults and violence, and the invention of new and unprecedented torture. And before now I have heard of some persons who, in their ferocity and unequalled fury, have not spared even the dead; but have been so brutal as even to venture to beat the dead corpses with goads; (95) and when some one blamed their brutality, in that not even death, that relief and real end of all miseries, could prevent their victims from being insulted by them, but that, instead of a grave and the customary funeral rites, they were exposed to continued insult, they made a defence worse even than the accusation brought against them, saying that they were insulting the dead, not for the sake of abusing the dumb and senseless dust, for there was no advantage in that, but for the sake of making those who through ties of blood or of friendship were nearly connected with them feel compassion for them, and so inducing them to pay a ransom for their bodies, thus doing them the last service in their power.

XX

XX. (96) Then, O you most worthless of all men! I would say to them, have you not first learnt what you are now teaching? or do you know how to invite other people to compassion even by the most inhuman actions, and yet have you eradicated all merciful and humane feelings from your own souls? And do you act in this way in spite of not being in want of good advisers, and especially of our laws, which have released even the earth from its yearly burdens, giving it a relaxation and a respite? (97) and it, although it seems to be inanimate, is nevertheless fully prepared to make a requital and to recompence favours, hastening to pay back any gift which it has received; for as it receives an exemption every seventh year, and is not forced to exert itself that year, but is set wholly free for the whole circle of the year, in the subsequent year produces double, or sometimes, many times, larger crops than usual from its great productiveness. (98) And in like manner you may see the trainers acting in the same way towards the athletes; for when they are exercising them with continual and uninterrupted practice, before they are wholly knocked up, they refresh them, giving a respite not only from their exertions in training, but also from their strict regimen of eating and drinking, relaxing the severity of their diet so as to produce a cheerfulness of soul and good condition of body. (99) And yet they are not to be looked upon as teachers of indolence and luxury, inasmuch as their professed business is to train men to the endurance of labours, but by a certain method and artificial system they add to their natural strength a strength more powerful still, and to their innate vigour a more energetic vigour still, increasing their previous powers by reciprocal remission and exertion, as by a well-regulated harmony. (100) And I have learnt all this from all-wise nature, which, knowing the industrious and laborious condition of our race, has distributed them into day and night, giving to us the one for wakefulness, and the other for sleep; (101) for she felt a natural anxiety, like a careful mother, that her offspring should not be worn out with toil; for by day she excites our bodies, and rouses them up to all the necessities and duties belonging to life, compelling those to work who would gladly be accustomed to cultivate the leisure of idleness, and an effeminate and luxurious life. But by night, as if she were sounding a retreat in time of war, she invites us to rest, and to take care of our bodies. (102) And those men who have laid aside a heavy weight of business, which has lasted from morning till evening, do now lay their burdens aside and return home and devote themselves to ease, and indulging in profound sleep, refresh themselves after the labours of the day. (103) This long interval between sleeping and waking nature has allotted to men, that they may by turns labour diligently and by turns rest, so as to have all the parts of their bodies more ready for action, and more active and powerful.

XXI

XXI. (104) And the lawgiver, who is a prophetic spirit, gave us our laws, having a regard to these things, and proclaimed a holiday to the whole country, restraining the farmers from cultivating the land after each six years' incessant industry. But it was not only on account of the motives which I have mentioned that he gave these injunctions, but also because of his innate humanity, which he thinks fit to weave in with every part of his legislation, stamping on all who study the holy scriptures a sociable and humane disposition. (105) For he commands his people every seventh year to forbear to enclose any piece of land, but to let all the olive gardens and vineyards remain open, and all their other possessions, whether they be seed-land or trees, that so the poor may be able to enjoy the spontaneously growing crops without fear, in a greater, or at all events not in a less degree than the owners themselves. (106) On which account he does not allow the masters to cultivate the land, having in view the object of not causing them any annoyance from the feeling that they are at all the expense, but that they do not receive any revenue from their lands to make up for the expense, while the poor enjoy all the crops as their own; and he permits those who appear to be strangers to enjoy all these things, raising them from their apparent lowly condition, and from the reproach of being beggars. (107) Is it not then fit to love these laws which are full of such abundant humanity? by which the rich men are taught to share the blessings which they have with and to communicate them to others: and the poor are comforted, not being for ever compelled to frequent the houses of the indigent to supply the deficiencies by which they themselves are oppressed; (108) but there are times when the widows and orphan children, as if they had been deriving a revenue from their own properties, namely the spontaneously growing crops, as I have said before, and all other classes of person who are disregarded from not being wealthy do at last find themselves in the possession of plenty, being on a sudden enriched by the gift of God, who has called them to share with the possessors themselves in the number of the sacred seven. (109) And all those who breed flocks and herds lend their own cattle with fearlessness and impunity to graze on the land of others, choosing the most fertile plains, and the lands most suitable for the feeding of their cattle, availing themselves of the license of the jubilee; and they are not met by any ill-will or illiberality on the part of the masters, as having the property in these lands by old custom, which having prevailed for a very long time, so as to become familiar, has now prevailed even over nature.

XXII

XXII. (110) Having laid down these principles as a kind of foundation of gentleness and humanity, he then puts together seven sevens of years, and so makes the fiftieth year an entirely sacred year, enacting with reference to it some ordinances of especial honour beyond those which relate to the ordinary years of communication of property. (111) In the first place he gives this commandment. He thinks it fitting that all property that has been alienated should now be restored to its original masters in order that the inheritances originally apportioned to the different tribes may be preserved, and that no one who originally received an allotment may be wholly deprived of his possessions. (112) Since it often happens that unforeseen circumstances come upon men by which they are compelled to sell what belongs to them. And so he provided in a suitable manner for their necessities, and prevented those who purchased the lands from being deceived, allowing the one to sell their lands, and teaching the others very plainly the conditions on which they are going to purchase. (113) For the law says Do not give a price as if for an everlasting possession, but only for a definite number of years, which must be less than fifty; for the sale effected ought not to be a sale of the lands owned, but a sale of the crops, for two most weighty reasons; one, that the whole country is called the possession of God, and it is impious for any one else to be recorded as the masters of the possessions of God; and secondly, because a separate allotment has been assigned to each land-owner, of which the law does not choose the man who originally received the allotment to be deprived. (114) Therefore, the law invites the man who is able to recover his original property within the period of fifty years, or any one of his nearest relations, to use every exertion to repay the price which he received, and not to be the cause of loss to the man who purchased it, and who served him at a time when he was in need of assistance. (115) And at the same time it sympathises with the man who is in too great a state of indigence to do so, and bestows its compassion on him, giving him back his former property with the exception of any fields which have been consecrated by a vow, and are so placed in the class of offerings to God. And it is contrary to divine law that any thing which has been offered to God should ever by lapse of time become profane. On which account it is commanded that the accurate value of those fields shall be fully exacted, without showing any favour to the man who dedicated the offering.

XXIII

XXIII. (116) These are the commandments which are given with respect to the divisions of the land and the inheritances so portioned out. There are others also enacted with respect to houses. And since of houses some are in cities, being within walls; while others are open abodes in the country, and not within any walls; the law has directed that those in the country shall always be redeemed with money, and that those which are not redeemed before the fiftieth year shall be restored without any payment to their original owners, just as their other possessions;[1246] for the houses are a portion of the man's possessions. (117) But those which are within walls shall be liable to be redeemed by those who have sold them for a full year;[1247] but if they be not redeemed within that year, then after that year they shall be confirmed to those who had bought them, the jubilee of the fiftieth year not injuring the claim of the purchasers. (118) And the reason of these enactments is that God wills to give even to strangers an opportunity of becoming firmly established in the land. For since they have no participation in the land, inasmuch as they are not numbered among those to whom the inheritances have been apportioned, the law has allotted to them a property in houses, being desirous that they who have come as suppliants to the laws, and who have taken refuge under their protection, should not be homeless wanderers in the land. (119) For the cities, when the land was originally portioned out in inheritances, were not divided among the tribes, nor indeed were they originally built together in streets, but the inhabitants of the land preferred to make their abode in their open houses in the fields. But afterwards they quitted these houses and came together, the feeling of a love of fellowship and communication, as was natural, becoming stronger after a lapse of time, and so they built houses in the same place, and cities, of which they allowed a share also to the strangers, that they might not be destitute of every thing both in the country and in the cities.

XXIV

XXIV. (120) And concerning the tribe which was set apart as consecrated for the priesthood, the following laws are established. The law did not bestow upon the keepers of the temple any portion of the land, considering the first fruits of it a sufficient revenue for them. But it allotted them eight and forty cities to dwell in, and a suburb of two thousand cubits around each City.[1248] (121) Therefore, it did not confirm the houses in these cities in the same manner that it did those in the other cities which are built within walls, to the purchasers, if those who had sold them were not able to redeem them within the year, but it permitted them to be redeemed at any time, like the open houses in the country taken from the gentiles, to which they corresponded. Since the Levites had received only houses in this district, of which the lawgiver did not think it fit that those who received them should be deprived any more than those to whom the allotments of the open houses in the country had fallen. And this is enough to say about the houses.

XXV

XXV. (122) But the laws established with respect to those who owed money to usurers, and to those who had become servants to masters, resemble those already mentioned; that the usurers shall not exact usurers' interest from their fellow countrymen, but shall be contented to receive back only what they lent; and that the masters shall behave to those whom they have bought with their money not as if they were by nature slaves, but only hirelings, giving them immunity and liberty, at once, indeed, to those who can pay down a ransom for themselves, and at a subsequent period to the indigent, either when the seventh year from the beginning of their slavery arrives, or when the fiftieth year comes, even if a man happen to have fallen into slavery only the day before. For this year both is and is looked upon as a year of remission; every one retracing his steps and turning back again to his previous state of prosperity. (123) But the law permits the people to acquire a property in slaves who are not of their own countrymen, but who are of different nations; intending in the first place that there should be a difference between one's own countrymen and strangers, and secondly, not desiring completely to exclude from the constitution that most entirely indispensable property of slaves; for there are an innumerable host of circumstances in life which require the ministrations of Servants.[1249] (124) Sons shall inherit their parents' property, but if there should be no sons, then the daughters would inherit. For just as in their nature men take precedence over women, so also in families they shall have the first share, inheriting property and filling the station of those who have died, being held by a law of necessity that lets no earthborn mortal live forever. (125) But if virgins are left behind with unmarried, no dowry having been set apart by the parents while they were still living, they shall receive a share equal to that of the males. But the presiding power must take care to watch over those who are left behind and of their growth and of the expenses for sustenance and the training that is appropriate for girls, and, whenever the time should come, for appropriate marriage, husbands approved in all things having been selected by merit. (126) Preferably they should be relatives, but if not, they should at least be of the same deme and tribe, so that the lots assigned as dowries will not be alienated through marriages but remain in the tribal allotments as ordered from the beginning. (127) But if someone should have no offspring, then let the brothers of the deceased succeed to the inheritance. For the place in the family after sons and daughters belongs to brothers. And if someone who has no brothers should die, the uncles on the father's side should succeed to the property, and if there are no uncles, then the aunts, the closest of the remaining household members and other relatives. (128) But if scarcity should seize the family, so that no blood relations are left, then let the tribe be the heir. For the tribe is also a kind of family, if we draw a larger and more complete circle. (129) The perplexity raised by some, however, should be laid to rest: Seeing that the law mentions all members of the family, the deme, and the tribe in the order of succession to inheritances, why did it remain silent only about parents, who, it would seem, should be just as eligible to inherit their children's property as the children are to inherit theirs? Here is the answer, my good fellow! Since the law is divine, and since it always aims at following the logic of nature, it did not wish to introduce any ill-omened provisions; for parents pray to leave behind living offspring who will have succeeded to their name, their lineage, and their property, while their worst enemies call down the opposite on them as a curse, namely, that the sons and daughters should die before their parents. (130) Therefore in order to avoid making explicit provisions for a situation that would be illfitting and discordant with the harmony and concord that characterize the administration of the whole cosmos-- namely, the case where children die and parents survive--the law both necessarily and fittingly omitted ordering that mothers and fathers should inherit the property of sons and daughters, knowing that this outcome was out of accord with life and nature. (131) So then, the law was careful not to say in so many words that parents inherit when their children die, in order not to seem to reproach grieving parents by allotting to them a benefit that no one would want, and in order not to call misfortunes to mind; but it allotted the property to them in another way, as a small consolation for a great evil. (132) How, then, does it do this? It puts down the father's brother as the heir of his nephews, no doubt rewarding the uncle for the father's sake--unless anyone is so silly as to suppose that one who honors someone for the sake of someone else thereby chooses to dishonor the latter. Those who pay attention to their friends' acquaintances do not thereby neglect their friends, do they? Do not those who show the most solicitous care for those whom they honor also welcome their friends? In precisely the same way, when when the law names the father's brother to share in the inheritance on account of the father, how much more does it name the father! It does not do this explicitly, for the reasons cited, but it makes clear the will of the lawgiver with surer force than an explicit mention. (133) The eldest son does not share equally with those who came after him but is considered worthy of a double portion, since two people who were previously husband and wife became father and mother on account of the first offspring, and once he came along he was the first to call those who engendered him by these names. Furthermore--and this is the most essential point--the household that was previously childless became one blessed with a son for the continuance of the human race. The seed of this continuance is marriage, and its fruit is the begetting of children, of whom the eldest is the head. (134) I suppose that it is for this reason that the firstborn sons of the enemies who had given no quarter, as the holy scriptures reveal, were all cut off in their youth in one night, while the firstborn of the people of the nation were dedicated to God as a thank-offering and were thus consecrated. For it was necessary to weigh down the former with a heavy and inconsolable grief, the destruction of those who held first place, but to reward the savior God with the firstfruits, whose lot was the preeminence among the children. (135) But there are some men who after getting married and having children have at length unlearned prudence and drifted into incontinence. Lusting after other women, these men have wronged their first wives and behaved toward their children from them no longer as fathers but as uncles, imitating the impious behavior of stepmothers toward previously born children. They have given themselves and their property over entirely to their new wives and to their sons, having been overcome by pleasure, the most shameful passion. The law would not have hesitated to bridle these lusts somehow if it had been possible, lest they kick up their heels even more; (136) but since it was difficult, or rather impossible, to cure this wild frenzy, the law abandoned the man as being in the grip of an incurable disease. It did not, however, overlook the son of the woman wronged on account of the new love but commanded that he should receive a double share of the distribution left for the brothers. (137) There are many reasons for this. For in the first place it punishes the guilty man by compelling him to do something good for the son whom he has chosen to treat badly; and it makes clear the invalidity of his inconsiderate judgment in that it profits the one who was in danger of suffering loss at his hands by putting itself in the role of the parent--the role abandoned by the natural father with regard to the firstborn son. (138) Secondly, it shows mercy and compassion on those who have been treated unjustly, whose burden of distress it lightens by giving them a share in grace and gift; for the double portion of the inheriting son was no less likely to please the mother, who will be encouraged by the kindness of the law, which did not permit her and her offspring to be totally overcome by their enemies. (139) In the third place, being a good referee of justice, it considered in itself that the father had freely lavished provisions upon the sons of the beloved wife due to his affection for her, while he considered the sons of the hated wife to deserve nothing due to his hatred for their mother. Thus the former had inherited more than their equal share during his lifetime, while the latter were in danger even upon his death of being deprived of the whole patrimony. So then, in order to equalize the distribution to the sons of both wives, it set aside a double portion as the rightful inheritance of the eldest, the son of the wife who had been put away. This is enough regarding these things.

THE THIRD FESTIVAL

XXVI

XXVI. (140) Following the order which we have adopted, we proceed to speak of the third festival, that of the new moon. First of all, because it is the beginning of the month, and the beginning, whether of number or of time, is honourable. Secondly, because at this time there is nothing in the whole of heaven destitute of light. (141) Thirdly, because at that period the more powerful and important body gives a portion of necessary assistance to the less important and weaker body; for, at the time of the new moon, the sun begins to illuminate the moon with a light which is visible to the outward senses, and then she displays her own beauty to the beholders. And this is, as it seems, an evident lesson of kindness and humanity to men, to teach them that they should never grudge to impart their own good things to others, but, imitating the heavenly bodies, should drive envy away and banish it from the Soul. [1250] (142) The fourth reason is that of all the bodies in the heaven, the moon traverses the zodiac in the least appointed time: it accomplishes its orbit in a monthly interval. For this reason the law has honored the end of its orbit, the point when the moon has finished at the beginning point from which it began to travel, by having called that day a feast so that it might again teach us an excellent lesson that in the affairs of life we should make the ends harmonious with the beginnings. This will happen if we hold the reins on our first impulses with the power of reason and do not permit them to refuse the reins and to run free like animals without anyone in charge of the herd. (143) With regard to the benefits which the moon provides to all on earth, why is it necessary to run through and detail them? Their proofs are obvious. Or isn't it by its waxings that rivers and springs overflow, and again by its wanings that they diminish; that seas sometimes retreat and are drawn down through their ebb and flow, and at other times suddenly run full through the tide; that the air experiences all sorts of shifts in the form of clear weather, cloudy weather, and other changes? Don't the fruits of cultivated crops and trees grow and come to maturity through the orbits of the moon which nurses and ripens each of the growing crops through dewladen and very gentle breezes? (144) But this is not the appropriate occasion, as I said, to speak at length about the praise of the moon by running through and enumerating the benefits which it provides to animals and to all on the earth. For these reasons and others similar to them, the new moon has been honored and taken its place among the feasts.

THE FOURTH FESTIVAL

XXVII

XXVII. (145) And after the feast of the new moon comes the fourth festival, that of the passover, which the Hebrews call pascha, on which the whole people offer sacrifice, beginning at noonday and continuing till evening. (146) And this festival is instituted in remembrance of, and as giving thanks for, their great migration which they made from Egypt, with many myriads of people, in accordance with the commands of God given to them; leaving then, as it seems, a country full of all inhumanity and practising every kind of inhospitality, and (what was worst of all) giving the honour due to God to brute beasts; and, therefore, they sacrificed at that time themselves out of their exceeding joy, without waiting for priests. And what was then done the law enjoined to be repeated once every year, as a memorial of the gratitude due for their deliverance. These things are thus related in accordance with the ancient historic accounts. (147) But those who are in the habit of turning plain stories into allegory, argue that the passover figuratively represents the purification of the soul; for they say that the lover of wisdom is never practising anything else except a passing over from the body and the passions. (148) And each house is at that time invested with the character and dignity of a temple, the victim being sacrificed so as to make a suitable feast for the man who has provided it and of those who are collected to share in the feast, being all duly purified with holy ablutions. And those who are to share in the feast come together not as they do to other entertainments, to gratify their bellies with wine and meat, but to fulfil their hereditary custom with prayer and songs of praise. (149) And this universal sacrifice of the whole people is celebrated on the fourteenth day of the month, which consists of two periods of seven, in order that nothing which is accounted worthy of honour may be separated from the number seven. But this number is the beginning of brilliancy and dignity to everything.

THE FIFTH FESTIVAL

XXVIII

XXVIII. (150) And there is another festival combined with the feast of the passover, having a use of food different from the usual one, and not customary; the use, namely, of unleavened bread, from which it derives its name. And there are two accounts given of this festival, the one peculiar to the nation, on account of the migration already described; the other a common one, in accordance with conformity to nature and with the harmony of the whole world. And we must consider how accurate the hypothesis is. This month, being the seventh both in number and order, according to the revolutions of the sun, is the first in power; (151) on which account it is also called the first in the sacred scriptures. And the reason, as I imagine, is as follows. The vernal equinox is an imitation and representation of that beginning in accordance with which this world was created. Accordingly, every year, God reminds men of the creation of the world, and with this view puts forward the spring, in which season all plants flourish and bloom; (152) for which reason this is very correctly set down in the law as the first month, since, in a manner, it may be said to be an impression of the first beginning of all, being stamped by it as by an archetypal Seal. [1251] (153) Although the month in which the autumnal equinox occurs is first in sequence according to solar orbits, it is not considered first in the law. The reason is that at that time, after all the crops have been harvested, the trees lose their leaves and everything that springtime produced in the height of its glory is withering under dry winds after it has been made dry by the flaming heat of the sun. (154) Therefore he thought that to apply the name "first" to the month in which the hill country and the plain become barren and infertile, was incongruous and unfitting. For it is necessary that the most beautiful and desirable phenomena belong to those things which are first and have received the position of leadership, those phenomena through which the reproduction and growth of animals and fruit and crops take place, but not the ominous destructive forces. (155) And this feast is begun on the fifteenth day of the month, in the middle of the month, on the day on which the moon is full of light, in consequence of the providence of God taking care that there shall be no darkness on that day. (156) And, again, the feast is celebrated for seven days, on account of the honour due to that number, in order that nothing which tends to cheerfulness and to the giving of thanks to God may be separated from the holy number seven. (157) And of the seven days, Moses pronounces two, the first and the last, holy; giving, as is natural, a preeminence to the beginning and to the end; and wishing, as if in the case of a musical instrument, to unite the two extremities in harmony. (158) And the unleavened bread is ordained because their ancestors took unleavened bread with them when they went forth out of Egypt, under the guidance of the Deity; or else, because at that time (I mean at the spring season, during hich this festival is celebrated) the crop of wheat is not yet ripe, the plains being still loaded with the corn, and it not being as yet the harvest time, and therefore lawgiver has ordained the use of unleavened food with a view to assimilating it to the state of the crops. For unleavened food is also imperfect or unripe, as a memorial of the good hope which is entertained; since nature is by this time preparing her annual gifts for the race of mankind, with an abundance and plenteous pouring forth of necessaries. (159) The interpreters of the holy scriptures do also say that the unleavened food is a gift of nature, but that barmed bread is a work of art. (160) Since, therefore, the vernal festival is a commemoration of the creation of the world, and since that it was inevitable that the most ancient persons, those formed out of the earth, must have used the gifts of the world without alteration, pleasure not having as yet obtained the dominion, the lawgiver ordained that food which was the most suitable to the occasion, wishing to kindle every year a desire to walk in the paths of a holy and rigid way of Life. [1252] (161) The setting out of twelve loaves--the same number as the tribes--on the sacred table especially guarantees the things which have been said. For they are all unleavened, the clearest example of an unmixed food which has been prepared not by human skill for pleasure but by nature for the most essential use. These things are sufficient for this topic.

THE SIXTH FESTIVAL

XXIX

XXIX. (162) There is also a festival on the day of the paschal feast, which succeeds the first day, and this is named the sheaf, from what takes place on it; for the sheaf is brought to the altar as a first fruit both of the country which the nation has received for its own, and also of the whole land; so as to be an offering both for the nation separately, and also a common one for the whole race of mankind; and so that the people by it worship the living God, both for themselves and for all the rest of mankind, because they have received the fertile earth for their inheritance; for in the country there is no barren soil but even all those parts which appear to be stony and rugged are surrounded with soft veins of great depth, which, by reason of their richness, are very well suited for the production of living Things. [1253] (163) The reason is that a priest has the same relation to a city that the nation of the Jews has to the entire inhabited world. For it serves as a priest--to state the truth--through the use of all purificatory offerings and the guidance both for body and soul of divine laws which have checked the pleasures of the stomach and those under the stomach and [tamed] the mob [of the Senses] [1254] by having appointed reason as charioteer over the irrational senses; they also have driven back and overturned the undiscriminating and excessive urges of the soul, some by rather gentle instructions and philosophical exhortations, others by rather weighty and forcible rebukes and by fear of punishment, the fear which they brandish threateningly. (164) Apart from the fact that the legislation is in a certain way teaching about the priesthood and that the one who lives by the laws is at once considered a priest, or rather a high priest, in the judgment of truth, the following point is also remarkable. The multitude of gods, both male and female, honored in individual cities happens to be undetermined and indefinite. The poetic clan and the great company of humans have spoken fabulously about them, people for whom the search for truth is impractical and beyond their capability of investigation. Yet all do not reverence and honor the same gods, but different people different gods. The reason is that they do not consider as gods those belonging to another land but make the acceptance of them the occasion for laughter and a joke. They charge those who honor them with great foolishness since they completely violate sound sense. (165) But if he is, whom all Greeks together with all barbarians acknowledge with one judgment, the highest Father of both gods and humans and the Maker of the entire cosmos, whose nature--although it is invisible and unfathomable not only to sight but also to perception--all who spend their time with mathematics and other philosophy long to discover, leaving aside none of the things which contribute to the discovery and service of him, then it was necessary for all people to cling to him and not as if through some mechanical device to introduce other gods into participation of equal honors. (166) Since they slipped in the most essential matter, the nation of the Jews--to speak most accurately--set aright the false step of others by having looked beyond everything which has come into existence through creation since it is generate and corruptible in nature, and chose only the service of the ungenerate and eternal. The first reason for this is because it is excellent; the second is because it is profitable to be dedicated and associated with the Older rather than those who are younger and with the Ruler rather than those who are ruled and with the Maker rather those things which come into existence. (167) For this reason it amazes me that some dare to charge the nation with an anti-social stance, a nation which has made such an extensive use of fellowship and goodwill toward all people everywhere that they offer up prayers and feasts and first fruits on behalf of the common race of human beings and serve the really self-existent God both on behalf of themselves and of others who have run from the services which they should have rendered. (168) These are the things they do for the entire race of human beings. On the other hand they give thanks for themselves for many things. The first is that they are not perpetually wandering here and there among islands and continents and like foreigners and those without a permanent abode who have settled the lands of others and occupy others' wealth are reproached since they have acquired no portion of land from lack of means, but have acquired a land and cities and for a long time have been in possession of their own inheritance, for which reason it has been a sacred duty for them to offer the first fruits. (169) The second is that they did not receive a worthless and common land, but a good and fertile land both for the breeding of domestic animals and the abundance of unspeakably great crops. For there is no poor soil in it, and even the parts that seem to be stony and hardened are broken up with soft and especially deep veins which because of their richness are good for crop production. (170) In addition to these things, they did not receive a desolate land, but one in which there was a populous nation and great cities abounding in men. Yet the cities were emptied of their inhabitants and the entire race disappeared except for a small part: some as a result of wars and others as a result of divinely sent attacks because of their new and strange practices of wrongs and all of the impieties they used to commit through their great efforts to demolish the laws of nature. These things happened so that those who replaced them might be sobered by the calamities of others, and learn from their deeds that those who become devotees of evil deeds will suffer the same fate but those who have honored a life of virtue will possess their assigned portion, numbered not among emigrants but among the native residents. (171) That the first fruit is a handful for their own land and for all lands, offered in thanksgiving for prosperity and a good season which the nation and the entire race of human beings were hoping to enjoy, has been demonstrated. We should not be unaware that many benefits have come by means of the first fruit: first, memory of God--it is not possible to find a more perfect good than this; then, the most just recompense to the real Cause of the fruitfulness. (172) For the things which occur as a result of agricultural skill are few or none at all: to build up furrows, to dig and spade all around a plant, to deepen a trench, to cut off excessive growths, or to perform any similar task. But the things which come from nature are all essential and useful: the most fertile ground, a land well-watered by springs and both spring-fed and seasonal rivers and sprinkled with annual rains, mild temperatures of air moved by breezes which are most conducive for life, countless types of crops and plants. For which of these has a human either discovered or engendered? (173) Nature which has engendered these things has not begrudged a man its own goods, but considered him to be the governing part of mortal animals because he has a share in reason and good sense. She therefore chose him on the basis of his merit and summoned him to participate in her own goods. For these things it is right that the host, God, be praised and admired since he sees to it that the truely hospitable earth, all of it, is always full of not only the necessities but even of the things which make for a luxurious life. (174) In addition to these things, we should not fail to pay our regard to benefactors. For the person who is thankful to God who needs nothing and is selfsufficient, will also make it a habit to be thankful to humans who are in need of how many countless things. And there are many meanings intended by this offering of the first fruits. In the first place they are a memorial of God; secondly, they are a most just requital to be offered to him who is the real cause of all fertility; (175) and the sheaf of the first fruits is barley, calculated for the innocent and blameless use of the inferior animals; for since it is not consistent with holiness to offer first fruits of everything, since most things are made rather for pleasure than for any actually indispensable use, it is also not consistent with holiness to enjoy and partake of any thing which is given for food, without first giving thanks to that being to whom it is becoming and pious to offer them. That portion of the food which was honoured with the second place, namely, barley, was ordered by the law to be offered as first fruits; for the first honours were assigned to wheat, of which it has deferred the offering of the first fruits, as being more honourable, to a more suitable season.

THE SEVENTH FESTIVAL

XXX

XXX. (176) The solemn assembly on the occasion of the festival of the sheaf having such great privileges, is the prelude to another festival of still greater importance; for from this day the fiftieth day is reckoned, making up the sacred number of seven sevens, with the addition of a unit as a seal to the whole; and this festival, being that of the first fruits of the corn, has derived its name of pentecost from the number of fifty, (penteÂkostos). And on it it is the custom to offer up two leavened loaves made of wheat, as a first fruit of the best kind of food made of corn; either because, before the fruit of the year is converted to the use of man, the first produce of the new crop, the first gathered corn that appears is offered as a first fruit, in order that by an insignificant emblem the people may display their grateful disposition; [1255] (177) We must disclose another reason. Its nature is wondrous and highly prized for numerous reasons including the fact that it consists of the most elemental and oldest of the things which are encased in substances, as the mathematicians tell us, the rightangled triangle. For its sides, which exist in lengths of three and four and five, combine to make up the sum twelve, the pattern of the zodiac cycle, the doubling of the most fecund number six which is the beginning of perfection since it is the sum of the same numbers of which it is also the Product. [1256] To the second power, it seems, they produce fifty, through the addition of 3 x 3 and 4 x 4 and 5 x 5. The result is that it is necessary to say that to the same degree that fifty is better than twelve, the second power is better than the first power. (178) If the image of the lesser is the most beautiful sphere of those which are in heaven, the zodiac, then of what would the better, the number fifty, be a pattern than a completely better nature? This is not the occasion to speak about this. It is sufficient for the present that the difference has been noted so that a principal point is not considered to be subordinate. (179) the feast which takes place on the basis of the number fifty has received the name "the feast of the first produce" since during the feast it is customary to offer two leavened loaves made from wheat as the first fruit of grain, the best food. It is named "the feast of the first produce" Either [1257] because before the annual crop has proceeded to human use, the first produce of the new grain and the first fruit which has appeared are offered as first fruit. (180) For it is just and religiously correct that those who have received the greatest gift from God, the abundance of the most necessary as well as most beneficial and even the sweetest food, should not enjoy it or have any use of it at all before they offer the first fruits to the Supplier. They are giving him nothing since all things and possessions and gifts are his, but through a small symbol demonstrate a thankful and God-loving character to the one who needs no favors but showers continuous and ever-flowing favors. (181) Or else because the fruit of wheat is most especially the first and most excellent of all productions. (182) And the bread is leavened because the law forbids any one to offer unleavened bread upon the altar; not in order that there should be any contradiction in the injunctions given, but that in a manner the giving and receiving may be of one sort; the receiving being gratitude from those who offer it, and the giving an unhesitating bestowal of the customary blessings on those who offer. [...] [1258] Not indeed to that [...] [1259] (183) For those for whom it is lawful and permissible will use what has once been consecrated; and it is lawful for those who are consecrated to the priesthood, who have received the right given by the humaneness of the law to share in the things offered on the altar which are not consumed by the unquenchable fire, either as a wage for their services or as a prize for contests in which they compete on behalf of piety or as a sacred allotment in view of the fact that with regard to the land they have not acquired their appropriate part in the same way as the other tribes. (184) And it is permitted to the priests; and the leaven is also an emblem of two others things; first of all of that most perfect and entire food, than which one cannot, among all the things of daily use, find any which is better and more advantageous; and the fruit of wheat is the best of all the things that are sown; so that it is fitting, that that should be offered as the most excellent of first fruits, for the most excellent gift. (185) The second is a more figurative meaning, implying that every thing which is leavened is apt to inflate and elate; and joy is an irrational elation of the soul. Now man is not by nature disposed to rejoice at anything that exists more than at an abundant and sufficient supply of necessaries; for which it is very proper to give thanks joyfully, making a display of gratitude, for the invisible happiness affecting the mind, which shall be perceptible to the outward senses through the medium of the leavened loaves; (186) and these first fruits are loaves, not corn, because when there is corn there is no longer anything wanting for the enjoyment of food, for it is said that the wheat is the last of all the grains which are sown to ripen and to come to harvest. (187) And there are thus two most excellent acts of thanksgiving having a reference to two distinct times; to the past, in which we have been saved from experiencing the evils of scarcity and hunger while living in happiness and plenty; and to the future, because we have provided ourselves with supplies and abundant preparations for it.

THE EIGHTH FESTIVAL

XXXI

XXXI. (188) Immediately after comes the festival of the sacred moon; in which it is the custom to play the trumpet in the temple at the same moment that the sacrifices are offered. From which practice this is called the true feast of trumpets, and there are two reasons for it, one peculiar to the nation, and the other common to all mankind. Peculiar to the nation, as being a commemoration of that most marvellous, wonderful, and miraculous event that took place when the holy oracles of the law were given; (189) for then the voice of a trumpet sounded from heaven, which it is natural to suppose reached to the very extremities of the universe, so that so wondrous a sound attracted all who were present, making them consider, as it is probable, that such mighty events were signs betokening some great things to be accomplished. (190) And what more great or more beneficial thing could come to men than laws affecting the whole race? And what was common to all mankind was this: the trumpet is the instrument of war, sounding both when commanding the charge and the retreat. ... There is also another kind of war, ordained of God, when nature is at variance with itself, its different parts attacking one another. (191) And by both these kinds of war the things on earth are injured. They are injured by the enemies, by the cutting down of trees, and by conflagrations; and also by natural injuries, such as droughts, heavy rains, lightning from heaven, snow and cold; the usual harmony of the seasons of the year being transformed into a want of all concord. (192) On this account it is that the law has given this festival the name of a warlike instrument, in order to show the proper gratitude to God as the giver of peace, who has abolished all seditions in cities, and in all parts of the universe, and has produced plenty and prosperity, not allowing a single spark that could tend to the destruction of the crops to be kindled into flame.

THE NINTH FESTIVAL

XXXII

XXXII. (193) And after the feast of trumpets the solemnity of the fast is celebrated, [1260] Perhaps some of those who are perversely minded and are not ashamed to censure excellent things will say, "What sort of a feast is this where there is no eating and drinking, no troupe of entertainers or audience, no copious supply of strong drink nor the generous display of a public banquet, nor moreover the merriment and revelry of dancing to the sound of flute and harp, and timbrels and cymbals, and the other instruments of music which awaken the unruly lusts through the channel of the ears? (194) For it is in these and through these, it seems, that they think good cheer consists. They do this in ignorance of the true good cheer which the all-wise Moses saw with the most sharpsighted eyes and so proclaimed the fast a feast and named it the greatest of feasts in our ancestral language, "a Sabbath of Sabbaths," or as the Greeks would say, a seven of sevens and a holier than things holy. He did this for many reasons. (195) The first reason is the temperance which the lawgiver is continually exhorting men to display at all times, both in their language and in their appetites, both in and below the belly. And he most especially enjoins them to display it now, when he devotes a day to the particular observances of it. For when a person has once learnt to be indifferent to meat and drink, those very necessary things, what can there be of things which are superfluous that he would find any difficulty in disregarding? (196) The second reason is, that every one is at this time occupied in prayers and supplications, and since they all devote their entire leisure to nothing else from morning till evening, except to most acceptable prayers by which they endeavour to gain the favour of God, entreating pardon for their sins and hoping for his mercy, not for their own merits but through the compassionate nature of that Being who will have forgiveness rather than punishment. (197) The third is an account of the time at which this fast is fixed to take place; for by this season all the fruits which the earth has produced during the whole year are gathered in. And therefore to proceed at once to devour what has been produced Moses looked upon as an act of greediness; but to fast, and to abstain from touching food, he considered a mark of perfect piety which teaches the mind not to trust to the food which it may have prepared as the cause of health or life. (198) Therefore those who, after the gathering in of the harvest, abstain from the food, do almost declare in express words, "We have with joy received, and we shall cheerfully store up the bounteous gifts of nature; but we do not ascribe to any corruptible thing the cause of our own durable existence, but we attribute that to the Saviour, to the God who rules in the world, and who is able, either by means of these things or without them, to nourish and to preserve Us.[1261] (199) At all events, behold, he nourished our forefathers even in the desert for forty Years.[1262] How he opened fountains to give them abundant drink; and how he rained food from heaven sufficient for each day so that they might consume what they needed, and rather than hording or bartering or taking thought of the bounties received, they might rather reverence and worship the bountiful Giver and honour him with hymns and benedictions such as are due him." (200) The day of the fast is always celebrated on the tenth day of the month by order of the law. Why is it on the tenth? As we have specified in our treatments of it,[1263] it is named complete perfection by wise Men[1264] and encompasses all the proportions, the arithmetical and the harmonic and the geometric, and in addition the harmonies: the 4:3 ratio through four notes, the 3:2 ratio through five notes, the 2:1 ratio through the octave, the 4:1 ratio through the double octave, and it also has the 9:8 ratio so that it is the most perfect summation of musical theories. From this fact it is named complete Perfection.[1265] (201) Therefore God has ordained that abstinence from food should take place in accordance with the perfect number, for the sake of affording the best nourishment to the best thing which is in us; that no one may suppose that the interpreter of God's word is enjoining hunger, the most intolerable of all evils, but only a brief cutting off of the stream which flows into the channels of the body. (202) For thus the clear stream which proceeds from the fountain of reason was likely to be borne smoothly and evenly to the soul, since the uninterrupted use of food inundating the body contributes also to confuse the reason. But if the supply of food be checked, then the reason getting a firm footing as in a dry road, will be able to proceed in safety without stumbling; (203) and besides it was fitting that when the supply of all things had turned out according to the wishes of the people and become completed, they should, amid the abundance of their harvest, preserve a commemoration of their previous want by abstinence from food, and should offer up prayers, in order that they might never come to a real experience of a want of necessary food.

THE TENTH FESTIVAL

XXXIII

XXXIII. (204) The last of all the annual festivals is that which is called the feast of tabernacles, which is fixed for the season of the autumnal equinox. And by this festival the lawgiver teaches two lessons, both that it is necessary to honour equality, the first principle and beginning of justice, the principle akin to unshadowed light; and that it is becoming also, after witnessing the perfection of all the fruits of the year, to give thanks to that Being who has made them perfect. (205) For the autumn (metopoÂron), as its very name shows is the season which comes after (meta) the fruits of the year (teÌn opoÌran) are now gathered into the granaries, on account of the providence of nature which loves the living creatures upon the earth. (206) And, indeed, the people are commanded to pass the whole period of the feast under tents, either because there is no longer any necessity for remaining in the open air labouring at the cultivation of the land, since there is nothing left in the land, but all ... is stored up in the barns, on account of the injuries which otherwise might be likely to visit it from the burning of the sun or the violence of the Rains. [1266] (207) For when the crops which provide nourishment are in the fields, you act as a manager and guard of those necessities not by having cooped yourself up like a woman who belongs at home, but by having gone out to the fields. If severe cold or summer heat befalls you as you live in the open air, the overgrowths of the trees are handy shelters. If you get under their protection, you will be able to escape easily the harm from each. But when all the crops are in, go in with them to look for a more substantial abode for rest in place of the toils which you endured as you worked the land. Or again, it may be a reminder of the long journey of our ancestors which they made through a wide desert, living in tents for many years at each station. (208) And it is proper in the time of riches to remember one's poverty, and in an hour of glory to recollect the days of one's disgrace, and at a season of peace to think upon the dangers that are past. (209) In addition to the pleasure it provides, a not inconsiderable advantage for the practice of virtue comes from this. For people who have had prosperity and adversity before their eyes and have pushed the latter away and are enjoying the free use of the better, of necessity become thankful in disposition and are being urged on to piety by fear of a change of state to the contrary condition. As a result they honor God in songs and words for their present wealth and persistently entreat and conciliate him with supplications that they will no longer be tested with calamities. (210) Again, the beginning of this festival is appointed for the fifteenth day of the month, on account of the reason which has already been mentioned respecting the spring season, also that the world may be full, not by day only but also by night, of the most beautiful light, the sun and moon on their rising opposite to one another with uninterrupted light, without any darkness interposing itself between so as to divide them. (211) And after the festival has lasted seven days, he adds an eighth as a seal, calling it a kind of crowning feast, not only as it would seem to this festival, but also to all the feasts of the year which we have enumerated; for it is the last feast of the year, and is a very stable and holy sort of conclusion, befitting men who have now received all the produce from the land, and who are no longer in perplexity and apprehension respecting any barrenness or scarcity. (212) Perhaps, however, the first cubic number, the number eight, was assigned to the feast for the following reason. It is in its Capacity [1267] the beginning of solid substance at the transition from the incorporeal, the end of the intelligible. The intelligible [make the Transition] [1268] to a solid nature through the scale of ascending powers. (213) And in fact, the autumnal feast, just as I said, as a kind of summation and end of all the feasts in the year seems to be more stable and steadier since people have already received the revenue from the land and are no longer in a state of fear and baffled by doubts about productivity or dearth. For the anxious thoughts of farmers are not settled until the crops are in because of the losses just waiting to happen from so many people and animals. (214) I have spoken in this way about the sacred week and the sacred number seven at more than usual length, wishing to show that all the feasts of the year are, as it were, the offspring of the number seven, which stands in the relation of a mother. [...] [1269] Follies and joys; and because in such assemblies and in a cheerful course of life there are thus established seasons of delight unconnected with any sorrow or depression supporting both the body and the soul; the one by the pleasure and the other by the opportunities for philosophical study which they Afford. [1270]

XXXIV

XXXIV. (215) There is, besides all these, another Festival [1271] sacred to God, and a solemn assembly on the day of the festival which they call castallus, [1272] from the event that takes place in it, as we shall show presently. Now that this festival is not in the same rank, nor of the same importance with the other festivals, is plain from many considerations. For, first of all, it is not one to be observed by the whole population of the nation as each of the others is. Secondly, none of the things that are brought or offered are laid upon the altar as holy, or committed to the unextinguishable and holy fire. Thirdly, the very number of days which are to be observed in the festival are not expressly stated.

XXXV

XXXV. (216) Nevertheless, any one may easily see that it has about it some of the characteristics of a sacred festival, and that it comes very near to having the privileges of a solemn assembly. For every one of those men who had lands and possessions, having filled vessels with every different species of fruit borne by fruit-bearing trees; which vessels, as I have said before, are called castalli, brings with great joy the first fruits of his abundant crop into the temple, and standing in front of the altar gives the basket to the priest, uttering at the same time the very beautiful and admirable hymn prescribed for the occasion; and if he does not happen to remember it, he listens to it with all attention while the priest recites it. (217) And the hymn is as follows:--"The leaders of our nation renounced Syria, and migrated to Egypt. Being but few in number, they increased till they became a populous nation. Their descendants being oppressed in innumerable ways by the natives of the land, when no assistance did any longer appear to be expected from men, became the supplicants of God, having fled for refuge to entreat his assistance. (218) Therefore he, who is merciful to all who are unjustly treated, having received their supplication, smote those who oppressed them with signs and wonders, and prodigies, and with all the marvellous works which he wrought at that time. And he delivered those who were being insulted and enduring every kind of perfidious oppression, not only leading them forth to freedom, but even giving them in addition a most fertile land; (219) for it is from the fruits of this land, O bounteous God! that we now bring you the first fruits; if indeed it is a proper expression to say that he who receives them from you brings them to you. For, O Master! they are all your favours and your gifts, of which you have thought us worthy, and so enabled us to live comfortably and to rejoice in unexpected blessings which thou hast given to us, who did not expect them."

XXXVI

XXXVI. (220) This hymn is sung from the beginning of summer to the end of autumn, by two choruses replying to one another uninterruptedly, on two separate occasions, each at the end of one complete half of ten years; because men cannot all at once bring the fruits of the seasons to God in accordance with his express command, but different men bring them at different seasons; and sometimes even the same persons bring first fruits from the same lands at different times; (221) for since some fruits become ripe more speedily, and others more slowly, either on account of the differences of the situations in which they are grown, as being hotter or colder, or from innumerable other reasons, it follows that the time for offering the first fruits of such productions is undefined and uncertain, being extended over a great space. (222) And the use of these first fruits is permitted to the priests, since they had no portion of the land themselves, and had no possessions from which they could derive revenue; but their inheritance is the first fruits from all the nation as the wages of their holy ministrations, which they perform day and night.

XXXVII

XXXVII. (223) I have now said thus much respecting the number seven, and the things referring to it among the days, and the months, and the years; and about the festivals which are connected with this number seven, following the regular connection of the heads of the subject, which I proposed to myself according to the order in which they are mentioned in the sacred history. And I shall now proceed in regular order to consider the commandment which comes next, which is entitled the one about the honour due to Parents. [1273]

XXXVIII

XXXVIII. (224) Having already spoken of four commandments which, both as to the order in which they are placed and as to their importance, are truly the first; namely, the commandment about the lenity of that sovereign authority by which the world is governed, and that which commands that man should not look upon any representation or figure of anything as God, and that which forbids the swearing falsely, or indeed the swearing carelessly and vainly at all, and that concerning the sacred seventh day--all which commandments tend to piety and holiness. I now proceed to the fifth commandment, relating to the honour due to parents; which is, as I showed in the mention I made of it separately before, on the borders between those which relate to the affairs of men and those which relate to God. (225) For parents themselves are something between divine and human nature, partaking of both; of human nature, inasmuch as it is plain that they have been born and that they will die; and of divine nature, because they have engendered other beings, and have brought what did not exist into existence: for, in my opinion, what God is to the world, that parents are to their children; since, just as God gave existence to that which had no existence, they also, in imitation of his power, as far at least as they were able, make the race of mankind everlasting.

XXXIX

XXXIX. (226) And this is not the only reason why a man's father and mother are deserving of honour, but here are also several other reasons. For among all those nations who have any regard for virtue, the older men are esteemed above the younger, and teachers above their pupils, and benefactors above those who have received kindnesses from them, and rulers above their subjects, and masters above their slaves. (227) Accordingly, parents are placed in the higher and superior class; for they are the elders, and the teachers, and the benefactors, and the rulers, and the masters. And sons and daughters are placed in the inferior class; for they are the younger, and the pupils, and the persons who have received kindnesses, and subjects, and slaves. And that every one of these assertions is correct is plain from the circumstances that take place, and proofs derived from reason will establish the truth of them yet more undeniably.

XL

XL. (228) I affirm, therefore, that that which produces is always older than that which is produced, and that that which causes anything is older than that of which it is the cause; but those who beget or bring forth a child are in some sense the causes and producers of the child which is begotten or brought forth, and they stand in the light of teachers, inasmuch as all that they know themselves they teach to their children from their earliest infancy, and they not only exercise and train them in the supernumerary accomplishments, impressing reasonings on the minds of their children when they come to their prime, but they also teach them those most necessary lessons which refer to choice and avoidance, the choice, that is to say, of virtues, and the avoidance of vices, and of all the energies in accordance with them. (229) For who can be more completely the benefactors of their children than parents, who have not only caused them to exist, but have afterwards thought them worthy of food, and after that again of education both in body and soul, and have enabled them not only to live, but also to live well; (230) training their body by gymnastic and athletic rules so as to bring it into a vigorous and healthy state, and giving it an easy way of standing and moving not without elegance and becoming grace, and educating the soul by letters, and numbers, and geometry, and music, and every kind of philosophy which may elevate the mind which is lodged in the mortal body and conduct it up to heaven, and can display to advantage the blessed and happy qualities that are in it, producing an admiration of and a desire for an unchangeable and harmonious system, which they will afterwards never leave if they preserve their obedience to their captain. (231) And in addition to the benefits which they heap upon them, they have likewise authority over the children of whom they are the parents, not as is the case in cities, in consequence of some drawing of lots or election, so that any one can find fault with his governor as having become so either by some blunder of fortune and not by reason, or it may be by the impetuosity of the multitude, the most inconsiderate and foolish of all things, but being established in this post by the most excellent and perfect wisdom of the sublime nature, which regulates all divine and human affairs in accordance with justice.

XLI

XLI. (232) For these reasons it is allowable for parents even to accuse their children, and to reprove them with considerable severity, and even, if they do not submit to the threats which are uttered to them by word of mouth, to beat them, and inflict personal punishment on them, and to imprison them; and if they behave with obstinacy and resist this treatment, becoming stiff-necked through the greatness of their incurable wickedness, the law permits them to chastise them even to the extent of putting them to Death. [1274] But still this permission is not given to either the father by himself, or to the mother by herself, by reason of the greatness of the punishment, which it is not fitting should be determined by one, but by both together, for it is not probable that both the parents will agree about putting their child to death unless his iniquities are very grievous, and weigh down by a certain undoubted preponderance that firm affection which is firmly implanted in the parents by nature. (233) But parents have received not only the power of a ruler and governor over their children, but also that of a master, according to both the very highest characteristics of the possession of servants, namely, possessing them as born in the house, and also as purchased with money, for they expend a price many times greater than their real value on their children and for the sake of their children, in wages to nurses, and instructors, and teachers, besides all the expenses which they incur for their dress and their food, and their other care of them when well and when sick, from their earliest infancy till the time that they are full grown. And not only are those looked upon as servants born in the house who have actually been brought forth within the walls, but those also are so regarded who by the laws of nature receive from the masters of the house a sufficient support to maintain them in life after they are born.

XLII

XLII. (234) Since this, then, is the case, those who do honour their parents are not doing anything worthy of praise, since even any single one of the commandments already mentioned is sufficient to invite them to regard their parents with reverence. But are not those men worthy of blame, and accusation, and the very extremity of punishment, who neither respect them as older than themselves, nor listen to them as their teachers, nor think them worthy of any requital as their benefactors, nor obey them as their rulers, nor fear them as their masters? (235) Therefore the law says, "Honour thy father and thy mother next after God;" [1275] assigning to them the second place in honour, on the same principle as nature herself has ranked them in her decision of their proper place and duties. And you will not honour them more by any line of conduct than by endeavouring and appearing to be virtuous persons. As the being such is a seeking of virtue without pride and without guile, and appearing such aims at virtue in connection with a good reputation and praise from one's associates; (236) for parents, thinking but little of their own advantage, think the virtue and excellence of their children the perfection of their own happiness, for which reason it is that they are anxious that they should obey the injunctions which are laid upon them, and that they should be obedient to all just and beneficial commands; for a father will never teach his child anything which is inconsistent with virtue or with truth.

XLIII

XLIII. (237) And any one may conjecture that pious respect is due to parents, not only from what has been said above, but also from the manner in which persons behave to those who are of the same age with their parents; for the man who shows respect to an old man, or to an old woman, who is no relation to him, must appear in some degree to be remembering his own father and mother, and, out of this consideration, to be looking upon them as the images of his parents, who are the real models. (238) On which account, in the sacred scriptures, it is not only commanded that young men should rise up and give the best seats to their elders, but also that they should rise up before them when they pass by; [1276] showing honour to the grey hairs of old age, to which there is a hope that they may come themselves if they now yield precedence to them. (239) And this commandment also seems to me to have been enacted with exceeding beauty and propriety; for the law says, "Let each man fear his father and his Mother," [1277] enjoining fear rather than affection, not as being more advantageous and profitable with reference to the present occasion, for the first of these feelings affects foolish persons when they are being instructed or reproved, and folly cannot be cured by any other means than fear. But the second feeling, namely, affection towards their parents, it is not fitting should be inculcated on children by the injunctions of a lawgiver, for nature requires that that should be spontaneous. For it has implanted it so deeply from very infancy in the souls of those who are so completely united by blood, and by the services done by the parents to the children, that it is always selftaught and spontaneous, and has no need of commandments to enforce it. (240) But the law has enjoined fear, because children are accustomed to feel an easy indifference. For though parents attend to their children with an exceeding violence of affection, providing them with necessary things from all quarters, and bestowing all good things upon them, and shrinking from no labour and from no danger, being bound to them by love stronger than any oaths, still some persons do not receive their affection as if it aimed solely at their good, being full of luxury and arrogance; and coveting a luxurious life, and becoming effeminate both in body and soul, permitting them in no respect to entertain proper dispositions as through the native powers of their minds, which they are not ashamed to overthrow, and to enervate, and to deprive of each separate energy, and so they come not to fear their natural correctors, their fathers and mothers yielding to and indulging their own private passions and desires. (241) But we must also urge on the parents of such persons that they employ more weighty and severe admonitions in order to cure this impetuous obstinacy of their children, and we must warn the children to reverence their parents, fearing them as their rulers and natural masters; for it is with difficulty even by these considerations that they will be brought to hesitate to act unjustly.

XLIV

XLIV. (242) I have now then gone through all the five heads of laws in the first table, and have noticed also all the particular points which had any reference to any individual. I must also now point out the punishments affixed to the transgression of these laws. (243) Now there is one common penalty affixed to them all, namely, death, through which all such offences have a kind of relationship to one another. But the causes of this sentence being pronounced in such cases are different, and we must begin with the last, the one that relates to parents, since it is in reference to this one that the words are still ringing in our ears, "If any one shall beat his father or his mother, let him be Stoned." [1278] And very justly, for it is not fit that that man should live who insults those who are the causes of his living; (244) but some of the men of high rank, and some of the lawgivers, looking rather at the vain opinions of men than at the truth, have softened this commandment, and instituted as a penalty, for those who beat their fathers, that their hands should be cut off; and for the sake of bearing a good reputation in the eyes of hasty and inconsiderate persons, they profess to them that it is becoming, that the parts with which such men have struck their parents should be cut off; (245) but it is a piece of folly to be angry with the servants rather than with those who are the causes of such folly; for it is not the hands that behave with such insolence, but insolent men perform their actions with their hands, and it is the men who must be punished, unless indeed it can be called fitting to let men go who have committed murder with the sword, and to content one's self with throwing away the sword; and unless, on the contrary, one ought not to give honour to those who have shown preeminent valour in war, but to the inanimate coats of armour, by means of which they have behaved themselves valiantly; (246) and unless again it is reasonable, in the case of those who have gained the victory in the gymnastic games, in the stadium, or the double race, or the long straight course, or in the contest of boxing, or in the pancratium, to attempt to crown only the legs and arms of the conquerors, and to let the whole of their bodies remain unhonoured. Surely it would be a ridiculous thing to lay down such principles as these, and to abstain in consequence from punishing or honouring those who were the real causes of the results in question; for we do not pass over a man who has given a splendid exhibition of musical skill, playing exquisitely on the flute or the lyre, and think the instruments themselves worthy of proclamations and honours. (247) Why, then, should we deprive of their hands men who beat their fathers, O you most noble lawgivers? Is it that they may for the future be wholly useless for any purpose whatever, and that they may exact as a tribute, not once a year but every day, from those whom they have treated with iniquity, compelling them to supply them with necessary food, as being unable to provide for themselves? For their father is not so wholly hard-hearted as to endure to see even a son who has so grievously offended against him dying of hunger, after his anger has been blunted by time. (248) And even if he has not laid hands upon his parents, but has only spoken ill of those whom he was bound to praise and bless, or if he has in any other manner done anything which can tend to bring his parents into disrepute, still let him Die. [1279] For since he is a common enemy, and if one may tell the plain truth, he is a public enemy of all men, to whom else can he be kind and favourable when he is not so to the authors of his being, by whose means he came into this world, and of whom he is a sort of supplement?

XLV

XLV. (249) Again, let the man who has profaned the sacred seventh day as far as it may have lain in his power, be liable to the punishment of death. For, on the contrary, it is proper rather to provide whatever is profane, be it a thing or be it a person, with means of purification, in order to induce a change for the better, since "envy," as some one has said, "goes forth out of the divine company." But to dare to adulterate or to deface the holy coinage is an act which displays an extraordinary degree of impiety. (250) In that ancient migration which took place when the people of Israel left Egypt, and when the whole multitude was travelling through the pathless wilderness, when the seventh day came all those myriads of men which I have described before rested in their tents in perfect tranquillity; but one man, and he not one of the most despised or lowest class of the people, disregarding the commands which were laid upon the nation, and ridiculing those who attended to them, went forth to pick up sticks, but in reality to show his contempt for and violation of the law. (251) And he indeed came back bearing with him a faggot in his arm, but the men who remained in their tents although inflamed with anger and exasperated by his conduct, nevertheless did not at once proceed to very harsh measures against him that day by reason of the holy reverence due to the day, but they led him before the ruler of the people, and made known his impious action, and he having committed him to prison, after a command had been given to put him to death, gave the man up to those who had originally seen him to execute. As therefore, in my opinion, it was not permitted to kindle a fire on the seventh day for the reason which I have already mentioned, so likewise it was not lawful to collect any fuel for a fire.

XLVI

XLVI. (252) Against those who call God as a witness in favour of assertions which are not true, the punishment of death is ordained in the law; [1280] and very properly, for even a man of moderate respectability will never endure to be cited as a witness, and to have his name registered in support of a lie. But it seems to me that he would look upon any one who proposed such a thing to him as a thoroughly faithless enemy; (253) on which account we must say this, that him, who swears rashly and falsely, calling God to witness an unjust oath, God, although he is merciful by nature, will yet never release, inasmuch as he is thoroughly defiled and infamous from guilt, even though he may escape punishment at the hands of men. And such a man will never entirely escape, for there are innumerable beings looking on, zealots for and keepers of the national laws, of rigid justice, prompt to stone such a criminal, and visiting without pity all such as work wickedness, unless, indeed, we are prepared to say that a man who acts in such a way as to dishonour his father or his mother is worthy of death, but that he who behaves with impiety towards a name more glorious than even the respect due to one's parents, is to be borne with as but a moderate offender. (254) But the lawgiver of our nation is not so foolish as, after putting to death men who are guilty of minor offences, then to treat those who are guilty of heavier crimes with mildness, since surely it is a greater iniquity than even to speak disparagingly or to insult one's parents, to show a contempt for the sacred name of God by means of perjury. (255) And if even he who swears in an unbecoming manner is guilty and blameable, of what punishment is that man worthy who denies the one only true and living God and now honours the creature above the Creator, and chooses to honour not only the earth and the water, or the air, or the fire, the elements of the universe, or again the sun and moon, and the planets and fixed stars, and the whole of heaven, and the universal world, but even stocks and stones, which mortal workmen have fashioned, and which by them have been shaped into human figures? (256) Therefore, let such a man be himself likened to images carved by the hand; for it ought not to be that that man should have any soul himself who honours things destitute of soul or life, and especially after he has been a disciple of Moses, whom he has often heard announcing to him and under the influence of divine inspiration declaring those most sacred and holy admonitions, "Take not the name of any other gods into thy soul for a remembrance of them, and utter not their names with thy voice, but keep both thy mind and thy speech far from all other interpositions, and turn them wholly to the Father and Creator of the universe, that thus thou mayest cherish the most virtuous and godly thoughts about his single government, and mayest speak words that are becoming and most profitable both to thyself and to those that hear Thee." [1281]

XLVII

XLVII. (257) We have now then mentioned the punishments which are ordained against those who neglect the five commandments. But the rewards which are offered to those who keep them, even though the law has not set them forth in express words of injunction, are nevertheless figuratively intimated. (258) Therefore the fact of not thinking that there are any other gods but the true God, nor imagining that things made by the hand of man are gods, and the fact of not committing perjury, are things which have no need of any other reward, for the mere fact, in my opinion, of practising these virtues is itself a most excellent and most perfect reward. For at what circumstance can a lover of truth feel more really delighted than at the devotion of himself to one God, and attending in a guileless and pure manner to his service? (259) And when I speak of witnesses, I mean not such persons as are slaves to pride, but such as are devoted to an admiration of goodness free from all error, by whom the truth is honoured. For wisdom itself is the reward of wisdom; and justice, and each of the other virtues, is its own reward. And truth, as being the most beautiful in the whole company, and as being the chief of all the holy virtues, is in much greater degree its own recompense and reward, affording as it does happiness to all who practise it, and blessings of which they cannot be deprived to their children and descendants.

XLVIII

XLVIII. (260) Again, those who properly keep the sacred sabbath are benefited in two most important particulars, both body and soul; as to their body, by a rest from their continual and incessant labours; and as to their soul, by forming most excellent conceptions respecting God as the Creator of the universe and the careful protector of all the things and beings which and whom he has made. And he made the whole universe in one week. It is plain, therefore, from these things that the man who honours the seventh day will himself find honour. (261) In the same way let not him who honours his parents dutifully seek for any further advantage, for if he considers the matter he will find his reward in his own conduct. Not but what, since this commandment is inferior in importance to the first five commandments, which have a more divine character, inasmuch as this is concerned with mortal subjects, God has given an inducement to obey this one, saying, "Honour thy father and thy mother, that it may be well with thee, and that thy days may be long in the Land;" [1282] (262) affixing thus two rewards to this injunction, one being in fact the participation in virtue, for "well" means virtue, or at least cannot subsist without virtue; while the other is, if one is to say the truth, immortality by length of days, and a life of long duration, which thou wilt preserve even in the body living with thy soul, purified with a perfect purification. These things have now been discussed at sufficient length. Let us after this, since the opportunity offers, consider the commandments in the second table.

Footnotes:

1233. Yonge's title, A Treatise on the Special Laws, Which Are Referred to Three Articles of the Decalogue, Namely the Third, Fourth, and Fifth; About Oaths, and the Reverence Due to Them; About the Holy Sabbath; About the Honour To Be Paid to Parents.

1234. Lev 5:21.
1235. Deut 19:16.
1236. Lev 27:3.
1237. Lev 10:3.

1238. Yonge's translation includes a separate treatise title at this point: On the Number Seven. His next division begins and ends with roman numeral I (= X in the Loeb). The publisher has elected to follow the Loeb numbering.

1239. Yonge's translation includes a separate treatise title at this point: To Show That the Festivals Are Ten in Number. This "treatise" begins with roman numeral I (= XI in the Loeb), enumerates each of the ten festivals individually, and extends through Loeb number 214. The publisher has elected to follow the Loeb numbering.

1240. Lev 23:2.
1241. Gen 18:10.
1242. Exod 20:9.
1243. Deut 15:1.
1244. Deut 15:12.
1245. Lev 25:4.
1246. Lev 25:31.
1247. Lev 25:19.
1248. Lev 35:5..

1249. sections 124-139 were omitted in Yonge's translation because the edition on which Yonge based his translation, Mangey, lacked this material. These lines have been newly translated for this edition.

1250. sections 142-144 were omitted in Yonge's translation because the edition on which Yonge based his translation, Mangey, lacked this material. These lines have been newly translated for this volume.

1251. sections 153-154 were omitted in Yonge's translation because the edition on which Yonge based his translation, Mangey, lacked this material. These lines have been newly translated for this volume.

1252. section 161 was omitted in Yonge's translation because the edition on which Yonge based his translation, Mangey, lacked this material. These lines have been newly translated for this volume.

1253. sections 163-174 were omitted in Yonge's translation because the edition on which Yonge based his translation, Mangey, lacked this material. These lines have been newly translated for this volume.

1254. there is a clear problem with the text here, i.e., the noun ochlon lacks a verb.

Philo Judaeus

1255. sections 177-180 were omitted in Yonge's translation because the edition on which Yonge based his translation, Mangey, lacked this material. These lines have been newly translated for this volume.

1256. literally, "being the sum of its own parts to which it is equal." In mathematical notation: $1 + 2 + 3 = 6 = 1 \times 2 \times 3$.

1257. the "or" is in section 181.

1258. the whole of this passage appears corrupt and unintelligible. Mangey especially points out that what was forbidden was not to offer unleavened bread, but leavened bread upon the altar. See Exodus 28.23:18.

1259. part of section 183 was omitted in Yonge's translation because the edition on which Yonge based his translation, Mangey, lacked this material. These lines have been newly translated for this volume.

1260. part of sections 193-194 was omitted in Yonge's translation because the edition on which Yonge based his translation, Mangey, lacked this material. These lines have been newly translated for this volume.

1261. part of sections 199-200 was omitted in Yonge's translation because the edition on which Yonge based his translation, Mangey, lacked this material. These lines have been newly translated for this volume.

1262. Deut 8:2.

1263. this is probably a reference to the tractate Concerning Numbers mentioned in QG 4.110 and Mos. 2.115.

1264. panteleia is a Pythagorean name for the number ten.

1265. the text literally says: "the 11/3 through four, the 11/2 through five, the doubled through the octave, the quadrupled through the double octave, and it also has the 11/8 ratio ..." Philo has a fuller statement in Opif. 48. In each instance he is following the Pythagoreans who applied number theory to music. For similar treatments see Plutarch, Moralia 1139D (Mus. 23) and Sextus Empiricus Adv. Math. 7.94-95.

1266. portions of sections 207, 209, 212, 213 were omitted in Yonge's translation because the edition on which Yonge based his translation, Mangey, lacked this material. These lines have been newly translated for this volume.

1267. the term dynamei is problematic here. It normally means "squared"--as Colson recognized--but is here understood more generally.

1268. there is no verb in the text. The translation follows one of Cohn's conjectures [metabainei] which matches metabasin nicely.

1269. I have translated this as it is printed in Schwichest's edition. Mangey makes the treatise end at "mother."

1270. Yonge's translation includes a separate treatise title at this point: On the Festival of the Basket of First-Fruits and notes that it is not given in Mangey's edition. Accordingly, his next paragraph begins with roman numeral I (= XXXIV in the Loeb). Yonge's "treatise" concludes with number IV (= Loeb XXXVII). The publisher has elected to follow the Loeb numbering.

1271. Deut 26:1.

1272. castallus is interpreted "a basket with a pointed bottom."

1273. Yonge's translation includes a separate treatise title at this point: On the Honour Commanded To Be Paid to Parents. Accordingly, his next paragraph begins with roman numeral I (= XXXVIII in the Loeb). Yonge's "treatise" concludes with number XI (= XLVIII in the Loeb). The publisher has elected to follow the Loeb numbering.

1274. Deut 21:18.
1275. Deut 5:16.
1276. Lev 19:32.
1277. Lev 19:3.
1278. Exod 21:15.
1279. Exod 21:16.
1280. Deut 19:19.
1281. Exod 23:13.
1282. Exod 20:12.

www.ingramcontent.com/pod-product-compliance
Lightning Source LLC
Chambersburg PA
CBHW021834220426
43663CB00005B/242